Business to Business Marketing Management

Business to business markets are considerably more challenging than consumer markets and demand specific skills from marketers. Buyers, with a responsibility to their company and specialist product knowledge, are more demanding than the average consumer. The products themselves may be highly complex, often requiring a sophisticated buyer to understand them.

Increasingly, B2B relationships are conducted in a global context. However all textbooks are region-specific – except this one. This textbook takes a global viewpoint, with an international author team and cases from across the globe. Other unique features of this excellent textbook include:

- placement of B2B in a strategic marketing setting;
- full discussion of strategy in a global setting including hypercompetition;
- full chapter on ethics early in the text;
- detailed review of global B2B services marketing, trade shows, and market research.

This new edition has been completely rewritten, and features expanded sections on globalization and purchasing, plus brand new sections on social media marketing and intellectual property. More selective, shorter, and easier to read than other B2B textbooks, this is ideal for introduction to B2B and shorter courses. At the same time, it's comprehensive enough to cover all the aspects of B2B marketing any marketer needs, be they students or practitioners looking to improve their knowledge.

Alan Zimmerman is Professor and Area Co-ordinator for the International Business (IB) program at City University of New York, College of Staten Island, New York, USA.

Jim Blythe is Professor of Marketing at Westminster University and Visiting Professor at Plymouth Business School, UK.

Business to Business Marketing Management

A global perspective

SECOND EDITION

**Alan Zimmerman and
Jim Blythe**

Routledge
Taylor & Francis Group

LONDON AND NEW YORK

First edition published by Thomson Learning 2004

Second edition published
by Routledge 2013
2 Park Square, Milton Park, Abingdon, Oxon OX14 4RN

Simultaneously published in the USA and Canada
by Routledge
711 Third Avenue, New York, NY 10017

Routledge is an imprint of the Taylor & Francis Group, an informa business

© 2013 Alan Zimmerman and Jim Blythe

British Library Cataloguing in Publication Data
A catalogue record for this book is available from the British Library

Library of Congress Cataloging in Publication Data
Zimmerman, Alan S., 1942–.
 Business to business marketing management: a global perspective/
 Alan Zimmerman and Jim Blythe. – 2nd ed.
 p. cm.
 Blythe's name appears first in the earlier edition.
 Includes bibliographical references and index.
 1. Marketing – Management. I. Blythe, Jim. II. Title.
 HF5415.13.B565 2013
 658.8′04 – dc23
 2012036653

ISBN: 978-0-415-53702-5 (hbk)
ISBN: 978-0-415-53703-2 (pbk)
ISBN: 978-0-203-06758-1 (ebk)

Typeset in Berling and Futura
by Florence Production Ltd, Stoodleigh, Devon
Printed and bound by CPI Group (UK) Ltd, Croydon, CR0 4YY

To my late parents, Alice and Roy Zimmerman, whose love of learning and world view inspired my intellectual curiosity. And to my brother, Steve, who has always cheered me on.

Contents

11 Supply chain management   254

12 Managing distribution channels   274

Case studies

Figures

Tables

Exhibits

Acknowledgements

Alan Zimmerman

First, I would like to acknowledge my friend and co-author, Jim Blythe, who continues to make this process so rewarding. While many people have made contributions to the material through their advice over the years, several individuals should be named. First I would like to thank my wife, Lori, for her consistent love and encouragement as well as her endless supply of brownies for quick energy. I would also like to acknowledge our editor at Routledge, Amy Laurens, and her colleague Rosie Baron for their help. We are also indebted to the anonymous reviewers of the text who made very valuable critical contributions and helped us improve the material. Any errors which remain are ours alone.

Of all of the business people I have known over many years, I would like to single out Michael Ferrara, Executive Chairman of Adlens, a former colleague, boss and client whose observations are reflected in many areas of this text. I would also like to recognize my teaching colleagues and my department chair, Tom Tellefsen, at the College of Staten Island, as well as Wilma Jones and her staff at the Library for their consistent support. In addition, I thank my current and past students at the College, especially Alexandra Doronina whose assistance was invaluable.

Jim Blythe

I would like to thank Alan for his friendship and collaboration on this book. Maintaining a good working relationship with 3,000 miles of water in between isn't always easy, especially as I was in Japan for a good part of the process which meant we had some rather surreal conversations due to the time difference.

I would like to endorse Alan's acknowledgement of Amy and Rosie, and the reviewers who picked us up on some omissions that we should have seen for ourselves. I would also like to thank Sue, my wife, who brings me tea from time to time and listens to me fretting about deadlines.

Finally, I would like to thank my students, past and present, for making me think before I open my mouth. Without them, I would not have been able to write this, or any other, book.

Chapter 1

Introduction to business to business marketing

INTRODUCTION

Marketing has its roots in understanding consumers, and because we are all consumers it has become altogether too easy to concentrate on using consumer-based examples and theories when discussing marketing concepts. However, business markets are far larger: businesses buy and sell more goods than do consumers, and the transactions that take place between organizations have a greater impact on the economy and on the welfare of people than do the transactions between businesses and consumers. Understanding the differences between marketing to consumers and marketing to professional buyers in commercial organizations is the first step in developing a successful business marketing program.

CHAPTER OBJECTIVES

After reading this chapter, you should be able to:

- define the B2B market
- discern the differences between real marketing and "trappings"
- understand the size and scope of the market
- describe the differences between B2B and consumer marketing
- explain B2B goods classifications
- understand the importance of relationships in B2B marketing.

DEFINING THE BUSINESS TO BUSINESS MARKET

The business market has been defined to include organizations that buy products and services for use in the production of other products and services that are sold, rented or supplied to others. It also includes retailing and wholesaling firms that acquire goods for the purpose of reselling or renting to others (Kotler and Armstrong, 2001). But this definition is far too narrow for our purposes. The full B2B market includes customers who are institutions like hospitals and charities and all levels of government. This is especially true across the globe where quasi-government operations like the Mexican oil supplier Pemex may be the biggest customer in a country. The business market not only includes physical products but it includes services as well. In fact, as we will see, large institutions, governments and businesses buy virtually every type of product and service.

Business buyers generally buy to increase their company's profits. Institutional buyers have the same concerns but they may be focused on providing an adequate surplus. There are only two basic ways to increase profits (or surplus): boost sales or lower costs. These objectives may be achieved by increasing efficiency or purchasing lower-cost products/services. Sometimes B2B buyers also buy to avoid penalties from government regulators or negative publicity from activist groups. The most effective marketing programs directed at business buyers are always based on one of the following three basic appeals:

■ increasing sales;
■ reducing costs;
■ meeting government regulations/avoiding negative PR.

Especially when taking a marketing strategy from a domestic to an international setting, experience shows that the appeal must be simple to explain. Appeals that do not fall into one of the three basics above often fail when translated to foreign markets.

Exhibit 1.1 is an advertisement which clearly shows how the use of a rather uninteresting-looking product can improve company productivity. The message is simple and can easily be translated to any number of languages.

TRAPPINGS VS. SUBSTANCE

As is illustrated by the Talking Point below, many B2B firms *appear* to adopt the marketing concept, but more often than not they are stuck in what has been called the "Rugged Engineering Trap." This is a warmed-over version of production-orientation where a firm is convinced (usually by its engineers) that if "we build a better widget, the world will beat a path to our door." These firms are only giving lip service to the marketing concept especially where technology is emphasized over customer needs. This disease is chronic in B2B marketing and continues among many firms as you read these words. Michael Porter (2001) wrote that some companies "have used Internet technology to shift the basis of competition away from quality features and service toward price" because they

EXHIBIT 1.1 Cisco Systems advertisement

Source: Cisco Systems. Reproduced with permission from Cisco Systems.

Talking Point

A product known as an auto diode is a key component in the alternators used in virtually every automobile in the world. One old line electrical products manufacturer was supplying an attractive product at a cost of nearly one dollar per unit. Competitors developed a much simpler product which eliminated the outer layer of packaging and could be offered to automotive manufacturers at less than $0.20. The engineers at the older firm were convinced that buyers at General Motors, Ford, and Toyota would be willing to pay more for the better packaged product, even though both met the same functional requirements. One engineer even remarked, "they can see the better quality – it looks better!"

Is price the only consideration in B2B markets? Are we living in a world where manufacturers can only survive by being the cheapest? Or is the real issue value? And how do you define that?

forgot to satisfy customers. Many B2B firms adopt what appears to be a marketing orientation, but they are simply using the "trappings" of marketing rather than the substance. Trappings include activities like:

- declarations of support from top management;
- creating a marketing organization complete with product management;
- new strategic or marketing planning approaches;
- complete marketing information (MIS) systems;
- increasing marketing expenditures for advertising, research and training.

(The above adapted from Ames, 1970). With tongue in cheek, Cova et al. (2006) listed more than 70 "marketing panaceas." These included phrases like "authenticity marketing, cause-related marketing, customer-centric marketing, expeditionary marketing, geo-marketing, multilevel marketing, network marketing, one-to-one marketing, relationship marketing, societal marketing, symbiotic marketing, and value marketing." These appear to be further "trappings."

The trappings do not address the central need for a B2B firm to focus on the critical purpose of its existence. More than 30 years ago, Peter Drucker said that "there is only one valid definition of business purpose: to create a customer" (Drucker, 1973). And yet Lou Gerstner stated that IBM's major problem when he took over was that the firm had forgotten to satisfy customers and was more interested in promoting technology (Gerstner, 2002).

No amount of sparkling technology, management dictums, new plans or systems can replace the basic understanding exhibited by the most effective B2B firms. The key task doesn't sound very exciting, but it is absolutely vital to success. That is to determine what customers really want and to put all the resources of the firm on the task of delivering it. A firm that can accomplish this (no mean feat) is really a marketing-oriented firm, not one with just the "trappings" of marketing. As we shall see, there are major differences between consumer and B2B marketing. Yet, the basic concept of satisfying customers' needs remains the same. Experience has shown that B2B marketers must be generalists. They are far more involved with customers' individual needs and must often adapt their product and service offerings to meet those needs. Sales people for B2B firms frequently need to have the same skills as general managers, for they often select the most important customers or customer segments, design products and service packages to satisfy those customers, develop marketing plans for them, set the prices, and perform the follow-up service required to keep the customers happy.

The consumer sale in most products consists of only one transaction compared to the many transactions that take place before that one final sale is made in the business to business world. The conversion sequence shown below gives an idea of the number of steps required to make any product.

Since businesses, institutions and governments buy every product, simply looking at a product cannot tell us whether it is a consumer or B2B product. Consider the humble hairdryer. If we trace this product through the stages in the production chain, we will see that many B2B transactions must take place in order for a final sale to a consumer to happen. (See Figure 1.1.)

Now, let us apply the hairdryer to this process. (See Figure 1.2.)

If we examine the hairdryer, we can see that it is made up of about five major elements, including a plastic shell, a heating element, a motor and fan, controls and switches, and a wire and plug. The

FIGURE 1.1 Conversion sequence

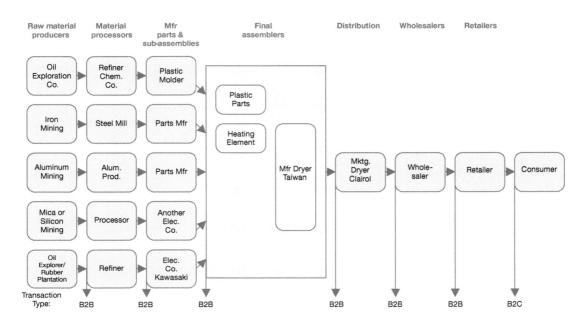

FIGURE 1.2 Transactions to make a hairdryer

diagram above shows how many possible transactions there are from the original gathering of the raw materials to the final sale to the consumer. We can count 18 transactions which fall into the B2B category as compared to one final transaction to the consumer. To make this simple electric hairdryer requires raw materials from oil, steel, aluminum and rubber producers, materials processors who turn the raw ores into usable products, manufacturers of parts, and sub-assemblies who put together materials of various kinds and deliver several components to another firm who would be a final assembler. In this case, we have assumed the final assembler is in Taiwan. The final assembler then delivers the product to the distributor, a private brander who may be a firm like Clairol. This firm then sells the product to a wholesaler, who in turn sells to a retailer and only then does the consumer have the opportunity to purchase it.

IMPACT OF THE INTERNET

The advent of the Internet is fundamentally changing the way firms address their production or supply chain. IBM buys 95 percent of its requirements using e-procurement. In 2000, Daimler-Chrysler, Ford and General Motors launched a joint procurement service. The service, now called Covisint, grew rapidly from about 22,000 users at the end of 2001 to over 77,000 users at the end of 2002. It was divested in 2004, but by 2012 Covisint had become cloud-based, had over 500 global customers with 22 million users worldwide, and was processing over 1 billion transactions per annum (Covisint, 2012). Both IBM and Ford report hundreds of millions of dollars in savings by using e-procurement methods.

Both in the US and in Europe some firms have fully adopted e-procurement while others have not. This seems to depend on industry category and/or cultural values (Pearcy et al., 2008; Batenburg, 2007).

A study of corporate facilities managers shows they are far more willing to purchase low-risk products like supplies than expensive capital items via the Internet. This study shows, on average, only 3 percent of capital items but 10 percent of maintenance and repair supplies were purchased by these buyers over the Internet (Tellefsen and Zimmerman, 2004). The study also showed that buyers are more likely to use the Internet for data gathering than order placement. Recent proprietary research conducted by one of the authors confirms this finding. Architects and specifiers overwhelmingly use manufacturer's websites to gather general product information or specific specifications. Most of the respondents to these studies begin their search with a product or manufacturer or brand name.

SIZE OF THE MARKET

As we can see from the number of transactions that take place to provide our simple hairdryer, the B2B market is far larger than the consumer market. The purchases of governments alone dwarf the purchases of any collection of companies and consumers. For example, in 2010 the US Department of Defense alone spent $365.9 billion on purchasing goods and services, whereas the Ford Motor Company only spends $65 billion a year, globally (United Nations Global Compact, 2012).

CONCEPTUAL DIFFERENCES BETWEEN B2B AND CONSUMER MARKETING

While on the surface the basics of marketing are the same for attracting consumers, businesses, governments or institutions, there are a number of differences which make the marketing of products and services in the B2B market quite different from marketing to consumers. The 12 major differences in consumer versus B2B marketing are spelled out in the table below.

Internal to company

In business marketing, it is not possible for one department alone to develop or make a change in an offering and gain the approval of a large number of customers. In a business marketing firm, a product manager usually must act like a mini-general manager. He/she faces every product manager's problem of responsibility without authority. The business marketing manager must be able to gain cooperation from all the other functions including engineering, information resources, and manufacturing. Especially in the manufacturing of B2B products there are often long lead times.

An office furniture product manager takes the needs of the marketplace (gained from market research), and working with an internal or external industrial designer develops concepts for a product. At the same time, the product manager must involve engineering, finance, and manufacturing to develop initial feasibility studies and cost estimates for the product. The lead time for tooling (the forming equipment used to make the product pieces) may be close to one year. This product manager must make decisions, finalize the design, gain cooperation from all other departments, and then approve the order for the tooling while planning to introduce a product one

TABLE 1.1 Twelve major differences

Twelve major differences: consumer vs. business to business marketing

- Internal to company
  - Interdependence of departments
  - Differences in product management responsibilities
  - Marketing strategy=corporate strategy

- Customer/marketing
  - More rational decision
  - Narrower customer base
  - More buying influences and locations
  - Different segmentation
  - More markets and channels
  - Personal customer contact more important

- Uncontrollables/environment
  - Technology
  - Derived demand
  - Less end-user info

year in advance. While consumer product managers are usually graduates of advertising agencies or corporate advertising departments, business product managers often have technical backgrounds. The reason for this is that advertising plays such a small role in business marketing when compared to consumer marketing. In addition, product managers are frequently required to make customer visits. These visits not only give these managers important feedback, but the product managers are active members of the sales team, providing expertise and the authority from headquarters on pricing and special packages of product and service.

In business marketing, the marketing strategy often is the same as the overall corporate strategy. For reasons already cited, many of the firms' functional areas must be involved in the marketing strategy. For instance, a small security division of a large corporation was faced with an opportunity to develop special security equipment for the White House in Washington, D.C. The sales person presented his ideas to engineering, manufacturing and the finance department and the entire division decided to pursue this exciting strategic opportunity, changing the corporate strategy from commercial to governmental target market segments. The investments required to make this product were significant. In addition, other departments had to change their priorities with the new product forcing a new strategy. The gestation period from time of suggestion to actual sales involving this large government contract was well over two years, and therefore, the entire division had to change its strategy to be successful.

Customer/marketing

While emotion plays some role in the purchasing process, generally speaking buying decisions are more rational in non-consumer markets. It is hard to justify the purchase of a new company-wide computer system based on the color of the machine housings or the social relationship between the purchaser and the sales people. Some rationale must be developed in order for this decision to be accepted by all members of the purchasing team. This will be described in more detail in Chapter 2.

Consumer markets generally consist of millions of individuals. Far fewer customers make up most non-consumer markets. For instance, a provider of jet engines need call on only a few potential customers such as Airbus and Boeing, who manufacture the majority of commercial airliners. In business marketing, Pareto's Law is often strongly in effect. In other words, a small percentage of the customers account for a very large percentage of all the business in a particular segment. For instance, in the United States, about 4 percent of all corporations account for 70 percent of all exports. This narrow base means that in many markets, the buyers have more power than the sellers.

While in consumer marketing families and other reference groups play key roles in the purchasing decision, in business markets the decision-making unit or buying center is the key. There are a number of individuals who take specific roles and make decisions based on these roles. This will be discussed in detail in Chapter 2. In addition to a number of individuals in this decision-making unit, one finds a number of locations involved. One large credit card firm assembled a team who were located in various cities throughout North America, Europe, and Asia. These individuals rarely met, but communicated by e-mail, voice mail and fax. In making a buying decision about a new computer software program, these people took various roles and came to the decision without physically ever being in the same room.

Business buyers are characterized in different ways than are consumer buyers. Consumers can be segmented by demographic or psychographic methods while customers in business markets are segmented by factors such as industry classification codes, product applications, price sensitivity, location, importance of product to the buying firm and customer size. This segmentation is discussed in far more depth in Chapter 5.

While consumer goods are often sold directly or through only one or two steps of distribution, business equipment and services providers often use many different channels. Most large producers sell directly to large customers, while also selling through various other channels at the same time. For instance, a roofing shingle firm is likely to sell directly to large home builders, contractors and "big box" retailers like Home Depot in the US or B&Q in the UK, while at the same time selling through distributors who in turn sell to smaller lumber yards, builders' merchants, and other outlets. Each effort through different distribution channels reaching different customers requires a different marketing strategy.

The largest portion of a business marketing budget is often accounted for by the sales force. Personal contact is extremely important to the success of a business marketer. In some firms, highly trained sales people with engineering or medical degrees are required to make a convincing case to sophisticated customers. In consumer markets, television, publications, radio and other non-personal information sources are critical. Proprietary research completed with architects and specifiers over the last 15 years shows that they consistently place equal value on the manufacturer's salesperson and the Internet as sources of information, compared to advertising, catalogs, or any other source.

Over the last few years some have questioned whether this "marketing dichotomy" is justified. Cova and Salle (2007) use Sun Microsystems as an example of a firm dealing with some customers with a traditional B2B approach while also providing "open source" products which require the support and encouragement of a developer "brand" community. These authors believe that the IMP and Consumer Culture Theory (CCT) approaches have blurred the differences between B2B and B2C marketing. The arguments rest on the definition of the customer as a passive responder to marketing techniques. While this approach offers interesting concepts many of the major differences listed continue to be important for managers attempting to develop B2B marketing plans.

Uncontrollables/environment

While some final consumers find technology exciting, it is not usually the telling attribute with consumers. With business customers, the application of proper technology often has significant effects on the financial results. One only need imagine the production line of a computer manufacturer to see the importance of particular circuit boards. A circuit board provider would need to be intimately familiar with the technology used by Dell, Acer or Hewlett-Packard in order to serve these firms most effectively. Should an error be made and the wrong type of board be provided, these computer manufacturers' assembly lines would shut down and the loss of revenue would be significant. Technology is also very important in improving the sales success ratio. Since salespeople can carry laptop or tablet computers into a customer's location, they can often make very effective presentations and at the same time tap into head office databases to answer important questions on the spot.

Perhaps the best known difference between consumer and business marketing is the concept of derived demand. This simply means, as we have seen in the hairdryer example, that the demand for business marketers' products is derived from sales to the consumer. A firm supplying personal security systems to home builders would be affected significantly by the number of new homes or apartments built in a particular area. Should demand for these homes slacken, no amount of convincing marketing will force a home builder to purchase more personal security systems than he can install in newly built residences. Business marketers must look beyond their own customers to the ultimate consumer to understand trends which may have a significant effect upon their business. The disposable income in a particular market has a significant effect on the demand for automobiles. A firm supplying seats or GPS equipment to automobile manufacturers would do well to review the disposable income trends in a particular market to predict future sales of their product.

In consumer markets, there are well-established government and private firms supplying specific market data. For instance, in the United States, the AC Nielsen Company supplies frequent data about supermarket sales by product and brand. In addition, models exist which can predict the success of a consumer marketing activity based on small experiments. Here exposing a test market to advertising then examining the results can allow a firm to predict nationwide sales since well-established formulas are commercially available to make this prediction. No such formulas exist in B2B markets and frequently the data required by a particular business marketer is difficult to find. A firm which manufactures access flooring (a product which provides a false floor on top of an original floor to allow a plenum for housing wiring and passing air conditioning) was attempting to determine the size of its market in the Far East. The firm looked first at the United States and found that no government data was available which specifically identified the sales of this type of product. The closest identification was "metal fabricated products, nec." "NEC" means not elsewhere classified, the bane of any marketing research person. This means that data concerning many kinds of fabricated metal parts was included in the category and the access flooring manufacturer could only know the absolute largest possible size of his market but was really no closer to identifying the real size. In looking for data in Hong Kong, China and even Japan, he ran into the same problem. No data of this definition was available. This kind of problem is often true for business marketers and the solution to this problem is described in further detail in Chapter 4.

RELATIONSHIP BUILDING

A vital part of success in business marketing is the development and maintenance of customer relationships. Instead of simply looking at a series of transactions between a customer and a supplier, the successful marketer attempts to establish a relationship. This is not always a long-term relationship, but the interchange should be seen as more than a simple transaction. In fact, one definition of marketing is "to establish, maintain, enhance, and commercialize customer relationships so that the objectives of the parties involved are met. This is done by a mutual exchange and fulfillment of promises" (Grönroos, 1990). The seller gives a set of promises related to products, services, financing, administration, information, social contacts and other commitments. The buyer gives a set of promises related to payment and use of the product. When the promises are kept on both sides both parties gain benefits and the relationship is enhanced. Once past promises are fulfilled new sets of promises can be made on both sides to continue the building of the relationship (Calonious, 1986, 1988).

Research shows that not every customer either needs or desires a long-term relationship (Day, 2000 and Cannon and Perreault, 1999). Some business marketers should segment their customers according to their relationship needs. For a fuller explanation of this, see Chapter 14.

Talking Point

Consumer marketing is almost the same as B2B marketing. After all, aren't these customers and multiple buying influences and environmental forces present in each market? Shouldn't a person who was in charge of marketing for toothpaste be able to adapt to selling oil well drilling equipment?

Or are we saying that people stop being human when they become industrial buyers?

THE IMP APPROACH

The Industrial Marketing and Purchasing Group was formed in the mid-1970s by researchers from five European universities. IMP sees B2B marketing not just from the point of view of firms forcing their marketing programs on buyers but as an ongoing interaction between buyers and sellers. This research stream implies that buyers and sellers are dependent on each other and that the interactions themselves create new value for both (About the IMP Group, 2012). This approach is based on relationship marketing pioneered by Grönroos as described in the section above. Four major differences between traditional and IMP approaches have been identified (Cova and Salle, 2007). These are whether customers are engaged in a series of single purchases or a long-term complex relationship, whether the customer takes an active or passive role in these interactions, whether markets are stable or unstable and whether focus should be given individually to the supplier or customer or to the supplier–customer interaction over time. Some researchers state that a shift is necessary from studying marketing to studying markets (Venkatesh and Penaloza, 2006). A key criticism of the IMP approach has been the difficulty of applying it to everyday management problems (Ankers and Brennan, 2004 and Golfetto et al., 2007). Nevertheless the insights into networks and relationships are valuable and have been incorporated into this textbook where appropriate.

BUSINESS GOODS CLASSIFICATIONS

There are a number of ways of classifying B2B goods. All are entirely different than consumer goods classifications, which are usually divided into convenience, specialty and shopping goods. From a B2B point of view, goods are divided by the use to which they will be put. The most widely accepted classification of business products is as follows:

- *Entering goods and services* – products and services that become part of other products – raw materials, component parts and materials. Examples of these kinds of products are taillights for an automobile, lumber or metallic ores, formed parts of aluminum or plastic or electronic products like integrated circuits. These are usually expensed rather than capitalized.

- *Foundation goods and services* – products that are used to make other products. This includes installations and accessory equipment. The former are items like offices and buildings and the latter are machine tools. Foundation goods do not become part of the finished products. While most of them are capital items, some foundation goods can also be expensed.
- *Facilitating goods and services* – products and services that help an organization achieve its objectives. These goods also do not enter the product or even the production process. Generally speaking, facilitating goods and services are expensed rather than capitalized. Examples of facilitating goods and services are market research services, cleaning supplies and services, copiers and small hardware. Facilitating goods are usually divided into supplies and business services. In this category are items which are often characterized as MRO (maintenance, repair, and operations).

As will be seen, the goods classification aids in developing strategy for the business marketer. While it is only one important aspect of strategy development, the type of good gives basic direction to the strategy.

ROAD MAP THROUGH THE TEXT

As you read through the text, you will see it is uniquely oriented, with a global perspective. While it contains all the basics of B2B marketing, including the latest research in various areas, our goal has been to focus on the entire world since most B2B marketers must take advantage of opportunities wherever they arise. In addition, we believe that marketing is essentially a practical discipline. So, while theory is introduced, we attempt to focus the student on real tools which can be used in the day to day management of a B2B firm.

The book is organized into four main sections. First is the Business Market Environment. This section provides the context for B2B marketing and includes the current chapter as well as a discussion of business organization buying behavior and strategic planning for global markets. We have placed strategic planning at an early stage in the book since this overview is necessary to put the rest of the text into proper context. This is true for ethical considerations as well. Chapter 4 reviews ethical issues for business marketers, especially important when dealing with the global marketplace.

The second major section, called Evaluating Market Opportunities, which includes market research and information systems, discusses ways of gathering information which are unique to the B2B marketer; segmentation, targeting, and positioning, which is designed to show marketers how to group customers across the world into like segments; and market entry tactics describing how the strategic planning you have accomplished in the earlier portions of the text can be applied to ways of entering new markets with an emphasis on foreign markets.

The third major section is Formulating the Marketing Mix, which focuses on the specific tactical activities involved in business to business marketing. First is a discussion of product strategy and development, which describes new product development for the global B2B market, the product lifecycle and the management of products for business markets. Next is a discussion of business services, describing the differences between the marketing of products and the marketing of services. Chapter 10 describes pricing in a global context. Here we review the basics of business product pricing and the major issue of transfer pricing. Chapter 11 deals with supply chain management, the strategic management of distribution channels including logistics and physical distribution, getting goods to the right location in the right quantities and in the right condition.

Chapter 12 looks at distribution. The discussion here includes power relationships in distribution and the special problems of the global distribution of B2B products. Chapter 13 examines current communications theory as it applies to B2B marketing. Customer relationships and key account management is a critical aspect of B2B marketing and Chapter 14 will review this in a global context. Chapter 15 focuses on sales promotion, especially on the often neglected area of exhibitions and trade fairs, so important especially to B2B marketers throughout the world. Chapter 16 discusses corporate reputation management, the most up-to-date way of looking at this, which includes public relations and corporate advertising as well as crisis management.

The final section of the text, Managing the Marketing Program, describes the specific management issues faced by B2B marketers. First is marketing planning, implementation and control in Chapter 17, which discusses combining the elements of a marketing mix in the correct way and overcoming difficulties of implementation. Next, Chapter 18 describes various ways of organizing the marketing function, including staff empowerment and the management of functional groups within the firm as well as change management. The final chapter describes the future of business marketing, including the continued rise in importance of the Internet and other communications technologies (including social networking), and possible changes in globalization.

CASE STUDY

Rising Sun

Toyo Ichiura had recently been transferred from the Consumer Electronics to the Business Solutions Division of Rising Sun Electronics. The firm is a US $10-billion company, manufacturing every kind of electronic product from TVs to portable CD players. Rising Sun is a household name throughout the world, known for quality consumer electronics products. Recently they have also become interested in serving business markets and established the Business Solutions Division to take their electronic know-how into business markets. Their first segments will be related to business communications and on-site security. Last year they sold about $500 million in products and services to business markets but top management expects these markets to grow in excess of 20 percent per year. In addition, the margins on business products are at least double those in the consumer markets.

After only about three months on the job as vice president of marketing for Business Solutions, Ichiura was wondering how he could carry out his assignment from the CEO. When the CEO hired him, he had said "the

. . . continued

marketing in our B2B operations just isn't what it should be. Since you have extensive experience in marketing for consumer electronics products, I assume you will be able to determine what we can do to improve our marketing for Business Solutions."

As Ichiura began to study the Business Solutions Division, he came to a few tentative conclusions. First, advertising and promotion received little emphasis in this division. Second, marketing for each business seemed to be relevant only to that business, a self-contained unit. Third, the product managers in these businesses were deeply involved with their customers, sometimes spending weeks at a time working on one large customer rather than focusing one common appeal to the largest number of consumers.

Ichiura decided to discuss his observations with some of his more experienced B2B colleagues at RSE. When he described his tentative conclusions, his colleagues surprised him by disagreeing with them. So he decided to speak to a fellow graduate of Tokyo University he knew was now working in a B2B position in the steel industry. He was in for another surprise. After some reminiscing, Ichiura broached his subject with his friend Yoichiro Watanabe. He reiterated his three major conclusions and asked for advice. Watanabe took a moment to look at the busy traffic in the Tokyo streets below before responding.

"Well, it is difficult. While marketing is called marketing with consumers and is also called marketing in the B2B world, there are so many differences it is hard to know where to begin. The kinds of tools you used in your previous position are just the opposite in many cases to what should be done in your current position. It might be prudent to put off your deadline for reporting to your CEO and spend some time with the major customers of your division. I believe I know you very well and I know you will be able to learn the nuances of this new field."

CASE STUDY QUESTIONS

1   Was Watanabe wrong? Were the B2B marketing executives at RSE just protecting their past decisions?
2   What major differences do you think Ichiura will find if he follows Watanabe's advice?
3   Is it a good idea to promote consumer marketing executives to senior B2B marketing positions?
4   Why do advertising and promotion play a subsidiary role in B2B marketing?
5   What are the major differences between B2B buyers and consumer purchasers?

CHAPTER SUMMARY

Business to business marketing is substantially larger and very different from consumer marketing. The business market includes all businesses, institutions and governments who buy virtually every product and service to help them in turn provide products and services to other businesses and to consumers. Marketing to these customers requires a different orientation than that used in consumer marketing.

The key points from this chapter are as follows:

- The most effective B2B marketing programs focus on one of three basic appeals: increasing sales, reducing costs, meeting government regulations.
- "Trappings" such as new technology, planning approaches or management dictums cannot substitute for a true customer orientation – finding out what customers really need and focusing the organization on providing it to them.
- There are far more B2B than consumer marketing transactions and the B2B market is far larger than the consumer market.
- The Internet is changing how customers buy but the need for a basic marketing orientation remains.
- There are 12 major differences between B2B and consumer marketing which include those which are related to the company, customers and the environment.
- Building relationships is critical to the business marketer since an in-depth understanding of the customer processes is the main ingredient in B2B processes.
- Business goods/services are classified as entering – items which become part of the product/service of the customer company, foundation – usually large capital items that are used to make products and facilitating – which help the customer's organization achieve its objectives.

REVIEW QUESTIONS

1   What are the main characteristics of B2B marketing?
2   What are the most important tools a B2B product manager would use to achieve his/her objectives?
3   What are the 12 major differences between B2B and consumer marketing? How would these differences affect formulating a B2B strategy?
4   How can a manager avoid the "trappings" of marketing?
5   What defines the relationships which are so important to B2B marketers?
6   What are the major goods classifications of B2B products?

REFERENCES

About the IMP Group (2012). Accessed 8 June at http://www.impgroup.org/about.php

Ames, B. Charles (1970). "Trappings vs. Substance in Industrial Marketing." *Harvard Business Review*, Vol. 48, Iss. 4, 93–102.

Ankers, Paul and Brennan, Ross (2004). "A qualitative study of IMP researchers' perceptions of 'managerial relevance'." IMP Annual Conference, Copenhagen Business School.

Batenburg, Ronald (2007). "E-procurement adoption by European firms: A quantitative analysis." *Journal of Purchasing and Supply Management*, Vol. 13, Iss. 3, 182–92.

Calonius, Henrik (1986). "A Market Behavior Framework" in *Contemporary Research in Marketing*. Moller, K. and Paltschick, M. (eds), Proceedings from the XV Annual Conference of the European Marketing Academy, Helsinki, Finland.

Calonius, Henrik (1988). "A Buying Process Model" in *Innovative Marketing – A European Perspective*. Blois, K. and Parkinson, S. (eds), Proceedings from the XVII Annual Conference of the European Marketing Academy, University of Bradford, England.

Cannon, Joseph P. and Perreault, William D., Jr. (1999). "Buyer–Seller Relationship in Business Markets." *Journal of Marketing Research*, Vol. 36, Iss. 4, 439–60.

Cova, Bernard and Salle, Robert (2007). "The industrial/consumer marketing dichotomy revisited: a case of outdated justification?" *Journal of Business and Industrial Marketing*, Vol. 23, Iss. 1, 3–11.

Cova, Bernard, Badot, Olivier, and Bucci, Ampelio (2006). "Beyond Marketing: In Praise of Societing." Accessed 22 June 2012 at http://www.futurelab.net/blogs/marketing-strategy-innovation/2006/07/sneak_preview_beyond_marketing.html

Covisint. Accessed 18 March 2012 at http://www.covisint.com

Day, George S. (2000). "Managing Market Relationships." *Journal of the Academy of Marketing Sciences*, Vol. 28, Iss. 1, 24–30.

Drucker, Peter F. (1973). *Management: Tasks Responsibilities Practices*. New York: Harper & Row.

Gerstner, Louis (2002). *Who Says Elephants Can't Dance?* New York: Harper Collins.

Golfetto, Francesca, Salle, Robert, Borghini, Stefania, and Rinallo, Diego (2007). "Opening the network: bridging the IMP tradition and other research perspectives." *Industrial Marketing Management*, Vol. 36, Iss. 7, 844–8.

Grönroos, Christian (1990). "Relationship Approach to Marketing in Service Contexts: The Marketing and Organizational Behavior Interface." *Journal of Business Research*, Vol. 20, Iss. 1, 3–11.

Kotler, Philip and Armstrong, Gary (2001). *Principles of Marketing*. Upper Saddle River, NJ: Prentice-Hall.

Pearcy, Dawn H., Parker, Devlon B. and Guiinipero, Larry C. (2008). "Using Electronic Procurement to Facilitate Supply Chain Integration: An Exploratory Study of US-based Firms." *Mid-American Journal of Business*, Vol. 23, Iss. 1, 23–35.

Porter, Michael E. (2001). "Strategy and the Internet." *Harvard Business Review*, Vol. 79, Iss. 3, 62–78.

Tellefsen, Thomas and Zimmerman, Alan (2004). "The Impact of Buyer Perceptions and Situational Factors on Internet Usage." *International Journal of Internet Marketing and Advertising*, July/Sept, Vol. 1, No. 3, 268–82.

United Nations Global Compact (2012). Sustainable Supply Chains: Resources and Practices. Accessed 17 January 2013 at www.unglobalcompact.org/docs/issuesdoc/supplychain/SupplyChainRepspread.pdf

Venkatesh, A. and Penaloza, L. (2006), "From Marketing to Markets: A Call for Paradigm Shift" in Sheth, J.N. and Sisodia, R.S. (eds), *Does Marketing Need Reform?: Fresh Perspectives on the Future*, Armonk, N.Y.: M.E. Sharpe, pp. 134–50.

Chapter 2

How business organizations buy

INTRODUCTION

Organizational buying is often supposed to be more rational and less emotional than consumer purchasing behavior. However, it would be wrong to assume that organizational buying is always entirely rational: those responsible for making buying decisions within organizations are still human beings, and do not leave their emotions at the door when they come to work, so it seems unrealistic to suppose that they do not have some emotional or irrational input in their decision-making.

CHAPTER OBJECTIVES

After reading this chapter, you should be able to:

- ■ explain the main influences on buyer decision-making
- ■ describe the main techniques that industrial buyers use
- ■ describe some of the internal processes that organizations use to manage and control the buying function.

THE DECISION-MAKING UNIT

There are very few cases where an industrial purchasing decision is made by only one person. Even in a small business it is likely that several people would expect to have some influence on or input into the purchase decision. Because of this, the decision-making process often becomes formalized, with specific areas of interest being expressed by members of the decision-making unit (DMU), and with roles and responsibilities being shared. This group which cannot be identified on any company organization chart, also called the buying center, varies in make-up from one buying situation to another. Individuals may participate for a brief time only or be part of the group from conception to conclusion.

The decision-making unit is thought to contain the following categories of member (Webster and Wind, 1972):

- Initiators. These are the individuals who first recognize the problem.
- Gatekeepers. These individuals control the flow of knowledge, either by being proactive in collecting information, or by filtering it. They could be junior staff who are told to visit a trade fair and collect brochures, or a personal assistant who sees his or her role as being to prevent salespeople from "wasting" the decision-maker's time.
- Buyers. The individuals given the task of sourcing suppliers and negotiating the final deal. Often these are purchasing agents who complete the administrative tasks necessary for buying. These people often work to a specific brief, and may have very little autonomy, even though they may be the only contact a supplier's salespeople have at the purchasing organization.
- Deciders. These are the people who make the final decisions, and may be senior managers or specialists. They may never meet any representatives of the supplying companies. Deciders generally rely heavily on advice from other members of the DMU.
- Users. These are the people who will be using the products which are supplied: they may be engineers or technicians, or even the cleaning staff who use cleaning products. Their opinions may well be sought by the deciders, and in many cases the users are also the initiators.
- Influencers. These people "have the ear of" the deciders. They are trusted advisers, but from the supplying company's viewpoint they are extremely difficult to identify. Influencers may be employed by the purchasing firm (for example, engineers, information systems managers or research managers) or they may be consultants (for example, architects, acoustics and safety consultants). An influencer might even be the decider's golf partner, old college friend, or teenage son.

These categories are not, of course, mutually exclusive. A User might also be an Influencer, or a Gatekeeper might also be an Initiator. The categories were originally developed to explain purchasing within families – which may be an example of the apparent similarities between business to business marketing and consumer marketing.

In fact, the members of the decision-making unit are affected both by rational and emotional motivations. Salespeople are well aware that buyers are affected by their liking or dislike for the suppliers' representatives, and buyers will often be working to their own agendas: for example, a buyer might be seeking a promotion, or might feel threatened in terms of job security, or may be conducting a vendetta with a colleague. Any of these influences might affect the buyer's behavior, but all of them would be difficult or impossible for a supplier's salesperson to identify correctly and act upon.

In general, members of a decision-making unit tend to be more risk-averse than do consumers. This is because the buying center (DMU) members have more to lose in the event of a wrong decision: for a consumer, the main risk is financial, and even that is limited since most retailers will replace or refund goods purchased in error. For the industrial purchaser, however, a serious purchasing mistake can result in major negative consequences for the business as well as loss of face at work, shattered promotion dreams, or even dismissal in serious cases. The professional persona of the industrial buyer is liable to be compromised by purchasing errors, which in turn means that the buyer will feel a loss of self-esteem.

Determining the relative power of each member of the buying center (DMU) for each purchasing situation is a difficult task. Ronchetto et al. (1989) identify these characteristics of individuals who may be most influential in a DMU:

- important in the corporate and departmental hierarchy;
- close to the organizational boundary;
- central to the workflow;
- active in cross-departmental communications;
- directly linked to senior management.

It should be obvious that purchasing managers are most important in repetitive purchases while the CEO will become heavily involved in unique, costly and risky buying decisions.

As a result of this increased risk, industrial buyers use a variety of risk-reducing tactics (Hawes and Barnhouse, 1987). These are as follows, and are presented in order of importance:

1　Visit the operations of the potential vendor to observe its viability.
2　Question present customers of the vendor concerning their experience with the vendor's performance.
3　Multisource the order to ensure a backup source of supply.
4　Obtain contract penalty clause provisions from the potential vendor.
5　Obtain the opinion of colleagues concerning the potential vendor.
6　Favor firms that your company has done business with in the past.
7　Confirm that members of your upper management are in favor of using the vendor as a supplier.
8　Limit the search for, and ultimate choice of, a potential vendor only to well-known vendors.
9　Obtain the opinion of a majority of your co-workers that the chosen vendor is satisfactory.

Buyers are affected by individual, personal factors as well as environmental and organizational factors. Personally they exhibit many of the same influences on the buying decision that consumers have: the desire to play a role, for example, may cause a buyer to be difficult to negotiate with as he or she tries to drive a hard bargain. The desire for respect and liking may cause a buyer to want to give the order to a salesperson who is exceptionally pleasant or helpful, and to deny the order to a salesperson who is regarded as being unpleasant or pushy. Business buyers are likely to be affected by some or all of the environmental influences in Figure 2.1 (Loudon and Della Bitta, 1993):

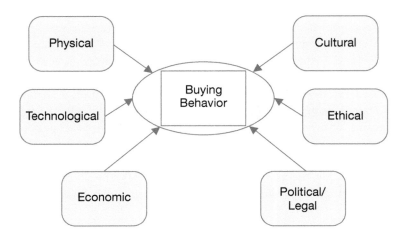

FIGURE 2.1 Environmental influences on buyer behavior

■ *Physical influences.* The location of the purchasing firm relative to its suppliers may be decisive, since many firms prefer to source supplies locally. This is especially true in the global marketplace, where a purchasing company may wish to support local suppliers, or may prefer to deal with people from the same cultural background. In many cases, buyers seem almost afraid to source from outside their own national boundaries, even when rational considerations of cost and quality would make the foreign supplier the better bet.

■ *Technological influences.* The level of technological development available among local suppliers will affect what the buyer can obtain. The technology of the buyer and the seller must also be compatible: in global markets this often presents a problem, since international technical standards remain very different for most products. Despite efforts within the European Union to harmonize technical standards, Europe still does not have standardized electrical fittings, plumbing fittings or even computer keyboards. Many European firms find it easier to trade with former colonies thousands of miles away than deal with countries within the EU, simply because the technical standards of the former colonies are identical with their own.

■ *Economic influences.* The macroeconomic environment is concerned with the level of demand in the economy, and with the current taxation regime within the buyer's country. These conditions affect buyers' ability to buy goods as well as their need to buy in raw materials: if demand for their products is low, the demand for raw materials to manufacture them will also be low. On a more subtle level, the macroeconomic climate affects the buyer's confidence in the same way as it affects consumer confidence. For example, a widespread belief that the national economy is about to go into a decline will almost certainly make buyers reluctant to commit to major investments in stock, equipment and machinery. In a global context, the fact that countries enter and leave recessions at different times will affect the timing of marketing efforts on the part of vendors. At the microeconomic level, a firm experiencing a boom in business will have greater ability to pay for goods and a greater level of confidence.

- *Political and legal influences.* Governments frequently pass laws affecting the way businesses operate, and this is nowhere more true than in international trade. Trade sanctions, trade barriers, specifically non-tariff barriers, preferred-nation status and so forth all affect the ways in which buyers are permitted or encouraged to buy. In some cases, governments specifically help certain domestic businesses as part of an economic growth package. The political stability of countries is also a factor that vendors need to take account of. Laws often lay down specific technical standards, which affect buyer decisions. Buyers may be compelled to incorporate safety features into products, or may be subject to legal restrictions in terms of raw materials. Often, vendors can obtain competitive advantage by anticipating changes in the law.
- *Ethical influences.* In general, buyers are expected to act at all times for the benefit of the organization, not for personal gain. This means that, in most cultures, the buyers are expected not to accept bribes, for example. However, in some cultures bribery is the normal way of doing business, which leaves the vendor with a major ethical problem – refusing to give a bribe is likely to lose the business, but giving a bribe is probably unethical or illegal in the company's home country, especially now that the OECD Anti-Bribery Convention has been widely adopted. As a general rule, buyers are likely to be highly suspicious of doing business with a salesperson who they perceive as acting unethically – after all, if the salesperson is prepared to cheat on his or her employer, he or she cannot be trusted not to cheat on the buyer.
- *Cultural influences.* Culture establishes the values, attitudes, customary behavior, language, religion, and art of a given group of people. When dealing internationally, cultural influences come to the forefront: in the UK it might be customary to offer a visitor a cup of tea or coffee, whereas in China it might be customary to offer food. Dim Sum originated as a way for Chinese businessmen to offer their visitors a symbolic meal, as a way of establishing rapport. Beyond the national culture is the corporate culture, sometimes defined as "the way we do things round here." Corporate culture encompasses the strategic vision of the organization, its ethical stance, and its attitudes toward suppliers among other things. In addition, many businesspeople act in accordance with their professional culture as well (Terpstra and David, 1991). Each of these will affect the way business is done.

Organizational factors derive from the corporate culture, as well as from the strategic decisions made by senior management within the firm. Organizational policies, procedures, structure, systems of rewards, authority, status, and communication systems will all affect the ways buyers relate to salespeople. Figure 2.2 shows the main categories of organizational influences on buyers' behavior.

Buying tasks differ greatly between firms, but may also differ significantly within firms. For example, the buying task for a supermarket clearly differs from that for a manufacturing company, since the supermarket intends to sell on the vast majority of its purchases unchanged whereas the manufacturer is largely concerned with sourcing components and raw materials. Within this generalized structure the supermarket has other variations in the buying task: the buyer's approach to buying canned goods will be totally different from the approach used to buy fresh produce such as vegetables or fresh fish. Equally, the manufacturer will have a different approach when buying basic raw materials vs. buying components, and a different approach again when buying lubricating oil or business services or new factory premises. The purchasing tasks will affect the buyer's thinking and negotiating approach, usually so seriously that firms will have separate buyers for each type of buying task.

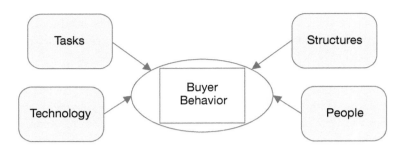

FIGURE 2.2 Organizational influences on buyer behavior

The structure of the organization falls into two categories: the formal structure, which is what shows on the organization chart, and the informal structure, which is actually what dictates staff behavior in most cases. The informal structure is the network of social obligations, friendships, and internal liaisons which influence day-to-day behavior. The formal organization structure determines such issues as the degree of centralization in purchasing decision-making, the degree to which buying decisions follow a formal procedure (i.e. how constrained by the rules the buyers are), and the degree of specialization in buying for different purposes or different departments in the organization. The informal structure dictates such issues as rivalry between buyers, "brownie points" (recognition by management for jobs done well), cooperation between buyers in maintaining each other's status in the eyes of the boss, and so forth. The maze of informal relationships can be extremely complex, especially for a salesperson observing it from the outside, but often forms a key element in the success or failure of key-account selling. In the global context, the informal structure is subject to many cultural influences – the Oriental concern with gaining or losing face, for example, can be a crucial factor in doing business. The informal structure is also important in determining who will be the influencers in the decision-making unit; some colleagues' opinions may be regarded as more trustworthy than others, for example.

The technology within the organization may act to control or circumvent much of the buyer's role. For example, computer-controlled stock purchasing, particularly in a just-in-time purchasing environment, will prevent buyers from being able to negotiate deals and in many cases removes the buyer from the process altogether. Models for inventory control and price forecasting are also widely used by buyers, so that in many cases the negotiating process is virtually automated with little room for maneuver on the part of the buyer. In these circumstances the selling organization needs to go beyond the buyer to the other members of the DMU in order to work around the rules.

The characteristics of the people involved in the organization will, in part, determine the organization culture, but will in any event control the interpretation of the rules under which the purchasing department operates. At senior management level, the character of the organization is likely to be a function of the senior management, and in many cases the organization's founder will have set his or her personality firmly on the organization's culture. Virgin is clearly an offshoot of Richard Branson's personality, as Bodyshop is an offshoot of Anita Roddick's.

Talking Point

We frequently hear about the global village, and about the convergence of cultures, and about a new world order in which we accept and understand each other's cultures. So why is it necessary to consider cultural issues when we are marketing products and services? Surely the goods themselves speak for themselves – does crude oil have a cultural value, or does a stamp mill have a cultural connotation?

Shouldn't buyers be prepared to accept and understand cultural differences? Otherwise how are we to do business? Or perhaps the buyers arrogantly believe that the sellers should adapt their approach to meet the buyers' culture – thus possibly missing out on getting the best deals for their organizations.

If we get clashes between corporate cultures within the same country, how much worse will the clashes be in globalized markets?

CLASSIFYING BUSINESS CUSTOMERS

A business customer is one who is buying on behalf of an organization rather than buying for personal or family consumption. For the purposes of discussion, we usually talk about organizations as the purchasers of goods, but of course this is not the case: business customers, in practice, are human beings who buy on behalf of organizations.

Organizations might be classified according to the types of buying and end-use they have for the products. Table 2.1 shows the commonly accepted classifications.

Business and commercial organizations

Business and commercial organizations can be segmented as original-equipment manufacturers (OEMs), users and aftermarket customers. OEMs buy foundation, entering and facilitating goods including machinery and equipment used to make products and which are incorporated directly into the final product. For example, computer manufacturers may buy machine tools to make computer cases and also buy silicon chips from specialist producers: the chips are incorporated into the final product, but the same type of chip might be incorporated into computers from several different OEMs. The Intel icore7 chip is an example.

For OEM buyers, the key issue will be the quality of the products or services. Such buyers are usually operating to fairly exact specifications laid down by their own production engineers and designers: it is unlikely that the supplying firm will be able to do very much to have the specification changed. This means that introducing a new product to an OEM will be a lengthy process, since the supplying company will need to establish a long-term relationship with the customer in order to become involved at the design stage for the new products.

User customers buy products, which are used up within the organization, either as components in their own equipment or to make the equipment perform properly, for example lubricating oils

TABLE 2.1 Classification of buying organizations

Type of organization	Description
Business and commercial organizations	These organizations buy goods, which are used to make other goods and those that are consumed in the course of running the organization's business. These organizations buy foundation goods and services used to make other products, facilitating goods and services, which help an organization achieve its objectives, and entering goods and services, which become part of another product.
Reseller organizations	Resellers buy goods in order to sell them on to other organizations or to final consumers. Typically, resellers will be wholesalers or retailers, but they may also be agents for services, for example travel agents or webmasters who act as facilitators for other firms.
Governmental organizations	Governments buy everything from paperclips to aircraft carriers through their various departments. Because national and local government departments operate under specific rules, a different approach from that for businesses is usually required.
Institutional organizations	Institutional organizations include charities, educational establishments, hospitals and other organizations that do not fit into the business, reseller or government categories. These organizations may buy any of the products but they are used to achieve institutional goals, usually to provide services.

or cleaning products. These products are not resold, but may be bought in considerable quantities. Obviously some of these are service products – accountancy or legal services, cleaning services, maintenance or building services are all contained within the firm and not resold.

Aftermarket customers are those involved in the maintaining, repairing and overhauling (MRO) of products after they have been sold. For example, in the elevator business, independent contractors not affiliated with the original manufacturer perform most MRO. These contractors buy the components, supplies and services they need wherever they can find them.

The classification split between OEM, users and aftermarket customers is only relevant to the supplier. OEMs can also be user customers for some suppliers. For example, a plastic molding company may sell components to an OEM and plastic tools to a user as well as plastic replacement parts to an aftermarket organization: in some cases these may even be the same organization. Buying motivations for each type of purchase are clearly very different.

Reseller organizations

The majority of manufactured goods are sold through reseller organizations such as retailers and wholesalers. Intermediaries provide useful services such as bulk breaking, assortment of goods, and accumulation of associated product types: due to increased efficiencies resulting from these services, intermediaries tend to reduce overall prices for the final consumer. Cutting out the middleman usually reduces efficiency and tends to increase prices as a result; although there is a popular view that disintermediation reduces prices by cutting out the intermediaries' mark-ups.

Reseller organizations are driven almost entirely by their customers. This means that they will only buy products which they perceive to have a ready market: there is therefore a premium on employing buyers who have a clear understanding of marketing. Unlike the OEM buyers, there is little need for resellers to understand the technical aspects of the products they buy – they merely need to feel confident that the ultimate consumers will want the products.

Reseller organizations carry out the following basic functions:

- negotiations with suppliers;
- promotional activities such as advertising, sales promotion, providing a salesforce, etc.;
- warehousing, storage and product handling;
- transportation of local and (occasionally) long-distance shipments;
- inventory control;
- credit checking and credit control;
- pricing and collection of price information, particularly about competitors;
- collection of market information about consumers and competitors.

For manufacturers, this places a premium on establishing close long-term relationships with resellers. Shared information, as part of an integrated channel management strategy, becomes crucial to forward planning.

Government organizations

Government and quasi-government organizations are major buyers of almost everything. In some markets, the government is heavily involved in industry. For instance, all insurance in India has been a government monopoly and the oil industry in Mexico is controlled by PEMEX, a quasi-government entity. Governments are thought to be the largest category of market in the world, if all levels of government are included in the equation. The structure of government varies from one country to another: for example, in Spain there is the national government based in Madrid, the regional governments (e.g. the Junta de Andalucia), the provincial governments (e.g. Provincia de Granada) and the local town halls (e.g. Ayuntamiento de Ugijar). Sometimes these local town halls group together to form an alliance which carries out mutually-beneficial activities such as tourism marketing or funding a local swimming-pool, but frequently they act independently of one another within the frameworks of their own jurisdictions.

Because of the strict rules under which most government organizations operate, special measures are often needed to negotiate deals. In particular, government organizations are characterized by the tendering system, in which firms are asked to bid for contracts, which are then usually offered to the lowest bidder. From a supplier's viewpoint, this can be seriously counterproductive since the lowest price is likely to be also the least profitable price, so selling firms will often try to circumvent the process by ensuring that they become involved before the tender is finalized. In this way it is often possible to ensure that the tender is drawn up in a way that favors the proactive firm over its competitors, thus ensuring that competitors either do not bid at all, or bid at too high a price.

In some cases, governments need to purchase items which are not available to the general public or to other businesses. Military hardware is an obvious example: clearly ordinary businesses are not allowed to buy tanks or fighter planes. On a more subtle level, goods such as handguns are not permitted for private organizations in the UK, but can be sold to the Army or the police force. Some types of computer software are only appropriate for use by the tax authorities, and academic research is, in general, paid for entirely by the government in the UK. From a marketing viewpoint, these specialist markets present an interesting challenge, since in some cases the products need to be tailored to a specific government or a specific government department. This may mean that there is considerable scope for negotiation, but since the contract might still have to go out to tender, the company may find that it has merely wasted time unless it can demonstrate that no other company can carry out the work.

In some circumstances, governments may issue a "cost-plus" contract, in which the organization is given a specific task to carry out, and bills according to the cost of the contract plus an agreed profit margin. In the early days of space research this type of contract was common, since it was impossible to predict what the costs might be when dealing with an unknown set of circumstances. More recently these contracts have fallen into disrepute since they reward inefficiency and waste.

Institutional organizations

Institutions include charities, universities, hospital trusts, schools, and non-profit organizations of all types, and so forth. In some cases these are government-owned but independent for purposes of purchasing and supply (for example, secondary schools), in other cases they are totally independent (for example, registered charities). The traditional view of these organizations is that they are chronically under-funded and therefore do not represent a particularly munificent market, but in practice the organizations actually have a very substantial aggregate spending power.

Because budgets are almost always very tight, the marketing organization may need to be creative in helping the institution to raise the money to buy. For example, a firm which produces drilling equipment may find that it has a substantial market at Oxfam, since Oxfam drills wells in many arid regions of the Developing World. Oxfam relies on public generosity to raise the money to buy

---

Talking Point

We are often told that marketing is about managing the exchange process, yet government departments and many institutions seem to lay down the ground rules from the start. Marketers have to play by the buyer's rules to be in the game at all – so how can they possibly be managing the process? Pushed from one set of constraints to the next, it would seem that the average marketer is just a pawn in the buyers' hands!

Yet maybe that is how it should be, if customers are at the center of everything we do. Not to mention that the management process itself could be construed as a clearing-house for pressures rather than as a directive force – in a sense, no manager is actually in control, so why should marketers be any different?

the equipment, so the manufacturer may find it necessary to part-fund or even manage a fundraising campaign in order to make the sale.

Suppliers are often asked to contribute to charities, in cash or in products. This may not always be possible, since the supplier's only market might be the charities, but in some cases firms may find it worthwhile to supply free products to charities in order to gain PR value, or sometimes in order to open the door to lucrative deals with other organizations. For example, a Developing World charity might be prepared to field-test equipment which could then be sold to a government department in the same country.

BUYERS' TECHNIQUES

Buyers use a wide variety of techniques according to the buying situation they are faced with. The buying situations are generally divided into three types:

1   Straight re-buy. This is a situation where the buyer is buying the same product in very much the same quantities from the same supplier. For example, an engineering company might buy the same quantity of components from its suppliers each month. In these circumstances the buyer needs no new information, and does not need to engage in much negotiation either. Prudent buyers may occasionally look at other possible sources of components in order to ensure that no new technology is available or that other suppliers are not able to supply the same components more cheaply, but in general the order placement is automatic. In many cases the buyer establishes an electronic data interchange (EDI) link with a supplier or establishes automatic buying procedures through the Internet and orders are handled without any human interface. If the product is of minor importance, or represents a low commitment in terms of finance or risk, the buyer will not undertake any information search and will probably simply order the goods. This is called causal purchasing, because it results automatically from a cause such as low stock level. For example, a buyer for a large engineering firm probably spends very little time deciding on brands of paper for the photocopier. On the other hand, buying copper cable might be a routine purchase, but the buyer might monitor the market for alternatives occasionally. Such buying is called routine low-priority buying because it has a lower priority than would be the case if an entirely new situation were being faced. The company is unlikely to get into serious trouble if it pays 10 percent more than it should for cable, for example.

2   Modified re-buy. In this situation, the buyer re-evaluates the habitual buying patterns of the firm with a view to changing them in some way. The quantities ordered, or the specification of the components, may be changed. Even the supplier may be changed. Sometimes these changes come about as a result of environmental scanning, in which the buyer has become aware of a better alternative than the one currently employed, or sometimes the changes come about because of marketing activities by the current suppliers' competitors. Internal forces (increases or decreases in demand for components) might trigger a renegotiation with suppliers or a search for new suppliers. In any event, the buyer is faced with a limited problem-solving scenario in which he or she will need to carry out some negotiation with existing or new suppliers, and will probably need to seek out new information as well. In a modified re-buy situation a buyer

may well require potential suppliers to bid against each other for the business: the drawback of this approach, however, is that it often results in damaging the relationship with existing suppliers that may have been built up over many years.

3 New task. This type of buying situation comes about when the task is perceived as being entirely new. Past experience is therefore no guide, and present suppliers may not be able to help either. Thus the buyer is faced with a complex decision process. Judgemental new task situations are those in which the buyer must deal with technical complexities of the product, complex evaluation of alternatives, and negotiating with new suppliers. Strategic new task situations are those in which the final decision is of strategic importance to the firm – for example, an insurance company in the market for new record-keeping software will be investing (potentially) hundreds of thousands of pounds in retraining staff, and in transferring existing records, not to mention the risks of buying software which is unable to cope with the tasks it is required to carry out. In these circumstances, long-range planning at director level drives the buying process, and the relationship with the suppliers is likely to be both long-term and close.

From the viewpoint of the business marketer, the main chance of winning new customers will come in the new-task situation. The risks for buyers involved in switching suppliers are often too great unless there is a very real and clear advantage in doing so: such an advantage is likely to be difficult to prove in practice. In the new task situation, potential suppliers may well find themselves screened out early in the process, and will then find it almost impossible to be reconsidered later.

THE BUYGRID FRAMEWORK

Organizational buying can be seen as a series of decisions, each of which leads to a further problem about which a decision must be made (Cardozo, 1983). From the viewpoint of the business marketer, it is possible to diagnose problems by examining the sequence of decisions – provided, of course, the decision sequence is known to the marketer. Marketers can identify the stage at which the firm is currently making decisions, and can tailor the approach accordingly.

The industrial buying process can be mapped against a grid, as shown in Figure 2.3.

The most complex buying situations occur in the upper left portion of the framework and involve the largest number of decision makers and buying influences. This is because new tasks require the greatest amount of effort in seeking information and formulating appropriate solutions, but will also require the greatest involvement of individuals at all levels of the organization, each of whom will have his or her own agenda.

The buygrid framework has been widely criticized, however. Like most models it tends to over-simplify the case. As in consumer decision-making, the sequence may not be as clear-cut and events may take place in a different order in certain circumstances. For example, a supplier might approach a firm with a solution for a problem which it didn't know it had, thus cutting out several stages of the process: the firm may well recognize the need and the problem, but will probably not need to acquire proposals and select a supplier since the supplier is already on board with a solution. Second, suppliers go to great lengths to differentiate themselves from competitors as effectively as they can,

	Buying Situations		
Stage	**New task**	**Modified Rebuy**	**Straight Rebuy**
Anticipation or recognition of a problem (need) and a general solution			
Determination of characteristics and quantity of needed item			
Description of characteristics and quantity of needed item			
Search for and qualification of potential sources			
Acquisition and analysis of proposals			
Evaluation of proposals and selection of supplier(s)			
Selection of an order routine			
Performance feedback and evaluation			

FIGURE 2.3 The buygrid framework

Source: adapted from the Marketing Science Institute Series, "Industrial Buying and Creative Marketing," by Patrick J. Robinson, Charles W. Faris, and Yoram Wind. Copyright 1967 by Allyn and Bacon, Boston.

so that the buyer may not have any other potential suppliers of the exact product on offer. Third, the model assumes a rational approach to purchasing which is often simply not there. Finally, the boundaries between new task, modified re-buy and straight re-buy are by no means clear-cut.

Because buyers are influenced by both rational and emotional considerations, the potential supplier needs to be aware of the buying motives of each member of the decision-making unit. What is more, each member of the DMU will apply different criteria for judging which suppliers should be included and which excluded (Kelly and Coaker, 1976): the finance director might emphasize low prices, whereas the chief designer might be concerned with product quality, and the production engineer with reliable delivery. The buyer might be concerned with the relationship with the supplier's sales people.

In the case of key-account management, this problem of dealing with different members of the DMU is often overcome by taking a team approach to the sale. While the key-account manager handles the initial contact and the management of the process, other specialists are brought in to deal with financial aspects, technical aspects, and so forth. In this way each member of the DMU is speaking to someone with whom he or she has a common language and a common understanding of the conceptual environment within which each specialty operates. In some cases the number of people working on the account can become large: when IBM were dealing with Lloyd's Bank (one of the Big Four UK banks) they had over 100 people working on the account, and set up a special branch office in the Canary Wharf area to be near Lloyd's head office.

VALUE ANALYSIS

Value analysis is a method of evaluating components, raw materials and even manufacturing processes in order to determine ways of cutting costs or improving finished products. Value-in-use is defined as a product's economic value to the user relative to a specific alternative in a particular application (Kijewski and Yoon, 1990). Value-in-use is the price that would equalize the overall costs and benefits of using one product rather than using another.

For example, consider long-life light bulbs. These bulbs are usually between five and ten times as expensive as ordinary tungsten-filament bulbs to buy, but last five times as long and use only 20 percent of the electricity. For a domestic consumer, this represents a considerable saving, more than enough to cover the initial outlay for the bulbs, but for a business customer the saving is even greater, since the cost of paying someone to replace the bulbs is significant. Assuming the life of a tungsten-filament bulb as being 1,000 hours on average, compared with 5,000 hours for a long-life bulb, the calculation would run as seen in Table 2.2.

Using this calculation, the company can make an immediate saving of just under £1,400 a year by switching to long-life bulbs. In fact, the capital cost of changing all the bulbs in the building would be recovered in the first year, although in practice the firm would probably only replace the tungsten-filament bulbs as they fail in use: in this way the labor cost of replacing the bulbs would be no higher than normal.

Because some buyers do use this type of calculation to assess alternative solutions to existing problems, the astute marketer will be prepared with the full arguments in favor of the new solution,

TABLE 2.2 Long-life bulb vs. tungsten-filament bulb	
1. Annual cost of existing product:	
250 replacement light bulbs x 45p	£112.50
Cost of electricity: @ 6.7p per kilowatt x 60 watts x 150 bulbs x 2,400 hours:	£1,447.20
Cost of replacing bulbs assuming 10 minutes per bulb @ £10 per hour:	£416.00
TOTAL COST PER ANNUM:	**£1,975.70**
2. Cost of using long-life bulbs:	
50 replacement bulbs per annum x £5 =	£250.00
Cost of electricity: @ 6.7p per kilowatt x 11 watts x 150 bulbs x 2,400 hours:	£ 265.32
Cost of replacing bulbs assuming 10 minutes per bulb @ £10 per hour =	£83.20
TOTAL COST PER ANNUM:	**£598.52**

TABLE 2.3 Assessing suppliers

Attribute	Assessment method
Technical capability	Visit the supplier to examine production equipment, inspect quality control procedures, and meet the engineering staff.
Managerial capability	Discuss systems for controlling processes, meet the managerial staff, and become involved in planning and scheduling supplies.
Financial stability	Check the accounts filed at Companies House or the SEC, or other public record office, run a credit check, examine annual reports if any.
Capacity to deliver	Ascertain the status of other customers of the supplier – would any of these take priority? Assess the production capacity of the supplier, warehouse stocks of the product, reputation in the industry.

including all the relevant factors, which make the product more attractive. On the other side of the coin, astute purchasers will involve potential suppliers in the discussions and in the value analysis process (Dowst and Raia, 1990).

EVALUATING SUPPLIER CAPABILITY

Purchasers also need to assess the capability of potential suppliers to continue to supply successfully. This is a combination of assessing financial stability, technical expertise, reliability, quality assurance processes, and production capacity. In simple terms, the purchasing company is trying to ensure that the potential supplier will be in a position to keep the promises it makes.

Table 2.3 illustrates some of the ways in which buyers can assess potential suppliers.

Whilst these methods are better than nothing, in most cases they rely on judgement on the part of the purchaser, who may not in fact have the necessary expertise to understand what the supplier's capability really is.

EVALUATING SUPPLIER PERFORMANCE

Even after the contract is awarded, the purchasing company is likely to need to review the supplier's performance periodically. In some cases, suppliers have been known to relax once the contract is awarded, and of course the circumstances of the buying organization are likely to change considerably in the course of what will be a lengthy relationship.

The basic evaluation methods are as outlined in Table 2.4.

All of these methods involve some degree of subjectivity; in other words each method requires buyers to make judgements about the supplier. The fact that the outcomes are expressed in numbers gives each method a spurious credibility: those involved in evaluation exercises of this nature should be aware that the evaluation exercise itself should be evaluated periodically, and the criteria used by the various individuals involved need to be checked.

Talking Point

The methods of assessment shown in the table all rely on some kind of judgement on the part of the buyer. Even the financial figures filed at the company record office require interpretation – and may even have been "massaged" to make the company look more financially viable than it actually is.

So why bother with what is, after all, a somewhat time-consuming exercise? Presumably a rogue supplier would have little difficulty in pulling the wool over the eyes of a buyer who probably lacks the engineering training to understand what is in front of him or her. On the other hand, an honest supplier would probably provide the "warts and all" picture that might well lose the contract. Maybe buyers would be better advised to go for the supplier who looks the worst – at least we know they are being honest with us!

TABLE 2.4 Evaluation approaches

Approach	Explanation
Categorical plan	Each department having contact with the supplier is asked to provide a regular rating of suppliers against a list of salient performance factors. This method is extremely subjective, but is easy to administer.
Weighted-point plan	Performance factors are graded according to their importance to the organization: for example, delivery reliability might be more important for some organizations than for others. The supplier's total rating can be calculated and the supplier's offering can be adjusted if necessary to meet the purchasing organization's needs.
Cost-ratio plan	Here the buying organization evaluates quality, delivery and service in terms of what each one costs. Good performance is assigned a negative score, i.e. the costs of purchase are reduced by good performance: poor performance is assigned a positive score, meaning that the costs are deemed to be greater when dealing with a poor performer.

Talking Point

Much of the emphasis in the preceding sections has been on the purchaser's evaluation of suppliers. But what about the other way round? Customers are not always plaster saints – some are late payers, some impose unreasonable restrictions, some reject supplies for the flimsiest of reasons, and some are just plain unpleasant to deal with.

So should suppliers have their own systems for assessing purchasers? Should we just grovel at the feet of any organization willing to buy our goods – or should we stand up and be counted? After all, without supplies no company can survive – so presumably we are equally important to one another.

Maybe this is really the purpose of segmenting our markets – and what is really meant by segmentation.

CASE STUDY

New ERP System

A large public university with more than 20 locations throughout a major city currently has nearly 100 different computer and software systems to manage functions such as student registration, billing and collections, purchasing, human resources and payroll. Some of these systems run on "legacy" mainframe computers while others can be accessed on personal computers throughout the university. The university has appointed a new Chancellor, Dr Lijuan Zhang, and she believes this is an area where huge savings might be realized. While she is no computer expert, Dr Zhang has read extensively about ERP systems and found a definition online – "enterprise resource planning (ERP) systems integrate internal and external management information across an entire organization." Major ERP system components include a central database that stores and manages the key information of the institution. It should also include report generators, and analytical tools. From her discussions with other administrators in large organizations it seems like this new system might cost as much as $500 million. Therefore she feels it will be important to involve all interested people to be sure that they feel involved in the decision.

During the past three years local and national governments have been cutting back on their expenditures for education. Tax revenues have been lower and legislatures have been less willing to appropriate funds or to raise tax rates. Just recently the press has been reporting that some students who are not citizens are attending classes and realizing the benefits that normally go to those who live in the city. This has focused more attention on university policies and procedures. Because the university is a public institution it has established strict ethical rules – no employee is permitted to receive anything of value from a potential supplier.

Since the university is a very large organization with more than 200,000 students, she also has a significant staff to help her. This includes a large Management Information

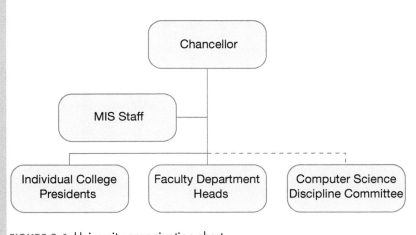

FIGURE 2.4 University organization chart

. . . continued

CASE STUDY ... *continued*

Systems Department who would probably take the lead in this kind of change. Dr Zhang understands that implementing a new ERP system will require major changes throughout the entire institution. The university has many component divisions, including each individual college and cross-college discipline committees. Naturally the Computer Science Departments in each college would want to have a say in any decision related to changing computer systems. A simple organizational chart is presented below. Since this is a university organization it is important to note that the faculty enjoy a high level of independence from both the individual college presidents and the Chancellor of the entire university.

Zhang has found from her reading that acquiring a new ERP is extremely complex. Especially important is the formation of the acquisition team. According to experts (Verville et al., 2007), the team should be multi-disciplinary. The head of this team may be chosen from inside or outside the organization and must be a strong leader. A steering committee consisting of senior level individuals should be selected from the acquisition team. Two of the major firms that provide ERP systems are Oracle and SAP. Assume that you are the director of marketing for the education division of SAP. Of course you see this as a very large potential client. The university will not only make a very large initial purchase but continue an ongoing relationship for the foreseeable future.

CASE STUDY QUESTIONS

1 How will the political environment affect the purchasing process?
2 Who might be included in the decision-making unit (DMU)?
3 Who would be the influencers, deciders, buyers, gatekeepers and users in the DMU?
4 Briefly describe how the environmental influences might come into play in the university buying decision?
5 How might the DMU go about evaluating your firm as a potential supplier?

CHAPTER SUMMARY

Buyers have a large number of influences on their decision-making. At the very least, buyers have their own personal agendas within the companies they work for: in the broader context, a wide range of political, environmental, and technological issues will affect their decision-making. The end result is likely to be a combination of experience, careful calculation, and gut feeling.

The key points from this chapter are as follows:

- Buyers are subject to many pressures other than the simple commercial ones: emotions, organizational influence, politics, and internal structures are also important factors.
- The decision-making unit (DMU) or buying center is the group of people who will make the buying decision. Roles and composition of DMUs vary widely.

■ Business and commercial organizations are likely to be swayed most by past experience with a vendor, product characteristics, and quality.

■ Resellers are driven by their customers.

■ Government markets are large, and almost always use a tendering system.

■ Institutional markets may need special techniques to help them afford to buy the products.

■ Markets can be divided into those buyers who buy products designed to make other products or who will incorporate the purchase into their own products (original-equipment manufacturers); those who consume the product in the course of running their businesses (user markets); or those who serve the aftermarket.

■ A purchase may be a straight re-buy, a modified re-buy, or a new task. These are given in order of increasing complexity, and do not have discrete boundaries.

■ A team approach to buying usually dictates a team approach to selling.

REVIEW QUESTIONS

1 How would you expect a government department to go about buying a new computer system?

2 How might internal politics affect a buyer's behavior?

3 What factors might be prominent in the buying decision for cleaning materials?

4 What factors might a supplier take into account when evaluating a purchasing company?

5 How might the directors of a company go about setting standards for evaluating suppliers? What objective criteria are available?

REFERENCES

Cardozo, Richard N. (1983). "Modelling organisational buying as a sequence of decisions." *Industrial Marketing Management*, Vol. 12, Iss. 2 (Feb.), 75.

Dowst, S. and Raia, E. (1990). "Teaming up for the 90s." *Purchasing*, Vol. 108, No. 2 (Feb.), 54–9.

Hawes, J.M. and Barnhouse, S.H. (1987). "How purchasing agents handle personal risk." *Industrial Marketing Management*, Vol. 16, No. 4, 287–93.

Kelly, P. and Coaker, J.W. (1976). "Can we generalise about choice criteria for industrial purchasing decisions?" in Bernhardt, K.L. (ed.), *Marketing 1776–1976 and Beyond*. Chicago: American Marketing Association, pp. 330–3.

Kijewski, V. and Yoon, E. (1990). "Market-based pricing: beyond price-performance curves." *Industrial Marketing Management*, Vol. 19, No. 1 (Feb.), 11–19.

Loudon, David L. and Della Bitta, Albert J. (1993). *Consumer Behavior: Concepts and Applications*. New York: McGraw Hill.

Ronchetto, John R., Jr., Hutt, Michael D., and Reingen, Peter H. (1989). "Embedded Influence Patterns in Organizational Buying Systems." *Journal of Marketing*, Vol. 53, Iss. 4, 51–62.

Terpstra, Vern and David, Kenneth (1991). *The Cultural Environment of International Business*. Cincinnati, OH: South-Western Publishing Company.

Verville, Jacques, Palanisaimy, Ramaraj, Bernadas, Christine, and Halington, Alannah (2007). "ERP Acquisition Planning: a Critical Dimension for Making the Right Choice." *Long Range Planning*, Vol. 40, Iss. 1, 45–63.

Webster, F.E. and Wind, Y. (1972). *Organisational Buying Behaviour*. Englewood Cliffs, NJ: Prentice Hall.

Chapter 3

Strategic planning for global business markets

INTRODUCTION

Strategy is concerned with moving the organization from where it is now to where we would like it to be. It is the business process concerned with planning the long-range activities, character, and underlying values of the organization.

Strategy differs from tactics in that strategic decisions are far more difficult to reverse, they usually involve the decision-makers in rejecting other options, and they tend to dictate the long-term nature of the organization as well as its activities.

CHAPTER OBJECTIVES

After reading this chapter, you should be able to:

- explain the main dimensions of strategy as they apply in B2B markets
- describe various approaches to strategy
- explain the importance of the planning process
- explain the relationship between strategy and tactics
- describe ways of developing competitive advantage in a rapidly-changing global economy.

STRATEGIC PLANNING PROCESS

Strategic planning starts with the firm's full understanding of the business it participates in. No better approach has been developed than that offered by Peter Drucker (1973). Drucker advised businesses to ask three basic and two sub-questions:

- What is our business?
    - Who is the customer?
    - What is value to the customer?
- What will our business be?
- What should our business be?

Asking "what is our business?" is the way to get to the firm's vision and business mission and two of the most important questions in determining the answer to that first question are "who is the customer?" and second, "what is value to the customer?" These we have shown in later steps of the strategic planning process (choice of segments). Answering the question "what will our business be?" means to project the current trends and business practices into the future with no change – how will the business look if it keeps operating the same way for years into the future? The third question is where strategic planning really takes place. In this case, management thinks about what the business should look like and what changes need to be made so that the business will be addressing the proper markets with the proper products and services at a future time.

Figure 3.1 shows an overview of the strategic planning process.

MISSION, VISION AND OBJECTIVES

All organizations need to coordinate the attitudes and activities of staff. In order to do this, most firms try to develop a corporate culture in which the overall strategic direction of the organization is the driving force. This strategic direction is most often communicated via a corporate vision, a corporate mission, and corporate objectives. Some firms have only one of these: some have all of them. They are not mutually exclusive, in other words.

Vision is the management's view of what the organization should be. Often the vision comes from the founder of the organization: charismatic individuals such as Anita Roddick of Body Shop, Richard Branson of Virgin, and Steve Jobs of Apple imprinted their personalities on the companies they founded. Everyone within those companies shares the corporate vision, at least in some degree, and understands the intended "personality" of the organization – it is not necessary to produce a vision statement, although many firms do this.

The lack of a vision statement does not mean that there is no vision. The characteristics of an organization can be very clear to its members without having anything at all in writing. One of the difficulties faced by companies led by visionaries such as Roddick or Branson is that there is a lack of continuity. As we have seen in the case of Body Shop, if the founder leaves, retires or dies the company can easily lose its way.

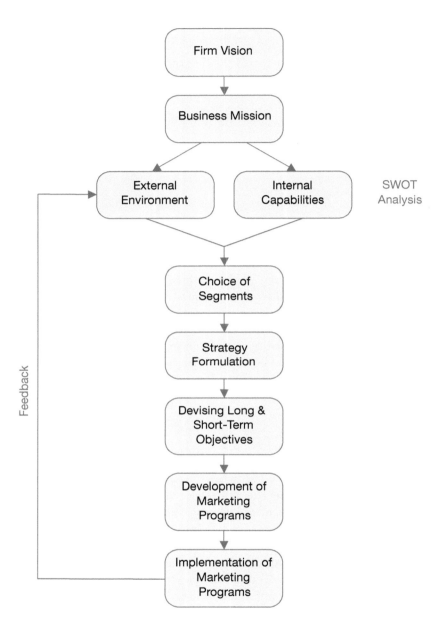

FIGURE 3.1 Strategic planning process

The corporate mission is the overriding reason for the organization's existence. It is the purpose of the organization. The mission statement is the formal document which outlines the reasons for the organization's existence, but frequently it is no more than a set of corporate platitudes which do little to inform staff, customers, and other stakeholders of what the organization is about.

A corporate mission statement has five characteristics (Ackoff, 1986):

- It contains a formulation of objectives that enables progress toward them to be measured.
- It differentiates the company from its competitors.
- It defines the businesses that the company wants to be in, not necessarily the ones it is already in.
- It is relevant to the stakeholders in the organization, not just to shareholders and managers.
- It is exciting and inspiring.

Mission statements must reflect corporate values in order to be of use in coordinating corporate activities (Campbell, 1989). Campbell goes on to argue that there are four key issues involved in developing a useful mission:

- Clarification of the purpose of the organization. Is it the organization's purpose to maximize shareholder value – or is the purpose to (for example) develop a worldwide network?
- Description of the business and its activities, and the position it wants to occupy in its field. For example, the business might want to "offer supreme value for money" or "be the industry leader in quality engineering."
- Statement of the corporate values. This would include the company's intentions toward its employees, customers, and suppliers.
- Organizational behavior should be controlled in such a way as to match with the mission statement. If this is not the case, the mission becomes mere empty rhetoric – it would be better to amend the mission statement to reflect actual behavior than to have a mission statement which does not match outcomes.

Cochran et al., (2008) add that mission statements should be tested for readability, connotative meanings and applicability. For readability, they suggest reviewing the number of words and sentences and eventually the "fog index." Connotative meanings relate to the emotional response engendered by the mission statement. They offer a questionnaire to be given to managers to measure their feelings generated by any potential mission statement. The applicability analysis means trying out the mission statement to see whether it is practical in particular situations and they suggest the use of mini-cases to measure this.

Examples of good or poor mission statements are easy to find. David and David (2003) found that a majority of the 95 firms they studied did not address several of the nine essential components required of a mission statement. As shown in Table 3.1, IBM's mission statement meets some of the requirements described above while that of a UK firm seems not to.

Mission statements have become an essential part of corporate life in the past 30 years or so. Banks expect companies to have mission statements, staff are often asked to explain how their activities relate to the corporate mission, and mission statements are often found in corporate end-of-year statements as a justification for corporate activities.

TABLE 3.1 Comparing mission statements

IBM company mission	Company mission of UK firm
At IBM, we strive to lead in the invention, development and manufacture of the industry's most advanced information technologies, including computer systems, software, storage systems, and microelectronics. We translate these advanced technologies into value for our customers through our professional solutions, services and consulting businesses worldwide.	To exceed expectations, add value and general prosperity for all stakeholders whilst contributing positively to the development and sustainability of the built and natural environment through the application of technical excellence and innovation.

Talking Point

"If we don't know where we're going, any road will do to take us there." This well-known saying implies that knowing where we want to be allows us to choose a route – yet the analogy with road transport is not a good one. Business life is infinitely more complex than driving between cities: the cities do at least stay in the same places relative to each other, and the roads do not suddenly turn to marshmallow or get taken over by competitors.

So is there really any point in spending much time putting together a mission statement? Can we realistically set out a corporate direction years in advance? And if we make the statement less rigid and therefore much more vague, does it have any value? Striking this balance may be the hardest part of producing a mission statement!

STRATEGY

The definition of strategy continues to be debated among scholars and managers. Some believe strategies are a series of actions and some that strategy cannot be formulated but comes about as a result of reactions to changes in environmental forces. Some believe that strategy should be defined as a plan and some combine the reactions and the plan in their definition. The most useful definition grows out of the thinking expressed by Peter Drucker (1994) nearly 20 years ago. Drucker explained that successful firms develop "the theory of the business." This includes assumptions about the overall environment including the customer and technology, assumptions about the mission of the organization and finally assumptions about core competencies needed to accomplish that mission. Building on this base, Peng (2009) offers a very useful definition of strategy: "a firm's theory about how to compete successfully." This definition allows firms to identify the key aspects of their theory using the SWOT Analysis described below, then develop specific programs and plans to take advantage of their theory.

PLANNING

Going through this process requires looking at both the external environment and the internal capabilities of the firm and performing a SWOT Analysis (strengths, weaknesses, opportunities, threats). The environment must be examined for opportunities and threats while the firm's internal capabilities are looked at for strengths and weaknesses. Here, managers must be entirely honest with themselves so the company's true capabilities can be assessed. The next most important step is the choice of market segments which is covered in depth in Chapter 6. This step is the most important strategic step a manager can take. Next comes strategy formulation, developing objectives, marketing programs, and implementation. A feedback loop must be established so that results can be compared with plans throughout the process.

Objectives are about where the company wants to be. An objective needs to be measurable and specific, however: many corporate objectives are couched in vague terms, perhaps talking about "providing products of the highest quality." This is not measurable, since it is impossible to say what is the highest quality – judgement of this will differ from one person to another. In other words, there is a difference between an aim (which is a general direction and is not measurable) and an objective, which is a destination point and is therefore measurable.

Long-term objectives relate to the desired performance and results on an ongoing basis: short-term objectives relate to the near-term performance targets that the organization desires to reach in progressing toward its long-term objectives (Thompson and Strickland, 1980). Some firms use management by objectives as a way of controlling and directing activities of staff members, but this can lead to a lack of initiative: what is not measured is not managed, and is therefore not done.

The main advantage of setting objectives is that the organization has a clear direction, and also a clear coordinating mechanism. Everyone in the organization either knows what they should be doing to achieve the objective, or can work out what they need to do when faced with new circumstances. The major drawbacks of objectives are first that achieving the immediate objective becomes paramount, at the cost of responding to environmental changes or to the overall direction of the firm, and second the difficulty of finding a new direction once the objective has been achieved. For example, if a firm has the objective of "becoming the world's largest supplier of ball bearings" written into its mission statement, the statement would have to be revisited if the firm actually becomes the world's largest supplier of ball bearings.

Strategy formulation involves three strands: planning, vision, and emergent strategies (incremental changes to the pre-determined plan). The strategy will need to steer a course consistent with the environment within which a firm operates, the firm's resources, and the values of the organization (EVR). The closer this EVR congruence, the more effective the organization will be.

Planning is the process of formulating responses to possible future events. Virtually everyone plans to a greater or lesser extent, and organizations are no exception: predicting the future, however, occurs with varying accuracy, so most plans require a considerable degree of flexibility in order to work successfully. In fact, Dwight Eisenhower once remarked that "plans are nothing, planning is everything." In other words, the process itself is at least as valuable as the output of that process.

Plans can be considered as part of an ongoing learning process within the organization (Idenburg, 1993). It is possible to distinguish between:

- Formal planning systems, through which clear objectives should lead to intended strategies. These systems are best suited to industries where change is slow and the environment is stable.
- Learning or real-time planning, which represents a formal approach to adaptive strategy creation. Regular meetings between managers will occur, in which new responses to environmental changes will be discussed and new strategies formulated.
- Incremental change and logical incrementalism. The organization operates within a clear mission, but with the recognition that there is a need for flexibility. Managers are encouraged to experiment.
- Emergent strategies, in which the organization in effect "muddles through" by reacting to environmental changes as they occur. This mode apparently involves little or no planning, but in fact the organization which follows this approach will have structures in place for coping. For example, an organization which exists in a turbulent environment in which rapid change is endemic is likely to adopt an organismic organization structure, is likely to have recruitment and training policies which allow for rapid shifts in personnel tasks, is likely to have administrative systems which are flexible, and is likely to have enhanced systems for monitoring the environment. Such organizations are therefore not as disorganized as they at first may appear.

Planning within a global environment is, of course, extremely complex because of the near-impossibility of monitoring every aspect of the global environment. Virtually all firms operate in a global context, even those which do not intend to operate outside their own national borders – unless the firm's home country operates in a protectionist manner, the firm is open to competitors entering the market from overseas. This can easily upset the most carefully-laid plans, since the EVR congruence will be lacking in circumstances where the environment has undergone a sudden shift.

Talking Point

It seems as if planning ahead is so difficult it is hardly worth bothering. The world is changing so fast, we can hardly keep pace – so why bother? Why not just take each day as it comes? After all, we can't predict the future – or can we?

And yet many things remain the same. Firms still need the same raw materials as they have for the past hundred years, they still need to produce things and sell things: even in fast-changing areas such as electronics the principles of physics on which circuitry works have not changed. Anybody who reads science fiction could have predicted the cellular telephone (from 1951) the communications satellite (1947) and the rise of conservationism (1950). Maybe what we should be doing is planning around the near-certainties and letting the uncertainties take care of themselves!

COMPETITIVE ADVANTAGE

The purpose of almost any strategy is to create competitive advantage. There are various approaches to this. One is the industry-based approach exemplified by Michael Porter's work (1985). Porter identified three basic competitive strategies.

- Cost leadership. In this strategy, the company minimizes its production, distribution and/or marketing costs so that it can compete on price without sacrificing profits. The low cost approach may be aimed at the entire industry across the world or to a particular segment (either global or local). This means sourcing factors of production from the cheapest possible sources, which may mean moving production to developing countries in order to save costs, or moving production closer to the markets the company serves.
- Differentiation. If the company's products stand out from competitors by being substantially different (from the customer's viewpoint) the firm is able to charge a premium. The firm may concentrate on differentiation across the entire industry or in just one segment. This relies on having strong segmentation and targeting strategies.
- Focus. Here the company concentrates on a few tightly-defined market segments, with low cost or differentiation strategies, avoiding the temptation to try to please everybody. Sometimes these markets are exclusive in the sense of involving very expensive or highly-technical products. For example, Novo Nordisk of Denmark specializes in producing industrial enzymes. Alternatively, the firm might provide for a given customer type – Wild Well Control Inc. of Texas specializes entirely in putting out oil-well fires.

According to Porter, the least effective approach is to try to be both a low cost and differentiated firm, which results in a firm being "stuck in the middle."

This approach has been criticized on several bases: however, the main problem is precisely defining an industry. A clear example is the photographic industry. Traditionally a firm like Kodak could place itself squarely in the photography industry and know exactly what that meant. Now we see camera manufacturers competing with firms in the mobile phone and electronics industries. Google, which dominates the Internet search industry, moved quickly into mobile communications when they believed phones would be the new vehicle for accessing the Internet. Kodak's failure to adapt to the market led directly to the company seeking Chapter 11 protection from its creditors in 2012, as a way of staving off bankruptcy while the company re-invented itself.

Another approach to strategy is based on company resources. This approach is based heavily on value chain analysis.

VALUE CHAIN ANALYSIS

Organizations operate by adding value to their inputs in order to create wealth. The outputs of a firm should be more valuable than the inputs, or there is really no point in carrying out the activities, and equally there is unlikely to be much chance for the firm to survive in the long run. This applies equally to non-profit organizations and even governments: a government which does not spend tax money in such a way as to improve the lives of its electorate is quickly voted out of office. Likewise a charity which does not contribute anything worthwhile to the community will find that its contributions from the public rapidly dry up.

Value creation will only happen if the suppliers, producers, wholesalers, retailers, and indeed everyone involved in moving from raw materials extraction through to consumers can cooperate in an effective manner. Along the way the basic raw materials acquire market values much greater than their original cost: crude oil extracted for $100 a barrel becomes plastic items worth 50 or 100 times as much, for example. Negotiation is the mechanism by which this wealth is divided amongst the various organizations involved.

The implications of this are as follows:

■ Value creation requires cooperation from all the members of the value chain. Whether this comes about through negotiated coordination of activities or through market forces does not matter: the organizations rely on each other either way.
■ Those in the chain must consider the needs of other chain members if the process is to work to mutual advantage.
■ Cost improvement and efficiency improvements will benefit everyone in the chain in the long run, but most especially will benefit the individual member because there is no need to renegotiate with other members in order to reap the benefits.
■ There is therefore a premium on managing the value chain within the firm itself.
■ There is a fundamental reliance on the contribution of people.

Within the firm, the basic structure of the value chain is as shown in Table 3.2 (Porter, 1985).

Each of the activities in the value chain might lead to competitive advantage. In some firms, it is only the marketing that really distinguishes the product: for example, lubricating oil is produced to standards laid down by engine manufacturers, so a trucking company will need to buy oil of a specific standard. All the oil companies supply oil to the same standard, so the only real difference is going to lie in the marketing of the product. In other firms, the reliability of the outbound logistics might be the deciding factor for customers (especially if the customer operates a just-in-time production system). Here considerations of outsourcing become extremely important. A basic concept is that firms should focus on what they do best and outsource to others activities where they do not add value.

The value chain is supported by four activities, as follows:

■ Procurement. This is the function of acquiring the inputs used in the value chain, and applies to inputs used at any stage. In other words, procurement is not only connected with the inbound raw materials or components: it is also concerned with anything used in the course of providing marketing inputs, servicing inputs, or materials used for outbound logistics.
■ Human resource management. This is the function of recruiting, training, and rewarding staff members in the organization.
■ Technology development. This includes know-how, research and development, product design, and process improvement work.
■ Infrastructure. This includes the working spaces (factories, offices, mines, etc.), the organizational structure of the firm, the financial and operational control systems, and the feedback systems used by management.

Growing out of the value chain analysis is the VRIO framework (Barney, 2002). Here a firm should examine each of its resources and capabilities for value, rarity, imitability and the ability of the firm's organization to exploit it. Firm capabilities that are valuable, rare, costly or difficult for competitors to imitate, and well exploited by the organization lead to sustained competitive advantage.

TABLE 3.2 Value chain

Primary activity	Explanation and examples
Inbound logistics	Inbound logistics is the study of movement of factors of production. For example, a manufacturer of inboard motors needs to ensure that stocks of component parts are always on hand. A failure to have sufficient fuel injection systems in stock means that production would cease, even if pistons, propellers, cylinder blocks, gears, and everything else needed were ready at hand.
Operations	These are the processes which convert inputs into finished products. For the inboard motor manufacturer, this would mean machining raw castings, manufacturing engine covers, painting, assembling motors, testing the finished motors, packaging the products.
Outbound logistics	Outbound logistics is concerned with the movement of finished products. It involves the shipping of products in a timely manner to customers in order to meet their needs: in the case of the inboard motor company, this means ensuring that boat builders are supplied on time, since they are in turn unable to complete the boat unless they have the motors, and also ensuring that boat chandlers and repair yards have supplies of replacement motors as necessary.
Marketing and sales	These activities ensure that the customers are aware of the products and favor them over competitors' products. For the inboard motor manufacturer this falls into two phases: first, the company needs to persuade boat builders, repair yards and the like that their motors are best, but also they may need to persuade the final consumer, the boat owner, of the same thing. In a sense this is part of the same process: boat builders are unlikely to specify a motor that boat owners have never heard of or distrust.
Service	After-sales activities for an inboard motor manufacturer would include supplying spare parts as necessary (and preferably promptly), warranty work on failed motors, training of service engineers at boat repair yards, and helplines for boat yards and boat owners.

VALUE NETWORKS

The concept of the value chain has a close relationship with supply chain analysis, with the addition of the support functions within the firm. Unfortunately, the dynamic nature of twenty-first-century markets means that supply chains are constantly breaking or changing their natures so that supply chain and value chain analysis is insufficient to describe the complex relationships that exist between firms in a given market. The implications of partnerships, strategic alliances, and relationship marketing need to be considered as well.

Value chain analysis implies a linear process, ignoring inputs from outside the chain: the reality is that many firms may input into the process at various stages and therefore the value chain becomes a value network, a group of interrelated entities which contribute to the overall creation of value through a series of complex relationships.

For a firm in a global market, this means that many relationships in many different countries need to be considered. The value network may be different for each major customer – for example, an international construction company such as Taylor Woodrow may form alliances with many other companies in order to carry out a major construction project. Perhaps the best example of this is the Channel Tunnel Project, in which Taylor Woodrow, Costain, Wimpey, Balfour Beatty and Tarmac joined together with five French construction companies (Bouygues, Dumez, Spie Batignolles, Société Auxiliaire D'Entreprises, and Société Générale D'Entreprises) to form Transmanche Link. Eurotunnel was, and still is, the largest construction project in history, and involved many hundreds of companies in a complex network of responsibilities, each having to make its own contribution at the right time and in the right way. Each of the companies involved in the Transmanche Link consortium also had other construction projects in process: for example, Wimpey was at the time Britain's biggest house builder, and also owned Morrison Homes, the United States' biggest house builder. In fact many advanced thinkers now propose that firms derive competitive advantage from their networks and these networks are competing against one another rather than individual companies (Cares, 2006).

Peng (2009) points out the shortcomings of both the resource and industry-based approaches and adds a third consideration to strategy formulation: institutions. Managers, especially in a global context, may make decisions forced on them by formal or informal institutions in a particular country. For instance the Chinese government did not allow foreign majority ownership of any banking institutions for many years. Firms wishing to do business in China may have believed the industry was attractive and that their firm provided unique capabilities which could be exploited best by a wholly-owned subsidiary. Nevertheless Chinese regulations prevented that strategy choice. Informal institutions relate to culture, ethics, and corruption. Managers must be cognizant of these factors as well when choosing a strategy.

In the global context, competitive advantage can be achieved in different ways for each market the firm operates in. A company which is the cost leader in its domestic market might very well find itself to be a differentiator in a foreign market, perhaps because its products are unknown there. Some firm's resources are more important in one country than another. In some places the firm may have to develop new resources. Because of the poor infrastructure in India an electronics

Talking Point

The competitive positions outlined by Peng, Porter, Barney, and others seem to offer firms a fine choice of approaches. Yet many firms (if we believe their mission statements) try to offer more and more to customers. Statements such as "We seek to offer the best products at the most realistic prices" imply a conflict in the strategic position – and one which is likely to prove fatal.

So where does that leave us? Are the mission statements mere idle rhetoric, promising things which the firm has no intention of delivering, or are firms trying to be all things to all men and thus heading for the bankruptcy court? Or can the firms take the best of all the competitive strategies offered? Does this give the firm's managers permission to do whatever they want to do and claim that it is part of a very clever combination strategy?

firm might have to offer standby power supplies to run its equipment during the frequent power failures, although the firm has no competitive advantage in the standby power generation business. Smart firms know when to compete and when to collaborate. Marketing alliances of all kinds have been developed to serve customers. These may focus on product or service, promotion, logistics or joint pricing (Kotler, 2003).

COMPETITION AND HYPERCOMPETITION

Competitive positions within markets become established over time, particularly in markets which are fairly stable. The competitive positions which evolve are as follows:

1   Market leader. This company has the largest market share, which may make it subject to the scrutiny of monopoly regulators. On the other hand, these firms can control the market because they have the largest buying power. Market leaders have two basic strategic options: they can try to win even greater share from the smaller firms in the market, or they can try to expand the overall market. The former course will probably lead to retaliation and/or investigation by monopoly regulators, so most market leaders seek to expand the overall market, even though this will also benefit the smaller firms. Some market leaders will try to squeeze more profit from the same market share by cutting costs, which is of course bad news for suppliers, who may well find themselves in a painfully weak bargaining position.
2   Market challengers. These are firms which seek to increase their share of the market, either at the expense of the market leader or (more likely, given the power relationships involved) at the expense of the smaller firms in the market. In order to attack the market leader, the challenger must have a substantial competitive advantage, whereas attacking smaller competitors may only involve running a powerful promotional campaign, a short price war, or a takeover policy.
3   Market followers. Market followers usually try to avoid any direct confrontation with the market leaders, since they are unable to sustain a competitive battle in the long run. The usual strategy for a follower is to allow the market leader to make most of the investment in developing a new market, then pick up any segments which are too small for the market leader to bother with. Although market followers will never become marketing leaders, they often have much the same profit levels since they do not have the expense of developing the markets (Haines et al. 1989).
4   Market nicher. These companies concentrate on small segments of the market, seeking to meet the needs of those customers as closely as possible. Since nichers operate on a low-volume, high-margin basis, they are often small to medium-size companies (Clifford and Cavanagh, 1985). The competitive strategy of a nicher is to get to know the segment so well that competitors are effectively shut out, so the key to success is to specialize.

Market leaders frequently need to defend their positions, as do other suppliers, albeit on a less frequent basis. Defense strategies are as shown in Table 3.3.

TABLE 3.3 Market leader defense strategies

Strategy	Explanation
Position defense	This involves building barriers which prevent or restrict competitors from entering the market. These barriers may be related to inputs – for example, cornering the market in raw materials – or to outputs, for example using a patent to protect a particular process.
Flanking defense	Since market leaders often ignore parts of the market which they feel are not worth approaching, competitors can sometimes find an opening without directly confronting the market leader.
Pre-emptive defense	The market leader will sometimes attack the other companies before they can move in, for example by using a massive price cut to stave off a threat of entry.
Counter-offensive defense	When attacked, the market leader launches an instant counter-attack. This can take the form of a promotional campaign, a price war or the development of a "me-too" version of the competitor's product.
Mobile defense	The market leader moves into new markets before the competitors can do so. In effect, the market leader takes a proactive approach.
Contraction defense	Sometimes the market leader finds itself unable to defend all its markets and withdraws to its core business. In some cases this has not proved sufficient, and the company has continued to retreat until it has nowhere left to go.

In most markets, the market challenger's best strategy would be to attack the market leader, unless of course the market leader can defend its position effectively. This means that market leaders need to be constantly vigilant, and must be able to mount a vigorous defense. More importantly, the market leader needs to make it clear to competitors that it has the capability to mount a vigorous defense, or even attack if circumstances warrant it.

Market challengers might use any of the strategies outlined in Table 3.4.

So far, this section has been about monopolistic competition in which firms jockey for position in a fairly gentlemanly manner dividing up the market into neat segments in which each company operates with little risk of attack from other companies. In some markets this has given way to hypercompetition in which "anything goes" (D'Aveni, 1994). In an extensive study of nearly 7,000 firms and 40 industries over a 25-year period, Wiggins and Ruelfi (2005) found that competitive advantage had become more difficult to sustain across a broad range of industries and that a single sustained competitive advantage is less common than a series of advantages.

To cope with this new reality, managers look for new ways to out-compete rivals. This goes further than merely staking out a claim in the market: in any market in which there is room for four companies, five or six will be competing, and the weakest will eventually disappear – only to be replaced by a newcomer. The philosophy underpinning hypercompetition is that managers need to concentrate on a new 7-S framework, rather than the Peters and Waterman (1982) 7-S framework popularized in *In Search of Excellence*. The 7 Ss are shown in Table 3.5.

The 7-S framework presented in Table 3.5 is not intended to be read as a series of generic strategies. It is a set of key approaches that might carry the organization in many different directions. The framework also encompasses three factors for effective delivery of tactical disruptions of the market: vision, capabilities, and tactics.

Within the hypercompetitive environment, traditional sources of strength no longer apply. Giants of industry are frequently brought down by relatively small competitors, able to adapt to new situations or able to bring new ideas to bear. Much of the success in a hypercompetitive environment is based on the strategy of finding and building temporary advantages through market disruption rather than sustaining advantage and building for equilibrium. In other words, success comes from initiating changes in the market rather than from responding to changes.

Of course, not all disruptions are successful. For a disruption to be successful, it must fulfill the first S – the creation of a temporary ability to serve stakeholders better than the competition can. Successful firms may well prioritize the customer as the most important stakeholder: customer satisfaction becomes the instrument by which the company seeks the satisfaction of other stakeholders such as employees and shareholders. For example, Intel have a process of concurrent engineering in which Intel designers visit every major computer manufacturer and every major software house around the world to ask them what they want in a chip. The company also provides early software simulations to computer manufacturers, thus allowing these customers to gain a first-to-market

TABLE 3.4 Market challenger strategies

Strategy	Explanation
Frontal attack	In a frontal attack the market challenger attacks the target company by matching its efforts across the board. The challenger attacks the competitor's strengths rather than its weaknesses, in effect entering into a war of attrition. The company with the greatest resources will usually win in these circumstances, but such frontal attacks are costly for all concerned.
Flanking attack	The flanking attack concentrates on the competitor's weaknesses, seeking out areas where the competitor is unable to compete effectively. The challenger will identify areas of the business which the competitor is serving badly. Sometimes the company under attack will simply retreat rather than fight for a market which is marginal for it, so this can be an effective strategy for a small firm attacking a larger one.
Encirclement attack	This strategy involves attacking from several directions at once. It works best when the attacker has more resources than the defender.
Bypass attack	Here the challenger bypasses the other firms entirely and targets totally new markets. This is particularly effective in a global context, where a new market may open up in which the leading competitors are not represented.
Guerrilla attack	The challenger makes occasional attacks on a larger competitor, using different tactics each time in order to confuse the target competitor. The constant switching of tactics does not allow the competitor time to formulate a response, in effect forcing the competitor to become a follower.

TABLE 3.5 The 7-S framework

Factor	Explanation
Superior stakeholder satisfaction	The ability to satisfy the firm's stakeholders more effectively than competitors are able to offers clear advantages. Customer satisfaction, much beloved by marketers, is only part of this process, since other stakeholders must also be kept happy or even delighted by the firm's activities.
Strategic soothsaying	This is about understanding the future evolution of markets and technology. Success in predicting future trends is clearly linked to success in making or responding to changes.
Positioning for speed	Preparing the company for a rapid change of approach is crucial to the firm's ability to initiate and respond to competitive shifts.
Positioning for surprise	Being able to make changes rapidly enough to take the competitors by surprise is a useful capability, as is being flexible enough to cope with surprises.
Shifting the rules of the game	As firms learn how to break down entry barriers quickly and cheaply, the "gentlemen's agreements" to avoid direct competition are breaking down. A firm which is successful at shifting the rules is likely to catch competitors flat-footed and thus gain competitive advantage quickly.
Signaling strategic intent	Letting competitors know what will happen if they follow a particular course may be a good way to slow down or negate their strategic actions.
Simultaneous and sequential strategic thrusts	Either carrying out a number of different competitive initiatives at once, or carrying them out in a rapid sequence, can confuse and disorientate competitors. Often, a "false start" along one course followed by a rapid change of direction to another course will be highly effective.

advantage over competitors, and also Intel produce software compilers which they supply to software companies in order to make the transition to the new chip run more smoothly. The ability to predict future trends in markets is clearly crucial to a firm such as Intel: the company not only needs to predict trends in its own business to business markets, but also needs to predict trends in the consumer markets that its customers serve.

To an extent, soothsaying is linked to vision: the corporate vision is likely to include some assessment of possible future trends and opportunities for disruption.

The capability for disruption is dependent on the next two factors. A company's ability to act fast and its capacity for surprising its competitors are crucial in causing disruption: if two companies see the same opportunity together, the one which is able to act the fastest will win the day. Equally, the firm which is able to create new opportunities which its competitors are unable to foresee will drive the market.

The final three elements are concerned with the tactics for disruption. Actions that shift the rules of competition will catch competitors out, but of course such changes are subject to retaliation as competitors readjust. Most planning takes account of possible competitor responses, but it is far less common for managers to attempt to shape the responses of competitors so as to maximize competitive advantage. Signaling the firm's likely competitive responses to competitors in advance can delay their plans while they consider the consequences, and can sometimes create surprise.

Simultaneous thrusts or a sequence of rapid moves can confuse and create surprise among competitors. Moving in several different directions at once makes it difficult for competitors to formulate a suitable response, since the competition is unlikely to be able to coordinate across all fronts in the same way as the initiating firm can coordinate.

In a hypercompetitive market, competitive advantage is gained by achieving four key goals, as shown in Figure 3.2.

Hagel et al. (2008) describe an approach called "shaping strategy" to respond to rapidly-changing environments. These researchers contend that an old historical pattern – disruption followed by stability – will no longer prevail. Instead, because underlying technologies are changing so quickly, stability will not be achieved. They believe managers, reacting to the constantly changing technology, institutions and relationships, tend to attempt to gain more control over their core capabilities and become more reactive. They reject the idea of adaptation as a successful strategy but instead recommend a much larger leap called a shaping strategy. This requires developing an entirely new platform

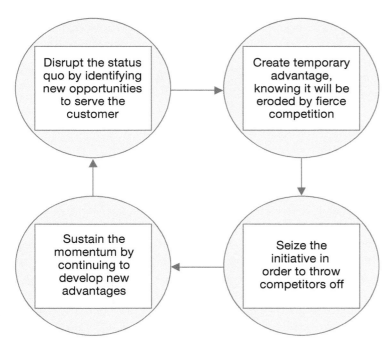

FIGURE 3.2 Key goals of hypercompetition

then attracting a critical mass of participants, using networks to amplify the effects. While they admit this is a high risk/high reward approach, this may be the only rational response to consistently turbulent environments.

In hypercompetition it is not sufficient to be able to build a static set of competencies, as has been the case in the past. It is also important to know how to use competencies to seize the initiative and maintain the flow of disruptive changes in order to maintain a lead. Successful hypercompetitors do not wait for a competitive response – they continue to innovate and upset the market equilibrium, keeping ahead by maintaining a balancing act which the competitors are unable to match.

Companies need to consider trade-offs, as with any other analysis pattern or scheme. However, the approaches are not mutually exclusive, and companies can (and do) select more than one approach at a time. There are of course many trade-offs (D'Aveni, 1995), and Table 3.6 shows only a few examples.

Talking Point

Frequently marketers use the language of warfare to describe what they do. We defend markets, we run advertising campaigns, we establish territories, we conquer a market, we attack a target. And at the same time we talk about nurturing the customers – rather like a military commander who claims to be liberating the people he's killing.

So how do we reconcile this apparent discrepancy? Do we change our terminology, to reflect the nurturing side of our nature? Or do we change what we do, so that instead of battling with our competitors for the pawns we call customers, we start to cooperate with our competitors to meet customer needs?

Or is it perhaps nearer to the truth to admit that actually we are out to please the shareholders – the customers are merely a means to an end?

Because firms have limited resources, they will be unable to acquire all the 7-S elements at once, and will therefore need to consider which ones to prioritize. This requires analysis of the competitors in order to play to the weaknesses of the competition. The trade-offs mean that firms cannot use all the elements at once anyway, although it is perfectly feasible to combine a few elements at any one time.

Hypercompetition should not be seen as a universal formula for all firms in all circumstances. Many firms operate in stable industries where competitive pressures are relatively low – the oil industry is an example. Change is slow in such industries, and the type of rapid disruption of the market described in hypercompetition is unlikely to be of any relevance. In the longer run, if all firms in a given industry adopt the hypercompetitive approach, anarchy is likely to be the result and a new paradigm will need to be found to establish an element of stability. The model also assumes that rapid change will continue indefinitely, and that the speed of change is increasing: both of these assumptions are subject to question.

TABLE 3.6 Trade-offs in the 7-S framework

Trade-off	Description
Speed vs. stakeholder satisfaction	Companies may sacrifice product quality (thus affecting customers) or may push employees too hard in order to increase speed of change. Rushing new products to market without proper testing may also reduce customer satisfaction.
Surprise vs. stakeholder satisfaction	Sudden changes of direction are unsettling for employees and may well confuse customers. Shifting the rules and simultaneous strategic thrusts also lead to confusion among staff and shareholders, and may weaken brand values which have taken years to establish.
Speed vs. soothsaying	Speed can easily leave too little time for reflection on future events, especially since the effects of change cannot be estimated if the changes themselves are happening too fast. The same is true of simultaneous strategic thrusts.
Shifting the rules vs. speed	Shifting the rules often requires strategic alliances to be formed with other firms (either competitors or members of the value chain) which means that negotiations will reduce speed. These negotiations also reduce the possibilities for surprise, since any such negotiations are likely to be public.
Sequential thrusts vs. surprise	Sequential thrusts commit the firm to a predetermined course of action which may be surprising in itself, but which will rapidly lose the element of surprise as the plans leak out.

GLOBALIZATION STRATEGY

Firms which adopt a global strategy will usually try to develop international competitive strengths that would not have been available to them had they remained purely domestic firms. They will also perceive key opportunities and threats on a worldwide basis. This does not, of course, preclude the firm from having a national strategic orientation in some areas of its operations. Here it is critically important that firms use the three-pronged approach recommended by Peng described above, considering industry, resource and institutional factors.

There are four main strategic options open to the globalizing company (Grosse and Kujawa, 1992).

- Aim for a high share of a global market.
- Aim for a niche in a global market.
- Aim for a high share of a national market.
- Aim for a niche in a national market.

The firms seeking a high share of a global market will need to begin by identifying high-volume segments which exist globally, in other words segments which cross national boundaries. Examples are the global computer business and the global telecommunications market. Secondly the firm will need to produce a wide range of products to meet the needs of that market segment or those market segments. In order to compete against global niche marketers, the global high-share company must seek those benefits which come from being able to supply a wide range of products. These include inbound logistics advantages such as being able to use the same raw materials to produce many products, and the ability to offer a wider range of choice to customers.

Global niche strategists target a single industry or a single type of problem. For example, Microbiological Systems Ltd. supply biologically-based environmental pollution detection systems to the chemical industry. The firm is at the cutting edge of research in the area, and is able to supply systems which are cheaper, more sensitive, and more reliable than anyone else's. Such firms protect their market niche by holding the key patents on the processes they use, and by spending large amounts on R&D in order to stay ahead of the competition.

Global nichers usually want to avoid head-on competition with the major firms, typically because they do not have the resources for a long-drawn-out battle. The policy works best for firms which have a global advantage (i.e. an advantage over all other firms in the industry wherever they are located), and which do not have to adapt their product to meet local conditions.

National high share strategists target countries where they think they can obtain a high share of the market. This may come about because of tariff barriers which prevent other foreign firms from entering the market (as in the case of a customs union or common market), or it may be that local firms are unable to supply the demand for the products. In some cases the production facilities for a firm may be located in a country where the raw materials are easily available: for example, Rio Tinto Zinc produces aluminum in Australia and New Zealand, copper in Papua New Guinea, and uranium in Namibia. In each case the company is well-placed to supply local or regional demand for the end product.

Choosing one country from another can be a difficult problem with more than 200 to pick from. A number of researchers have proposed using an adaptation of the well-known GE matrix. This market choice matrix is shown in Figure 3.3.

The Market Choice Matrix compares product/business strengths with a particular market's attractiveness. On the vertical axis, the product/business strengths relate to a specific set of factors which may be varied by the manager depending upon the analysis for his particular firm. A suggested list of factors for this axis include:

- business size;
- financial strength;
- technology superiority;
- brand perceptions;
- personnel.

The horizontal axis, market attractiveness, would include factors such as:

- trade barriers;
- competition;
- cultural acceptance;

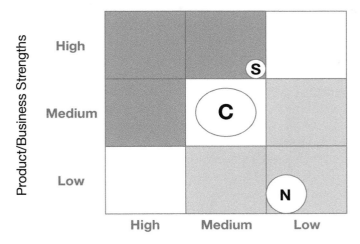

FIGURE 3.3 Market choice matrix

Source: adapted from GE Strategic Planning Grid.

- technological readiness;
- previous corporate establishment;
- availability of distribution.

Each of the factors for product/business and market attractiveness should be given a weight and then each sub-factor rated. When the weights and ratings are summarized, an overall number can be developed. From this number, the placement on the market choice matrix would be determined. The relative size of the market can be shown by varying the size of the circles representing each country market.

On the example attached, we have shown a firm with medium business strengths and medium market attractiveness for China, which is represented by a large circle since the market potential is large. Sweden is represented as a market where the business has high strengths, but the attractiveness is only medium since the market is crowded with competition. The size of the Swedish market is shown with a smaller circle. Finally, a medium-sized circle is shown in the lower right-hand corner for Nigeria where this firm has little strength and the market attractiveness is rather low. For this product, the market size in Nigeria is about the same as that of Sweden.

In some cases national high-share strategists are favored because they are prepared to allow the national government a share in the firm. This type of joint venture is favored in Sweden and in many developing-world countries, where the governments find it a useful way to raise revenue without increasing taxation.

National niche strategists exploit the advantages of specialization on a national basis to help defend their segments against local and international rivals. This approach works best where global product strategies are not compatible with local demands, and where a large amount of product adaptation is needed from country to country. Competitive advantage derives from the firm's ability to adapt to local needs: for example, a truck manufacturer will need to adapt the vehicles for climatic differences and infrastructure differences – the quality of the roads is likely to make a difference to suspension specifications, gear ratios, and so forth.

Recent work by Douglas and Craig (2011) describes a "semiglobal marketing strategy," instead of a "unified and integrated strategy for global markets." This idea results from the opportunities in many interesting places throughout the world, specifically the so-called BRIC countries, Brazil, Russia, India, and China, as well as a number of growing markets at the next tier such as Indonesia, Mexico, Nigeria, and Turkey. These markets are populated by different customers, competitors, and institutions that require various firm skills and resources. Companies must develop local market knowledge and learn to tailor products, promotions, and distribution to each country. While much has been written about pan-national segments, there are many individual country markets where extensive local adaptation is required. In some cases there are country clusters rather than global segments which can be exploited. So a firm must adapt a semiglobal strategy, meeting the needs of individual or clusters of country markets.

Garten (2000), in reviewing the requirements for global strategy advises:

- Rethink everything about the strategy – even what the strategy means in a fast and brutally competitive environment.
- The best strategies are developed by organizations that can gather and process massive amounts of information.
- Companies that succeed globally are constantly innovating.
- To succeed globally, firms need to create a culture which allows for extensive internal and external collaboration.
- Global change offers unprecedented opportunities to capture markets.

In general, globalization presents management with the key strategic choice between achieving economies of scale versus meeting local market requirements. To gain economies of scale requires concentrating production and other value-adding activities in one or a few locations, while meeting local needs often dictates establishing facilities in many markets, obviously adding to overall costs.

CASE STUDY

Case study: Tullow Oil PLC

Tullow Oil is a bit of a maverick in the oil exploration business. The company was founded in 1985 by an Irish accountant, Aidan Heavey, who thought there might be potential in small oil fields in Africa that large companies had overlooked. Heavey named the firm after the small town about 35 miles south of Dublin where he began the company. He started by talking to a friend at the World Bank who knew about a project in Senegal where he could rework some old fields. Tullow has been remarkably successful ever since. They strike oil in about 70 percent of their exploration and appraisal wells, double the industry average. In 2006 the firm discovered a more than 1-billion barrel field in the Lake Albert region of Uganda and now has operations in more than 20 countries. Tullow's geologists use their discoveries to look for similar geological areas for further exploration. For instance the firm drilled a well off French Guiana because they believe there are similar oil deposits in Latin America to those in West Africa, since the two continents once made up a single landmass. Tullow involved two major European oil firms in that exploration, Shell and Total, and announced that they had discovered a large quantity of oil.

Their 2011 financial results are impressive (2010 results are shown in brackets):

- Sales revenue ($m) **2,304** (1,090): Up 111 percent
- Operating profit ($m) **1,132** (262): Up 332 percent
- Profit before tax ($m) **1,073** (179): Up 499 percent
- Profit after tax ($m) **689** (90): Up 670 percent
- Basic earnings per share (cents) **72.5** (8.1): Up 795 percent
- Full year dividend per share (pence) **12** (6): Up 100 percent

As the company grows, it faces political, cultural, and environmental challenges. For instance, Uganda's government wants Tullow to join with other firms to build a refinery within the country. And the Ugandan government sent a $472 million tax bill to the firm. As the company begins to explore in Kenya it is moving into a location where there are many early hominid sites. Richard Leakey, the well-known anthropologist, says Mr. Heavey has a very good attitude toward the responsibilities an oil company should have in that area. Tullow issues an annual corporate social responsibility report measuring its CSR efforts.

Some problems have been discussed in the press. Oil industry analysts at Oxfam America, the global relief and development organization, said safety and environmental concerns weren't fully addressed before the project was approved. Even though Jubilee field production has started, Ghana has yet to update environmental laws governing extractive industries that were written a generation ago. Ghanaian officials said new legislation will be considered this year. Some are concerned that this first oil project was Ghana's first major one of any kind.

One report says the following:

. . . continued

For Tullow Oil and its partners, corporate social responsibility is no more business as usual. They appear bent on departing from the tokenistic approach of providing various forms of services needed or not, to local communities. Some say, the company is only responding to increased media attention, pressure from non-governmental organizations, and rapid global information sharing, which have led to a surge in demand from civil society, consumers, governments, and others for businesses to adhere to sustainable business practices.

But, Tullow says it is here to demonstrate that it is possible to conduct oil business in a way that benefits all, both companies and resource owners. The company recently organized a free health screening exercise for local people who were screened for diabetes, HIV, hypertension, breast cancer, dental care, ear, eye, nose, and throat infections.

Mr. Ken McGhee, the Corporate Social Responsibility Manager for the Jubilee partners [the operators of the large oilfield in Ghana], said the screening exercise was aimed at offering free medical services to inhabitants residing within its operational area adding that "the health needs of the people within their catchment area would remain paramount to the company and never be relegated to the background." A total amount of $1.6 million has been committed by the Jubilee partners to develop six coastal districts of the Western Region. Under a project tagged "Town Planning: an Imperative for Sustainable Oil economy in Western Region" the capacity of the six districts to professionally craft development plans to serve as the basis for both structural and human development in the short to medium term will be enhanced.

The company's website offers much information about its Vision and strategies.

Vision

To be the leading global independent exploration and production company.

Strategy

Tullow pursues a consistent and repeatable strategy which seeks to deliver sustainable long-term growth with a balance between funding, exploration and production spend, and major activities in core areas.

Strategic Priorities

1   Execute selective, high-impact exploration programmes funded by surplus cash flow or equity.
2   Deliver major projects, with a significant focus on increasing bankable reserves.

... *continued*

CASE STUDY ... *continued*

3   Manage our assets to high-grade the portfolio, replenish upside, and assist funding needs.

4   Ensure safe people, procedures and operations, and minimizing environmental impacts.

5   Build long-term relationships with governments, local communities and key stakeholders.

6   Continue to develop a strong team with excellent commercial, technical, and financial skills.

Overall, Tullow's approach seems responsive to the needs of the twenty-first century.

Case based on: Reed, Stanley. (2012). "Finding success on the oil frontier." *New York Times*, 4 July: B1; Code of Conduct. (2012). Tullow Oil. Accessed 4 July 2012 at http://digitalpages.digitalissue.co.uk/?userpath=00000082/00008126/00070465/; "Jubilee partners make corporate social responsibility address real needs (2012)". Accessed 4 July 2012 at http://ghanaclean.net/?p=694; *Badgley*, Christiane (2012). "Oil-industry regulation lags behind as Ghana ramps up production." 19 January. Accessed 4 July 2012 at http://www.iwatchnews.org/2012/01/19/7896/west-africa-oil-boom-overlooks-tattered-environmental-safety-net

CASE STUDY QUESTIONS

1   Do Tullow's vision and strategies meet the requirements described in the chapter?
2   How is Tullow's lack of a mission statement important to the future success of the firm?
3   How do resources, industry, and institutional considerations affect Tullow's strategy?
4   What type of globalization strategy do you think Tullow has adopted?

CHAPTER SUMMARY

Strategy is the guiding force of any organization. It allows every member of the organization to understand where the organization is heading, which means that decision-making by junior managers and even grass-roots workers becomes much easier. The framework created by an effective, and effectively-communicated, strategy is essential for the smooth running of the organization.

However, strategic planning is not a straightforward matter. Competition, hypercompetition, and the rapidly-changing environment all affect the firm's ability to plan ahead.

Key points from this chapter are:

■   Mission statements, vision statements, and objectives are all ways of communicating the overall strategy of the organization.

- Strategy revolves around environment, resources, and vision: the more congruent the EVR, the more successful the strategy.
- Value chains are not sufficient to analyze global businesses: the value network, containing all the partner organizations, also needs to be considered.
- Traditional strategic approaches are industry or resource-based. Formal and informal institutions need to be considered as well.
- Positions within the market are market leader, market challenger, market follower, and market nicher.
- Hypercompetition is about disrupting markets in order to out-compete other organizations.

REVIEW QUESTIONS

1 Why should firms consider industry, resource, and institutional factors in developing strategy?
2 How might a firm apply basic defense strategies in a hypercompetitive environment?
3 What is the difference between vision and mission?
4 How might a firm plan for entering a former communist country such as China?
5 What would be the most appropriate competitive strategy for a small firm wishing to enter a well-established national market?

REFERENCES

Ackoff, R.L. (1986). *Management in Small Doses*. New York: John Wiley.

Barney, J. (2002). *Gaining and Sustaining Competitive Advantage*. Upper Saddle River, NJ: Prentice-Hall.

Campbell, A. (1989). Research findings discussed in Skapinker, M. (1989). "Mission accomplished or ignored?" *Financial Times*, 11 January.

Cares, J. (2006). "Battle of the Networks." *Harvard Business Review*, Vol. 84, Iss. 2, 40–1.

Clifford, Donald K. and Cavanagh, Richard E. (1985). *The winning performance: How America's high–growth midsize companies succeed*. Toronto and New York: Bantam Books.

Cochran, D.S., David, F.R., and Gibson, C. (2008). "A Framework for Developing an Effective Mission Statement." *Journal of Business Strategies*, Vol. 25, Iss. 2, 27–39.

D'Aveni, R.A. (1994). *Hypercompetition: Managing the dynamics of strategic manoeuvring*. New York: Free Press.

D'Aveni, R.A. (1995). "Coping with hypercompetition: the new 7Ss framework." *The Academy of Management Executive*, Vol. 9, Iss. 3, 45–67.

David, Forest R. and David, Fred R. (2003). "It's Time to Redraft Your Mission Statement." *Journal of Business Strategy*, Vol. 24, Iss. 1, 11–14.

Douglas, Susan P. and Craig, C. Samuel (2011). "Convergence and Divergence: Developing a Semiglobal Marketing Strategy." *Journal of International Marketing*, Vol. 19, Iss. 1, 82–101.

Drucker, Peter F. (1973). *Management Tasks, Responsibilities, Practices*. New York: Harper & Row.

Drucker, Peter F. (1994). "The Theory of the Business." *Harvard Business Review*, Vol. 72, No. 5, Sept.–Oct., 1994, 95–104.

Garten, Jeffrey E. (2000). *World View: Global Strategies for the New Economy*. Boston: Harvard Business School Publishing, pp. xiii-xiv.

Grosse, R. and Kujawa, D. (1992). *International Business*. Homewood Ill: Irwin.

Hagel, John III, Brown, John Seely, and Davison, Lang (2008). "Shaping Strategy in a World of Constant Disruption." *Harvard Business Review*, Vol. 86, Iss. 10, 81–9.

Haines, D.W., Chandran, R. and Parkhe, A. (1989). "Winning by Being the First to Market . . . or Second?" *Journal of Consumer Marketing*, Vol. 6, Iss. 1, 63–69.

Idenburg, P. J. (1993). "Four styles of strategy development." *Long Range Planning*, Vol. 26, Iss. 6, 132–7.

Kotler, Philip (2003). *Marketing Management*. Upper Saddle River, NJ: Prentice-Hall.

Peng, Mike W. (2009). *Global Strategy*. Mason, OH: South-Western Cengage Learning.

Peters, T.J. and Waterman, R.H. (1982). *In search of excellence: lessons from America's best-run companies*. New York: Harper & Row.

Porter, M.E. (1985). *Competitive Advantage: Creating and Sustaining Superior Performance*. New York: Free Press.

Thompson, A.A. and Strickland, A.J. (1980). *Strategy formulation and implementation*. Homewood, Ill: Irwin.

Wiggins, Robert R. and Ruefli, Timothy W. (2005). "Schumpeter's ghost: is hyper competition making the best of times shorter?" *Strategic Management Journal*, Vol. 26, Iss. 10, 887–911.

Chapter 4

Ethical considerations for business marketers

INTRODUCTION

Establishing the proper ethical conduct for employees and managers is an important yet difficult task. Recently, both the business and general press have been filled with stories exposing ethical lapses in corporations across the world. In this chapter, we will attempt to clarify the most important issues in global ethics and provide tools to help you establish ethical guidelines for the marketing department.

CHAPTER OBJECTIVES

After reading this chapter, you should be able to:

- describe various approaches to corporate responsibility
- explain the concepts of ethical principles and business ethics
- describe how ethical standards impact the various functions of marketing
- understand the special considerations affecting ethical behavior in a global economy
- describe the best way to analyze ethical problems
- explain methods for making a firm more responsive to ethical matters.

ETHICAL ENVIRONMENT

Any marketing department is operating in many environments which affect its ability to establish and maintain ethical conduct. These various influences are shown in Figure 4.1.

Terpstra and David (1991) describe the corporate environment as including formal administrative structures such as organization charts and the assignment of authority, responsibility and information flow as well as formal administrative systems such as methods for controlling operations, evaluation and rewards systems, and the corporate culture. Corporate culture is defined by Terpstra and David as, "a learned, relatively enduring interdependent system of meanings that classify, code, prioritize and justify activity both within the organization and toward the external environments it has defined as relevant." They point out that the symbols and meaning of corporate culture are usually imperfectly shared by organizational members.

The societal environment includes social relationships and cultural definitions of life. Two of the most important aspects of this environment are the infrastructure, such as technical, educational, and research; and government regulation. Because doing business outside the home country can so often be dependent upon cultural differences, the diagram has specifically identified cultural influences as a separate item. The main elements of a definition of culture include these characteristics:

- shared set of beliefs;
- learned and passed on from one generation to another;
- used to distinguish one group from another;
- provides solutions to problems every individual faces – how he/she should properly relate to another individual of the same or opposite sex, the physical world and the universe.

(Terpstra and David, 1991; Keegan and Greene, 2010; and Czinkota and Ronkainen, 2006)

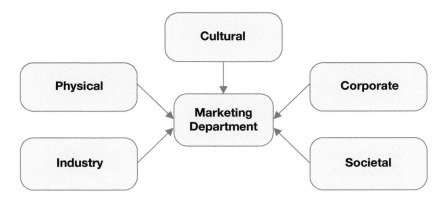

FIGURE 4.1 Firms' ethical environments

Source: adapted from Terpstra and David (1991).

The physical environment includes climate, geography, plant and animal life, and natural resources. The view of the physical environment has a major impact upon what is considered proper behavior. For instance, citizens of Western Europe are far more concerned about air pollution than are most individuals in the Peoples' Republic of China.

Finally, the industry environment is also an important influence on the ethical behavior of individuals. Acceptable behaviors which become industry norms are often considered to be the standards by which actions should be judged. Competitive forces are often at the heart of questionable actions taken by individuals.

BUSINESS ETHICS

Ethics means a standard of behavior, a conception of right or wrong conduct (Lawrence and Weber, 2011). Ethical principles are guides to moral or immoral behavior. Ideas of right and wrong are derived from religious beliefs as well as industry and professions, families, friends, school, and the media. All of these influences help an individual develop a specific concept of morality and ethics.

Business ethics is simply the application of the foregoing ideas to business settings. Developing the proper guiding principles for business ethics has been the subject of discussion over many years. Three basic competing views of corporate responsibility have been put forward (Goodpaster and Matthews, 1992). These can be defined succinctly as:

- the invisible hand;
- the hand of government;
- the hand of management.

The invisible hand, most strongly expressed by Milton Friedman, assigns to business the sole responsibility of making profits within the law. In this conception, the marketplace will punish immoral behavior and the overall common good results from each firm pursuing competitive advantage. Self-interest is the most important factor in this view.

The hand of government view, expressed by John Galbraith, describes a system in which corporations pursue economic objectives while governments and political processes force firms to set objectives which will result in the common well-being. As Goodpaster and Matthews explain, the similarities of these two views are interesting. In both, morality and ethics are the responsibility of rules and incentives rather than independent judgment by individuals or corporations.

The third view, called the hand of management, assigns the corporation an important role in setting moral behavior and developing a corporate conscience. This approach expects managements not to ignore profit and business survival but to "coordinate imperatives, not deny their validity." In this view, the presence of ethical or intelligent individuals will not ensure an ethical corporation. Therefore, these standards must be structured to coordinate and organize individuals for the purpose of achieving an overall moral responsibility.

Although there remain some who would take the Friedman, invisible hand, position, there appears to be a trend toward more corporate responsibility in nearly every part of the world. The reasons for this are self-evident. The negative publicity resulting from revealed unethical behavior is swift, and overwhelming negative reaction can boil up quickly in the form of protests and boycotts. Second, as will be explained later in this chapter, tighter regulations are being adopted by a number of countries. Third, some studies indicate that firms which emphasize ethical and socially responsible behavior have better financial performance (Nguyen and Cragg, 2012; Verschoor, 1998 and Kurschner, 1996) although the opposite is not always true.

Two basic approaches form the basis for ethical thinking. The first, deontology, embodies the view that ethical decisions follow absolute principles. Actions are inherently right or wrong, independent of their consequences. These principles are often derived from a religious base such as the traditions of Judaism, Christianity, and Islam or from philosophies such as Confucianism (Newton, 2004). The most familiar derivative of deontology is Kant's Categorical Imperative. The Categorical Imperative requires that for an action to be proper it would have be acceptable as general or a universal law, all people are respected and an individual considers the decision both as a rule-maker and a rule-follower.

Another approach is consequentialism (also known as teleology) which bases its judgment of any action on the goodness of its consequences. The most well-known form of this school is utilitarianism which favors actions that generate "the greatest good for the greatest number." Many managers use a version of the utilitarian principle in their ethical decision making, since it is similar to the familiar cost-benefit analysis.

In reality, managers find it difficult to make decisions based only on one school of ethics or another. It is easy to see that applying the utilitarian principle runs into problems in such simple decisions as attempting to decide whether to make a large investment in new plant and equipment versus paying dividends to shareholders. An analysis of costs and benefits is difficult when various stakeholders' interests are in competition. In addition, the utilitarian principle might lead a manager to operate an unsafe insecticide plant which might benefit a large population with better crops and therefore better nutrition while harming a few hundred people located nearby the plant site. Utilitarianism often leads managers to ignore minority rights.

Using deontology also creates problems. Jean Paul Sartre illustrated the problem which arises when two universal principles conflict with one another. During World War II, he was forced to choose between staying home to comfort his ill and ageing mother and fighting for the freedom of France (Donaldson et al., 2002).

A third approach is that of "virtue" theory ethics in which individual character plays a major role. The teachings of Aristotle are at the heart of this theory which states that individuals should learn good habits in order to live a virtuous life. Further, virtuous people should be role models as well. This approach has been criticized because it does not provide clear rules and decision-making methods. (Above based on Donaldson, et al., 2002; Whysall, 2000 and Schlegelmilch, 1998.)

Lawrence and Weber (2011) offer a slightly different view, describing four methods of ethical reasoning:

- virtue;
- utilitarian;
- rights;
- justice.

The utilitarian and virtue approaches have been explained above. The rights method says an action is ethical when basic human rights are respected. Here again, it is difficult to balance the various stakeholders' rights. In the justice method, an attempt is made to distribute benefits and costs fairly. The major problem with this approach is similar to that of utilitarianism in that it is difficult to measure benefits and costs and hard to agree on which group should be the recipient of each (Smith, 1995).

MARKETING AND ETHICS

Smith (1995) says that marketers often rely on simple rules or maxims such as those shown in Table 4.1.

By its very nature, B2B marketing places the buyer–seller relationship at its center. Many ethical issues arise from the dynamics of this relationship. In addition, there are issues related to product, pricing, marketing communications, channels of distribution, and market research. A list of possible ethical issues which face B2B marketers is presented in Table 4.2.

Talking Point

A salesperson for an etching machine manufacturer has placed his equipment with a firm in Singapore. After several weeks of attempting to get the equipment to operate properly, the customer demands that the machine be removed and replaced with a new one. Management decides to replace the machine with a refurbished model which is undetectable from a newly manufactured product.

Should the salesman tell the customer that this product is remanufactured? Would he risk losing the sale? Or his job? If the machine really is indistinguishable from a new one, who cares about being economical with the truth?

Or would that be the equivalent of a woman lying about her age to a man she is about to marry? Or a man lying about the fact that he already has a wife in another country?

TABLE 4.1 Ethical maxims for marketing

- Do unto others as you would have them do unto you.
- Would I be embarrassed if the media publicized my decision?
- Good ethics is in the firm's long-term best interest.
- Would colleagues view this action as proper?
- When in doubt, don't.

Source: adapted from Smith, 1995.

TABLE 4.2 Ethical issues in international B2B marketing

Selling

- Bribery
- Gifts/favors/entertainment
- Misrepresentation/overselling
- Conflicts of interest
- Compensation and bookings

Product

- Safety
- Obsolescence/Elimination
- Service/Warranty
- Manufacturing – environmental impact
- Disposal

Marketing Communications

- Deceptive/misleading advertising and/or sales promotion
- Violations of confidential information (direct, Internet marketing)

Pricing

- Price-fixing
- Reciprocity
- Violation of secrecy in bidding
- Unjustified price discrimination
- Unfair pricing
- Questionable invoicing
- Artificial transfer pricing

Distribution

- Discrimination
- Dishonesty
- Inflated "commissions"

Market Research

- Respondent participation
- Researcher responsibilities

Personnel

- Discrimination in hiring
- Unfair treatment of employees

Source: adapted from Smith (1995); Craig and Douglas (2000); Chan and Armstrong (1999).

Selling

In the selling function, many difficult ethical problems emerge. An obvious one is bribery. In some countries, bribery is practically non-existent and is legally and culturally frowned upon. But in others, payments ranging from small "dash" or "grease" payments to large special commissions have been the norm. The World Bank (2012) estimates the overall cost of corruption including bribery at over $1 trillion annually. A salesperson confronted with possible bribery has an ethical decision to make depending upon home country and host country laws and customs.

According to Terpstra and David (1991), both frontstage and backstage culture exist in every country. Frontstage culture includes the standard, normal, proper ways of doing things that insiders *are* willing to share with outsiders. It is easy for a visiting business person to determine what frontstage culture is all about. This includes the question of formality versus informality in addressing new acquaintances, gift-giving traditions, the relationship between social engagement and business negotiations and so on. What is more troubling is backstage culture, defined as knowledge that insiders see as standard ways of doing things that they are *not* willing to share with outsiders. Insiders may not want to share knowledge because the activities may be illegal or because the special knowledge gained gives the insider a competitive advantage. Very often, the most carefully guarded backstage cultural activity is the bribe or so-called "commission."

For many years, the United States was alone in enforcing strict anti-bribery regulations. The Foreign Corrupt Practices Act, which took effect in 1977, provides for fines up to $2 million for corporations and up to $250,000 for officers, directors, stockholders, employees, and agents in addition to a prison term of up to five years for those who bribe government officials to gain a marketing advantage. The immediate effect was a steep drop in US business in several developing countries. In 1997, the Organization for Economic Cooperation and Development (OECD) adopted the Convention on Combating Bribery of Foreign Public Officials in International Business Transactions. The Convention recommended that OECD members enact laws to criminalize bribery activity. As of 2012, all 39 countries had signed onto the Convention and the follow-up OECD Recommendation of 2009 and enacted the implementing legislation (OECD, 2012). Despite this the OECD continues to remind countries to improve enforcement of the anti-bribery convention. Recently Australia, Brazil, Canada, Mexico, South Africa, and Turkey were cited for "little or no enforcement." (Economist – "Supply-Side," 2011). It should be noted that both the OECD Convention and the FCPA do not relieve a firm from responsibility when managers use a third party such as an agent to actually deliver the "commission" to a government official. The OECD Convention also includes the proviso that legislation be adopted to eliminate the tax deductibility of bribes paid to public officials. See Table 4.3 for the complete list of signatories.

A distinction is made between "dash" or "grease" payments and large scale bribery. The former are small payments such as those made to customs officials in airports. These kinds of traditional payments are not violations of the laws in most countries.

In the case of bribery, regulations in developed countries may obviate the ethical issues. What is illegal is clearly unethical and this makes the manager's decision an easy one. Nevertheless, we have seen recent examples of questionable activity in many industries. Wal-Mart was accused of making illegal payments of about $24 million in Mexico and Siemens paid $800 million in fines for violating the FCPA. Criminal enforcement in the US has increased from just 2

TABLE 4.3 Signatory countries – OECD Anti-bribery Convention

Argentina	Italy
Australia	Japan
Austria	Korea
Belgium	Luxembourg
Brazil	Mexico
Bulgaria	The Netherlands
Canada	New Zealand
Chile	Norway
Czech Republic	Poland
Denmark	Portugal
Estonia	Russia
Finland	Slovak Republic
France	Slovenia
Germany	South Africa
Greece	Spain
Hungary	Sweden
Iceland	Switzerland
Ireland	Turkey
Israel	United Kingdom
	United States

Source: OECD Report on Anti-Bribery Convention (2012).

enforcement actions in 2004 to 48 in 2010 with 100 open investigations in 2012 (Savage, 2012). The U.S. SEC lists its FCPA enforcement actions on its website. These include actions against Biomet, a medical device company accused of bribing doctors in Argentina, Brazil, and China; the Noble Corporation, accused of bribing customs officials in Nigeria; and London-based medical device company Smith & Nephew, whose US and German subsidiaries were accused of bribing public doctors in Greece (SEC Enforcement FCPA, 2012).

Though Islamic nations are not members of the OECD, managers in these countries are prohibited from engaging in bribery or other forms of "marketing dishonesty" by religious principles (Saeed et al., 2001).

Research shows that gift-giving can be an effective tool for B2B marketers, with more expensive gifts relatively more effective in generating a positive and sustained increase in customer intent to repurchase and actual sales (Beltramini, 2000). A study of more than 300 industrial buyers showed that 50 percent had a firm policy to accept no gifts. Another 24 percent had policies which limited the value of a gift to under $50. Of those firms with no limits on gifts, most were smaller (under 200 employees) (Bird, 1989). Gifts are also fraught with danger in foreign markets. Reardon (1984) recites a number of embarrassing instances where an uninformed salesperson gave inappropriate gifts such as a gold bracelet from Tiffany to his Saudi customer's wife (acknowledging the wife is not acceptable), insisted that his Japanese counterpart open a gift in his presence (embarrassing since it is not customary) and provided a clock to a buyer in China (a symbol of bad luck). The US Institute for Supply Management recognizes that appropriate gift-giving levels differ in many cultures. They provide Principles and Standards of Ethical Supply Management Conduct to help firms develop their own codes of ethics (Baranowski et al., 2007). Judgment is also required in deciding upon entertainment or providing favors. Taking customers to lunch or dinner or to a concert or a sporting event certainly is within the ethical bounds of nearly every society. But other entertainments may tax the ethical limits and should be reviewed carefully.

The question of favors is more complex. In China, the concept of *guanxi* is culturally ingrained. This means developing personal relationships by doing favors for another party and thus obligating him/her. The other then feels he/she should do reciprocal favors. *Guanxi* is a fact of life in China and in a number of other societies as well and must be viewed as a necessary part of doing business. In a later part of this chapter we will discuss ways of responding to various ethical challenges such as this.

Misrepresentation and/or overselling a product, especially by puffing up specific aspects in a not entirely accurate way or by omitting possible critical problems also create ethical issues. In the selling function, individuals also face conflicts of interest, not only because they may be required to sell products which are not suited for a particular client but also because some agents and distributors may handle competing products. Finally, in the selling area, compensation and bookings can create ethical problems. Most salespeople are well aware of the most effective way to increase their compensation and this is certainly within the prescribed limits of any ethical system. However, when sales are manipulated to yield unjustified compensation, ethical issues come to the fore. In one case a firm owned by a single proprietor was about to sell to a large multinational. The owner instructed his salespeople to generate phantom orders to increase the order book and therefore the acquisition price by the multinational. Salespeople were compensated on unreal sales and therefore participated in this unethical behavior.

Product

Marketers must be primarily concerned with the safety of their products. Ethical issues often come to the fore when buyers are unaware of potential safety problems which may result from the use of a manufacturer's product. In B2B marketing, most governments do not establish laws and governmental agencies to protect buyers. The rule of caveat emptor (buyer beware) is generally applied to business buyers. This places an additional ethical burden on suppliers of business products to be sure their products are safe when used in the proper way. In some cases, instructions must be supplied in local languages and even in sign language when the installers or service people are illiterate.

A second product area is that of obsolescence or elimination. While "sloughing off" product has been recommended by Peter Drucker and others for many years, an ethical issue is how quickly products are eliminated or made obsolete. A corollary issue is that of follow-on service of these products. In some cases, a firm eliminates a product and also makes no arrangement for supplying spare parts or service. While it may seem obvious that this can create negative reactions in the marketplace, some firms neglect this important assurance.

One author experienced this problem in Chile. Local managers were angry at the multinational represented by the author because the firm had pulled out of Chile when the world copper price rapidly declined. The desertion left owners of mining equipment without spare parts or service, creating major problems for them. Here, an ethical approach would have also been good business as Chile rebounded and the firm wished to sell not only additional mining equipment but many other products in a market which was now holding quite a negative opinion of it. When a firm offers a warranty, it should be sure that any claims can be satisfied.

While not specifically a marketing problem, the environmental impact caused by manufacturing may be weighed in the decision by a customer to choose one product versus another. In the building products industry, for instance, some architects are now asking for detailed information about manufacturing processes of interior walls (drywall or gypsum board) in order to establish whether a particular product meets established "green" standards.

Disposal can also pose a difficult problem for marketers. In the EU, disposal is an integral part of the overall product cycle and products must be designed with disposal in mind. An interesting and difficult problem arose in the UK in 1995 (Zyglidopoulos, 2002). The Brent Spar, a very large floating oil storage buoy, had been decommissioned several years before. After reviewing the various alternatives, the Shell Corporation decided to dispose of the Spar through sinking it in deep water. However, Greenpeace, the environmental group, objected on a number of grounds and organized protests throughout continental Europe, including calling for a boycott. Faced with these protests and a negative reaction from the general public as well as governments, Shell had to change their disposal plans.

Marketing communications

Advertising is a large area in which ethics standards need to be applied. Ordinary "puffery" of product is expected in consumer advertising. But in business marketing, generally speaking, this will backfire. Nevertheless, some managers who have spent the majority of their careers in the consumer area have felt the need to overemphasize benefits in advertising.

A new area of concern is the violation of confidential information. Some business marketers have collected a great deal of personal information about customers and potential customers through the Internet. The use of this information must be carefully thought through if ethical standards are not to be violated.

Pricing

In the area of pricing, obvious illegal activities such as price fixing are prohibited by antitrust laws in most developed countries and price fixing is prevented in the developing world if harm comes to participants who make their homes in countries where antitrust laws are strictly enforced.

Reciprocity is an interesting problem. This simply means giving preference to a vendor who is also a customer. In a hypothetical example, General Electric may be selling plastics to an electronics manufacturer while also buying computers from that same firm. In this case, a salesman might be tempted to use that relationship to gain an advantage with the electronics firm. An unscrupulous buyer at GE might threaten to cut off computer purchases unless the electronics firm purchased plastics from the company. In many firms, this practice is frowned upon and even specifically prohibited by the firm's code of ethics. However, it is sometimes described as one of the marketing tools in basic texts.

Since business marketers often are required to provide sealed bids for a contract, they should have the confidence that these prices are not shared with others. However, in public bidding (tendering) it is expected that all bids will be revealed. The timing of these discussions is often a sticking point. An unethical buyer might share pricing with a supplier before bids are officially opened and an ethical problem may arise for the salesperson given this special look at the pricing of his/her competitors.

Unjustified price discrimination and unfair pricing occurs when a firm decides to price differently for the same class of customer buying the same quantity. While this kind of discrimination is illegal in the US and in other developed countries, problems can arise where pricing discrimination is used unfairly from one country to another. At the extreme, this can cause the shipment of gray goods back to an unwanted market.

International trade seems to be plagued by questionable invoicing resulting in money laundering. It is a rare international business person who has not been approached by some firm asking for inflated invoices as a way of transferring funds out of a particular country. A similar but not as frequently encountered problem is transfer pricing where prices are set artificially high in order to avoid taxation in a particular market.

Distribution

A vexing problem is attempting to set the same requirements of, and give the same benefits to, distributors around the world. Meeting local market conditions can often result in a hodgepodge of distribution policies. It is important that a firm apply its ethical standards to distribution policies in various markets. Finally, related to the bribery discussion above, inflated commissions should be viewed as suspect by any manufacturer's marketing department. The Foreign Corrupt Practices Act requires that accounting procedures be in place to detect unusually large commissions which may eventually result in bribes.

Market research

Craig and Douglas (2000) advise that respondents' participation in research must be entirely voluntary and that it is unethical to mislead them in order to gain their cooperation. Respondents must be told that their responses will be held in strict confidence and that their identity will be anonymous. Respondents must not be harmed in any way by the research process and should be informed if recording devices or other forms of observation, which may not be evident, are being used. Researchers should be truthful about their skills and experiences. They should take care to design and conduct research in the most cost-effective way. Researchers should be careful to provide security for the data and provide findings only supported by the data. Researchers also should clearly define work they are doing which is not related to research. Contracts should follow the guidelines provided by the European Society for Opinion and Marketing Research (ESOMAR), the American Marketing Association or other professional associations.

Personnel

Certainly a firm must be careful in applying requirements for hiring individuals. Discrimination is proscribed by law in many countries and yet discrimination may be the best course of action in particular markets. For instance, it would not be feasible to hire a woman as a salesperson in Saudi Arabia. Nevertheless, the proper application of law and ethics is required in choosing employees. Some firms in the quest to reduce cost have established unsafe or unfair working conditions. While this does not impact directly on an international marketing person's area of responsibility, it does affect the ability of the marketer to sell products in those markets where ethical concerns are important. Closer to the marketing responsibility is the treatment of local salespeople, other marketing specialists, and clerical staff. While personnel policies may not transfer completely from the home office, reasonable expectations of employees should be considered when setting local policies.

According to Chonko and Hunt (2000), ethical conflict occurs when individuals see their duties toward one group as inconsistent with their duties toward another (including one's own self). The most important conflicts found by these researchers were balancing corporate interests against the interests of: customers, self, society, and subordinates (in that order). In their study, Chonko and Hunt found the ten most difficult ethical problems identified by marketing professionals were (in frequency of mention):

- bribery;
- fairness;
- honesty;
- pricing;
- product;
- personnel;
- confidentiality;
- advertising;
- manipulation of data;
- purchasing.

Issues not identified by these authors but which also have received much attention are pollution, budget considerations, non-reporting of violations, and refusing to help customers.

ETHICS IN GLOBAL BUSINESS

Zyglidopoulos (2002) states that multinationals have to maintain higher levels of social and environmental responsibility because of the severe corporate reputation effects of lapses in these areas. He further states that matters impacting the firm's reputation should not be left to the discretion of national subsidiaries but should be coordinated centrally at headquarters who would set a global set of norms.

Chan and Armstrong (1999) identify problems by their importance in a study of 300 Australian and Canadian firms (150 each). The five most frequently *mentioned* international marketing ethical problems were ranked as follows:

- large-scale bribery;
- cultural differences;
- involvement in political affairs;
- pricing practices;
- illegal/immoral activities.

The five most frequently *occurring* categories of ethical problems were: cultural differences, gifts, favors and entertainment, pricing practices, questionable commissions to channel members, and large-scale bribery. Chan and Armstrong define cultural differences as those involving potential misunderstandings related to traditional requirements of the exchange process including what may be called a bribe by one culture but not by another, different practices related to gifts, payments, favors and entertainment, and political contributions. Interestingly, these authors found differences between Australian and Canadian managers in both their perceptions of the importance of ethical problems and in their listing of the frequency of the problems.

There is no question that there are different understandings of corruption in various markets. Transparency International, an independent non-governmental organization, publishes an annual corruption perceptions index. For 2011, this list is presented as Table 4.4.

TABLE 4.4 Transparency International Corruption Perceptions Index 2011

Country rank	Country	CPI 2011 score	Country rank	Country	CPI 2011 score
1	New Zealand	9.5	10	Canada	8.7
2	Denmark	9.4	11	Luxembourg	8.5
2	Finland	9.4	12	Hong Kong	8.4
4	Sweden	9.3	13	Iceland	8.3
5	Singapore	9.2	14	Germany	8
6	Norway	9	14	Japan	8
7	Netherlands	8.9	16	Austria	7.8
8	Australia	8.8	16	Barbados	7.8
8	Switzerland	8.8	16	United Kingdom	7.8

continued . . .

TABLE 4.4 . . . *continued*

Country rank	Country	CPI 2011 score	Country rank	Country	CPI 2011 score
19	Belgium	7.5	46	Mauritius	5.1
19	Ireland	7.5	49	Rwanda	5
21	Bahamas	7.3	50	Costa Rica	4.8
22	Chile	7.2	50	Lithuania	4.8
22	Qatar	7.2	50	Oman	4.8
24	United States	7.1	50	Seychelles	4.8
25	France	7	54	Hungary	4.6
25	Saint Lucia	7	54	Kuwait	4.6
25	Uruguay	7	56	Jordan	4.5
28	United Arab Emirates	6.8	57	Czech Republic	4.4
29	Estonia	6.4	57	Namibia	4.4
30	Cyprus	6.3	57	Saudi Arabia	4.4
31	Spain	6.2	60	Malaysia	4.3
32	Botswana	6.1	61	Cuba	4.2
32	Portugal	6.1	61	Latvia	4.2
32	Taiwan	6.1	61	Turkey	4.2
35	Slovenia	5.9	64	Georgia	4.1
36	Israel	5.8	64	South Africa	4.1
36	Saint Vincent and the Grenadines	5.8	66	Croatia	4
			66	Montenegro	4
38	Bhutan	5.7	66	Slovakia	4
39	Malta	5.6	69	Ghana	3.9
39	Puerto Rico	5.6	69	Italy	3.9
41	Cape Verde	5.5	69	Macedonia, FYR	3.9
41	Poland	5.5	69	Samoa	3.9
43	Korea (South)	5.4	73	Brazil	3.8
44	Brunei	5.2	73	Tunisia	3.8
44	Dominica	5.2	75	China	3.6
46	Bahrain	5.1	75	Romania	3.6
46	Macau	5.1	77	Gambia	3.5

continued . . .

TABLE 4.4 ... *continued*

Country rank	Country	CPI 2011 score	Country rank	Country	CPI 2011 score
77	Lesotho	3.5	100	Malawi	3
77	Vanuatu	3.5	100	Mexico	3
80	Colombia	3.4	100	Sao Tome & Principe	3
80	El Salvador	3.4	100	Suriname	3
80	Greece	3.4	100	Tanzania	3
80	Morocco	3.4	112	Algeria	2.9
80	Peru	3.4	112	Egypt	2.9
80	Thailand	3.4	112	Kosovo	2.9
86	Bulgaria	3.3	112	Moldova	2.9
86	Jamaica	3.3	112	Senegal	2.9
86	Panama	3.3	112	Vietnam	2.9
86	Serbia	3.3	118	Bolivia	2.8
86	Sri Lanka	3.3	118	Mali	2.8
91	Bosnia and Herzegovina	3.2	120	Bangladesh	2.7
91	Liberia	3.2	120	Ecuador	2.7
91	Trinidad and Tobago	3.2	120	Ethiopia	2.7
91	Zambia	3.2	120	Guatemala	2.7
95	Albania	3.1	120	Iran	2.7
95	India	3.1	120	Kazakhstan	2.7
95	Kiribati	3.1	120	Mongolia	2.7
95	Swaziland	3.1	120	Mozambique	2.7
95	Tonga	3.1	120	Solomon Islands	2.7
100	Argentina	3	129	Armenia	2.6
100	Benin	3	129	Dominican Republic	2.6
100	Burkina Faso	3	129	Honduras	2.6
100	Djibouti	3	129	Philippines	2.6
100	Gabon	3	129	Syria	2.6
100	Indonesia	3	134	Cameroon	2.5
100	Madagascar	3	134	Eritrea	2.5

continued . . .

TABLE 4.4 . . . *continued*

Country rank	Country	CPI 2011 score	Country rank	Country	CPI 2011 score
134	Guyana	2.5	154	Nepal	2.2
134	Lebanon	2.5	154	Papua New Guinea	2.2
134	Maldives	2.5	154	Paraguay	2.2
134	Nicaragua	2.5	154	Zimbabwe	2.2
134	Niger	2.5	164	Cambodia	2.1
134	Pakistan	2.5	164	Guinea	2.1
134	Sierra Leone	2.5	164	Kyrgyzstan	2.1
143	Azerbaijan	2.4	164	Yemen	2.1
143	Belarus	2.4	168	Angola	2
143	Comoros	2.4	168	Chad	2
143	Mauritania	2.4	168	Congo, Dem Rep	2
143	Nigeria	2.4	168	Libya	2
143	Russia	2.4	172	Burundi	1.9
143	Timor-Leste	2.4	172	Equatorial Guinea	1.9
143	Togo	2.4	172	Venezuela	1.9
143	Uganda	2.4	175	Haiti	1.8
152	Tajikistan	2.3	175	Iraq	1.8
152	Ukraine	2.3	177	Sudan	1.6
154	Central African Republic	2.2	177	Turkmenistan	1.6
154	Congo Republic	2.2	177	Uzbekistan	1.6
154	Côte d'Ivoire	2.2	180	Afghanistan	1.5
154	Guinea-Bissau	2.2	180	Myanmar	1.5
154	Kenya	2.2	182	Somalia	1
154	Laos	2.2	182	Korea (North)	1

Source: reprinted from Corruption Perceptions Index. Copyright 2011. Transparency International: the global coalition against corruption. Used with permission. For more information, visit http://www.transparency.org

A brief review of the table will show that corruption is perceived to be rampant in North Korea, Somalia, Myanmar, Afghanistan, Uzbekistan, Turkmenistan, Sudan, Iraq, Haiti, Venezuela, Equatorial Guinea, and Burundi. Each of these countries scored lower than 2.0 in this index. Markets which are perceived to have very low levels of corruption include New Zealand, Denmark, Finland, Sweden, Singapore, and Norway, each of which scored above 9.0 in the index.

The widely varying environments in countries throughout the world have led some to postulate that no one set of ethical guidelines can be established for marketing people which will be effective in every market. This leads inevitably to cultural/ethical relativism which contradicts the idea that there are universal moral truths. Rachels (2002) says cultural relativism is based on the idea that since cultures have varied practices, any one of these practices may be acceptable. For instance, if in one culture large bribes are a matter of course while in another no bribes are permitted in gaining contracts, cultural relativism would say that no rules regarding bribes would be proper. Cultural relativism says that if a society is living up to its own moral standards, that is all that is required of it. It does not allow for the idea of moral progress and change for the better.

It is obvious that managers in different cultures have different ethical attitudes toward the situations they face every day. For instance, MacDonald (1988) showed that Hong Kong managers believed that taking credit for another person's work was more unethical than bribery or gaining competitor information, a finding completely at odds with the beliefs of Western managers.

Donaldson and Dunfee (1999) say accepting "whatever prevails in the host country" is a mistake because this can result in both corruption and public relations disasters and "substitutes unmitigated relativism for good sense." As we have seen earlier in this chapter, absolute adherence to one theory

---

Talking Point

The *SS United States* was probably one of the swiftest and most luxurious ocean liners in the 1950s and 1960s. Because it was designed to be lightweight and fireproof, the ship probably contained more asbestos than any other. In 1992, it was purchased by a consortium planning to refurbish it for luxury cruising. However, the asbestos would have to be removed first. In the United States, this project would cost an estimated $100 million. So, the liner was towed to Turkey where the same jobs could be completed for about $2 million. The Turkish government refused to allow the removal there. Subsequently, the owners were looking at other locations such as Sevastopol in Ukraine, where laws about the environment were less strict.

If a country's laws don't prohibit a particular action, is it ethical to have the ship towed to Sevastopol and the asbestos removed in a way which might cause cancer among workers and nearby residents even if there aren't any laws against it in Ukraine? Shouldn't a corporation be able to take that action? How can a manager reconcile his beliefs with those in a particular nation?

And from a practical viewpoint, some of the countries where this work could be carried out are very poor. People are starving without the work (and foreign currency) that this type of job offers. Maybe we are willing to starve rather than compromise our ethics – but are we justified in letting others starve because of them? (This talking point based upon Satchell, (1994.)

or another does not provide a manager with the guidance required to face ethical problems he/she encounters in the conduct of business. This is especially true when varying cultural standards are at play as well.

Hunt and Vitell (1986) proposed a general theory of marketing ethics which takes into account the cultural, industry and organizational environments as well as personal experiences and both deontological and consequentialist considerations to arrive at the proper behavior. This framework, while useful, does not specifically address the problem of competing cultural norms.

Donaldson and Dunfee (1999) propose a theory based on the Integrative Social Contracts Theory (ISCT). These authors differentiate between pluralism, allowing for tolerance of other cultures' norms, and relativism in which any action undertaken by managers in a particular culture is acceptable simply because it has been undertaken by others in that culture.

Chan and Armstrong (1999) claim that international marketing relativism is becoming a dominant approach and that "experience and culture have become criteria of what is ethical." Yet, Husted et al. (1996) showed that there was a measure of agreement across various cultures related to questionable business and marketing practices. In the past, the concept of universal ethical standards was looked upon by some as a form of moral imperialism implying that one set of standards is inevitably more right than another. However, with the coalescing of universal standards, an emerging set of universal norms appears to be forming.

Donaldson and Dunfee (1999) describe three levels of ethical standards or norms. At the most basic level are *hypernorms* – fundamental rights acceptable to all cultures and organizations. Second are *consistent norms*, which are more culturally specific. They must be consistent with hypernorms, however. According to Donaldson and Dunfee, most corporations' ethical codes fall within this category. A third level is called *moral free space*. Here we find norms that are inconsistent with some of the legitimate norms described in the second level yet are often expressions of strongly held cultural beliefs. Moving even farther away are what these authors call *illegitimate norms*. These are the norms which are incompatible with hypernorms.

Using this approach, hypernorms relate to basic practices such as price gouging in markets where there are no alternatives or using slave labor to manufacture products. But, the existence of moral free space allows managers to adapt where the norms of a particular country conflict with consistent norms in the home country but not with the overriding hypernorms. One example given by these authors relates to nepotism. In India, firms often promise employees a job for one of their children when a child reaches the proper age. In the West, this might violate an anti-nepotism policy. But, this kind of action, quite acceptable in India, falls into the moral free space of the model proposed. This approach allows managers to avoid the dangers of ethical relativism which establishes no standards whatever while allowing for adaptation to local cultures when that adaptation does not violate basic moral standards.

ANALYZING ETHICAL PROBLEMS

When a manager faces a problem which may raise ethical issues, he/she should be able to apply guidelines which can help in decision making. Figure 4.2, Analyzing an ethical question, combines the thinking of Lawrence and Weber (2011) and Donaldson and Dunfee (1999).

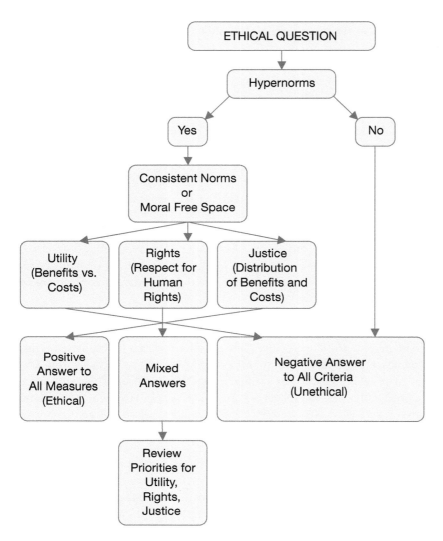

FIGURE 4.2 Analyzing an ethical question

Source: adapted from Lawrence and Weber (2011); Donaldson and Dunfee (1999).

An ethical question would first be tested against the hypernorms which form the bedrock of ethical thinking. Violation of these hypernorms would lead to rejecting a possible course of action as unethical. If the action is permissible when compared to consistent norms or falls into moral free space, it would then be subjected to a review in terms of utility (the benefits versus the costs), rights (whether human rights are respected), and justice (related to whether the benefits and costs are fairly distributed). Should the action provide positive answers when viewed from the basis of utility, rights, and justice, the action proposed would be ethical. Should the action create negative results when viewed from these three perspectives, it would be unethical. Should the answers be mixed, a manager would have to balance the concerns of all stakeholders as related to utility, rights, and justice before deciding on a course of action.

MAKING ETHICS WORK

In response to the need for more consistent ethical behavior, corporations have attempted to institutionalize basic corporate values. One very obvious response has been the development of codes of ethics. But the mere existence of codes of ethics is generally ineffective in implementing ethical behavior among managers (Chonko and Hunt, 2000). While it is important to have a code of ethics, it is more important that top management make ethical behavior a priority. Chonko and Hunt cite several studies confirming that the commitment of senior management to ethics is essential for promoting ethical behavior and that familiarity with the company code of ethics increases sensitivity to ethical decision making.

A number of firms have been cited for having useful codes of ethics and many, including Schneider Electric, Marriott International, and Caterpillar Inc. have been recognized as the most ethical firms worldwide (Ethisphere, 2011). Caterpillar has published excellent guidelines (see Figure 4.3). Their worldwide business code of conduct is summed up in four words: integrity, excellence, teamwork, commitment. In this code, the firm states "We hold ourselves to the highest standard of integrity and ethical behavior. We tell the truth" (Caterpillar, 2005).

Paine (1994) has described two approaches to corporate integrity strategies. The first approach emphasizes compliance which is based on avoiding litigation and liability. A firm pursuing this approach establishes rules for employees hoping to direct employee behavior through the threat of punishment. As Paine points out, however, the emphasis on legal restrictions may allow the perception that "if it's legal it's ethical." But actions which are lawful can be unethical, especially in developing countries.

Paine believes a more effective approach is based on individual integrity, emphasizing employee responsibility for proper conduct. In this approach, the firm supplies clear codes of conduct, training for employees, audits and controls to ensure that standards are being met. Paine stresses, as do others (Robin and Reidenbach, 1987; Chonko and Hunt, 2000) that top management has a critical role to play in establishing the proper ethical climate and behavior. Robin and Reidenbach further state that top management must integrate ethical core values into the organization's corporate culture.

Paine summarizes an effective integrity strategy as follows:

- The guiding values and commitments make sense and are clearly communicated.
- Company leaders are personally committed, credible, and willing to take action on the values they espouse.
- These values are integrated into the normal channels of management decision-making and reflected in the organization's activities.
- Company systems and structures support and reinforce core values.
- Managers throughout the company have the decision-making skills, knowledge, and competence to make ethically sound decisions on a day-to-day basis.

OUR VALUES IN ACTION

Caterpillar's Worldwide
Code of Conduct

Integrity
The Power of Honesty

Excellence
The Power of Quality

Teamwork
The Power of Working Together

Commitment
The Power of Responsibility

page_7

FIGURE 4.3 Caterpillar's worldwide code of conduct

Reproduced courtesy of Caterpillar Inc.

continued . . .

НАШИ ЦЕННОСТИ В ДЕЙСТВИИ

Международный кодекс деловой
этики компании Caterpillar

Добросовестность
Сила честности

Профессионализм
Сила качества

Работа в команде
Сила совместной работы

Ответственность
Сила ответственности

страница_7

FIGURE 4.3 . . . *continued*

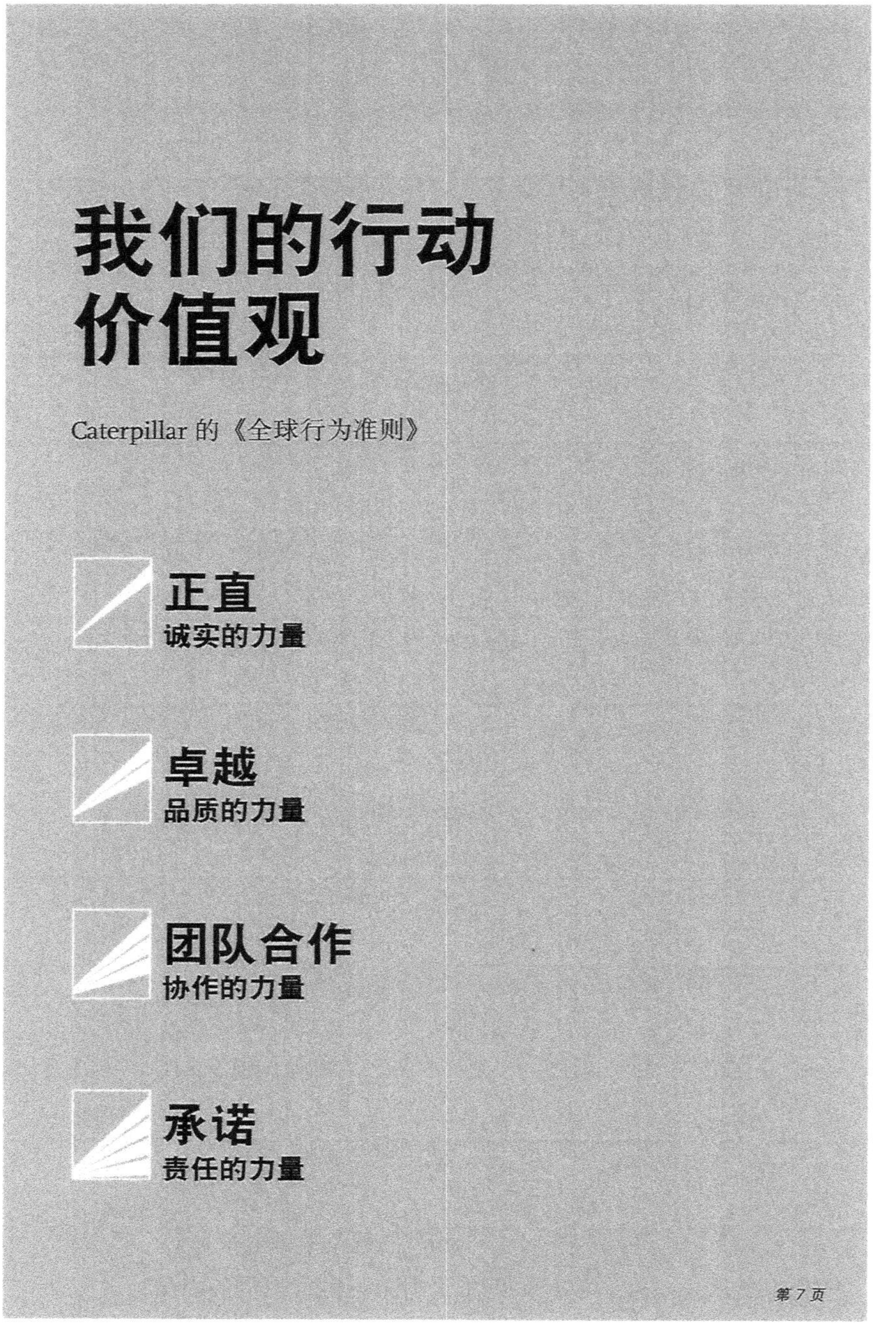

我们的行动
价值观

Caterpillar 的《全球行为准则》

正直
诚实的力量

卓越
品质的力量

团队合作
协作的力量

承诺
责任的力量

第 7 页

FIGURE 4.3 . . . *continued*

To make ethics work within a corporation, it is important that a training program be established. Some firms also have appointed an ethics officer and/or an ethics committee. Many firms conduct ethics audits to compare actual behavior with the established company standards. In order to implement truly ethical behavior, a firm must establish a comprehensive program including the code of ethics, employee training, and an ethics officer as well as audits of conduct. The Institute of Supply Management in the US reinforces many of Paine's ideas (Baranowski et al., 2007). It points out the importance of establishing an executive committee on ethical conduct with wide authority and responsibilities, and the need to communicate regularly with suppliers and conduct training sessions for them explaining a firm's ethics policies. It also adds that the firm should "quickly and decisively deal" with employees or suppliers who violate ethics policies.

Associations as well have established codes of ethics. ESOMAR, a worldwide market research association, has a long and detailed code of ethics as does the Chartered Institute of Marketing (CIM, 2012) and the American Marketing Association (AMA). The CIM is the largest marketing organization in the world, including students, and has branches in 11 nations as well as headquarters in the UK. The AMA includes about 30,000 members.

CASE STUDY

Taiwan Office Furniture

Jian Ching-yen is the vice president of marketing for Taiwan Office Furniture, a $50 million (US) manufacturer of office furniture located near Taipei. Today he is faced with a serious problem which needs to be handled properly. Over the past few years the firm has grown rapidly because of a new light-weight material they are using to manufacture binder bins or flipper door cabinets, which hang on office furniture panels and also can be mounted on drywall. Some disturbing news has recently reached Jian and today there will be a meeting to discuss the implications.

Since the new material was introduced for these cabinets, Taiwan Office Furniture had been able to lower its prices and is now at least 30 percent cheaper than its nearer competitors for the cabinets. Because the cost of the cabinets make up a good percentage of the overall selling price of an office furniture installation, Taiwan has been able to win many bids and therefore sales are growing rapidly.

On a recent trip to Jakarta and Manila where 25 percent of the furniture has been sold, one distributor mentioned to Jian that in a few instances the new material had lacked the strength to hold a fully loaded cabinet.

As a matter of course, Taiwan Office Furniture issues to its distributors guidelines for cabinet loading. The firm warns that placing more than 100lbs in a four-foot wide cabinet may overload its capabilities. Yet,

. . . continued

office workers rarely weigh what they put in a cabinet and binders filled with paper plus large inserts with office supplies like staples and CDs can easily bring the weight beyond that recommended by the company. During his trip, Jian was also told by distributors both in Malaysia and Indonesia that in a few installations, heavily-loaded cabinets had fallen off panels or walls. In no case was an office worker injured, but this seems to be raising a possible problem for the firm.

The meeting today will be with the executive committee, including Jian's boss, the president of the firm, as well as the manufacturing, engineering, and financial officers of the firm. Jian has talked to all of them privately and summarizes their positions as follows:

Manufacturing – we are making the product to the specifications given to us by engineering. There are no manufacturing defects.

Engineering – the standards we set are reasonable and when tested the product meets the standards we have set.

Finance – while this may be a problem, we can't get too carried away and cost ourselves a profitable quarter or year.

The company has approximately 20,000 of these cabinets in place. To fully test each unit at approximately US$50 per test would cost the company US$1 million. To replace all the units would cost a minimum of US$200 per unit or about US$4 million. That certainly would have a major impact upon the bottom line for at least one-quarter and possibly more.

Jian feels the cabinet situation may be an ethical problem since there are no laws regulating this kind of situation. Jian thinks about his options and sketches them on a pad:

1 Ignore the problem since very few instances have been reported.
2 Send out additional warnings to both distributors and office workers.
3 Test all installed units.
4 React to problems only, replacing those units which fail.
5 Replace all units.

Jian knows it's not going to be a pleasant meeting, but he believes something must be done.

CASE STUDY QUESTIONS

1 How can Jian Ching-yen apply ethical tests to this problem?
2 What are the possible consequences should the firm decide to do nothing?
3 What is the best course of action for Jian to take?
4 How should he present his case to the executive committee meeting that is about to take place?

CHAPTER SUMMARY

Establishing an effective ethics program, especially in a firm heavily involved in international business, is both a challenge and a necessity. Firms violating societal norms suffer major negative effects to their corporate reputation. Therefore, it is important that managers understand how to deal with ethical problems in all markets throughout the world. The key points from this chapter are:

■ The marketing department is operating within many influences. Corporate culture is an important part of the ethical tone of the firm.

■ Today, relying solely on the market's invisible hand or the hand of government leaves the firm vulnerable.

■ While philosophy gives us deontology (acting based on absolute principles) and utilitarianism as well as virtue ethics, none of these approaches nor the simple rules sometimes used in marketing departments give useful guidelines for managers.

■ There are ethical issues in many aspects of marketing, including selling, product, marketing communications, pricing, distribution, market research, and personnel.

■ Local markets range from highly corrupt to completely honest and in some cases lead marketers to the thought that no established ethical principles can be applied throughout the world – cultural relativism.

■ A most useful theory proposes that fundamental ideas called hypernorms can be accepted by all marketers. Once these are established, adapting to local cultures is less difficult.

■ Firms and associations have developed codes of conduct. But codes of conduct by themselves do not ensure ethical behavior. A full corporate program must be established to ensure ethical behavior by all stakeholders.

REVIEW QUESTIONS

1   Describe the environmental impacts on the marketing department's ethical decision-making.
2   What are the major competing views of corporate responsibility? Describe in detail.
3   Compare and contrast the deontological, consequentialist, and virtue theories of ethics.
4   List the key ethical issues in international B2B marketing and describe some key issues in at least three of these areas.
5   How important is the question of bribery in international business? What is being done on an international basis to counter it?
6   What are the most important international marketing ethical problems?
7   What is cultural/ethical relativism? What are the drawbacks to this approach and how can a manager adapt to local cultures while maintaining ethical standards?
8   What are the key elements of a successful corporate ethics program?

REFERENCES

Baranowski, Judy, Addler, David D., Kalin, Leah, Lallatin, Carla S., Smiley, Steve, and Turner, Gwen (2007). "Ethical Behavior – Boundaries of Influence." Institute of Supply Management. Accessed 25 June 2012 at http://www.ism.ws/files/Pubs/Proceedings/EKBaranowski.pdf

Beltramini, Richard F. (2000). "Exploring the Effectiveness of Business Gifts: Replication and Extension." *Journal of Advertising*, Vol. 29, No. 2, 75–8.

Bird, Monroe Murphy (1989). "Gift-Giving and Gift-Taking in Industrial Companies." *Industrial Marketing Management*, Vol. 18, Iss. 2, 91–4.

Caterpillar (2005). Worldwide Code of Conduct. Accessed 27 June 2012 at http://www.cat.com/cda/files/89286/7/worldwide_code.pdf

Chan, T.S. and Armstrong, Robert W. (1999). "Comparative Ethical Report Card: A Study of Australian and Canadian Managers' Perceptions of International Marketing Ethics Problems." *Journal of Business Ethics*, Vol. 18, Iss. 1, 3–15.

Chonko, Lawrence B. and Hunt, Shelby D. (2000). "Ethics and Marketing Management: A Retrospective and Prospective Commentary." *Journal of Business Research*, Vol. 50, Iss. 3, 235–44.

CIM (Chartered Institute of Marketing) (2012). Accessed 26 June at http://www.cim.co.uk/about/interoffices.aspx

Corruption Perception Index (2011). Transparency International. Accessed 26 June a http://cpi.transparency.org/cpi2011/results/

Craig, Samuel and Douglas, Susan P. (2000). *International Marketing Research*. Chichester, W. Sussex: John Wiley.

Czinkota, Michael R. and Ronkainen, Ilkka A. (2006). *International Marketing*. Mason, Ohio: Cengage.

Donaldson, Thomas and Dunfee, Thomas W. (1999). "When Ethics Travel: The Promise and Peril of Global Business Ethics." *California Management Review*, Vol. 41, No. 4, 45–63.

Donaldson, Thomas, Werhane, Patricia H., and Cording, Margaret (2002). *Ethical Issues in Business: A Philosophical Approach*. Upper Saddle River, NJ: Prentice-Hall.

Economist, The (2011). "Supply-Side." *The Economist*, Vol. 400, Iss. 8758 (5 November), 72.

Ethisphere (2011). 2011 World's Most Ethical Companies. Accessed 26 June 2012 at http://ethisphere.com/past-wme-honorees/wme2011/

Goodpaster, Kenneth E. and Matthews, John B., Jr. (1992). "Can a Corporation Have a Conscience?" *Harvard Business Review*, Vol. 60, Iss. 1, 132–41.

Hunt, Shelby D. and Vitell, Scott (1986). "A General Theory of Marketing Ethics." *Journal of Macromarketing*, Vol. 6, No. 1, 5–16.

Husted, Bryan W., Dozier, Janelle Brinker, McMahon, Timothy J. and Kattan, Michael W. (1996). "The Impact of Cross-National Carriers of Business Ethics on Attitudes about Questionable Practices and Forms of Moral Reasoning." *Journal of International Business Studies*, Vol. 27, Iss. 2, 391–411.

Keegan, Warren J. and Green, Mark C. (2010). *Global Marketing*. Upper Saddle River, NJ: Prentice-Hall.

Kurschner, Dale (1996). "Five Ways Ethical Business$$ Creates Fatter Profit$." *Business Ethics*, Vol. 10, Iss. 2, March–April, 20–3.

Lawrence, Anne T. and Weber, James (2011). *Business and Society: Stakeholders, Ethics, Public Policy*. New York: McGraw-Hill.

MacDonald, G.M. (1988). "Ethical Perceptions of Hong Kong/Chinese Business Managers." *Journal of Business Ethics*, Vol. 7, Iss. 11, 835–45.

Newton, Lisa H. (2004). *Ethics in America: Source Reader*. Upper Saddle River, NJ: Prentice-Hall.

Nguyen, A. and Cragg, W. (2012). "Interorganizational Favour Exchange and the Relationship Between Doing Well and Doing Good." *Journal Of Business Ethics*, Vol. 105, Iss.1, 53–68.

OECD (2012). Anti-bribery Convention. Accessed 25 June 2012 at http://www.oecd.org/document/24/0,3746,en_2649_34859_1933144_1_1_1_1,00.html

Paine, Lynn Sharp (1994). "Managing for Organizational Integrity." *Harvard Business Review*, Vol. 72, Iss. 2 (March–April), 106–17.

Rachels, James (2002). "The Challenge of Cultural Relativism" in *Ethical Issues in Business: A Philosophical Approach*. Donaldson, Thomas, Werhane, Patricia H. and Cording, Margaret (eds), Upper Saddle River, NJ: Prentice-Hall, pp. 410–19.

Reardon, Kathleen K. (1984). "It's the Thought that Counts." *Harvard Business Review*, Vol. 62, Iss. 5, 136–41.

Robin, Donald P. and Reidenbach, Eric R. (1987). "Social Responsibility, Ethics, and Marketing Strategy: Closing the Gap between Concept and Application." *Journal of Marketing*, Vol. 51, Iss. 1, 44–58.

Saeed, Mohammad, Ahmed, Zafar U., and Mukhtar, Syeda-Masooda (2001). "International Marketing Ethics from an Islamic Perspective: A Value-Maximization Approach." *Journal of Business Ethics*, Vol. 32, Iss. 2, 127–42.

Satchell, Michael J. (1994). "Deadly Trade in Toxics." *U.S. News and World Report*, 7 March, Vol. 116, Iss. 9, 64–6.

Savage, Charlie (2012). "With Wal-Mart Claims, Greater Attention on a Law." New York Times, 25 April. Accessed 25 June 2012 at http://www.nytimes.com/2012/04/26/business/global/with-wal-mart-bribery-case-more-attention-on-a-law.html

Schlegelmilch, Bodo (1998). *Marketing Ethics: An International Perspective*. London: International Thomson Business Press.

SEC Enforcement FCPA (2012). Accessed 25 June 2012 at http://www.sec.gov/spotlight/fcpa/fcpa-cases.shtml

Smith, N. Craig (1995). "Marketing Strategies for the Ethics Era." *Sloan Management Review*, Vol. 36, Iss. 4, 85–97.

Terpstra, Vern and David, Kenneth (1991). *The Cultural Environment of International Business*. Cincinnati, OH: South-Western Publishing Company.

Verschoor, Curtis C. (1998). "A Study of the Link Between a Corporation's Financial Performance and Its Commitment to Ethics." *Journal of Business Ethics*, Vol. 17, No. 13, 1509–16.

Whysall, Paul (2000). "Marketing Ethics – An Overview." *The Marketing Review*, Vol. 1, No. 2, 175–95.

World Bank (2012).The Costs of Corruption. Accessed 25 June 2012 at http://web.worldbank.org

Zyglidopoulos, Stelios C. (2002). "The Social and Environmental Responsibilities of Multinationals: Evidence from the Brent Spar Case." *Journal of Business Ethics*, Vol. 36, Nos 1–2, 141–51.

Chapter 5

Market research

INTRODUCTION

Market research is at the heart of any effective marketing program especially when a manager is planning to enter a foreign market. Research is the starting point for determining who the best customers are, how they go about making buying decisions and what the potential sales might be to each of them. Market research also helps a manager determine what competitors are doing and what they might do. It is critically important to develop as much information as possible before making financial commitments. While business decisions can never be made with absolute certainty, developing as much information as possible reduces the uncertainty to a manageable level.

CHAPTER OBJECTIVES

After reading this chapter, you should be able to:

- understand the need for market research
- differentiate between business to business and consumer market research
- list recent changes in the field including new pitfalls researchers face
- understand how to develop a market information system and describe the research process
- describe the role of market research in determining market potential and developing sales forecasts
- recognize when there is a need for and pinpoint the appropriate time for using outside specialists
- explain how to use each of the market research methods
- understand the uses of benchmarking.

Talking Point

How one approaches market research is often determined by the mindset of the individual conducting the research. A story is told about a young business person sent to Africa in the early nineteenth century to determine the potential market for shoes. Upon arriving, he traveled the continent back and forth and at the end of the month sent a cable to the home office in London which said, "No market for shoes in this continent . . . no one wears them." The chief of the company was unwilling to accept this verdict, so he sent out another "researcher." Observing the same state of "bare feet" in the continent, the replacement individual cabled, "Tremendous market for shoes since no one has them yet."

So does this mean that the perceptions of the researcher are more important than the facts? If so, is any market research truly objective?

THE NEED FOR MARKET RESEARCH

Market research is "the systematic and objective identification, collection, analysis, dissemination, and use of information for the purpose of improving decision making related to the identification and solution of problems and opportunities in marketing." (Malhotra, 2010). While other and more detailed definitions have been given, especially by the American Marketing Association, this definition is concise and focuses on the fact that information needs to be developed as it relates to specific business problems or opportunities. In business to business settings, market research is heavily used for forecasting, developing trends, finding market potential, studying the competition, and developing sales forecasts and sales quotas.

DIFFERENCES BETWEEN CONSUMER AND BUSINESS MARKET RESEARCH

While consumer and business marketers both conduct research related to product attributes and product acceptance, most consumer research focuses on these areas. Consumer market researchers also spend a good deal more on advertising and packaging research than do business marketers. Most business market research is aimed at market potential and determining members of the buying center (DMU) or the network. In addition, business market researchers are often faced by a different set of problems than are consumer researchers. Table 5.1 gives an overview of these differences.

CHANGES IN MARKET RESEARCH

While the basic techniques for completing market research have remained the same, the advent of the Internet has had a major impact on the gathering of both primary and secondary data. Now it

TABLE 5.1 Consumer versus business to business marketing research

Consideration	Consumer	Business to Business
Universe	Large. Dependent on category under investigation but usually unlimited.	Small. Fairly limited in total population and even more so if within a defined industry category.
Respondent accessibility	Fairly easy. Can interview in malls, at home, on the telephone, via the Internet or using mail techniques.	Difficult. Usually only during working hours at plant, office, or on the road. Respondent is usually preoccupied with other priorities.
Respondent cooperation	Over the years has become more and more difficult, yet millions of consumers have never been interviewed.	A major concern. Due to the small population, many respondents are being over-researched. The purchaser and decision makers in the business firm are the buyers of a variety of products and services from office supplies to heavy equipment.
Sample size	Can usually be drawn as large as required for statistical confidence since the population is in the hundreds of millions.	Usually much smaller than consumer sample, yet the statistical confidence is equal to the relationship of the sample to the total population.
Respondent definitions	Usually fairly simple. Those aware of a category or brand, users of a category or brand, demographic criteria, etc. The ultimate purchaser is also a user for most consumer products and services.	Somewhat more difficult. The user and the purchasing decision maker in most cases are not the same. Factory workers who use heavy equipment, secretaries who sit on office chairs, etc., are the users and, no doubt, best able to evaluate products and services. However, they tend not to be the ultimate purchasers and in many cases do not have any influence on the decision-making process.
Interviewers	Can usually be easily trained. They are also consumers and tend to be somewhat familiar with the area under investigation for most categories.	Difficult to find good B2B interviewers. At least a working knowledge of the product class is essential. Preferably more than just a working knowledge.
Study costs	Key dictators of cost are sample size and incidence. Lower incidence usage categories (for example, users of soft moist dog food, powdered breakfast beverages, etc.) or demographic or behavioral screening criteria (attend a movie at least once a month, over 65 years of age, and own a cat, etc.) can up costs considerably.	Relative to consumer research, the critical elements resulting in significantly higher per-interview costs are: lower incidence levels, difficulties in locating the "right" respondent (that is, the member of the correct buying center or network) and securing cooperation, time, and concentration of effort for the interview itself.

Source: adapted from Katz (1979).

is possible to reach respondents without the use of telephone or mail techniques. The danger of an unqualified respondent completing the survey is about equal for the Internet and mail techniques. The Internet has also made it possible to develop secondary data much more rapidly and efficiently. Virtually any data source is available to anyone in any part of the world once that person has made the connection to the web. This allows faster, more accurate development of information and the ability to compare sources at very low cost.

DEVELOPING A MARKETING INFORMATION SYSTEM

A marketing information system (MkIS) is a fully integrated approach to developing, storing and using information from all sources to help develop the most effective marketing strategies and plans.

An effective marketing information system uses not only information developed by market research but also information that exists both in internal and other data sources. All this information is placed in a so-called "data warehouse." The development and maintenance of the data warehouse is a key task for any marketing department. It requires excellent planning and organization and dedication to keep it up to date and usable. In order to use the information in the data warehouse, many firms have developed decision support systems (DSS). A decision support system is an interactive computer-based tool used by decision makers to help answer questions and solve problems. The function of a DSS is to change data (simply statistics about some particular item) into information which may show the relationship between one event and another.

Here again, diligence is required to develop and maintain the most effective DSS. A true competitive advantage can be developed through an effective MkIS and an easy to use DSS.

THE MARKETING RESEARCH PROCESS

The marketing research process follows six major steps outlined in Table 5.2.

The first and most important step is to determine clearly what information is needed. In order to do this, a firm must anticipate how the information will be used. Will the decision be strategic or tactical? Will it have major or minor cost ramifications? At this point, a quick review may suggest that the cost of potential research exceeds the cost of a mistaken decision. Some business marketing segments include only a few customers. It may be more effective to discuss questions with key customers than to develop a formal market research project. When marketing services, it is often less costly simply to try out an idea to see whether the market reacts positively rather than spend the time and money fielding research. Within this step, the researcher must also decide what kind of presentation will be required, whether highly technical or managerial in approach.

Clearly, the most important aspect of this stage of research is the definition of the problem. This is the step which causes the most problems and can lead a firm down an expensive path toward poor results. Specific discussions must be held with all decision makers to clearly understand the problem. In this step, managers often confuse symptoms with problems. A symptom might be

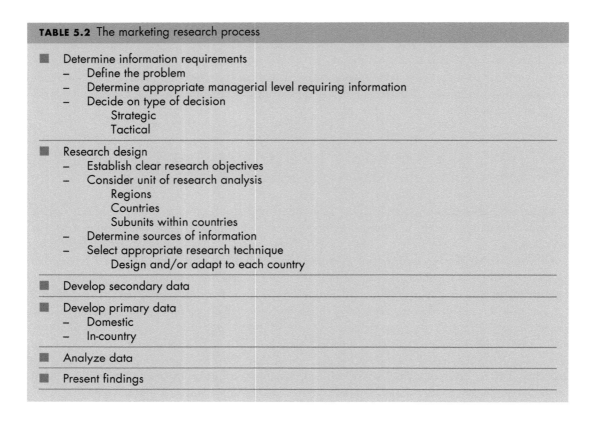

TABLE 5.2 The marketing research process

- Determine information requirements
  - Define the problem
  - Determine appropriate managerial level requiring information
  - Decide on type of decision
    - Strategic
    - Tactical

- Research design
  - Establish clear research objectives
  - Consider unit of research analysis
    - Regions
    - Countries
    - Subunits within countries
  - Determine sources of information
  - Select appropriate research technique
    - Design and/or adapt to each country

- Develop secondary data

- Develop primary data
  - Domestic
  - In-country

- Analyze data

- Present findings

declining sales in a particular product line or more customers telling a firm their prices are too high. But more work must be done to focus on what might be causing sales to decline or customers to complain about prices. Some of these symptoms are caused by problems not necessarily discoverable by market research. For instance declining sales could be caused by stock outages or resignation of the key distributor. Working to define the specific actionable problem is important here.

Once the problem is defined, we move to the next step – research design. The critical part of this step is to establish clear research objectives. Like any objectives, research objectives must be measurable. "To determine why sales of laser printers are declining" would be a poor research objective. A more specific research objective might be "to determine why buyers of laser printers are failing to trade in their printers for new ones" or "to determine the market potential of a specific office chair in the UK for next year."

Research will be designed differently if it is to be conducted across a number of countries. More careful design must be undertaken to be sure results are comparable from one culture to another.

Next, the researchers must determine how the information will be developed. The sources vary widely from secondary information to primary research techniques which will be discussed later in this chapter.

Once the first two steps have been completed, researchers should develop secondary data before moving ahead to custom or primary research. Secondary data are defined as those which have already been developed for some other purpose. These data are available from many sources, including governments, trade associations, and publications. Nearly all of it has been put on the Internet in some place. A good starting point is usually a Meta search engine such as Google. The main reason for proceeding with secondary data before embarking on primary research is quite simple: it costs less and is faster to complete than custom research. Once this step is completed, it may be that the researcher has developed all of the information necessary for a decision to be made. Therefore, no primary research would be undertaken.

However, especially when dealing with international research, one may find that secondary sources do not give a full and accurate picture. To begin with, secondary data are often out-of-date. It is often unclear how the data were collected and whether the respondents were relevant to the problem faced by the researcher. Especially using Internet sources, it would be prudent to have several independent sources of information giving the same relative answer before proceeding confidently. A list of sample business to business information sources on the Internet is shown in Table 5.3.

TABLE 5.3 Sample Internet business information sources

- http://www.corporateinformation.com – Select a country and/or an industry and develop in-depth information about companies, country and/or industry.

- http://www.frost.com – Frost & Sullivan; provides research information and consulting services.

- http://www.intelliquest.com – Millward Brown Intelliquest; provides technology and Internet companies with information-based marketing services.

- http://www.uspto.gov – United States Patent and Trademark Office, non-commercial federal entity; provides info on all aspects of patents including trade-related intellectual property issues.

- http://www.census.gov – United States Census Bureau; provides massive amounts of information including population facts and estimates.

- http://www.dnb.com – Dun & Bradstreet supplies business information; they have information on 75 million companies worldwide.

- http://www.comscore.com – Designed for obtaining market intelligence regarding an online category focusing on social media.

- http://www.topica.com – Email discussions, newsletters and publishing solutions.

- http://www.wilsonweb.com/webmarket – Internet marketing information center; provides information on web marketing.

- http://fita.worldbid.com – Federation of International Trade Association (FITA); Trade leads, International Buy/Sell exchange, business to business marketplace that helps a company find more business.

continued . . .

TABLE 5.3 ... *continued*

■ http://www.fita.org/tshows.html – Database of hundreds of trade shows, conventions, seminars and meetings worldwide. One can search by city, state, country, industry or month.

■ http://www.bizweb.com – Index of company websites; search by category.

■ http://www.business.com – Allows a firm to compare selected vendors.

■ http://www.europages.com – The European Business Directory; search for information on a supplier or service provider. A business to business directory published in 26 languages.

■ http://www.economist.com/countries – Basic info including economic data, political profiles, links to newspapers and government offices, for many countries.

■ http://www.trade.gov – US International Trade Administration information.

■ http://www.globaledge.msu.edu/ibrd/ibrd.asp – Provides an outline of the business climate, political structure, history, and statistical data for more than 190 countries. A directory of international business resources categorized by specific orientation and content, glossary of definitions and descriptions of terms and acronyms used in international business.

■ http://www.ustr.gov – Office of the United States Trade Representative; provides the latest news, report and publications, speeches and testimony, National Trade Estimate Report on foreign trade barriers, published annually and written by USTR staff, surveys significant foreign barriers to US exports.

■ http://www.unctad.org – United Nations Conference on trade and development based in Switzerland. Aims at the integration of developing countries into the world economy, schedules of events and meetings.

■ http://www.cia.gov/library/publications/the-world-factbook/ – the CIA World Factbook, a thorough annual compilation of history and data about every country in the world.

■ http://www.oecd.org – Organization For Economic Cooperation and Development; provides data and reports about the largest economies in the world.

■ http://www.direct.gov.uk – Business information for UK companies. Special section on trade and investment for British companies.

■ http://www.finfacts.ie/– Resource for Irish firms doing business abroad and for information about Ireland.

After a thorough review of secondary data a firm may identify missing pieces of information required to make decisions. At this point the firm will choose to use primary data gathering. Table 5.4 lists the primary data research methods.

There are three major ways to develop primary data: through surveys, observation, or experimentation.

Experimentation is not often used in business to business research. It involves developing matched sets of respondents and varying stimuli to each to determine what reactions might be obtained. This method is more often used in consumer market research. Test marketing is probably the main way

TABLE 5.4 Primary data methods

■ Survey
  – Personal interviews
  – Focus groups
  – Mail surveys
  – Telephone surveys
  – Internet surveys or focus groups

■ Observation
  – Watching how products are used, for example how factory workers use machine tools
  – Analyzing websites and other communications tools
  – Observing employee behavior

■ Experimentation
  – Test marketing
  – Trials of new systems or products at selected customers' premises

in which experimentation might be used in B2B research, but asking selected customers to use a product for a trial period (beta testing) is also a possibility, particularly when a close relationship exists between the firm and its customers.

Observation simply means "watching" either users or decision makers. A business to business firm might, for instance, use time-lapse photography in a factory to determine how workers use a color measuring device in a production line. Some firms have also been known to observe the number of containers flowing out of a competitor's factory to measure their sales rate.

By far the most common form of research is the survey. In business marketing, personal interviews (also known as desk-side interviews) are often used for determining customer requirements or to forecast future needs of key customers. Where questions are complex, personal interviews are often the best method.

If respondents are geographically concentrated, it can be less costly to conduct focus groups with five to ten individuals. Focus groups are best used with respondents who identify more readily with their profession than with their employer. For instance, placing marketing directors of competing firms in one focus group will usually yield no useful information, whereas assembling a group of architects who work for various companies can be quite successful. Focus groups are less costly per respondent than personal interviews, while maintaining many of the advantages. Frequently, business marketers need to show potential customers what a product looks like or how it works. Both personal interviews and focus groups allow for this and both allow for the gathering of a great deal of information in a limited amount of time. The key advantages to both interviews and focus groups is the ability to obtain answers to probing questions that get to the heart of a customer's thinking process. In addition, focus groups often give researchers special insight into the influence others have on the decision making processes of all the members of the buying center.

The disadvantages of both focus groups and personal interviews are the cost and relative time required to collect, analyze, and report the data. Since the number of persons interviewed must be limited by the market research budget, projecting results to a national or world market is problematic. Interviewer bias is also a possible disadvantage for these methods. Focus groups and in-depth interviews are particularly useful for finding out why people behave the way they do. However, surveys generally only tell us what people do or intend to do.

Telephone surveys are frequently used to get information from business respondents. When respondents are easy to identify and reach by phone, this method is far less costly than either focus groups or personal interviews. Telephone interviews can also be completed quickly and, if the sample is chosen properly, the results are projectable to the overall market. As must be obvious, it is difficult to ask in-depth, probing questions on the telephone and there is a limit to the length of interviews. Some interviewer bias may creep into the discussions, so that the opinions recorded reflect the interviewer's personality and beliefs more than the respondent's. In addition, it is not always clear that the respondent is identified correctly and so respondents may misrepresent themselves. One major disadvantage of telephone surveys is that the researching firm would be unable to show products, concepts or advertising to the respondents unless special arrangements are made to send information to them in advance of the interviews.

Mail surveys are the least expensive market research approach. Just about any respondent is a possible target for mail research and this method can completely eliminate interviewer bias. The major disadvantages to mail surveys are the low response rate and the complete lack of control over who actually responds. In other words, business marketers may receive surveys completed by secretaries or administrative assistants rather than the actual targeted individual. Mail surveys are also relatively slow and eliminate the possibility of showing products or concepts with a live demonstration.

The Internet is being widely used for both surveys and focus groups (Kursan and Mihic, 2010). The major advantages of using the Internet in this way are speed and low cost (see Figure 5.1). Internet surveys are far less expensive than telephone surveys and Internet focus groups are equally less expensive than "live" focus groups. The ability to show some products or advertising or software to respondents is an advantage for the Internet approach. However, there are some disadvantages. For B2B research the total cost of an Internet project can be the same or higher than for a telephone

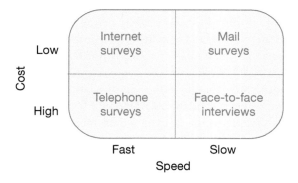

FIGURE 5.1 Cost vs. speed in surveys

project because of the lack of sources for e-mail addresses of respondents and the necessity to pay each respondent an incentive for participation. Since in most B2B segments readily available e-mail addresses of respondents do not exist, the approach is to recruit each respondent by telephone and then send him/her to a website to complete the survey. This requires an incentive to be paid, which can often amount to the same or more per respondent as the cost of a completed telephone interview. The additional cost of telephone recruiting can easily make the total cost prohibitive. In addition, many firms do not allow complete employee access to the Internet. This automatically limits the sample and may bias the results.

Both Internet surveys and Internet focus groups have the disadvantage that it is not clear who is responding and misrepresentation may occur. Internet focus groups have an additional disadvantage in that face-to-face reaction and the ability to read body language is eliminated. Brüggen and Willems (2009) conducted research comparing three focus group methods – traditional, online, and e-Delphi focus groups. The latter method is an e-mail discussion, an asynchronous research method, where a discussion leader e-mails open questions to selected respondents and they answer over a period of time. They concluded that each method has its advantages. Online focus groups are suitable for fast, spontaneous reactions to a new product or concept and are especially useful for testing ideas across international market segments. The e-Delphi approach can be applied to more respondents, is good for international research, and can gather both qualitative and quantitative information. A successor to the e-Delphi approach is the online discussion board or forum. In this method respondents reply to questions or statements at a specific website. Both Brüggen and Willems, and Kursan and Mihic conclude that the Internet is an effective research tool best used in combination with traditional offline research methods.

Some firms also undertake customer visits by firm personnel (rather than professional researchers) to gather various kinds of data. With this method, firm personnel may visit a customer's site or invite key customers to the firm's headquarters. Customer visits can reveal current and potential problems related to products or service, uncover unknown customer needs which may lead to new market opportunities, and also solidify customer relationships. This method can be as effective as formal market research using the methods described above if care is taken in the selection of respondents and the capturing of data. Firm personnel must be given training in interviewing techniques and be provided with discussion guides or questionnaires to manage the visits. When these precautions are not undertaken, this method is best used as a sales aid. One firm invited customers to view a new product at its headquarters. Customers were flown in on the company's aircraft and treated to extensive hospitality. While touring the models of the new product, the visiting customers made many useful comments. Unfortunately, the host company made no provision to capture the comments and the visits were far less valuable than they should have been. Table 5.5 presents an overview of survey methods.

Applying all of these research techniques to the international setting requires an increased level of sensitivity. While in the past some felt that qualitative research techniques such as personal interviews and focus groups could not be applied in many markets, studies by one of the authors show this not to be the case (Zimmerman and Szenberg, 2000). Nearly every qualitative research technique is employed in nearly every country, from the People's Republic of China to Mexico and desk-side interviews are employed nearly as frequently. Costs for business research vary widely by

TABLE 5.5 Comparing business to business survey methods

Research method	Characteristics of respondents	Advantages	Disadvantages
Personal (desk-side) interview	– Few – Geographically dispersed – Difficult to reach	– Ask complex questions – Show/demonstrate product or concept – Get qualitative (why) answers – High response rate	– Most costly method – The most time-consuming method – Risk of interviewer bias – Results usually not projectable to entire market
Focus groups	– Moderate number – Geographically concentrated – Somewhat difficult to reach – Identify with profession rather than employer	– Cost efficient compared to personal interviews – Show/demonstrate product or concept – Faster than personal interviews – Get qualitative (why) answers – Interaction can simulate real world decision making	– Relatively costly, though less per respondent than personal interviews – Possible moderator bias – Dominance by one/few respondents – Relatively time-consuming – Usually not projectable to entire market
Telephone surveys	– Few or many – Geographically dispersed – Relatively easy to identify and reach	– Lower cost than personal interviews or focus groups – Fast – Projectable with large enough sample	– Limits types and length of questions – Possible interviewer bias – Possible misinterpretation of respondent – Inability to show concept or demonstrate product
Mail surveys	– Any respondents who can receive mail	– Least costly of all methods – Eliminates interview bias	– Control of qualified respondents – Low response rate – Relatively slow – Inability to show concept or demonstrate product
Internet surveys	– Respondents with access to Internet	– May be lower cost than telephone surveys – Fast – Ability to show some concepts or products	– Possible invalid sample – Control of qualified respondents – Need to recruit and pay respondents
Internet focus groups	– Moderate number – Geographically dispersed – Difficult to reach	– May be lower cost than traditional focus groups – Faster than traditional focus groups – Ability to show some concepts or products	– Control of qualified respondents – Lack of face-to-face interaction – Others, same as focus groups above

country, with the most expensive country being Japan, where a typical project may cost twice as much as one completed in the US.

An important concept in international research is the debate between the so-called "emic" and "etic" schools of thought. The emic school believes that attitudes and behaviors are unique to a particular culture while the etic school attempts to find universal culture-free measures which may be applied across various markets. Differences of this nature tend to be minimized in business marketing since questions more often relate to technical problems than emotional and personal motivations. Nevertheless, a business marketer must be aware of these two schools of thought and carefully apply measures used in one culture to others, using suitable tests to be sure the measures are appropriate.

Talking Point

In reviewing secondary data, it is important to maintain a somewhat skeptical attitude, especially as it relates to data from various international and Internet-only sources. Key questions to ask are:

- Who collected the data?
- What methods were used to collect the data?
- Who were the respondents?
- When was the data collected?

So if secondary data is so fraught with risk, why use it at all? Why not go straight to collecting our own primary data, where at least we can maintain some semblance of quality control?

Or would this just get us in trouble with the finance director?

SAMPLING AND VALIDITY

A key part of gaining usable answers from research is developing the proper sample. In business markets, the number of individuals is usually limited. In addition, Pareto's Law often applies (simply put, about 80 percent of the results come from about 20 percent of the entities). So, in many markets a handful of corporations will buy most of the product. Because of this, random sampling, often used in consumer research where each individual is looked upon as a relatively equal customer, is not frequently used in business markets. Generally speaking, business marketers use stratified random sampling where a specific subset of potential respondents is selected and then specific respondents are chosen by chance from this subset. In some markets there are so few potential respondents who may purchase the product that a 100 percent review of the population is possible. For instance, a firm which sells products to the commercial air frame manufacturing business could interview Boeing, Airbus, Embraer, and Bombardier and have the answers covering most of the market potential.

Validity means a particular research measurement actually measures what it is supposed to measure. Problems with validity arise when questions are vague or misleading, or respondents attempt to be especially cooperative and answer questions even when they have no information. Pre-tests of research instruments can help improve validity.

Internationally, these questions are even more difficult because respondents in various cultures may give a different interpretation to a perfectly "obvious" concept. For instance, the word "family" is interpreted in Africa to include all of the extended family, while in Western societies it is often interpreted to include only the immediate family. Similar problems can arise in business markets and therefore survey instruments and focus group moderator guides must be pre-tested before being used across many cultures. Often it is useful to have interviewers define terms for respondents before proceeding with the interviews. Also, in some cultures respondents do not wish to disappoint the interviewer. This means that respondents may give an answer even when they have no idea what the true situation is, or may provide answers which they think will please the interviewer.

DEVELOPING QUESTIONNAIRES

To write a good questionnaire is an art as well as a skill. First, questions should be placed in a logical order, with the most sensitive questions at the end of the questionnaire. All questions should relate to research objectives. If questions are being asked which don't help produce the desired result, they add time and should be eliminated. For focus groups and personal interviews, open-ended questions (those that cannot be answered by a simple yes or no) are best because they start discussion and lead to explanation by the respondent. For telephone and mail surveys, closed-ended questions are best. These are questions which can be answered by selecting a measurement such as "always, sometimes, never" or by a yes–no or some other simple choice. Avoid double-barreled questions, that is, questions that ask for two answers at the same time. This is a common failing of even some sophisticated researchers. A question such as "have you bought electronic equipment from us and are you satisfied" might be answered yes. But in analyzing the results, one would not know whether the respondent was saying "yes, we have bought equipment" or "yes, we are satisfied with the equipment" or both. Do not use wording or jargon that the respondent may not know. This is especially a problem in business marketing where assumptions can often be made about those within the market. Frequently respondents are not familiar with the terminology the manufacturer considers quite basic. Rather than admit ignorance, respondents will often give answers which are completely misleading or uninformed.

Provide a succinct, but convincing introduction which tells the respondent why they should help the researcher gather the information needed. In some cases, respondents may be promised a summary of the results. If this isn't possible, simply stating that results will be used to help improve service can be effective. Allow for "don't know" responses rather than make the respondent answer a question he or she is unqualified to answer. Avoid hypothetical questions or examples which may confuse the respondent. Specifically asking a respondent if they would buy a product if it were priced at a particular level usually yields useless results. To estimate true buying potential, trade off or conjoint (sometimes also called forced-choice) analysis is usually used. This is a much more reliable indicator of future buying behavior. Asking respondents for specific suggestions for new products is also usually unproductive. It is more effective to ask respondents what problems they face in order to elicit ideas for new products or product improvements.

ANALYZING THE DATA

In analyzing quantitative data, researchers will assemble the information into cross-tabulated tables which allows the examination of the answers to the questions by sub-segment, such as years' experience or geographic location. Table 5.6 is a sample of a cross-tabulated page of research from a study of architects and Figure 5.2 shows the respondents' answers to a question about their Internet usage. As can be seen, the total of all respondents' answers is given as well as answers by region, by type of firm, size of firm, title of respondent, type of work, and whether they are heavily or not heavily involved in designing single-family residential homes. Three Internet usage columns are the same as the classification columns on the far left. In this case, we can see that 42.5 percent of respondents who work in large firms can be classified as heavy Internet users vs. only 30.7 percent of those who work in medium-sized firms.

Results may be analyzed using available software programs which describe data or help to develop forecasts. Significance tests (t-tests) are extremely important in determining how likely it is that the results from the sample represent the opinions and beliefs of the entire population. Sophisticated researchers also undertake factor analysis in order to determine whether one factor being measured is simply the same as another measured factor. The goal is to establish a list of important factors which would be independent from each other. Software available for personal computers allows fairly sophisticated statistical analysis to be performed quite simply and at low cost.

Qualitative data analysis is by necessity more subjective. Usually, transcripts are made of focus groups or interviews from recordings made during the interviews on focus groups. Powerful text analytics software, sometimes called computer-assisted qualitative data analysis software (CAQDAS) allows researchers to review word and phrase patterns in focus groups or interview transcripts. Sinkovics and Penz (2011) point out that CAQDAS can be employed to overcome the difficulties encountered when conducting qualitative research in multiple countries and can result in a more holistic understanding of multi-stakeholder perspectives. Some sophisticated researchers are applying these techniques to various Internet sources including social media sites. One successful example was Radian6 (Anderson 2011). In general, qualitative research can explain the thinking processes respondents are using to arrive at conclusions; extremely valuable marketing information. On the other hand, conventional wisdom dictates that qualitative results are not projectable because of the small sample sizes. However as we have seen in some business markets, dominated by very few major players, a limited sample will indeed deliver highly projectable results.

The final step is to present the findings. In most cases, a firm will request a written report as well as an oral presentation. The advent of the Internet and presentation software allows a firm to receive electronic copies of the written report and to view a presentation electronically which can then be used for further presentation within the firm. Experience shows that presentations must be carefully honed to keep the attention of top management. The use of graphics and even integrated "sound bytes" or video clips from focus groups or interviews (if available) enhance the impact of

TABLE 5.6 Electronic and print product information (December 2011)

Q. 13 Internet usage classification

	Region					Firm Type			Firm Size		Title			Work Type			Single Family Res.		Internet Usage		
	Total	West	Mid-West	North East	South	Gen. Contr	Home Bldr	Dsgn Bld	Med	Large	Cons. Mgr.	Esti-mator	Super/Pres/VP	Mostly Renov	Mostly New	50-50	<25%	25%+	Never Use	5 hrs/less	5+ hrs
Total	404 100%	90 100%	72 100%	85 100%	157 100%	289 100%	38 100%	77 100%	277 100%	127 100%	133 100%	151 100%	120 100%	67 100%	286 100%	51 100%	343 100%	61 100%	49 100%	183 100%	139 100%
Heavy User	139 34.4%	29 32.2%	25 34.7%	28 32.9%	57 36.3%	94 32.5%	15 39.5%	30 39.0%	85 30.7%	54 42.5%	47 35.3%	53 35.1%	39 32.5%	25 37.3%	101 35.5%	13 25.5%	119 34.7%	20 32.8%	– –	– –	139 100%
Light User	204 50.5%	43 47.8%	38 52.8%	44 51.8%	79 50.3%	149 51.6%	16 42.1%	39 50.6%	146 52.7%	58 45.7%	62 46.6%	80 53.0%	62 51.7%	31 46.3%	145 50.7%	28 54.9%	177 51.6%	27 44.3%	– –	183 100%	– –
Never Use	49 12.1%	15 16.7%	7 9.7%	10 11.8%	17 10.8%	36 12.5%	7 18.4%	6 7.8%	37 13.4%	12 9.4%	15 11.3%	18 11.9%	16 13.3%	8 11.9%	34 11.9%	7 13.7%	37 10.8%	12 19.7%	49 100%	– –	– –
Don't Know/ Refused	12 3.0%	3 3.3%	2 2.8%	3 3.5%	4 2.5%	10 3.5%	– –	2 2.6%	9 3.2%	3 2.4%	9 6.8%	– –	3 2.5%	3 4.5%	6 2.1%	3 5.9%	10 2.9%	2 3.3%	– –	– –	– –

Source: Architectural Research Associates.

the presentations. The most effective presentations last no longer than one hour, should concentrate on the conclusions to be drawn from the research, and should suggest potential actions resulting from these conclusions.

MARKET POTENTIAL AND SALES FORECASTS

Frequently, market research is used by managers to estimate the market potential for a particular product or product line and then to develop sales forecasts and quotas for the sales force. Two overall strategic approaches to sales forecasting exist; break-down and build-up. The break-down approach begins with the overall market for the product category and seeks to predict what the firm's share of that market will be. For example, a bank may have access to government economic forecasts which can be used to calculate the total loans market for the following year. The bank forecasters will know what the bank's share of the market was in previous years, and can use this information to make a reasonable estimate of what the bank's total lending will be in the ensuing year.

Obviously, the first and most important step is to define the market segment. This will be discussed at length in the next chapter. In order to develop sales forecasts, one must develop market potential. In order to develop market potential, various methods should be combined. The use of both primary and secondary data is usually essential to arrive at a meaningful answer. Figure 5.2 describes the development of the market potential for an office furniture firm.

Assuming the firm was examining the potential in several foreign markets, the first step would be to determine how many workers there are in each market, then reduce that number to administrative workers and further reduce it to desk workers who might be able to use the office furniture. Next, a percentage of desk workers who would be given new furniture each year must be determined. The resulting number would then be multiplied by a dollar figure spent per employee and this would yield the market potential in a particular market for office furniture. Market

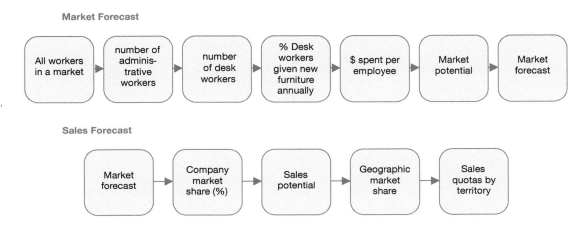

FIGURE 5.2 Development of market forecast and sales forecast

potential is the maximum possible sales of all firms of a particular kind of product in a market during a particular period, usually one year. The market forecast is a somewhat lower number management uses as a realistic basis for planning.

Starting from the market forecast, the sales forecast can then be developed. In order to do this, the market forecast would be multiplied by the company's expected market share in this particular country. This then yields the sales potential. The sales potential could then be reduced to territorial quotas by using the geographic market share. For example, let us assume a market forecast of $200 million was developed for office seating in Japan. This figure would then be looked at based on the market share for the firm developing the sales forecast. If this market share were 25 percent, sales potential would be $50 million. In order to assign sales quotas, management might increase the sales forecast over the sales potential, assuming that extra efforts by the sales force might increase market share. However, for this example, let us assume that $50 million would be used as a sales potential. If it is determined that Tokyo is 50 percent of the market, the sales quota for Tokyo would be $25 million.

As might be expected, some of this data is easily obtained through secondary sources. However, other data would need to be developed though other methods. Often, primary research is used to develop an estimate of these unknowns, such as the percent of desk workers to be supplied with new furniture annually or the dollars to be spent per employee on new furniture. Figure 5.2 shows the Chain-Ratio Method of developing a forecast. However, other methods are also used. Some firms have been able to use statistical series for comparison with sales of a particular product, for instance, one might determine that for every $10-million worth of automobiles shipped, $500,000 in brake lights will be sold. These kinds of relationships can be developed through time series analysis (see Table 5.7). Here again, a usage factor may need to be developed through primary research.

Some firms use the Delphi technique to forecast the future, especially for new products with no historical data. In the Delphi method, opinions of a panel of experts are gathered. Once all of the opinions have been summarized, they are circulated to the panel through several rounds with the

TABLE 5.7 Time series analysis

Type of Analysis	Description
Trend analysis	Focuses on aggregate sales data collected over a long period to determine whether sales are rising, falling, or staying level.
Cycle analysis	Here the forecaster examines the sales figures from a number of years to see whether there is a cyclical pattern; perhaps a response to the economic boom-and-bust cycle. This method has been largely discredited for most markets, since the cycles do not follow a regular pattern.
Seasonal analysis	Sales figures are analyzed on a monthly or even weekly basis to see whether there is a seasonal cycle operating.
Random factor analysis	In any analysis there will be figures that do not fit the pattern; random factor analysis seeks to attribute explanations for these abnormal findings. For example, a spell of unseasonal weather might have affected one month's figures.

goal of developing a consensus among the experts. The e-Delphi technique described above makes this method less time-consuming and more affordable.

In most forecasts, an important input is executive judgment. Frequently, senior managers who have been working in a particular industry or country for many years have very good ideas about the size of markets or the penetration of a particular product. Their input should be used in developing the final forecast.

Many firms also use the sales force composite method to develop a sales forecast. This is a bottom-up approach where individual sales people estimate their sales for the following year. Each of these forecasts is then summarized to develop territorial and national as well as international forecasts. While this is a valuable tool to be used in developing the final forecast, experience has shown that sales forces tend to be too optimistic. Using the sales composite forecast alone usually yields territorial objectives which turn out to be nearly impossible to achieve. In short, the best method for developing a sales forecast is the combination method, that is, using the results of several methods both quantitative and qualitative. This usually yields the most accurate market potential and sales forecasts.

In international research, some firms have turned to scenario analysis, recognizing that developments in international markets are often discontinuous. In this approach, scenarios are developed by experts through the Delphi technique and by senior management. Scenarios encourage firms to develop contingency plans should the sales forecast prove unreliable because of unpredictable events.

TABLE 5.8 Common sales forecasting techniques

Technique	Explanation
Customer survey	Typically, customers would be asked about their buying intentions over (say) the next 12 months. Often buyers would be unable to answer with any degree of certainty, but the average of the responses is often fairly accurate, depending on the industry involved.
Salesforce survey	Salespeople are asked how much they expect to sell. This has the drawback that they may be over-optimistic, or (on the other hand) may fear that they will be held to their forecast and will deliberately under-estimate.
Distributor survey	A variation on the salesforce survey, used when the company has a substantial network of distributors.
Delphi approach	This is a method of eliciting expert opinion from a panel of those involved (sales managers, marketing executives, distributors, etc.)
Time-series analysis	Using the company's past sales records to predict the future. Time-series is unable to take account of the unexpected, and of course looks at comparing the current situation with the past, rather than comparing the current position with a projection of where the company should be.
Test marketing	Launching the product in a limited market, either geographically or in terms of customer groups, can be very effective in developing an estimate of overall sales following roll-out to all customers. The main drawback is that it telegraphs the company's intentions to its competitors.

ORGANIZING FOR MARKET RESEARCH

Many different approaches to organizing the marketing information system have been employed by various firms. A basic decision must be whether all functions are to be performed within the firm or whether some will be contracted to independent vendors. The obvious advantage of holding all work within the firm is the absolute certainty that none of the information will be given to unauthorized people. A major disadvantage is the high cost, keeping experts on staff who may not be fully employed all of the time.

Some large firms maintain a centralized research function through which all projects are implemented. Others have decentralized their research functions so that Business Units are completely in charge of all of their own projects. The obvious benefit for the decentralized organization is that all research projects tend to be relevant to the specific needs of the divisions. However, the major drawback is that no firm-wide studies (such as image studies of the overall corporation) are ever undertaken. Therefore, many large firms have opted to have a centralized research function with localized, divisional researchers as well.

One fact is absolutely clear and that is no market intelligence unit can be successful without the support of top management. While the market intelligence function often reports to the marketing function, one might argue that it should report to general management rather than a functional area. In some firms, the information function reports to the financial organization.

A key question is the "make or buy" decision for market research. As mentioned before, some firms prefer to hold all information in-house and will continue to keep all research functions internal. However, this requires experts such as focus group moderators to be employed either at running focus groups throughout the year or in some other way. Very few industrial firms require the number of focus groups or interviews which would keep a moderator or interviewers busy all the time. Therefore, most business marketing firms opt to use outside vendors. Throughout the world there are experts in every aspect of market research ready to serve. Organizations like ESOMAR can provide lists of vendors by specialty and location.

An ongoing analysis is necessary to determine the level of centralization and in-house staffing required. But a successful project requires one point of contact within the firm. Usually this individual should know something about market research in order to manage the project successfully. Outside vendors will present specific proposals which should include the objectives of the study, methodology, completion schedule, and costs as well as deliverables.

Figure 5.3 is an example research proposal adapted for this text.

Not having a specific proposal can lead to misunderstandings and disappointment for the contracting firm. One large, multinational firm commissioned a study from a large consulting firm in Japan. At the conclusion of the study, the consulting firm presented the results on PowerPoint slides then scooped up the USB drive and left. The multinational firm had no written report and no record of the findings, except for notes taken during the presentation. A clear definition of deliverables would have avoided this problem.

ACME COMPANY

SYSTEM FOLLOW UP STUDY

INTRODUCTION

Recently completed focus groups indicated some buyer interest in a new computer-based system to be offered by Acme Co. But there were several reservations expressed by respondents. The firm has now advanced the development of the concept.

The firm has also improved the demonstration of this service and wishes to further test the general viability of the concept.

OBJECTIVES

- To test the acceptability of the new system with buyers.
- To help select participants for the in-market test.

METHODOLOGY

- Because we want detailed reactions to the new system and may want the participants to have hands-on experience, we recommend mini-focus groups be held to accomplish these objectives.
- Eight mini-focus groups will be held, four in London and four in New York. Each is planned for 1½ hours.
- ABC Research will develop all recruiting guides for the mini-focus groups, subject to the approval of Acme management. Individuals will be screened for size of firm, industry and other criteria to be determined.
- Lists for recruiting will be provided by Acme Co. and will be obtained by ABC Research.
- ABC Research will recruit seven (7) individuals for each group according to the requirements in the recruiting guide. We recommend that participants be paid an honorarium of $100–125 for their time. (Note: We have budgeted for five respondents per group, at $125.)
- John Smith will serve as impartial moderator at all groups.
- ABC Research will make all arrangements for focus group facilities.
- ABC Research will develop a detailed focus group discussion guide subject to the approval of Acme management. The discussion guide will be designed to elicit:

  - General reaction to the concept.
  - Insight into sellers and products most suited for the new system.
  - Perception of benefits of and objections to the new system.
  - Customer requirements for system tools including installation, training, ease of use and reporting.
  - Perspectives on fee structures and data security.

- An ABC researcher will be present at all groups to aid in arrangements and take notes.
- Acme *will* be mentioned as the sponsor of the research.
- After the focus groups are completed, ABC will develop a complete report summarizing the findings. This report will emphasize conclusions and recommendations based on our findings and experience.

NEEDED FROM ACME

- Proposed system concept statement and computer demo as agreed.
- Lists for recruiting.

DELIVERABLES

- Complete report of focus groups via email.
- PowerPoint presentation of findings (optional at extra cost).
- Audio tapes (if requested).
- Transcripts of focus groups (if requested).
- Video tapes (optional).

TIMING

Action	Complete By
Approval	January 10
Arrangements/Logistics	January 17
Approved Recruiting Guide	January 17
Discussion Guide	January 24
Recruiting	January 31

Focus Groups: (Recommended Schedule)

London	February 4 (Noon and 6:00 p.m.)
	February 5 (8:30 a.m. and Noon)
New York	February 8 (8:30 a.m. and Noon)
	February 9 (8:30 a.m. and Noon)
Debriefing	February 14
Complete Report	March 31

FIGURE 5.3 Sample research proposal

continued overleaf . . .

BUDGET

Professional Services		$ 22,500
Expenses (billed at cost)		$ 16,000

Facility rental (8 @ $600)	$ 4,800
Food (8 @ $100)	800
Travel	3,000
Transcripts (8 @ $175)	1,400
Incentives (8 X 5 X $125)	5,000
Telephone/copies	500
Clerical	500

TOTAL BUDGET   **$ 38,500**

Videotaping available at $350 per group additional (billed at cost).

TERMS

One half of budget less incentives due upon approval (January 10)	$ 16,750
Incentives due one week before first group (January 31)	$ 5,000
One quarter of budget less incentives due at midpoint of project (January 31)	$ 8,375
One quarter due upon completion of project (March 31)	$ 8,375

APPROVAL

_____   _____
John Smith, President   Date
ABC Research

_____   _____
Joe Jones,   Date
Manager, Market Research
Acme Co.

FIGURE 5.3 . . .*continued*

MANAGING RESEARCH PROJECTS

To summarize, the best way to manage a market research project is to clearly understand what the project is to accomplish. Research objectives should be clearly specified before any research is undertaken. At that time, the firm should identify what it knows and what it doesn't know and then do a thorough secondary data search. Once the firm decides it needs primary research, research vendors should be carefully chosen. The firm should check the references of any research vendor and that vendor should know both the industry and the market. Many firms issue project specifications so that research suppliers can provide proposals on the same set of guidelines. The contracting firm should require written proposals for review before choosing a vendor. Research, especially including many international markets, should not be underfunded. It is preferable to limit the scope of research than to complete partial research across many topics and markets. Finally, the research project must be managed in the domestic as well as in country markets. Table 5.9 lists these project management guidelines.

BENCHMARKING

Many firms see benchmarking as an important aspect of their overall information gathering program. Benchmarking began as a result of the reengineering movement and has often been focused heavily on processes such as engineering, purchasing, manufacturing, and human resources. But benchmarking can also be put to fruitful use by business marketers. The essence of benchmarking is identifying "best practices" for particular processes or functions, then learning from these practices and adapting them to the needs of your firm. Firms who wish to benchmark usually identify potential sources for information in non-competing industries where the processes involved show some commonality. The process is described in Figure 5.4.

The first step is to determine the processes to be benchmarked. Naylor et al. (2001) identify a method for choosing marketing processes which might be benchmarked by placing them on a matrix which attempts to measure each function's importance to business success and the urgency for the need for improvement. Vorhies and Morgan (2005) identify eight key marketing capabilities for benchmarking. Their study establishes a relationship between these marketing capabilities and firm performance. Once the processes to be benchmarked have been determined, a secondary research program should be undertaken to find firms which may be candidates for cooperation and to develop general knowledge about these processes. Vorhies and Morgan recommend the use of customer satisfaction and profitability measures in the search process.

TABLE 5.9 Managing research project (guidelines)

- Anticipate actions resulting from findings
- Clarify/specify research objectives
- Identify knowns vs. unknowns
- Develop secondary data first
- Choose research providers carefully
    - References – check
    - Knowledge of industry
    - Knowledge of market
- Review detailed proposals
- Do not underfund
- Manage domestically and in-country

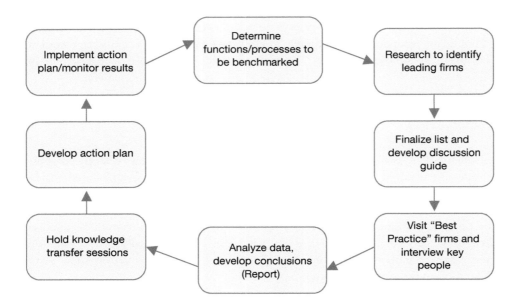

FIGURE 5.4 The benchmarking process

Source: based on Kotler and Keller (2009); Naylor et al. (2001); Fulmer et al. (2000); and Stork (2000).

The next step is to finalize the potential partner list and to develop a discussion guide to be used during site visits. Then the firm should arrange meetings where representatives of the benchmarking firm would visit firms known for best practices and ask the pre-developed questions. Here a guide more like a focus group moderator's guide would be best since the questions should be framed in an open-ended manner. The next step is to analyze the data and develop the conclusions, providing a report for all interested firm personnel. Following this, the benchmarking team should arrange for knowledge transfer sessions either by one-on-one discussions within the firm or by group meetings. Fulmer et al. (2000) describe a two-day knowledge transfer session in which management as well as the best-practice interviewees in addition to the benchmarking team all participate. Next would be to develop an action plan using the information learned from the benchmarking process. In this plan, Stork (2000) recommends setting goals then identifying work steps necessary to achieve these goals and methods of measurement to see whether progress is being made toward the goals. He also suggests a plan for "recalibration" as the action plan might have to be changed as a result of changing environments. He warns about writing a report and simply filing it. While the action plan is implemented, there should be a feedback mechanism to start the process over should that be required.

While benchmarking is certainly popular, with some reports of more than 70 percent of the 500 largest US firms practicing it (Naylor et al., 2001), Quinn (1999) warns against simply meeting best practices. He identifies "figures of merit which set targets above the normal so that the firm develops competitive advantages in its most important core competencies," thereby taking benchmarking one step further.

CASE STUDY

NG Electronics Corporation

The NG Electronics Corporation is a $250-million manufacturer of various electronic components, headquartered in Seoul, Korea. The firm had embarked on a long-term program of research and development with two university professors and had finally perfected a new high-speed, high-efficiency motor. Upon testing this small electric motor, NG discovered that it was far more efficient than competitors'. The firm wished to move ahead quickly and turned to Lonny Cho, the director of marketing, to determine whether or not they should commit to building a new production facility.

The bulk of NG's sales were to large OEMs, with the rest (about 25 percent) sold to small manufacturers and distributors. Lonny thought about the problem and realized that the firm could easily determine the acceptability of the new product with the larger OEMs. But the hundreds of other potential customers around the world presented a different picture. No one on Lonny's staff, including him, had any experience with market research. And since there was no budget for this they decided to move ahead on their own. After some thought, Lonny determined that the key questions were:

1   How many units would a particular customer wish to buy?
2   How big was each customer segment?
3   What were the customer segments?
4   Who at each firm made the buying decisions for these motors?
5   What were the most popular sizes?
6   From whom did they usually buy?
7   How did they learn about new products?

Lonny knew enough to perform some secondary data work on his office computer and determined that the key end-use market segments for this product were:

- pumps;
- industrial sewing machines;
- aircraft auxiliary equipment;
- fluid meters.

Lonny thought about the sample. Since NG already sold to two of the end-use segments, he had customer lists of the larger OEMs, but he would have to source lists of the smaller ones and the distributors. Because there was no budget, Cho selected a few of his junior employees who spoke English very well to conduct telephone interviews. He then developed a questionnaire (which is included as Exhibit 5.1). In addition to developing the survey and starting his employees on the project, Cho also thought about the possibility of calling an outside market research firm to handle the work.

. . . continued

CASE STUDY ... *continued*

Company Name _____   Industry Category _____

City _____   City and Country _____

Individual interviewed _____   Title _____

Good morning/afternoon. I'm _____, calling for NG Electronics. We are conducting a survey among knowledgeable executives like yourself about small high-speed motors and I'd appreciate your cooperation. I'll be as brief as possible.

1   To what extent are you involved in the _____ specifying _____ purchase of small, high-speed electric motors? (Check which ones)
_____ Very involved
_____ Somewhat involved
_____ Not involved (Ask to speak to the person most involved in that location and start interview again)
_____ Terminate
_____ Refused

2   What is the primary use of high-speed motors you buy?
_____
_____

3   What volume of small, high-speed motors would you normally purchase over a year's time?
_____ Current Purchases   _____ Peak   _____ Purchase activity next year

Units:
_____ Less than 100
_____ 100–300
_____ 300–500
_____ Over 500

4   What price do you usually pay?
_____
_____

5   What size high-speed electric motors do you mostly purchase?
_____
_____

6   What RPMs do you require?
_____
_____

7   What is the average life of the small, high-speed motors you build into your original equipment?
_____
_____

8   Where do you usually buy your small, high-speed motors? (Prefer names and locations if possible)

	Name	Location
From a distributor	_____	_____
Direct from the factory	_____	_____

9   What is the primary reason you would select one supplier over another?
_____ Competitive Pricing   _____ Technical capability
_____ Response time to quotes   _____ Fabrication capability
_____ Inventory availability   _____ Location
_____ Other (quality, service, delivery) _____

10   Do you usually buy your high-speed motors packaged with other components, or do you buy only the motor?
_____ Package   _____ Motor   _____ Both

11   In making your purchasing or recommendation decision for high-speed motors, please describe how important how the following are (check the appropriate items):

Factor:	No Importance		Somewhat important		Very important
	1	2	3	4	5
Manufacturer's reputation	____	____	____	____	____
Distributor reputation	____	____	____	____	____
Availability	____	____	____	____	____
Service after the sale	____	____	____	____	____
Price	____	____	____	____	____
Warranty	____	____	____	____	____

EXHIBIT 5.1 Customer market survey

. . . *continued*

CASE STUDY ... *continued*

12 Which of the following is most important (Check one)

_____ Manufacturer's reputation
_____ Distributor reputation
_____ Availability
_____ Service after the sale
_____ Price
_____ Warranty

13 How do you receive information on the products you consider? (May check more than one, but not more than three)

_____ Mailings from manufacturers
_____ Mailings from distributor
_____ Trade publications
_____ Internet
_____ Salespeople–distributor
_____ Salespeople–manufacturer
_____ Word of mouth
_____ Other _____

14 How would you prefer to receive information on new products? (Check no more than three)

_____ Mailings from manufacturers
_____ Mailings from distributor
_____ Trade publications
_____ Internet
_____ Salespeople–distributor
_____ Salespeople–manufacturer
_____ Word of mouth
_____ Other _____

15 For purposes of classification, how many employees are at this location?   _____

16 What is the approximate age of your manufacturing facility at this location? (in years) _____

EXHIBIT 5.1 Customer market survey

CASE STUDY QUESTIONS

1 What is your overall assessment of Lonny Cho's approach to his information needs?
2 Will the questionnaire Cho designed elicit the information he is seeking?
3 What modifications would you make on this questionnaire

   a. if it were used as an Internet or mail survey
   b. to be used as a telephone survey

4 If you were Lonny Cho would you prefer to use your own employees or attempt to get a budget to hire a market research firm?

   a. Why would you?
   b. How could you justify the use of an outside firm?

CHAPTER SUMMARY

Market research is critical to developing an effective business marketing program. Research used properly helps marketers identify and solve problems. While consumer research focuses most on advertising and packaging, business research is more often focused on developing market potential. Consumer research deals with a large number of consumers, each of whom is generally looked upon as equal, while business research generally deals with very small populations where a few respondents control the largest portion of sales volume. Understanding the make-up of the DMU or buying center is a critical task of market research and once this understanding is developed, market research can be far more effective. The Internet has made developing secondary data far easier since virtually all published information is available somewhere on the web. However one must be careful in using Internet information without confirmation from many sources.

Most sophisticated firms attempt to develop a complete marketing information system, including a decision support system to help managers use the information to make decisions. Developing both an effective marketing information system and a decision support system is a difficult project requiring consistent effort.

When developing market research, the most important step is to define exactly what information is needed. To do this, a firm must decide what use the information will be put to and who will be making decisions based on the information developed. Clear research objectives are critical if a research project is to be successful. After reviewing all secondary research, the firm then decides whether to move ahead with primary research. The Internet allows focus groups and interviews to be completed far less expensively. However it may be impossible to draw a representative sample through the Internet. Since there are far fewer members of any particular population in a market segment, it may be possible to interview a small number of individuals to develop realistic and projectable results using focus groups, desk-side or telephone interviews. The advantage of the personal approach is that products can be demonstrated and more in-depth questions can be used. Firms must be careful that instruments such as questionnaires or focus group moderation guides can be used in various markets across the world. While all qualitative market research techniques have been used successfully in various countries, pre-testing of these instruments is necessary to be sure of the validity of the responses. When analyzing quantitative data, cross-tabulated tables are used to show the differences between various sub-segments of the respondent pool. Qualitative research is analyzed using software which can identify words or groups of words used frequently or by old-fashioned reading and discussion methods.

Market research is used often by business marketers to develop market potential. Once a market segment is developed, research is often used to develop critical ratios, such as the percentage of individuals who may decide to buy a new software product within the next year. These ratios are then applied to known data to develop a market potential. Once the market potential is developed, sales forecasts and sales quotas are usually determined. Since in business marketing the sales force is so critical, developing attainable sales quotas is important. Some firms use the Delphi technique to forecast the future, requiring a group of experts to give their opinions in several rounds. Firms also use the sales force composite method, using a bottom-up approach from the sales force. However, this approach tends to give very optimistic forecasts. Scenario analysis is also useful, especially in international research where unpredictable events happen quickly.

While a few firms hold all market information functions within the firm, most outsource at least data collection, hiring focus group moderators or telephone or Internet researchers when required. Keeping all research within the firm obviously protects sensitive data. However, the extremely high cost of keeping specialists on staff who may not be fully employed deters most firms from doing this. Many firms have a combined centralized and decentralized approach to research, the centralized function developing projects affecting the entire firm and the decentralized function completing research which focuses only on a particular division or product line. When hiring an outside research vendor, specific proposals must be obtained. A firm must qualify the vendor's expertise in market, product and method. When commissioning a research project, a firm must be careful not to underfund the project. To be successful, a project must have the support of top management. Where management understands the role of market research and the costs involved, the most successful projects are completed.

Benchmarking is the process of identifying best practices in organizations and then attempting to emulate these to improve the way things are done within a firm. The benchmarking process resembles the market research process in many ways and care must be taken to select the proper candidates and to develop the correct research instruments. Once best practices are identified, the firm must have an action plan to make sure these practices are implemented. The most successful firms try to exceed these best practices to establish real competitive advantage.

REVIEW QUESTIONS

1   What are the major differences between consumer and business to business market research?
2   What are the advantages and disadvantages of using the Internet for market research?
3   If you were the marketing director for a keyboard manufacturer whose major customers are personal computer manufacturers, how could you design the most effective market research program? What are the key steps in the process for you?
4   When would you choose the personal interview method versus the focus group method to gather data?
5   Suppose you were to be assigned to develop a sales forecast for tempered glass to be used in office buildings in Singapore. What are the major steps you might take to get to an acceptable forecast?
6   What are the advantages and disadvantages of in-house versus outside vendor completion of market research?
7   Suppose you were the marketing communications manager for a company in India developing software. What steps might you take to implement a benchmarking program to improve your department's results?

REFERENCES

Anderson, T.C. (2011). "Text Analytics." *Marketing Research*, Vol. 23, Iss. 3, 6–7.

Brüggen, E. and Willems, P. (2009). "A critical comparison of offline focus groups, online focus groups and e-Delphi." *International Journal of Market Research*, Vol. 51, Iss. 3, 363–81.

Fulmer, Robert M., Gibbs, Philip A. and Goldsmith, Marshall (2000). "Developing leaders: how winning companies keep on winning." *Sloan Management Review*, Vol. 42, Iss. 1, Fall, 49–59.

Katz, Martin (1979). "Use same theory, skills for consumer, industrial marketing research." *Marketing News*, Vol. 12, Iss. 14, January, 16.

Kotler, Philip and Keller, Kevin Lane (2009). *Marketing Management 13th edition*. Upper Saddle River, NJ: Prentice-Hall.

Kursan, I. and Mihic, M. (2010). "Business intelligence: the role of the internet in marketing research and business decision-making." *Management: Journal Of Contemporary Management Issues*, Vol. 15, Iss. 1, 69–86.

Malhotra, Naresh K. (2010). *Marketing Research: An Applied Orientation, 6th ed.* Upper Saddle River, NJ: Prentice-Hall.

Naylor, John, Hawkins, Nick, and Wilson, Carina (2001). "Benchmarking marketing in an SME: the case of an Italian kitchen furniture manufacturer." *The Marketing Review*, Vol. 1, Iss. 3, 325–39.

Quinn, James Brian (1999). "Strategic outsourcing: leveraging knowledge capabilities." *Sloan Management Review*, Vol. 40, Iss. 4, Summer, 9–21.

Sinkovics, R.R. and Penz, E. (2011). "Multilingual elite-interviews and software-based analysis." *International Journal of Market Research*, Vol. 53, Iss. 5, 705–24.

Stork, Ken (2000). "Getting payback from benchmarking." *Purchasing*, Vol. 129, Iss. 11, 22 December, 30

Vorhies, D.W. and Morgan, N.A. (2005). "Benchmarking marketing capabilities for sustainable competitive advantage." *Journal Of Marketing*, Vol. 69, Iss. 1, 80–94.

Zimmerman, Alan S. and Szenberg, Michael (2000). "Implementing international qualitative research: techniques and obstacles." *Qualitative Research: An International Journal*. Vol. 3, Iss. 3, 158–164.

Chapter 6

Segmentation, targeting, and positioning

INTRODUCTION

Choosing the most rewarding market segments is probably the most important strategic decision a firm must make. It is also perhaps the most demanding of decisions. When a firm chooses the market segment(s) it wishes to pursue, by necessity it is also eliminating a number of potential market segments from its customer base. However, segmentation is often carried out ineffectively by business marketers.

CHAPTER OBJECTIVES

After reading this chapter, you should be able to:

- understand the importance of market segmentation
- differentiate between consumer and business segmentation techniques
- describe the segmentation process
- differentiate between segmenting by identifiers and by response profile
- understand the basics of segmenting across countries
- explain how market targeting may be used to implement market segmentation
- describe the positioning process
- describe the relationship between positioning, market targeting, and segmentation.

IMPORTANCE OF SEGMENTATION AND TARGETING

Even the wealthiest firm cannot afford to serve all potential customers in the same way: no firm has unlimited resources. Since 1956 when Wendell Smith described the idea of market segmentation, firms have known that they should target those groups of customers who are most likely to help the firm reach its objectives, whether maximizing profit, maximizing market share, or entering a new strategic market. As we have seen in Chapter 3, unless a firm chooses overall cost leadership as its basic strategy, strong segmentation is required for success in both differentiation and niche strategies. Sophisticated marketing managers have developed the idea of "cost to serve." This simply means determining what it costs to provide products and services to particular market segments. It may seem obvious that supplying many small customers with small quantities of custom-made product is more costly than supplying a few large customers with large quantities of standard product, but often this simple truth may be lost in an avalanche of data. The basic tenet behind the idea of segmentation is to find and serve the most rewarding customers: if a firm is able to offer a unique set of benefits to a particular market segment it will have achieved a significant competitive advantage.

Effective segmentation offers a number of advantages to any firm that successfully completes the task. First, the very act of analyzing all potential customers and narrowing the list to those deemed potentially most responsive is in itself a worthwhile undertaking. By doing this, the firm can develop specific marketing strategies for one or a number of identified segments, so that the product/service offering, the pricing, the promotion, and the distribution will be tailored to satisfy each segment. By identifying the most rewarding segments a firm will be able to allocate its budgets properly, making the largest expenditures on the most lucrative and responsive market segments. Once the segments are clearly identified and the marketing process begins, the firm can monitor the success of these efforts and reallocate resources or re-segment as necessary.

The work in developing market segments usually relies on detailed analysis of market research, and sales data of specific product lines, but there is a danger in over-reliance on the latter. Many firms define a market segment by product type or product size. This overly simplistic approach can have dire consequences, because it is product-focused rather than customer-focused. For example, aircraft manufacturers might segment according to the size of aircraft purchased, on the assumption that smaller airlines buy smaller, cheaper aircraft and larger airlines buy larger ones. The choice may, however, be more dependent on the routes flown since the length of the destination runways may be the deciding factor, and airlines flying those routes may switch to short take-off and landing aircraft should the designs become available.

Another common error business marketers make in segmenting is simply accepting the definition of an entire industry as one segment. For instance, a manufacturer of train control equipment might say "we sell to electrified railroads" and classify the Santiago Subway or the London Underground in the same category as a surface electrified railroad in India. The fact that underground railways protect the control equipment from the weather would thus be ignored. Some managers go the other way, defining their segments too narrowly and thus missing out on potential customers. They may focus on a few major firms, ignoring new segments which are unrelated to the primary target segment.

Talking Point

If a whole industry is not a segment, then what is? If we define our segment as smaller than the whole industry, how do we decide who we are NOT going to sell to?

And isn't that a little stupid anyway? If another firm in the same industry wanted to buy our products, are we going to throw them out on their ears?

Or if a firm from another industry wants to buy, what do we say? Do we tell them their money isn't good enough for us? Obviously not – so what are we saying?

Is segmentation about who spends their money with us – or is it about how we spend our money?

CONSUMER VERSUS B2B SEGMENTATION

According to Kotler (2003), the major segmentation bases for consumer markets are geographic, demographic, psychographic, and behavioral. Geographic segmentation includes aspects such as city or state, climate or landscape: demographic segmentation includes factors such as age, family size and lifecycle, gender, income, occupation, education, religion, race, generation, nationality, and social class. Psychographic segmentation includes lifestyle and personality characteristics, while behavioral segmentation includes purchase occasion, benefits sought, user status, usage rate, loyalty status, readiness stage, and attitude toward the product. Some of these variables can be applied in business marketing as we shall see. Certainly geographic segmentation is important, as are the "demographics of the firm" and, in some cases, the demographics of the buyers. There is less importance placed on the race, religion or nationality of buyers of business products, although cultural factors will be important in global markets, while psychographics are generally inapplicable in business markets. Of the behavioral variables, many can be adapted to business markets and this has been done with some success. Business marketers should be careful about applying consumer segmentation techniques directly to business markets. Unrefined use of consumer segmentation techniques can lead a business marketer in the wrong direction.

RELATIONSHIP BETWEEN SEGMENTATION, TARGETING, AND POSITIONING

Segmentation, targeting, and positioning are part of a single process as shown in Figure 6.1.

The first step is to group customers together along common variables: the next step is to choose the most attractive segments for the marketing effort. The third step is to develop a position which attempts to place the marketing firm uniquely in the mind of the buyers. The firm will then implement its marketing strategy around the position it has developed.

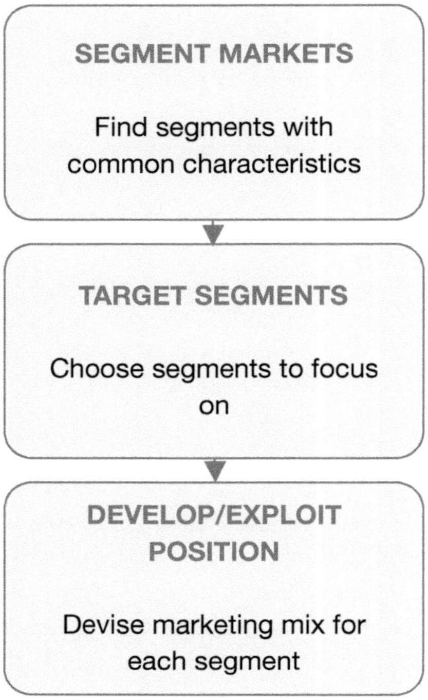

FIGURE 6.1 Segmentation/targeting/positioning process

Source: adapted from Kotler (2003).

EFFECTIVE SEGMENTATION

A market segment has been defined as a group of customers who can be reached with a distinct marketing mix. That is, these customers have certain traits in common which helps to explain (or predict) their reaction to a firm's marketing program. Since, of course, the marketing mix consists of the seven Ps of marketing – price, product, promotion, place, people, process, and physical evidence – a market segment would react to a unique mix of these marketing stimuli.

While segmenting is always a possibility, it is not always a most rewarding course to follow. For example, a security firm might segment its customer base into supermarkets and drug store chains. However, if there was no difference in the requirements of these customers nor in their reaction to the firm's offerings as represented by the marketing mix, this kind of segmentation would be unproductive. Hlavacek and Ames (1986) warn that firms may find themselves in one of two extreme situations: either they have not identified enough market segments, or they have found too many. The tests of a good market segment are listed in Table 6.1.

First, a segment must be measurable. That is, specific information about the size and expenditures and characteristics of any segment can be determined through primary or secondary research. Second,

TABLE 6.1 Tests of a good segment

- Measurable
- Substantial
- Accessible
- Differentiable
- Stable

the market segment must be substantial, that is, large enough to justify a firm's expenditures of manpower and capital. Third, the segment must be accessible. The firm must be able to reach the segment through marketing efforts. For instance, it would be of no use to know that left-handed purchasing managers are more inclined to buy cleaning solvents from a particular firm, since there is no clear way to reach this segment through sales effort or established media. Some analysts add the term "actionable" to this list of segmentation tests but accessible and actionable really describe the same attribute. A good segment must be differentiable which means it is homogeneous within and heterogeneous between. In other words, the group targeted reacts in a particular way to marketing stimuli and that reaction is different from the reaction of other segments. This variable should also be reviewed for the level of response. If a segment is more responsive than another, it may make it more attractive for a particular marketer. Finally, the best segments are somewhat stable. Although segments can change as product offerings and marketing stimuli are changed, the best segments are relatively stable justifying the investment by a firm in targeting that particular segment.

COMPETITION

When a firm chooses which segment to serve it is in essence choosing its competitors as well (Zahra and Chaples, 1993). Competitive analysis consists of finding the relevant market segment, identifying competitors, determining their strengths and weaknesses, and anticipating their future actions. Although segmentation defines the competition, sometimes new competitors who were not identified as serving that segment will enter the market. Since competitors may define a segment in a different way, it is helpful to understand the competitor's definition of segments and then to re-examine the segmentation approach for new insights.

SEGMENTATION VARIABLES

Business marketing segmentation variables can be divided into two main categories.

In the first category called *identifiers* by Day (1990), firms try to pre-establish segments *a priori*, that is before any data are collected. This is done by using traditional segmentation variables because the data are easier to obtain through observation of the buying situation or from secondary sources.

TABLE 6.2 Segmentation variables

Identifier (a priori)	Response profile (a posteriori)
■ Demographic – Industry classification – Firm type – OEM, end user, aftermarket (MRO) – Company size – Geographic location – Financial info/credit rating	■ Vendor product attributes – Overall value – Product quality – Vendor reputation – Innovativeness – On-time delivery – Lowest cost
■ Operations – Technologies used – Level of use – heavy, light, non-user – Centralized/decentralized purchasing	■ Customer variables – DMU (buying center) make-up – Purchase importance – Attitude toward product – Corporate cultural characteristics (innovativeness)
■ Product required – Custom ←→ standard	■ Application – End use – Importance of value in use
■ Purchasing situation – Buying situation – new task, modified rebuy, straight rebuy – Current attitude toward our firm – Relationships	■ DMU/buying center personal characteristics – Risk tolerance – Loyalty to current vendor – Age – Experience – Education – National culture

Source: adapted from Kotler (2003); Day (1990); Rao and Wang (1995); Malhotra (1989); Cardozo (1980).

Some researchers call these macro variables. As can be seen from Table 6.2, they include demographic factors, operations factors, product required, and purchasing situation variables, related to current or potential customer market segments. Day (1990) also identified *response profile* characteristics, "unique to the product or service . . . based on attributes and behavior toward the product category or specific brands and vendors in that category." These include specific vendor attributes such as overall value offered, product quality, vendor reputation, on time delivery and so on. In addition, customer variables such as the make-up of the decision-making unit (or buying center), the importance of the purchase to the subject segment, and the innovativeness of the firms in this potential segment are examined. The response profile technique also involves reviewing the user's applications of the product to determine how products are used – for example, a construction company might use detergent for cleaning the offices, or it might be used as an additive to concrete to make it easier to mix. Finally, personal characteristics may be included to define a particular segment. These include variables related to individuals in the buying center such as national culture, risk tolerance, loyalty, age, education, and experience. There is a great deal of evidence that an individual's national culture has an impact on his or her decision-making. Gupta (2012) identified over 30 Cultural Value Dimensions (CVDs) to help explain behavior. While a detailed discussion of the effect of each of these CVDs is beyond the scope of this section, a few examples will illustrate these cultural effects. Individuals who are members of a culture which enjoys uncertainty tend to prefer informal interactions between people while high uncertainty avoidance cultures prefer formalized interactions. Those from cultures with long-term orientations find relationships more important than those from cultures with a short term orientation who focus more on tasks than relationships.

The response profile variables are often referred to as *a posteriori*, or after-the-fact variables, in which a "clustering approach" is used to gather similar customers together based on their needs. Some researchers call these micro variables.

Looking at the usefulness of the two basic segmentation approaches as measured against the tests for a good segment, Malhotra (1989) claims the identifier approach is better than the response profile approach in terms of measurability and accessibility since it is easier to find and reach the segments which already have established data classifications. He feels this method is particularly good for institutional markets, where the number of establishments is small and the number of variables is large. On the other hand, Malhotra believes that using the response profile or clustering approach will produce more responsiveness from a particular segment since the marketing mix will be closely tailored to the specific needs of the segment identified.

Generally speaking, business marketers have used identifiers to segment markets. The major reason for this is simplicity. The Internet has made it easy to get the information needed to segment markets this way.

The use of the response profile approach is a subject of much discussion in the literature. While there is general agreement that the customer's view of vendor attributes, or how the decision-making unit is constituted, or the risk tolerance of key members of the DMU, is invaluable segmentation information, there is little agreement about how widespread this approach is.

Dibb and Simkin (2001) point out that although much has been written about segmentation, there is limited guidance for managers trying to put the theory into practice. They identified three major categories of barriers to effective segmentation: infrastructure, process, and implementation. These can be further subdivided into culture, structure, and resources.

Infrastructure barriers include support (or lack of it) from senior management, lack of intra-functional communications, entrenched organizational structures, and the lack of financial and human resources. Process issues include the lack of practical advice on how to implement segmentation, unwillingness to share ideas and information, lack of fit with corporate strategy, and misuse of the process due to poor understanding of it. Implementation barriers include the difficulty of changing present segmentation in the firm. Since industries are often organized around product categories or distribution channels, it can be difficult to develop segments which are not congruent with those existing divisions. Barriers also include poor identification of responsibility, poor communications, and lack of senior management involvement. The acid test comes when managers try to align budgets and assignments with segmentation solutions. If this isn't accomplished, the entire process is a waste of time. A summary of the key segmentation barriers and recommended treatments is shown in Table 6.3.

Dibb and Simkin recommend solutions to the problems identified. Managers need to identify the information, people and skills required to get the segmentation process done. Senior management

TABLE 6.3 Diagnosing and treating key segmentation barriers

Problems	Infrastructure	Process	Implementation
Culture	• Inflexible, resists new ideas • Not customer focused • Doesn't understand segmentation rationale	• Not committed to sharing data/ideas • Lack of "buy in" • No fit with corporate strategy planning	• Product focus • Insufficient belief in the process • Unwillingness to change current segmentation
Structure	• Lack of intra-functional communications • Low senior management interest or involvement • Entrenched organizational structures	• Misuse of segmentation process	• Poor demarcation of responsibility • Ineffective communications of segmentation solution • Poor senior management involvement
Resources	• Too few or untrained people • Insufficient budgets	• Inadequate data available • Insufficient budgets • Too few or untrained people	• Lack of alignment of budgeting with segmentation • Insufficient time allowed
Solutions	Prior to process: • Find available data • Identify people/skills • Get senior management support • Develop communications • Establish adequate budgets • Train people – basic segmentation skills	During process: • Specify segmentation steps • Fill gaps in education/skills • Collect data – internal and external • Establish regular communications meetings • Review for fit with corporate strategy	Facilitate Implementation: • Identify and communicate findings • Make changes to plans and programs • Identify changes required to culture and structure • Specify budgets, responsibilities and timing to roll out solutions • Develop method for monitoring roll out

Source: Based on Dibb and Simkin (2001).

must support the process, develop proper communications channels, establish adequate budgets, and set up training for people who will be assigned to do the process but may not have the necessary education or skills.

During the process, it is important to identify the segmentation steps, get the education gaps filled, then collect the data through internal and external sources (here a firm may employ a number of secondary and primary data techniques). It is also important to establish regular meetings for communications or progress, and for senior management to be sure that the segmentation is going to fit into the overall corporate strategy.

Finally, to facilitate implementation the authors recommend identifying the specific audiences to whom the findings will be communicated and then to do that, to make changes to plans and programs congruent with the new segmentation solutions, to identify changes that are required in the culture and the structure of the firm, then to specify responsibilities, budgets, and timing to make the segmentation work. Finally, managers need to set up a monitoring process to see whether the segmentation process is being implemented, and whether this implementation is effective.

SEGMENTATION PROCESS

While the process can be described, there is no one correct way to go about segmentation. Finding customers who can be served with a particular marketing mix is both an art and a science. A creative marketing executive will see combinations of potential customers which his competitors may not see. This alone yields a strong competitive advantage. A mix of data analysis and judgment based on industry experience is often necessary to achieve really effective segmentation.

The most widely accepted approach to segmentation is that proposed by Bonoma and Shapiro (1984). They describe the nested approach, starting with very general, easily available information and moving to the most specific variables which, incidentally, are the most difficult to obtain information about. See Figure 6.2.

The first and most obvious step is to group companies by industry classification. In the United States, the most common industry classification has been the Standard Industrial Classification (SIC), which was replaced in 1997 by the North American Industrial Classification System (NAICS). The NAICS was created to rationalize data among the three NAFTA countries – the United States, Canada and Mexico – and is updated regularly. The last update was in 2007, when some minor changes were made in parts of the information sector. Other classification systems include the Standard International Trade Classification (SITC), established by the United Nations in 1950, and revised several times since. The US also participates in the Harmonized Commodity Description System, known simply as the Harmonized System which has been used to classify goods in international trade since 1 January 1989. This system is in common use in more than 50 countries.

Industry classifications give a firm a start on the grouping of customers and prospective customers into potential segments.

Many firms simply divide their customers into heavy, medium, and light users, the so-called A-B-C division. This may be useful for assigning sales persons to particular accounts, but it is a poor substitute for the full segmentation process since it only partly takes account of customer needs. Using firm demographics also includes dividing customers into types – OEM, end user, and aftermarket (MRO) – and also grouping them by company size, geographic location, and by specific financial factors such as credit worthiness.

Classifying customers according to OEM, end user or aftermarket gives useful clues to their commonalities. An OEM or original equipment manufacturer buys components, systems, equipment, and materials. In the case of components, these enter the OEM's final product while materials are consumed in the manufacturing of their products. Systems and equipment are used to make the

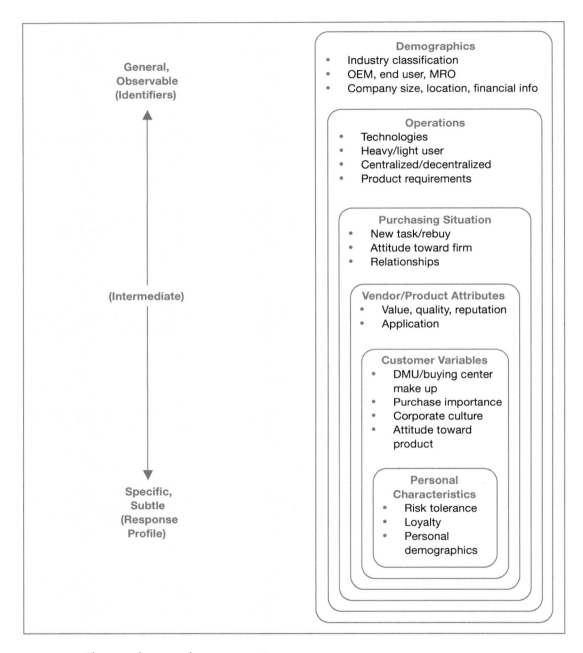

FIGURE 6.2 The nested approach to segmentation

Source: adapted from Bonoma and Shapiro (1983).

TABLE 6.4 Classification of customers

Type of customer	Description
OEM	Original Equipment Manufacturer. These customers buy manufacturing equipment, raw materials, and components to make into finished products. Examples would be car manufacturers or consumer durables manufacturers.
End user	These customers use the product in the course of running the business. For example, a company will use cleaning materials, energy, copier paper, office furniture, and so forth without incorporating any of these items into the finished products which it sells.
Aftermarket (MRO)	Maintenance, repair, and operations companies provide services to companies and consumers. For example, a computer repair company will use spare parts, tools, and transport to repair or replace defective parts.

products. OEMs often purchase many different items to develop a particular product (see the hairdryer example in Chapter 1) and frequently brand the product with their own name. Users obviously put the product to use. For instance, John Deere tractors are used by farmers while Deere itself is an OEM (Hlavacek and Ames, 1986). The after market, also called MRO, includes firms who offer add-on products, repair services or replacement parts. Often, a producer may sell his product or services to all three of these firm types, but each is a separate and different segment since requirements will probably be quite different.

A second step involves more understanding of customer operations. In this step, the marketer would determine what technologies potential customers are employing, whether they are heavy or light users of the product to be offered, whether they purchase in a centralized or decentralized way, and specifically what product requirements customers have, ranging from standard to custom products.

A third step is to look at the purchasing situation – whether this purchase is a new task for this firm, a straight rebuy or a modified rebuy, whether the potential customer has positive attitudes toward the firm, and what relationships have been established by the marketing firm with potential customers.

A fourth step is to determine what commonalities there are among potential customers related to the particular attributes of an offering firm. For instance, one customer group may be quite price sensitive while another emphasizes delivery and a third demands product quality defined in some specific manner. For example, a firm supplying chemicals to an ink maker may find that color consistency is of primary importance and far outweighs price or delivery as a purchasing attribute. Another aspect of the vendor attribute would be the application in which the product may be used.

A more refined and more difficult set of variables to gain is identified in Figure 6.2 as customer variables. First and most important would be the make-up of the buying center or DMU. Included here would be the importance of this purchase to the firm, the corporate culture (including the attitude toward innovation), and the attitude toward the product area. A final (and most difficult) set of characteristics which may be used for segmentation are personal characteristics of individuals in the DMU. These include national culture, age, experience and education, loyalty to current vendor, and risk tolerance. A common saying in many firms is "no one ever got fired for buying IBM." Individuals with low-risk tolerance would tend to choose a vendor like IBM since chances of negative consequences for an individual when choosing the pre-eminent supplier in any market are far lower than if that individual had chosen a rather unknown supplier. Research by the authors shows that in nearly every industrial market, firms tend to stay with vendors who have satisfied them. Therefore an important segmentation characteristic is the attitude toward the firm, as well as loyalty and tolerance for risk.

Robertson and Barich (1992) proposed a simple approach to segmentation based only upon the purchase decision process. In this case, the authors claim that identifying potential customers as first time prospects, novices and sophisticates yields all the segmentation information needed. First time prospects are firms who see a need for the product, have started to evaluate possible suppliers, but have not yet purchased. Novices are customers who have purchased the product for the first time within the last 90 days and sophisticates have purchased the product before and are ready to rebuy or have recently repurchased. First time prospects are seeking honest sales reps who know and understand their business, a vendor who has been in business for some time, and the availability of a trial period. Novices are looking for technical support, training, and knowledgeable sales reps. Sophisticates are seeking compatibility with existing systems, customized products, a successful record from the vendor, speed in fixing problems, and post-sales support. The main advantage of this simplified approach is the ability to implement it with the sales force, which is often the major hurdle for effective segmentation implementation.

Segmenting by customer benefits is often recommended as the most effective approach and Rao and Wang (1995) found that identifiers do not correlate very well with profile or benefit sought variables. While these authors endorsed the nested approach to segmentation, they emphasized the importance of understanding specific customer benefits for the most effective segmentation.

Talking Point

A firm in Costa Rica developed a new technique for inexpensively testing blood samples for a number of potentially contagious diseases. The founder of the firm is a doctor with extensive experience in this field. In only a few years, the firm had established itself as the leading supplier to large, city-based hospitals in its native country as well as Venezuela, Columbia, and Ecuador. The founder felt the firm should continue to serve large, city-based hospitals in Latin America.

Is the founder correct? Does the identifier segmentation approach give the firm its best competitive position? Would it be worth the effort for the firm to try to use the response profile approach as well?

Since the firm is so small, and is in such a niche market anyway, why not let the world beat a path to its door? Why worry about segmenting at all?

SELECTING THE BEST SEGMENTS

Freytag and Clarke (2001) offer a segment selection process illustrated in Figure 6.3.

This process requires that a firm compare potential segments it may serve, estimating future attractiveness, resource demands, and fit with firm strategy. First, the firm should decide whether this particular segment will be growing at a suitable rate, is large enough and profitable enough to serve. Second, the firm should assess the competition and the risk, understand any governmental

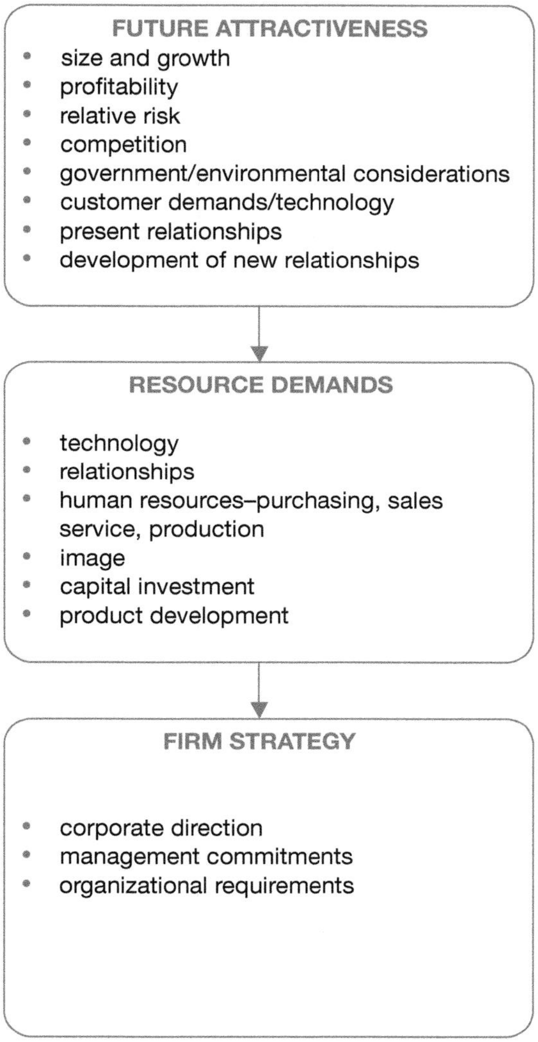

FUTURE ATTRACTIVENESS
- size and growth
- profitability
- relative risk
- competition
- government/environmental considerations
- customer demands/technology
- present relationships
- development of new relationships

RESOURCE DEMANDS
- technology
- relationships
- human resources–purchasing, sales service, production
- image
- capital investment
- product development

FIRM STRATEGY
- corporate direction
- management commitments
- organizational requirements

FIGURE 6.3 Segment selection process

Source: adapted from Freytag and Clarke, 2001.

or environmental concerns, what demands customers may have, and how serving this particular segment may affect present and future relationships with current and future customers. Third, the firm must look at demands on its resources in technology, relationships, human resources in each of the functional areas, image, capital investment, and product development required. Finally, the firm should examine whether this new segment is congruent with its present or future strategy related to the overall corporate direction, management's commitment, and organizational requirements required to implement the strategy.

Bonoma and Shapiro (1983) recommend choosing segments using two major criteria: Customer Conversion Analysis and Segment Profitability Analysis. The first simply means the attempt by a manager to determine how many potential prospects in a particular segment can be converted to customers and how large that served segment will be. This is based upon the number of prospects in a market (the density) which can be reached for a particular marketing expenditure.

Segment Profitability Analysis is an attempt to determine the contribution margin per dollar invested to serve that segment. They recommend combining these approaches to determine which segments a firm ought to serve.

NEED TO RE-SEGMENT

Since business market segments change quickly, managers should re-segment frequently. Some have suggested re-segmenting at the beginning of a new stage of the product lifecycle, but this is too difficult to determine. Nevertheless, changes in competition, technological advances, economic downturns or upswings, and consolidation of an industry make re-segmentation very important, and the pace at which these factors change means that segment instability is becoming a very real problem. If managers are not proactive in anticipating segment instability, they will only react to change when it is too late and will find themselves playing "catch-up" with more astute competitors (Blocker and Flint, 2007).

Once a firm begins to look at its existing segmentation on a regular basis, managers may find it necessary to establish new segments for the most effective use of its marketing efforts. Managements should avoid being "married" to the current segmentation, and should hold open the possibility of re-segmenting. It is a management task to ask questions regularly, reexamining the basic assumptions which underlie the current segmentation.

In some cases firms develop the segments themselves. This is often the case with radical new technology: there is no established need for the product, so new customers develop ideas as they adopt the product. This was the case for Biacore, a Swedish manufacturer of affinity biosensors. The technology was so new, the company was able to develop the market segments from scratch using its experience with early adopters of the product (Harrison and Kjellberg, 2010).

GLOBAL SEGMENTATION

Segmentation strategy is not limited to any one country. Sophisticated business marketing firms look across countries for commonalities of market segments. For instance, Nobel Enterprises offers mining explosives across various countries to similar customer types, coordinating its activities in each country by segment and offering product and sales activities accordingly (Gillespie et al., 2004). The same segmentation procedure described in Figure 6.2 can be used across various countries except that the data is much more difficult to get, and developing common measures is often a real obstacle. Despite this, Schuster and Bodkin (1987) found that more than 40 percent of the firms they surveyed gathered segmentation information for the following macro variables: geographic location, company size, usage, buying strategy, end market, and decision-making stage. More than 40 percent of firms gathered data for the following micro variables: product attributes, purchase importance, attitudes, and personal characteristics.

In business markets, it is not unusual to find commonalities among customers throughout the world. Electric utilities require the same products whether they are located in Kuala-Lumpur or Caracas. A firm selling switchgear to electric utilities must look to a worldwide customer base in order to get the economies of scale necessary to be a global competitor. According to Yip (2003), customers can be segmented according to their purchasing patterns. *Global customers* are quite willing to purchase products outside their domestic markets and tend to have global control of purchasing from headquarters. *National global customers* use suppliers from around the world, but employ the products in one country. *Multinational global customers* buy from suppliers in many countries, but they use the products in many countries as well. Management should look for commonalities among customers, using the segmentation process described in the earlier part of the chapter rather than accept that minor differences make serving one segment across countries too difficult to achieve. There are many benefits to serving multinational customer segments, not only including economies of scale but also rapid movement to world class product and service offerings, making further expansion even easier.

A study of the purchasing decision process in a region of the United States, Sweden, France, and five southeast Asian countries found some differences in the decision-making process and the structure of the buying center (Mattson and Salehi-Sangari, 1993). This study also found differences in the most important purchase decision variables used by the decision-making unit for the same products. In short, this study serves as a caution that care must be taken in segmenting markets across countries. However, the benefits of international segmentation are worth the effort required.

MARKET TARGETING

Once the segmentation process is nearly complete, the firm must choose the target market segments it wishes to serve. A target market is a set of buyers with common characteristics which a company decides to serve. To decide on which market segments to target, a firm would decide whether a segment is attractive, whether the firm has the resources to serve that segment, and whether serving that segment fits with the company's overall objectives.

A firm may choose to apply *undifferentiated marketing* which means focusing on commonalities among all segments, but in essence attempting to serve the entire market with only one marketing mix. This is found most often in the earliest stages of a product lifecycle when undifferentiated product will be accepted by customers because there is no other choice. For example, early personal computers were heavy, slow, expensive, and had limited software capabilities yet firms bought large numbers of these personal computers because the productivity increases of their employees outweighed the difficulties of finding specific computers which satisfied their corporate needs. Undifferentiated marketing usually only lasts as long as competition is limited.

When a firm decides to use *differentiated marketing*, it designs specific marketing mixes to serve each segment. Obviously, differentiated marketing costs more than undifferentiated marketing and can only be justified when the results outweigh the cost. The easiest way to picture differentiated marketing is to conceive of the marketing machine as shown in Figure 6.4.

In this machine, each lever represents one of the 7 Ps. In using differentiated marketing, these levers would be set to best satisfy a particular segment. For the next segment, the levers would be set differently. However, it is important to remember that not all levers have to be changed to serve each segment. In many cases the same product, price, and promotion, etc. may serve two different segments where the only variation required is distribution or service (included under place).

For firms with very limited resources the only choice may be *concentrated marketing.* In this case a firm concentrates on one or very few segments. The idea is to build a dominant position in that segment. For example, a firm manufacturing highly sensitive, low-light level television cameras focuses its efforts on industrial applications such as unauthorized entry or pilferage. Here again, the marketing machine must be carefully set to serve the specific segment(s) chosen. This is perhaps the most risky targeting strategy since the possibility exists that the segment may experience economic difficulties, or choose to use a substitute product. Firms using the concentration strategy must be vigilant about the possibility of new segments evolving.

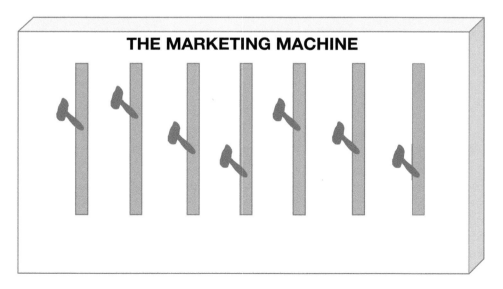

Price   Product Promotion Place People   Process   Physical evidence

FIGURE 6.4 The marketing machine

POSITIONING

Positioning essentially means developing a theme which will provide a "meaningful distinction for customers" (Day, 1990). The concept of positioning was strongly advanced by Ries and Trout (2001). They state that many products already have a distinctive position in the mind of the customer. These positions are difficult to dislodge. For instance, IBM would be thought of as the world's largest and most competent computer company. Trout and Ries say that competitors have three possible strategies they may follow. First, the firm may choose to strengthen its current leadership position by reinforcing the original concepts that led to the first position in the mind of the customer. Second, the firm might establish a new position – "*cherchez le creneaux*" – looking for new openings in a market. Third, the firm might try to de-position or re-position the competition. Ries and Trout claim that customers establish a ladder for each product category in their minds. On these ladders, buyers establish possible suppliers as first, second or third level. This can offer an opportunity for positioning. Their most famous example of this comes from the auto rental business and the rental company, Avis. When Avis entered the market, Hertz held an unassailable position as the premier car rental firm. Avis was one of many other competitors, but Avis chose to position themselves as "#2" which at that time was an unoccupied position. This immediately catapulted Avis to a position as an important competitor despite the reality that it was no larger than any of the other competitors fighting for a piece of the market with the pre-eminent Hertz. Avis established itself as the first alternative to Hertz in the minds of customers. This is also known as establishing the "against" position – Avis placing themselves against Hertz.

Treacy and Wiersema (1993) offer three value disciplines – operational excellence, customer intimacy or product leadership. They recommend a firm become a "champion" in one of these areas while simply meeting industry standards in the other two.

Often, positioning is based upon a series of perceptual maps. An example is shown in Figure 6.5.

This example shows two important variables, the horizontal axis for initial price and the vertical axis for technical assistance. It is obvious that the lower right-hand corner of this matrix is probably a poor position to be in. In this quadrant, a firm would be offering a high initial price with only adequate technical assistance.

Let us assume that three firms are in the market. Firm A is a low-priced firm offering little technical assistance. Firm B is a higher-priced firm with very good technical assistance. The management of Firm C may see an opportunity to stake out a position as a somewhat lower price offering than B with somewhat better technical assistance than A. (Of course, a firm which could occupy the upper left quadrant offering low initial price and very good comprehensive technical assistance might win many more customers than either A, B, or C. However, in the real world it is usually impossible to offer this combination because the cost of offering a high level of service precludes offering a low price as well.)

A critical point is that customers must place value on the variables being examined. In our example, if the customers had little need for technical assistance this perceptual map would be virtually useless. However, if Firm C's market research shows that technical assistance and initial price are critical variables in the decision-making process this map is quite useful in helping develop a position which can be clearly communicated to potential customers.

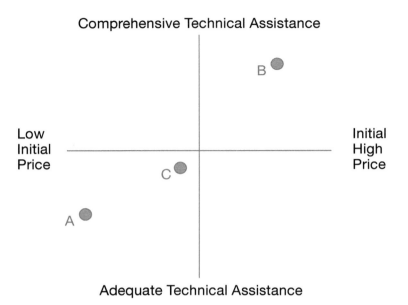

Comprehensive Technical Assistance

FIGURE 6.5 Perceptual map

A special consideration for international positioning is the country of origin effect. Buyers often have established perceptions of country capabilities, i.e. "German engineering" develops positive associations. For example, a US-based office furniture firm decided to make products for the EU in a new, state-of-the-art factory in Kells, Ireland. The products were equal in quality in every way to those produced in the US factory, yet Continental buyers often rejected the Irish-made product for competitive brands made in their home countries. Country of origin effect seems to be reduced as buyers become more informed, but it is important a manager knows what perceptions already exist so that they can be addressed.

RE-POSITIONING

If a current position has been rendered useless by competitor pressure or customer indifference or because the results are disappointing, new positioning is necessary. Day (1990) offers the four-step process for reassessing a positioning theme as shown in Table 6.5.

The main test of this approach is to be sure that alternatives are meaningful to customers, are feasible, and are superior to what the competition offers or may offer in future.

Designing the programs to implement the chosen position can be a complex task requiring cooperation from all functional areas in the firm and sometimes requiring product and service modifications as well. Once a position is chosen, a firm must clearly communicate this position in a consistent way. The best positioning is simple to communicate – "the fastest, the oldest or the most technically competent" – are easy messages to communicate through advertising, public relations, and especially through the sales force. It is especially important that a simple position be established when a firm is to communicate in many languages and across many cultures. Stating the position in its irreducible simplest form will make it easy for the sales force to communicate what the company stands for and this is a critical ingredient in global success. Choosing the right position is the culmination of all the market segmentation and targeting work which has been discussed in this chapter.

TABLE 6.5 Developing a new positioning theme

1. Identify alternative positioning themes.

2. Screen each alternative according to whether it is:
    –   Meaningful to customers;
    –   Feasible given the firm's competencies and customer perceptions of the firm;
    –   Superior/unique vs. competition; difficult for them to match;
    –   Congruent with company objectives.

3. Choose the position that best satisfies the criteria, and generates the most enthusiasm and commitment within the organization.

4. Design the programs needed to implement the position. Compare costs of these programs with likely benefits.

Source: adapted from Day, 1990.

CASE STUDY

Banco Portugues de Investimento

Northern Portugal is the cradle of the nation's entrepreneurial spirit. Business people in the region consider themselves to be the real wheeler-dealers of the Portuguese economy, running mainly small- to medium-size businesses, and having a certain air of contempt for their counterparts in Lisbon and further south. According to the northern Portuguese, Lisbonites are mere employees of multinationals who spend their time on politics and parties while the real deals are done in the North.

Of course, in common with most other capital cities, Lisbon is where the power and money gravitates; like the multinationals, banks have a strong presence there. However, the Portuguese have a saying that banks are born in Oporto and die in Lisbon, where deal-making skills become blunted and attention to detail becomes lax. For this reason, Banco Portugues de Investimento keeps its headquarters in Oporto.

BPI is an exclusive merchant bank set up in 1981 by Artur Santos Silva; Senhor Silva subsequently set up or acquired a string of subsidiary banks between Oporto and

. . . continued

Lisbon. Two of these, Banco de Fomento e Exterior and Banco Fonsecas & Burnay, have head offices in Lisbon, while a third, Banco Borges & Irmao, remained in Oporto. Borges & Irmao was focused toward Northern Portugal, which is where the bulk of its branches were, and Fonsecas & Burnay was focused in the south. Later these banks were subsumed into the overall brand of Banco BPI, but since Allianz Bank (a German bank) bought part of the bank, BPI has also traded as Allianz Portugal.

Bank managers have been briefed to develop consumer lending niches such as credit cards and car purchase loans, segments where BPI claims it has developed key products. The business in the North has the added bonus of using its retail activities to scout for corporate finance – so many of its retail customers are business people running small and medium enterprises. Typically, banking groups in Portugal divide their markets into three main segments; small and medium enterprises, universal banking, and large corporations. BPI believe that the delivery of tailor-made services to specific segments is the key to success in domestic banking.

Banking executives are painfully aware that there is a lot of work to be done in restructuring the industries of Northern Portugal – they talk in terms of identifying products and standardizing them, of joint marketing projects, and of pooling companies together for research and testing of projects. Aiding management buy-outs and merger and acquisition deals are seen as ways of ensuring continuity in businesses, and banks are looking toward cross-border transactions with companies in Northern Spain as a way of consolidating businesses. So far progress has been slow – obviously the economic problems faced by Portugal have called a halt to business expansions, but also there have been few large enterprises emerging from the spate of mergers and acquisitions. Most firms are still engaged in traditional industries such as leather production, agriculture, and textiles, all of which face stiff competition from lower-cost producers in other countries.

Meanwhile, BPI has developed a strong position in Africa: the former Portuguese colonies of Angola and Mozambique are among the economic powerhouses of Southern Africa, and BPI has a stake in their growth through shareholdings in local banks there. This has helped cushion the bank from the 2008 world financial crisis: Mozambique is among the world's fastest-growing economies, with burgeoning chemical and manufacturing industries as well as traditional agriculture and mining, and Angola has great mineral wealth (including diamonds) which will eventually catapult the country into becoming one of the wealthiest in Southern Africa. BPI is well-placed to take advantage of this, once the current political troubles are over, and in November 2010 the bank signed an agreement with the Bank of China under which BPI will assist China in creating inward investment by Chinese companies in Portugal and Portuguese Africa. The two banks will also cooperate on cross-border trade settlements, funding of major projects, and day-to-day banking issues such as letters of credit, documentary collections, and capital management.

. . . *continued*

CASE STUDY ... *continued*

CASE STUDY QUESTIONS

1   How does BPI appear to have segmented its market?

   a.   What variables have they used?

2   Why should an investment bank look to have a foothold in the consumer market?
3   What do you think are the drivers behind Bank of China's interest in BPI?
4   How might the company segment the African market?
5   Which segments should BPI avoid?
6   What could an effective positioning strategy be for BPI?

CHAPTER SUMMARY

The most important strategic decision a business marketing firm must make is choosing the most rewarding market segments. Segmentation is the first of the three step process, followed by choosing the most effective segment, called targeting, and positioning the firm in the most attractive way toward that market segment.

   The key points from this chapter are as follows:

- Consumer marketers segment by geographic, demographic, psychographic, and behavioral characteristics. Only some of these are applicable to business market segmentation.
- It is dangerous to simply apply consumer marketing segmentation techniques to business markets.
- A good segment is measurable, substantial, accessible, differentiable, and stable.
- Identifiers fall into demographic, operations, product, and purchasing situation variables.
- Response profile variables include product attributes, customer application, and buying-center personal characteristics.
- Infrastructure barriers, process issues, and implementation barriers are the major problems encountered by firms attempting to segment their markets effectively.
- Segmentation should be continually re-examined to be sure that market conditions have not changed.
- Each group requires different capabilities from a firm.
- Future attractiveness of the segment, demands on the resources of the firm, and the fit with the firm strategy are the three major tests to be applied.

REVIEW QUESTIONS

1   What are the major differences between consumer and business to business segmentation techniques?
2   Describe how segmentation, targeting and positioning are related to one another.
3   Enumerate the tests of a good market segment.
4   List identifier segmentation variables and response profile segmentation variables.
5   What might be the problem of applying segmentation across different cultures and countries?
6   Apply the nested approach to segmentation to a multinational bank.
7   In selecting a market segment, what are the three major criteria?
8   How do the settings on the "marketing machine" and the identification of market segments tell you whether a company is using undifferentiated, differentiated, or concentrated marketing?
9   How do perceptual maps help in positioning?
10 What obstacles might a firm expect in implementing its segmentation, targeting, and positioning procedures?
11 Assume you are the marketing vice president for a firm selling interior lighting equipment. How might you go about segmenting your markets on a worldwide basis?

REFERENCES

Blocker, Christopher P. and Flint, Daniel J. (2007). "Customer Segments as Moving Targets: Integrating Customer Value Dynamism into Segment Instability Logic." *Industrial Marketing Management*, Vol. 36, Iss. 6, 823–33.

Bonoma, Thomas V. and Shapiro, Benson P. (1983). *Segmenting the Industrial Market*. Lexington, M.A.: D.C. Heath.

Bonoma, Thomas V. and Shapiro, Benson P. (1984). "Evaluating Market Segmentation Approaches." *Industrial Marketing Management*, Vol. 13, Iss. 4, 257–68.

Cardozo, Richard N. (1980). "Situational Segmentation of Industrial Markets." *European Journal of Marketing*, Vol. 14, No. 5/6, 264–76.

Day, George S. (1990). *Market-Driven Strategy: Process for Creating Value*. New York: Free Press.

Dibb, Sally and Simkin, Lyndon (2001). "Market Segmentation: Diagnosing and Treating the Barriers." *Industrial Marketing Management*, Vol. 30, Iss. 8, 609–25.

Freytag, Per Vagn and Clarke, Ann Hojberg (2001). "Business to Business Market Segmentation." *Industrial Marketing Management*, Vol. 30, Iss. 6, 473–86.

Gillespie, Kate, Jeannet, Jean-Pierre, and Hennessey, H. David (2004). *Global Marketing: An Interactive Approach*. Boston: Houghton Mifflin.

Gupta, S. (2012). "A Framework Development Process to Integrate Cultural Value Dimensions in a Managerial Decision Making Context." *Journal Of Business & Economic Studies*, Vol. 18, Iss. 1, 1–53.

Harrison, Debbie and Kjellberg, Hans (2010). "Segmenting a Market in the Making: Industrial Market Segmentation as Construction." *Industrial Marketing Management*, Vol. 39, Iss. 5, 820–31.

Hlavacek, James D. and Ames, B.C. (1986). "Segmenting Industrial and High-Tech Markets." *Journal of Business Strategy*, Vol. 7, Iss. 2, 39–50.

Kotler, Philip (2003). *Marketing Management*. Upper Saddle River, NJ: Prentice-Hall.

Krauss, Michael (2003). "New Tech Still Suffers Old Marketing Woes." *Marketing News*, Vol. 37, Iss. 5, 12.

Malhotra, Naresh K. (1989). "Segmenting Hospitals for Improved Management Strategy." *Journal of Health Care Marketing*, Vol. 9, No. 3, 45–52.

Mattson, Melvin R. and Salehi-Sangari, Esmail (1993). "Decision Making in Purchases of Equipment and Materials: A Four-Country Comparison." *International Journal of Physical Distribution and Logistics Management*, Vol. 23, No. 8, 16–30.

Rao, Chatrathi P. and Wang, Zhengyuan (1995). "Evaluating Alternative Segmentation Strategies in Standard Industrial Markets." *European Journal of Marketing*, Vol. 29, No. 2, 58–75.

Ries, Al and Trout, Jack (2001). *Positioning: The Battle For Your Mind*. New York: McGraw-Hill.

Robertson, Thomas S. and Barich, Howard (1992). "A Successful Approach to Segmenting Industrial Markets." *Planning Review*, Vol. 20, No. 6, 4–48.

Schuster, Camille P. and Bodkin, Charles D. (1987). "Market Segmentation Practices of Exporting Companies." *Industrial Marketing Management*, Vol. 16, Iss. 2, 95–102.

Treacy, Michael and Wiersema, Fred (1993). "Customer Intimacy and Other Value Disciplines." *Harvard Business Review*, Vol. 71, Iss. 1, 84–93.

Yip, George S. (2003). *Total Global Strategy II*. Upper Saddle River, NJ: Prentice Hall.

Zahra, Shaker A. and Chaples, Sherry S. (1993). "Blind Spots in Competitive Analysis." *Academy of Management Executive*, Vol. 7, No. 2, 7–28.

Chapter 7

Market entry tactics

INTRODUCTION

Entering new markets is both challenging and rewarding. A manager must weigh a number of variables to get the decision right. This is especially true when a firm is thinking about getting into international markets. Segmentation, which we discussed in the last chapter, is an important prerequisite for determining the best new market to enter. Once the decision is made, there are many choices for market entry. These are based on specific considerations which will be described in this chapter.

CHAPTER OBJECTIVES

After reading this chapter, you should be able to:

- understand the key considerations in market entry decisions
- explain the role of management in an internationalizing firm
- describe the foreign market entry strategy alternatives
- show how foreign market entry decisions are made
- prescribe the cure for blocked markets
- describe the special characteristics of strategic alliances.

MARKET ENTRY CONSIDERATIONS

Many factors in the environment affect the market entry decision. As described in Figure 7.1, these so-called uncontrollables include economic, demographic, competitive, political/legal, technological, and social/cultural aspects.

Obviously the economic environment has a major impact on the market entry decision. Growth in an economy or particular segment may also attract competitors and make an entry decision more difficult. On the other hand, an economy or segment that isn't growing may cause firms to leave the market and enter new, more promising segments. The demographic trends include shifts and growth in population. These trends have major effects on consumer spending which in turn affects derived demand in business markets.

The competitive environment both in a firm's current served segment and in a market under consideration has an important effect on the entry decision. Firms already in the target market will need to be dislodged, but at the same time the firm entering the market cannot afford to neglect its existing markets.

Changes in the political/legal environment may cause a firm to see a new market as attractive or a current market as unattractive. A new government planning decision to expand military spending might cause an electronics firm to pursue the government market for the first time.

The technological environment has a profound effect on market entry decisions. Technology can force a firm to leave a market or make it possible to enter a new one. In addition, Internet services have radically reduced the cost of communications to any market throughout the world; they also allow buyers instant access to competing product and service offerings from vendors in many locations and enable them to increase the number of firms they consider while making a buying decision

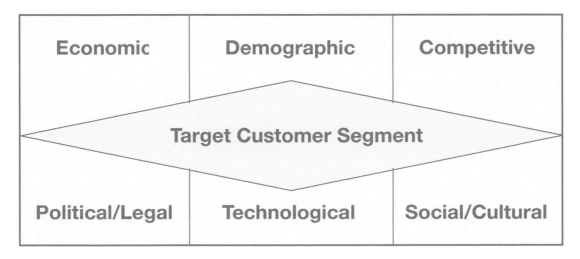

FIGURE 7.1 Environmental factors

	Current product	New products
Current markets	Market-penetration strategy	Product-development strategy
New markets	Market-development strategy	Diversification strategy

FIGURE 7.2 Product market expansion guide

Source: Ansoff, 1957.

(Heide and Weiss, 1995). Some believe technology is the major driving force pushing firms into new markets.

Finally, the social/cultural environment is important to entry decisions. Changes in social mores have a major effect on business to business marketers, since their demand is derived from consumer markets. For instance, the addition of women to the workforce has meant more meals eaten in restaurants, creating major markets for producers of restaurant equipment and suppliers of every type.

Ansoff's well-known Matrix (Figure 7.2) helps firms to decide whether they wish to provide current products to current markets or take those same products to new markets. The other basic alternative is to take new products to current markets or new products to new markets (Ansoff, 1957).

Market penetration and product development strategies are outside the scope of this chapter. Market development occurs when a firm uses its current products to approach a new market segment. A market segment is a group of customers which react in a specific way to a marketing mix (see Chapter 6). So, while market development allows a firm to take its current products to a new segment, it will more than likely be required to change other aspects of the mix – pricing, promotion or distribution.

Day (1990) adds a third alternative (Related) to each axis. This is placed between Current and New on each axis of the grid – products and markets. Taking Related products to Present or Related markets through product improvements or line extensions is a less risky way to expand than Market Development or Diversification. Needless to say, Diversification into markets completely unrelated to the firm's current segments with products or services completely new to the firm is the riskiest path to take. If a firm excels in some activity, management might feel it can expand into new areas to exploit these skills in some new way but as Day says, "in practice these prospective synergies are often illusions."

An example of this can be seen in the business interiors industry. Hauserman, Inc. was the dominant producer of ceiling-high movable metal walls, primarily used as room dividers in offices. Hauserman decided to move into a new but related product area, manufacturing less-than-ceiling-high panels with essentially the same function of space division and storage. The firm had well-established customers in most of the largest corporations in the US, Europe, and Asia and believed it would be easy to sell additional products to these current customers. While Hauserman thought it was pursuing a market penetration or possibly a product development strategy, the truth turned out to be quite different. The market segment the firm was approaching included an entirely different buying center (DMU). Instead of selling to plant engineers and maintenance people, the firm now found itself addressing architects, interior designers, and facilities managers employed by these same large firms. While it was not clear to Hauserman when their planning was taking place, the company wound up in a diversification strategy, facing a completely new set of customers and competitors with new products. After a prolonged, expensive, and unsuccessful effort, the firm chose to leave this market segment.

Strategic planning is reviewed in depth in Chapter 3. As described in that chapter management needs to consider industry, resource, and institutional factors when entering a new market.

SUCCESS FACTORS

Chesbrough (2003) examined variables related to the entry of sub-markets in the hard disk drive industry. He concluded that a number of factors are important to success when moving into a new market segment. These are presented in Table 7.1.

The capital structure of the firm has an important influence on success in new market entry. Firms with more traditional capital sources tend to focus more on current markets than on new markets. Chesbrough also identified the importance of securing the required technical skills through acquisition, licensing, or hiring of highly skilled employees as an important factor in successfully moving into a new segment. Another important factor is the forecast growth of the new market.

TABLE 7.1 New market entry factors

- capital structure;
- technical skills;
- customer relationships;
- competition in new market;
- competition in current market;
- forecast growth of the new market;
- management attitudes.

Source: adapted from Chesbrough (2003).

Firms who move quickly into markets where the growth was forecast to be significant had more success. The Strategic Planning Institute's conclusion based on the Profit Impact of Market Strategy (PIMS) database reinforces these findings (Strategic Planning Institute, 2012). Customer relationships are also a key success factor. A firm can use its existing customers to try out new technologies and gain rapid feedback to improve its offerings. As might be expected, management attitudes are also important to the success of a firm moving into a new market. As we will see, this is especially true in international market entry.

The competition in both new and current markets has an effect on a firm's entry. That heavy competition in a current market would make a firm wish to move to a new segment is obvious. A lack of competition in a new market would make it attractive.

ROLE OF TECHNOLOGY

Geroski (1999) points out that technological competence combined with good planning is essential to successful market entry. An example can be taken from the airline industry in the US where the replacement of older DC9s and 737s (which were unable to fly coast-to-coast) by newer aircraft allowed low-cost airlines to compete with established carriers on these very profitable, long-haul routes. He also points out that technology alone will not guarantee success. Other competencies are prerequisites for success in new markets – improved customer service, developing new products, strong brand names or reputations or better management of suppliers are all examples.

Talking Point

For many years, research showed that firms who got into a market first were the most successful firms. The well-known PIMS database showed a correlation between firms who were first movers and high market share. Consulting companies like Boston Consulting Group pushed the idea of getting into a market first with low prices to keep out the competition.

But what happened to the old saying, fools rush in where angels fear to tread? What happens if all the predictions are wrong, and the product flops? Why not let someone else take all the risk, and make all the mistakes, then come in with a better product that builds on their experience?

FIRST MOVERS VS. FOLLOWERS

When moving into a new market, a firm would consider whether it wishes to be a first mover or a follower. Many of the same new market entry factors identified by Chesbrough (2003) would be relevant to this decision. First movers usually end up with the largest market shares, and they erect high barriers to entry by other firms through the early establishment of their brand name or economies of scale in production or marketing, the commitment of distribution channel members and customer loyalty (reinforced by high switching costs); also by establishing social ties and new networks ahead of competitors. It has been well established that manufacturing firms realize first mover advantages. Magnusson et al. (2009) find that service firms benefit from these advantages as well. For first-mover service firms the ability to secure the best human resources before rivals is quite important. These first movers also profit from the development of long-term relationships with customers, and the creation of an effective company culture and organization. Studying firms entering India and China, Johnson and Tellis (2008) find that "earlier entrants enjoy greater success." First movers are often believed to have a head start that cannot be overcome by later entrants into a market (Varadarajan and Jayachandran, 1999). They learn about their customers' preferences and can even shape their customers' beliefs as the market develops.

On the other side of the ledger, these pioneers incur large cost disadvantages compared to firms who follow them into a market. Boulding and Christen (2001) found pioneers to be substantially less profitable than followers in the long run. Specifically in their study, the return on investment (ROI) of first movers was more than 4 percent lower than followers in industrial markets. Later entrants learn from the first movers and avoid costly mistakes and may be more flexible in their processes. Varadarajan and Jayachandran (1999) suggest that firms use a contingency approach to the first mover decision – that is, consider factors such as product type, advertising intensity or minimum scale required in the industry before deciding to be a pioneer in a market. One need only think back to RIM and the BlackBerry for a good example of a pioneer who did not reap ultimate real rewards by being first.

ENTERING FOREIGN MARKETS

Of all new market entry decisions, a foreign market entry decision is the most difficult. Long-term commitment on the part of management is essential: without commitment of resources and manpower the market entry will fail, since existing competitors in the target country are often totally committed to what is, for them, the home market. In their study of marketing organizations in three countries, Hult et al. (2007) emphasize the importance of senior management in both the financial and marketing performance of a firm's globalization efforts. They find that management is vital in formulating global strategy and building the proper organizational culture which can handle the complexities and challenges of various international markets.

Major motivations to globalize are shown in Table 7.2.

A firm with proactive motivations especially looking for additional profits will often "stay the course" when expected profits take longer to be realized. According to one experienced international manager, global business "takes longer, is harder and costs more" than everyone in the firm expects.

A firm with real or perceived advantages in technology or product may achieve long-term success. Having exclusive information about customers, distribution or competitors in foreign markets can also be a proactive reason to move ahead internationally. Since we have already discussed the importance of management commitment, a management which wishes to push a firm in an international direction will certainly do so and will have a lasting effect as long as that management is employed by the corporation.

Governments frequently offer tax breaks to exporters, but these can easily be removed by subsequent finance ministers, so they usually only provide a temporary incentive. For instance in

TABLE 7.2 Major motivations to globalize

Proactive reasons	Reactive reasons
Profit advantage	Competitive pressures
Unique products	Overproduction
Technological advantage	Declining domestic sales
Exclusive information	Excess capacity and/or saturated domestic markets
Managerial commitment	Maturity/decline stage of PLC
Economies of scale	Proximity to customers and ports
Market size	Managerial fads

Source: adapted from Czinkota and Ronkainen (2010).

the United States, Foreign Sales Corporation provisions were in conflict with World Trade Organization agreements, because they were seen to be an unfair subsidy on US exports. The WTO requested that the US Congress amend the tax laws to bring them into compliance with WTO regulations, as a result of which some firms withdrew from export markets.

Economies of scale are another proactive motivator. The home market, especially in a small country, may not be large enough to support entry into a particular product market. Manufacturing large numbers of products in a centralized factory may be necessary to compete with other large firms. Finally a large market may be an important reason to move ahead. China offers such a large market for many products that managers overlook the difficulties of entering in order to take advantage of the remarkable incremental sales.

Reactive motivations usually do not have long-lasting effects. A reactive motivation such as competitive pressure makes a firm think internationally simply to exclude its competitors from a foreign market. Some firms move too quickly into these situations and find themselves unprepared for the difficulties they encounter. Overproduction, saturated domestic markets, declining domestic sales, and excess capacity are similar reactive kinds of motivators. The underlying idea is that when the domestic market declines, the foreign markets are used as "safety valves" to take up the slack for declining domestic sales. In these cases, the effects are not long lasting and when domestic market activity improves managements not committed to international business often reduce or terminate their foreign market activities.

This can lead to negative feelings and reluctance to purchase again from any of those same corporations in the future. A specific example occurred in Chile where Westinghouse Electric Corporation sold heavy equipment to the Chilean copper mining industry. After Westinghouse withdrew to the USA following an upswing in demand there, some Chilean firms took the attitude "You left us when things got better in the US. How do we know you won't do it again?"

When a product reaches the end of its lifecycle in the home market, some managers become tempted to sell the product in what they perceive as a less sophisticated market. This tactic might have worked 20 or 30 years ago, but innumerable web outlets, satellite TV, improved education, and travel opportunities mean that prospective buyers have seen, and want, the latest technology and are often offended by being offered less. Even in cases where the older technology would be more appropriate, buyers often want the latest model. Another reactive motivation is closeness to customers and ports. This is often given as the reason why US companies trade more heavily with Canada than with any other country. The final reactive motivation may result from investor, media, or peer pressure – a managerial fad. Alexander and Korine (2008) point out that "the belief that companies must become more global is . . . a generally unquestioned assumption that can undermine the rational behavior of companies." They believe, before a firm embarks on a globalization strategy, management must carefully review three questions:

- Are there potential benefits for the company?
- Do we have the necessary management skills?
- Will the costs outweigh the benefits?

Generally speaking, the most successful firms in international markets are those with proactive motivations. They attempt to secure a market position internationally rather than simply react to orders from outside their domestic market or pressure from others.

CHOOSING FOREIGN MARKETS

Experience has shown that a marketing program in a new location has the best chance of success if the firm can present simply one clear advantage. A number of these are summarized in Table 7.3.

A firm will have the easiest time convincing customers to try its product if there is a clear reason to do so. Lower cost is obviously a most compelling reason. In the table we have specified lower *landed* cost. It is important for a firm to understand all customer costs, including import duties and VAT, when comparing what a customer would pay to acquire its product or service versus the competitive offering.

More cost-effective technology means a purchasing firm will realize savings through reduced labor or increased output, either in production or marketing. Some firms succeed because they have a certain cachet, either through strong branding or through the reputation of the country of origin. In some markets, American, German, or Japanese technology may be perceived as the best. Whether

TABLE 7.3 Critical competitive advantage

Lower landed cost
Most cost-effective technology
Style or fashion cachet
Higher quality
More environmentally acceptable

TABLE 7.4 Major considerations in choosing a particular international market

Macro	Micro
Country	Market
– Economic	– Customer
– Political/legal	a) Key segments
– Cultural	b) Purchase criteria
– Technological/infrastructure	– Market size and growth
– Geographic	– Competition
	– Product acceptance

this is true or not isn't important to the success of the firm if it can successfully position itself as providing the latest for the technologically-advanced culture. Another obvious benefit which can be easily communicated is higher quality. Quality must be defined in customer terms for each product or service. Some customers may see quality as durability while others may feel quality relates to the appearance of the final product. The only definition of quality which matters is the customer's. The final, simple to explain, competitive advantage is environmental acceptability. In the EU where environmental concerns are more important than in the US, recycle-ability or biodegradability may be a key selling point.

The major considerations in choosing a particular market are shown in Table 7.4. These fall into two major categories, macro (or country-specific considerations) and micro (or market-specific factors).

Of critical importance are the needs of the customer; the exact relationship which the customer requires for successful sales and service by the marketing firm.

The choice of which foreign market to enter cannot easily be separated from the choice of entry mode. Most firms will perform an iterative process while looking at the attractiveness of a particular market and thinking about ways of entering and weighing factors in each area before making a final decision. We have chosen to present the considerations related to particular markets first, followed by the entry mode choices, to more clearly delineate the considerations a firm must make when choosing foreign market entry. An overview of the considerations in this complex decision is presented in Figure 7.3. It should be noted that some of the factors described relate to the markets under consideration, some relate to company capabilities and still others relate to the benefits or drawbacks from particular entry strategies. This diagram, intended as an overview, describes all the factors which affect the final decision to enter a foreign market through a particular entry strategy.

Figure 7.1 described most of the environmental factors which affect a market entry decision. These same economic, demographic, competitive, political/legal, technological, and social/cultural factors are at work in any foreign market. But some specific characteristics of the overseas market should be mentioned here. Obviously, countries differ in their economic situations. In some particular locations, there may be a number of well-financed firms who are looking for a product offered by a particular firm. But in others, the weak finances and/or lack of hard currency may force a marketing firm to offer an unusual approach to a market. In some cases, a particular market may be extremely small and a firm may not be able to serve it profitably.

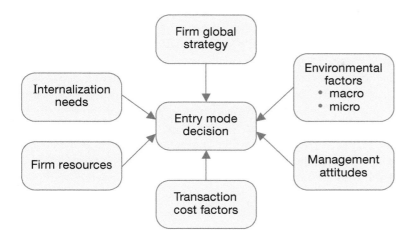

FIGURE 7.3 Foreign market entry considerations

Source: adapted from Kim and Hwang (1992); Bradley and Gannon (2000); Czinkota and Ronkainen (2004); Buckley and Casson (1998).

In the political/legal arena, a firm may encounter obstacles both in the home country and the host country. For instance, the Foreign Corrupt Practices Act, in effect in the United States since the 1970s, forbids company payments to government officials for securing a favorable decision on product sales or other possible advantages. In countries where bribery is the normal way of doing business, this may handicap US firms (see Chapter 4).

Host country governments often impose trade barriers of various kinds. These may take the form of tariffs or non-tariff barriers which may make the market difficult or impossible to enter. In India the government prevented firms from entering the insurance market until very recently. A special section on these so-called "blocked markets" is included at the end of this chapter.

Technologically, markets vary widely. Appropriate technology for groups of markets may be required, or (as stated earlier) buyers may demand the latest technology even when it is not appropriate.

In some cases, cultural differences can make doing business in a particular place quite difficult. Terpstra and David (1991) describe the triple socialization of managers, meaning they are operating in three different cultures – national, professional, and corporate – and they must balance the values they hold in each of these cultures while functioning in a foreign market.

Terpstra and David also introduce the concept of "frontstage" and "backstage" culture. Frontstage culture consists of the normal ways of doing things that insiders are willing to share with outsiders while backstage culture represents the normal ways of doing things that insiders are not willing to share with outsiders. A marketer attempting to enter a new market should find a mentor who can reveal to him the commonly accepted ways of doing things, whether they are part of the frontstage or backstage culture.

Geographic considerations are often overlooked. For instance, a shipment of high-tech X-ray equipment was held in storage at a port in Saudi Arabia. Because the shipping firm did not consider the very high temperatures that would be experienced by this equipment while it was being shipped, some of the machines literally exploded before the shipping containers could be opened.

Micro factors focus on the particular market or markets under consideration. First, of course, it is necessary to identify the segment or segments. As we have seen, some segments transcend national borders, especially in business markets. If this is the case, a firm may consider a number of national markets together while looking at these micro factors. The second and most important factor here is determining market size and growth. Many of the techniques described in Chapter 5 would be used here. Competition is a critical factor in deciding whether or not to enter a market. One additional variable which may be present especially in smaller international markets is the ability of competition to dominate the distribution channels. In many industrial markets, there are very few knowledgeable, qualified distributors for particular products. If a firm was marketing scientific instruments for laboratories, it would be surprising to find more than one or two qualified distributors in smaller or emerging markets. This may mean a marketing firm reconsiders its approach to a particular market or the firm may consent to using a competitor's distributor since there is no other entry strategy. We have described product acceptance in various sections of this chapter. Suffice it to say that individuals must be comfortable with the technology required to operate equipment being offered or knowledgeable enough to take advantage of the services being offered.

FOREIGN MARKET ENTRY STRATEGY

There are three schools of thought about how firms enter international markets. The first is the gradual involvement or Uppsala model which believes that firms enter international business at first using low resource commitment modes such as licensing or exporting. As the firm gains more knowledge and experience, it moves to higher levels of market entry alternatives in terms of resource commitment and accepts higher levels of risk.

A second approach is based on transaction cost analysis. In this approach, firms keep to themselves functions which they can perform at lower cost and contract out to other firms activities which can be completed by those other firms at lower cost. Firms consider all costs when making these decisions, including the costs of checking quality and managing marketing, production, sourcing and so on.

The third approach focuses on location specific factors as described above.

As we will see later in the chapter protection of proprietary information is a key consideration in today's world.

Pan and Tse (2000) showed that in the People's Republic of China firms made discrete decisions in two main steps. First, they chose between equity (joint and sole venture) and non-equity (export and contract) alternatives. In this decision, country-specific factors are most important. Next, managers made the decision about the kind of equity venture they would pursue, and here firm-specific factors are more important than country (or environmental) factors.

Buckley and Casson (1998) developed a comprehensive model summarizing the effect of a number of variables on the market entry decision. Their variables included: location costs, internalization factors, financial variables, cultural factors (trust and psychic distance), market structure, competitive strategy, adaptation costs, and the costs of doing business abroad. They conclude that firms take into account different sets of variables in deciding upon local production or local distribution activities. In addition, they emphasize the importance of competition and market structure in the entry decision.

Many researchers have found that "cultural distance" between home market and target market is an important factor for choosing one particular market instead of another. Some studies call into question the importance of cultural distance as a determining factor in the choice of foreign markets. Mitra and Golder (2002) found that, in the large multinational consumer products companies they studied, knowledge gained by the corporation from working in similar cultural and economic environments around the world was a most important determinant for firms choosing to enter particular markets. In other words, firms learn from operating in countries which are close culturally or economically to a particular target market and then use that knowledge to increase their confidence for moving forward into a selected market. In this study executives placed more importance on economic than cultural factors. These executives feel they can hire or transfer managers with experience in similar foreign markets to overcome any cultural problems.

Emerging markets such as India and China offer tempting opportunities but also special problems. In these markets, the legal system is often underdeveloped and corruption can pose a major hurdle to success. The infrastructure – both physical and financial – may be inadequate for a modern multinational. Brand recognition may be minimal for products which are well established in more advanced countries. In fact, all the uncontrollable or environmental factors may be quite different in these emerging markets. A manager must more carefully assess these factors in emerging markets and then tailor a marketing mix which will be successful in each emerging country.

IMPORTANCE OF NETWORKING

A basic assumption of the industrial or B2B network approach is that an individual firm is dependent for its success on resources controlled by other firms (De Búrca, 1994). In this approach there are no distinct boundaries between the firm and its environment. The network is made up of three components: actors, activities, and resources. Actors perform activities and/or control resources (Hakansson and Johanson, 1992). Firms interact with one another exchanging resources, products, and services. These interactions affect all the actors, making the networks themselves dynamic groupings. Growing from this theory, an internationalizing firm is not working on its own but is attempting to establish or develop network positions in foreign markets (Johanson and Mattsson, 1988). In globalizing, a firm may be finding new counterparts, developing already established networks or increasing coordination between various country-based networks. In this approach foreign market entry is not seen as an event but as a process that takes place over time as interaction between the actors in the network increases. Research distinguishes between social networks, those involving personal relationships, and business networks which evolved from repeated economic exchanges (Vasilchenko and Morrish, 2011). These researchers find that entrepreneurs exploit social and business networks for international opportunities and influence firms' selection of markets and entry mode. It is the relationships themselves which open often random and unpredictable opportunities. New research casts an interesting light on the "born global" phenomenon, meaning firms which jumped quickly to internationalization. Chandra et al. (2012) find that the processes are the same for firms moving quickly or more slowly into globalization. "Born globals," according to these researchers, have really been learning and developing resources over a period of time before they move to internationalize. Networks play a key role as sources for information, referrals, and even chance encounters which offer opportunities.

COMPARING THE ENTRY STRATEGY ALTERNATIVES

There are three basic ways to enter foreign markets: exporting, investment or contract. While much has been made in international marketing literature about a step-by-step process of international market entry, many of the most sophisticated firms do not move in a step-by-step process but instead they see themselves as "born global." Especially for services or technology firms where "brick and mortar" investments are often not required, firms tend to use the most effective entry strategy rather than moving through a step-by-step approach. The necessity to establish economies of scale quickly or to capture market share have led to immediate acquisitions by firms in the telecommunications business, to name one example.

Experience has shown that before moving into a foreign market, a firm should ask itself at least two key questions:

■ First, why have we succeeded domestically? (What are the critical success factors that have made our firm successful?)
■ Second, can these key success factors be duplicated in foreign markets?

Examining each of the alternatives more closely, let us first look at exporting. As Table 7.5 shows, there are a number of export alternatives with various names.

TABLE 7.5 Export alternatives

Domestic (indirect)	Foreign (direct)
■ Customers (domestic locations)	■ Customers (foreign locations)
Agents	
■ Brokers	■ Brokers
■ Export agents	■ Manufacturers' reps
■ Export management companies	■ Factors
	■ Managing agents
Merchants	
■ Domestic wholesalers	■ Distributor/dealers
■ Export trading companies	■ Import jobbers
■ Export management companies	■ Wholesalers/retailers

Source: adapted from Zimmerman and Fitzpatrick (1985).

Indirect exporting means selling a product to a customer or an intermediary located within the same domestic market. Direct exporting means selling that product to a customer or an intermediary located in a foreign market. It should be noted here that large customers often purchase products or services from the provider domestically or outside the country without involving any intermediary. For instance, Texas Instruments purchased office furniture from a large manufacturer. All the furniture was sent to a central warehouse where Texas Instruments personnel sorted, packaged and shipped it to the offices where it was required.

The table also shows the difference between agents and merchants. Rather than the specific terminology used for each type of firm, the most important distinctions between all of these intermediaries are whether they are located in the same country as a manufacturing firm and whether they are agents or merchants. Agents are firms which aid in finding and selling customers but do not take ownership of the product. Merchants do take title, own the product and can resell it. The importance in this difference relates to control. A manufacturing firm selecting an agent will have far more control over his subsequent marketing activities than it will over a merchant. While selling to a merchant is attractive, since a firm will receive payment and no longer have the risk of loss of a product, merchants can sell products in unauthorized markets leading to the problem of "gray goods," the unauthorized shipment of products from their intended market.

In reviewing Table 7.5 it should be noted that export management companies are listed twice, once under indirect agents and then again under indirect merchants. Export management companies are generally small firms with expertise in a particular industry or geographic area or both. They can serve as agents in finding customers and distributors without buying and reselling products. But they also can serve as merchants where they take on an ownership role and they do buy and resell. The same export management company may perform both roles for the same client in different markets.

The second and third foreign major market entry strategies are shown in Table 7.6.

Using investment, a firm may choose to pursue a sole venture in which it owns all aspects of the foreign business entity, establish a joint venture or enter into a consortium. Wholly owned or sole venture entry modes may be so-called greenfield enterprises in which the firm establishes a branch office or subsidiary from the ground up. Or a firm may choose to make an acquisition of an existing firm. This is often a fast way to buy market share and expertise in a foreign market. Of course, the investing firm would expect to pay a premium for the speedy entry afforded by the acquisition

TABLE 7.6 Investment and contract alternatives

Investment	Contract
■ Wholly owned or sole venture	■ Licensing
– Greenfield	■ Franchising
a) Branch offices	■ Strategic alliances (non-equity)
b) Subsidiaries	■ Management contract
– Acquisitions	■ Contract manufacturing
■ Joint ventures/strategic alliances	
■ Consortia	

process. A firm may choose to establish a joint venture. Some researchers see equity investment joint ventures as one form of strategic alliance but strictly speaking, a joint venture occurs when two firms invest to start up a third, new entity. A consortium is a group of firms formed to complete a particular large project. A consortium of engineering, train equipment, and construction firms was formed to build the Rio de Janeiro subway, for instance.

The third major form of market entry is contract, which takes many forms. In licensing, one firm lets another use its intellectual property for a fee, usually a royalty on sales. Franchising, related to licensing, takes place when a franchiser grants the franchisee the right to do business in a particular way in exchange for a similar fee. More popular and important today are non-equity or non-investment strategic alliances. In this case, two firms decide to work together in a particular area, setting limited objectives which are usually spelled out in a memorandum of understanding. For instance, two pharmaceutical firms signed a strategic alliance which allowed a US firm to market in the US a Japanese firm's blood pressure medicine while allowing the Japanese firm to market in Japan the US firm's ulcer medicine. Strategic alliances take many forms and may just focus on production, marketing, or research and development. A special section on strategic alliances is included in this chapter.

Finally, contracts for manufacturing or management are also an alternative. Under a management contract, a firm asks another to manage an effort for them. This could be the management of marketing or production and there would be a fee paid by the contracting firm to the manager. In contract manufacturing, one firm simply issues a purchase order to another to make products. For example, an office furniture firm wishing to serve a local market in Mexico chose a supplier to make desktops and assemble other simple furniture products. This was an arms-length arrangement, not a joint venture or even a strategic alliance but simply the selecting of one firm to manufacture products for another.

The most important considerations for each of the major market entry alternatives are presented in Table 7.7.

As can be seen, indirect export is an easy way to begin to explore international business which requires little in the way of resources, either capital or human. Risks are low as are returns, and a firm would gain little experience in an international market using this approach. Direct export gives a firm somewhat more experience while requiring more in the way of people. Direct export also allows for less control by the firm. Licensing can yield excellent returns since the investment is small. Licensing requires some human resources to be sure that intellectual property registrations are kept up-to-date and that the licensees are performing properly. This is also true of franchising. While licensing presents a rather attractive picture since royalties seem to go right to the bottom line of the licensor's financial statement, there are a number of hidden costs as described above. The key worry of the licensor is the possibility of establishing a competitor. This happened to an elevator manufacturer who had licensed a large Japanese electronics firms to make elevators according to specifications from the US company. After ignoring the licensee for many years, this US firm was surprised to see the Japanese company bidding on contracts in Saudi Arabia. Some vigilance is required to be sure that the licensee is meeting quality and marketing standards and audits are required of the books to be sure that the proper royalty payments are being made.

Minority joint ventures require less investment than majority joint ventures and in some countries may be the only way to enter through investment. The minority partner may be a much larger firm

TABLE 7.7 Comparing entry alternatives

	Resources required	Potential risk(s)	Experience gained	Return on investment	Host gov. reaction	Control capabilities	Other considerations
Indirect export	Very little	Low risk of any kind	Limited	Limited	None	Limited	Easy way to explore int'l business
Direct export	Minimum capital – must manage effectively	Low risk of loss	Some experience in foreign market(s)	Good	Limited	Possible loss of control of marketing	Good first learning step
Licensing/ franchising	Minimum capital – human resources may be significant	Risk of establishing competitor (licensing)	Limited	High but gross margin limited	May be unfavourable	Possible loss of control of quality and/or marketing	May be only way into market – need to keep I.P. registered
Minority joint venture	Significant, but less than majority j.v. or sole venture	Significant for investment; differences between partners	May be limited – take advantage of local knowledge	May be good	Generally favourable	Less than majority j.v. or sole venture	May be required by government
Majority joint venture	High for capital and human resources	Significant for investment; differences between partners	High – some local knowledge	May be excellent	May be unfavourable	High	Many firms prefer this
Sole venture	Highest level of any alternative	Assume all risk for investment	High – no local knowledge in ownership position	May be excellent	May be unfavourable	Highest possible	Protect company secrets
Contract	No capital – can be significant human resources	Low	Limited	N/A	None	High	Meets specific needs

and may feel uncomfortable in a minority position. The relationship between the minority owners and majority owners is the key to seeing that local knowledge is used to the fullest extent while the possibly more experienced and larger minority partner can also bring its skills to bear. Host governments generally favor minority positions for large multinationals. It should be said that host governments in many markets have the right to review both license and joint venture agreements and to reject those they consider unfair as to up-front payments or royalty levels. Some firms that take the minority position do not use the possibility to gain experience about a local market. A minority partner must be proactive to get as much knowledge and experience as possible in this situation.

Many multinationals favor the majority joint venture approach in which they enter into business with a minority partner who has the local knowledge to help develop a particular market. In some cases host governments are displeased by that kind of arrangement, but this does give the multinational control over all aspects of the business. The danger is that the majority partner may impose its will on the minority partner, thereby losing the valuable local input. Both majority joint ventures and sole ventures pose the highest possible risk since the investments are usually the largest and most inflexible of any alternative.

When a firm decides to go it alone and create a sole venture, it has complete control of all aspects of a business. This approach may provide the highest return on investment. Of course the risk of this approach is higher than any other alternative since the firm is basically entering a foreign market by itself without any input from local ownership partners.

Contracting will be used to meet specific needs in a particular market. Since very little or no capital is invested, risks are generally low. Host firms can protect their intellectual property by not sharing very much with a contract manufacturer or manager. On the other hand the firm will gain little experience from this kind of arrangement unless it is extremely proactive in seeking it out. The firm can exercise the highest possible control with this kind of arrangement.

VIRTUAL MARKET ENTRY

The maturing of the Internet and communications technologies has opened a new entry possibility – virtual market entry (Jeannet and Hennessey, 2004). In this case, a firm can take advantage of its ability to establish a detailed website, plus its own Intranet – the ability to share files among employees and selected members of the distribution channel – e-mail and sophisticated smart phones. Using all of these communications devices, a firm may choose to enter a market without a physical presence. This can be an effective way to avoid government restrictions. Proprietary research completed by one of the authors shows that, for many products, the Internet is primarily a tool used in searching for product information. However for some products purchases are frequently made in this way. For instance Microsoft routinely allows downloads of software from its website.

It should be noted that the simple establishment of a website does not make a business successful. Evidence shows that significant conventional promotional efforts are required to direct customers toward a site. In addition, while the cost of establishing a website is relatively low, the cost of updating and maintaining the site, especially if the firm is planning to take orders directly, can be significant. Underfunding of websites is a chronic problem in business markets.

STRATEGIC ALLIANCES

A strategic alliance is a formal or informal arrangement between two or more companies with a common business objective (Czinkota and Ronkainen, 2010). There are many ways in which firms cooperate with one another, covered by this definition, including joint ventures and other contractual arrangements. But often these alliances are less formal and involve the agreement by two or more firms to pursue particular objectives in order to help each another. At a time when the cost to serve all markets throughout the world has become prohibitive, smart managers are deciding where and when to compete and where and when to cooperate.

These alliances may be formed within a country or across diverse, international markets. One leading thinker on the subject, Kenichi Ohmae (Ohmae, 1989) said, "with enough time, money and luck you can do everything yourself. But who has enough?" In April 1992, Mitsui entered into a cooperative alliance with Baosteel, a relatively new Chinese steelmaking enterprise (Mitsui, 2012). Since that time the agreement has led to a network of steel service centers throughout China and by August 2010 the network consisted of 12 plants in total.

Keegan and Green (2013) identify three characteristics of strategic alliances:

- The participants remain independent after forming the alliance.
- The participants share the benefits of the alliance as well as control over performance.
- The participants make ongoing contributions in technology, products, and other key strategic areas.

Alliances are growing rapidly in popularity. In a recent survey by Deloitte (Byrne, 2012), 54 percent of managers predicted an increase in strategic alliances during the next two years. According to the survey, "companies are learning from industries like technology and life sciences that use strategic alliances very effectively to manage risk and capital."

Alliances take many forms. They often focus on joint R&D or marketing efforts. The main reasons for the popularity of strategic alliances are shown in Table 7.8. As can be seen in the table, strategic alliances are often used to develop global markets. No one firm has the ability to develop every market simultaneously around the world, so it will frequently agree to local help in one or a number of particular markets. The very high cost of developing new products and producing them for worldwide consumption also leads firms to establish alliances for completing research or setting up production.

Sometimes, it may be a good idea to cooperate with another firm or a network of firms who may be ready to establish a dominant position in a particular market. This can be done by developing a strategic alliance with a competitor or with a third firm who would be able to block your competitor. Some alliances are developed on the basis of learning new skills. Some firms wish to acquire technology. This is particularly true in the biotechnology business where the larger pharmaceutical firms have often partnered with very small but highly skilled biotechnology firms. In some cases, a particular resource may be critical to the success of a firm and it may be necessary to develop an alliance to protect the supply of that resource. Alliances are also formed to procure products around the world, in order to reduce the cost of doing so, and in some cases alliances are formed so that firms can share technology rather than develop it on their own.

TABLE 7.8 Reasons for strategic alliances

- Develop markets/especially global
- Spread very high cost/risk of R&D/production
- Block or co-opt competitors
- Enhance important skills
- Control critical resources
- Cost-effective procurement
- Share technology
- Provide learning opportunities

Source: adapted from Varadarajan and Jayachandran (1999); Czinkota and Ronkainen (2010); Keegan and Green (2013).

In choosing an alliance partner, it is important to take the time to be sure the firm you wish to work with will prove reliable over time. Table 7.9 is a profile instrument which allows assessment of a potential partner based on the most important characteristics a firm may establish for selection.

The main areas to be assessed relate to the past performance of the firm, its current capabilities, the reputation and relationship that the firm has established, the goals and strategies and overall compatibility of the two firms. It might be noted that this partner profile may be used for potential distributors, agents or joint venture partners as well as alliance partners. Using this approach, a firm can choose one potential partner from another. First, management would establish weights for each characteristic and then rate each potential partner on these characteristics. The weights and ratings would be multiplied, the total tallied, then divided by the total weights to gain an overall rating for a particular firm.

The factors for the success of one alliance versus another have been studied by a number of researchers. Generally speaking, success factors have been summarized in Table 7.10.

First and most important is careful selection of both the partner and the projects. Research has found that similar organizational cultures are more important than similar national cultures (Pothukuchi et al., 2002). Also important is a relative balance of power and management between the partners. This will be discussed below in some detail. Leadership from senior management is necessary so that all members of the alliance know what is expected of the organization and of the relationship. Also important is communications, not only at top management level but also at the operational and the worker level of the organization. Very important is the careful negotiation of the agreement. The more formal the alliance may be, the more time must be given to negotiations. In other words, the negotiation of a joint venture agreement would take far longer than the negotiation of a simple letter of understanding between two firms for a strategic alliance. One most important factor for success is the clear division between knowledge to be shared and knowledge that is not to be shared. Research also shows that successful alliances are based on complementary skills. If each firm has the same skills, the reasons for alliance are often hard to sustain. Researchers

TABLE 7.9 Partner profile

Characteristics	Weight (1–10)	Rating (1–10)	Total
PAST PERFORMANCE			
Sales growth			
Market share			
Cooperation with other partners			
Experience with market/product			
Financial strength			
CAPABILITIES			
Facilities			
Marketing/sales			
Design/technological			
Size of firm			
Language			
After sales			
Knowledge of local business customs			
REPUTATION/ RELATIONSHIPS			
With suppliers			
With customers			
With financial institutions			
With government(s)			
GOALS AND STRATEGIES			
Short-term			
Long-term			
COMPATIBILITY			
Product lines			
Markets			
Style/personalities			

Source: adapted from Moriarty and Kosnik (1989).

TABLE 7.10 Alliance success factors

- Careful selection of projects and partners – similar organizational cultures
- Detailed review of new alliance effects on existing firm relationships
- Relative balance of power/management between partners
- Leadership of senior managements
- Communications at all levels of organization
- Careful negotiation of agreement – clear "divorce" provisions
- Clear definition of shared vs. proprietary knowledge
- Complimentary skills in each partner
- Built-in flexibility

Source: adapted from Keegan and Green (2013); Peng (2009); Varadarajan and Jayachandran (1999); Pothukuchi et al. (2002); Bleeke and Ernst (1995).

recommend built-in flexibility since markets develop quickly, technology changes and, especially looking at worldwide industry, the ability to quickly change is vitally important. In addition, it is important that clear "divorce" provisions be included in any agreement between two parties.

Bleeke and Ernst (1995) warn that joint ventures formed for the wrong reasons often fail and end up with one partner selling itself to another. They reinforce the point that alliances of complementary equals are the only path that leads to a "marriage for life." This requires partners who have different product, geographic, or functional strengths.

Apple has been using strategic alliances to its benefit over many years (Grant and Baden-Fuller, 2004). Since its founding the firm developed alliances with Microsoft, Kodak, and HP. Recently they announced an alliance with Clearwell (2010) to offer e-discovery capabilities on the iPad. This is especially useful for law firms – Clearwell's market focus.

SELECTING THE ENTRY STRATEGY

In making the decision about which investment alternative to use, Dunning (2001) developed the eclectic paradigm (also known as OLI) in which he identified three important considerations for making decisions: ownership advantages, location advantages, and internalization considerations. A first consideration is ownership advantages accruing to the firm from its intellectual property. Here a firm feels it is vital to keep proprietary information within the firm. For instance, the company may own patents or have developed specific ways of doing business which it does not wish to share with a partner. This would preclude the use of export or joint venture forms and focus the firm more strongly toward a sole venture entry strategy.

Internalization advantages derive from classic transaction cost analysis, meaning that some forms of ownership yield higher returns to a firm and therefore that firm does not wish to contract with

TABLE 7.11 Major considerations for entry strategy

- Profit
- Risk
- Control
- Non-profit objectives

Source: adapted from Root (1994).

another to perform particular functions. In addition the firm may feel a compelling need to control specific aspects of its value chain such as production inputs, marketing programs or quality. Finally, according to Dunning, firms look at a particular location to decide whether it has the right environmental conditions for success. These include trade barriers, natural resources, costs and availability of key production inputs, transportation and communications costs, and market characteristics like per capita income, size of product market, political risk, and cultural distance.

Root (1994) developed strategy decision rules for choosing the most appropriate entry alternative: maximize profit over the strategic planning period subject to constraints imposed by company resources, risk, and non-profit objectives. Obviously, profit will vary with each alternative. Risk is a critical alternative. Various kinds of risk must be faced, ranging from the risk of starting a competitor through licensing through the risk of a loss of investment because of political changes in a particular market. Control is also a key consideration in choosing the correct strategy. If a firm must control information or quality or manufacturing processes, or even marketing strategies, to be successful, several of the possible entry strategies would be unsuitable. Here considerations of intellectual property will come into play. Non-profit objectives may include market share or reversibility of a decision as well as other corporate considerations. One of these might be the need to market a particular product in a market in order to secure orders for a more important product. In one instance, a division of a large multinational was asked to market office furniture in South Korea despite a 200 percent import duty so that this firm would be able to secure large contracts for nuclear power plants. Considerations like this for large multinationals do not fall into the control, profit or risk categories but can be important in the decision process. These considerations are summarized in Table 7.11.

BLOCKED MARKETS

Governments often erect trade barriers to protect local industry. These barriers can range from tariffs to restrictions on operations or entry through various forms of discriminatory rules and regulations called non-tariff barriers. These non-tariff barriers are especially common in services industries and are described in detail in Chapter 9. Large multinationals can take advantage of blocked markets. For example, some years ago, the Saudi Arabian government decided it would buy large transformers based on local content, the percentage of local input included in the final manufactured product.

The supplier quickly arranged in-country assembly, shipping these transformers in a knocked-down form so that the pieces could be joined inside Saudi Arabia. This essentially amounted to bolting the parts together and painting the product. Because the firm was able to show a higher local content than any competitor it essentially took a monopoly position for a significant period of time.

CASE STUDY

Case study: Fraport AG

Wilhelm Bender thought back on his involvement in the Philippines with Fraport AG. He had left Fraport after many years but recent decisions made him wonder what could be learned from the experience. The investment had spawned some time-consuming lawsuits including the initial rejection by the International Center for the Settlement of Investment Disputes (ICSID) in 2007 of Fraport's $425 million claim. That ICSID decision said Fraport had concealed an "unlawful investment," based on secret agreements with its Filipino shareholders. But at the end of December 2010 that decision was overturned by a new tribunal at the ICSID. These decisions brought back memories of the day in 2003 when he had made one of the most difficult decisions of his business career.

Bender remembered looking out the window of the Lufthansa flight back to Frankfurt and reviewing the events leading up to the disappointing week he had just experienced. Fraport AG had made the decision to write off its complete investment in the Philippines as a result of the failure of the final negotiations undertaken by him.

Fraport is a Frankfurt-based company whose main business is to operate the Frankfurt airport. With sales of about $2 billion, the company had recently gone public and decided to expand internationally. In 2003, Fraport was operating airports in Hannover and Saarbrücken as well as in Turkey and Peru. As part of its aggressive international expansion, Fraport decided to target Manila in the Philippines. In wanting to operate an airport in the Philippines, the company considered a number of market entry strategies. They finally decided on a joint venture and formed the Philippines International Air Terminal Company with one of the smaller and less prominent ethnic Chinese trading families that play a central role in the Philippine economy, the Cheng family.

In order to make this project work, the joint venture needed to gain a contract from the Philippine government and was awarded one by then-president Fidel Ramos. He was succeeded by President Joseph Estrada and the contract was expanded in size and scope. Unfortunately, Mr Estrada had to leave office after a popular uprising in 2001. He was succeeded by Gloria Macapagal Arroyo, who gained prominence by promising to fight corruption.

The project members had been accused of bribing some officials under the Estrada regime. Mrs Arroyo requested that the contract be changed significantly. Especially important to the success of Fraport's joint venture were provisions giving them exclusive rights to operate duty-free shops in the new

. . . continued

CASE STUDY ... *continued*

terminal, requiring that all airlines move to the new terminal and pay higher fees than they had paid with the old terminal. The joint venture members built a huge new Terminal Three at a cost of nearly $400 million. But the joint venture was constantly suffering from a shortage of capital. Most of the money was put up by Fraport. Then Fraport was told that the agreement they had made with the government had been declared null and void. The current government, especially, disputed the rights to the duty-free stores and the higher fees charged to airlines. Only a month later the Philippine Supreme Court upheld the cancellation. The new terminal finally opened and is being operated by the Philippine government.

Bender wondered whether there had been a better way to enter the Philippine market or whether his choice of partner had been flawed. For now, he only knew his firm had been forced to take a US $318 million charge, resulting in an overall US $132 million loss for the year.

* This case is based upon Landler, Mark, "A Bitter Exit From a Philippines Airport." *New York Times*, 30 April 2003, p. W1; International Centre for Settlement of Investment Disputes (2007). Fraport AG Frankfurt Airport Services Worldwide v. Republic of the Philippines accessed 2 July 2012 at http://italaw.com/documents/FraportAward.pdf; Fraport wins NAIA 3 appeal Lala Rimando, abs-cbnNEWS.com

01/03/2011.

CASE STUDY QUESTIONS

1   What environmental considerations would Fraport need to have carefully examined before deciding to move ahead in the Philippines?

2   What other market entry strategies might have been available to a firm like Fraport in the business they are in?
   a. What was the role of networking in this enterprise?

3   What are the key considerations one might use in choosing a potential joint venture partner?

4   How is the role of government different in international markets?

5   If you were Mr Bender, what would your next step be?

CHAPTER SUMMARY

Perhaps the most perplexing decision a manager must make is when and how to enter new markets. A manager must first clearly decide upon the segments to be addressed and then, taking into account all the environmental factors and his/her company resources, choose the most effective market entry strategy. The key points from this chapter are as follows:

■ A range of environmental factors, including economic, demographic, competitive, political/ legal, technological, and social/cultural are all at work affecting the new market entry decision.

■ Firms can take their current products to current or new markets or develop new products for their current or new markets. The latter is the riskiest strategy. Firms who do not realize which alternative they are choosing can often experience severe difficulties.

■ Technology is often a key factor in driving firms to new markets and is also a critical success factor.

■ While traditionally first movers into markets have been seen as gaining major benefits, they also experience major cost disadvantages when compared to followers. A follower strategy can be successful as well.

■ Firms who are successful in moving into foreign markets usually have proactive reasons. Rather than simply reacting to declines in their domestic market, they see foreign markets offering new opportunities. Positive management attitudes toward foreign market entry are critical to success.

■ The most successful firms in foreign markets have at least one clear competitive advantage they can translate to their new market.

■ Choosing the correct market and the correct market entry strategy is an iterative process requiring thorough knowledge of the environmental factors in a market as well as the company's resources and requirements.

■ The three basic ways of entering foreign markets are exporting, investment or contract. While some believe firms move through stages in their international efforts, newer research tends to reinforce the idea that many firms just choose the proper strategy even if they have no past international experience.

■ Deciding on the correct entry strategy requires a firm decide how it can maximize profit subject to company resources, risk, control requirements, and non-profit objectives.

■ Many firms encounter blocked markets and need to take a long-term approach to opening these markets.

■ Strategic alliances offer a firm an opportunity to work with other firms who have complementary strengths without the need for a formal relationship like a joint venture. But careful selection of the partner and clear goals and communications are prerequisites to success.

REVIEW QUESTIONS

1 What are the key environmental factors to be considered when entering a new market?
2 Describe the product market expansion guide using both Ansoff's and Day's approaches.
3 What are the advantages and disadvantages of being a first mover into a market?
4 Describe the proactive and reactive reasons for entering foreign markets.
5 Why is it important to have a clearly communicated competitive advantage in a foreign market? List those given in the text.
6 What are the major macro and micro considerations in choosing a particular market?
7 What are the three schools of thought about how firms enter international markets? Describe each in detail.
8 Describe the role of networking in foreign market entry.
9 What are the three basic ways to enter foreign markets?

  a.   What are the main differences between agents and merchants?

10 Describe the advantages and disadvantages of the various investment and contract market entry strategies.
11 What are the strategy decision rules for choosing the most attractive foreign market entry alternative?
12 What are the main reasons for strategic alliances?

  a.   What are the critical factors in choosing one partner versus another?
  b.   What are the most important factors for success in an alliance?

13 If you were faced by a blocked market, what actions would you take?

REFERENCES

Alexander, Marcus, and Korine, Harry (2008). "When you shouldn't go global." *Harvard Business Review*, Vol. 86, Iss. 12, 70–7.

Ansoff, Igor (1957). "Strategies for Diversification." *Harvard Business Review*, Vol. 35, Iss. 5, 113–24.

Bleeke, Joel and Ernst, David (1995). "Is Your Strategic Alliance Really a Sale?" *Harvard Business Review*, Vol. 73, Iss. 1, 97–105.

Boulding, William and Christen, Markus (2001). "First Mover Disadvantage." *Harvard Business Review*, Vol. 69, Iss. 9, 20–1.

Bradley, Frank and Gannon, Michael (2000). "Does the Firm's Technology and Marketing Profile Affect Foreign Market Entry?" *Journal of International Marketing*, Vol. 8, No. 4, 12–36.

Buckley, Peter J. and Casson, Mark C. (1998). "Analyzing Foreign Market Entry Strategies: Extending the Internationalization Approach." *Journal of International Business Studies*, Vol. 29, No. 3, 539–62.

Byrne, Allana (2012). "Executives expect increase in mergers, strategic alliances in 2012." Inside Counsel, 23 May 2012. Accessed 1 July 2012 at http://www.insidecounsel.com/2012/05/23/executives-expect-increase-in-mergers-strategic-al

Chandra, Y., Styles, C., and Wilkinson, I. (2012). "An Opportunity-Based View of Rapid Internationalization." *Journal Of International Marketing*, Vol. 20, Iss. 1, 74–102.

Chesbrough, Henry W. (2003). "Environmental Influences Upon Firm Entry into New Sub-Markets: Evidence from the Worldwide Hard Disk Drive Industry Conditionally." *Research Policy*, Vol. 32, Iss. 4, 659–78.

Clearwell Systems (2010). "Apple Enters Strategic Partnership with Clearwell to Bring E-Discovery to the iPad." Accessed 2 July 2012 at http://www.clearwellsystems.com/ediscovery-news/pr_04_01_10.php

Czinkota, Michael and Ronkainen, Ilkka A. (2010). *International Marketing 9th ed.*, Mason, OH: Southwestern Publishing.

Day, George S. (1990). *Market Driven Strategy*. New York: Free Press.

De Búrca, Seán (1994). "The Network Perspective – Theoretical Foundations, Assumptions and Characteristics." Working paper. University College Dublin.

Dunning, John H. (2001). "The Eclectic (OLI) Paradigm of International Production: Past, Present and Future." *International Journal of Economics of Business*, Vol. 8, No. 2, 173–90.

Geroski, Paul A. (1999). "Early Warning of New Rivals." *Sloan Management Review*, Vol. 40, No. 3, Spring, 107–16.

Grant, Robert M. and Baden-Fuller, Charles (2004). "*A Knowledge Accessing Theory of Strategic Alliances.*" *Journal of Management Studies*. Vol. 41, Iss. 1, January. Accessed 2 July 2012 at http://www.baden-fuller.com/Resources/a%20 knowledge%20accessing%20theory%20of%20strategic%20alliance _pdf1.pdf

Hakansson, H. and Johanson, J. (1992). "A Model of Industrial Networks" in *Industrial Networks – A New View of Reality*. Axelsson, B.A. and Easton, G. (eds), London: Routledge, 1992.

Heide, J.B. and Weiss, A.M. (1995). "Vendor consideration and switching behavior for buyers in high-technology markets." *Journal Of Marketing*, Vol. 59, Iss. 3, 30.

Hult, G., Cavusgil, S., Kiyak, T., Deligonul, S., and Lagerström, K. (2007). "What Drives Performance in Globally Focused Marketing Organizations? A Three-Country Study." *Journal Of International Marketing*, Vol. 15, Iss. 2, 58–85.

International Centre for Settlement of Investment Disputes (2007). Fraport AG Frankfurt Airport Services Worldwide v. Republic of the Philippines. Accessed 2 July 2012 at http://italaw.com/documents/FraportAward.pdf

Jeannet, Jean-Pierre and Hennessey, H. David (2004). *Global Marketing Strategies*, New York: Houghton-Mifflin.

Johanson, Jan and Mattsson, Lars-Gunnar (1988). "Internationalisation in Industrial Systems – a Network Approach" in Hood, N. and Valhne, J.E. (eds), *Strategies in Global Competition*, New York: Croom-Helm.

Johnson, J. and Tellis, G. (2008). "Drivers of Success for Market Entry into China and India." *Journal Of Marketing*, Vol. 72, Iss. 3, 1–13, doi:10.1509/jmkg.72.3.1

Keegan, Warren J. and Green, Mark C. (2013). *Global Marketing 7th ed.* Upper Saddle River, NJ: Prentice-Hall.

Kim, W. Chan, and Hwang, Peter (1992). "Global strategy and multinationals' entry mode choice." *Journal of International Business Studies*, Vol. 23, No. 1, 29–53.

Landler, Mark (2003). "A Bitter Exit From a Philippines Airport." *New York Times*, 30 April 2003, p. W1.

Magnusson, P., Westjohn, S., and Boggs, D. (2009). "Order-of-Entry Effects for Service Firms in Developing Markets: An Examination of Multinational Advertising Agencies." *Journal Of International Marketing*, Vol. 17, Iss. 2, 23–41.

Mitra, Debanjan and Golder, Peter N. (2002). "Whose Culture Matters? Near-Market Knowledge and its Impact on Foreign Market Entry Timing." *Journal of Marketing Research*, Vol. 39, Iss. 3, August, 350–65.

Mitsui and Company Homepage (2012). Accessed 1 July 2012 at http://www.mitsui.com/jp/en/business/challenge/1191101_1856.html

Moriarty, Rowland T. and Kosnik, Thomas J. (1989). "High-Tech Marketing: Concepts, Continuity and Change." *Sloan Management Review*, Vol. 30, Iss. 4, 7–18.

Ohmae, Kenichi (1989). "The Global Logic of Strategic Alliances." *Harvard Business Review*, Vol. 67, Iss. 2, March/April, 143–54.

Pan, Yigang and Tse, David K. (2000). "The Hierarchical Model of Market Entry Modes." *Journal of International Business Studies*, Vol. 31, No. 4, 535–54.

Peng, M.W. (2009). *Global Business*. Mason, OH: Cengage.

Pothukuchi, Vijay, Damanpour, Fariborz, Choi, Jaepil, Chen, Chao C., and Park, Seung Ho (2002). "National and Organizational Culture Differences and International Joint Venture Performance." *Journal of International Business Studies*, Vol. 33, No. 2, 243–65.

Rimando, Lala (2011). "Fraport wins NAIA 3 appeal." Accessed 2 July 2012 at abs-cbnNEWS.com

Root, Franklin R. (1994). *Entry Strategies for International Markets*. New York: Lexington.

Strategic Planning Institute (2012). Accessed 1 July 2012 at http://pimsonline.com/pims-strategy.htm

Terpstra, Vern and David, Kenneth H. (1991*). The Cultural Environment of International Business*. Cincinnati, OH: South-Western Publishing.

Varadarajan, Rajan P. and Jayachandran, Satish (1999). "Marketing Strategy: An Assessment of the State of the Field and Outlook." *Journal of the Academy of Marketing Science*, Vol. 27, No. 2, 120–43.

Vasilchenko, E. and Morrish, S. (2011). "The Role of Entrepreneurial Networks in the Exploration and Exploitation of Internationalization Opportunities by Information and Communication Technology Firms." *Journal Of International Marketing*, Vol. 19, Iss. 4, 88–105.

Zimmerman, Alan S. and Fitzpatrick, Peter (1985). *Essentials of Export Marketing*, New York: AMACOM.

Chapter 8

Product strategy and product development

INTRODUCTION

No market remains the same forever and marketing managers are always looking for new and better ways of doing things to generate satisfaction for their customers and increase return to their shareholders. Competitors lurk in every market, trying to think of more attractive products and services. All of this means a firm must engage in a formal new product development (NPD) process. The firm needs to develop an overall product strategy and then manage a process which will keep its offering as attractive as possible to customers.

CHAPTER OBJECTIVES

After reading this chapter, you should be able to:

- differentiate between business to business and business to consumer product strategy
- understand the product life cycle and how it applies to B2B and global markets
- describe the diffusion of innovation process
- outline and explain the new product development process
- discuss the considerations in global brand strategy
- understand the make or buy decision and how global sourcing and subcontracting relate to this decision.

DEFINITION OF PRODUCT

A product is an offering of a firm which satisfies the needs of customers. Customers are seeking to purchase benefits and they are willing to part with items of value (including money and time) in exchange for gaining these satisfactions. This includes the core product and benefits, essentially the value the customer is actually purchasing, plus the product attributes which include the brand name, the design, the country of origin, and price and packaging, as well as support services such as delivery, installation, warranty, and after-sales service. Since many business marketers began their careers as engineers they often focus too strongly on the tangible core product and functions, rather than the total package that the customer considers when he/she buys.

The customer looks at the total product as shown in Figure 8.1.

PRODUCT STRATEGY

The product strategy of a firm relates to making decisions about the features, quality, and the entire offering shown in Figure 8.1. In addition, product strategy involves developing a rational relationship between and among product offerings. For instance, an office furniture product manager must decide upon the features, functions and benefits of a particular seating line, the quality level which will affect the pricing and all of the ancillary items under his control including packaging, design, country

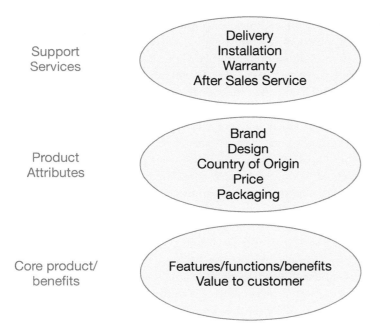

FIGURE 8.1 The total product

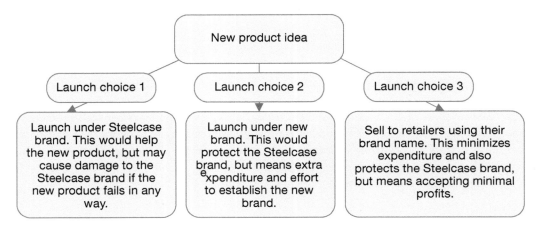

FIGURE 8.2 Trade-offs in launching new products

of origin, delivery, installation, warranty, and after-sales service. He or she also has to make decisions about the brand. If one assumes that this product manager is employed by Steelcase, the world's largest office furniture manufacturer, he or she may choose to offer the product as a Steelcase-branded product or to develop a new brand name not associated with Steelcase, so that this product stands on its own. A third choice might be to private-brand the product for some other outlet such as Office Depot or Staples. These three choices are illustrated in Fig 8.2.

The issues involved in this type of trade-off are complex, since the marketing manager is unable to predict the future accurately. The balance between investment and risk is always a difficult one for managers, since there are few ways to obtain a high return without taking some risk. On the other hand, taking risks does not, of itself, generate high returns. Usually these conflicts are resolved by internal negotiations between marketing and other functional managers within the firm. In deciding upon the entire product offering, the manager must distinguish between an individual product which has a unique set of the attributes seen in Figure 8.1, a product line, which is a group of these individual products which are related to one another, and the overall product assortment which is all of the product lines together.

In the global context, product lines tend to expand to accommodate the varying requirements of national markets. Each country requires slightly different product characteristics, leading to a proliferation of models. It is critical for a manager of the product line to attempt to limit the number of products and product lines to the minimum which will satisfy the requirements of most of his customers. Pruning the product line to remove unprofitable or underperforming products should be a regular activity for marketers.

While consumer product strategy is similar to business product strategy, there are a few major differences. First, consumer products focus more heavily on brand identity and product appearance than do strategies related to business products. Since most business products are sold with related services like installation, training, after-sales service, and maintenance, in almost every case a business product must be offered as a total package. As mentioned earlier, business buyers attempt to minimize the emotional content of their decisions. In most cases, they are concerned with specific tangible benefits which can be measured when they make a buying decision. Therefore, designing a business product requires a full understanding of the customer's value-creating activities so that the product can be positioned as an important contributor to the customer's value chain.

THE PRODUCT LIFECYCLE

The product lifecycle dictates that a firm engages in a dedicated product development process (see Figure 8.3).

The product lifecycle posits that there are four major stages through which most industries advance. The first is Introduction, marked by start-up sales growth. Generally in this stage a firm is spending more on producing and marketing the product than it is receiving in revenue from sales. In the Growth stage the product begins to be accepted and sales climb, with a consequent improvement in the relationship between revenue and expenditure. The initial investment in developing the product and preparing to produce it has probably been met, and the firm should begin to see a positive return on the investment. The longest period is the Maturity stage in which sales begin to level off since penetration in the market is high. Even though sales level off, so that revenue remains fairly constant, profits can continue to rise throughout this stage, depending upon competitive pressure and efficiencies the firm may realize.

The Maturity stage is the point at which the investment really pays off. Expenditure on marketing is usually relatively low as a percentage of the revenue received, and the initial start-up investment should have been recouped. The final stage is Decline in which sales of the product gradually fall off as it is supplanted by some newer solution. Here profits may continue to be positive even though

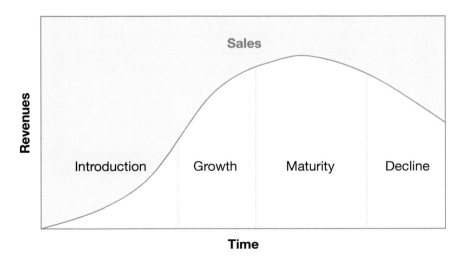

FIGURE 8.3 Product lifecycle

sales revenue may decrease sharply. Eventually, the product will cease to be viable as competing products enter the market, or as newer versions of the product are produced by the firm.

The product lifecycle concept has been criticized because it presents too specific a pattern of stages for industries which don't always follow a smooth curve. In addition, those who are marketing the product seldom know what stage the product is in. A key criticism is that the product lifecycle may be the result of marketing efforts rather than a course followed by products regardless of the effort placed behind them, in other words marketers act in ways which make the product life cycle inevitable. For example, whenever Intel develop a new computer chip they publicize the product heavily, they carry out major sales campaigns with the computer manufacturers, and they price competitively. Inevitably this means that the new chip has a rapid growth rate, but loses money at first – just as the product lifecycle model predicts. As the chip becomes established, Intel invariably begin developing the next generation of chip, thus ensuring that the current model must go into a decline when the new chip hits the market. Thus the product lifecycle becomes a self-fulfilling prophecy. A further criticism of the PLC is that there is no way to determine the timescales, so there is no way of knowing whether the product still has another year to go in the Growth stage or whether it is heading into maturity. The Maturity stage might last anything from a few weeks (in the case of some electronic products) to a period of centuries (in the case of, say, iron ore). Also, there is no doubt that the lifecycle is affected by marketing activities. A product which is heading into a decline might be repositioned into a new market (commonly a foreign one), or might be nursed back to life with some clever promotional campaigns. Finally, the product lifecycle is nearly irrelevant for particular brands. Thus the product life cycle is a better descriptor than it is a predictor.

Despite the criticisms, the product lifecycle is a useful short-hand tool for considering the most effective strategy at a particular time.

As can be seen from Table 8.1, in the Introduction stage, by necessity, only a few product variations are offered. Pricing can be high to recoup large investments (skimming) or low to establish market share (penetration). A marketer in this stage attempts to build channels of distribution. He or she uses promotion to build primary demand, that is, to explain to customers why they need this particular innovation. The overall objective here is to create awareness and have individuals try the product. An example of this can be seen from the computer industry. There are many software houses producing desktop publishing suites, but most have a problem when it comes to publishing on the Internet. The software used to create the website content needs to be compatible with the software used by the potential users of the website, or they will be unable to read the content. Adobe overcame this problem by giving away free copies of their Acrobat Reader software (free being the ultimate low price), allowing web users to read material produced by Adobe customers. In turn, this encourages firms to use Adobe's desktop publishing systems and other software. In order to use the Adobe approach, a firm must be very well funded, since the cost of developing software simply to give it away is high, and of course there is no reason why competitors should not copy the tactic and thus negate the benefits. Therefore, most B2B firms would probably be forced to use a skimming approach in order to recoup heavy development costs. Worldwide competition and opening markets make imitators of the new product a foregone conclusion. Firms who cannot afford to use a penetration strategy may look for a strategic alliance with an established firm in order to gain access to an established distribution network.

TABLE 8.1 Product lifecycle and marketing strategies

Variable	Introduction	Growth	Maturity	Decline
Product	Basic, little choice	Some extensions, services	Many offerings serving many segments	Far fewer competitors
Price	Skimming or penetration	Meet competition	Meet competition or cut with specific deals	High or low depending on competition
Place	Build channels	Continue to build channels	Move toward intensive distribution	Selective or direct sales
Promotion	Build primary demand	Begin to build selective demand	Persuading and reminding, stressing differences between brands	Reduced to necessary minimum
People	Potentially an important differentiator in the early, missionary phase of the launch	Probably need a higher input to monitor progress and solve teething problems	Less input needed as the product is familiar to customers	Expensive people element likely to be withdrawn from the mix as far as possible
Process	Many teething problems likely	Teething problems reduce, but process will need to adapt to greater volumes of sale	Process should be well-established and need little attention.	Process will need to adapt to reducing sales and corporate commitment.
Physical evidence	Extremely important in reassuring customers	Extremely important for retaining customers	Lesser importance as customers are confident of the product	Useful in retaining customers who might otherwise defect
Overall objective	Create awareness and trial	Maximize market share or return on investment	Hold market share or maximize profits	Reduce costs, maximize remaining sales and profits

Source: adapted from Kotler, 2003.

In the Growth stage, the firm tries to add some extensions and accompanying services to the basic product, as a way of differentiating the product from those of competitors entering the market. Pricing may continue at either a skimming or penetration level but in general firms are forced to respond to new competitors who come into the market, so prices will need to reflect the new competitive environment. Distribution continues to be a key aspect of growth and firms look to build channels of distribution, possibly by forming strategic alliances. Promotion changes in this stage from convincing a customer that his firm needs this product type to establishing the benefits of one particular brand versus another. The overall objective in this stage is to maximize market share through low pricing and heavy promotion or to maximize return on investment through a high price strategy.

In the Maturity stage, competition is rampant with many different kinds of product and service offerings serving many different segments. In this stage, firms usually don't have much choice in setting prices because the price is set by the market – in other words, the interplay between suppliers and customers is what sets the prices, not the decisions of the marketing managers. Distribution tends to become intensive in many markets where the most important thing is to sell through as many channels as possible. Intensive distribution for global B2B products will often mean finding one qualified distributor in each country market, rather than selling through discount stores on every corner as it does in consumer marketing. Promotion focuses on persuading and reminding customers, stressing the differences between brands. In this stage the firm's overall objective is to hold market share through aggressive pricing, communications, and distribution or to maximize profits by focusing on key segments.

In the Decline stage, there may be fewer competitors as many firms drop out of a slowing market. Price may be kept high or low depending on the number of competitors. Once only a few competitors exist, a firm may have the capability to raise prices on products nearing obsolescence. Place moves toward selective distribution, or in many cases, direct sales through an Internet website or catalog. Promotion is reduced to the absolute minimum. The overall objectives here are to reduce costs and to maximize the remaining sales and profits in this product market. In some countries (especially in the Developing World) older technology serves the needs of many customers – a firm must decide how to provide parts and service for these markets in order to maintain a positive reputation with customers who may later wish to user newer products.

It is, of course, dangerous for a firm to have all of its products in one stage of the life cycle. Many start-up firms find themselves in this position, since they often only have one product to sell, but if all products are in the Introduction stage, the firm has no sources of cash to finance growth. On the other hand, if all products are in the Maturity stage, there are no oncoming new products to replace those heading toward decline.

Products move differently through stages of the product lifecycle in various countries' markets. For example, one might surmise that the progress of the iPhone through the various stages was quite different in the US, the countries of the EU, and Africa during 2007 and 2008. This was due to the launch date in each region being different – the iPhone launched in the US in July 2007, in Europe in November that year, and in Africa in late 2008. This is shown graphically in Figure 8.4.

It is extremely important that a manager understands where in the product lifecycle a particular product is when entering any market since this position strongly affects the entire marketing strategy for the firm. It is not infrequent that a firm may bring a new, technologically-advanced product to a market and find virtually no distribution capable of installing and servicing the product. This is exactly what happened with PCs in China in the late 1980s and early 1990s.

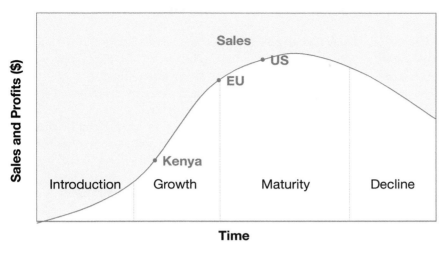

FIGURE 8.4 Product lifecycle – example of iPhone in late 2008

Talking Point

The product life cycle gives us a model of what should happen to a product after it is introduced – but the emphasis here is on the word "should." Some products simply flop as soon as they are launched – others grow rapidly, then disappear without trace as a smart competing product appears.

So how can we time the launch of the next new product? How do we know for sure that the last product launch will go according to plan? Or that the current one will? The answer is of course that we have no way of knowing, because we can't predict the future. So what's the point? Why not just launch when we feel like it, or when the product is ready for market, and let the products take their chances?

Or maybe any planning is better than no planning? An educated guess is better than a stab in the dark?

DIFFUSION OF INNOVATION

The product lifecycle is based upon findings by Rogers (1962) which showed that innovations move through markets in an orderly manner. Customers can be classified according to their willingness to accept new ideas. These firms can generally be classified following Rogers as follows:

■ *Innovators* – These are companies who will be willing to try new products or services and are willing to be the first ones. Rogers identified 2.5 percent of companies as falling into this category. These firms are the ones who accept the product during the earliest stages of the product lifecycle.

■ *Early Adopters* – After the innovators try a product, these companies will also try it. They are generally open to new ideas but want some proof that the product will work. These firms would be responsible for the growth seen in the Growth phase of the product lifecycle.

■ *Early Majority* – Firms who will buy the product once it is thoroughly tried and tested. These firms form the backbone of the Maturity phase of the product lifecycle.

■ *Late Majority* – Firms who generally do not wish to try new services or products and wait until many other firms have accepted the innovation. Firms like this would be responsible for maintaining the growth of the product in the latter stages of the Maturity phase of the product lifecycle.

■ *Laggards* – Those who would adopt the product only under duress or not adopt at all.

Rogers identified attributes of innovations which affect the speed of their acceptance:

■ *Relative advantage*: the perception that the idea is better than the one it supersedes.
■ *Compatibility*: consistency with existing values, past experience and the needs of a firm's buyers and influencers.
■ *Complexity*: more complex ideas are adopted more slowly.
■ *Trialability*: if a firm can try out a small aspect of a new idea it will be accepted more quickly than if a firm has to make a major switch. For instance, the trialability of a new company-wide computer system would be extremely low and therefore acceptance would be very slow.
■ *Observability*: if the effects of an innovation can be easily seen this innovation may be adopted more quickly.

The underlying reason for the product lifecycle is the constant development of new technologies and processes which create opportunities but also pose threats to firms established with the currently accepted technology. In addition, the globalization of trade throughout the world, including the lowering of barriers to market entry, has allowed new technologies to penetrate into markets which were formerly blocked. No firm can succeed without assuming that its current approach to products and services is in danger of being replaced by newer, better and less costly alternatives, and research shows that firms which have vigorous research and development programs are more successful in the marketplace (Song and Noh 2006). The same research showed that competitive advantage depends on the following factors:

1   Project environment. Creating an atmosphere of innovation and a culture of change will foster new development.
2   Skills and resources. Firms which can make full use of the skills of their employees, and the research facilities at their disposal, will produce more effective new products.
3   Project leadership. The ability to motivate staff to give of their best, and to direct the process effectively, is crucial to the successful completion of any project.
4   Strategic fit. New products which have a good fit with the overall strategy of the firm will have more chance of success than those which lie outside the firm's strategic direction.

5   Efficient NPD processes. If the company has set up systems for new product development, the results are likely to be a great deal better than they would be if NPD is left as an ad-hoc activity.
6   Effective product positioning strategies. Ensuring that the new products actually fit into a suitable niche in the market is essential for any market-oriented firm.

Geoffrey Moore (1995) introduced the idea of the technology adoption lifecycle. Here he showed that in the early stages of a market, technology enthusiasts and visionaries who represented the innovators and early adopters in the adoption process are willing to accept new technologies enthusiastically. But moving to the next step in the Early Majority phase requires convincing what he called the *pragmatists* to accept the innovation. Moore identified a huge "chasm" which stopped products from crossing over from minimal acceptance by the enthusiasts and visionaries into the mainstream market dominated by the pragmatists and the next group (Late Majority, he called the *conservatives*). The "chasm" is defined by Moore as a "time of great despair when the early market's interest wanes but the mainstream market is still not comfortable . . . with the solutions available." In order to get over the chasm, Moore recommends a focus on vertical market segments which have specific needs for this particular technological innovation, convincing those in the majority, mainstream market that the new solution will be beneficial to them. He reiterates the basic idea that only a full understanding of the customer's business can enable a firm to successfully sell a new technology to this customer.

The fact that the new product has advantages over the existing ones does not necessarily mean that it will be financially rewarding, however. The costs of developing a new product might well damage profits for a long time, and there is research which shows that while product advantage relates positively to market performance it does not relate well to financial success (Hsieh et al., 2008).

It is obvious that many firms understand this lesson and are assigning considerable resources to the product development process. In 2008, companies based in the United States reported research and development expenses of $330 billion worldwide (against worldwide sales of $11 trillion). This

TABLE 8.2 New product development times

Company	Product	Development time in years	
		1980	1990
Honda	Automobiles	8	3
Volvo	Trucks	7	5.5
Rank Xerox	Copiers	5	3
Brother	Printers	4	2
Apple	Computers	3.5	1
AT&T	Telephone Systems	2	1

Source: adapted from Topfer (1995).

means that the average firm spent around 3.3 percent of sales on developing new products (National Science Foundation, 2009). Manufacturing firms accounted for 71 percent of this figure, and (perhaps surprisingly) small firms spent almost double the amount larger firms spent, expressed as a proportion of sales.

New product development time has been reduced radically over the last few years. Topfer (1995) showed the difference in development time for selected products as seen in Table 8.2. In many cases, development time has been cut in half and in some cases even to one-third. Managers are well aware of this trend and are organizing to move more quickly to get from idea to market.

NEW PRODUCT DEVELOPMENT PROCESS

Product development is defined succinctly as "the transformation of market opportunity and a set of assumptions about product technology into a product available for sale" (Krishnan and Ulrich, 2001). Crawford (2003) has been a pioneer researcher in the new product development process. He first poses the question "what is a new product?" and provides these categories:

- *New-to-the-world products* – These are inventions such as the first automobile or computer. These are very rare: most new products are in fact simply improvements on existing products.
- *New category entries* – Products introduced by firms into a product category where the firm had not been doing business up to this time.
- *Additions to product lines* – These are line extensions in the firm's current markets such as a tablet computer introduced by Apple.
- *Product improvements* – Current products made better in some way.
- *Repositioning* – Taking a current product and attempting to find a new use for it. Although not a B2B example, the most famous example of this is Arm and Hammer Baking Soda which was repositioned many times as a refrigerator deodorant or carpet cleaner.

Some simplify this by saying that new products are simply any product new to the firm providing it. In any event, as we have seen, it is important to have a formalized new product process.

Crawford identified five phases in the new product process:

1 *Opportunity identification and selection* –Where new product opportunities are identified and selected for further development.
2 *Concept generation* –Where an attractive opportunity includes research with customers and preliminary analysis takes place.
3 *Concept evaluation* – Careful review of new product concepts on technical, marketing, and financial variables. This phase also requires ranking to choose the most promising concepts to move forward to the next phase.
4 *Development* – In this phase, both technical and marketing development take place. Prototypes are designed and tested and the production process must be established. Marketing must develop a full marketing and business plan, including all additional services and products required by this concept.

5   *Launch* – In this final phase, the product is commercialized. Distribution and sale of the product begins and the marketing launch plan is put into effect.

Underlying the entire new product development process is the overall strategic direction of the firm. The firm must be sure that the new product development is congruent with its strategy. For instance, an aerospace firm decides that it has a high level of software expertise. However, before beginning the development process to offer a software product the firm must fully understand the differences between the market for software and the current aerospace business it is familiar with.

When business marketing firms attempt to find sources for new ideas, they can look to unmet needs or problems. Table 8.3 presents some ideas for approaching unmet needs.

First, routine market contacts often unearth areas where a firm may provide a product or service not available currently. Second, the firm may undertake specific problem analysis through discussions with experts or with users themselves through surveys, focus groups or observation. Finally, a firm may employ scenario analysis, attempting to establish the most likely scenarios for the future and to anticipate what problems their customers may face because of new developments identified in the scenarios.

Von Hippel et al. (1999) say firms fail to develop breakthrough products for two reasons: (1) companies have built-in incentives to focus on the short-term and (2) developers really don't know how to get to product breakthroughs. These researchers arrived at an approach to gaining excellent new ideas by studying 3M Corporation. A most important source of new ideas for 3M is lead users. The process encompasses four major steps:

1   *Laying the foundation* – A team is formed which identifies the markets to target and the kinds of innovations they may wish to pursue. In this stage the team must gain the support of key managers within the company.
2   *Determining the trends* – In this step, the team talks to experts in the field and attempts to understand the newest technologies and applications in the area.

TABLE 8.3 Approaches used to discover unmet needs and problems

■ Routine Market Contacts
  * sales call reports
  * service department
  * complaint files

■ Problem Analysis
  * list of user problems
  * expert opinion
  * published sources
  * direct inquiry of heavy users, individually or in focus groups
  * user panels
  * user observations

■ Scenario Analysis

TABLE 8.4 Checklist of idea stimulators for business to business products

- ◼ Change the physical, thermal, electrical, chemical, or mechanical properties of this product.
- ◼ Any new electrical, electronic, optical, hydraulic, mechanical, or magnetic way of performing a function?
- ◼ Is this function really necessary?
- ◼ Can we change the power source to make it work better?
- ◼ Can standard components be substituted?
- ◼ How might the product be made more compact?
- ◼ What if it were heat-treated, hardened, alloyed, cured, frozen, plated?
- ◼ Who else could use this operation or its output?
- ◼ Has every step been computerized as much as possible?
- ◼ How can we use the Internet to improve this product/service?

Source: adapted from Crawford, 2003.

3 *Identifying lead users* – The team identifies the most important users who are on the leading edge of a particular target market. They will then gather information from these lead users and develop preliminary product ideas.

4 *Developing the breakthroughs* – The final step is to move the preliminary concepts through toward completion. The first portion of this step is hosting a workshop with several lead users and in-house marketing and technical people. During these workshops, all participants work to design final concepts which will fit the company as well as the customers' requirements.

Crawford and DiBenedetto (2003) have supplied a checklist of idea stimulators for B2B products. An abbreviated version of this list is presented in Table 8.4.

The key to a successful new product process is that a few real winners emerge while most of the potential losers are eliminated. However, no process can eliminate all failures. Many managers are quite wary about the highly visible step of introducing a new product. If a manager is hoping to have 100 percent success then this process will eliminate most of the potential successes while eliminating every potential failure.

DETERMINANT ATTRIBUTES

Hansotia et al. (1985) described a determinant attribute as one which is both important and differentiating. The task of the business marketer is both to understand the importance of each attribute of a product and/or service as it is perceived by his customers and whether a particular attribute differentiates the offering from those of the competitors. As can be seen in Figure 8.5, attributes must be important and differentiating in order to be determinant.

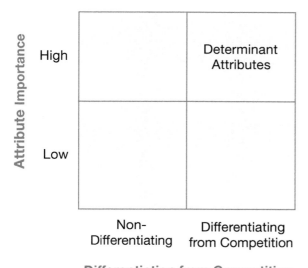

FIGURE 8.5 Attribute analysis

Source: adapted from Hansiota et al., 1985.

A determinant attribute is one on which customers will base their choices about which products or services to purchase. To design products effectively, the manager must know which aspects of a particular offering are important to customers. But that is not enough information. In addition, the manager must determine whether one or a group of attributes makes a particular competitor stand out from others. Only this combination of high importance and differentiation will yield the determinant attributes, the upper right corner of the matrix shown in Figure 8.5.

Research projects for industrial firms have shown clients' rating very high on unimportant attributes shown in the upper left hand corner of the matrix, or very low on the most important and differentiating attributes, placing the firm in the lower right portion of the matrix. Neither of these ratings will result in a firm offering products with determinant attributes which are clearly preferred by its customers.

TESTING THE NEW PRODUCT CONCEPT

Crawford and DiBenedetto (2003) define a new product concept as a statement which describes the benefits the new product will give to customers versus other products or solutions they are currently using, with the description of the form and/or technology through which these benefits will be realized. Once the new product concept has been honed it is ready for testing by customers. In business products, as in consumer markets, radical new technologies are difficult to test when customers cannot visualize the benefits. Customers are often not equipped to react to product concepts which solve problems they are not aware of. A better approach for developing product concepts would be working with customers to find new ideas, based on potential or possible problems. Generally speaking, concepts are tested using some form of market research. If the product is easily visualized, mail or web surveys may suffice. But when the product needs to be experienced by potential customers, actual prototypes may be required and personal experience through focus groups may be the best method for concept testing. In some cases, web-based surveys may be used where a product may be seen but direct experience with it is not required to understand customers' reactions. (For a more detailed discussion, see Chapter 5).

After the concept testing, detailed screening of the concept is necessary to see whether it should be moved into the next step. When a firm wishes to examine the attractiveness of various new product alternatives, it will review each of these alternatives using some form of a scoring model. A brief example of this is included in Table 8.5.

TABLE 8.5 Scoring model factors and scales

Factor	Scale				
Technical Aspects:	*1*	*2*	*3*	*4*	*5*
Technical task difficulty	Very difficult				Easy
Research skills required	Have none required				Perfect fit
Development skills required	Have none required				Perfect fit
Technical equipment/processes	Have none required				Have all
Rate of technological change in market	High/erratic				Stable
Design superiority assurance	None				Very high
Security of design (patent)	None				Have patent
Manufacturing equipment/processes	Have none required				Have them now
Vendor cooperation available	None in sight				Current relationship
Likelihood of competitive cost	Well above competition				Over 20% less
Likelihood of quality product	Below current levels				Leadership
Speed of market	Two years or more				Under six months
Team people available	None right now				All key ones
Investment required	High				Low
Commercial Aspects:	*1*	*2*	*3*	*4*	*5*
Market volatility	High/erratic				Very stable
Probable market share	Fourth at best				Number one
Probable product life	Less than a year				Over 10 years

continued . . .

TABLE 8.5 . . . *continued*

Factor	Scale				
Commercial Aspects:	*1*	*2*	*3*	*4*	*5*
Similarity to product line	No relationship				Very close
Sales force requirements	Have no experience				Very familiar
Promotion requirements	Have no experience				Very familiar
Target customer segment(s)	Perfect stranger(s)				Close/current
Distribution channels	No relationship				Current/strong
Target cost	Very unsure of meeting				Meet target
Importance of task to user	Trivial				Critical
Degree of unmet need	None/satisfied				Totally unmet
Likelihood of filling need	Very low				Very high
Competition to be faced	Tough/aggressive				Weak
Technical/field service requirements	No current capability				Ready now
Environmental effects	Only negative ones				Only positive ones
Global applications	No use outside nat'l mkts				Fits global
Market diffusions	No other uses				Many other areas
Probable profit	Break even at best				ROI > 40%

Source: adapted from Crawford and DiBenedetto, 2003.

A firm should develop its own scoring model relevant to its own business and past successes and failures realized through the new product process. The factors and the scales should be adapted for each particular firm's situation, but the process should be used to determine which is worthy of further effort and which should be abandoned. Ames and Hlavacek (1984) offered a figure similar to Figure 8.6, showing how 100 new product ideas might yield only one new product.

In evaluating potential products, Crawford and DiBenedetto have pointed out the possible errors which could be made, summarized in the risk/payoff matrix. This is seen in Figure 8.7.

As they point out, the AA decision (stopping development of a product which would fail as soon as you can) and the BB decision (continuing the development of a product which would succeed) are obviously correct decisions. The incorrect decisions are AB and BA. AB means a product which would succeed is stopped before it has a chance to enter the market: BA allows a product which will fail to continue through the process. Often, the worst error is not the BA which obviously can waste resources on a possible failure, but the AB-type error which aborts successes before they reach the market. In many business marketing firms, managers have been trained to avoid making losses and therefore they often make the AB error so that hardly any new products reach the market. At a certain point, aggressive competitors make these managers pay dearly for this too-restrictive product innovation program.

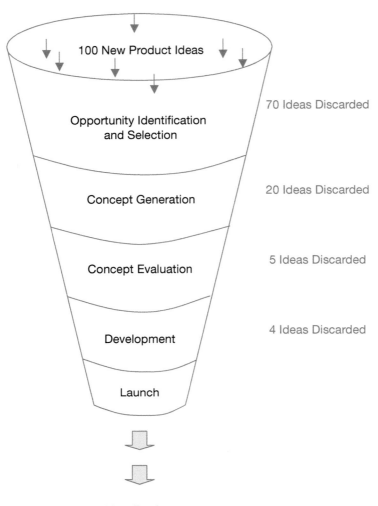

100 New Product Ideas

70 Ideas Discarded

Opportunity Identification and Selection

20 Ideas Discarded

Concept Generation

5 Ideas Discarded

Concept Evaluation

4 Ideas Discarded

Development

Launch

New Product

FIGURE 8.6 New product funnel

Source: adapted from Ames and Hlavacek, 1984.

Decision is to:	A Stop the project immediately	B Continue product development process
If the product were marketed:		
A. It would fail	AA	BA
B. It would succeed	AB	BB

FIGURE 8.7 Risk payoff matrix

Source: adapted from Crawford and DiBenedetto (2003).

PROJECT TEAMS

It is important that the marketing plans work with the development plans on parallel paths toward launch. This is represented graphically in Figure 8.8.

As can be seen, product and marketing plans have to be developed together. A firm which wishes to move quickly must arrange for the simultaneous creation of the product and the marketing plan. In fact, this is an iterative process since the product marketing, especially pricing, is highly dependent upon the cost and features that make up the product offering.

The evaluation of a global product concept presents additional difficulties. Cross-functional teams must be established, which include representatives from a firm's most important markets through-

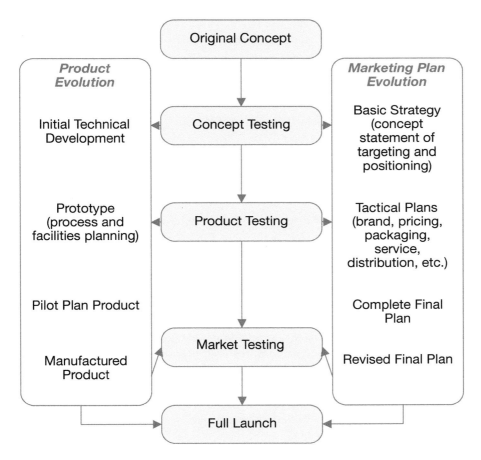

FIGURE 8.8 The twin streams of development

Source: adapted from Crawford and DiBenedetto, 2003.

out the world. Despite electronic communications such as Skype, some face-to-face meetings are probably necessary and there is no question that this can slow down the new product process. Nevertheless, complete "buy-in" is required from all concerned country organizations in order to ensure that the product will be successful throughout the world.

Project teams are the heart and soul of success for B2B new products. These teams generally include engineers, pure scientists, finance experts, and marketing people, most often product managers. In some large firms, members of the market research team may also be included. Both manufacturing and design engineers are generally on the team and many teams include outside consultants such as independent product designers or consulting engineers. Setting up a multi-function team for a global corporation can be complex. Problems of language and culture sometimes interfere with communications on these teams (Garrett et al., 2006), but one cure is to initiate cross-functional meetings with representatives from various country markets on a regular basis to increase trust and understanding.

For example, US firms are more likely to use a formal NPD process than are firms based in Hong Kong, and US firms have also used formal systems for longer, on average (Ozer and Cheng, 2006). Some Asian cultures rely heavily on interpersonal relationships, which can hinder innovativeness (Atuahene-Gima et al., 2006): this is because such relationships tend to lead to a market-driven, reactive approach to NPD, whereas a market-driving approach is often more successful (Beverland et al., 2006).

McDonough (2000) found that 97 percent of the firms in his study have used cross-functional teams and that one-third of the teams used them 100 percent of the time. The study further showed that the use of this approach did not depend upon size of firm or revenue, that cross-functional teams were widely used across many different kinds of organizations. McDonough et al. (2001) found the use of global NPD teams is increasing. They define global NPD teams as those including individuals who work and live in different countries and are culturally diverse. Companies in the study reported that they expect at least one out of five of their NPD teams to be global. Achieving and sustaining trust between team members, developing effective interpersonal relationships, and fostering effective communications between members are more difficult with global teams than with other kinds of teams. In addition, there are some indications that global teams find it more difficult to identify customer needs and ensure that project goals remain stable and stay on budget, keep on schedule and have sufficient resources. These researchers also found that teams of people at one location realize better performance than global teams.

McDonough (2000) identified three major categories which contribute to the success of cross-functional teams. First is stage setting: developing appropriate project goals, empowering the team with needed decision-making power, then assigning the required human resources and creating a climate which will be productive. Appropriate project goals are the most important of these factors associated with success. The second category of factors relates to enablers. These are team leaders, senior managers, and product champions. Team leadership is the most important of these factors. Finally, team behaviors such as cooperation, commitment to the project, ownership of the project, and respect and trust among team members are important to cross-functional team success. Cooperation is the most important of these factors. Of all of the factors mentioned, the one most frequently cited in the research as important to cross-functional team success is cooperation among team members. Setting appropriate goals was second in relative importance. As mentioned, obtaining cooperation and trust among those with vastly different cultural backgrounds can be a challenge, yet it is a worthwhile goal since cross-functional teams do create projects with higher success rates. In view of these findings, firms need to spend more time training managers to handle the problems which arise with global teams, and to be sure that the organizational structure provides these teams with the proper resources.

These cross-functional teams enable a firm to respond to the shortening global product lifecycles and quicker time to market exhibited by most competitors. Instead of approaching the new product development process in a sequential way where one stage needs to be totally completed before the second stage begins, more sophisticated firms are using an overlapping approach, the so-called "rugby" approach to new product development (Takeuchi and Nonaka, 1986). In this approach, teams are self-organized and have substantial freedom. This process avoids rigid controls and encourages transfer of knowledge through the team as well as throughout the organization. Here, while one function of a firm may be leading one stage, another function has already taken up task. For instance, while marketing may be developing and testing concepts for a new roofing product, the technical staff would be working simultaneously at examining the feasibility of the new roofing material formulation. At specific checkpoints, all functional participants must review their progress in order to determine whether to move toward the next stage.

In many cases, new product development will take place in conjunction with customers. In the B2B arena, such co-development projects are very much more likely to happen than would be the case in consumer markets, simply because any firm developing a new product will need to work with suppliers to develop the new components necessary. In some cases customer companies will delegate the development of components to the suppliers (in other words, will issue a detailed specification for the component and expect the suppliers to develop it from there). In other cases the customer company will seek to cooperate in the process, discussing the development with the supplier as the new component is created (Johnsen and Ford, 2007). Such cooperation is not always successful: customer firms can, and do, differentiate between situations where they need to supply "know-how" and situations where they need to help with capability (Wagner and Hoegl, 2006). However, in most situations cooperation between supplier and customer is very much more likely to lead to successful outcomes than in cases where suppliers simply develop something new in the hope of interesting the market – provided the correct processes and preconditions are in place (van der Valk and Wynstra, 2005). Many firms tap into their networks to develop something new, enlisting their customers, suppliers and developers, and using their expertise to create something which will suit the whole network.

Managing the process when customers and suppliers work together can be complex, because the team members are actually working for different organizations, with different agendas and different working practices (not to mention different reward systems). Clearly managers in each company need to have some control over the process, even when it is intended to be a creative activity: research shows that a control system based on rewards for outputs increases cooperation, whereas a system based on control of the process will tend to reduce cooperation (Bonner, 2005). Even so, conflicts will arise: the most important factors for resolving such conflicts are communication management, trust, and commitment to the collaboration (Lam and Chin, 2005). Clearly a system of rewarding the team for a successful outcome will help to develop commitment to the collaboration, which in turn will engender communication and greater trust.

THE INTERNET AND NPD

Global teams rely heavily on the instant communication available through the Internet. Ozer (2000) offered a number of propositions related to the use of the Internet in the new product development process. A summary of some of the key ideas offered by Ozer is seen in Table 8.6. Among these suggestions, there is no question that the increased collaboration available through the Internet is critical to the success of global cross-functional teams.

TABLE 8.6 Use of Internet in the NPD process

NPD Activity	Internet Role
■ Opportunity identification	■ More ideas from more sources
■ Concept generation and screening	■ Improve flexibility of process ■ More comprehensive screening process
■ Development	■ Improve quality and efficiency of manufacturing development ■ Facilitates collaboration among team members
■ Launch	■ Faster feedback of results ■ Quicker changes of tactics

Source: adapted from Ozer, 2003.

GLOBAL PRODUCTS

Yip (2003) identifies common customer needs and global customers as key drivers for firms attempting to develop global products. By common customer needs he means "the extent to which customers in different countries have the same needs and taste." Global customers are those who wish to have the same products in all their locations throughout the world. In addition, high product development costs and fast changing technologies as well as scale economies are driving firms to

---

Talking Point

What is so important about the new product development process for globalized business to business firms? Most firms just react to what customers ask for and then cobble together something new. It seems to work for most small to medium-sized firms, so why should they spend all their time and effort developing a process including a scoring model and also doing research to find out what customers really want? Why not do it like we always did it – make a new product when we need it?

consider developing global products. Yip advises firms to begin by identifying the most important strategic markets and then attempting to find commonalities rather than differences in the needs of these customers in various markets around the world.

EXTENSION VERSUS ADAPTATION

For many years a key discussion in international marketing has been the question of whether a product can be taken to international markets in its original form or whether the product must be modified. In the case of business products, generally speaking, products are not acceptable without modification throughout the world. The fact that electrical systems vary and there are differences between the metric and non-metric measurement systems and the costs of fuel and space availability almost always makes some modifications necessary. Keegan and Greene (2013) have identified three major strategies for product development:

- *Extension strategy* – offering a product virtually unchanged from its home market version to all other markets throughout the world.
- *Adaptation strategy* – changing design, function, or packaging for particular countries.
- *Product invention* – inventing new products from scratch for the world market.

The decision to extend, adapt or invent depends upon many factors including cultural, economic, and political environments as well as the internal capabilities of the firm. Keegan and Greene believe that product decisions are linked with marketing communications decisions. For instance a firm may devise a strategy in which a product offering is not changed while a communications offering is. This they call Product Extension/Communication Adaptation. In this case, a firm would use its existing product, but position it differently for the market segment to be approached. Similarly, a firm may use the same communication strategy, but change the product. This occurs where technical requirements mandate changes, but the marketing strategy is otherwise similar. For example, a firm offering the fastest micro computer would not have to change its marketing appeal simply because the product is designed to run on 50 Hz electricity instead of 60 Hz. Firms may also adapt both communications and product or invent new approaches to both.

INTELLECTUAL PROPERTY

Although it is common to see counterfeit watches, handbags, and other products in nearly every major city around the world, counterfeit products are not limited to consumer items. There is also a large market for counterfeit industrial products. The OECD (2007) reports that more products than ever are being counterfeited and the types are expanding. Even military products have been widely counterfeited. After a 14-month investigation, the US Senate Armed Services Committee found many counterfeit parts installed in US military equipment including thermal night vision sights, memory chips, and even a complete traffic alert and collision avoidance system (Capaccio, 2012).

Other studies have identified counterfeit wiring, circuit breakers, auto parts, batteries, sewer pumps, aircraft bolts, and helicopter blades creating major problems for purchasers (Griffin, 2012; UNODC, 2010; and Naim, 2005). The truth is any product may be subject to counterfeiting.

According to the World Intellectual Property Organization (WIPO) intellectual property "refers to creations of the mind: inventions, literary and artistic works, and symbols, names, images, and designs used in commerce" (WIPO, 2007). This includes all forms of IPR: copyrights, patents and trademarks. The US State Department defines counterfeiting as "the act of producing or selling a product containing a sham mark that is an intentional and calculated reproduction of the genuine

FIGURE 8.9 Results of pirated product.

Source: Copyright, National Electrical Manufacturers Association. Reprinted by permission.

mark," and defines piracy as "the act of exact, unauthorized, and illegal reproduction on a commercial scale of a copyrighted work or of a trademarked product" (USINFO, 2006).

A distinction between "knockoffs," gray goods, and counterfeit goods must be made. Knockoff products may seem the same as branded products, but they do not abuse the copyrights, patents or trademarks (intellectual property) of any manufacturer. Gray goods are products which are offered by the owner of the intellectual property. These products are genuine and legitimate, but have found their way into unintended markets through channel diversion. This will be discussed in Chapter 12.

It is extremely difficult to determine the real magnitude of the counterfeit market. In 1982 the International Trade Commission estimated the worldwide sales of counterfeit goods at $5.5 billion (Abbott and Sporn, 2002). Since that time many estimates have been made. In 2006, the US government estimated the global market value of the counterfeit industry at $500 billion with a growth rate of 1,700 percent over the past ten years (IPR, 2009). The OECD (2007) put the worldwide volume of tangible counterfeit *products* at about $200 billion, an amount larger than the GDPs of 150 countries. However even the OECD estimates are based on incomplete information. The OECD itself says, "available information on counterfeiting and piracy falls far short of what is needed for robust analysis and policymaking." Frontier Economics estimated the value of the worldwide counterfeit product market at $465 to $650 billion in 2008 (Frontier Economics, 2011). Their approach is also based on customs seizure ratios developed by the OECD.

The amount of counterfeit product intercepted by Customs Services around the world is a tiny percentage of the overall estimated size of the counterfeit goods market. The OECD (2007) offered the value of seizures by Customs Services in 35 countries at about $769 million in 2005, representing 0.01 percent of total imports for these countries. A study by the US General Accountability Office (GAO, 2007) suggests that the percentage of the US market accounted for by counterfeit product may be much smaller than previously estimated. Inspecting 287,000 randomly selected shipments from 2000 to 2005 the GAO found counterfeiting violations in only 0.06 percent. The GAO also stated that customs seizures in 2005 amounted to only .0017 percent of the value of the goods in product categories likely to be subject to counterfeit. The OECD (2009) updated their work claiming that the total of counterfeit product had reached $250 million and accounted for 1.95 percent of world trade in 2007.

Researching the size of the counterfeit market unearths the same numbers from very few original sources repeated frequently. Managers should realize that while it is impossible to determine the actual size of this market because of the uncertainty of measurement methods, product counterfeiting is a serious and growing problem. (GAO, 2007; OECD, 2009; Croxon, 2007; IACC, 2007, EC-europa, 2011).

According to the OECD (2009) counterfeiting is taking place in just about all economies. Their data show counterfeit products intercepted from more than 130 economies including 27 of the OECD's 34 member countries. Reviewing EU member customs data shows China as the number one source of counterfeit products, with 85 percent of the articles seized. Other source countries by this measure include Hong Kong, India, Moldova, Turkey, Greece, and the United Arab Emirates. US customs data shows the same pattern. Since 1998, China has accounted for the largest percentage of counterfeit products seized, ranging from a low of 16 percent in fiscal year 1999 to a high of 81 percent in fiscal years 2006 through 2008 and continuing at 62 percent for 2011. Other important source countries for counterfeit products seized in the US are Hong Kong, Pakistan, India, and Taiwan (CBP, 2012).

Although there are many governmental and nongovernmental agencies dedicated to fighting the counterfeiting problem managers must take action to protect their rights. Chaudhry and Zimmerman (2009) recommend the following seven major steps:

1   *Develop IP protection strategy* involving many if not all of the company's functions and clearly communicate the IP policy throughout the organization as well as to contractors, distributors, retailers, and government officials.
2   *Establish a formal and/or informal brand integrity team.* Some firms have large sophisticated antipiracy organizations while smaller firms may have to develop an ad-hoc committee of senior managers.
3   *Manage the registration of all copyrights, trademarks, and patents.* This step is absolutely critical and requires management. Although 185 countries belong to the Paris convention (WIPO, 2012), all of which recognize patent claims made in a firm's home country, it is necessary to register patents in various jurisdictions. The same is true for copyrights and trademarks. The company must set up a system to determine where its IP must be registered and when the registrations need to be renewed.
4   *Create a monitoring program to quickly funnel any information about counterfeits to a central information repository.* This program should gather all counterfeiting developments. This information should be reviewed on a regular basis by top management to monitor conditions, and to adapt tactics to the latest pirate actions.
5   *Develop a multi-pronged action plan, with programs directed at employees, the distribution channel, local law enforcement, and international organizations.* Educating employees and channel members, as well as local law enforcement authorities, is crucial. Management should tell distributors and retailers that it will take action to protect its intellectual property and actions taken should be widely publicized within the channel.
6   *Prepare to fight pirates on every level including investigating retailers and distributors as well as manufacturing sources, pursuing injunctions, and working with local law enforcement authorities.* Educating the local police while building good relations will help pave the way for effective action when necessary (Chang, 2011). Some firms are seeking injunctions in US courts for seizing the overseas bank accounts of pirates in the US.
7   *Develop an evaluation and feedback system.* Since it is clear counterfeiters adapt to keep their operations going, managers must continue to review the effectiveness of their programs using financial and non-financial measurements to get a clear idea of their success or lack of it.

COUNTRY OF ORIGIN

In marketing international products, an additional factor is quite important. This is the country of origin. Buyers' perceptions of a product may relate strongly to the source of that product. Many years ago the Westinghouse Electric Corporation was virtually forced to make an acquisition of a circuit breaker manufacturer in Germany. German buyers were convinced that only German manufacturers made circuit breakers of the quality they required.

According to Anholt (2000), countries often represent particular aspects of a brand. But perceptions are not held forever. The most striking turnaround has been for Japan, which in only one generation changed the meaning of the words "Made in Japan" from a negative to a positive. Any firm marketing a product which is made in Japan will have a slight benefit because buyers believe Japanese products embody advanced technology and quality. Korea is making the same transformation. Some countries evoke no response in the minds of buyers. Anholt cites Slovenia which elicits no perceptions at the present time. When a product manufactured in a particular country is successful it can aid other manufacturers in that country. For instance, Nokia has given Finland the opportunity to establish itself as a high-quality source of electronic products.

Choosing the location of various activities related to new product development in a global corporation is a difficult decision. It is important that a particular managing unit be established. But this managing unit, wherever it is located, must work with all the affected divisions and subsidiaries in order to develop a fully acceptable product.

MANAGING THE GLOBAL PRODUCT

A brand is a set of perceptions which a consumer has about a particular product from a particular manufacturer. A brand is essentially a promise from a manufacturer to a customer about the benefits his firm will receive from a particular product. While there are many local brands known only in a particular market, there are also international brands which have been successful in several markets or in a region. A global brand has the same name and positioning throughout the world (Keegan and Greene, 2013). A key product strategy decision is the branding decision. First, a marketer must decide whether or not the product will have a brand name. This is especially important for products which are ingredients or components of other products. The well-known "Intel inside" is an example of the branding of a component which has been successful. Kotler (2003) identifies four major branding decisions:

- *Brand sponsor decision* – whether the brand will be a manufacturer, distributor, or licensed brand.
- *Brand name decision* – whether to have individual names, one overall, a "family" name, or several family names.
- *Brand strategy decision* – whether to extend the line or develop new brands.
- *Brand repositioning decision* – when a firm needs to change the perceptions of customers about a particular brand.

Court et al. (1996) report that the brand was responsible for as much as 26 percent of the purchase decision for various business to business products. Brand importance is far more significant for consumer products (in the same study the brand of computer was responsible for 39 percent of the purchase decision by consumers). Nevertheless one can see that the brand is responsible for one-sixth to one-fourth of the purchase decision in the study conducted by these McKinsey consultants (see Figure 8.10).

For business to business firms, the development of a global brand is not always appropriate. Where strong local brands exist a global firm may be able to take advantage of the benefits these strong

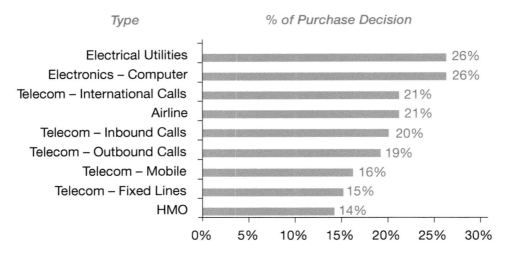

| Type | % of Purchase Decision |

FIGURE 8.10 Relative importance of the brand
Source: adapted from Court et al., 1996.

local brands offer through acquisition or strategic alliances. The establishment of a global brand is usually only cost effective for firms who can afford very high marketing communications investments. Generally speaking, business to business firms would not be in this position. If a firm cannot realize major economies of scale from a global brand they should avoid the effort.

PACKAGING AND LABELING

In worldwide markets, packaging and labeling assume a high level of importance. Packaging serves three major functions: protection, promotion, and convenience for the user. It also serves as an important impediment to counterfeiters. Changing packaging frequently is a key tool to keeping one step ahead of illicit suppliers (Genuario, 2006). For worldwide marketers, a critical aspect is protection. Since product is often transferred through various transportation modes, it usually requires special packaging. In many facilities, this special packaging can cause manufacturing output to slow down considerably. In some cases, pilferage is a problem and products must be packaged to prevent this.

A special consideration related to packaging is a need for waste reduction mandated by governments. In some cases, firms are responsible for disposal both of the packaging and the product after its useful life is completed. This focus on waste reduction has caused many managers to rethink their approach to packaging. For instance, the typical delivery of an office building full of furniture would create several container loads of cardboard packaging. Many office furniture manufacturing firms have now switched to plastic shrink wrap to reduce the very large amount of cardboard left over once new office furniture is installed.

Labeling is also important as business products are shipped around the world. Managers must be aware that they face both language and literacy problems. A box clearly labeled in English would be of relatively little use in Saudi Arabia. In addition, the Filipino workers in Saudi Arabia who might be unloading and installing a particular product may be illiterate, even in their own language. Therefore, clever use of sign language is required to communicate clearly such important messages as "this side up" or "do not puncture with a forklift."

QUALITY

Much has been written about the concept of quality. Research shows that customers always value quality but are not always specific about what the term means to them. It is most important to define the determinant attributes which usually make up a particular buyer's definition of quality. Internationally, firms are relying on the standards established by the International Standards Organization (ISO). Frequently, buyers request that vendors meet particular ISO standards in the 9000 series. When a firm receives certification it can meet the needs of buyers who use ISO 9000 as a basic requirement. The term TQM, total quality management, is used to mean that the firm is dedicated to focusing on customer needs and delivering the quality customers want. Firms who practice marketing as we understand it will meet TQM standards. For Intel corporation, total quality means "level of service to the customer, responsiveness to the customer, delivery performance, competitive pricing, comprehension or anticipation of where the customer is going in the marketplace – all of the things that define your worth in the mind of the customer," according to Thomas Hogue, VP Materials and Services, Intel Corporation (Porter, 1996). Hogue goes on to say that Intel asks their customers to tell them how they are doing in the customers' supplier rating system. In fact, a recent study reported by *Purchasing* showed that 67 percent of 700 firms surveyed believed their supplier measurement system noticeably improved the performance of suppliers who were measured. Nearly three-quarters of those surveyed thought these improvements were worth the time and money spent developing, deploying and maintaining the measurement system (Porter, 1999).

General Electric Corporation applies the Six Sigma approach to quality to its vendors. Six Sigma means that a product would have a defect level of no more than 3.4 parts per million. GE Medical Systems asks its suppliers to use the Six Sigma approach to reduce product defects. In fact, GE even provides what they call Six Sigma "black belts" who are experts in the methodology to help suppliers find problems in their manufacturing process and correct them in order to move toward the Six Sigma level of defects (Purchasing, 1999).

GLOBAL SOURCING

Sophisticated buyers understand that in almost every case they have a "make or buy" decision. That is, a firm can choose to internally develop and produce all necessary products and services or it can outsource those not considered part of their core competencies. Firms look to outsource in order to lower their costs or gain access to better technologies. Outsourcing of services will be discussed in some detail in the next chapter. A survey by *Purchasing* shows that nearly two-thirds of firms have been outsourcing for more than five years. In this survey, 60 percent of buyers said they outsourced to avoid expensive capital investments and more than half said they outsourced to gain the technical expertise of a contract manufacturer. Respondents found on-time delivery and detailed knowledge of the product to be problems they experienced in the outsourcing process.

Core competencies relate importantly to outsourcing decisions. Core competencies are areas in which the firm will be able to outperform its competition. But the firm must be careful to choose just a few of these activities for management attention. For instance, 3M has focused on four critical technologies which it supports with a very effective innovation system. As has been noted earlier, managers should focus their efforts on activities which affect the determinant attributes, those customers use to choose one vendor over another. Once these core competencies are selected, the company must focus its efforts on maintaining superiority, so it is obvious that outsourcing of core competencies will not be acceptable. However, a clear definition of these competences allows a firm to look to outsourcing as a way of cutting costs and letting management focus more of its efforts on what is really important to the company's success. While outsourcing involves costs for seeking and managing firms, where these costs are exceeded by benefits the firm should look closely at an outsourcing alternative.

The question of outsourcing becomes critical in the global setting. Cost to manufacture, package, transport and install products as well as training, relevant import duties, and value added taxes must all be included to determine a final landed price for any product in any market. Once this price is determined, the marketing plan may be profoundly affected. In fact, product sourcing and marketing should be viewed as an iterative process since a firm may arrive at the conclusion that domestic manufacturing and an export market entry strategy will yield uncompetitive pricing in a selected market. A solution to this may be outsourcing of some portions of the product manufacturing or changing the location of manufacture while revising the marketing plan. For instance, a firm manufacturing water purification plants may find that shipping large and bulky components from its home market may make it uncompetitive in the Middle East. Therefore the firm might review the manufacturing of these components in a lower-cost Eastern European nation such as Hungary to reduce both manufacturing and shipping costs. Since this firm may not have an ongoing need for this manufacturing, the firm may choose contract manufacturing for selected components.

Quinn and Hilmer (1995) say three questions should be answered when considering outsourcing:

■ What is the potential for obtaining competitive advantage?
■ What is the potential vulnerability from outsourcing?
■ What can be done to alleviate this vulnerability through arrangements with suppliers?

These three questions affect the option to be chosen by managers. In some cases a firm may choose to make a product or component in a partnership such as a strategic alliance. Where vulnerability is lower and tight control is not as important, a firm may choose to simply contract with a manufacturer to get the products completed.

A dissenting view of the importance of core competencies is presented by Khanna and Palepu (2000). These researchers point out that while focusing on key competencies may be a correct strategy in Western economies, in emerging markets firms may do better by diversifying. In emerging markets, there are information gaps between labor, investors and consumers and the firm, misguided and poorly enforced government regulations and inefficient contract enforcement. Therefore, firms must take on a number of basic functions which normally would be left to other institutions in well-developed markets. Firms who do take on these functions can ensure that their marketing efforts are successful.

CASE STUDY

Case study: Toshiba

In 1875, a new engineering company was founded in a newly industrializing Japan. The company, Tanaka Sheizo-sho, began by making telegraph equipment. Under the brand name of Shibaura Seisaku-sho the company became a manufacturer of heavy electrical equipment, eventually merging in 1939 with Tokyo Denki, Japan's largest manufacturer of domestic electrical products. The new company's official name, Tokyo Shibaura Denki, quickly became shortened to Toshiba, and the company adopted this as their official name in 1978.

During World War II, Toshiba was cut off from world markets and sources of raw materials: the company developed the first Japanese radar systems during this period, but it was not until after the war that it was able to begin expanding again. This time, in common with other Japanese companies, the shortage of raw materials became a spur to invention. Toshiba developed transistor technology from a laboratory novelty to a fully fledged set of techniques: it developed the first transistor TV set in Japan, the first microwave oven, and was involved in developing space communications equipment. In 1970, it unveiled the world's first video telephone, and in 1971 the world's first expanded integrated circuit TV.

Toshiba was not slow to see the possibilities of computer and communications technology, either. In 1978 it unveiled the first Japanese word processor, and launched a communications satellite; the following year saw it release the world's first optical-disk data storage system (the first CD, in other words). In 1985, Toshiba launched the world's first laptop, a combination of its engineering brilliance and its ongoing parsimony with raw materials.

During the 1990s a further stream of new devices appeared from the Toshiba labs: the world's smallest transistor, the first sub-notebook PC, the microfilter colour TV tube, the DVD, the flat TV screen, the DVD video player and recorder, and the first MPEG device.

The twenty-first century saw Toshiba developing high-definition TV and high-definition DVD recording devices, as well as NAND flash memories and broadband processors.

The company's basic commitment is stated in its corporate documentation:

> We, the Toshiba Group companies, based on our total commitment to people and to the future, are determined to help create a higher quality of life for all people, and to do our part to help ensure that progress continues within the world community.

Toshiba manufactures a wide range of electronic products for industrial use. Its high-definition cameras are used in food sorting, security systems, inspection of inaccessible places such as pipelines, and in aircraft systems. Because the cameras are extremely small and light, and yet provide high definition, they

. . . continued

are extremely useful anywhere where weight and size are a problem.

The company has a policy of running regular research sessions with customers to uncover new needs and refine existing products. This research ranges from interviews to questionnaires, and the results are taken very seriously indeed – as a direct result of Toshiba's discussions with customers, the following changes were made in recent years:

■ Exposure to X-rays from Toshiba medical equipment was halved.
■ Shock-resistant mobile PCs were developed following observation of how people handled the equipment.

■ A 0.85-inch hard disk drive was developed for use in miniature computers (palm tops) and portable GPS units.

Recently, the company has started to use questionnaires sent to mobile telephones of customers. This has increased response rates dramatically – often several thousand responses come in from each questionnaire, giving the company some extremely rapid feedback on new products. As in its new product development, Toshiba wants to be at the forefront of technology in its customer research. For the past 130 years, Toshiba has maintained engineering excellence without losing sight of customer needs.

CASE STUDY QUESTIONS

1 What type of innovation strategy is Toshiba pursuing?
2 What is the role of customer input in developing new products?
3 How might Toshiba improve its innovation strategy?
4 What have been the main drivers of innovation at Toshiba?
5 What is the role of the brand in Toshiba's success?

CHAPTER SUMMARY

It is highly important that every firm has a new product development process. Managers must decide what their core competencies are and develop programs to improve their products and services for customers while carefully considering outsourcing non-essentials. The key points from this chapter are:

■ A product is an offering of the firm which satisfies the needs of customers. It is a bundle of benefits including brand name, design, country of origin, price, packaging, and services.
■ The product lifecycle is the underlying reason for the necessity of a product development process since products are usually replaced by newer technologies over some period of time.

The logic for the product lifecycle is based on the diffusion of innovation which specifies various customer types who are more or less willing to accept new products in more or less time.

- Managers must develop a product strategy which includes understanding how many products should be included in a line and how many product lines are necessary.
- Various products may be in different stages of the product lifecycle in specific countries. Managers must understand where each product stands along that curve in order to manage its marketing properly.
- New product development times are shrinking and global customers are looking for the latest technology throughout the world.
- A firm must work hard to excel on the determinant attributes, ones which customers use to make decisions about products or services to purchase.
- A good new product development process will weed out the poor ideas while allowing the successful ones through. A too-tight process will eliminate all new ideas and a too-loose process will allow costly failures to come to market.
- Marketing plan development and product development must be simultaneous. The forming and managing of new product teams across world markets is a challenging task which requires team leadership and cooperation.
- Country of origin can have a significant effect upon a product's success. A manager must develop an overall world strategy for his brands, seeking global brands only where economies may be realized.
- Packaging and labeling are especially important in international business because of shipping requirements and the need to recycle packaging.
- Quality plays a key role in business purchasing decisions. ISO 9000 is a basic requirement in many industries and the Six Sigma approach is becoming more important to many buyers.
- Firms must decide whether to make or buy all the products and services they use. Global outsourcing requires sophisticated analysis of all costs. Where vulnerability from outsourcing is low and tight control of particular suppliers is not important, outsourcing may be the best choice.

REVIEW QUESTIONS

1 Describe the total product including support services, product attributes, and core product benefits.
2 Describe the differences between consumer product strategy and business to business product strategy.
3 How does diffusion of innovation relate to the product lifecycle?
4 What are the strategic choices a firm can make in each stage of the product lifecycle?

5   What are the main factors which affect the speed of acceptance of an innovation?

6   Describe the differences between the product lifecycle and the technology adoption lifecycle.

7   Name the five phases in the new product process and describe each.

8   What are some ways of getting ideas for new products?

9   What is a determinant attribute and why is it important to a firm in the new product development process?

10 Describe a scoring model. What role does it play in the new product development process?

11 What is meant by AB and BA decisions? How can you tell if a new product development process is working correctly through this approach?

12 How do product evolution and marketing plan evolution relate to one another?

13 What are the rules for developing effective global cross-functional project teams and how does the Internet relate to this?

14 What is a global product and what kinds of strategies may be employed for global product development?

15 Describe country of origin and its effect on global products.

16 List the most important branding decisions. Should a firm always have a global brand?

17 Draw a country market portfolio for any products and countries you may choose.

18 Describe the strategies you might undertake based on the placement of country/product on this matrix.

19 Why are packaging and labeling especially important in global business to business markets?

20 How do customers define quality and what role does ISO 9000 play?

21 Relate core competencies to global sourcing. What costs must be included in this decision and what major problems would a firm possibly encounter in outsourcing?

REFERENCES

Abbott, George W., Jr. and Sporn, Lee S. (2002). *Trademark counterfeiting.* New York: Aspen Law and Business: § 1.03 [A] [2].

Ames, B. Charles and Hlavacek, James D. (1984). *Managerial Marketing for Industrial Firms.* New York: Random House.

Anholt, Simon (2000). "The Nation as Brand." *Across the Board*, Vol. 37, Iss. 10, 22–7.

Atuahene-Gima, Kwaku, Li, Haiyang, and De Luca, Luigi M. (2006). "The contingent value of marketing strategy innovativeness for product development performance in Chinese new technology ventures." *Industrial Marketing Management*, Vol. 35, Iss. 3, April 2006, 383–93.

Beverland, Michael B., Ewing, Michael T., and Matanda, Margaret Jekanyika (2006). "Driving-market or market-driven? A case study analysis of the new product development practices of Chinese business-to-business firms." *Industrial Marketing Management*, Vol. 35, Iss. 2, 116–27.

Bonner, J.M. (2005). "The influence of formal controls on customer interactivity in new product development." *Industrial Marketing Management*, Vol. 34, Iss. 1, 71–83.

Capaccio, Tony (2012). "China Counterfeit Electronics Found in Weapons, U.S. Panel Says." Bloomberg. 22 May. Accessed 5 June 2012 at http://www.sfgate.com/cgi-bin/article.cgi?f=/g/a/2012/05/22/bloomberg_articlesM4DTXZ6KLVR701-M4F3M.DTL

CBP (US Customs and Border Protection) (2012). Intellectual Property Rights – fiscal year 2011 seizure statistics. Accessed at http://www.cbp.gov/xp/cgov/newsroom/news_releases/national/01092012.xml on 3 May 2012.

Chang, Jack (2011). Personal Interview. Shanghai, 5 January 2011.

Chaudhry, Peggy and Zimmerman, Alan (2009). *The Economics of Counterfeit Trade.* Berlin: Springer-Verlag.

Court, David, Freeling, Anthony, Leiter, Mark, and Parsons, Andrew J. (1996). "Uncovering the Value of Brands." *McKinsey Quarterly*, No. 4, 176–8.

Crawford, C. Merle and DiBenedetto, Anthony (2003). *New Products Management.* New York: McGraw-Hill/Irwin.

Croxon, S. (2007). Personal interview. London 19 October 2007.

EC-europa (European Commission – Taxation and customs union) (2011). Report on EU customs enforcement of intellectual property rights: Results at the EU border – 2010. Web. Accessed 24 May at http://ec.europa.eu/taxation_customs/resources/documents/customs/customs_controls/counterfeit_piracy/statistics/statistics_2010.pdf

Frontier Economics (2011). *Estimating the Global Economic and Social Impacts of Counterfeiting and Piracy.* London: Frontier Economics, February 2011. Accessed at http://www.iccwbo.org/uploadedFiles/BASCAP?Pages/Global%20Impacts%20-%20Final.pdf

GAO (2007). Better data analysis and integration could help U.S. customs and border protection improve border enforcement efforts. Accessed at *http://www.gao.gov/new.items/d07735.pdf.* Cited 21 November 2007.

Garrett, Tony C., Buisson, David H., and Chee, Meng Ap (2006). "National culture and R&D and marketing integration mechanisms in new product development: A cross-cultural study between Singapore and New Zealand." *Industrial Marketing Management*, Vol. 35, Iss. 3, April 2006, 336–47.

Genuario, L. (2006). "Fight Counterfeits – A Four-Tiered Approach To Help Fight Against The Global Problem Of Counterfeiting." *Beauty Packaging Magazine.* March. Accessed 28 March 2012 at http://www.beautypackaging.com/articles/2006/03/fight-counterfeits

Griffin, Jeff (2012). "High-Risk Products: Know when you may be in a counterfeit situation." Accessed 18 May 2012 at http://www.counterfeitscankill.org/news/?fa=show&id=3338&cms=1

Hansiota, Behram J., Shaikh, Muzaffar A., and Sheth, Jagdish N. (1985). "The Strategic Determinancy Approach to Brand Management." *Business Marketing*, Vol. 70, Iss. 2, 66–83.

Hsieh, Ming-Hung, Tsai, Kuen-Hung, and Wang, Jun-Ren (2008). "The moderating effects of market orientation and launch proficiency on the product advantage–performance relationship." *Industrial Marketing Management*, Vol. 37, Iss. 5, 593–609.

IACC (International AntiCounterfeiting Coalition) (2007). "The negative consequence of international intellectual property theft." Accessed at http://www.iacc.org

IPR enforcement report (2009). Commission of the European Communities. Accessed 24 May 2012 at http://trade.ec.europa.eu/doclib/docs/2009/october/tradoc_145204.pdf

Johnsen, Thomas E. and Ford, David (2007). "Customer approaches to product development with suppliers." *Industrial Marketing Management*, Vol. 36, Iss. 3, April 2007, 309–21.

Keegan, Warren J. and Green, Mark C. (2013). *Global Marketing*, Upper Saddle River, NJ: Prentice-Hall.

Khanna, Tarun and Palepu, Krishna (2000). "Why Focused Strategies May Be Wrong For Emerging Markets" in Garten, Jeffrey E. (ed.), *World View: Global Strategies for the New Economy.* Cambridge, MA: Harvard Business Review Books.

Kotler, Philip (2003). *Marketing Management.* Upper Saddle River, NJ: Pearson-Prentice-Hall.

Krishnan V. and Ulrich, Karl T. (2001). "Product Development Decisions: A Review of the Literature." *Management Science*, Vol. 47, No. 1, January, 1–21.

Lam, Ping-Kit, and Chin, Kwai-Sang (2005). "Identifying and prioritizing critical success factors for conflict management in collaborative new product development." *Industrial Marketing Management*, Vol. 34, Iss. 8, 783–96.

McDonough, Edward F. III (2000). "Investigation of Factors Contributing to the Success of Cross-Functional Teams." *Journal of Product Innovation Management*, Vol. 17, No. 3, 221–35.

McDonough, Edward F. III, Kahn, Kenneth B., and Barczak, Gloria (2001). "An Investigation of the Use of Global, Virtual and Collocated New Product Development Teams." *Journal of Product Innovation Management*, Vol. 18, No. 2, 110–20.

Moore, Geoffrey A. (1995). *Inside the Tornado*. New York: Harper-Collins.

Naim, M. (2005). *Illicit: How smugglers, traffickers and copycats are hijacking the global economy*. New York: Doubleday.

National Science Foundation (2009). *Science and Engineering Indicators 2009*. Arlington VA: National Science Foundation.

OECD (2007). The economic impact of counterfeiting and piracy. Accessed at http://www/oecd.org/dataoecd/11/38/38704571.pdf cited 18 June 2007.

OECD (2009). Magnitude of counterfeiting and piracy of tangible products: an update. Accessed 22 May 2012 at http://www.oecd.org/dataoecd/57/27/44088872.pdf

Ozer, Muammer (2000). "Process Implication of the Use of the Internet in New Product Development: A Conceptual Analysis." *Industrial Marketing Management*, Vol. 32, No. 6, 517–530.

Ozer, Muammer and Cheng, Ziguang (2006). "Do the best new product development practices of US companies matter in Hong Kong?" *Industrial Marketing Management*, Vol. 35, Iss. 3, 293–307.

Porter, Anne Millen (1996). "Intel Corp Takes on Big Q." *Purchasing*, Vol. 119, January 11, 54–5.

Porter, Anne Millen (1999). "Quality Report – Raising the Bar." *Purchasing*, Vol. 127, January 14, 44–50.

Purchasing (1999). "Using Six Sigma to Manage Suppliers." *Purchasing*, Vol. 127, January 14, 90.

Quinn, James Bryan and Hilmer, Frederick G. (1995). "Strategic Outsourcing." *McKinsey Quarterly*, No. 1, 48–70.

Rogers, Everett M. (1962). *Diffusion of Innovations*. New York: MacMillan.

Song, Michael and Noh, Jeonpyo (2006). "Best new product development and management practices in the Korean high-tech industry." *Industrial Marketing Management*, Vol. 35, Iss. 3, 279–92.

Takeuchi, Hirotaka and Nonaka, Ikujiro (1986). "The New New Product Development Game." *Harvard Business Review*, Vol. 64, Iss. 1, 137.

Topfer, A. (1995). "New Products – Cutting the Time to Market." *Long Range Planning*, Vol. 28, No. 2, 61–78.

UNODC (2010). *The Globalization of Crime: A Transnational Organized Crime Threat Assessment*. UNODC, Chapter 8, accessed at http://www.unodc.org/documents/data-and-analysis/tocta/TOCTA_Report_2010_low_res.pdf on 3 May 2012.

USINFO (2006). USINFO glossary of intellectual property terms. Accessed at http://www.america.gov/st/econenglish/2008/April/20080429233718eaifas0.3043067.html. Cited 16 May 2007.

Van der Valk, Wendy and Wynstra, Finn (2005). "Supplier involvement in new product development in the food industry." *Industrial Marketing Management*. Vol. 34, Iss. 7, 706–13.

Von Hippel, Eric, Thomke, Stefan, and Sonnack, Mary (1999). "Creating Breakthroughs at 3M." *Harvard Business Review*, Vol. 77, No. 5, 47–57.

Wagner, Stephan M. and Hoegl, Martin (2006). "Involving suppliers in product development: Insights from R&D directors and project managers." *Industrial Marketing Management*, Vol. 35, Iss. 8, 961–73.

WIPO (2007). Member States. Accessed 29 May 2012 at http://www.wipo.int/members/en/

Yip, George S. (2003). *Total Global Strategy II*. Upper Saddle River, NJ: Prentice-Hall.

Chapter 9

Services for business markets

INTRODUCTION

On the surface there appear to be many similarities between the marketing of tangible products and the marketing of intangible services. But there are a number of important differences as well. Nearly every successful B2B firm offers a combination of products and services, and often the services are more profitable than the products are. This chapter will help you understand the differences and improve your skills in marketing services.

CHAPTER OBJECTIVES

After reading this chapter, you should be able to:

- understand the differences between tangible products and intangible services
- explain how these differences affect the management and marketing of services
- outline the important considerations in product support services
- understand the role of corporate culture in services marketing
- describe how service quality is measured
- explain the process of blueprinting
- describe the best way to develop new services
- describe the pitfalls and opportunities in transitioning from a product to a service orientation
- know how to deal with international services trade barriers.

SERVICES AND INTERNATIONAL TRADE

According to the World Trade Organization (WTO, 2012), commercial services accounted for about 19 percent of world exports in 2011. Exports of commercial services totaled $4.2 trillion – a significant increase from about $1.5 trillion in 2001. The leading exporters of services are shown in Table 9.1.

It is clear that services are an important part of global business. And services are becoming a more important component of every firm's offerings, even if the firm's main business is physical products.

As the largest clients become more global, they often seek to reduce the number of suppliers from whom they purchase services. They also wish to standardize these services. Yip (2003) says that large firms may wish to reduce the number of auditors they use and choose only the largest accounting firms who can apply a "consistent world wide approach (within the contexts of national rules within each country of operation)." These large global customers want common procedures and standards.

International services are "traded" in four different ways according to the General Agreement on Trade in Services (GATS, 2001). The GATS "modes of supply" are:

- services supplied from one country to another (e.g. international telephone calls), officially known as "cross-border supply";
- consumers from one country making use of a service in another country (e.g. tourism), officially known as "consumption abroad";
- a company from one country setting up subsidiaries or branches to provide services in another country (e.g. a bank from one country setting up operations in another country), officially known as "commercial presence";

TABLE 9.1 Leading exporters of services in 2011 (%)

United States	13.9
United Kingdom	6.6
Germany	6.1
China	4.4
France	3.9
India	3.6
Japan	3.4
Spain	3.4
Netherlands	3.1
Singapore	3.0

Source: WTO, 2012.

TABLE 9.2 Unique services characteristics

Factor	Description
Intangibility	Services cannot be touched, felt or even tried out.
Consumed when produced	Production and consumption of services take place at the same time.
User participation	Even when the user is not required to be at a location where the service is performed, users participate in every service production.
Perishability	Services cannot be inventoried.
Variability	Because of the labor-intensive nature of services, there is a great deal of difference in the quality of service provided by various providers, or even by the same providers at different times.

Source: adapted from Shostack, (1977); Lovelock, (1992).

The unique characteristics of services add considerably to the risk perceived by customers in buying services. In some cases, customers do not possess the technical knowledge required to make adequate judgments in the services area (Zeithaml and Bitner, 1996). In fact, customers are often unable to judge the quality of the service even after using it (Choi and Scarpa, 1994).

MANAGEMENT IMPLICATIONS

As a business moves toward the intangible side of the Goods/Services Continuum, new management concerns become paramount. The table below summarizes the implications growing from each of the factors unique to service businesses. Since the fact that services are intangible makes it difficult for customers to evaluate the quality of a proposed service, management should attempt to focus on "tangible clues" of the service to give messages to potential customers about what to expect. These clues can be in the form of uniforms, written contracts, guarantees, and brochures describing the service or a consistent logo to be used in promotion.

Since services are consumed when they are produced, the role of the so-called "part-time marketers" becomes critical (Gummesson, 1991). Part-time marketers are people who carry out marketing activities but do not belong to the marketing or sales department. But they are the people who handle the "moments of truth" (the moment when the buyer–seller interaction takes place). These part-time marketers often outnumber the full-time marketers who report to sales and marketing departments. Careful selection and training for these people is critical to managing these moments of truth. More recent research has pointed out the importance of word-of-mouth in the internal marketing toward part-timers to create a more satisfying service encounter (Lundberg, 2008).

TABLE 9.3 Service characteristics/management implications

Factor	Implications
Intangibility	Enhance and differentiate the "tangible clues," establish tangible evidence of service.
Consumed when produced	Careful selection of and training for "part-time marketers." Must handle "moment of truth" correctly the first time.
User participation	Fully understand customer expectations of service. Involve customer more in service performance where appropriate.
Perishability	Work to alter demand or supply to avoid extremes of "chase demand" or "level capacity" strategies. Plan capacity at a high level of demand. Use marketing tools (price, promotion) to control demand. Use part-time employees, cross-training or other methods to control supply.
Variability	Either standardize completely for low cost, low-skilled employees or recruit higher-cost, higher-skilled employees and allow them latitude to deliver customer satisfaction.

Sources: Source: Shostack (1977); Grönroos (1990b); Sasser (1976).

Because the user participates in the production of the service along with the provider of the service, it is critical to understand customer expectations for the particular service. In addition, in some cases in order to manage demand, some firms ask customers to do more. An example would be self-service shopping in an office supply superstore such as Staples, which has implications for reducing the satisfaction of the clients as well.

Since services are perishable and cannot be inventoried, management must work to alter the demand or supply side of the equation to attempt to keep customers satisfied. Sasser (1976) described two extremes of services management, one called "chase demand," and the other "level capacity." The first approach requires consistently adding or subtracting equipment and people to meet an unpredictable flow of demand. The second requires that provisions be made at the highest possible demand level with resulting periods of non-productivity. A better approach is the attempt to control either demand or supply. Managers can use price as well as promotion to shift demand from peak periods to non-peak periods, as airlines and hotels do. Some manufacturers even create reservation systems so that customers can reserve a firm's service production capacity in advance.

On the supply side, managers may use part-time employees to fill in during peak demand periods or attempt to maximize efficiency and ignore non-essential tasks during peak times. Another suggestion is to cross-train employees so that they can perform more than one job and relieve bottlenecks during peak periods. Mudie and Pirrie (2006) reinforce these ideas. They add outsourcing or improving productivity from employees to increase capacity. Some industries such as airlines use various levels of yield management based on sophisticated computer models of capacity and customer willingness to pay.

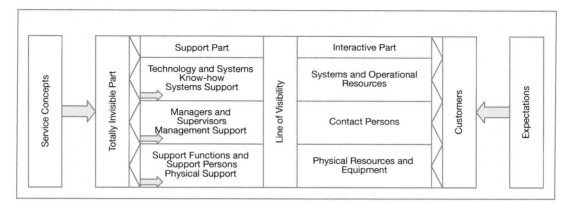

FIGURE 9.2 Interactive vs. invisible aspects of service

Source: adapted from Grönroos (1990, 208).

Finally, services are variable by their very nature. Each performance of a service by an employee, whether a full-time or part-time marketer, will not be perceived in the same way by the customer. Each moment of truth is unique. Managers have reacted to this in two different ways. Some attempt to standardize the operations as completely as possible and then use low-cost, low-skilled employees. In some cases, automating as much of the service as possible is an additional attempt to standardize. Another approach, depending upon the complexity of the service, is to recruit higher-cost, higher-skilled employees, allowing latitude for these employees to provide customer satisfaction. The latter is seen in the case of Marriott, where employees are "empowered" to give customer satisfaction. These employees are given a wide range of authority to gain this overall result.

Lovelock (1992) describes the service management trinity, the three key functional areas actively involved in making services work: marketing, operations, and human resources. The operations function includes the people, facilities, and equipment that run the service operation. Much of this is invisible to the customer. The marketing system shares with operations the delivery of the service, but marketing, in addition, provides other components such as billing, advertising, sales personnel, and research.

As has been mentioned, much of the customer interface in services is handled by part-time marketers who normally report to an operations department. Therefore, operations must understand the importance of the interfaces with the customer and human resources must be able to recruit and train individuals who will meet the overall objectives of the corporation for satisfying customers. Grönroos (1990b) identifies the interactive portion of a service, in other words, the portion where customers interact with the firm in contrast to the invisible support portion of the service.

PRODUCT SUPPORT SERVICES

Product support is an often overlooked marketing tool. In many B2B markets, the support of the equipment sold is at least as important as the equipment itself. In addition, the support services offered can frequently set a vendor apart from its competitors. As we have seen, the failure to provide service can create major problems for providers in international markets.

Frequently customers use a lifecycle approach to the purchasing of equipment and related services. In this area, customer needs can be defined as follows (Lele and Karmarakar, 1983):

- frequency of failure;
- downtime experienced;
- cost of the downtime;
- uncertainty about all of the aspects listed above.

Lele and Karmarakar point out that a customer's reaction to particular events is non-linear. For instance, a farmer might accept a downtime of four hours for a combine harvester. But by the time this downtime reached eight hours during harvesting season, the farmer might actually be compelled to buy a new combine to keep the harvest going. Customers react in the same way to the frequency of failure. Using Lele and Karmarakar's example, a farmer may accept an average of one or two failures per season but react negatively to three or four failures. Customers incur costs to repair items as well as lost wages for idle employees during failures.

In a later article, Lele (1986) identifies three major support service strategies: design-related strategies, support-system-related strategies, and strategies that reduce customer risks. The design-related strategies include increasing product reliability or changing the product to make it more modular in construction or to build in redundancy. As Lele points out, product design and product support service need to be considered at the same time. Support-system-related strategies attempt to change how service is provided to customers. This may include improving response time by adding more technicians or improving repair time by better training or built-in diagnostics. Strategies that reduce customer risks include warranties and service contracts. In choosing a specific service strategy, manufacturers must weigh speed and cost of product development, manufacturing and service costs as well as the needs of customers and their willingness to pay for services.

CORPORATE CULTURE

A critical aspect of the success of a service business is the overall corporate culture established by top management. Studying exemplary public service organizations in Canada, Somerville and Elliott (2011) found commonality despite differences in size, structure, and services provided by each organization. They concluded that the leadership in each one created "a culture of innovation, trust, collegiality, empowerment and appropriate risk taking that enabled exemplary client service." They also stress that effective communication and human resources practices, especially recruitment, training, and mentoring are important.

As described above, a strong and well-established corporate culture which enhances an appreciation for good service and customer orientation is critical. The firm must establish a service-oriented culture so that employees know how to respond to any situation. In addition, internal marketing is critical to the success of any service firm. Internal marketing means communicating to each employee the importance of his or her role in the provision of customer satisfaction. In addition, employees should be encouraged to have the broadest possible view of their own jobs.

Heskett et al. (1994) show a direct relationship between employee satisfaction, employee retention and productivity, and customer satisfaction; which directly relates to financial performance. Inherent in the success of marketing services is the idea of relationship marketing (Grönroos, 1990b). The foundation of this concept is that customer relationships, whether long- or short-term, are the essence of success in marketing. The basis of a successful relationship is a mutual exchange and fulfillment of promises. The seller makes certain promises related to the goods and services it will provide and the buyer gives a set of promises as well. If the promises are kept on both sides, the relationship grows and strengthens. Successful relationship marketing will rely strongly upon the leadership and corporate culture established by top management. This will be explored in depth in Chapter 14.

MEASURING SERVICE QUALITY

The subject of service quality has been studied extensively over the last 20 years. The leading thinkers have reduced the measurement of service quality to five major dimensions. These are seen in Table 9.4.

A critical point to note here is that customers measure satisfaction based on their *expectations* versus their *perceptions* of the actual service performance. This re-emphasizes the need for cooperation between marketing, operations, and human resources. Where the marketing and/or sales department over-promise, the customer may perceive the service as unsatisfactory, therefore marketing and operations should agree on the capabilities of the service and should be working together on this service from planning through execution.

Research completed over many years by Radley Resources (a B2B market research firm owned by one of the authors) for a major business travel firm reinforces the idea that promises made by the sales force can often lead to customer dissatisfaction. Raising the expectations of customers to an unsustainable level means that no amount of hard work can make these customers satisfied,

TABLE 9.4 Service quality dimensions

Dimension	Description
Tangibles	Appearance of physical facilities, equipment, personnel, and communications materials.
Reliability	Ability to perform the promised service dependably and accurately.
Responsiveness	Willingness to help customers and to provide prompt service.
Assurance	Knowledge and courtesy of employees, ability to convey trust and confidence.
Empathy	Caring, individualized attention to customers.

Source: Berry et al. (1992).

whereas making promises at a more reasonable level and then out-performing those promises would yield very satisfied customers.

Repeated testing of these dimensions has shown that reliability is most important. In business marketing, reliability means delivering what was promised on time. It may be noted here that studies completed by Radley Resources in various industries confirm that this factor is most important in customer satisfaction. Jayawardhena et al. (2007) determined that customer perception of service encounter quality in a B2B context is defined by four dimensions: professionalism, civility, friendliness, and competence. Since, as has been established by earlier research, interpersonal relations are critical in B2B exchanges, their work also supports the idea that service quality and satisfaction builds customer loyalty not only to the employee involved in the encounter but also to the firm providing the service.

When customers judge the quality of a service, they examine two aspects of the experience: the process and the outcome. The outcome, or the result, may be satisfactory, but the customer will judge the overall service as unsatisfactory if the process they have been exposed to is unsatisfactory. Grönroos (1998) gives an example of elevator repair and maintenance. The largest repair and maintenance provider in the Scandinavian market completed some research to determine why, despite being the largest firm with the best products, they were losing business to competitors. After two rounds of research (quantitative and qualitative), the company found that although the customers were satisfied with the end result of the work being done, they were uncomfortable with the manner in which the work was completed. Grönroos observes, "top management and the marketing and sales group thought that the company provided products (the results of repair and maintenance) whereas the customers considered the company to be offering processes." Both the product (the outcome) as well as the process has to be well executed to gain complete customer satisfaction for services. In fact, some say that any firm engaged in relationship marketing is essentially providing services marketing in which products are only a means to an end and the processes are most important to building and sustaining the customer relationship which leads to long-term profitability.

Research by Xerox Corporation found that there was an extreme difference in the attitudes toward the company between customers who said they were merely satisfied and those who said they were *completely* satisfied. The latter were six times more likely to repurchase Xerox products over the next 18 months than were merely satisfied customers (Jones and Sasser, 1995). High levels of satisfaction lead to increased customer loyalty and according to Jones and Sasser, increased customer loyalty is "the single most important driver of long-term financial performance."

A final note on measurement: should there be problems in executing a service, prompt problem resolution not only satisfies the customer, but can strengthen the relationship. One way to make this happen is to designate specific employees to handle customer problems and to give these employees authority to resolve those problems.

QUALITY OF E-SERVICES

Measurement of customer perceptions of services delivered through the Internet shows that somewhat different dimensions form the core of customer perceptions of website services. These are differentiated between a "no problem" setting and a situation where problems have occurred. These dimensions are listed in the table below.

TABLE 9.5 e-Service quality dimensions

Dimension	Description
No problem	
Efficiency	Ability to get to website, find desired product/info and check out.
Fulfillment	Accuracy of service promises, product in stock, on-time delivery.
Reliability	Availability and proper functioning of the site.
Privacy	Assurance that shopping and credit card info is secure.
After a problem	
Responsiveness	Providing necessary info, mechanisms for returns, on-line guarantees.
Compensation	Return of payment, shipping, and handling costs.
Contact	Ability to contact live customer service agent by phone or e-mail.

Source: adapted from Zeithaml et al. (2002).

As can be seen, efficiency, fulfillment, reliability, and privacy are the key e-service quality dimensions when no problem has occurred in a transaction. Zeithaml et al. (2002) show that after a problem has occurred, three new factors become important in a customer's assessment of a website. These include responsiveness, compensation, and contact.

Other differences exist between the measurement of the quality of services in general and the measurement of e-service quality. Customers do not have well developed expectations for service from websites. Where providing more of any dimension in a non-Internet based service results in greater satisfaction, this does not appear to be true with an e-service. There appears to be a satisfaction point beyond which customers find providing more service intrusive. For example, customers want to have an e-mail acknowledging an order and another notifying them that a shipment has taken place. More e-mails than this decrease satisfaction rather than increase it.

The research completed by Zeithaml et al. (2002) has shown three major gaps in planning Internet sites. The first is the information gap, which is the discrepancy between "customers' requirements concerning a website and management's beliefs about those requirements." The second gap identified is the design gap, which means "the failure to fully incorporate knowledge about customer requirements into the structure and functioning of the website." The final gap is the communication gap, which comes about because marketing does not clearly understand a website's features, capabilities, and limitations. This gap often occurs because of a lack of understanding between marketing and operations, a problem identified above. As we have seen, customers judge service based on expectations and these expectations are often raised or lowered by promises made by the firm (especially through the marketing people). It seems a frequent occurrence that marketing people do not understand what a website can or cannot do and tend to over-promise.

Overall, there is a final gap, the fulfillment gap, which is the net result of the gaps in information, design, and communication and is the overall discrepancy between a customer's expectations and their actual experiences. No research has yet been conducted which attempts to apply these general e-service quality dimensions to the business to business setting. So, for now we must adapt these general findings. The authors believe it is fair to expect business and institutional customers to judge an e-service using these same dimensions. Eid et al. (2006) find that perceptions of B2 B e-commerce quality seem to vary by industry. All the managers they interviewed agreed that ease-of-use was an important factor. Also identified are clear organization, easy to navigate Web pages, accurate information (adapted to the needs of various nationalities and cultures), and download speed. "Good design" is important in some industries but not as important as relevant information.

BLUEPRINTING

An important part of developing or improving a service is the development of the blueprint. The basic idea is to lay out all the steps required to make a service successful so that a firm can understand who is involved in the service and most importantly where the service passes the "line of visibility" which divides the backstage, or invisible portions of the service performance, from the front stage portions of the process that are visible to the customer. By developing a blueprint, one can estimate the time required to complete each process and isolate possible bottlenecks or fail points which need to be strengthened before the service is implemented (Shostack, 1984). While some observers have developed a horizontal method for blueprinting, others have used a vertical method. Included here (Figure 9.3) is an example of a simple blueprint for a car rental process developed by Lovelock (1992).

DESIGNING NEW SERVICES

Blueprinting is a key part of developing a new service. However, often new services result from trial and error. Heskett (1986) has suggested steps to enhancing new service development:

- establish a culture for entrepreneurship;
- create an organization to foster new service development;
- test ideas in the marketplace;
- monitor results;
- reward risk takers.

While it is difficult to develop a prototype of a service, many of the same steps used in developing new products can be applied to developing new services. Once the service is blueprinted, it should be possible do a detailed business analysis to estimate the potential profitability of the service. The service can then be organized and introduced in a limited way for market testing before moving on to full commercialization. Berry (1989) established four rules for the development of a new service:

Front Stage   **Back Stage**

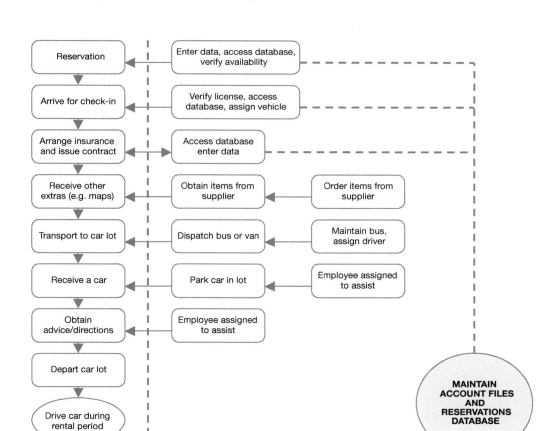

FIGURE 9.3 Flow chart of rental car process

Source: Lovelock (1992). Lovelock, Christopher. *Managing Services: Marketing, Operations And Human Resources,* 2nd Edition, © 1992. Reprinted by permission of Pearson Education, Upper Saddle River, NJ.

- give people a good reason to change;
- start strong;
- market to employees;
- make the service real.

The first rule is based on the idea that customers perceive higher risks for new services because of the very nature of services, explained earlier. They are intangible and un-testable by the purchaser. Therefore, a simple and clearly explainable reason for trying out the new service is required to get customers to use it.

A firm must "start strong" because first impressions are lasting impressions, especially when it comes to services. Word of mouth is critically important, especially in international business markets where industries are small and professional associations dominate. It is most important to test the service performance before offering it to customers so that the first impression will be an excellent one and create positive word of mouth.

Since, as we have seen, employees are critical to the success of any service, it is vital that the firm market to its employees, letting the employees know exactly what the service is designed to do, giving them clear limits of authority, and encouraging them to do their best. Once again, the importance of corporate culture cannot be over emphasized.

Since services, as we know, are intangible, they should be made "real" as much as possible. One strategy is to emphasize tangible benefits as much as possible or create tangibles and connect them to the service. As mentioned, specially designed packages, brochures, and guarantees can help in this regard.

De Brentani (1995) described certain types of service projects that generally succeed while others usually fail in business to business markets. Types that succeed are:

- the Customized Expert Service;
- the Planned Pioneering Venture;
- the Improved Service Experience.

The Customized Expert Service is one that leverages the firm's capabilities, but is customized to fit the needs of customers. Expert personnel who can find out from buyers what they require in order to tailor the service to them are crucial to the success of this strategy. De Brentani found this to be the most successful new service offering. An example of this strategy is a model used to select media developed by a marketing communications firm.

In the Planned Pioneering Venture, a firm develops a new service around its core competencies but in an unfamiliar competitive environment. This is usually complex and expensive and requires a formal and carefully planned service development process. Tangible evidence is required here to convince customers to try the new venture. An example of this service is a PC-based system payroll managers could use to input salary payments.

In the Improved Service Experience, a firm makes improvements to a current service offering using new equipment to enhance the speed and reliability of the service process. While responding to the needs of customers, this scenario is based upon the established facilities and resources of the firm. An example of this service is a new high-speed cargo loading system provided by a shipping company.

New service projects that often fail fall into two categories:

- the Peripheral Low Market Potential Service;
- the Poorly Planned Industrialized Clone.

The first of these is just what it sounds like, peripheral to the firm's core capabilities and not yielding any visible value-added for a customer. This is the proverbial "quick and dirty" addition to the line made with little effort to understand customer needs. This approach is a common type of service failure in business to business markets.

The second failure mode is based on equipment that is too complex. These are also often clones of competitive service offerings and usually do not meet customer requirements nor match very well with the capabilities of the offering firm. These are the "me-too" projects launched without the research and planning necessary to fully understand customer needs and to deliver the extra benefit vs. competition.

To sum up, new service offerings that are successful meet the needs of customers, leverage a firm's capabilities, and are introduced through a careful and well-thought-out process.

MARKETING SERVICES

As in tangible products, the most important first step in marketing services is to identify the relevant segment. There is some evidence that service segments tend to be narrower than product segments. In addition, business services may have to be customized for individual customers yielding a segment of one. Some segmentation may be accomplished along with a level of expectation since this is a key determinant of the perceived success of a particular service (i.e. those with lower expectations versus those with higher expectations may be placed in different segments).

The product is the service offering, including all of the processes and outcomes which customers will see. Earlier discussions emphasize the importance of bringing together human resources, operations and marketing in developing the proper approach to the service offering.

Distribution of services is often not possible. In fact, customers will often travel to the supplier's location to obtain a very important service from a highly differentiated vendor. While tangible goods are often sold throughout the world through intermediaries, highly intangible services like management consulting or architecture are nearly impossible to pass through steps of distribution.

Pricing for services revolves around managing demand, as has been explained above. Moorthi (2002) says that pricing the most intangible of services (like consulting) is difficult. Despite very strong competition, a renowned consultant might receive a premium price. In the case of the most intangible services quality becomes more important than price. In fact, price is often seen as a surrogate for quality.

Promotion for services has some unique aspects. The most important is the need for internal marketing to employees. This must be a key part of the success of any services offering. To customers, Moorthi (2002) emphasizes the need for education. Word of mouth is also critical among customers and developing satisfied customers who will speak positively to others is very important. This point cannot be emphasized enough. In less populated countries like Denmark or

Chile, the communities of specialists in various industries are especially small. Poor service for one customer can easily sour an entire country's market on a service provider. A firm that wishes to develop loyalty creates, as Jones and Sasser (1995) call them, "apostles," who can convert others to the firm's product or service offering. A firm needs to avoid creating so-called "terrorists," those who are so dissatisfied that they will give negative feedback to colleagues. This is especially easy with the advent of social networking, blogs, unauthorized websites, and mass e-mail.

THE TRANSITION FROM PRODUCT TO SERVICE ORIENTATION*

Many managers see the intriguing possibilities in moving their firm from a product-centric orientation to more concentration on the services aspects of their business. Services seem attractive because they often require less capital investment and provide higher margins. Many B2B firms are now embracing the idea of Solutions Marketing, by offering services to accompany products to help solve customer problems (Maddox, 2012). Motorola divided its company into two – consumer products and Motorola Solutions for business to business products and services. Dow Chemical developed a new branding campaign, "Solutionism: The New Optimism," focused on the interplay of science and humanity to develop solutions for global problems. In a study of more than 100 self-identified solutions marketers, 85 percent said this would be extremely or very important to the future of their business. Raddats and Easingwood (2010) build upon their typology to suggest new service areas for product-centric B2B firms. Firms which currently offer no services can begin by offering "product attached services" like installation, training, and other support for their own products. Those who are already offering services for their own products might enhance the kinds of services offered on those products or add services to third-party products. Firms already offering enhanced services on their own products may move to offering those services on other products as well. This strategy will require that the firm develop strong relationships and management of an extensive network of vendors and customers. Some are using the term "servitization," which originated 20 years ago (Vandermerwe and Rada, 1988) but is used more frequently now. The term originally meant that a manufacturing firm would add services to its offering. A current definition is "the management of information, processes, capacity (people, equipment and facilities), products, services and funds from the earliest supplier to the ultimate customer" (Johnson and Mena, 2008).

No matter the terminology, the difficulties of moving from product to service orientation can be daunting. Tuli et al. (2007) warn that selling solutions is complex, must take into consideration many stakeholders within a customer organization, and may take up to two years to finalize. As described above a first step many firms take is to offer warranties, installation or maintenance services for their basic products. In this case, competitors quickly match the offerings. Then, when faced with a large sales opportunity a firm often sacrifices margins in a bundled offering, thereby setting

---

* This section is based upon information provided by IBM Institute for Business Value and IBM Business Consulting Services.

a dangerous precedent of essentially giving away services. Changing to a services orientation is a real challenge and many firms have found it difficult to succeed in this transformation because of poor strategy or execution.

IBM has built their company strategy around solutions marketing, business outcomes for customers, for some years. Currently this includes cloud computing, business analytics, and what they call "smarter commerce" (Maddox, 2012). Greenberg (2000) recommends that instead of becoming a "solutions provider," meaning adding a range of services to traditional products, a firm should seek to become a customer value provider (CVP). A CVP attempts to aid its clients in providing value to *its* customers throughout the value chain. The firm may look "up-chain" in procurement or research and development. Examples are vendor-managed inventory and electronic data interchange (EDI) order capability. A new up-chain area for helping customers create value is collaborative product design. There are obvious benefits including the new knowledge of the customer's business and establishing strong relationships.

"In-chain" aspects of the business relate to manufacturing and include asset management. Down-chain aspects of customer value include marketing/sales and distribution/logistics. In one case cited by Greenberg, a firm that produced custom designed packaging offered to receive its customers' products, package them and distribute the goods to retailers. In changing the firm from a product provider to a CVP, management must realize that important transformations must be made in corporate culture, organization design, and metrics (ways of measuring success for individuals and groups). In addition, the firm may have to change the way it measures return on assets and its technology infrastructure. In implementing this strategy, Majewski and Srinivas (2003) point out that managers often underestimate the resources necessary to change their firm's orientation.

In moving from product-centric to service-oriented, firms often come upon the following issues: operational inefficiencies, offering development problems, channel conflict, sales redesign, and pull-through issues. To overcome these problems a firm will need to develop a formalized product development system for the service business and the ability to develop clear assignments for channel members based on capabilities. Often, firms fail to redesign their sales forces in the proper way. Consultative selling may be required, but this requires a major cultural shift for a sales force which is comfortable selling products only. In addition, the firm must change its incentive program to be sure the goals of the salespeople are congruent with the goals of the new organization. Pull-through often requires that a member of the firm use products not manufactured by the firm in order to satisfy customer needs. Again, cultural change is required to make this work. Storbacka (2011) points out that managing a solutions business requires cross-functionalities not only between marketing and sales but also with finance, manufacturing, supply, engineering, and servicing. This research points out that success in providing customer solutions requires the firm to develop processes which are scalable and repeatable. The firm doesn't just provide solutions that deliver value to customers but participates "in long-term collaboration and co-creates value with the customer." Finally the research details 64 capabilities and management practices for solution businesses, falling into 12 major categories related to commercialization, industrialization, and solution platforms.

In short, moving from a product-centric to a service-oriented business is difficult and requires understanding the customer's entire business and attempting to become a CVP to help your customer provide more value to its customers.

INTERNATIONAL SERVICES DELIVERY

Service delivery in foreign markets is dictated by the nature of the service and the customers, the attitudes of the host governments and the frequent need for high control of operations. Vandermerwe and Chadwick (1989) developed a six-sector matrix based on the relative involvement of goods and the degree of consumer/producer interaction. For services with a high consumer/producer interaction level and a low involvement of goods, these authors find that the internationalization strategy is to gain high control through direct investment, mergers or acquisitions. In most instances, the management of the people who provide the service by the "exporting" company is the critical factor for the success of the business.

In addition, since services cannot be protected through patents, they can be imitated and therefore speed is essential in finding and moving into foreign markets (Nicolaud, 1989). Carman and Langeard (1980) argue that internationalization is more risky for a service firm than for a goods manufacturer since host governments tend to view these firms as taking from the host country and leaving little. Grönroos (1990b) adds that service firms have to enter foreign marketing "all at once" rather than moving through various stages like a goods producing firm.

Since services are perishable, responsiveness to demand is critical. Unsold services "perish"; they cannot be inventoried, or stored for later. Therefore, the service manager must use all marketing tools at his command to adjust for increases and decreases in demand. An early study of services managers found that "successful services managers are managing the capacity of their operations and the unsuccessful ones are not" (Sasser, 1976). The main implication here is the freedom to add or lay off workers if needed, including bringing in home country management or workers on short notice. The ability to manage demand also means pricing flexibility is critical. Short channels of distribution to keep close to the customer as well as tight control over personnel selection are also required (Czinkota and Ronkainen, 2004). These characteristics of managing services tend to make service firms prefer the establishment of their own subsidiaries or branch offices and mergers and acquisitions to joint ventures, licensing or franchising (Erramilli and Rao, 1993; Vandermerwe and Chadwick, 1989). However a study of the insurance industry (Zimmerman, 1999) indicates that managers are sophisticated in finding ways into markets without the need for establishments. The Internet is an especially powerful way for a services firm to enter a market without a physical

Talking Point

How is it that a $20 billion Italian-based company with very good products failed to gain any real market position in the United States despite an effort lasting over 15 years? Olivetti Corporation, maker of many technical products which were well accepted throughout the EU failed to overcome its US- and Japanese-based competition.

Management focused on aggressive pricing and product quality. But when a customer buys a number of copiers, what is most important to the customer? What is the customer really buying? How could a firm like Olivetti have better established itself in the US market?

presence. Ekeledo and Sivakumar (2004) find that e-commerce changes the market entry strategies for services firms. They divide services based on the level of digitization possible for the service act: full-digital and partial-digital services. For services that can be fully digitized a firm may be able to divide up the service provision and offer some portions from a distance, i.e. export. This could yield economies of scale and also protect intellectual property. For partial-digital service some tasks of production as well as accounting and billing might be centralized in one location through e-commerce. An interesting finding is that, in the e-commerce world, rather than jeopardizing intellectual property, licensing of customers can actually protect it.

OVERCOMING TRADE BARRIERS

The rapid growth in services has caused governments to react. While tariff barriers have declined, non-tariff barriers (NTBs) against services have increased. The barriers take any number of forms ranging from establishment requirements to restrictions on ownership to limitations on services to be offered to different tax treatment. Table 9.6 presents a sample of services trade barriers.

The General Agreement on Trade in Services (GATS), part of the Uruguay Round GATT agreement, is the first multilateral agreement covering trade and investment in service sectors. The GATS also provides a specific legal basis for future negotiations aimed at eliminating barriers that discriminate against foreign services providers and deny them market access. While the GATS agreement is attempting to reduce services trade barriers, the agreement includes many loopholes and exceptions (White, 2002). Therefore, firms are often faced with the task of getting around these barriers through their own ingenuity. Managers wishing to overcome barriers generally approach the problem in two major ways – international negotiations and management actions.

Basche (1986) found that service company executives favored negotiations through existing general multilateral organizations like GATT or bilateral industry-specific negotiations for overcoming barriers.

Kotler (1986) identified "blocked" markets as those with high entry barriers caused by governments, labor unions, and other interest groups. He prescribed the use of "megamarketing" to overcome blocked markets, adding two Ps (power and public relations) to the familiar four Ps of marketing. Kotler described five bases of power a firm might use to influence critical decision makers in its favor – reward, coercion, special expertise, legitimacy, and prestige. He recommended that international executives map the existing power structure and develop a strategy and an implementation plan. The firm should choose one of three broad strategies: neutralize opponents, organize allies, or turn neutral groups into allies. Kotler also specifically mentions "at home" lobbying – using the home government to pressure a foreign government into opening a market.

Dahringer (1993) suggested five key management actions which can be taken to combat barriers to international trade in services. These are:

- Embodying – including services in physical goods, to move the total product toward the more tangible domain.
- Superior management – developing strategic alliances, most particularly franchising, which permit a partnership between a locally knowledgeable partner and the foreign organization.

TABLE 9.6 Some trade barriers to services

General:

- prevention of foreign investment in particular sectors
- minimum capital requirements
- limits on operating or administrative locations
- special fees or taxes on foreign firms
- compulsory joint ventures with local partners
- operating permits or licenses for foreign firms.

Professional Services:

- barriers to certain forms of establishment (incorporation or partnerships)
- foreign professionals required in ownership
- nationality required for membership in professional organization or to practice
- limits or requirements on residency.

Banking:

- restrictions on number of bank licenses
- requirements for joint ventures
- prohibitions on other lines of business (insurance or securities)
- restrictions on residency of employees
- limits/restrictions on domestic deposits
- limits/directions for types and sizes of loans
- restrictions on number of branches
- limits on foreign participation in boards of directors.

Distribution Services:

- land acquisition
- government requirements – zoning, environmental, employment, operating hours
- prohibition of large-scale stores
- restrictions on people's movements
- limited/no import licenses available for wholesalers.

Source: adapted from Deardorff and Stern (2004); Dee, Philippa (2005).

- Customizing – developing the most attractive package of benefits so that customers will pay a higher price or move to the service rather than have the service brought to them.
- Technology – using communications and computer technologies (technology transfer is another way of overcoming barriers).
- Micromarketing – working with governments to relieve discrimination through government actions.

Dahringer also includes superior services quality as a management action. This seems better included in customizing and superior management rather than a separate category.

A manager's choice of market entry strategy is affected by the trade barriers he/she sees. Thoughtful managers may elect not to enter a market or to modify their strategy. These successful international services executives take a long-term view of their effort (Zimmerman, 1999). They engage in multiple levels of strategic actions, making use of technology and working with home and host governments as well as other local decision-makers.

CASE STUDY

ColorRight

ColorRight Corporation, based in Switzerland, is a marketer of color measurement equipment. The firm was the inventor of a particular approach using special technology invented by the company which is now more than 50 years old. At the beginning of its history, the firm concentrated on equipment for medical laboratories, film processors, and printing firms. For instance, the firm supplies equipment to measure the color on film and presses for newspapers and other printers and provides equipment to the largest automobile manufacturers so that they can be sure the paint on one part of the automobile matches the paint on another or on replacement parts. At the present time, ColorRight is doing business in more than 60 countries and serves many of the largest multinationals throughout the world.

The new CEO appointed just last year, Mervin Lacroix, reviewed the results for the latest fiscal year. He saw flat or declining year-on-year turnover for each of his five major end-use market segments:

- graphic arts;
- printing and packaging;
- digital printing;
- photo processing;
- retail color matching;
- industrial color;
- medical/dental.

Lacroix contemplated the results and also some disturbing news from the sales force. Apparently, SunColor, a Japanese-based competitor, had proposed to a number of large customers that they offer some new services such as reviewing the product requirements so that color measuring equipment could be

. . . continued

CASE STUDY ... *continued*

tailored to the assembly line of an automotive plant. These offers were made at no cost to the customers.

Lacroix assembled his management team and asked each to comment on this new development and also to assess ColorRight's current problems which were resulting in no growth. Each department head spoke in turn. The engineering manager spoke about improving the response time of the equipment, lowering the weight, and improving portability. The manufacturing manager talked about increasing reliability and low-ering manufacturing costs. The director of marketing asked for six new salespeople for North America, three for Europe, and ten for Asia as a way of solving the problem. The chief financial officer warned everyone that budgets could not be expanded unless sales began to rise.

Lacroix thanked his staff and pondered their answers. He had recently come upon the idea of services as the main driver of the firm and he wondered what would be involved in changing ColorRight from a product-centric to a service-oriented firm.

CASE STUDY QUESTIONS

1   If you were Lacroix, which of the department heads' advice would you find most useful?
2   How would you respond to the moves of your competitor, SunColor?
3   What possible obstacles might Lacroix face if he moves forward on changing ColorRight from a product-centric to a service-oriented business?
4   What steps could he take to move in that direction?
5   Assume you were hired by Lacroix and asked to start a services business. What advice would you give him as you began to establish this business?
6   What motivation do you think SunColor has in offering services to some of its major customers?

CHAPTER SUMMARY

While there appear to be many similarities between the marketing of tangible products and the marketing of intangible services, there are quite a number of differences. Managers must be aware of the unique characteristics of services, which make their marketing quite different. The key points from this chapter are:

■   Services are intangible, consumed, and produced at the same time, perishable, and variable in the quality provided at various times. In addition, users participate in the production of the service.

- There are few pure goods or services. Usually in business markets, goods are offered with attendant services.
- Managing the service aspect of the business can be very profitable and can help the firm secure a very favorable position with the customer.
- To manage services, marketing, operations, and human resources must plan and operationalize services together.
- Successfully changing a firm from product-centered to service-oriented requires leadership by management, especially in the area of corporate culture.
- The assessment of service quality has been well-established, however measurement of B2B e-service quality varies by industry.
- Firms often introduce "me-too" services with no value added. This usually results in a failure of the services business.
- While some researchers claim services businesses must have establishments in-country to market services internationally, there is some evidence to suggest that that is not true. The Internet allows services to be marketed throughout the world with no "bricks and mortar" investment.
- Governments attempting to protect local businesses have been very creative in developing barriers, creating major problems for services marketers. Marketers must use technology, take a long-term view, and approach various constituencies to get these barriers lowered.

REVIEW QUESTIONS

1 What are the unique aspects of services and how does this affect the management and marketing of these services?
2 List the various combinations of services and goods which may be offered by a firm.
3 How do marketing, operations, and human resources work together in a services business?
4 Describe the most important customer needs in product support services.
5 What is the role of corporate culture in services marketing?
6 Name the five key dimensions used to measure service quality and describe each.
7 How do process and outcome relate in customer judgment of service satisfaction?
8 What are the most important e-service quality measurements?
9 Describe blueprinting. Develop a blueprint for a local service business.
10 If you were developing a new service for an oil field lubricant firm, what are the key steps you might use and what rules would you apply to make this new service successful?
11 Name the major differences in marketing services versus products.
12 What are the key problems in moving from a product-centric to a service-oriented business and how would you overcome them?
13 What are the critical problems in marketing services internationally and how would you deal with them?

REFERENCES

American Marketing Association (2012). *Dictionary of Marketing Terms.* Accessed 4 July 2012 at http://www. marketingpower.com/_layouts/Dictionary.aspx?dLetter=S

Basche, James R. (1986). *Eliminating Barriers to International Trade and Investment in Services.* Research Bulletin, No. 200, New York: The Conference Board.

Berry, Leonard L. (1989). "How to Sell New Services." *American Demographics,* Vol. 11, Iss. 10, October, 42–3.

Berry, Leonard L., Zeithhaml, Valarie A., and Parasuraman, A. (1992). "Five Imperatives for Improving Service Quality" in Lovelock, C. *Managing Services.* Englewood Cliffs: Prentice Hall.

Carman, James M. and Langeard, Eric (1980). "Growth Strategies for Service Firms." *Strategic Management Journal,* Vol. 1, Iss. 1, 7–22.

Chase, Richard and Stewart, Douglass (1995). *Mistake Proofing: Designing Errors Out.* Portland, OR: Productivity Press.

Choi, C.J. and Scarpa, C. (1994). "A Note on Small vs. Large Organizations." *Journal of Economic Behavior & Organization,* Vol. 24, Iss. 2 (July), 219–24.

Czinkota, Michael R. and Ronkainen, Ilkka A. (2004). *International Marketing* (7th Edition), Mason, Ohio: Thomson-Southwestern.

Dahringer, Lee D. (1993). "Marketing Service Internationally: Barriers and Management Strategies." *Journal of Services Marketing.* Summer, Vol. 5, No. 3, 5–17.

Deardorff, Alan V. and Stern, Robert M. (2004). "Trade in Services and International Trade Agreements: the Development Dimension." Accessed 3 July 2012 at http://siteresources.worldbank.org/INTRANETTRADE/ Resources/WBI-Training/Deardorff-Stern_Barriers2IntlServices.pdf

De Brentani, Ulricke (1995). "New Industrial Service Development: Scenario for Success and Failure." *Journal of Business Research,* Vol. 32, 93–103.

Dee, Philippa. (2005). "A compendium of barriers to services trade." Accessed 2 July 2012 at http:// siteresources.worldbank.org/INTRANETTRADE/Resources/Topics/Services/Report.pdf

Eid, Riyad, Elbeltagi, Ibrahim, and Zairi, Mohamed (2006). "Making Business-To-Business International Internet Marketing Effective: A Study of Critical Factors Using a Case Study Approach." *Journal of International Marketing,* Vol. 14, Iss. 4, 87–109.

Ekeledo, Ikechi and Sivakumar, K. (2004). "International market entry mode strategies of manufacturing firms and service firms: A resource–based perspective." *International Marketing Review,* Vol. 21, Iss. 1, 68–101.

Erramilli, M. Krishna and Rao, C.P. (1993). "Service Firms' International Entry-Mode Choice: A Modified Transaction-Cost Analysis Approach." *Journal of Marketing,* Vol. 57, Iss. 3, 19–38.

GATS (2001). *GATS – Fact and Fiction.* Geneva, Switzerland: World Trade Organization.

Greenberg, Dan (2000). *Product Provider to Customer Value Provider: Escaping the Services Maze.* Somers, NY: IBM Institute for Business Value, IBM Global Services.

Grönroos, Christian (1990a). "Relationship Approach to Marketing in Service Contracts: The Marketing and Organizational Behavior Interface." *Journal of Business Research,* Vol. 20, Iss. 1, 3–11.

Grönroos, Christian (1990b). *Services Management and Marketing.* Lexington, Mass: Lexington Books.

Grönroos, Christian (1998). "Marketing Services: The Case of a Missing Product." *Journal of Business and Industrial Marketing,* Vol. 13, No. 4/5, 322–38.

Gummesson, Evert (1991). "Marketing-orientation Revisited: The Crucial Role of the Part-Time Marketer." *European Journal of Marketing,* Vol. 25, No. 2, 60–75.

Heskett, James L. (1986). *Managing in the Service Economy.* Boston: Harvard Business School Press.

Heskett, James L., Jones, Thomas O., Loveman, Gary W., Sasser, W. Earl, Jr. and Schlesinger, Leonard A. (1994). "Putting the Service-Profit Chain to Work." *Harvard Business Review,* Vol. 72, Iss. 2, 164–74.

Jayawardhena, Chanaka, Souchon, Anne L., Farrell, Andrew M. and Glanville, Kate (2007). "Outcomes of Service Encounter Quality in a Business-To-Business Context." *Industrial Marketing Management*, Vol. 36, No. 5, 575–88.

Johnson, Mark and Mena, Carlos (2008). "Supply Chain Management for Servitized Products: a Multi-Industry Case Study." *International Journal of Production Economics*, Vol. 114, Iss. 1 (July), 27–39.

Jones, Thomas O. and Sasser, W. Earl, Jr. (1995). "Why Satisfied Customers Defect." *Harvard Business Review*, Vol. 73, Iss. 6 (Nov/Dec), 88–99.

Kotler, Philip (1986). "Megamarketing." *Harvard Business Review*, Vol. 64, No. 2 (March/April), 117–24.

Lele, Milind M. (1986). "How Service Needs Influence Product Strategy." *Sloan Management Review*, Vol. 28, Iss. 1 (Fall), 63–70.

Lele, Milind M. and Karmarakar, Uday S. (1983). "Good Product Support is Smart Marketing." *Harvard Business Review*, Vol. 61, Iss. 6, 124–32.

Lovelock, Christopher H. (1992). "A Basic Toolkit for Service Managers" in Lovelock, C. *Managing Services*. Englewood Cliffs: Prentice Hall.

Lundberg, M. (2008). "A word-of-mouth approach to informal information sharing among part-time and short-term employed front-line workers in tourism." *Journal of Vacation Marketing*, Vol. 14, Iss. 1, 23–39.

Maddox, K. (2012). "Solutions marketing a complex mix for b-to-b." *B To B*, Vol. 97, Iss. 5, 1.

Majewski, Brigitte M. and Srinivas, Singu (2003). *The Services Challenge: Operationalizing Your Services Strategy*. Somers, NY: IBM Global Services.

Moorthi, Y.L.R. (2002). "An Approach to Branding Services." *Journal of Services Marketing*, Vol. 16, No. 3, 259–74.

Mudie, Peter and Pirrie, Angela (2006). *Services Marketing Management*. Burlington, MA: Butterworth-Heinemann, 171–5.

Nicolaud, B. (1989). "Problems and Strategies in the International Marketing of Services." *European Journal of Marketing*, Vol. 23, No. 6, 55–66.

Raddats, Chris and Easingwood, Chris (2010). "Services Growth Options for B2B Product-Centric Businesses." *Industrial Marketing Management*. Vol. 39, Iss. 8, 1334–45.

Sasser, W. Earl Jr. (1976). "Match Supply and Demand in Service Industries." *Harvard Business Review*, Vol. 54, Iss. 6, 133–40.

Shostack, G. Lynn (1977). "Breaking Free From Product Marketing." *Journal of Marketing*, Vol. 41, Iss. 2 (April), 73–80.

Shostack, G. Lynn (1984). "Designing Services that Deliver." *Harvard Business Review*, Vol. 62, Iss. 1, 133–9.

Somerville, K. and Elliott, C. (2011). "Strategies to improve client service: Exemplars in the Canadian federal government." *Innovation Journal*, Vol. 16, No. 2, 1–16.

Storbacka, Kaj (2011). "A solution business model: Capabilities and management practices for integrated solutions." *Industrial Marketing Management*, Vol. 40, Iss. 5 (July), 699–711.

Tuli, K.R., Kohli, A.K., and Bharadwaj, S.G. (2007). "Rethinking customer solutions: from product bundles to relational processes." *Journal of Marketing*, Vol. 71, Iss. 3, 1–17.

Vandermerwe, S. and Rada, J. (1988). "Servitization of Business: Adding Value by Adding Services." *European Management Journal*. Vol. 6, Iss. 4, 314–24.

Vandermerwe, Sandra and Chadwick, Michael (1989). "The Internationalisation of Services." *The Service Industries Journal*, Vol. 9, Iss. 1, 79–93.

White, Lawrence J. (2002). Unpublished Paper. "International Trade in Services: More than Meets the Eye."

WTO (2012). Accessed 2 July 2012 at http://www.wto.org/english/news

Yip, George S. (2003). *Total Global Strategy II*. Upper Saddle River, NJ: Pearson-Prentice Hall.

Zeithaml, Valarie A. and Bitner, M.J. (1996). *Services Marketing*. Singapore: McGraw-Hill.

Zeithaml, Valarie A., Parasuraman, A. and Malhotra, Arvind (2002). "Service Quality Delivery Through Web Sites: A Critical Review of Extant Knowledge." *Journal of the Academy of Marketing Science*, Vol. 30, No. 4, 362–75.

Zimmerman, Alan S. (1999). "Impacts of Service Trade Barriers: A Study of the Insurance Industry." *Journal of Business & Industrial Marketing*, Vol. 14, Iss. 3, 211–26.

Chapter 10

Pricing

INTRODUCTION

Price is the only activity marketers engage in that produces revenue for the firm. All other marketing activities represent expenditures while pricing managed properly can make a major difference in the firm's revenue and income. Pricing for products and/or services must be congruent with the rest of the marketing plan. Managing price properly also means thoroughly understanding costs as well as customers.

CHAPTER OBJECTIVES

After reading this chapter, you should be able to:

- describe how organizational buyers look at price from a value point of view
- understand the most important factors in business to business pricing
- list the factors impacting upon pricing strategy development
- understand the importance of cost to pricing decisions
- describe how firms manage the competitive bidding process
- describe key factors affecting customer price sensitivity
- explain the issues in transfer pricing
- describe the competitive bidding powers.

THE MAGIC OF PRICE

As has been pointed out above, price is the only place where marketers have a chance to directly improve the bottom line. They do this by carefully pricing products for maximum profitability. Let us look at the simplified example shown in Table 10.1.

With the original price of $10 a firm sells one million units for a total revenue of $10 million. The direct cost for manufacturing the product (including all of the variable costs) at $6/unit adds up to $6 million. Administrative costs are $3 million. In this case, as can be seen from our simple example, the profit to the firm is $1 million. Now let us assume that the marketing vice-president decides to raise the price by 5 percent. Therefore, the product will now be sold at $10.50. If one million units are sold, the total revenue would be $10.5 million. The direct cost for making one million units remains $6/unit for a total of $6 million and the administrative costs also remain the same at $3 million. This example shows how a 5 percent increase in price results in a 50 percent increase in profit from $1 million to $1.5 million.

This example is given only to show how a small movement in price can result in very large benefits to the firm. However, this example has some obvious flaws. First, the example boldly assumes that the firm will still sell one million units at the higher price. Basic economics teaches us that demand curves slope downward toward the right as seen in Figure 10.1.

If one raises the price, the quantity sold declines. This demand curve certainly holds true for commodity products where all the offerings are exactly the same, such as sand or milk. However, in some consumer markets and in almost all B2B markets, the demand curve actually looks more like that shown in Figure 10.2.

Here we see a "stepped" demand curve. This illustrates the point that there are ranges of prices at which the demand will not change. If our marketing director is clever enough to determine that customers are not price sensitive to a difference between $10 and $10.50, he/she would realize the increased revenue from changing the price.

A second possible criticism of our example is that the increased price may require increases in administrative expenses such as hiring more salespeople or increasing advertising or trade show promotion. Here again our example would fail. So, while we see that the simple example in

TABLE 10.1 The magic of price		
	Original Price	New Price (increase price 5%)
Sales Revenue (1 million units @ $10)	$10,000,000	$10,500,000
Direct Costs (Labor, materials, etc) (@ $6.00 per unit)	$6,000,000	$6,000,000
Administrative Costs (Overhead)	$3,000,000	$3,000,000
Profit	$1,000,000	$1,500,000

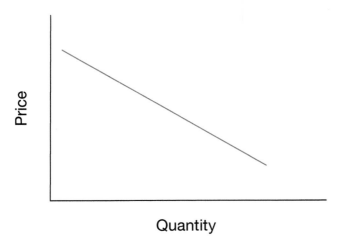

FIGURE 10.1 Standard demand curve

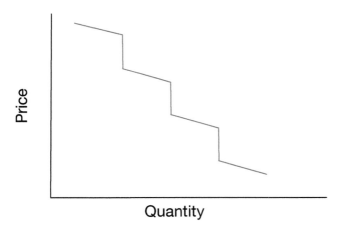

FIGURE 10.2 Stepped demand curve

Table 10.1 is an oversimplification of most situations, it does serve to illustrate the point that business marketers must be fully aware of their capability to increase the profitability of their firm through the judicious use of pricing.

THE PRICING PROCESS

Figure 10.3 shows an overview of the pricing process. First, the firm must set pricing objectives in line with its corporate objectives. Second, the manager will develop the pricing strategy to be used in each relevant segment. Then the manager will determine what the demand will be at various

FIGURE 10.3 The pricing process

Talking Point

There is a lot of data to support the idea that a firm which has the largest market share also is the most successful in a particular industry. And what is the most effective way to gain the largest market share? Certainly to lower prices below the competition. If this is true, wouldn't a smart marketing manager always lower his prices below the firm's competitors to get the biggest market share possible? What could possibly prevent him from taking this action?

pricing levels. Following this, he or she will estimate costs then review the competition, select a pricing method and policy and finally determine the exact prices to be assigned to each individual product and product line.

PRICING OBJECTIVES

Generally speaking, pricing objectives can be divided into three major types (Perrault et al., 2010): profit-oriented, sales-oriented or status quo-oriented. Profit-oriented objectives include pricing to realize a target return on investment or to maximize profits. Sales-oriented objectives aim to increase sales either in currency or unit terms or to penetrate markets and increase share. Status quo-oriented pricing includes meeting competition or choosing to compete on a non-price basis. In some cases, a firm does not have the luxury of pricing to maximize its profits but only to survive in the face of an industry with very strong competition and overcapacity.

Some firms set an internal rate of return for particular product lines and price to achieve this. Others seek a particular margin on sales. The choice depends upon the nature of the industry. In a business where few sales are made per year, the target return on investment is most likely the best approach, whereas in a high volume business the margin on sales becomes more important. These accepted versions of pricing strategies do not include the most favorable approach which is to establish pricing based on the value customers place on the product. As has been described above, this requires an in-depth knowledge of the customer's business and the ways in which the product is put to use by the customer.

PRICING STRATEGY

To develop a pricing strategy, the manager must consider many factors. An overview of pricing strategy development is seen in Figure 10.4.

The major factors relate to the firm, the environment, distribution channels, competitors, and customers. Firm considerations are first the corporate objectives that the firm has established. In addition, costs are critical. In this case, we mean costs not only of the product but the costs of marketing as well, including the market entry costs of various foreign locations. One very important factor in the cost of production is where the production facility is located. Sourcing is very important to the overall decision in marketing products outside the home country, as we have seen. A key factor will be the costs realized by a foreign factory and the shipping costs inherent in that location.

Finally, the firm marketing program is critical since price must be congruent with the rest of the marketing. For instance, a firm decides that it wishes to offer a laptop computer which will withstand the rigors of a construction site. If the firm designs the product to be the most durable available, then advertises it as such and trains its distribution channels to place the product in the most difficult environments, it would hardly make sense to price the product below ordinary competing laptops.

One important consideration which should not be overlooked is the relationship of the selected price to the pricing of other products in the line and to other product lines. For instance, a firm may choose to price a large order of ink jet printers at very low prices in order to realize large margins

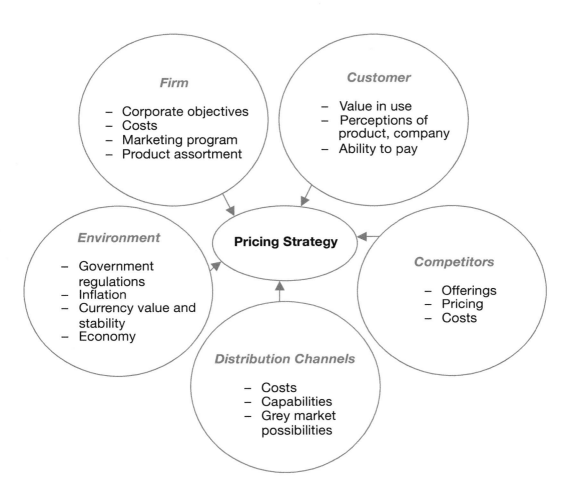

FIGURE 10.4 Pricing strategy development
Source: adapted from Hollensen, 1998; Cavusgil, 1996.

from the sales of exclusive ink cartridges to be contracted for by the customer over a significant period of time. When pricing electric motors, specific horsepower to price ratios may be established by long tradition in the industry and therefore prices must be set to match these customer expectations even though they are not based on costs.

The environment impacts the pricing strategy in many ways: government regulations including price controls, import duties and quotas as well as taxes will have a major effect upon pricing possibilities. Inflation is another important factor in pricing strategy. In countries with hyperinflation where governments do not allow rapid price increases, a firm should be most aggressive, assigning the highest possible price to any product which is new or modified. The value of a currency in a particular market and the stability of that value will again impact whether a firm can feel comfortable with a particular price level or whether the firm must be vigilant about changing the price as often as possible. Finally, the relative growth or decline in a particular economy will have an obvious effect on pricing.

Distribution channels also have a large impact on the pricing strategy. The costs associated with the services performed by distributors will have a major effect upon the final price paid by the customer. Therefore, a marketing manager must be fully aware of the costs to be added by the distribution channel and take actions to reduce those costs or even move the services in-house in order to meet required pricing on the customer level. This relates to the capabilities of distribution. Should they be unable to install, train, and service a particular product, those costs would be passed to the manufacturer and this would be included in the overall pricing approach. Finally, some distributors may see an opportunity for gray market re-export. This occurs when a manufacturer prices a product at a very low level in a particular country to meet competition. But sharp distributors in that market overbuy and sell the excess in another market, undercutting the latter market's much higher prices and turning a neat profit. Dealing with these "gray market" products is an ongoing problem for many international marketing managers.

Of course competitors have a major effect upon pricing strategy. First, one must examine their offerings in detail to understand the benefits and drawbacks of their approaches versus the firm's approach. For products sold in markets where bidding is not required to be made public and sales are infrequent it may be difficult to obtain competitors' pricing. Nevertheless, an effort should be made. Finally, competitors' costs are a very important factor in your pricing strategy. Here again it may be quite difficult to obtain these costs, but the manager should attempt at the very least to estimate.

The most important factor in the pricing strategy is obviously the customer. As has been pointed out, it is vital for marketing managers to understand how customers go about doing their business. This will enable the marketing manager to establish true value-in-use price. Also important in this mix are the perceptions customers have of both the product and the manufacturer. And, of course, the ability to pay is important. In some cases, a customer may wish to acquire a product but be unable to secure the necessary funds to obtain it. In this case, a marketing manager may have to resort to alternative payment schemes, accept goods or services in payment (countertrade) or establish long-term payment programs to aid the customer in getting the product he/she needs.

DETERMINING DEMAND – CUSTOMER PERCEPTIONS OF PRICE

As we have seen in Chapter 8, customers perceive a total product including core benefits, product attributes, and support services yielding a package of benefits they need. These benefits must be balanced against the costs customers will experience to gain them. Of course, the most important cost is the net outlay of funds required from the customer firm to gain these benefits. This outlay is perceived by the customer not simply in terms of the initial price, but in terms of the value received for the expenditures over the useful life of the product. Customer firms are rather sophisticated in their application of discounted cash flow to pricing offered by vendors and they understand the net difference between one offer and another. Here also, customers may choose to lease rather than own products, thereby increasing the value of the offering to them. Customer perceptions of costs and benefits are shown graphically in Table 10.2.

TABLE 10.2 Customer perceptions of costs and benefits

Benefits	Costs
Functional (physical aspects of product, service benefits)	Acquisition (initial price, less discounts, plus freight, installation, taxes)
Operational (reliability/durability)	Operational (internal coordination, switching costs, downtime, training, disposal)
Financial (payback period)	
	Potential Risks (to operations, personal)
Personal (commendation for choosing right product)	
Relational (joint working, trust in, commitment of supplier)	

Source: adapted from Menon et al., 2005; Shapiro and Jackson (1978); and Cespedes (1994).

CUSTOMER PERCEPTIONS OF COSTS AND BENEFITS

As can be seen in Table 10.2, customer benefits fall into functional, operational, financial, personal, and relational categories. The functional are those that come to mind most readily, related to the physical aspects of the product, specific benefits of the service or the total benefits derived from the package of products and services. But also important are operational benefits such as reliability and durability, financial aspects such as the payback period, and personal benefits which some member of the buying center may realize because of his or her choice of a particular product. Newer research (Menon et al., 2005) adds relational benefits. Strong business relationships and joint working arrangements increase the customer's perception of value. These in turn are derived from customers' trust in the supplier and their perception of the supplier's commitment to them. Customer costs include acquisition costs, which include the initial price less discounts plus freight, installation and taxes, operational costs, including internal coordination, training, possible downtime, switching costs (discussed below), and eventual disposal of the products purchased, and finally, costs related to risk. These include both the risk to the firm which might be caused by a product which did not function correctly and personal career-related risks. Menon et al. believe that supplier trust reduces acquisition costs. In order to price a product correctly, a manager must understand exactly how the customer perceives all these costs and benefits. Menon et al. find that customers focus more on overall benefits in this calculation than they do on the costs.

As we have mentioned in earlier chapters, it is critical for the marketer to fully understand the customer's business, to be aware of the risks the customer faces and the ways in which the customer realizes success. Pricing in this way means setting price based on *value-in-use*. Shapiro and Jackson (1978) give an example of a DuPont pipe made of a particular resin. The pipe was introduced at a far greater price than its competition based on the fact that its life expectancy was much higher than the competitor's pipe. Since this product is buried below ground in many applications the cost to the customer of failure is significantly higher than the difference between DuPont's and the competitor's offerings. The company could then price the product based on its value to the customer or its value-in-use. Value-in-use pricing means the vendor captures some of the benefits realized by the customer. Macdonald et al. (2011) emphasize that value-in-use is a complex proposition and depends very much on the context. They question whether value is delivered solely by a single provider. In their conception, the customer is a co-creator of value and can define value-in-use in terms of their goals or objectives. Achieving these objectives requires employing internal as well as external assets throughout the customer's network. In addition the definition of value-in-use by the customer changes as the customer's goals change. They find two types of goals – preventative and promotional. The former focuses on solving problems and the latter on increasing organizational productivity or effectiveness. Sharma and Iyer (2011) show that traditional pricing strategies may not be useful in solution marketing since solutions often require special capabilities and knowledge for which costs are not easily determined for each transaction, economies of scale may not be realized, and customized solutions are unique and difficult to compare to competition. It is difficult for the solution provider to know what value the customer places on the solution. Supplier firms often believe they are selling solutions when in fact they are only selling bundled products and services which the customer can easily de-bundle. They conclude that most firms are using traditional pricing approaches and that value pricing models are being very infrequently used.

PRICE SENSITIVITY

We have already discussed the importance of segmentation in market planning. It should be obvious that establishing the needs of each segment is a precursor to developing appropriate pricing for each segment. In some cases, a product can be customized to meet the specific needs of a segment and priced quite profitably because of the customization. In setting prices for specific segments, the marketing director must estimate the price sensitivity of that particular market segment. Dolan (1995) listed factors that affect customer price sensitivity. See Table 10.3.

The major categories are customer economics, search and usage, and competition. Customers will be more sensitive, therefore decreasing the ability of the marketing manager to change his price, if the percentage expenditure for the particular item is large in comparison to the total expense that the customer is making to achieve a particular end. Pricing flexibility will also be reduced if the customer has to resell the product into a very competitive market. Should the item be of extreme importance to the successful operations of the customer's firm, price sensitivity will tend to decline because reliability becomes paramount.

Reviewing the search and usage category, customers will be more price sensitive if information search is easy and inexpensive and competitive offerings are easily compared. In addition, the customer's price sensitivity is increased substantially where switching costs are low. Switching costs are all the costs associated with changing from one particular product or service to another. For example, a firm might be standardized on a particular IBM computer system. A competing manufacturer, let us say Fujitsu, offers the customer a new computer system with demonstrably better features. However, the customer would hesitate to change knowing that the switching costs, including down-time, training, and the inevitable problems caused by such a major change would

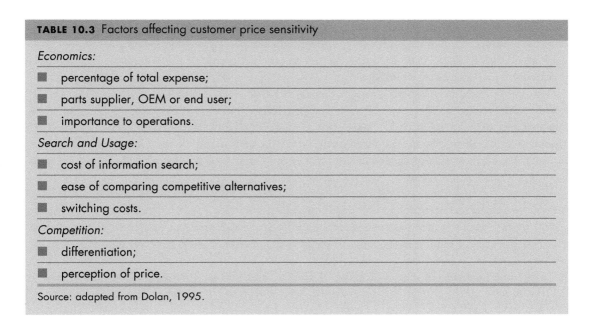

TABLE 10.3 Factors affecting customer price sensitivity

Economics:

■ percentage of total expense;

■ parts supplier, OEM or end user;

■ importance to operations.

Search and Usage:

■ cost of information search;

■ ease of comparing competitive alternatives;

■ switching costs.

Competition:

■ differentiation;

■ perception of price.

Source: adapted from Dolan, 1995.

be substantial. These costs may, indeed, outweigh the benefits seen from a potential new system. Finally, price sensitivity is decreased where the manufacturer's offering is clearly differentiated from its competition and where price perception gives an aura of quality to a particular product.

In Chapter 5, we discussed methods of estimating the total demand by market segment. One should employ these methods to develop an aggregate number for demand based on various pricing levels using the techniques described in that chapter.

COSTS

For marketing managers, developing reliable costs to use in pricing decisions is often a frustrating process. Often, many products are made in the same factory and the allocation of costs by the finance department is often arbitrary. Products which are easy to manufacture and have low material costs often assume too much of the overhead of a facility, making the marketing manager's task in pricing to meet market conditions quite difficult. In this regard, marketing people are advised to study the costing process used at a particular facility in-depth so that they can convincingly present their case for proper costing of particular product lines.

Activity based costing (ABC) allows a firm to more accurately determine what costs should be assigned to particular product lines and customers. According to Narayanan and Sarkar (2002), under ABC managers separately keep an account of expenses required to produce individual units and batches, to design and maintain and produce, and to keep the manufacturing facility running. ABC requires that costs be allocated not only to products but also to customers so that a manager can determine the cost to serve a particular customer. In Narayanan and Sarkar's study, Insteel

Corporation tracked overhead needed to serve special customer needs including packing and loading, order processing and invoicing, post-sales service, and the cost of carrying receivables. These costs were attributed to each customer and allocated to product based on the volume of each product purchased by a particular customer.

Through the ABC approach, Insteel discovered that at a particular plant studied, freight represented 16 percent of the total people and physical resources cost. After the detailed analysis, management decided to increase the weight shipped per truck load, resulting in a 20 percent reduction in freight expense. The visibility of the ABC system also allowed Insteel to change the product line and increase prices for less profitable products. As described above, developing costs for integrated solutions is much more difficult.

Although the high risks associated with it have been well-established, the idea of "pricing down the learning curve" is one which has persisted for at least two decades. Learning curve (or experience curve) theory simply states that costs decline rapidly with each doubling of output of a particular product. Experience curve effects come from three major sources (Day and Montgomery, 1983):

- Learning: increased efficiency because of practice and skill or finding new and better ways to do things.
- Technological improvements: new production processes and product changes which improve yield.
- Economies of scale: increased efficiency resulting from larger operations.

These improvements are especially relevant to investment and operating costs. Day and Montgomery found significant limitations of the strategic relevance for experience curve approaches and they warn against an all-out dedication to this approach. While it may give some advantages in some markets, it also introduces rigidity that may make the firm slower and less flexible in its ability to respond to customer or competitive changes. The experience curve will only be strategically relevant when the three major effects identified above are important in the strategic environment of a particular firm. Ames and Hlavacek (1984) point out that slavishly following the experience curve approach has yielded disastrous results, especially for established or mature products where gains through experience diminish rapidly.

Generally the aggressive (penetration) pricing approach to gain market share is justified in three circumstances. First, in new or underdeveloped markets where customers are very price sensitive, price may be the weapon of choice to establish a secure market presence before competitors can move. Second, where fixed and variable costs will assuredly drop with a rapid increase in volume. And finally where competitors are weak or have rigid high costs a firm may use pricing to place a severe strain on its competitors who will probably not be able to match the firm's lower prices (McKinsey Quarterly, 2003).

COMPETITION

Needless to say, understanding competitive offerings, including their prices, is critical. To begin with, a firm must be careful about setting its prices higher than the competition. This obviously depends upon the strategic position the firm finds itself in. Should the company be a leader in its market, it probably will price higher than its competitors. In monopolistic competition situations, smaller firms would realize no benefit by attempting to price lower than the dominant competitor since the large firm could easily match the smaller firm's prices or even retaliate by lowering prices further, putting a much larger financial strain on the smaller firm than it would realize itself.

In high growth or hyper-competitive markets, some firms may attempt simply to disturb the status quo as we have seen in Chapter 3. An important tool in these markets is the race to the next price point. While this is more common in consumer markets, there is a strong effect in B2B markets as well. Moore (1995) points out that when workstation prices were lowered to under $50,000 and then under $10,000 the result was "huge boosts in sales volumes." He continues, "the vendor who hits the next lowest price point engages a large new market segment who previously could not afford to take advantage of a particular product or technology. When a market leader does not move toward that price point rapidly, new aggressive competitors will do so." This is true even in the case where these smaller competitors have to sell below their costs. In the hyper-competitive situation, the learning curve has its most telling effect.

Countering direct competitive efforts requires creativity to differentiate the firm's offering from its competitors'. In Chapter 9, we described the transition from a product-centric company to a solutions provider and beyond that, too, a customer-value provider. One commodity chemical firm set up a new business unit to provide solutions selling to its customers. While expenses increased (selling, general, and administrative costs rose 5 percent), gross margins rose to 20 percent from 9 percent (Johanssen et al., 2003).

Understanding your competitors' current position is an important factor affecting the price but an equally important aspect of this decision is competitor reaction. Certainly, this aspect of pricing requires experience and knowledge. A correct assessment of competitors' reaction to increasing or decreasing price may determine whether the strategy chosen by the company is the correct one. Sophisticated companies are able to include in their data warehouse information about past competitive reactions to pricing moves. This knowledge can help the manager make more informed decisions about potential competitive actions.

Talking Point

International marketing director James Calvano suddenly received a phone call from Ahmed Markat, his sales manager in Istanbul. "Jim, what's going on? I just visited our customer, Cukuroba Electric, and they have been able to source transformers in Croatia at a 25 percent reduction from the prices we charge. Please let me know what to do." Calvano had been faced by this problem before. The company had a good distributor in Croatia who was taking advantage of the rebuilding in the Balkans. To get the business, Calvano had offered a very low price and the distributor had bought 100 large transformers.

Why doesn't the company just have the same price everywhere? Surely this type of price discrimination damages the reputation of the firm – so why make problems for yourself? Or maybe the new market makes it worth the small risk that someone will take advantage!

PRICING METHODS

Pricing methods are closely related to pricing objectives. Firms who wish to assure short-term profits start their pricing on the basis of cost. This is often true of firms in the earliest stages of internationalization. Some research shows that management pricing decisions vary by country of origin (Raymond, 2001). Some firms may elect to use a standard worldwide price based on all their fixed, variable, and export costs. Other exporters choose to differentiate pricing in various markets. In that case the firm uses three basic pricing methods (Cavusgil, 1996; Czinkota and Ronkainen, 2010):

- Rigid cost plus pricing: where the price is set simply by adding all the costs incurred for serving an international customer to the costs of manufacturing the product plus a margin.
- Flexible cost plus pricing: is similar to rigid cost plus pricing but allows for some price variation, such as discounts for large orders or to meet local competition.
- Dynamic incremental (market differentiated) pricing: assumes that fixed costs are incurred whether the firm sells outside its home market or not, so that the exporter seeks only to recover international variable costs.

Although many exporters use either the rigid cost plus or flexible cost plus approach, focusing on costs and competition rather than customer value in their pricing method, more sophisticated firms analyze cost and demand and develop prices for a target return on investment. This method generally assumes demand at a certain level and does not sufficiently take into account the changes in demand resulting from changes in price or potential competitive moves.

Firms using sales-oriented objectives attempt to set prices which will grow their sales in units or currency or increase market share. These approaches have been discussed in some depth above. Those with status quo objectives generally set prices to meet competition. Finally, firms who attempt to use value-in-use pricing base their pricing decision upon extensive work with customers. While it would be naïve to say that they should ignore costs entirely, marketing managers who wish to be successful must price from the market in, knowing customer needs and willingness to pay as well as competitors' offerings, current and future possible pricing. Should market prices in a particular country fall below the costs to serve customers in that country, management must reexamine the entire marketing strategy for that particular market and take steps to lower costs or decide not to serve customers in that particular market at that particular time.

A comprehensive study of research on export pricing completed by Tan and Sousa (2011) points out inconsistency and contradictory results in the 98 studies reviewed. One of their most important findings is the lack of convincing conclusions related to export performance resulting from the price adaptation versus standardization approach.

A special consideration for exporters is the escalation of price which can take place because of the additional costs of exporting, the import duties, and value added taxes (VAT) applied in various markets.

As can be seen from Table 10.4, a domestic product which is sold at the factory for $5 and is subject to the normal mark-ups by distributors and retailers might be sold to consumers for $9.38. This same product sent to an export market may be subject to the various costs escalations shown

TABLE 10.4 Escalation in export markets

Cost Factors	Domestic	Export Markets
Manufacturer's price at factory	5.00	5.00
+ Insurance, shipping (15%) (CIF)	–	0.75
Landed costs (CIF Value)	–	5.75
+ Tariff (20% of CIF Value)	–	1.15
Importer/distributor's cost	–	6.90
+ Importer/distributor's margin (25% of cost)	1.25	1.72
Subject to VAT (Full cost + margin)	–	8.62
+ VAT (18% on cost + margin)	–	1.55
Retailer's cost	6.25	10.17
+ Retailer's margin (50% on cost)	3.13	5.08
+ VAT (18% on margin)	–	0.91
Consumer price (Retailer's cost + margin + VAT)	9.38	16.16
% Escalation over domestic price	–	72%

Source: adapted from Becker (1980).

in Table 10.4, resulting in a consumer price 72 percent higher than that of the domestic price. (This table makes the assumption that the domestic market has no VAT.) Even adding VAT for the domestic market, export pricing can often be much higher. Managements can take several actions to reduce this price escalation, recommended by Czinkota and Ronkainen (2010). First the firm may attempt to eliminate some steps of distribution. In the example shown in Table 10.4, for simplicity, a number of wholesale steps were eliminated. But in some markets, especially in Japan, multiple steps of wholesaling are the norm. A marketer must examine eliminating some of these steps to keep the price escalation within reason.

A second method to reduce a final price in exporting is to adapt the product using lower cost components or ingredients and taking out costly additional features which can be made optional in particular markets. A third way to reduce escalation is to change tariff or tax classifications. This may require local lobbying of the taxing or importing authorities. A final method would be to assemble or produce overseas. Once foreign sourcing is established with far lower cost components, all costs applied to the product will be reduced. Shipping components to the local market for assembly is often a good cost-cutting approach. For instance, in Venezuela completed furniture products were subject to a punitive tariff of over 50 percent. An office furniture manufacturer decided to ship the product unassembled and then contract with a local assembler to put the pieces together. Unassembled components were subject to a tariff of only 10 percent. So, while assembly costs had to be added, the resulting market price was far lower than that realized when shipping in completed product.

PRICING POLICIES

Pricing policies include deciding upon list price and discount levels, allowances, rebates, and geographic differences (standardization vs. differentiation).

The question of list price varies by industry. In some industries, list prices are set in such a way that no customer ever pays that price. The list prices for a product line are set in order to provide various levels of discounts. Discounts can be given for volume purchases, whether cumulative or based on individual order, or based on time of order. As we have seen in Chapter 9, pricing for services is often used to manage demand.

Allowances and rebates are simply price reductions given to dealers or distributors to help them promote a particular manufacturer's product. Some firms give advertising allowances to their distributors in order to encourage them to promote their particular product or even for identifying their facilities such as showrooms or service vehicles with a particular brand name. A firm may choose to offer a trade-in allowance for older products in order to replace them with newer versions. A rebate is a fee paid to a purchaser once the product is bought and installed.

A firm must decide on its geographic policies. First and foremost will be whether one standard price will be established in all markets with the final local price determined by varying import duties, currency, and local laws. Differentiated pricing allows local distributors or sales agents to set prices.

LEGALITY OF PRICING POLICIES

Many nations regulate pricing in various ways. The most obvious controls relate to anti-competitive actions. In the EU and the United States, firms cannot collude to set prices and these kinds of laws are widely enacted although intermittently enforced in various other markets throughout the world. In the United States, a manufacturer must generally treat each class of customer equally. That is, the customer who buys a particular quantity of product should receive the same discount as another customer buying that same quantity. However, some exceptions to this rule are allowed. Manufacturers can use discriminatory pricing to meet a competitive threat in a particular market or if it can be proved that their costs to serve one customer are lower than another.

In setting international prices, another important issue is that of dumping. Dumping simply means that a product is sold in a particular market at a level less than its cost of production plus a reasonable profit margin. Anti-dumping penalties have increased in the United States, the EU, Canada, and Australia and this will continue to be a key issue in international marketing. Managers must be careful that their pricing decisions can be defended against anti-dumping accusations.

TRANSFER PRICING

Transfer pricing can have an important effect on pricing decisions. Transfer prices are those set for goods or services which are bought by one division of a firm from another division. These are inside or intra-corporate prices. As might be expected, local tax authorities are quite interested in the transfer prices set inside corporations. Creating artificial profits by pricing high from a low-tax jurisdiction may raise the attention of taxing authorities in the receiving higher tax nation.

Transfer pricing can also have a significant affect upon the motivation of local partners. If for tax reasons prices are set in such a way as to reduce the profits of a local subsidiary or joint venture, managers of this entity may become demotivated. This "softer" portion of the pricing decision between entities of a particular firm must also be taken into account.

DETERMINING PRICES FOR PRODUCTS AND PRODUCT LINES

The final step in our pricing process is to determine the actual prices. This requires an alchemy of customer perception, company needs, competition, environmental factors, and distribution. As seen in Figure 10.4, managers must decide how prices within a product line relate to one another and how total product line pricing relates to another product line's pricing. Setting the price for a product and attendant service requires a full analysis of all factors which may affect the customer decision and profitability as has been described above. Of course, a manager must be ready to react to competitive pricing moves. A useful exercise is to establish possible scenarios of competitive pricing moves, develop cost and customer information needed to make a decision in reaction to a competitor and then make a hypothetical decision.

TERMS OF SALE AND PAYMENT

Key items which can affect the pricing internationally are the terms of sale and terms of payment. Incoterms are standard terms of sale set by the International Chamber of Commerce. A new set of Incoterms went into effect 1 January 2011.

Incoterms specifically define the responsibilities of the buyer and the seller in any transaction. Table 10.5 shows some selected terms along with their explanations. As can be seen, EXW means Exworks. This is the minimum obligation of the seller to the buyer. In this case, the seller just makes the goods available, usually at his factory loading dock, and the buyer is responsible for all costs and risks from that point on. Other terms parcel out the risks and costs to the buyer and the seller in different ways as can be seen in Table 10.5. DDP – delivered duty paid – is the maximum obligation that the seller can take. In this case, the seller pays all the costs and assumes all the risks until delivery is made to the buyer. In addition, the seller is responsible for getting the product through customs, paying import duties, related taxes and so on. As one might guess, these terms of shipment and risk can be a source of competitive advantage and must be part of the overall equation used to determine pricing, including the charges for the product and/or service as well as the export payment method offered.

FINANCING FOREIGN TRADE

Although there are many terms of payment in international business, Table 10.6 shows those most often used.

TABLE 10.5 Selected Incoterms

Term	Explanation
EXW	Exworks – the seller needs only to make the goods available to the buyer at a specific place, usually the seller's factory. The buyer takes on all costs and risks from that point on.
FAS	Free Alongside Ship – seller delivers the goods alongside a vessel at a particular port and clears the goods for export. The buyer takes on all costs and risks from that point.
FOB	Free on Board – seller is responsible to load the goods on board the vessel chosen by the buyer. In this new rule, cost and risk are divided when the goods are actually on board the vessel. Some mistakenly use FOB as a synonym for EXW but according to Incoterm definitions it is quite different.
CIF	Cost, Insurance, Freight – seller pays transportation, freight, and insurance costs to the destination. The buyer has the risk of loss once delivery to the ship is made.
DDP	Delivered Duty Paid – seller delivers when the goods arrive at destination. Seller pays all costs and assumes all risks until delivery is made. The seller is responsible for import duties, taxes.

Source: Incoterms, 2010.

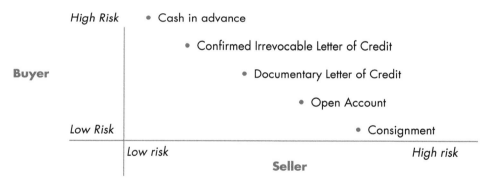

FIGURE 10.5 Export payment methods

In Figure 10.5, the buyer's risk has been placed on the vertical axis and the seller's risk on the horizontal axis. As can be seen, cash in advance reduces the risk of the seller while increasing the risk of the buyer, while consignment or open-account are high-risk strategies for the seller but low-risk for the buyer. Open account terms include payment by check, direct debit, electronic funds transfer or any other method that relies heavily on the buyer's eventual willingness to settle the debt after the goods have arrived. From the seller's viewpoint this is risky, since the buyer is in a foreign country and therefore enforcing the debt by legal action would prove extremely difficult. Once a relationship of trust has been established between a buyer and a seller, or in cases where the seller has reliable representation in the importing country, open-account is simple to use and may become inevitable.

A large percentage of international business is completed using letters of credit. With a documentary letter of credit, the importer's bank will pay for goods providing certain conditions are met, in most cases the presentation of a bill of lading or air waybill. There may be other requirements: an insurance certificate, pre-inspection certificate, dangerous goods notice, bank indemnities, and so forth. The drawback of this method is that the bank can, and indeed must, refuse payments unless all the conditions have been met exactly, even if the goods have been delivered on time and in perfect condition. The most common type is a confirmed, irrevocable letter of credit in which both the seller's bank and the buyer's bank are involved in the transaction. This allows the seller full confidence that his firm will be paid regardless of the creditworthiness of the buyer or the buyer's bank. Of course, the buyer will have to apply for a confirmed, irrevocable letter of credit and the issuing bank in the buyer's country will have to be sure that the buyer will have sufficient funds to cover it. Since the buyer often must borrow the funds to insure the letter, this approach, while comforting to the seller, may be a commercial drawback to completing a negotiation and may have a strong impact upon the price the seller can command from a buyer.

EFFECT OF THE INTERNET

Because the Internet has become so pervasive, a marketing manager must assume that any facts placed on the Internet will quickly be obtained by buyers throughout the world. Because there are price-oriented search engines, many firms are wary about putting their prices on the Internet so that comparisons are easily made. Where prices are posted, the Internet makes comparisons quite easy and therefore would dictate a standardized pricing policy rather than a differentiated one. If differentiated prices must be used, the website should explain why there is a price difference in a particular market based on additional costs for freight or distribution.

COMPETITIVE BIDDING

B2B sales are often completed through competitive bids. This is especially true for government institutions and non-profits such as hospitals. Some non-governmental firms also use competitive bids. In some cases, a firm may require a bid to a particular specification and then reserve the right to negotiate further with the winning bidder. Firms use specification buying especially for large projects. These firms develop detailed specifications based on the performance or description of a particular product or service or a combination of both. Firms supplying products or services to the military or large power plants or other major projects need to develop an expertise not only in the bidding process, but also in the specification process. "Specmanship" means a firm's sales force is expert at helping a customer develop specifications which will limit the bidders. The most successful salespeople can develop specifications with requirements that can be met only by their firm. When faced with a potential competitive bidding situation based on specifications to be developed by a large customer, it is necessary to spend the required time to influence the design of the specifications to ensure the most favorable specifications possible before bidding documents are released. As noted earlier in the chapter successful solutions marketing requires a supplying firm to develop a unique offering.

It takes as much work to develop a competitive bid as to create a business plan. It is not unusual for a firm to spend well over €100,000 to complete the analysis required to provide responsive bids to a particular customer. Before a firm decides to take on this major effort, a screening procedure should be completed. Table 10.6 shows a procedure for evaluating bid opportunities.

In this procedure, eight pre-bid factors should be examined. These factors are shown in Table 10.6. An analysis tool can be used to assign a weight to each factor and then rate the firm's capability for this particular bid. Multiplying the weights by the ratings gives a value for each factor and adding all of the values together gives the firm some idea of whether they should pursue this particular bid. Of course if there are other opportunities, these can be compared using this same tool.

The factors include plant capacity. The firm must consider whether winning this bid will place an unusual strain on the plant required to make the product or whether the plant is running at a relatively low level and can use additional work. Competition must be considered as well, both in terms of the number of competitors and their possible bids. Past experience with competitors will serve as a guide here. A third and most important area is the possibility for follow-up opportunities. In some cases, a firm winning a bid will be placed on a preferred supplier list (such as with a government) and many additional orders may follow. In addition, a firm may receive orders for associated products or services. Here, the marketer must be careful because many sophisticated purchasers will indicate a large follow-up to a particular order with the goal of pushing the supplier to reduce the initial price. The next factor is quantity. Obviously, a very large order is more attractive than a smaller one. Large orders for standard product with the same features is more attractive than an order for a mix of product. If the quantity can create economies of scale for a supplier, it will be more attractive than one which simply pushes a supplier past a point of diminishing returns. Delivery is a key consideration as well. In some cases, a large quantity of product is required to be delivered all at once. This may put an undue strain on the manufacturer's facilities.

TABLE 10.6 Evaluating bid opportunities

Pre-bid Factor	Weight (%)	Rating (1–10)	Value
Plant capacity	20	10	200
Competition	10	8	80
Follow-up opportunities	10	7	70
Quantity	10	7	70
Delivery	10	5	50
Profit	20	9	180
Experience	10	9	90
Bid capability	10	8	80
TOTAL	100%	N/A	820

Source: adapted from Paranka (1971).

Another important consideration is the effect of accepting this order on other customers, both from a delivery and plant capacity point of view. If a large order has the potential of reducing the manufacturer's capability to satisfy loyal customers in the future, it may not be as attractive. Obviously, profit is critical in deciding whether or not to move ahead. While this analysis must take place before final prices are determined, a general idea of the prices required to gain this order should be employed so that the firm can make an estimate of the possible profit to be realized. In some cases, a firm may decide that profit is not the overriding concern and that in order to fill the plant it will move ahead with a relative unprofitable bid. Another key factor is experience. As has been said, developing a winning bid for a particular project may take as much effort as an entire business plan for a new venture. If the firm has experience in developing bids of this particular kind, it should be looked upon more favorably. Finally, the bid capability means the availability of people and financial resources to actually complete the work. There may be times when the firm simply does not have the capability to do the required work and therefore the project becomes less attractive.

Table 10.7 shows a hypothetical bid situation where the firm has assigned weights to each of these factors and then rated the attractiveness of this bid along each one of the factors. The total value is then added and as can be seen for this particular bid opportunity the number is 820. It may be that the firm has set a minimum hurdle for proceeding with a bid. If we assume that hurdle might be 700 for this firm, it would proceed with the bidding process based on this score.

Once a firm has decided to move ahead, the firm must develop a pricing strategy. Pricing strategy for bids is the same as the general pricing strategy shown above. In some cases, a firm may price simply for survival in order to get some business to keep the plant running. In most cases, the firm will decide whether it wishes to gain market share, increase profitability or use any of the other strategies described above.

Internationally, insisting on competitive bidding can be a problem in a high-context culture, where the project will probably be given to the firm the buyers feel is best positioned to do it based on the past establishment of trust. However, in a low-context culture a firm would develop specifications and push the supplier to meet the specifications as written (Hall, 1976).

CASE STUDY

Crystal Components

Czech glass is a particularly attractive product in the chandelier industry. In northern Bohemia, glassworks have been in existence since the mid-fourteenth century and Czech crystal, which is colorless and ideal for engraving and cutting, has been particularly attractive to chandelier makers. In 1724, Josef Palme began making chandeliers in northern Bohemia. These chandeliers were acquired by King Louis XV, Maria Theresa, and the Russian Czarinas and some have been placed in La Scala in Milan and Versailles.

Thomas Klaus, president of Crystal Components, had established his firm as a major supplier of Czech glass components to the chandelier makers in the Czech Republic.

. . . continued

Now, he was thinking of moving into foreign markets. Preliminary research showed large numbers of chandelier makers in the EU, the US, and China. While they were quite capable of making chandeliers to equal the quality of those made in the Czech Republic, they would need the Czech glass to make these chandeliers world class in quality. So, he is most interested in establishing relationships with chandelier manufacturers as quickly as possible. A key question in his mind is the proper pricing for these components. He has established costs for spheres and ovals in the crystal formations used in the chandeliers and also has determined the import duties into each of the target markets. These are seen in Exhibit 10.1.

He knows that final prices of chandeliers range from €500 up to many thousands and each chandelier uses anywhere from 10 to 100 spheres, ovals or a combination of both. Since Crystal Components is a small firm, he also knows that he will need distributors to import the product into each of these markets and may have to provide some type of technical expertise to the chandelier manufacturers in their own languages. A quick analysis of the marketplace shows existing suppliers providing alternative product (not from the Czech Republic). Klaus has determined that competitors in general have the following prices for a 1 centimeter sphere – US$ 4.25, EU€ 4.50, China 30 yuan – and, in most cases, these firms are located within the markets he is concerned about.

Costs (all labor and materials)

Size:	Spheres:	Ovals:
1 cm	3.00 euro	4.00 euro
3 cm	5.00 euro	6.00 euro
5 cm	7.00 euro	8.00 euro

Import Duties

EU	15%
US	10%
China	25%

EXHIBIT 10.1 Crystal Components

CASE STUDY QUESTIONS

1 Which market(s) should Klaus move into first?
2 How should Klaus price his product in each of these markets based on the final pricing for his products?
3 How will this pricing affect the rest of Klaus's marketing strategy?

CHAPTER SUMMARY

As we have seen, price is a critical aspect of the overall marketing plan and must be totally congruent with the rest of the levers of the marketing machine. The most important points from this chapter are the following:

■ Marketing managers should attempt to give the highest possible price along the "stepped" demand curve to maximize the revenues for their firm.

■ Exceptions to this occur only in high tech, fast developing markets, where the quick race to the next price point is critical.

■ The overall pricing process moves through eight steps, starting with setting the pricing objective and ending with determining prices.

■ Pricing objectives may be profit-oriented, sales oriented, or status quo-oriented.

■ The pricing strategy must be developed considering firm, customer, competitor, distribution, and environmental variables.

■ Customers weigh functional, operational, financial, relational, and personal benefits against acquisition and internal costs as well as potential risks in determining whether a price is fair.

■ Some customers are more price sensitive than others. This is affected by the economics of the particular purchase, the cost of search and usage including switching costs, and competitive offerings available.

■ Developing reliable costs for product pricing is a difficult task for marketing people. Activity based costing helps assign costs to particular product lines and customers to get more accurate costs for their pricing.

■ Experience curve pricing is a dangerous strategy except in very limited circumstances.

■ Countering lower competitive costs may require the firm to look creatively at its offering and dictate that the firm attempt to become a customer-value provider rather than a product-centric company.

■ Many firms have taken the value-in-use approach one step further to solutions marketing, providing a package of product and services to help customers solve problems. Pricing of these solutions is complex.

■ International exporters generally use rigid cost plus or flexible cost plus approaches, but more sophisticated firms market differentiated pricing, working from the customer and using value-in-use pricing.

■ The firm must set pricing policies related to list price and discounts, allowances, rebates, and standardization versus differentiation for geographic areas. Pricing strategies seem to vary by culture.

■ When pricing, a firm must be careful to understand local laws regarding competition and dumping.

■ Transfer or intra-corporate prices are often scrutinized by local taxing authorities and may have a significant effect upon the motivation of local partners.

■ In setting prices, the marketing manager must decide upon the terms of sale and terms of payment. Standard terms of sale are provided by the International Chamber of Commerce. Frequently in international business, letters of credit are used to assure suppliers they will be paid. But other approaches may be required by commercial necessity.

■ Competitive bidding is a major factor in B2B markets. A wise firm employs knowledgeable salespeople to influence the specifications on which bids will be made.

■ Firms should employ an evaluation procedure to decide whether or not to move ahead with a particular bid.

REVIEW QUESTIONS

1 Describe the "magic of price" as it is explained in the text.
2 List the factors in the pricing process.
3 What are the three major types of pricing objectives firms may use?
4 In developing a pricing strategy, what factors should a manager consider?
5 How does the customer perceive costs and benefits in weighing whether a price seems fair?
6 How can a firm use value-in-use and solutions marketing in developing pricing?
7 What affects a customer's price sensitivity?
8 Explain the concept of switching cost.
9 How can a manager develop accurate costs to be used in his pricing decision?
10 When should the experience curve be used as a basis for pricing and when not?
11 What are the most common pricing methods used by international exporters? What are the benefits and drawbacks to these methods?
12 In developing pricing policies, what should an international firm consider?
13 How can transfer pricing affect the results realized by local partners?
14 List the most common Incoterms and the most common export payment methods.
15 What are the advantages and disadvantages of each and how do they relate to one another?
16 When a firm enters a competitive bidding situation, how might they analyze the attractiveness of entering a particular bid?

REFERENCES

Ames, B. Charles and Hlavacek, James D. (1984). *Managerial Marketing for Industrial Firms*. New York: Random House.

Becker, Helmut (1980). "Pricing: An International Marketing Challenge" in Thorelli, Hans and Becker, Helmut (eds), *International Marketing Strategy*. New York: Pergamon Press.

Cavusgil, Tamer S. (1996). "Pricing for Global Markets." *Columbia Journal of World Business*, Vol. 31, Iss. 4, Winter, 66–78.

Cespedes, Frank V. (1994). "Industrial Marketing: Managing New Requirements." *Sloan Management Review*, Vol. 35, Iss. 3, Spring, 45–60.

Czinkota, Michael and Ronkainen, Ilkka A. (2010). *International Marketing*, 9th ed. Mason, OH: Southwestern Cengage Learning.

Day, George S. and Montgomery, David B. (1983). "Diagnosing the Experience Curve." *Journal of Marketing*, Vol. 47, Iss. 44, Spring, 44–58.

Dolan, Robert J. (1995). "How Do You Know When the Price is Right?" *Harvard Business Review*, Vol. 73, Iss. 5, 174–83.

Hall, Edward T. (1976). "How Cultures Collide." *Psychology Today*, July, 66–97.

Hollensen, Svend (1998). *Global Marketing: A Market Responsive Approach*. Hertfordshire, UK: Prentice-Hall Europe.

Incoterms (2010). *Incoterms 2010*. Paris: ICC Publishing, S.A. Accessed at http://www.iccwbo.org/products-and-services/trade-facilitation/incoterms-2010/

Johanssen, Juliet E., Krishnamurthy, Chandru, and Schlissberg, Henry E. (2003). "Solving the Solutions Problem." *McKinsey Quarterly*, Iss. 3, 116–126.

Macdonald, Emma K., Wilson, Hugh, Martinez, Veronica, and Toossi, Amir (2011). "Assessing value-in-use: A conceptual framework and exploratory study." *Industrial Marketing Management*, Vol. 40, Iss. 5, July, 671–82.

McKinsey Quarterly (2003). "Penetration Pricing." *McKinsey Quarterly*, Iss. 3, 46–7.

Menon, A., Homburg, C. and Beutin, N. (2005). "Understanding Customer Value in Business-to-Business Relationships." *Journal Of Business-To-Business Marketing*, Vol. 12. Iss. 2, 1–35.

Moore, Geoffrey A. (1995). *Inside the Tornado*. New York: Harper Collins.

Narayanan, V.G. and Sarkar, Ratna G. (2002). "The Impact of Activity-Based Costing on Managerial Decisions at Insteel Industries – A Field Study." *Journal of Economics and Management Strategy*, Vol. 11, No. 2, Summer, 257–88.

Paranka, Stephen (1971). "Competitive Bidding Strategy." *Business Horizons*, Vol. 14, Iss. 3, June, 39–43.

Perrault, William D., Jr., Cannon, Joseph P., and McCarthy, E. Jerome (2010). *Essentials Of Marketing: A Marketing Strategy Planning Approach* (12th ed.), New York: McGraw-Hill.

Raymond, Mary Anne, Tanner, John F., Jr., and Jonghoon, Kim (2001). "Cost Complexity of Pricing Decisions for Exporters in Developing and Emerging Markets." *Journal Of International Marketing*, Vol. 9, No. 3, 19–40.

Shapiro, Benson P. and Jackson, Barbara B. (1978). "Industrial Pricing to Meet Customer Needs." *Harvard Business Review*, Vol. 56, Iss. 6, Nov.–Dec., 119–27.

Sharma, Arun R. and Iyer, Gopalkrishnan (2011). "Are pricing policies an impediment to the success of customer solutions?" *Industrial Marketing Management*, Vol. 40, Iss. 5, July, 723–9.

Tan, Q. and Sousa, C. (2011). "Research on Export Pricing: Still Moving Toward Maturity." *Journal Of International Marketing*, Vol. 19, Iss. 3, 1–35.

Chapter 11

Supply chain management

INTRODUCTION

Ensuring that the goods arrive at the customer's premises at the right time, in the right quantities, and at the right price is at the heart of marketing. In the past, simply ensuring that the delivery truck was reliable and the driver knew where to go was sufficient, but in recent years a much wider-ranging view has been taken of the process of taking raw materials and converting them to customer satisfaction.

Particularly in the global context, this process involves many different companies, often in different countries, each with their own needs. Managing this complex chain of supply efficiently is one of the ways firms can improve their profit margins and competitive position.

CHAPTER OBJECTIVES

After reading this chapter, you should be able to:

- explain the difference between logistics and physical distribution
- describe the key elements in managing the supply chain
- describe the key terms in exporting
- explain the role of relationships in supply chain management
- explain how to maintain relationships in the supply chain
- describe some of the difficulties inherent in managing global supply chains.

MANAGING THE SUPPLY CHAIN

Supply chain management has been described as the integration of business processes from end user through original suppliers to provide products, services, and information that add value for customers (Cooper et al., 1997). The critical element in managing the supply chain is to ensure that value is added for customers: in order to do this, the supply chain needs to be coordinated and needs to become as seamless as possible.

For business to business marketers this has two implications. First, it implies that the marketer needs to work at establishing relationships with both suppliers and customers, and in most cases will need to be prepared to change the firm's working practices in order to accommodate the needs of other firms in the supply chain. Second, it means that seeking new customers will mean fitting into an existing supply chain, where the rules and practices are already well-established.

In order for relationships to work at optimum efficiency within the supply chain, the members need to share information about strategic plans, new product development, and customer profiles and much else. This information is commercially sensitive, so a great deal of trust is necessary. Goods flow down the supply chain, but information flows up it, enabling the various members of the chain to plan around the reality of existing market conditions. Effective supply chain management is a powerful tool for creating competitive advantage for the following reasons (Quinn, 2000):

- It reduces costs.
- It improves asset utilization.
- It reduces order cycle time, thus speeding up delivery of customer satisfaction.

Effective supply chain management can also shut out competitors by denying them access to sources of components or raw materials. For example, when CD players were first marketed the only sources of supply for the CD drives were three factories in Taiwan, all of whom were under exclusive contract to Japanese electronics manufacturers. This effectively shut out European and US manufacturers until they could develop the manufacturing capacity themselves – a somewhat ironic position for the Europeans, since the technology was originally developed in the UK.

The goals of supply chain management are shown in Table 11.1.

If the supply chain is properly managed, it should create tangible benefits for customers in terms of reduced waste, more flexible and reliable deliveries, and improved costs. For the members of the supply chain, it should increase security of supply, make planning easier, reduce costs, and reduce competitive pressures. There have been many studies which have demonstrated the advantages of integrating the supply chain: Ferguson (2000) demonstrated that best-practice supply chain management (SCM) companies have a 45 percent cost advantage over median supply chain competitors. On the other hand, supply chain glitches have been shown to cause an average 9 percent drop in the value of the company's shares on the day the problem is announced, and up to 20 percent decline in the six months following the announcement (Bowman, 2001). In global supply chain management, there are four strategic marketing challenges (Flint, 2004). These are:

1   Customer value learning. Finding out what customers regard as valuable is complex in the global environment, because supplying firms need to consider differing decision-making processes,

TABLE 11.1 Goals of supply chain management

Waste reduction	By minimizing duplication, harmonizing operations and systems, and reducing inventories waste is reduced. For example, harmonizing materials handling equipment reduces the need for loading and unloading components and also creates economies of scale in purchasing equipment and containers.
Time compression	Improved information flows about market conditions enable supply chain members to predict demand more accurately and thus make response times quicker. Also, preferred-customer status within the supply chain means that each member responds more quickly to the needs of other members than to the needs of non-members. Reducing response times improves cashflow for all members because deliveries happen faster so invoices are paid sooner.
Flexible response	Ensuring flexibility in the supply chain means that all the members are able to adjust more quickly to changing market conditions. This can lead to major improvements in competitive advantage.
Unit cost reduction	Good supply-chain management seeks to reduce unit costs, which will either allow the firms in the chain to make more money or will allow them to reduce the price to the end consumer, which again offers a competitive advantage. Cost is not necessarily the same as price: a customer operating a just-in-time manufacturing system may accept a slightly higher price for receiving small daily deliveries rather than paying a lower price for one large monthly delivery, because the savings in terms of holding stocks will outweigh the extra outlay.

differing decision-maker values, different importance rankings of service versus physical attribute values, and so forth. The value chain may span several different cultures, so that each link in the chain must be considered separately as well as how it fits into the whole.

2 Understanding customer value change. Customers often change what they value as changing circumstances dictate. Because changes happen at different times in different countries, customer value is a moving target.

3 Delivering value in a world of uncertainty. Because change is constant, and may even be accelerating, it is virtually impossible to integrate the strategies of firms which are often thousands of miles apart and being pulled in different directions by local changes in the business environment.

4 The customer value process. In order to meet the problems raised by the first three challenges, marketers may need to shift from a functional toward a process orientation. This may be difficult, in that shareholders believe that they have invested in a company rather than in a supply chain, which makes it difficult for the process to be seamless.

These challenges will differ in importance from one firm to another, and the solutions will be widely varying, but these are not challenges which a global firm can ignore. Success in integrating the supply chain provides an important competitive advantage, and, given that globalization also provides the best opportunities for minimizing total costs, managing the global supply chain effectively is a powerful route to growth.

LOGISTICS VERSUS PHYSICAL DISTRIBUTION

Physical distribution is concerned with the movement of goods via road, rail, sea, and air. It is the process of organizing transportation which will move the goods in a timely, secure manner within a reasonable budget, taking all factors into account.

Logistics is a word borrowed from military terminology. The logistics approach takes a holistic view of the movement of goods, examining the whole process from raw materials through to final consumer. The intention behind the logistics approach is to integrate the various transport systems involved in order to ensure a smooth flow of goods.

The advantages of taking a logistics approach can be spectacular. For example, until the 1970s goods being transported by sea would often be loaded by hand onto a truck at the factory, taken to a train station where they would again be loaded by hand onto a railway truck, then taken to the docks where they would be handled again onto the ship. At the destination port, the reverse procedure would apply. Working each hold on a ship required a total of eighteen men, not counting the ship's crew: one gang of eight men on the dock, another gang of eight in the hold, and two men operating winches. One ship's officer would also be needed to supervise loading, in order to ensure that the ship's trim was not disturbed.

Looking at the problem from a logistics viewpoint led to the widespread introduction of containers. These are filled at the factory, then transported by train, truck or ship to the destination warehouse in the foreign country. Loading onto a ship now requires only five men: two on the dock to attach the lifting gear, one man in a container hoist, and two more men in the hold to detach the lifting gear. In some container ports the lifting cranes are designed to eliminate the need for the men on the ground, thus reducing the former eighteen men to only one, who is able to load several hundred tons an hour. The result of this has been a dramatic drop in the number of ships needed, since ships only spend hours in port instead of days, and a corresponding drop in the number of dock workers needed.

The concept of supply chain management is central to logistics. Place, time, and value are central features of logistics management, with transport and warehousing functioning as the intermediate links rather than the central concern. It is in the transport and warehousing operations that costs can be reduced, and the recent rapid development of information technology has greatly increased the possibilities for doing this. For a logistics operation to be successful on the international scale, two main criteria must be satisfied: firstly, the people working in the various countries need to be coordinated in an effective and professional manner, and secondly there must be a high level of specialist knowledge of the laws, conventions, product quality controls, and regulations in each country the goods must pass through.

Coordinating the professionals requires the following factors to be in place:

- Data communication needs to be transparent, with all those involved being kept informed as to what is happening to the goods.
- There must be a coordinating philosophy or set of rules to which all those involved should subscribe.

IT systems have enabled logistics coordinators to track consignments in real time wherever they are in the world. This enables effective use of resources: aircraft can always fly full, ships can be loaded swiftly and spend more time at sea, warehouses can be smaller because goods stay for shorter periods of time. For example, Solaglas (the UK's largest glass transporting company) uses TruckStops technology to manage the movements of its 125 trucks. Glass transportation is highly specialized, due in part to the fragile nature of the product and in part to the wide range of types of glass carried. Delivery requests are managed by a central computer system which tells loaders at the depots which products need to go where in each truck in order to facilitate unloading. Drivers carry a small computer in the cab which tells them which delivery is to go to which customer, and the delivery time and location is sent back to the company's central computer via GPS: the truck's satnav then gives the driver directions to the next drop. The system was tested at the firm's Dudley depot, and resulted in a reduction in the size of the fleet from 11 trucks to 7, at a saving of £60,000 per truck. The system reduced the distance driven by 1,000 kilometers per week (about 625 miles) and 100 liters of fuel (worth around £130). (Source: http://www.truckstopsrouting.com).

Another use of IT has been to minimize wasted journeys or part-full journeys. An example of how IT has been successful in facilitating this is the Delego company of Sweden. Delego was started by two truck drivers who met by chance on a ferry from Denmark to Germany. Chatting to other drivers over a few beers, the two truckers realized that several of their erstwhile colleagues were travelling between the same two points, but with only half-full or even empty trucks. The two truckers planned a new system for organizing part-loads, and eventually gave up their trucking jobs, borrowed some capital, and started the Delego website. The system works through the Internet: when a transport company has an empty or part-empty truck on a given route, the company enters its details on the Delego website (or by telephone), and Delego tries to match up the truck with a cargo, providing an estimate of the financial return for the trucker. Interestingly, use of IT does not necessarily improve supply chain management (even if it does improve logistics), largely because the individual firms' systems are often incompatible, and coordinating them throughout the supply chain is almost impossible as a result (Wu et al., 2006).

Talking Point

Whenever firms talk about becoming more efficient they seem to regard job losses as inevitable. In fact, many go further – they actively try to get rid of staff. And yet business is about people. Without people nothing happens – and if people are not earning money, how are they going to buy the goods that the manufacturers produce?

Furthermore, if firms keep on firing their staff, the company is shrinking – yet isn't it part of the imperative for companies in a capitalist world that they should grow?

Or maybe it's about restructuring – shifting people from inefficient jobs into efficient ones, and from jobs which are basically "make-work" into jobs which produce real value for everybody – company, customers and yes, even the workers! One thing's for sure – continual changes in working practices make for interesting times.

A recent technological development in tracking deliveries is the use of radio-frequency identification (RFID). This works by using a tag which can be identified automatically by radio equipment (rather like the smart card technology used on some city transportation systems, e.g. the Oyster cards used by London Transport or the Clipper ticket on the San Francisco BART). The RFID system knows when a shipment has passed through a warehouse or has been loaded onto a ship, without the need for a human operator to check it off against a list. At present, the main problem with RFID is that it requires all the operators in the logistics system to use the equipment – something that is still somewhat in the future (Kim et al., 2008).

Logistics has become widely adopted by global firms. Shipping and trucking companies are therefore redefining themselves as logistics facilitators. This means that such companies take responsibility for the whole process, moving goods from the factory gates to the final destination by whatever means are available. This leads to even greater savings for the businesses involved, since the process operates much more smoothly.

Logistics managers are responsible for some or all of the following interfaces:

- collaboration with physical distribution, which involves selecting transportation methods such as road, rail, sea, or air
- optimization of the material flow within the work center
- planning and organizing the storage area layouts, and the type of handling equipment involved
- selection of suppliers for raw materials, price levels, and specifications
- selection of subcontractors to perform specific tasks
- organizing after-sales activities, including problem resolution with supplied products
- verifying that sales forecasts accord with the real needs of the client
- developing delivery schedules
- developing packaging to meet the need for physical strength and security.

Logistics managing firms appear to be more successful if they have a market-oriented culture, with coaching and staff training having important roles in improving corporate performance (Ellinger et al., 2008).

Not all elements of the logistical system are controllable by the logistics manager. Transport delays, changes in legislation requiring new documentation, the bankruptcy of distribution channel members, or even the weather can play havoc with the best-laid logistical systems. This means that even greater care should be taken with those elements which are controllable.

Table 11.2 shows the elements which are controllable.

As with many other complex decisions, each element of the logistics system impacts on every other element. If the supplier is unreliable, the customer may have to bear the extra cost of holding large buffer stocks: additionally, if supplies fail, the customer may lose production or even customers. Clearly customers in many markets will favor reliable suppliers, and will even pay premium prices for this, so a good logistics system is likely to have pay-offs on the bottom line in terms of improved profits and possibly improved competitor advantage.

In practice, two main variables must be traded off against each other (see Fig 11.1). The first is the total distribution cost, which would generally be regarded as something which should be kept to a minimum. The second variable is the level of logistical service given to customers. As service

TABLE 11.2 Controllable elements in a logistics system

Element	Description
Customer service	Customer service is the product of all logistics activities. It relates to the effectiveness of the system in creating time and place utility. The level of customer service provided by the supplier has a direct impact on total cost, market share, and profitability. Service effectiveness has been shown to be the most important factor in third-party logistics supply, with price in second place (Tsai et al., 2007).
Order processing	This affects costs and customer service levels, because it is the starting point for all logistics activities. The speed and accuracy of order processing clearly affects customer service: this is particularly true in global markets, where errors or delays become multiplied by distance, and by the time it takes to make corrections.
Logistics communications	The way in which information is channeled within the distribution system affects the smooth running of the logistics. For example, a good progress-chasing system will allow deliveries to be tracked and therefore customer reassurance will be greater.
Transportation	The physical movement of the goods is often the most significant cost area in the logistics process. It involves the most complex decisions concerning carriers and routes, and is therefore often most prone to errors and delays.
Warehousing	Storage space serves as the buffer between production and consumption. Efficient warehousing reduces transportation costs by ensuring that (for example) containers are shipped full, and transport systems are fully utilized.
Inventory control	This ensures that the correct mix of products is available for customers, and also ensures that stocks are kept at a reasonable level to avoid having too much capital tied up.
Packaging	The purpose of packaging is primarily to protect the contents from the environment and vice versa. It also serves as a location for some shipping instructions, e.g. port of destination.
Materials handling	Picking stock to be included in an order is potentially a time-consuming and therefore expensive activity. Some warehouses have the capacity to automate the system, so that robots select the products and bring them to the point from which they will be shipped.
Production planning	Utilized in conjunction with logistics planning, production planning ensures that products are available in the right quantities and at the right times.
Plant and warehouse location	The location of the firm's facilities should be planned so as to minimize delivery times (and therefore minimize customer response times) as well as ensure that the costs of buying or renting space are minimized. This will often result in difficult decisions, since space near customers is likely to be more expensive than space in (for example) remote rural locations.

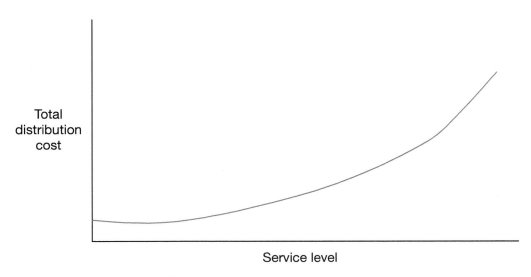

Total
distribution
cost

Service level

FIGURE 11.1 Logistics trade-offs

improves, costs will rise, and there is likely to be a diminishing return for extra expenditure: in other words, there is a point at which further expenditure is unlikely to make a material improvement in service levels.

Firms need to trade off these cost and service level considerations in such a way as to maximize the firm's ability to achieve its strategic objectives. The total-cost approach to logistics management attempts to balance these by assuming that all logistical decisions impact on all other logistical problems, so management needs to look at the efficiency of the system as a whole rather than only concerning itself with individual elements of the structure. The interactions between the elements are described as cost trade-offs, because an increase in one cost may be matched by a decrease in another. Reducing overall costs is the aim of this approach, but there are difficulties.

For example, the separate elements of the logistical system will almost certainly be controlled by different firms, each with its own cost structure and strategic aims. Thus an increase in cost for one element of the system will not be offset by a reduction in cost elsewhere, since the gainer and the loser are actually different firms. Even within a single firm, different departments will have their own budgetary constraints – managers may not be prepared to lose out so that someone else in the organization can gain. Any attempt to organize the logistical system as a seamless whole must take account of these problems, which of course places a premium on supply chain integration.

In some cases, the business must maintain the highest possible service levels whatever the cost. For example, delivery of urgent medical supplies is not cost-sensitive, but it is highly service-sensitive. At the other extreme, delivery of paper for recycling is unlikely to be service-sensitive, but almost certainly will be cost-sensitive.

Determining the level of service is a complex problem because it is difficult to calculate the possible revenue gains from an improvement in customer service levels. This calculation needs to be made in the light of competitive pressures, customer preferences, industry norms and so forth.

The cost element is much easier to calculate, and the net result needs to be a trade-off between the two elements. One study found that a 5 percent reduction in customer service levels resulted in a 20 percent decrease in sales (LaLonde et al., 1988).

ESTABLISHING AND MAINTAINING RELATIONSHIPS

Relationships exist not only between suppliers and purchasers, but also across several other categories of partner. Morgan and Hunt (1994) offered the following categorization:

- supplier partnerships

  - goods suppliers
  - services suppliers

- lateral partnerships

  - competitors
  - non-profit organizations
  - government

- buyer partnerships

  - intermediate customers
  - ultimate customers

- internal partnerships

  - business units
  - employment
  - functional departments.

From a marketer's viewpoint, the most important set of relationships here will be the buyer relationships, but this does not mean that the other relationships can safely be ignored. In terms of supply-chain management, these relationships are important as they ensure that the firm's place in the supply chain and its ability to contribute effectively are assured. For Morgan and Hunt (1994), relationship marketing refers to all marketing activities directed toward establishing, developing, and maintaining successful relational exchanges. This led them to develop the commitment–trust theory, which states that those networks characterized by relationship commitment and trust engender cooperation, a reduced tendency to leave the network, the belief that conflict will be functional rather than damaging, and reduced uncertainty.

All relationships (whether business or personal) are affected by the degree of trust which exists between the parties. Establishing a relationship of trust between businesses can be a complex affair, since many different individuals will need to be part of the process and consequently part of the outcome. There is more on this in Chapter 12.

CHANNEL SYSTEM ORIENTATION

In order to overcome some of the problems inherent in having a logistical system made up of several companies, supply-chain management seeks to synchronize channel activities through a series of negotiations which divide up the overall profits between members. At least in theory, this should make all members better off, since overall costs will fall and service levels will rise. In this scenario, relationships between the channel members must be seen as long-term, permanent, totally honest, and highly cooperative if savings are to result. The system also needs to be flexible, and it has been argued that purchasing and supply needs to become entrepreneurial (Guinipero et al., 2005). The main mechanism for dividing up the revenue gained from selling goods is price: pricing between chain members will determine the proportion of the overall profit each member gets, but it has been argued that pricing should be a joint tool, agreed by all members in order to optimize the marketing outcomes. This approach, it is argued, should replace the internal pricing processes which usually occur in firms (Christopher and Gattorna, 2005; Voeth and Herbst, 2006).

Companies with effective logistics systems grow 8 percent faster than those without, realize a 7 percent price premium, and are 12 times as profitable as firms with inferior service levels (Novich, 1992). Setting the service level may or may not be a function of profitability: much depends on the strategic aim of the company involved. This means that it may be possible to help a partner firm to achieve a strategic aim in exchange for a concession on profitability.

Key elements in welding the channel into a single system are as follows:

- Develop information systems which provide realistic sales forecasts for channel members.
- Standardize packaging and handling systems (for example by using palletization or containerization).
- Provide services (e.g. warehousing or data handling services) which improve efficiency for everyone (usually provided by the channel leader).
- "Pool" shipments to avoid the "empty truck" problem.

Since the service level is sometimes the only strategic advantage the channel has, there are obvious advantages in coming to an agreement and integrating the system. Unfortunately, such integration may take some years to achieve, since relationships of trust take time to establish. Supply chain management implies a greater degree of integration than does logistics management: SCM implies integration of all the business systems of the channel members, whereas logistics is only concerned with integrating the systems relating to the movement of goods. Inertia in the supply chain can reduce service levels – the inability to respond quickly to shifts in demand can result in poorer service, and firms often have difficulty in responding to customer pressure (Smith et al., 2005).

Managing the supply chain needs to include managing reverse logistics – the return of faulty or unwanted goods. Formalizing the reverse logistics systems tends to increase profitability and reduce inventory levels, since (for example) the return of a faulty product for repair or replacement will be completed more quickly. This in turn increases customer satisfaction, which is always a good thing (Autry, 2005). Given that most suppliers nowadays tend to have very liberal returns policies, reverse logistics has become a hot issue.

INVENTORY MANAGEMENT

Inventory management is the buffer in the logistical system. Inventories are essential in business to business markets because production and demand never quite match. This means that there are times when the producers need to stockpile product, and times when the demand outstrips supply and stockpiled products are released onto the market. This ensures a smooth flow of goods to the final users.

Operating deficiencies in the system will sometimes result in delays in delivery, in which case stocks can be used: also, industrial buyers cannot predict demand accurately because they are themselves relying (ultimately) on consumer demand, which is volatile. As we saw in Chapter 1, demand in business to business markets is much more volatile than that in consumer markets because of derived demand.

The attempt by some firms to introduce just-in-time purchasing in which the purchasing firm does not hold stocks, but instead shifts the responsibility for maintaining inventories onto the suppliers, does not accord with the systems approach to logistics, since it does not take account of the whole supply chain. Some have questioned the efficiency of JIT recently because of the tendency for it to contribute to traffic congestion as trucks make more frequent deliveries, and also its tendency to increase costs for suppliers since they frequently need to make smaller deliveries, as well as provide more warehouse space. See Table 11.3 for a summary of the impact of just-in-time on the marketing firm.

Estimates of future sales are the key element in controlling the logistics system. These estimates need to be far more accurate than the general ones used for planning sales promotions or other long-term marketing plans: the logistics and inventory forecast needs to be flexible enough to operate on a day-to-day basis if necessary. This requires some fairly sophisticated computer technology, which should be linked throughout the supply chain so as to enable firms further up the chain to

Talking Point

Just-in-time inventory management means arranging for components to arrive almost exactly at the moment when they are needed at the customer's factory. This obviously results in savings for the customer – but what about the supplier? Suppliers need to deliver small amounts frequently rather than large amounts periodically – so they use smaller vehicles, and more of them, and often park just outside the customer's gates until the exact minute for delivery.

Fine for the customer, of course, but wouldn't the supplier pass those costs on? Somebody has to keep the inventory – and somebody has to pay for it. Ultimately it's the end customer who pays. And what about the impact on the environment? All those extra vehicles clogging the streets and parking spaces cannot be a good thing!

Yet if ALL firms could arrange the logistics in a JIT manner, wouldn't the flow of goods from raw materials to finished products be a real process, instead of a lot of starts and stops? Maybe JIT has something to offer after all!

TABLE 11.3 Effects of JIT on marketing firms

Activity	Impact
Transportation	Because the number of shipments increases, the quantity ordered each time decreases. The shipments also need to meet the exact demands of the customer, and are non-negotiable, so the supplier must be flexible. In one study, 49 percent of companies using JIT said that the inability of suppliers to deliver to their specifications was a problem (Celley et al., 1986).
Field warehousing	Shipping over long distances may not be feasible because of the inherent unreliability of transportation, so smaller, more numerous warehouses will be needed. In addition, the use of third-party warehousing may be unsuitable because the customer will require absolute reliability: the supplier may not feel that a third party can be trusted sufficiently.
Field inventory control	Inventory levels of producers may need to be increased as customers will be totally unable to tolerate stockouts under any circumstances. Because of the need for 100 percent control of inventory, the producer may need to take over all the distribution functions.
Protective packaging	Packaging may be changed or even eliminated in some cases because the goods will be used immediately in production. This is a rare case where just-in-time might benefit the vendor.
Materials handling	There may be few changes here, but because quantities delivered are much smaller, it may not be feasible to use (for example) containerization as a way of reducing handling.
Order processing	The simplest way of dealing with this is electronically. The situation will inevitably become more complex as more frequent deliveries, at clearly-specified times, become necessary.

predict demand. Falling inventory at the retailer means increased demand at the wholesaler, the manufacturer, the component supplier, and the raw material supplier in that order, but delays in the system mean that increased demand at the retail level will perhaps take several months to filter through to the raw material level.

INTERNATIONAL TRADE

Table 11.4 shows the most common documents used in international trade.

This comprehensive list of paperwork may not be necessary for all shipments. There is considerable duplication, in other words. Having said that, trucks travelling through Europe may need to carry large amounts of paperwork to satisfy the formalities at each border, once the truck has left the European Union. Standardizing the documentation for trucks was a major issue within the EU in its attempts to maximize the free flow of goods throughout the Union, but of course the system is not perfect because member states are still permitted to ban imports from other member states if their Governments believe that the imports represent a threat to human or animal life. This was the justification for the French ban on British beef imports during the late 1990s, and is the justification for the British restrictions on the import of live shellfish from the rest of the European Union. In the United States virtually all border controls between the states have been abolished, but differences in state taxation mean that some products (especially cigarettes) are still worth smuggling internally. A pack of cigarettes which sells for $13 in New York would retail for $4.50 in Virginia – a difference making it well worthwhile to drive 350 miles each way. California maintains restrictions on imports of plants and fruit, for fear of importing an epidemic which would damage the state's lucrative fruit farming.

TABLE 11.4 Trade documentation

Export document	Description
Ocean bill of lading	The contract between the shipper and the carrier. The bill of lading is a receipt given by the carrier (often issued by the ship's purser) which proves that the goods were loaded. It has often been used as proof of ownership, so that it matches with the cargo unloaded, and can be bought and sold.
Export declaration	This includes complete particulars of the product and its destination, and is used to control exports and compile statistical information about exports.
Letter of credit	This is a financial document issued by the importer's bank, guaranteeing payment to the exporter subject to certain conditions (often the presentation of a bill of lading to prove that the goods were shipped).
Commercial invoice	The bill for the goods from the seller to the buyer. Often used by customs officials to determine the true value of the goods.
Certificate of origin	This document assures the buyer that the goods have not already been shipped from a country with which, for example, a trade embargo applies. These certificates are often provided by a recognized Chamber of Commerce in the exporting country.
Insurance certificate	This assures the importer that insurance is in place to cover the loss of, or damage to, the goods in transit.
Transmittal letter	A list of the particulars of the shipment and a record of the documents being transmitted, together with instructions for disposition of documents.
Customs entry	This provides information about the goods, their origin, estimated value, and destination. This is for the purpose of assessing customs duty.
Carrier's certificate and release order	A document to advise customs of the details of the shipment, its ownership, port of loading, and so forth. This certificate proves the ownership of the goods for customs purposes.
Delivery order	The consignee, or his customs broker, issues this to the ocean carrier as authority to release the cargo to the inland carrier. It includes all the data necessary to ascertain that the cargo may be released.

Talking Point

Obviously world trade is important. We can each make what we are good at making, and we can profit from ideas from other countries. Also, of course, more trade usually means less war – it is not a good idea to shoot the grocer. So why not just remove all trade restrictions immediately? Certainly there would be a painful period of readjustment, but after that, wouldn't life be so much easier? After all, poor countries frequently complain that they don't have fair access to rich markets while wealthier countries complain that they are paying too much for goods.

Or is free trade just a rich country's response? Do we only consider this approach because we know we have the economic power to clobber any opposition? A 10 percent drop in our standard of living during a period of readjustment would hardly be noticed – but in Mali or Ethiopia it would mean millions of deaths. So how DO we control trade? Simply by more paperwork? Or by a controlled and calculated regime of duties and documents? And if so, who does the controlling and calculating?

The most important document from the international marketer's viewpoint is the bill of lading, since this is proof of ownership. It is a document of possessory title, which means that only the holder of the bill of lading can collect the goods. There are exceptions to this general rule: if perishable goods arrive before the bill of lading has arrived (for example if the bill of lading has been sent by surface mail but the goods were sent via airfreight) the shipper can release the goods to a third party on receipt of a letter of indemnity from the party collecting the consignment. Possession therefore passes when the bill of lading is transferred, but ownership only passes when the parties intend it to pass, as evidenced by the sales contract.

As receipts, bills of lading provide only prima facie evidence that a certain quantity was received on board, that packaging marks were in order and that the goods were apparently in good condition. Nevertheless it is up to the carrier to prove that the items stated were not put on board, or that they were loaded in good condition. Obviously a ship's master is only required to attest that the goods appeared to be in good condition: with a few exceptions the ship's officers are not expected to carry out detailed internal inspections of cargoes to investigate their inner qualities.

Another problem in international transport is ensuring that everyone involved is clear about what is meant by specific terms. As discussed in Chapter 9, Incoterms have been agreed upon internationally to describe specific types of shipping conditions, so that importers and exporters know exactly who is paying for what.

TRANSPORTATION METHODS

Selecting a transportation method for a global market can be complex. As a general rule, the faster the shipment, the higher the cost, but standby air freight (in which the shipment is sent on the next available aircraft with spare capacity) can be relatively cheap, and when the costs of having capital tied up in goods in transit is also taken into account, can actually be cheaper than surface transportation. Obviously for perishable or highly valuable goods such as computer chips air freight is almost always cheaper, because there is less spoilage and the capital is tied up for a shorter period.

Five basic modes of transportation are used in business to business marketing. Goods are shipped by road, by rail, by air freight, by water, or in some cases by pipeline. Often combination systems are used, for example the ro-ro (roll on, roll off) ferries which transport lorries (or even just the trailers) across the English Channel, Irish Sea, and North Sea routes.

Figure 11.2 shows the factors which a marketing manager will typically take into account when choosing a transportation method.

In most cases, each of the factors will trade off against each of the others in some way. For example, sea transport (or indeed inland waterway transport) will be substantially cheaper than air freight, but it will be much slower. Equally, the reliability of rail transport may compare unfavourably with road transport, but may protect the goods better.

In some circumstances accessibility is an issue. The city of Iquitos, in Peru, is only accessible by water or air – there are no rail or road links into the city. This obviously limits the choices somewhat. Less obviously, some towns in Australia which are accessible by rail may only see one freight train a week, and are much better-served by road transport since Australian buses tow trailers for limited amounts of freight and usually offer a daily service.

Costs obviously vary in different countries. Inland waterways are widely used in Continental Europe, but are not commercially viable within the UK. Railway systems are heavily subsidized in Switzerland and the United States for environmental reasons, but not in the UK, where the system has deteriorated dramatically in the last 15 years or so.

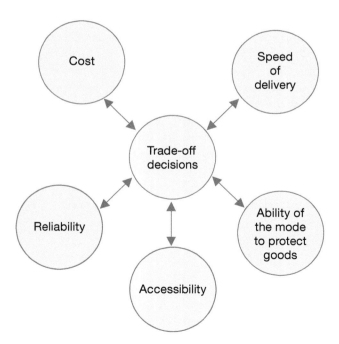

FIGURE 11.2 Trade-offs in transportation

Sea freight includes scheduled services (liners) which operate according to a fairly strict schedule, visiting specific ports at specific dates, and tramp services which sail once they have a full cargo for a specific destination. Liner services charge fixed rates, tramp ships (which are frequently modern, fast vessels) have variable rates which are almost always cheaper than the scheduled rates. Sea freight charges are based on either volume or weight, with extra charges for extra services, for example tallying cargo on and off (tallying means that a ship's officer counts the units of cargo as they are loaded).

Shipping agents will carry out all the functions of booking space on the ship and arranging for the loading of the cargoes: they are paid commission by the ship owners. The details of the shipment are contained on a standard shipping note (SSN), which advises the shipping company on what is to happen to the goods on arrival at the foreign port.

As mentioned earlier, airfreight used to be an expensive option, but is now much cheaper due to the increased efficiency of aircraft and the introduction of standby airfreight. Speedy delivery means less stockholding, more rapid settlement of invoices, less insurance, and therefore faster turnover of working capital. International airlines' cargo rates are fixed through IATA (International Air Transport Association) but carriers such as DHL are free to fix their own prices, and of course it is feasible to charter a cargo aircraft for a particularly large shipment. For air transport, the air waybill is the equivalent of the bill of lading, but it does not prove title to the goods. One of the problems with air transport, however, is that aircraft do not carry the standardized containers used by road and sea transport, so cargo has to be repacked, increasing handling costs.

Road transport is usually very flexible in that goods can be collected and delivered door-to-door, a factor which offsets the sometimes high costs per mile (when compared with sea or even air). In combination with roll-on-roll-off ferries truckers can operate throughout Europe, much of the United States seaboards, the Far East and North Africa, but for longer distances containers are more useful. Many countries restrict cabotage (the collection of cargoes en route) so that a vehicle may make a delivery in one country and be unable to pick up a return cargo. Road cabotage restrictions have been abolished within the European Union, but they still exist in most of Africa and non-EU countries.

Rail transport varies greatly between countries, largely due to the differences in rail and road infrastructure. In some countries (e.g. Germany) rail transport is well-developed and competes well with road transport. In other countries (e.g. Thailand) the rail network is by no means national, but is effective and efficient over the routes it does cover. In yet other countries (e.g. India) the rail network is capable of carrying only a tiny fraction of the freight transport needs of the country, due to an aging and poorly-maintained infrastructure and an emphasis on passenger transportation, which pushes the system close to or over capacity on many routes. The main drawback of rail transport in a small country like the UK is that the goods need to be loaded onto a truck, unloaded onto a train, then reloaded onto a truck at the other end. Normally it is simpler and quicker to drive the truck directly to the customer's premises. Within Continental Europe, the United States, and Australia distances are great enough to make transferring cargoes worthwhile, although in all three cases the long-distance truck (or road-train, in Australia) is much more widely-used.

CASE STUDY

Eddie Stobart

Eddie Stobart is something of a household name in the UK. The company's distinctive trucks, each with its smartly-dressed driver (they are required to wear shirts and ties) appear on motorways throughout the country, and in Continental Europe. Each truck is individually named (after real women) and each one is spotlessly clean. The company even has a dedicated fan club, with its own website, merchandize, and £18 membership fee (£20 for members outside Europe, which of course implies that there ARE members outside Europe).

The company's rise has been rapid, for a transport company. The original firm was started as an agricultural supply company in the 1950s, but in 1970 Eddie Stobart took over the family business and turned it into a haulage company. Operating from Cumbria, a rural area in the north of England, the company rapidly grew: the low costs associated with its location, plus being fairly central for the UK as a whole, gave the fledgling company some advantages but the main thrust of its success came from Stobart's unique vision of what a haulage company should be like. Stobart insisted that his trucks and drivers should be immaculate: the vehicles themselves were always spotless, and any driver caught not wearing a tie would face disciplinary action. Stobart also insisted that drivers should wave back and honk the horn should they be greeted by any passing motorist – an instruction which may have seemed bizarre to the average tough-guy truck driver, but which paid off in establishing word of mouth about the brand.

Eddie Stobart was also fortunate in that the new M6 extension motorway was built during the early 1970s, completing the connection between the Midlands and Scotland and passing close by Cumbria. As the company grew, Stobart established depots nearer to the customers, in the industrial Midlands (in 1987). During 2002, the company suffered a setback due to the fuel crisis, and Eddie sold out to his brother William (who already held 45 percent of the company) through a holding company owned by William and his brother-in-law. During the early part of the century, the directors considered moving everything to Warrington in Lancashire, to be nearer to the major Northern cities of Liverpool and Manchester, but dropped the idea because it would mean job losses in their beloved Cumbria: instead, the company bought Carlisle Airport with a view to turning it into an air freight center.

In a somewhat complicated deal, Eddie Stobart Limited was launched on the London stock exchange and became independent of its original parent company, eventually buying out the parent company (as well as acquiring other hauliers). In 2008, a spate of acquisitions created the Stobart Group, which now owned the inland ports of Widnes and Runcorn, London Southend Airport, Carlisle Lake District Airport, and several logistics companies. In 2010 Stobart bought a share in Irish airline Aer Arann, shortly after which Aer Arann announced that it would commence flights from Southend to Dublin and Galway.

. . . continued

CASE STUDY ... *continued*

In 2009, Stobart agreed to open a new depot in the East Midlands, near Leicester, in collaboration with chocolate manufacturer Nestlé. Stobart now distributes 75 percent of Nestlé's products throughout the UK and Ireland. The company is now able to operate a full logistics service: it has 40 depots around the UK and Ireland, offers warehousing and cross-docking facilities, has a rail division, a ports division and an air freight division, and (importantly) it owns at least part of the infrastructure – inland ports and airports, as well as vehicles and warehouses. Despite the company's size, it still retains a family-business style: the tradition of naming trucks dates back to Eddie Stobart himself, who named his first trucks Twiggy (after the model), Dolly (after Dolly Parton), Tammy (for Tammy Wynette), and Suzi (after Suzi Quattro).

Stobart died of heart failure at the age of 56, in 2011, but the business he and his brother built from scratch still carries on.

CASE STUDY QUESTIONS

1 How does the relationship with Nestlé help Nestlé's supply chain management?
2 How has Stobart moved from being a haulage company to being a logistics company?
3 What is the purpose of owning ports and airports?
4 What advantages might a customer see in dealing with a family business?
5 Why might Stobart have sought a joint venture with Nestlé?

CHAPTER SUMMARY

The physical distribution of products has marketing implications. Managing the supply chain effectively enables all of its members to maximize their efficiency, and hence their profits – or of course to pass on savings to customers and therefore be more competitive.

The key points from this chapter are as follows:

- Logistics takes a holistic view: physical distribution refers to particular elements of the process.
- The main trade-offs in logistics are cost and service level.
- Just-in-time purchasing may be counterproductive unless the supply chain is well-run.
- Airfreight can be cheaper than other forms of transport when all costs are taken into account.
- Documentation can be extremely complex for road transport across several international borders.
- Relationships exist across several categories of partner, not just buyers and sellers.

■ Balancing organizational and personal needs is crucial for establishing commitment in business relationships.

■ The crucial elements in welding together the supply chain are information systems, packaging and handling, effective services, and pooling of shipments.

■ Accurate sales estimates are the key to successful supply chain management.

REVIEW QUESTIONS

1 Why might the European Union have standardized cross-border paperwork?
2 What are the main advantages of air freight over rail freight?
3 Why might just-in-time be damaging to a logistics approach?
4 Why might an exporter use a tramp ship rather than a scheduled liner?
5 What are the main problems in establishing a logistics approach?

REFERENCES

Autry, Chad W. (2005). "Formalization of reverse logistics programs: A strategy for managing liberalized returns." *Industrial Marketing Management*, Vol. 34, Iss. 6, August, 566–76.

Bowman, Robert J. (2001). "Does Wall Street really care about the supply chain?" *Global Logistics and Supply Chain Strategies* (April), 31–5.

Celley, A.F., Clee, W.H., Smith, A.W., and Vonderembese, M.A. (1986). "Implementation of JIT in the United States." *Journal of Purchasing and Materials Management*, Vol. 22, Iss. 4 (Winter), 13.

Christopher, Martin and Gattorna, John (2005). "Supply chain cost management and value-based pricing." *Industrial Marketing Management*, Vol. 34, Iss. 2, February, 123–31.

Cooper, Martha C., Lambert, Douglas M., and Pugh, James D. (1997). "Supply chain management: more than a new name for logistics." *International Journal of Logistics Management*. Vol. 8, No. 1, 1.

Ellinger, Alexander E., Ketchen Jr., David J., Hult, G., Thomas M., Elmadao, Aybe Banu, and Richey Jr., Glenn R. (2008). "Market orientation, employee development practices, and performance in logistics service provider firms." *Industrial Marketing Management*. Vol. 37, Iss. 4, June, 380–93.

Ferguson, Brad (2000). "Implementing supply chain management." *Production and Inventory Management Journal*, Vol. 41, Iss. 2, 64.

Flint, Daniel J. (2004). "Strategic marketing in global supply chains. Four challenges." *Industrial Marketing Management*, Vol. 33, No. 1, January, 45–50.

Guinipero, Larry C., Denslow, Diane, and Eltantawy, Rehan (2005). "Purchasing/supply chain management flexibility: Moving to an entrepreneurial skill set." *Industrial Marketing Management*, Vol. 34, Iss. 6, August, 614–28.

Kim, Eun Young, Ko, Eunju, Kim, Haejung, and Koh, Chang E. (2008). "Comparison of benefits of radio frequency identification: Implications for business strategic performance in the U.S. and Korean retailers." *Industrial Marketing Management*, Vol. 37, Iss. 7, October, 807–18.

LaLonde, B. J., Cooper, M.C., and Noordweir, T.G. (1988). *Customer Service: A Management Perspective*. Oak Brook Ill: Council of Logistics Management.

Morgan, Robert M. and Hunt, Shelby D. (1994). "The commitment-trust theory of relationship marketing." *Journal of Marketing*, Vol. 58, No. 3 (July), 20–38.

Novich, N.S. (1992). "How to sell customer service." *Transportation and Distribution*, Vol. 33, No. 1, 46.

Quinn, Francis J. (2000). "A supply chain management overview." *Supply Chain Yearbook 2000*, Mason, OH: McGraw Hill, p. 15.

Smith, Michael F., Lancioni, Richard A., and Oliva, Terence A. (2005). "The effects of management inertia on the supply chain performance of produce-to-stock firms." *Industrial Marketing Management*, Vol. 34, Iss. 6, August, 629–40.

Tsai, Ming-Chih, Wen, Chieh-Hua, and Chen, Chiang-Shin (2007). "Demand choices of high-tech industry for logistics service providers – an empirical case of an offshore science park in Taiwan." *Industrial Marketing Management*, Vol. 36, Iss. 5, July, 627–35.

Voeth, Markus, and Herbst, Uta (2006). "Supply-chain pricing – A new perspective on pricing in industrial markets. *Industrial Marketing Management*, Vol. 35, Iss. 1, January, 91–102.

Wu, Fang, Yeniyurt, Sengun, Kim, Daekwan, and Cavusgil, S. Tamer (2006). "The impact of information technology on supply chain capabilities and firm performance: A resource-based view." *Industrial Marketing Management*, Vol. 35, Iss. 4, May, 505–21.

Chapter 12

Managing distribution channels

INTRODUCTION

Finding and managing distributors and dealers around the world can be a time consuming task for a B2B marketing manager. On the other hand, the distribution network is a key strategic resource which provides a strong competitive advantage. This chapter describes the process of discovering and managing channel partners in a global setting.

CHAPTER OBJECTIVES

After reading this chapter, you should be able to:

- explain the main issues in designing a suitable distribution policy
- explain the role of distribution in gaining competitive advantage
- describe ways of integrating the distribution network
- describe the advantages of different types of distribution system
- show how "cutting out the middleman" reduces efficiency and increases costs
- describe some of the techniques used for efficient customer response.

STRATEGIC ISSUES IN DISTRIBUTION

Strategy is about creating competitive advantage. The following factors are the key issues in the ways that distribution affects strategy:

■ A good distribution network adds value to the product by increasing utility.
■ The channel is the firm's major link to its customers.
■ Choice of channel influences the rest of the marketing mix, thus affecting overall strategy.
■ Building appropriate channels takes time and commitment, particularly in a global context, so distribution decisions are difficult to change.
■ The distribution system determines segmentation and targeting issues in many cases.
■ Conflicts may arise between the firm's strategic goals and those of the distributors, particularly in global markets where timescales may be very different.
■ Intermediaries in foreign countries may weaken the control of the supplier over the way the product is marketed.

Distribution adds utility to the product in the ways shown in Table 12.1.

The distribution system often determines the targeting rather than the other way round. This is particularly true in Developing World countries where the transport infrastructure means that some parts of the country are inaccessible: there is more on this in Chapter 11.

TABLE 12.1 Added utility

Utility	Explanation and Examples
Place utility	Making the product available in a place which is convenient for the customer. For example, Snap-On Tools offers a tool service to light engineering companies, using large Mercedes vans as mobile tool warehouses and calling on the firms on a weekly basis.
Time utility	Making goods available at a time which suits the customer's needs. Just-in-time ordering and delivery is an example of this : deliveries are planned in such a way that stocks of components arrive at regular intervals, thus eliminating the need for the purchaser to hold stocks.
Ownership utility	Goods are transferred to the purchaser rapidly after ordering, so that the purchaser can benefit immediately from ownership. This can involve the supplier in stockholding, however, which may be counterproductive: equally, the fact that stocks have to be held in a foreign country rather than delivered from the home country has allowed several companies to gain a competitive advantage in a foreign country, where the local competitors manufacture to order instead.
Information utility	Distributors are able to answer questions directly, providing faster answers than can be obtained from the supplying company. For example, a firm may set up a helpline for its users, but arrange for the distributors to operate the helpline so as to take advantage of local knowledge and experience.

Strategic advantage can be derived from the way distributors serve customers. Although it is part of received wisdom that "cutting out the middle man" reduces costs because the "middle man" profit is removed from the equation, it turns out that the services provided by the middle man are actually useful and necessary, and would have to be carried out by someone else. For example, a motor mechanic needs rapid delivery of spare parts: ordering each part for each car directly from the manufacturer would mean complex ordering and some very lengthy delays. Carrying out a routine service on someone's automobile might need 10 or 15 different spare parts, from light bulbs to brake linings, all manufactured by different companies in different parts of the country (or even different parts of the world). So the motor mechanic orders all the parts from a motor factor, who keeps stocks of the commonest parts and can deliver within an hour or so. The middle man's profit is almost always covered amply by the savings in time made by using the service.

Distributors serve customers in some or all of the following ways:

- Provide fast delivery. Local distributors will hold buffer stocks of products, so they should be able to supply customer needs rapidly.
- Provide a segment-based product assortment. Like the motor parts factor mentioned above, a distributor may well be able to supply a wide range of products which are suitable for the needs of a specific market segment.
- Provide local credit. A distributor may be able to provide credit facilities for firms. Having local knowledge, the distributor will be able to decide who is creditworthy and who is not. An overseas manufacturer may have no idea where to start obtaining credit ratings.
- Provide product information. Local distributors may have knowledge of other products which are useful to the customer and which are complementary to the firm's products.
- Assist in buying decisions. Distributors are often able to advise on the availability of components, or are able to research availability from among the manufacturers they act for. This can backfire from the manufacturer's viewpoint, since distributors may (and often do) carry several alternative components, some of which are likely to be "generic" components which are substantially cheaper than the manufacturer's own offerings.
- Anticipate needs. Because the distributors know the local market, they are often able to anticipate the needs of their customers and advise manufacturers accordingly.

Choosing the right distributor creates access to an existing group of committed customers. The distributor adds value to the product offering by giving advice, assistance, and rapid response. Distributors also serve manufacturers in the following ways:

- Buy and hold stocks. Distributors are the customers of the manufacturers, since they select, buy, and pay for the goods. The manufacturer is thus relieved of much of the financial and logistical responsibility of holding stocks.
- Combine manufacturers' outputs. Since customers almost always buy from a number of manufacturers, they will be exposed to the firm's products when they order products from a distributor. This in effect provides a "piggy back" promotional method.
- Share credit risk. Distributors may offer credit to their own customers, and carry the risk for this: even though the manufacturer will offer credit to the distributor in order to allow them to stock the products, this is a much smaller risk.

- Share selling risk. The distributors have a stake in making the sales, since they have committed to purchasing the products. Obviously there is an assumption that the products are saleable, and an assumption that the manufacturer will play a part in marketing the products, but both parties have a clear stake and commitment in the success of the product.
- Forecast market needs. Distributors are much closer to the market than the manufacturers are, and are therefore in a much better position to forecast demand.
- Provide market information. Likewise, the distributors are a good source of information about possible new needs of their customers. This can be helpful in new product development.

Setting up the right channels for getting the product from its source to the customer involves a combination of direct selling and the use of various intermediaries and facilitators. Intermediaries include distributors, wholesalers, and retailers who are classified as merchants. The channel also may include manufacturers' representatives or sales agents who find customers and even negotiate for the supplying firm. This group is classified as agents. The major difference between agents and merchants is that merchants purchase and resell product while agents do not. As has been pointed out in Chapter 7, a manufacturing firm will have far more control over an agent than over a merchant since the merchant owns the product. In formulating the firm's channel design, a marketing director must take into account a number of environmental influences as well as company resources and capabilities. These are shown in Figure 12.1.

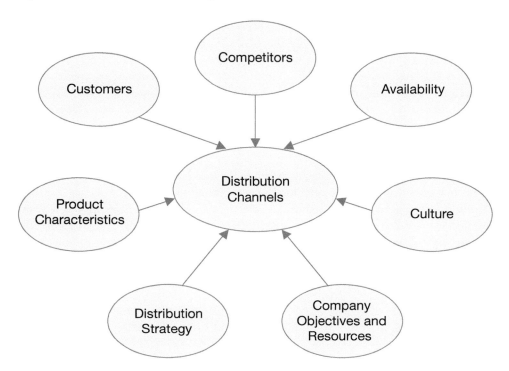

FIGURE 12.1 Influences on channel design

Source: adapted from Czinkota and Ronkainen, 2010.

Talking Point

How can customers require different levels of service? Why shouldn't everybody get the best service we can provide? Surely if we're truly customer-oriented, we should be providing the best service we can for everybody all the time!

Or maybe some customers are not as valuable as others. Maybe we don't make enough money out of some of them, so they get second-class service.

Or just maybe we have some customers who actually prefer us to leave them alone? Maybe they aren't prepared to pay for all that extra service – and would just like a basic, cheap arrangement.

First and foremost, the firm must look at customer segment requirements. Is the segment sophisticated enough to deal with remotely-located distribution outlets or is training and maintenance a necessity requiring local, on-the-scene distributors? As we will see later in this chapter, various kinds of customers require different levels of service.

For firms selling software, this may mean direct sales to large multinational corporations wherever they are located, one-step wholesale distribution to local small computer centers, direct sales to large computer retailers, and two-step distribution through distributors and retailers or direct sales through the Internet to the smallest clients. The way customers are segmented will have a major effect upon the distribution alternatives chosen. For instance, customers who are highly price-sensitive and can place large orders will not buy through even one step of distribution and will demand direct sales from the manufacturer.

Competitors may also determine channels to be chosen. If an entrenched competitor has already set a pattern of distribution which customers have become accustomed to, it will be difficult for a newcomer to change that pattern unless it can show efficiencies and cost savings to its customers as a result of these changes. The functions handled by distributors may also be set by the competitors. Here again, a newcomer would have difficulty changing what customers have come to expect.

Competition also may affect the next influence shown in Figure 12.1 – availability. In many small markets, there are few qualified distributors for products requiring technical knowledge. Most or all of these distributors may have already established agreements with competitors. If a new firm moves into a particular market, it may find that the most desirable distributors are not available. In this case, the marketing manager is faced with the difficult choice of offering his/her product to a distributor who is already handling a competitive product or finding a distribution firm in a related field and training that distributor to represent the product. In many countries the lack of qualified distribution is the rule rather than the exception.

Culture can have an important effect upon channel design as well. In some countries, an established way of distributing all products has grown up and become the norm. For example, in Japan there are many levels of distribution firms, which sell to one another before the product reaches the final consumer: this is a daunting challenge for non-Japanese marketers. In some markets, there is vertical integration whereby distribution firms are owned by manufacturers or close relationships have been established. Changing these culturally-driven distribution patterns will be difficult, especially since trust between channel members is lower when there are cultural differences between the players (Mehta et al., 2006).

Company objectives and resources also have a significant effect upon distribution choices. Clearly, distribution strategy must be in congruence with the marketing strategy which, in turn, should be in agreement with the overall company objectives. Equally important will be company resources. Should the firm decide to establish a large network of distributors in over 100 countries, the management of this network will require a large commitment of human resources. Since most distributors need to be trained and motivated by headquarters staff, frequent visits are usually necessary. Because of the travel time required to reach all parts of the globe, it is impossible for a limited staff to supervise and motivate a worldwide distribution network in multiple countries. A common problem is over-reliance on electronic communication as a substitute for personal training and motivation – a meeting conducted via Skype might be a very useful thing to do, but sometimes a face-to-face meeting is necessary, if only to put the relationship on a human level. Disappointment with distributor results can usually be traced to under-resourcing selection, training, and motivation of distributors.

Distribution strategy will also have an important influence on channel design. A firm must decide whether it requires intensive, selective or exclusive distribution. Intensive distribution means selling through as many outlets as are available and qualified. Selective distribution means choosing a limited number of firms as intermediaries. Exclusive distribution means choosing one intermediary in each market. Products that have few customers, such as nuclear power plants or aircraft engines, are obviously candidates for exclusive distribution. Choosing individual firms who can represent the manufacturer both in follow-up service as well as customer training is critical. A firm selling stationery to be used in offices will probably choose intensive distribution, hoping to market the product to as many users as possible through as many channel types as is practical.

Finally, product characteristics must be a part of the equation. If a firm has decided to market its product as a high-priced, high-service product, this will dictate choosing exclusive or selective distribution through well-financed, prestigious outlets, while a firm which identifies its product as a "value alternative" using lower prices will probably opt for the "warehouse" approach. The distribution strategy is directly related to the product characteristics as well (again, as for nuclear power plants or aircraft engines).

Although directors of marketing hope to see neat looking distribution charts, they often find that their actual distribution patterns are quite messy. Figure 12.2 shows how a manufacturer might distribute its product depending upon the considerations discussed above and shown in Figure 12.1.

Most firms use multiple distribution channels to reach customers in order to deliver the required satisfaction to any particular customer segment (Perry 1989). This can be helpful in meeting different market segments, but has the major drawback that the various distributors may resent the existence of the others, and may feel that their own positions are being undermined. Care needs to be taken to ensure that the segments really are clearly-defined and overlap is kept to a minimum.

Having said that, many firms manage to operate successfully through multiple distribution channels for different segments: for example, 3M have a total of five separate channels just for audio-visual equipment. In each case the distribution channel addresses a specific customer group, so that the different members of the distribution network do not compete with each other even though they all carry the same product lines. Evidence from Taiwan indicates that including the Internet as a distribution channel enhances the overall performance of firms (Ming-Sung et al., 2007). This finding should, of course, be considered in terms of its cultural context – the same finding may not apply elsewhere, especially if distributors are prone to view Internet distribution as a breach of trust. Using multiple channels appears to work best if the supplying company has a strong internal marketing orientation: internal and external channel conflicts also appear to be closely related (Webb and Lambe, 2007).

In some cases, firms inherit distribution channels when they take over other firms, or when there is a merger of firms in the same industry. Rationalizing the distribution channels can be daunting, with firms needing to assess which channels are most effective, and at the same time having to discard trusts which have sometimes been built up over many years. Firms should triangulate on the problem using multiple perspectives – assessing distributors by historical performance, sales management, strategic fit, and customer preference – before making a final choice about which distributors to keep and which to drop (Palmatier et al., 2007).

In Figure 12.2, we see a manufacturer selling directly, either through its own salesforce or through the Internet to certain customers. These might be the largest or the smallest customers. In addition, the manufacturer is using an agent, and while agents do not take title to the product, they may be the main intermediary in a particular market. This manufacturer also uses a distributor (wholesaler) who sells to customers as well as dealers (retailers), who also sell to customers. Also shown is a relationship between the agent and the distributor. A manufacturer may choose to have independent sales agents who call on distributors helping with the sale. Any one manufacturer may very well have distribution patterns that look like Figure 12.2. Firm management must frequently re-evaluate its choices, changing the distribution patterns to suit the needs of new market segments that it identifies.

Many firms divide their customers into A-, B- and C-type customers, with the A list comprising the top 10 percent by number and accounting for up to 50 percent of the firm's volume. The B-type customers are medium-sized, accounting for 25 percent of customers by number and perhaps

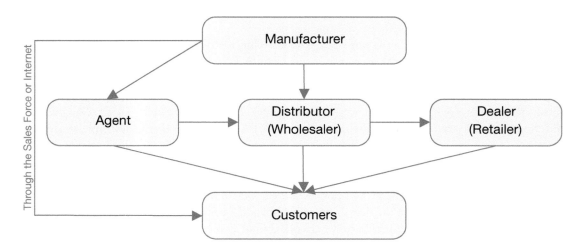

FIGURE 12.2 Marketing channels

TABLE 12.2 Agent/distributor agreements

Key Contract Areas:

- Type of Relationship
- Corporation vs. Individuals
- Taxes
- Duration of Agreement
- Termination
- Product Sale or Service Agreement
- Territory/Exclusivity
- Arbitration and Governing Law
- Payment and Compensation

- Terms/Conditions of Sale
- Facilities and Personnel
- Inventory
- Confidentiality
- Proprietary Information (Trademarks, Tradename, and Copyright)
- Records and Communications
- Advertising/Promotion
- Other Provisions

Source: Fitzpatrick and Zimmerman, 1985.

25–30 percent of all sales. The remaining nearly two-thirds of customers in the C category probably account for the smallest percentage of sales and their per-order volume is small. Of course, these customers may eventually move up into buying in greater volume, so they are still worth looking after. If a firm uses this approach, its distribution alternatives will be clear. The A-types will be served by direct sales from the manufacturer, the B-types through some form of distribution, and the C-types through the Internet or mail order.

In selecting a distributor, the first step is to use the Partner Profile shown in Chapter 7, Table 7.9. This can easily be applied to any possible distribution partner to determine whether this particular partner is the best choice. Unfortunately, choosing intermediaries is often approached under unrealistic deadlines during quick trips to multiple markets. Experience has shown that spending one day in a country and finding a firm through informal discussions over dinner or at a local pub usually results in a poor choice. A marketing executive then finds that the intermediary signed on in haste is very difficult to remove.

Because many countries have passed legislation steeply in favor of local distributors, the marketing manager should be sure that all distribution partners sign carefully drawn agreements. A list of the most important contract areas which should be included in any agent or distributor agreement is seen in Table 12.2.

The type of relationship refers to whether a firm will be taking title to the product or not, in other words, if the distribution partner is an agent or a merchant. The second contract area describes the type of entity the intermediary will be. It is preferable to make agreements with corporations rather than individuals. The latter leaves a firm open to the interpretation that the firm has an employer–employee relationship which is entirely different from that of an arm's length distributor, and allows far less protection in the event of disagreement. Indeed, in some countries (notably France) agents are regarded as employees, and have the full protection of employee legislation regarding termination of the contract.

In the case of taxes, the location of the establishment will determine the tax jurisdiction. It is best to appoint an intermediary with multiple lines so that it does not appear to be a branch of a manufacturing firm. The duration of the agreement should be limited – one to two years – and not indefinite. New agreements should be developed and signed periodically to show that the relationship is being renewed. Next, termination: should the agreement say that an intermediary can be terminated with or without cause as is permitted in the United States, this clause will usually be unenforceable in most other countries. The most solid basis for termination will be failure to reach goals. These goals must be established on a periodic basis by agreement of the manufacturer and the intermediary. Should the agreement be terminated, it is important to include in the document how the termination will take place. Important items such as disposition of inventory, return of literature and other materials, ownership of customer lists and so on should be described in this agreement. It is sometimes possible to specify the country under whose laws the contract will be enforceable, but this can lead to complex (and expensive) litigation.

The product sale or service agreement identifies what product or service areas the intermediary will be responsible for. Territory refers to the areas where the intermediary is to represent the manufacturer. Sophisticated manufacturers will retain the right to distribute the product independently of the distributor, but most distributors will want exclusivity in a particular country. In some cases, this will be the only logical course since a market may be too small to support multiple distributors. However, this course also leaves the manufacturer with no other alternative should the intermediary prove to be inadequate. The next area to include is whether or not disputes will be submitted to arbitration and what jurisdiction will be governing. It is always better to pre-establish an arbitration method in these agreements so that disputes can be settled without going to court. Payment and compensation relates to the way commissions will be calculated for agents and the way payments will be made through distributors. Because of anti-corruption laws, more fully discussed in Chapter 4, it is necessary to establish clear accounting pathways to trace payments.

Other important items listed above include the terms of sale such as ownership of the goods, the facilities and personnel to be applied to the distribution of the particular product line, and the inventory to be carried. An important clause to include in an agreement is confidentiality – intermediaries should be prevented from using sensitive information they may discover during the relationship – and confidentiality should survive the termination of the agreement. The intermediary should be required to acknowledge that the manufacturer retains the rights to all proprietary information. The intermediary should be granted limited use of this intellectual property, especially trademarks and copyrights. Records and communication should be specified so that the intermediary

TABLE 12.3 Guidelines for successful international distribution

1.	Select Distributors – don't let them select you.
2.	Find distributors with market development capabilities.
3.	Treat distributors as long-term partners.
4.	Fully resource the market entry effort.
5.	Keep control of marketing strategy.
6.	Require detailed market and financial data.

Source: adapted from Arnold (2000).

will know the reporting requirements of the manufacturer. Some manufacturers describe carefully the kinds of advertising and promotion to be used and even retain a right of approval before advertising is placed. Some other provisions may also be necessary in the agreement. The most important one is the so-called *force majeure*, which allows a firm freedom from the provisions of the agreement because of so-called "Acts of God." One may also wish to include a section requiring dealers to comply with all local laws.

This listing, while a good starting point, is not complete for every situation and a marketing director developing a distributor or agent agreement should take legal advice to be sure all clauses required for his/her particular business are included.

Arnold (2000) has identified many problems which surface in international distribution. While his research focused on developing markets, the problems identified are often experienced in developed countries. The multinational corporations Arnold studied wanted control over their businesses and often used distributors just to get started in a particular area. The managers had the idea that these distributors would be replaced or acquired as the business expanded. However, in many cases a more efficient and economical means of getting to market is through local distributors. These international distributors must be carefully chosen and managed. Based on Arnold, some rules of international distribution are listed in Table 12.3.

As has been mentioned, many firms do not spend enough time choosing distributors. Often, distributors are chosen simply because they make contact with the manufacturer, asking for the line. As Arnold (2000) says, "in fact, the most eager potential distributors may be precisely the wrong people to partner with." Carefully identifying the needs of the segment and the capabilities required in a particular country will lead a manufacturer to spend the required time to select the best possible candidate. Above all, this is the most important task in distribution management. Distributors who have key contacts in a country but are unable to develop a market usually are not the best long-term partners. Having said that, most distributors will spend only a limited amount of time developing a market. A manufacturer must understand its commitment to market development and cannot rely entirely upon the distributor to "pioneer" in a new market without significant help.

Although many multinational firms see distributors as simply market entry vehicles, a more effective strategy will be to choose distributors who will become partners. When a large firm shows that it will not partner with the local distributor on a long-term basis, the local distributor management often become defensive and look to short-term gains rather than long-term market development. On the other hand, research shows that a committed partner will become even more so in times of business uncertainty, when trust is at a premium (Lai et al., 2008).

As has been mentioned above, a full effort is required to enter a new market. Resources of all kinds, including people, are required to make a distributor successful. Training in selling and the technical aspects of the product is usually at a minimum and on-site visits to help in real situations are often what make the difference between success and failure. Arnold suggests that some multinationals have taken minority equity stakes in distribution companies. While this increases a multinational's exposure to market downturns and political risk, it also signals a level of commitment to local distributors. It can be a very effective way to gain cooperation and full effort from local intermediaries.

While distributors can implement strategy, adapting it to the local culture, the multinational should maintain control over the marketing strategy. In some cases, employees from the manufacturer should be sent to work in the distributor's business to ensure the implementation is following the strategy.

The need for market and financial data is obvious. Where cooperation has been established, distributors will be more forthcoming with these data. However, should the distributor suspect that the manufacturer is not committed to a long-term relationship, information flow is usually the first aspect of the relationship to dry up.

Some have suggested the setting up of distributor councils to increase cooperation among national or regional distributors, but this should be approached with caution. While they can serve as a vehicle for increasing cooperation, they can also reinforce dissatisfactions among distributors, especially in periods of downturn or where a manufacturer experiences product problems. A less formal approach may achieve the same results. In other words, holding annual or semi-annual meetings with regional or even worldwide distributors (should the number not be unwieldy) can serve as a good vehicle for education and motivation.

Supplier relations are important for any organization, not least because around 50 percent of the average firm's turnover is channeled back to suppliers of one sort or another (Hakansson, 1992). These relationships are dynamic, because they are built up through human contact and human effort. In fact, business is about people – only people buy and sell, hire and fire, and make decisions on behalf of their organizations. From the perspective of the buyer, the seller's salesperson actually is (in effect) the selling company. Likewise, from the salesperson's perspective the buyer is the buying company. This means that any sign of dishonesty or even unpleasantness on the part of the individuals concerned will affect the other party's perception of the company as a whole. Since the relationships a firm has are actually interrelated, a bad reputation can spread extremely quickly: salespeople, engineers, customers, and others meet each other at forums outside the organization and pass on opinions and information about their own firm and others.

Here is a checklist for selecting and motivating distributors.

1   Ask potential customers to recommend possible distributors. This will help ensure a smooth logistical flow.
2   Determine which distributor best fits the company's overall strategy. Goals and strategic aspirations of the distributor should be close to those of the company, so that the relationship remains close. For example, a conflict might arise between an aggressive company seeking rapid growth and a distributor which prefers high profit margins at the expense of growth.
3   Visit the distributor regularly. This helps to build the relationship by keeping the company up-to-date with developments in the market, and allows the distributor to raise issues. It is probably also advisable to allow the distributor access to staff at all levels in the organization – technical people, administrators, and financial managers – as well as marketers, since this will also strengthen the relationship.
4   Visit the overseas customers with the distributor. Provided the distributor or agent has no objection, joint visits to the overseas customers also help to support the distributor and build the relationship. Customers usually welcome the opportunity to have direct contact with the company.
5   Provide training and support. If the distributor's staff can be trained at the company's premises this will make a major difference to the smooth running of the relationship, since the distributor will make useful contacts for informal resolution of minor problems, and will develop a better understanding of the corporate culture.

However, economic factors should not be overlooked entirely. Some studies show that reciprocity in the importer–exporter relationship tends to be more heavily influenced by economic factors than by social factors, even though social factors remain important (Lee et al., 2008).

MANAGING DISTRIBUTION CHANNELS

Channels can be led by any of the channel members, whether they are producers, wholesalers, or retailers, provided the member concerned has channel power. This power comes from seven sources (Bitner, 1992), as shown in Table 12.4.

Channel cooperation is an essential part of the effective functioning of channels. Since each member relies on every other member for the free exchange of goods down the channel, it is in the members' interests to look after each other to some extent. Channel cooperation can be improved in the following ways:

- The channel members can agree on target markets, so that each member can best direct effort toward meeting the common goal.
- Define the tasks each member should carry out. This avoids duplication of effort, or giving the final consumer conflicting messages.

A further development is co-marketing, which implies a partnership between manufacturers, intermediaries, and retailers. This level of cooperation involves pooling of market information and full agreement on strategic issues (Marx, 1995).

Channel conflict arises because each member wants to maximize its own profits or power. Conflicts also arise because of frustrated expectations; each member expects the other members to act in particular ways, and sometimes these expectations are unfulfilled. For example, a retailer may expect a wholesaler to maintain large enough stocks to cover an unexpected rise in demand for a given product, whereas the wholesaler may expect the manufacturers to be able to increase production rapidly to cover such eventualities.

Channel management can be carried out by cooperation and negotiation (often with one member leading the discussions) or it can be carried out by the most powerful member laying down rules which weaker members have to follow. Table 12.5 shows some of the methods which can be used to control channels.

Restricting sales territories results in greater perception of both role performance and business performance on the part of both manufacturers and distributors: in other words, when a distributor is given an exclusive territory, both the distributor and the manufacturer believe that the performance of the other party is improved (Gonzalez-Hernando et al., 2005). Obviously a distributor who is excluded from that territory might feel differently.

Most attempts to control distribution by the use of power are likely to be looked on unfavorably by the courts, but of course the abuse of power would have to be fairly extreme before a channel member would be likely to sue.

Sometimes the simplest way to control a distribution channel is to buy out the channel members. Buying out members across a given level (for example, a wholesaler buying out other wholesalers in order to build a national network) is called horizontal integration; buying out members above or below in the distribution chain (for example a retailer buying out a wholesaler) is vertical integration. An example of extreme vertical integration is the major oil companies, which extract crude oil, refine it, ship it, and ultimately sell it retail through petrol stations. At the extremes, this type of integration may attract the attention of Government monopoly regulation agencies, since the integration may cause a restriction of competition.

TABLE 12.4 Sources of channel power

Economic sources of power	Non-economic sources of power	Other factors
Control of resources; the degree to which the channel member has the power to direct goods, services or finance within the channel.	Reward power. The ability to provide financial benefits, or otherwise favor channel members.	Level of power. This derives from the economic and non-economic sources of power.
Size of company. The bigger the firm compared with other channel members, the greater the overall economic power.	Expert power. This arises when the leader has special expertise which the other channel members need. Distributors in this situation tend to communicate more collaboratively, cooperate more, and rely on behavioral issues rather than outcomes (Sahadev, 2006).	Dependency of other channel members.
Referent power emerges when channel members try to emulate the leader.		Willingness to lead. Clearly some firms with potential for channel leadership prefer not to have the responsibility, or are unable to exercise the potential for other reasons.
Legitimate power arises from a superior–subordinate relationship. For example, if a retailer holds a substantial shareholding in a wholesaler, it has legitimate power over the wholesaler.		
Coercive power exists when one channel member has the power to punish another.		

TABLE 12.5 Channel management techniques

Technique	Explanation	Legal position
Refusal to deal	One member refuses to do business with one or more other members; for example, hairdressing wholesalers sometimes refuse to supply mobile hairdressers, on the grounds that this is unfair competition for salons.	In most countries suppliers do not have to supply anybody they don't wish to deal with. However, grounds may exist for a lawsuit if the refusal to deal is a punishment for not going along with an anti-competitive ruling by a supplier, or is an attempt to prevent the channel member from dealing with a third party with whom the manufacturer is in dispute.
Tying contracts	The supplier (sometimes a franchiser) demands that the channel member carries other products as well as the main one. If the franchiser insists that all the products are carried, this is called full-line forcing.	Most of these contracts are illegal in the UK, but are accepted if the supplier alone can supply goods of a given quality, or if the purchaser is free to carry competing products as well. Sometimes they are accepted when a company has just entered the market. They are generally acceptable in franchise situations (e.g. McDonald's) on the basis that the franchiser is looking to protect its brand values.
Exclusive dealing	A manufacturer might prevent a wholesaler from carrying competitors' products, or a retailer might insist that no other retailer be supplied with the same products. This is often used by retailers to ensure that their "price guarantees" can be honored – obviously consumers will not be able to find the same product at a lower price locally if the retailer has prevented the manufacturer from supplying anybody else.	Usually these are legal provided they don't result in a monopoly position in a local area; in other words, provided the consumer has access to similar products, there will not be a problem.
Restricted sales territories	Intermediaries are prevented from selling outside a given area. The intermediaries are often in favor of this idea, because it prevents competition within their own area.	Courts have conflicting views about this practice. On the one hand, these deals can help weaker distributors, and can also increase competition where local dealers carry different brands; on the other hand, there is clearly a restraint of trade involved.

Producers need to ensure that the distributors of their products are of the right type. The image of a distribution agent can damage (or enhance) the image of the products sold (and vice versa). Producers need not necessarily sell through the most prestigious distributor, and in fact this might be counter-productive for many cheap, everyday items such as office stationery or nuts and bolts. Likewise a prestigious product should not be sold through a downmarket distributor.

This is particularly important in global markets, where the producing company may not be familiar with the distribution methods in the target country. For example, manufacturers' agents in Germany tend to be highly professional and committed, and expect the same level of commitment from the firms they represent: they will expect regular visits from the selling company, marketing support, and above all reliability of delivery. In most cases a German agent will make a thorough investigation of the foreign company before accepting the task of selling its products. In other countries (notably the UK) manufacturers' agents are rarely as assiduous in checking out the client company – they are much more likely to take on the product, see if it sells, and if it fails to sell the agent will simply drop it from the range. For the German agent, the company he or she represents is integral to his or her reputation: for the UK agent, the relationship is not regarded as being as direct.

Talking Point

Presumably vertical integration greatly increases the efficiency of the supply chain. After all, if each stage of the supply chain is operated by a separate firm, with its own strategies and agendas, conflict is inevitable.

So why not run everything this way? Why don't monopolies regulators encourage vertical distribution rather than investigating it and punishing it? And if we argue that a vertically-integrated industry concentrates too much power in a few hands, is it really any different from the kind of integration that happens with a well-run supply chain? We ban oligopolistic collusion – why not ban the very open, bare-faced collusion that happens between members of a supply chain?

EFFICIENT CUSTOMER RESPONSE

Efficient customer response seeks to integrate the activities of manufacturers and distributors using computer technology; the expected result is a more responsive stocking system for the distributor, which in turn benefits the manufacturer. Some of the features of ECR are as follows:

- *Continuous replenishment* under which the supplier plans production using data generated by the distribution network.
- *Cross-docking* attempts to coordinate the arrival of suppliers' and retailers' trucks at the distribution centers so that goods move from one truck to the other without going into stock. Although transport efficiency falls because a supermarket truck collecting (say) greengrocery

might have to wait for several suppliers' trucks to arrive, the overall speed of delivery of products improves, which can be crucial when dealing with fresh foods.
- *Roll-cage sequencing* allows storage of products by category at the factory or warehouse; although this adds to the labor time at the factory, it greatly reduces labor time at the customer's warehouse, or the retail store, since the roll cages can be moved directly into position.

The main problem with ECR is that it relies on complete cooperation between members of the distribution chain. In any channel of distribution where the power base is unequal, this is less likely to happen; despite the overall savings for the channel as a whole, self-interest on the part of channel members may lead to less-than-perfect cooperation.

Using distribution networks strategically will always involve consideration of the strategies of the distributors themselves. These may conflict with the strategy of the supplying firm: harmonizing these strategic differences, and generating synergies from them, is a challenge for most firms.

CASE STUDY

Case study: General Sales Agents

General Sales Agents (or GSAs) act for airlines in places in which the airline does not have, and perhaps cannot afford, its own direct presence. GSAs typically act for several airlines, and are responsible for all types of sale within their geographical region – passenger tickets, air freight, and onward ticketing through other airlines. A GSA will charge between 3 and 5 percent commission for all business it brings in.

Airlines use GSAs for several reasons. First, if the airline does not want to establish its own offices in the GSA's country the GSA will provide a presence. For airlines this is a common occurrence – airlines fly to a great many different countries, but may only have a few flights a week, making it extremely inefficient to maintain an office in that country. Second, GSAs will often have local contacts with freight forwarding and logistics companies, making it easy for them to sell air

freight – note that the GSA will welcome the opportunity to offer more choice to potential customers, both in terms of destinations and of flight times.

One such GSA is Aviareps. Founded in Germany in 1994, Aviareps now has 40 subsidiaries worldwide. Each office is operated as an independent company, incorporated in the host country, but each reports back to corporate headquarters in Germany.

During the 1990s the company grew rapidly, not only in terms of expanding its direct business with airlines but also diversifying into tourism representation. Aviareps is able to represent hotels, cruise lines, railway companies, car rental companies, tourist attractions, and tourist resorts, and even tourist boards, as well as airlines, and is thus able to offer a seamless service to any company wanting to make bookings or provide services for most travel options.

There are, of course, countries where Aviareps does not have a presence. The

. . . *continued*

CASE STUDY ... *continued*

company has therefore concluded reciprocal agreements with GSAs in those countries, so that through bookings can be made and organizations such as tour operators can do business through Aviareps without needing to contact separate GSAs in each country where they want to do business.

For a relatively young company, Aviareps has done extremely well – it has 80 airlines and 90 tourism entities in its portfolio, and operates in every continent. Turnover in 2010 was €82 million, and the company handled over a billion euros' worth of business for its clients in that year. Equity in the company amounts to €14 million. The company remains in private hands, with 46 percent of the

equity held by its founder and chief executive, the rest being held by the other directors and a small amount by the investment company that helped finance the firm in its early days. The company does not allow clients or potential clients to hold shares: if Aviareps was publicly traded, it might happen that an airline would buy into the company, which would compromise its independent and impartial status.

The company's vision is to "bring people to the world, and bring the world to people." This they are achieving by acting as the catalyst that brings together many players in the travel industry – moving far beyond what most GSAs can do.

CASE STUDY QUESTIONS

1 What are the advantages of using Aviareps rather than other GSAs?
2 What sources of channel power does Aviareps have?
3 What advantages, from a customer's viewpoint, are there in the fact that Aviareps has its own offices in 40 countries?
4 What might an airline expect from a German agent such as Aviareps?
5 Why should a major airline such as Delta or KLM use a GSA?

CHAPTER SUMMARY

Distribution policy is a major contributor to strategy in business to business marketing. The purpose of the exercise is to ensure that goods arrive in the right condition, at the right time, and in the right place: good distribution makes it easy for potential customers to buy.

The key points from this chapter are:

- Distributors provide a wide range of services to both customers and to suppliers. These services have to be provided by somebody.
- Distribution can be a critical success factor in business to business markets.

- Distribution might be intensive, selective or exclusive: each has its advantages in specific markets.
- Distributors should be treated as partners.
- Conflict within distribution networks is inevitable, since the firms involved all have separate agendas.
- Channel management is carried out by cooperation and negotiation.
- Cutting out the middlemen is likely to increase costs and reduce the efficiency of the network as a whole.

REVIEW QUESTIONS

1 How might a company evaluate a relationship with a distributor?
2 What types of conflict are most likely in distribution networks?
3 What are the main ways of controlling distributors?
4 What are the main features of efficient customer response?
5 Negotiation implies power. What power might a distributor have when dealing with a supplier?

REFERENCES

Arnold, David (2000). "Seven Rules of International Distribution." *Harvard Business Review*, Vol. 28, No. 7, Nov–Dec, 131–7.

Bitner, M.J. (1992). "Servicescapes: the impact of physical surroundings on customers and employees." *Journal of Marketing*, Vol. 54, Iss. 2, April, 57–71.

Czinkota, Michael R. and Ronkainen, Ilkka A. (2010). *International Marketing* (9th Ed.). Mason, Ohio: South-Western Cengage Learning.

Fitzpatrick, Peter B. and Zimmerman, Alan S. (1985). *Essentials of Export Marketing*. New York: AMACOM.

Gonzalez-Hernando, Santiago, Iglesias, Victor, and Trespalacios, Juan A. (2005). "Exclusive territories and performance dimensions in industrial distribution channels." *Industrial Marketing Management*, Vol. 34, Iss. 4, May, 305–12.

Hakansson, H. and Gadde, L-E. (1992). *Professional Purchasing*. London: Routledge.

Lai, Kee-hung, Bao, Yeging, and Li, Xiaotong (2008). "Channel relationship and business uncertainty: Evidence from the Hong Kong market." *Industrial Marketing Management*, Vol. 37, Iss. 6, August, 738–51.

Lee, Dong-Jin, Jeong, Insik, Tark Lee, Hyoung and Jin Sung, Hye (2008). "Developing a model of reciprocity in the importer–exporter relationship: The relative efficacy of economic versus social factors." *Industrial Marketing Management*, Vol. 37, Iss. 1, January, 23–36.

Marx, W. (1995). "The co-marketing revolution." *Industry Week*, Vol. 244, Iss. 18, 2 October, 77–9.

Mehta, Rajiv, Larsen, Trina, Rosenbloom, Bert, and Ganitsky, Joseph (2006). "The impact of cultural differences in U.S. business-to-business export marketing channel strategic alliances." *Industrial Marketing Management*, Vol. 35, Iss. 2, February, 166–77.

Ming-Sung, Julian, Tsao, Show-Ming, Tsai, Wen-Hsien, and Hill, H-J Tu (2007). "Will eChannel additions increase the financial performance of the firm? – The evidence from Taiwan." *Industrial Marketing Management, Vol. 36, Iss. 1*, January, 68–80.

Palmatier, Robert W., Miao, C. Fred, and Fang, Eric (2007). "Sales channel integration after mergers and acquisitions: A methodological approach for avoiding common pitfalls." *Industrial Marketing Management, Vol. 36, Iss. 5*, July, 604–16.

Perry, D. (1989). "How You'll Manage your 1990's Distribution Portfolio." *Business Marketing*, Vol. 54, No. 46, June.

Sahadev, Sunil (2005). "Exploring the role of expert power in channel management: An empirical study." *Industrial Marketing Management, Vol. 34, Iss. 5*, July, 504–14.

Webb, Kevin L. and Lambe, C. Jay (2007). "Internal multi-channel conflict: An exploratory investigation and conceptual framework." *Industrial Marketing Management, Vol. 36, Iss. 1*, January, 50–7.

Chapter 13

Business to business marketing communications

INTRODUCTION

This chapter is about ways of communicating in business to business markets. The major difference between business to business and consumer marketing communications is the lack of mass media for businesses. Consumer marketing communications are heavily dominated by Internet, television, radio, and press advertising, but business to business advertising is less likely to use these media due to the much smaller number of buyers involved.

CHAPTER OBJECTIVES

After reading this chapter, you should be able to:

- describe communications theory
- describe the main problems in planning a campaign
- explain how attitude change models can be used in planning a campaign
- describe the factors that impact the marketing communications mix
- explain the use of models in business to business communications
- understand the role of the company website.

B2B VS. CONSUMER COMMUNICATIONS

Because business to business markets are smaller than consumer markets, some restrictions will apply. Table 13.1 shows the main differences.

Of course, business to business and consumer advertising also have a great deal in common. Advertising aims to reach people with its message, and change its target market in some way – changing attitudes or behavior, increasing the level of knowledge, or whatever the advertiser hopes to achieve. Ultimately advertisers hope to change behavior, because they hope to influence the audience to buy the products on offer. Other marketing communications are intended to have a similar effect.

There is a greater emphasis on personal selling in business to business markets than there is in consumer markets, largely due to the bigger order values and the smaller numbers of buyers in each market segment. Because the buyers and sellers are much more likely to establish a long-term relationship in a B2B environment, there is also a greater emphasis on the personal contact which selling entails.

COMMUNICATIONS THEORIES

Communications theory has been dominated by the Schramm model of communications (see Figure 13.1), a model which is familiar to most students of communication.

TABLE 13.1 Differences between B2B and consumer communications

Consumer markets	Business to business markets
Availability of mass media.	Mass media of little use.
Greater use of emotional appeals.	More rational approach used.
Greater tendency on the part of consumers to avoid the message.	Greater preparedness to seek out information.
Selective retention means that communications are quickly forgotten.	Communications are frequently stored for future reference – brochures, advertisements, and leaflets may be filed away.
Copy is almost always short and punchy, usually just ten or a dozen words.	Copy is frequently long, even a thousand words or more.
Communication is aimed at individuals, who are in most cases solely responsible for purchasing decisions.	Communication is aimed at groups, who in most cases need to agree on purchasing decisions.
Characterized by mass media, reaching broad market segments.	Characterized by industry-specific media, widely-read by decision-making unit members.

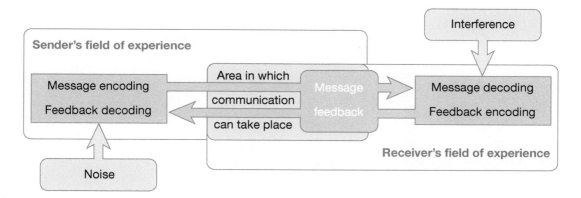

FIGURE 13.1 Conduit model of communications

In this model, the sender of a message first needs to code the message in order to send it. The code will need to be something the receiver can understand, for example it must be in a language the receiver knows. There must be a medium for the message to travel through (for example Internet, television or print), and the recipient must be able to decode the message. Interference and noise will affect the way the message is transmitted and interpreted (Schramm, 1948, 1971).

The problem with this model is that it implies that communication is something that is done to people, rather than a cooperative process. A more modern view of communication is that it is a co-construction of meaning in which the person receiving the message interprets it in the light of previous experience. In this model, communication is an active process on both sides: the input from the receiver is at least as great as that from the transmitter, and the message is likely to be interpreted in many different ways by each different receiver.

The model implies that communication creates a pool of meaning between the parties. Each person puts something into the pool, each person takes something out, and the pool changes slightly each time (see Figure 13.2).

To stretch the analogy further, when either party puts something into the pool the new input mixes with everything that is already in the pool. What the other party draws from the pool therefore includes some of what already existed. Provided the new material is not wildly at odds with what is already in the pool, the shared meaning will remain close: if the new material is very different from that which already exists between the parties, the person who put the material in may have to add a lot more before the meaning becomes clear.

This model of communications is particularly relevant to personal selling. The personal selling function is, by its nature, a dialogue in which the seller may control the process, but the bulk of the communication comes from the buyer. Salespeople who lose sight of this end up doing most of the talking and lose the sale.

The model also explains another phenomenon in communication, which is that some communications are actively sought out by customers, whereas others are not (Blythe, 2003). Unsought communications are those which the seller sends out in the optimistic hope that a buyer will respond: unsought mass e-mailings, display advertising, TV advertising, billboards, etc. Sought communications

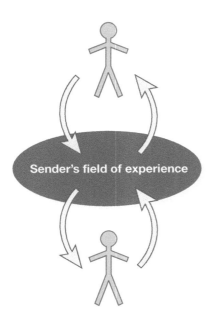

FIGURE 13.2 Pool of shared meaning

are those which a buyer specifically looks for: classified advertising, exhibitions, brochures, and even sales pitches. It is important to distinguish between the two, since the approach needs to be very different: an unsought communication needs to be persuasive and attention-grabbing, whereas sought communication should be informative and factual, because the buyer is already persuaded to a large extent.

Considered in terms of the decision-making process (see Chapter 2), buyers who are at the need-identification stage may be approached using unsought communication. A business publication advertisement, suitably placed, may make companies realize that they have a problem which had not previously been identified. For example, in the wake of the September 11 attacks on New York, British Airways ran a highly successful campaign on UK television aimed at encouraging business travellers back onto BA North Atlantic services. The advertisements contrasted one company pitching for business by sending a beautifully-produced glossy brochure to its New York customer, with another company whose executive arrives in person. The executive making the personal visit is quickly on first-name terms with the customer, and is greeted as a friend: the brochure is left on the table. The executives who sent the brochure, meanwhile, are congratulating themselves because, in the course of a telephone call, the New York customer said that he "liked the spreadsheets."

This advertisement was unusual in several respects. First, it appeared on television, which is rare for B2B advertising. Second, it was aimed at a general problem for any business, which is the failure to attach enough importance to personal contacts. Third, the product itself is generic – airplane rides across the Atlantic are provided by a very large number of airlines, any of whom might benefit from BA's advertising, since all it did was flag up the problem. Later BA advertising became much more brand-specific, delineating the advantages of using BA rather than its rivals.

Buyers who are at the information search stage may use display advertising because they will be sensitized to look out for it, but will rapidly move toward seeking out communications such as websites, brochures or sales presentations in order to obtain hard facts on which to base decisions. At this point an emotive sales pitch is likely to be of a lot less interest than a factual presentation.

SIGNS AND MEANING

A sign is anything that stands for something (its object) to somebody (its interpreter) in some respect (its context) (Pierce, 1986). Signs fall into three categories: icon, index, and symbol.

An icon is a sign that looks like the object, or represents it visually in a way that most people would relate to. For example, an agricultural machinery manufacturer might use a stylized picture of a tractor as a symbol, or might use a picture of a head of wheat (Figure 13.3).

An index is a sign that relates to the object by a causal connection. A man dressed in a checked shirt wearing a hard hat represents construction or possibly lumberjacking. Most people are familiar with the image of a manual worker.

A symbol is an artificial sign which has been created for the purpose of conveying meaning. The intertwined arrows used to indicate recycled or recyclable materials are familiar to most people: they convey an impression of greenness or environmental friendliness. Likewise many global companies use symbols to identify their brands. For example, the diamond logo of the Hong Kong and Shanghai Banking Corporation is familiar worldwide.

In fact, communication is carried out in many other ways than simply the words themselves. Only around 30 percent of communication uses words: companies communicate by using pictures, non-verbal sounds (e.g. the Intel four-note jingle), smell, touch, numbers, artefacts, time, and kinetics. Sales people know the value of body language and non-verbal communication: facial expressions and gesture are widely used to create meaning in advertising. Silent communication may take place through any of the following media:

FIGURE 13.3 Agricultural icons

- Numbers. Brand names frequently use numbers to imply that the brand is the latest in a long series. Boeing use this method to identify their aircraft models.
- Space. Images of people standing close together imply that they have a close relationship: some companies have placed their logos in close juxtaposition to indicate that they have a close relationship.
- Artefacts. Small gifts and free samples convey a sense of obligation to the recipient.
- Time. Images of a person in a hurry might convey an image of success and energy to Northern Europeans or Americans, but might convey arrogance, or someone who has no time for anyone else, to an African audience.
- Kinetics. Gesticulating, facial expressions, and body language all convey meaning.

Meaning is conveyed not just by words, but by the way the words are used, and by the peripheral cues that surround them. Much human communication is made for effect, rather than as a literal statement: people become adept at reading between the lines.

The main problem with silent languages is that they are not culturally universal. Body language and gesture does not transfer well to other cultures, even when the cultures are relatively close. Some well-known examples are the two-finger sign used in the UK, which means nothing to people elsewhere in Europe; the circle of forefinger and thumb which means "OK" in the US but is a rude gesture in Brazil; and showing the soles of the feet in Thailand.

More subtly, Japanese people tend to show their emotions less in public than do Americans, Indians tend to regard shabby clothes as denoting poverty whereas Northern Europeans associate this with freedom and independence, and numbers which are considered lucky in some cultures are considered unlucky in others (Costa and Pavia, 1992). Unfortunately, these cultural differences often go unrecognized because people tend to regard body language as universal. While a foreigner might easily be forgiven for an error in speaking the language (in fact such errors might even be seen as charming), the same courtesy does not usually extend to errors of body language or behavior.

The problem of misunderstanding arises because of ethnocentrism, which is the belief that one's own culture is the "right" one and everyone else's is a poor copy. Ethnocentrism is one of the few features of human behavior that belongs to all cultures (Shimp and Sharma, 1987). In practice marketing communications can be applied worldwide only with great care.

ATTITUDE AND ATTITUDE CHANGE

Attitude is a learned tendency to respond in a consistent way to an attitudinal object. Attitudes are made up of three components: cognition (which is what is consciously known of and thought about the attitudinal object), affect (which is what is felt emotionally about the attitudinal object), and conation (which is the intended behavior toward the attitudinal object). Provided these three components are in balance the attitude is stable and is therefore unlikely to change much. For example, a buyer might say, "I like Corus Steel. They are nice people to deal with, the products are always up to specification, and I think we'll probably always buy from them rather than from anyone else." The first part of this statement is affective (I like them, they are nice people), the second part is cognitive (the products are always up to specification), and the third part is conative (we'll probably always buy from them). Note that conation is only *intended* behavior – other factors may intervene to prevent the behavior being carried out.

Because attitudes tend to be stable, the first essential for attitude change is to destabilize the attitude. This means changing one or more elements of the attitude.

The cognitive element of attitude comes about because the individual develops salient beliefs about the company and its products. Salient beliefs are those which are the most important to the buyer, and which relate to the products concerned. For example, a buyer may believe that a company is 100 percent reliable on its delivery times, and because this is important to the buyer it will be a salient belief. The buyer may also believe that the same company provides very good working conditions for its staff, but may not care about this particularly and therefore the belief is not salient. If the company subsequently becomes unreliable, the salient belief will change and thus the attitude will change: if the company behaves badly toward its staff, this will not affect the buyer's attitude.

There are three ways to change attitudes, as follows:

- Add a new salient belief. For example, the BA advertisement mentioned earlier tried to add the belief that a personal contact is worth far more than even the glossiest brochure.
- Change the strength of a salient belief. If the belief is a negative one, it can be discounted or played down. If it is a positive one, it can be given greater importance. For example, a buyer may believe that a firm is reliable, and this may be important, but a set of statistics showing that the firm is 99.7 percent reliable will strengthen the belief by providing factual evidence.
- Change the evaluation of an existing belief. The importance of an existing belief can be strengthened. Using the reliability example, a buyer may accept that the firm is reliable, but has not realized that this in turn means that the buying firm's production has never been halted due to a failure on the part of the supplier – unlike other suppliers whose unreliability has resulted in large losses of production. This type of argument moves reliability much higher in the buyer's perception.

Changing a salient belief is not always about factual presentations aimed at cognition. Changes in salience can also come about through emotive appeals. For example, in the BA advertisement mentioned earlier, the executive who travelled to New York appeared smart, confident, young, organized, and generally admirable. The group who did not travel were huddled round a table in a poorly-lit room and appeared disorganized, unattractively-dressed, overweight, and lacking in confidence. This was clearly intended as an emotional appeal, implying that all the sensible people use British Airways. This type of association would help in some ways to overcome the problem of promoting travel generally rather than the BA brand (there is more on modeling later in the chapter).

Obviously new information does not always change attitudes. As the inconsistency between the existing attitude and evidence brought about by reality increases, there will come a point where the individual buyer needs to re-evaluate the attitude and go through some kind of mental readjustment to restore stability. This can come about through three main mechanisms:

- Stimulus rejection. The individual discounts the new information or rejects it entirely. This can easily come about if the new information is presented by an incompetent sales person who manages to come across as unreliable.

■   Attitude splitting. This involves only accepting that part of the new information which does not cause an inconsistency. The individual might accept that the new information is true, but that the firm's own circumstances are exceptional.

■   Accommodating the new attitude. Essentially this means accepting the new attitude in its entirety.

The three elements of attitude are so closely linked that a change in one is likely to lead to a change in both the others (Rosenberg, 1960). Attitudes can basically be changed via two routes (Petty and Caccioppo, 1983). The first route (the central route) involves an appeal to the rational, cognitive element of attitude. This generally will be more prevalent in business marketing than in consumer marketing (see Chapter 2). The second route is the peripheral route, which involves an appeal to the affective element, usually by associating the brand with another attitudinal object. For example, business to business marketers often refer to their products as the Rolls Royce (or Cadillac) of the product category, in order to tap into buyers' perceptions of the quality and reliability of Rolls Royce or Cadillac. Presumably younger marketers might begin tapping into the reputation of BMW, Lexus or Mercedes. In the BA example, the peripheral route is used by associating the brand with the smart-looking individual who is using it. No-one would believe that flying with BA will make someone more confident, better dressed, and thirty pounds lighter, but the emotional association is clearly drawn. Because of the interdependence of the elements of attitude, the peripheral route is effective in changing attitudes.

Obviously new information may conflict with the information the buyer already holds. Cognitive dissonance theory states that if an individual holds two conflicting cognitions, he or she will experience discomfort and will try to resolve the dissonance either by changing one or other of the views, or by introducing a third viewpoint which will reconcile the differences (Festinger, 1957).

The most interesting aspect of dissonance theory is that attitudes can apparently be changed more easily by offering low rewards than by offering high ones. Festinger and Carlsmith (1959) induced students to lie to each other by telling them it was part of a psychological experiment, and offering them payment varying from $1 to $20. The students who were offered the lower amount actually began to believe the lie, whereas those offered the higher amount tended not to. The higher-paid students were able to justify lying on the basis that they were receiving a substantial reward (at 1959 prices). The lesser-paid students had no such external justification, and therefore had to resolve the dissonance by believing the lie themselves.

The reason for the power of cognitive dissonance is that the arousal of dissonance always contains personal involvement. Therefore, the reduction of dissonance always involves some form of self-justification (Aronson et al., 1974). Self-justification is necessary because the individual usually feels that the dissonance has arisen as a result of an action or thought which is immoral or stupid or both. In the marketing context, cognitive dissonance may reveal itself as post-purchase dissonance. Here, the buyer of the product may find that information previously gathered about the product is inaccurate – the cognition based on the pre-purchase information search conflicts with the direct experience of using the product. In these circumstances the buyer can take one of four general approaches to reducing the dissonance:

■   Ignore the dissonant information and look for positive (consonant) information about the product. This means that it is important for sales people to call back on customers after the order has been delivered in order to check that all is well: if the customer is experiencing post-purchase dissonance, this is an opportunity to provide reassuring information.

▪ Distort the dissonant information, perhaps by considering the source of the information as unreliable.

▪ Play down the importance of the issue. Buyers may decide that the particular aspect of the product which causes the problem is really not very important after all.

▪ Change the behavior or the situation. From the marketer's viewpoint, this can be the most dangerous, since the buyer may change behavior by placing future orders elsewhere.

In most cases, post-purchase dissonance can be eliminated entirely by the intelligent use of salespeople. In extreme cases, buyers may take action against the vendor. These responses fall into three categories (Singh, 1988): voice responses (complaints to the supplier), private responses (complaints to colleagues, business contacts, and even family), and third-party responses (complaints through the Web, trade associations or litigation). Of the three, private responses are likely to be the most damaging, because these damage corporate reputation without the supplier having the opportunity to put their side of the case. The least damaging is a voiced response, so it may be advisable for companies to encourage customers to complain if anything is even remotely wrong with the products (see Chapter 2).

DEVELOPING THE MARKETING COMMUNICATIONS PROGRAM

In order to devise a marketing communications program which will meet the needs of the firm, the steps shown in Figure 13.4 should be followed. First, as can be seen from the figure, marketing communications objectives must be completely congruent with the overall corporate objectives and the marketing objectives of the firm. Some managers make the error of stating marketing communications objectives in imprecise terms. For example, some have offered objectives such as "help the salesforce increase market share considerably or "find new distributors in the European Union." A marketing communications manager who offers these kinds of objectives will be at a disadvantage after he/she has spent the budget because it will be unclear whether the objectives have been met. Marketing communications objectives should therefore be measurable. Examples are: "increase market share for high-powered semiconductors from 7 to 10 percent in the transportation market segment" or "develop ten new distributors in the EU for financial software products."

Target audiences and marketing communications objectives are really established simultaneously. In order for the objectives to be set, the audiences must be identified. Once the objectives and the audiences have been established, the proper media must be chosen. In business marketing, media may be electronic but is often web-based, print (either business or trade publications), exhibitions, brochures or mailings. An effective website is an absolutely essential component in the communications effort. Next, messages must be established. While business marketing communications focus on transmitting more fact than emotion, well-turned, interesting phrases will always attract more attention than simple declarative statements. Therefore, as much creativity must be applied

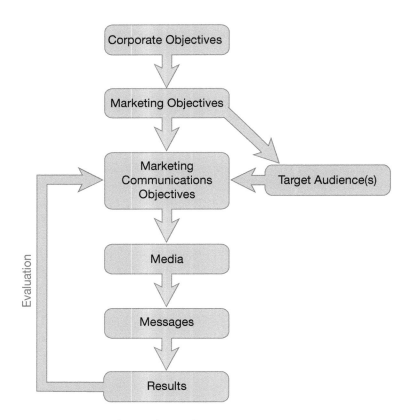

FIGURE 13.4 Developing the marketing communications program

to business marketing communications as is applied to consumer marketing communications. Proprietary research conducted by one of the authors confirms that the website is the first source for most information required by architects and specifiers when they are choosing building products.

Once the messages have been established and placements made, results must be measured. If the objectives have been set as has been described above, the manager will be able to compare the results with the objectives, evaluate any shortfalls and change the objectives, audiences, media or messages in order to improve results. Approaching business marketing communications in this way makes the effort an investment rather than simply an expense.

Marketing communications consists of advertising, public relations, sales promotion, and personal selling. How the effort is divided between these tools relates to the budget available. As can be seen in Figure 13.5, other important factors also have an effect upon the mix of tools to be used.

An important area is media and/or services availability and cost. While a firm might feel comfortable placing ads in a trade publication in large markets such as the United States or Brazil, it may find that no such publication exists in a particular foreign market. For instance, while there may be a publication focusing on hospital waste disposal in the large markets, it might not be possible to find such a publication in Swedish or Danish. Also to be considered are services availability and cost. For example, a firm might be comfortable with rapid public relations help or the ability to hire a firm to make videos. In Nigeria, firms like this might be far less available. The cost of these media or services may also be prohibitive where there is little competition in smaller markets.

A key factor determining the marketing communications mix is channel preferences. Distributors and agents often have strong opinions about how communications should be conducted. In some cases, these individuals wish to review and rewrite advertising messages. While they often have technical knowledge, many are not capable of clear communications using the written word. Nevertheless, a prudent manager will take into account the opinions of agents and distributors in local markets. Another determining factor is competition. Should a major competitor advertise heavily in a particular journal or establish a presence at a particular trade exposition, a marketing manager may be forced to match that competitor. Government regulations have some effect upon communications, although they are more prevalent in the consumer area. In some countries, direct comparisons between products are not permitted and some kinds of promotion are not allowed (for example, up until 2007 retailers were not allowed to advertise on French TV, and there are severe restrictions on advertising financial products such as hedge funds in the United States). The marketing manager must be acutely aware of these regulations so that he/she would not violate one of them. The next influence is the nature of the product itself. Some products are easily explained in print media while others need direct demonstration either at an exposition or through the salesforce. Using inappropriate media is simply a waste of expenditure.

Target audiences are not the same as target segments. Segments are those to whom the firm will sell. But target audiences also include those who influence the purchase. For instance, a firm may

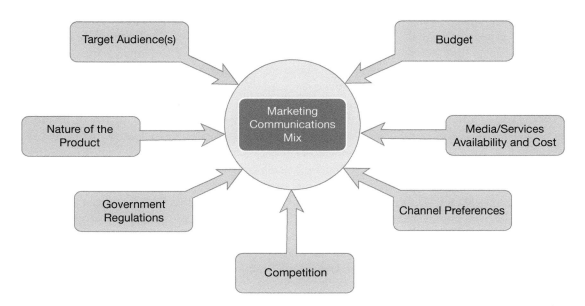

FIGURE 13.5 Determining the global B2B marketing communications mix

have decided its target segment for computer access flooring products is information systems managers in large multinational corporations. However, the firm may also find that independent consultants, whether for interiors, security or computer design may be equally important in making the buying decision. In other words, these are influencers in the buying center. These consultants must be included as target audience members, even if they are not identified as part of the segment design. The target audience is obviously of critical importance. Should a particular target audience in a particular market seem to gather all its information from one source, a marketing manager would be intelligent to place heavy emphasis on that source in his/her communications budget. Determining the preferences of target audiences is often somewhat difficult but can be accomplished through primary research.

The firm may also face some other obstacles in its global communications program. First, language can have a major effect upon the size and shape of print ads and catalogs. English is an economical language which takes up less space on a page than most others. Should the firm choose to develop television commercials for a global audience, no on-screen spokesman should be used. Also, adequate time must be allowed for translation and insertion of "voice over material" with no spokesman on-screen.

ADVERTISING

Advertising is a non-personal communication inserted in a medium. This means that it is not personal selling, or word-of-mouth communication, or messages on T-shirts. It is characterized by its impersonal quality, and also by its one-way approach: it is not interactive except in a very limited way.

Business advertising is aimed at organizations rather than at individuals. As we have seen, though, organizations do not make purchasing decisions: people do. Business advertising therefore needs to appeal to a wide spectrum of people, each with differing personalities and attitudes, and most especially each with a different role within the organization. This means that any advertising may need to have a wide appeal to reach people operating to different agendas. Organizational buyers rarely buy goods and services through advertising alone so advertising generally acts as a support mechanism rather than a primary means of communication.

If the cost of advertising is calculated on the basis of the cost of campaign divided by the number of people it reaches, it is very much cheaper than any other communication method, with the possible exceptions of company websites, PR and word-of-mouth. On the other hand, it is considerably less effective than, for example, personal selling. Since each communications medium has its particular strengths and weaknesses, it is important to integrate the marketing communications so as to build on the strengths of each. The sales manager who fails to realize that advertising is essential to support his sales team, and the advertising manager who fails to realize that advertising cannot do everything, will each be heading for disaster, yet often these two managers might be in conflict as they fight for budgets. There is more on this later in the chapter.

Advertising has the following roles in business to business marketing:

■　To create a favorable climate for personal selling. Salespeople whose companies advertise widely rarely have a problem with making appointments: a prime example of this is IBM. Their salespeople can arrive at a firm without an appointment and still be shown the way to the IT manager's office. In fact, McGraw-Hill magazines division ran a highly-successful press advertisement which showed a grumpy-looking buyer saying

> I don't know who you are. I don't know your company. I don't know your company's products. I don't know what your company stands for. I don't know your company's customers. I don't know your company's record. I don't know your company's reputation. Now – what was it you wanted to sell me?

It is easy to imagine the discomfort of a salesperson faced with this situation.

- To reach inaccessible buying influences. Some of the members of the buying unit are inaccessible to salespeople (see Chapter 2). In some cases the salesperson may never meet the final decision maker (see Chapter 14). One estimate states that salespeople may only reach an average of three out of ten buying influences that should be reached (*Sales and Marketing Management*, 1984). These people may, however, read the business press and may well have formed an opinion about the company and its products. Clearly advertising can help the process of establishing the brand in the minds of people who have little or no contact with salespeople.
- To reach unknown buying influences. In many cases it is impossible to know who the influencers in the buying decision are. The managing director's golf partner might be a stronger influence than the chief engineer, but the salesperson might be concentrating attention on the engineer. Again, the golf partner may well become aware of the company and its products through the firm's advertising activities.
- To generate leads for salespeople. Particularly in the case of sought communications the buyer may well contact the company for more information as a result of seeing an advertisement. These leads need to be qualified as serious leads, not merely casual enquiries. The advantage of these leads is that the salesperson can spend more time on visiting live prospects and less time on cold-calling or other lead-generating devices.
- To supplement field sales communications. Sales people often cannot call on their customers as often as they would like. In many cases, advertising is able to keep the company and its products fresh in the minds of buyers in between calls from sales people.
- To inform channel intermediaries. Both present and prospective channel intermediaries can be stimulated by advertising. These advertisements might be used to promote new products or to remind the distributors of the firm's existence and product lines.
- To stimulate derived demand. Because demand in B2B markets is derived from consumer markets, it may sometimes be worthwhile for a supplier to stimulate demand among its customers' markets in order to create a derived demand. An example of this was the UK's glass manufacturers who ran a joint campaign apparently aimed at consumers (but in reality aimed at canners and bottlers in the food industry), the strap line for which was "You can see what you're getting with glass." This helped to slow down the trend toward using steel cans, but did not help much in the parallel switch to plastic bottles.
- To project a favorable corporate image. Sometimes a firm which only supplies other firms may need to improve its public image. For example, a firm may need to re-establish its environmental credentials, or may wish to stimulate a consumer demand to include its products in the final product. An example of this is Intel, a firm which does not supply the public but which has

established its brand name in the public consciousness in such a way that most computer users want an Intel chip in their machines. This means, in turn, that computer designers and manufacturers are compelled to include Intel chips in their machines.

■ To provide the most economical promotional mix. Advertising can be much more cost-effective at the need recognition and information search stages than a sales call or even an exhibition (see Chapter 14).

MEDIA IN BUSINESS ADVERTISING

One of the major advantages of business to business marketing is that each industry has its own trade publications. This makes targeting easy, especially since members of the industry tend to read the publications (and the advertisements) more assiduously than most consumers read consumer magazines. Some trade journals are vertical, in other words they are read by all firms in the same industry, while other journals are horizontal (for example *Advertising Age*) and are read by a specific group of professionals across a wide range of industries. Most trade journals are also available online.

Trade journals tend to be kept, sometimes for long periods. Any regular visitor to corporate waiting rooms will have noticed that some of the trade journals on the table are several years out of date. Buyers frequently save articles from trade journals for future reference, and in some cases (notably professionals such as architects) the trade journals become part of the corporate library, used for information searches sometimes years later.

Selecting an appropriate trade journal follows the sequence shown in Table 13.2.

Trade journal advertising is a relatively low-cost form of advertising. Also, it is usually fairly closely-targeted, which means that less of the advertising budget is wasted in advertising to people who are not interested in the product category and never will be. Trade journals also have considerable credibility with their target audiences, and are often used as the main source of information for buyers. Trade journals have the advantage of being a sought communication, so advertising is often read.

DIRECT RESPONSE ADVERTISING

Direct response advertising involves a communication from the selling company to the purchasing company in a personalized and often tailored manner. The intention of direct response advertising is to open a dialogue between buyer and seller, so the medium needs to communicate effectively. Its main appeal is that it is easily monitored and controlled: databases help the monitoring process in the following ways (O'Malley et al., 1999):

■ tracking responses;
■ recording speed of fulfillment of the sale;
■ tracking responses in different sectors;
■ comparing conversion rates to response rates;
■ assessing the effectiveness of media in reaching the target audiences;
■ comparing response levels in different media;
■ recording customer data captured in the course of the campaign.

TABLE 13.2 Sequence of choosing trade journal

Stage of process	Explanation
Determine target markets	Use industrial classifications or trade directories to identify targets. Brainstorming with sales people and other marketers may be helpful at this stage.
Define members of the DMU (Buying Center)	Job titles, professional qualifications, and sometimes trade association membership can help in defining the membership of the DMU.
Determine what DMU members seek in the publications they read	This may be determined as a result of formal market research, or of simply asking people from the professions concerned. There is unlikely to be a definitive answer to this question, however, since different people will have different aims, and indeed any individual DMU member will have different needs at different times.
Develop messages to communicate to the DMU members	The problem here is that different DMU members will have different needs and therefore different messages. On the other hand, the messages should have a common theme since DMU members will need to speak with each other in order to arrive at a decision.
Determine which journals best fit the needs of the campaign	This can be determined using rating services such as BRAD (British Rate and Data).
Rank the publications	This can be done using the cost of advertising, the circulation figures, the editorial content and article value, and the degree of fit with the needs of the campaign.
Select the appropriate publication for each DMU member group	This will involve a judgment regarding the best penetration of buying influence for the money expended.
Evaluate the effectiveness of each publication	This is a complex area. Unless the firm is prepared to spend large amounts on formal market research, much of the evidence is likely to be hearsay. Also, given that many DMU members will keep trade journals for a long period, it may be some years before the impact of the advertising is felt. This is, of course, a general characteristic of advertising.

Unfortunately, much direct mail is poorly targeted so it is frequently destroyed without even being read. The key to success in direct response advertising is to target carefully and to make the message itself appropriate and worthwhile for the recipient. The main media used for direct response advertising are the Internet, telesales, and direct mail.

Direct marketing has been defined as "A cybernetic marketing process which uses direct response advertising in prospecting, conversion and maintenance." (Bauer and Miglautsch, 1992). Direct marketing is therefore neither a more sophisticated mail-order system, nor is it merely a communication device in the manner of mailshots.

Direct marketing is not a mass medium: it communicates with consumers as individuals, rather than as a group of segments (Bird, 1993). It is interactive, meaning that prospects respond directly (and measurably) to direct communications. Provided the communication is targeted accurately, responses will result.

The rapid growth of direct marketing in recent years has been the result of the falling cost of information technology, and also the fragmentation of markets.

The impact of technology on direct marketing is shown in Table 13.3.

Databases come in three basic varieties:

■ Hierarchical databases. Data is stored under a single criterion, for example an account number. This makes it easy to call up details on a specific individual, but hard to generate lists of (for example) customers who are habitual late payers. Hierarchical databases are essentially derived from manual filing systems: they are quicker, but not much more sophisticated.

TABLE 13.3 Impact of technology

Technological factor	Explanation and examples
Addressability	This is the ability to identify and reach individuals (Vavra, 1992). Computers allow marketers to record thousands of names and addresses, and also to search for information about firms rapidly in order to identify the appropriate recipients for mailings.
Measurability	Computers enable marketers to record the purchasing behavior of companies and to analyze purchasing patterns in order to tailor communications (Vavra, 1992).
Flexibility	The ability to approach each customer with a uniquely-tailored approach, using desktop publishing or data mining (Vavra, 1992).
Accountability	The ability to track expenditure and monitor returns (Vavra, 1992). Computer technology allows marketers to track each mailing individually if necessary, and record follow-ups.
Increased processing power	The ever-increasing data-processing capabilities of equipment allow faster and more detailed analysis of customers and their purchasing behavior.
Analytical software	The availability of analysis software has made statistical analysis of customer records extremely simple.
Telephone systems	Until the mid-1980s telephones could only realistically be used for outbound telesales. With the advent of 0800 numbers, respondents to mailings can call free. This greatly improves response rates. Another labor-saving innovation for firms has been the advent of IVR (interactive voice response) systems which allow many calls to be handled entirely by computer. Most callers find these systems irritating, however: business is about people, not economics

- Network databases. These use "tags" to identify records needed for analysis. For example, a customer's records might include a tag for the postcode (so that records can be sorted geographically), another tag for the date of the last transaction (so records can be sorted by recency of use), and a set of tags for other business variables such as type of customer or industry. Network databases are generally more useful than hierarchical databases, but are more expensive and harder to operate since the user must understand the structure of the data in order to manipulate it.
- Relational databases. Currently the dominant system, relational databases store the data in two dimensions: the data for a given customer lies in one dimension, the data on a given attribute across all customers lies in another. For example, a bank might store information on a loan under both the customer's records and the bank's loan records, including a record of late payment or extra borrowing. A relational database allows the information to be added to both records at once and be accessed either way.

When deciding on database design, managers should ask themselves the following questions (Linton, 1995):

- How will the database support business objectives?
- What is expected from the system?
- What are the main requirements?
- What applications will it be used for?

Sometimes a firm might find it worthwhile to outsource management of the database, although this is less common nowadays than previously, because powerful computers are cheap enough for firms to be able to manage the database in-house. The advantages of outsourcing database management are as follows:

- The database will not affect the capacity of the firm's internal systems.
- There will be no need to recruit or train extra staff.
- The database will be managed by specialists, who may be able to make useful suggestions for its management.
- Outsourcing may be more cost-effective due to economies of scale.

Populating the database may come from internal sources, such as the firm's own sales records (also form returns, exhibition enquiries, sales promotions and so forth), or it may come from bought-in databases. Lists of names can be bought from list brokers, and electronic directories can be used to identify prospects.

It is tempting to use market research records to populate the databases, but unless the respondents have specifically agreed to allow this, it is extremely dangerous to do so. Within the UK such practices may be illegal under the Data Protection Act, and many countries have enacted similar laws to prevent invasion of privacy. In any event, use of information which was provided under an assurance of confidentiality is unethical, and will result in greater refusals by respondents to take part in market research, which would of course be detrimental to the accuracy of research.

Cleaning the list will result in greater levels of response. Respondents can easily be irritated by misspellings of their names, wrong addresses, and so forth. The commonest errors are shown in Table 13.4 (Bradford, 1995).

Cleaning the list can be difficult. Visual checking of the list might remove some of the more obvious errors, but checking whether someone has left a company may be harder. The sales force may be able to assist with this.

De-duping (removing duplicate names) can be carried out in six stages (Mander, 1995).

1   Identify and examine key elements of the name and address. For example, title, initials, surname, position in the company, and each line of the address.
2   Form access keys. When two or more records share the same combinations of parts of names and addresses they should be identified and "pulled."
3   Develop a scoring system for potential duplicates. The higher the score, the greater the similarity. This allows the machine to compare records for similarity and "pull" the most similar ones.
4   Identify the acceptable level of duplication. This gives the machine a cut-off point beyond which the records are regarded as suspect.
5   Prioritize duplicates. If two people from the same company are receiving mailings, for example, the company can decide which of them should receive the mailing, or whether both of them should continue to do so.
6   Change the records. Delete unwanted records, merge data from duplicated records, and so forth.

TABLE 13.4 Common errors in databases

Error	Explanation
Incorrect name	Even minor errors such as wrong initials might result in someone else with the same surname receiving the mailing. In a large organization, this is likely to result in the mailing being destroyed, since the mailing may well go to the wrong division.
Titles	In some cases the recipient might be offended by the omission or addition of a title. For example, the medical profession is often touchy about being addressed as Doctor, and in the international context it is considered polite to use all the individual's titles (this is typical in Germany, where someone might be addressed as Frau Professor Doktor Schmidt, for example).
Duplicate entries	Sometimes the same person is listed under different versions of the same name. Someone might be listed as Alan Reynolds, A.J. Reynolds, Mr A. Reynolds, or any of several other combinations. Multiple mailings are not only wasteful for the company, they are irritating for the recipient and also give the impression that the company sending the mailing is careless and impersonal.
Gone-aways	Sometimes mail continues to be sent to individuals who have left the firm, retired, or even died. People change jobs on average every four or five years, so it is difficult for marketers to keep track of them.

The first three stages of this process can be carried out by computer: the final three require intervention by a human being. For small lists, the de-duping process is probably more easily carried out manually: a small engineering firm might only have a mailing list of a few hundred, whereas an airline frequent-flyer program might have a list running into thousands.

Segmentation in direct marketing also operates differently from that in traditional marketing. Traditionally, segmentation is a top-down process, beginning with a mass of possible customers and breaking them down into suitable groups. In direct marketing segmentation is often carried out by examining the characteristics of customers on the database and then aggregating them into segments. This means that each supplying company will develop its own segmentation approach, often behaviorally-based. In common with other forms of marketing, direct marketing has two main aims: customer acquisition, and customer retention. Customer acquisition can be aided by database combination, in which prospects are identified by mining the databases for information about them and their companies. Hot prospects can be identified by their propensity to respond to the mailings.

Customer retention is a process of first finding out why customers defect (Reichheld and Sasser, 1990). There is an assumption that satisfied customers will be loyal and dissatisfied customers will defect, but research shows that this is not always the case. Attitude is not necessarily a clear guide to behavior: conditions may prevent someone from carrying out intended behavior. Loyalty has been defined as "the relationship between the relative attitude toward the entity and patronage behaviour" (Dick and Basu, 1994). There are four categories of loyalty: no loyalty, in which the relative attitude is low and there is no consistent patronage behavior; spurious loyalty, in which the patronage behavior is high but the customer does not really believe that there is any real difference in product offerings; latent loyalty, in which the high relative attitude to the brand is not reflected in patronage; and loyalty, in which high patronage and high relative attitude go together.

Business to business marketers should be aiming to create relationships in which loyalty is high. Direct marketing can help here by ensuring that the customer is regularly contacted at all stages of the relationship in order to maintain a two-way flow of communication. According to proprietary research by one of the authors, unsought e-mail is particularly unpopular with business buyers. Most receive hundreds of e-mails per day and are only irritated by the additional volume.

STANDARDIZATION VS. ADAPTATION

The basic problem facing the global marketer is whether to seek to standardize the marketing communications, or tailor them to local cultural differences. The advantages of standardizing are cost, consistency across borders, and avoidance of creep in terms of brand values. The disadvantages are that the campaign will probably be produced to the "lowest common denominator," in other words it will have to offend nobody rather than please everybody.

Obviously marketing managers prefer standardization to adaptation. It is far less expensive to produce a single advertisement, publication or website than to develop specific versions for multiple markets. However few companies are able to standardize across all of their target markets. Most managers need to look carefully at each element of the marketing mix for possible standardization but must be ready to adapt to maximize the chances for success in any particular market.

In international marketing communications a key problem may be that the media available in one market may not be available in another. There will also be differences in the quality of the media and audiences they address. For instance in the United States there are highly specialized publications and websites focused on specific industries such as *Security Sales & Integration* for the commercial and residential security industry. In Nigeria or Thailand no such publication will exist.

Key factors encouraging standardization include economies of scale in marketing, the need for global control of marketing programs and buying center similarities across markets. Factors encouraging adaptation include government rules and regulations, divergent product use conditions and differing buying center behavior.

There are four basic strategies for international communications (Keegan and Green, 2013):

1   Same product, same communication. This can be used where the need for the product and its use are the same as in its home market. This applies to most engineering products such as nuts and bolts or sheet steel.
2   Same product, different communication. This can be used when the need for the product differs in some way in each of its target markets, or when cultural differences mean that the product has a different connotation. This may be the case with finished products such as (for example) drilling equipment, which may be used in Africa to drill water wells or in Europe to drill drainage holes. Although the basic function of the equipment is to poke holes in the ground, the conditions under which it is used and the advantages of using it will differ considerably.
3   Different products, same communication. Sometimes the product formula has to be changed to meet local conditions, but the promotion can remain the same. For example, safety regulations may differ between countries, but the basic product remains the same. An agricultural tractor may need to be adapted to run on the local fuel, but remain the same to all outward appearances.
4   Different products, different communications. Many markets require products which are unique to that market, and also have cultural differences which dictate changes in the communications mix. For example, computer software for Arabic markets needs to adapted for language and keyboard configuration, and also the marketing communication needs to be changed entirely for language and cultural parameters.

Translating advertising copy, brochures, leaflets, and other promotional materials is also prone to error and misunderstanding. Table 13.5 shows a checklist for translating advertising copy (Majaro, 2012):

Provided that a universally-recognized icon is available, and it is possible to produce meaningful hooks in each language, it should be possible to produce good international copy. Factual communications and sought communications are much more likely to translate successfully than are emotional communications.

INTEGRATING MARKETING COMMUNICATIONS

Currently, there is considerable interest in seeking to integrate marketing communications. The reasons for this are as follows:

TABLE 13.5 Translating advertising copy

Rule	Explanation
Avoid idiom, jargon or buzz-words	These can be difficult to translate, and easily adopt different meanings in the foreign language. Translators are rarely perfect in both languages, so such problems are likely to occur.
Check local legal requirements and codes of conduct	Foreign countries frequently have unfamiliar regulations. Sometimes these seem unreasonable or unlikely, but it is their country – you need to play by their rules.
Ensure that translators speak the everyday language of the country	Spanish spoken in Spain differs from that spoken in Latin America, just as American English and British English differ. Portuguese differs between Portugal, Brazil, Angola, and Mozambique, and French differs between France, Belgium, Côte D'Ivoire, Réunion, and so forth. For obvious reasons, people who are not native speakers should never be used.
Brief the translators thoroughly	Translating copy is not a one-for-one proposition. Phrases, style, and even content may need to be adapted in order to read well in the foreign language. A good translator will need to understand what your company and products are about in order to know how to translate.
Check the translation with customers and distributors in the local market	This gives the local users the chance to become involved, and also gives the opportunity to raise any criticisms of the material before it goes into production.
Re-translate the material back into the original language	This provides a final safety check. This is especially important, since the translators are almost certainly not part of your company and therefore probably do not understand the company philosophy, culture, and style, and may therefore use inappropriate phraseology.

- Greater consistency of message will increase the impact of the communication.
- Communications can reinforce each other.
- Different people respond more, or less, positively toward some media than to others.
- Economies of scale in terms of message formulation and delivery can be achieved.
- Integrated communications have a strategic effect: members of the organization become clearer about what the organizational aims are.

The aim of integration is to ensure that the basic messages which are sent out by the organization are consistent throughout, and that everyone is "singing from the same songsheet." In practice, integration is difficult to achieve, for the following reasons:

- The salesforce members may not be able, or prepared, to deliver the corporate message if they do not think that it meets the needs of the specific customer they are talking to.

- Employees often talk about their work when they go home, and may not always deliver the corporate message: this can result in damage to the corporate reputation.
- Firms in a global environment will need to adapt the message for different cultures.
- Communication is not a magic bullet: recipients interpret messages, and often confuse the message with the medium. This is a result of the "pool of meaning" model discussed earlier in the chapter.

There may even be an argument for NOT integrating communications. If a company is dealing with several different market segments, some of which exist in overseas markets, it may actually be more desirable to differentiate the communications and offer a different message to each group. The problem with this approach, of course, is that different groups may have very different perceptions of the messages, since it is almost impossible to ensure that the messages only reach the specific segment and no-one else.

One of the most useful ways of integrating marketing communications is through the use of a good website. Websites are frequently the first point of contact between a firm and its customers, and have the advantage that they represent a sought communication: people visiting a company's website frequently have an existing interest in that company's products and services. A good website will integrate communications because the other media the firm uses will drive potential customers to the website – and in some cases, the website drives customers to other communications media such as directories, call centers, or sales publications such as brochures.

Below is a checklist for establishing a successful website:

- The objectives for establishing the site must be clear from the outset.
- The site itself should be informative rather than persuasive, since it is a sought communication – people do not go online to be sold to.
- Graphics should be kept simple if possible; not everyone has a broadband connection, particularly if the potential customer is in a remote area or a country with a poor infrastructure. Many people have slow connections or slow computers.
- The impact of the communication should not depend entirely on the graphics; if the connection to the Internet is poor, downloading complex graphics or video clips might take too long.
- The site must be integrated with other communications; cross-marketing will encourage subscribers to visit the site.
- The site should be set up to gather information from those who visit it, either through requesting contact details from visitors or through downloading a tracking cookie (a piece of software which records and feeds back customer activity) onto the visitor's computer.
- The site should encourage interactivity by the use of offers, competitions, sales promotions and other incentives: people prefer interactive communications, in general (Vlasic and Kesic, 2007).
- Hyperlinks need to be fast, so that users can access the information they really need quickly.

Websites should always be easily navigable, since visitors can easily be put off and interrupt the search if they find that the site is hard to use.

Case study: Call Centers

Call centers have become the communications phenomenon of the decade. The huge increase in the ownership of mobile telephones, plus the desire for rapid (indeed instant) communication with companies, has generated a corresponding increase in the number of firms using a dedicated call center, staffed by dozens of operators ready to answer queries from customers. At the same time, the rising costs of putting salespeople on the road have forced companies down the road of using outbound call centers to telephone prospective customers with offers.

Many companies see the call center as being the front line for relationship marketing. Having an actual human being to talk to about new purchases, problems, or simply for advice is far more powerful (and human) than relying on letters and e-mails. Outbound call centers can follow up on purchases, can offer upgrades and sales of peripherals, and can follow up on referrals by satisfied customers.

Of course, call centers do have a downside. For one thing, they are often disliked by members of the public – the Telephone Preference Service, which arranges for people to be removed from calling lists, has been a runaway success: in a Parliamentary reply in July 2006, the Secretary of State for Trade and Industry reported that 12.7 million numbers were registered with TPS. This amounts to more than half the private telephones in the UK – although it is difficult to be specific, as the TPS confidentiality systems mean that there is no way to check whether consumers

have registered the same number more than once. For businesses, the situation is somewhat different – for one thing, TPS cannot block calls from a company with whom one already has a relationship, so calls from a supplier would not come under their control. Also, buyers exist to buy goods – if a supplier calls, it may very well be to the buyer's benefit to answer, and certainly an emergency shortage of goods might mean that the ability to make a quick call to the call center might make all the difference.

Call centers suffer from high staff turnover. The job itself is stressful, even when only dealing with inbound calls: customers can be abusive, or may ask difficult questions, or may simply be stupid. Call center staff still need to approach each new call with a positive attitude. Outbound call center staff face even greater stress: many people find the calls irritating, and even when they are happy in principle with being called without warning, the call may come at an inconvenient time, leading to a sharp response from the customer. Staff in Indian call centers have reported racist abuse, sexual harassment, and general rudeness from callers as being the main reasons for leaving the job altogether. 'I wanted to cry, but I had to take the next call' one female call center worker said.

For most business buyers, being able to call a supplier is a useful additional service: being called by a call center may be less appealing, although clearly salespeople do need to make telephone calls to set up appointments, and call centers might be helpful in doing this. Call centers are also used in

. . . continued

CASE STUDY ... *continued*

B2B marketing for selling advertising – again, not always something the media buyer might relish, but call centers certainly make full use of the opportunity when selling to small businesses.

From the supplier's viewpoint, a call center is a cost-effective way of serving smaller customers, those who do not warrant regular visits from salespeople. One-man businesses might only see a salesperson once or twice a year, other sales calls being made by telephone, or possibly e-mail.

Ultimately, call centers are here to stay. Love them or hate them, they exist to make communication between companies more effective and efficient: communication is one of the main building blocks of developing relationships, so call centers are likely to be in the forefront of relationship marketing for years to come.

CASE STUDY QUESTIONS

1   Why might people be resentful of call centers?
2   Given that 12 million telephone numbers are registered with TPS, why do firms continue to use outgoing calls?
3   How might a call center owner reduce staff turnover?
4   Why do callers become abusive with the only person who can help them?
5   How might call centers help in establishing good relationships?

CHAPTER SUMMARY

Communication is rather more complex than it at first appears. The communication that the company intends to send often bears little relationship to the communication which is actually received: this is because communication takes place in a large number of ways, and at many different levels. The medium often has as much effect as the message itself, and the way the message is conveyed alters the meaning. Finally, the message combines with the recipient's existing knowledge and prejudices to create an entirely new (and possibly unintended) message.

The key points from this chapter are as follows:

- Business buyers actively seek out information, whereas consumers are less likely to do so.
- Messages are not a magic bullet: communication is a cooperative process, and meaning is co-created.
- Sought communications are those which the buyer looks for: unsought communications are those which the seller sends out.
- Attitude consists of conation, cognition, and affect. Attitude change begins by changing one of these.

- Cognitive dissonance causes breakdowns in communication.
- Business buyers rarely buy as a result of advertising alone.
- Direct mail must be carefully targeted if it is not to end up in the bin.
- The main trade-off in international communications is the decision whether to standardize or to tailor.

REVIEW QUESTIONS

1 How might advertising be used as a catalyst for attitude change?
2 Why might a firm wish to tailor its international marketing communications?
3 How might a supplier company measure the effectiveness of its marketing communications?
4 What are the main differences between B2B and B2C marketing communications?
5 What is the difference between the peripheral and central routes to attitude change?

REFERENCES

Aronson, E. Chase, T., Heinrich, R., and Ruhnke, R. (1974). "A two-factor theory of dissonance reduction: The effect of feeling stupid or feeling awful on opinion change." *International Journal of Communication Research*, No. 3, 340–52.

Bauer, C. and Miglautsch, J. (1992). "A conceptual definition of direct marketing." *Journal of Direct Marketing*, Vol. 6, Iss. 2 (Spring), 7–17.

Bird D. (1993). *Commonsense Direct Marketing* (3e). London: Kogan Page.

Blythe, J. (2003). *Essentials of Marketing Communication*. Harlow: Financial Times Prentice Hall.

Bradford, G. (1995). "Targeting technology." *Admap*, Vol. 30, Iss. 1, January, 32–4.

Costa J.A. and Pavia, T.M. (1992). "What it all adds up to: Culture and alpha-numeric brand names" in Sherry, J.F. and Sternthal, B. (eds), *Advances in Consumer Research*, Vol. 19, 40, Provo, Utah: Association for Consumer Research.

Dick, A.S. and Basu, K. (1994). "Customer loyalty: Towards an integrated conceptual framework." *Journal of the Academy of Marketing Science*, Vol. 22, Iss. 2, 99–103.

Festinger L. (1957). *A Theory of Cognitive Dissonance*. Stanford, CA: Stanford University Press.

Festinger L. and Carlsmith, J.M. (1959). "Cognitive consequences of forced compliance." *Journal of Abnormal and Social Psychology*, Vol. 58, Iss. 2, 203–10.

Keegan, Warren J., and Green, Mark C. (2013). *Global Marketing*, Upper Saddle River, NJ: Prentice Hall.

Linton, I. (1995). *Database Marketing: Know what your customer wants*. London: Pitman.

Majaro, S. (2012). *International Marketing: A Strategic Approach to World Markets*. London: Routledge.

Mander, G. (1995). "De-duplication." *Journal of Database Marketing*, Vol. 1, Iss. 2, 150–61.

O'Malley, L., Patterson, M., and Evans, M.J. (1999). *Principles of direct and database marketing*. London: Financial Times Pitman.

Petty R.E. and Caccioppo, J.T. (1983). "Central and peripheral routes to persuasion: application to advertising" in Percy, L. and Woodside, A. (eds), *Advertising and Consumer Psychology*, Lexington, MA: Lexington Books.

Pierce, C.S. (1986) in Mick, D.G. "Consumer research and semiotics: exploring the morphology of signs, symbols and significance." *Journal of Consumer Research*, Vol. 13, Iss. 2, September 196–213.

Reichheld, F.F. and Sasser, W.E. (1990). "Zero defects: quality comes to service." *Harvard Business Review*, Vol. 66, Iss. 5, September/October, 105–11.

Rosenberg, M.J. (1960). "An analysis of affective-cognitive consistency" in Rosenberg et al. (eds), *Attitude Organisation and Change*. New Haven, CT: Yale University Press.

Schramm, W.A. (1948). *Mass Communications*. Urbana, Ill: University of Illinois Press.

Schramm, W.A. (1971). "The nature of communication between humans" in Schramm, W.A. and Roberts, D.F. (eds), *The Process and Effect of Mass Communication*, Urbana, Ill. Illinois University Press.

Shimp, T. and Sharma, S. (1987). "Consumer ethnocentrism: Construction and validation of CETSCALE." *Journal of Marketing Research*, Vol. 24, No. 3, August, 280–9.

Singh, J. (1988). "Consumer complaint intentions and behaviour: Definitions and taxonomical issues." *Journal of Marketing*, Vol. 52, Iss. 1, January, 93–107.

Vavra, T. (1992). *Aftermarketing*. Homewood, Ill: Irwin.

Vlasic, Goran and Kesic, Tanja (2007). "Analysis of consumers' attitudes towards interactivity and relationship personalization as contemporary developments in interactive marketing communications." *Journal of Marketing Communications*, Vol. 13, Iss. 2, 109–29.

Chapter 14

Customer relationships and key-account management

INTRODUCTION

Business is largely about personal relationships. Even though business people often aim to be totally rational in their buying behavior, the personalities of the people they see convey an image about the personality of the supplying corporation: for the buyer, the sales representative IS the corporation.

Personal selling has a special place in business to business transactions. Because of the higher order values and fewer number of buyers, suppliers feel the need to offer a personal service, supplied by the salesforce.

CHAPTER OBJECTIVES

After reading this chapter, you should be able to:

- describe the key issues in buyer–seller relationships
- explain the role and function of personal selling
- describe the sales process
- structure a sales presentation
- describe ways of motivating the salesforce
- describe the basic remuneration packages for salespeople, with their advantages and drawbacks.

BUYER–SELLER RELATIONSHIPS

Figure 14.1 shows the key issues in relationships between buyers and sellers.

■ Trust versus formality refers to the degree to which the relationship is bounded by contractual agreements. This issue can be affected by culture in the global context: most negotiators are less likely to trust foreigners than they are to trust people from their own cultural background, but also different cultures have different attitudes toward the role of trust in business. Often this comes from the legal codes of the countries involved: in the UK, for example, trust is of high importance because written contracts are not always enforceable – parties to the contract can claim that they were induced to sign by verbal reassurances which subsequently did not materialize. This means that a written contract is not the whole story, and may prove to be unenforceable. In Japan, written contracts are enforceable, but only after expensive and prolonged litigation, which means that written contracts are not regarded as highly as good relationships of trust. In Germany and the United States the written contract forms the basis of the agreement, so business relationships tend to be more formal.

■ Power and dependence refers to the degree to which either party can make life difficult for the other party. If one firm is heavily dependent on the other, the second firm can dictate the terms of the relationship.

■ The complexity of the relationship is likely to be a function of the closeness of the relationship. The more points of interaction which exist between the buyer and the seller, the more complex the relationship becomes, but at the same time the relationship also becomes closer.

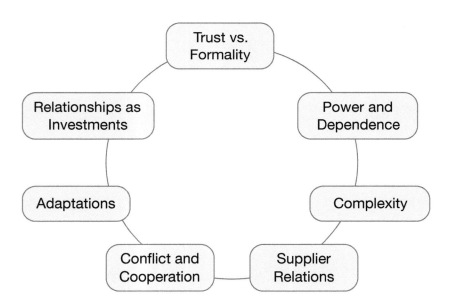

FIGURE 14.1 Issues in relationships

- Supplier relations concern the coordination of suppliers with each other, and the relationships which may develop therefrom.
- Conflict and cooperation are the opposite ends of a spectrum. Conflict is inevitable when companies with different aims, backgrounds, and agendas attempt to work together: if the conflict is resolved in a reasonable manner, cooperation is the end result.
- A longer-term result of conflict resolution is adaptations. As the relationship develops, the parties will need to adapt their business practices in order to cooperate better.
- A relationship might be considered a long-term investment. Each party will need to expend effort which is not immediately rewarded in order to enjoy longer-term benefits.

Business transactions may differ greatly from one another. At one end of the scale, there may be a one-off transaction involving relatively little decision-making and only limited contact between the buyer and the seller (for example, if the office manager needs to buy some emergency photocopier paper from a local office supplies company, and simply sends a junior member of staff out with some petty cash). At the other end of the spectrum a purchase decision might involve establishing a long-term relationship between the firms, operating at many levels and with frequent contact between members of both organizations. For example, a major insurance company might switch its business from IBM to Unisys, and consequently need to retrain its staff, establish a training program for new staff, alter its internal systems, establish new protocols for dealing with its existing customers, and so forth. Such a relationship would be expected to continue at all levels within the organization for the foreseeable future, as new software and hardware are developed and introduced, and internal systems adapt to external environmental changes.

Within this complex relationship there will be distinct interactions between the parties: these are called episodes (Hakansson and Gadde, 1992). The way each episode is handled will depend largely on the past history between the organizations (if any). If the parties know and trust each other, the episode will be handled in a different way from the way it would be handled if the parties have no previous relationship, or have reasons for mistrust. The possible cases for handling episodes can be broadly categorized as follows:

1   Simple episode with no previous relationship. These episodes would involve simple purchases, often in small quantities, or regular purchases of basic raw materials which are of a fairly standard nature (for example, sales representatives buying petrol).
2   Simple episode in a well-developed relationship. Here the relationship facilitates the process: for example, a firm's relationship with its bankers may mean that borrowing money becomes much simpler because the firm already has a track record.
3   Complex episode with no previous relationship. This type of transaction involves the most negotiation, because complexity in itself generates uncertainty and this is exacerbated by the unknown qualities of the other party to the transaction (see Chapter 1). Often these purchases are one-offs: for example, a power generating company may only buy one hydroelectric dam in its entire existence, so there is no opportunity to build a long-term relationship with the civil engineers who build the dam.
4   Complex episodes in well-developed relationships mean that many people from both organizations will need to interrelate (as in the case of the insurance company and the IT supplier

mentioned earlier). Again, the previous relationship will inform the progress of events, and the nature of the interaction.

Investing in a long-term relationship will therefore almost certainly pay dividends in reducing transaction costs, since there is little or no time wasted on learning about the other party. It also reduces risk by reducing complexity. The difference between an investment and a cost is simple: a cost is expected to yield returns within the same accounting period, whereas an investment is expected to yield a stream of returns spread across several accounting periods.

Relationships clearly have at least some of the characteristics of investments. In the early stages of the relationship, the main costs of establishing the relationship will be most evident. In the first few years, outgoings are likely to exceed revenues for the selling firm. In one study, this situation prevailed for the first four years of the relationship, and the selling firm only moved into profit in the relationship after seven years. This means that it is far more profitable to retain and improve existing relationships than it is to seek out new ones, and it is well-known that firms which expand too rapidly frequently encounter cashflow problems. From the purchasing firm's viewpoint, there are costs attached to dealing with a new supplier, particularly when the purchase is complex, whereas savings are likely only to accrue over long periods.

Where relationships differ from most other investments is that the relationship is not transferable in the way that (for example) an investment in plant and machinery would be. If one firm acquires another firm and takes over its operations, the relationship may continue as part of the package, but this in itself poses an obstacle to implementing change.

One of the major advantages of establishing a relationship is the possibility for making adaptations. Classical economics assumes that all products are identical, but of course this is not the case in the real world, and firms adapt their offerings in order to accommodate purchasers. To a lesser extent, purchasers sometimes adapt their requirements in order to take advantage of special offers from suppliers. An example of this is the Land Rover, originally designed in the late 1940s as a utility vehicle for farmers and landowners. The vehicle was designed around the availability of aluminum, which was then in oversupply in comparison to steel, which was strictly rationed. The rust-free qualities of aluminum quickly became a major selling-point for the vehicle, but this was a side-effect of the Rover Car Company's ingenuity in making use of a plentiful material to replace a scarce one.

From the seller's viewpoint, adaptation may take place in order to satisfy one purchaser's or a group of purchasers' needs. If the adaptation is intended to meet the needs of a group of purchasers, this is an example of segmentation and targeting. If the adaptation is intended to meet the needs of one purchaser, this is customization. Research shows that the commonest type of adaptation is in technological collaboration with materials suppliers (Hakansson, 1989). Adaptations involving components, equipment, and processes are less common.

Knowledge-based adaptation gains in importance as development issues increase in importance. Buyers who encourage their suppliers to learn about their systems and applications of technology will give the suppliers the opportunity to make potentially useful suggestions: the downside of this is that the buyer becomes more committed to the suppliers, and may find it harder to switch suppliers at a later date; for example, to take advantage of better deals elsewhere. In addition, the differences between supplier and purchaser are likely to lead to creative solutions for mutual problems.

Research shows that, at least in some cases, firms are not always aware of the extent of contacts made between themselves and their suppliers (Hakansson and Gadde, 1992). In some cases, engineering staff might meet regularly to discuss technical issues, or marketing people might consider joint promotional campaigns, without necessarily bothering to notify other departments that this is happening. Some interactions occur informally – individuals might meet at seminars or trade fairs, or on training courses, or even on the golf course. Such informal contacts are extremely important, and will only happen in cases where employees are satisfied with their employer and loyal to their companies: it is impossible for social relationships to flourish when employees are unwilling to put in the effort, or are disaffected to the point where they become critical of their employer, or (of course) where staff turnover is high (Theoharakis et al., 2009). Particularly in the case of key-account management, situations in which account managers leave the firm need careful handling. The evidence is that it need not be a disaster if an account manager leaves, but firms need to have effective handover systems in place for this eventuality (Madill et al., 2007).

The result of this is that many long-term relationships between firms rely much more strongly on mutual trust than on formality. This approach is strongly evidenced in Japanese firms, where contracts are regarded as an adjunct to the business agreement rather than as its main pillar: Japanese executives spend a great deal of time establishing informal relationships with suppliers and purchasers, and try to create an atmosphere of trust before being prepared to do business. This can be frustrating for American executives, and to some Northern European executives, who are used to doing business at a much faster pace and even (in the case of Americans especially) involving their legal advisers from the outset. Partly this difference in attitude is rooted in the Japanese culture, which is strong on issues such as duty and honesty, and partly it is a result of the Japanese legal system, which actively discourages corporate lawsuits by making them expensive and extremely long-drawn-out.

Even in Western business relationships, social interaction is important. Many firms will arrange corporate hospitality for important clients, and salespeople frequently take clients for lunch or invite them to corporate events. This is not an attempt at bribery: few professional buyers would be swayed by an expense account lunch or a trip to the races. What such hospitality is intended to achieve is the establishment of a feeling of trust between the buyers and sellers, and to put the business relationship on a human footing. This can only be achieved outside the office setting (Geiger and Turley, 2005).

Talking Point

Business is a risky business. Firms make mistakes, run out of money, buy the wrong goods, go broke with monotonous regularity. And yet we are apparently being advised to rely on trusting someone who is trying to sell us something – trying to get money from us, in other words!

If business is risky, shouldn't we be getting everything nailed down as tight as possible in a contract? And yet, if the Japanese don't worry too much about contracts (and they are, after all, the world's third largest economy, despite having virtually no natural resources), shouldn't we be learning from them, and relying on goodwill and a low golf handicap? Maybe we can all trust each other – but equally, we may be kidding ourselves!

Power and dependence are important aspects of buyer–supplier relationships. The most important supplier relationships are likely to involve large volumes of goods or materials, but may involve relatively low volumes of key supplies. From a purchaser's viewpoint, establishing a long-term relationship with a supplier carries the risk of becoming over-dependent on that supplier. Spreading the risk by using several suppliers means diluting the advantages of establishing a relationship.

Power-dependence relationships are seldom symmetrical. In many cases the purchaser will be holding most of the power, but in some cases the reverse is true – suppliers may even band together in order to exercise power over purchasers, as is the case with OPEC, the Organization of Petroleum Exporting Countries. OPEC operates by controlling the supply of oil to the rest of the world, and was originally set up (at the instigation of Venezuela) to redress the power balance between the largely Developing World oil producers and the industrialized countries who are the main users of oil. Sellers may have more power during a boom, when supplies may be limited, whereas buyers have more power in a recession. Abuse of the situation may very well lead to reprisals when the positions are reversed, of course, so maintaining a long-term relationship may rely on looking after good customers (or suppliers) when times are hard.

Although a good business relationship is characterized by cooperation, conflict will inevitably arise. The traditional view of conflict is that it is dysfunctional, so that all conflict is seen to impact negatively on both organizations and should therefore be avoided at all costs. In other words, conflict is a bad thing, reducing the efficiency of organizations by focusing attention on the conflict rather than on getting the job done.

An alternative view is that conflict is inevitable where people have a diversity of backgrounds, interests, and talents. The interactions or functional view of conflict is that it can be a positive force which helps effective performance and encourages creativity, and that far from diverting attention away from the aims of the organization, conflict ultimately generates more effective ways of achieving those aims.

If the degree of conflict is low, the relationship is probably not particularly meaningful or important to either party. Low conflict probably means low interaction: as interaction between the organizations increases, it seems likely that conflict will also increase. Equally, there should be a high degree of collaboration. Table 14.1 illustrates the trade-offs involved.

TABLE 14.1 Trade-offs between conflict and collaboration

	High degree of conflict	Low degree of conflict
High degree of collaboration	Well-developed relationship, probably highly-productive and highly-creative in solving mutual problems.	Pleasant, easy relationship with no exciting synergies. Low-risk, low-return environment.
Low degree of collaboration	Poor environment for achieving anything: a relationship which is probably short-lived.	Hardly a relationship at all. Not productive in any sense, this relationship is also unlikely to last.

Note from the table that the relationships with low degrees of collaboration are unlikely to be long-lived, and relationships with low degrees of conflict are unlikely to be creative or dynamic.

Overall, the most desirable outcome is one in which conflict is handled constructively, so that the outcomes are achieved which are acceptable to both parties. Conflicts should not be smoothed over, nor should they be allowed to escalate, so there is a premium placed on maintaining routes of communication.

In short, conflict is inevitable when there are two or more organizations which are independent of each other and therefore have different goals. The problem is exacerbated when one considers that the profits from the encounter will be divided according to negotiation. Increased openness will reduce the conflict, and create an understanding that the relationship is dependent on mutual profitability. Provided all parties accept this, agreements which allow for mutual gain will be more likely to occur.

THE ROLE OF PERSONAL SELLING

Personal selling is probably the largest single budget item in most business to business markets. Salespeople earn high salaries, and need expensive back-up: company cars, administration assistance, expensive computers, and other sales materials. Allowing for travelling time, preparation time, and so forth sales people spend only a fraction of their time actually making sales presentations. This therefore begs the question: why have we not been able to find a cheaper way to get business?

The reason is that sales people provide a personal touch. A salesperson is able to meet a buyer (or indeed anyone else in the buying corporation), discuss the buying corporation's problems, and develop a creative solution. The buyer understands the corporation's problem, the salesperson understands the capabilities of the supplier and their products, and (usually) the two share knowledge about the industry and the environment in which it operates. Even in the age of social media and highly-developed company websites, proprietary research conducted by one of the authors shows that buyers continue to consider the salesperson a vital resource. This relationship is illustrated in Figure 14.2.

The key point in this is that selling is about establishing a dialogue: it is not about persuading people to buy things they don't really want, it is not about fast-talking a buyer into making a rash decision, and it is most definitely not about telling lies about the firm's products.

Salespeople exist to carry out the following functions:

- identify suitable possible customers;
- identify problems those customers have or might have;
- establish a dialogue with the potential customer;
- refine the view of the problem to take account of the dialogue;
- identify solutions which are within the supplying firm's capabilities;
- explain the solution;
- represent the customer's views to the supplying company;
- ensure a smooth process of supply which meets the customer's needs;
- solve any after-sales problems which may arise.

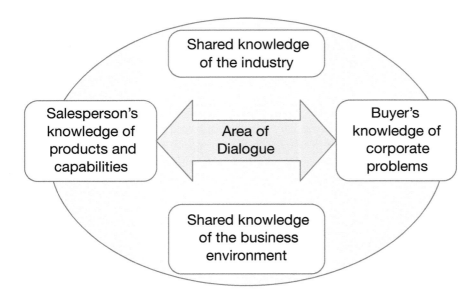

FIGURE 14.2 The function of selling

In the context of relationship marketing, the day-to-day activities of salespeople will include the following (Moncrief and Marshall, 2005):

- Customer retention and deletion. Salespeople not only need to keep the customers the firm wants, they also need to identify which customers are more trouble than they are worth.
- Database and knowledge management. Salespeople are in a prime position to gain information about customers, and will do so if they are supervised effectively and supported by senior management (Liu and Comer, 2007).
- Nurturing the relationship. Salespeople are in the front line for looking after customers and ensuring that they remain loyal.
- Marketing the products. Salespeople usually see this as their main function, but in fact it derives from effective completion of all the other functions.
- Problem-solving. Good salespeople solve customers' problems, even if this does not result in an immediate sale.
- Adding value and satisfying needs. Good salespeople add value by giving good advice, providing useful contacts, and even explaining how the products can be used more effectively.
- Customer relationship maintenance. Good salespeople should represent the customer's interests back to the firm.

Marketers usually think of personal selling as part of the promotional mix, along with sales promotion, advertising, and publicity. Personal selling is different from the other elements in that it always offers a two-way communication with the prospective customer, whereas each of the other elements is usually a one-way communication. This is partly what makes personal selling such a powerful instrument; the salesperson can clarify points, answer queries, and concentrate on those issues which seem to be of greatest interest to the prospect. More importantly, the salesperson is able to conduct instant "market research" with the prospect and determine which issues are of most relevance, often in an interactive way which allows the salesperson to highlight issues which the prospect was not aware of.

As with other forms of marketing communication, selling works best as part of an integrated campaign. Salespeople find it a great deal easier to call on prospects who have already heard something about the company through advertising, publicity, or exhibition activities, and many salespeople regard it as the main duty of the marketing department to deliver warm leads (or even hot ones). Equally, marketers regard it as part of the salesperson's responsibility to "sing the same song" by communicating the company's core message, in conjunction with the other communications methods. Salespeople have a strong role in developing brand values, since they are in a position to represent the company in a very real and tangible way (Lynch and de Chernatony, 2007).

Salespeople and marketers often have divergent views about the relationship between selling and marketing, and this is occasionally a source of conflict between them (Dewsnap and Jobber, 1998).

A MARKETER'S VIEW

Salespeople are able to find, inform, and persuade customers in a way that has yet to be bettered by any other communications medium.

This view of personal selling emphasizes the provision of information, and the element of persuasion. Personal selling is one of several possible options available to the marketer for communicating the company's messages to the customers; its major advantage over other communications is that the message can be tailored to fit the prospect's need for information. This is very much a marketer-oriented view; marketers appear to be working to the model shown in Figure 14.3.

In Figure 14.3, marketers make marketing mix decisions: pricing and product decisions in their turn impact on promotion decisions, and those promotion decisions subdivide into promotional mix decisions. These impact on the firm's publics: marketing intelligence is gathered from those publics through marketing research and salesforce feedback, enabling the marketers to fine-tune their decision-making. In this model, salespeople are seen as a part of the marketing mix, mere mouthpieces for the marketers.

Marketers and writers about marketing seem to be unanimous in their belief that personal selling is the most powerful promotional shot in the locker; equally, they seem to be unanimous in believing that it is the most expensive. Because of the supposed high cost of personal selling, and the knowledge that there are many other ways of communicating effectively with customers, marketers will sometimes look for ways of eliminating the salesforce.

To summarize the marketers'-eye view, the salesforce functions and their potential replacements are shown in Table 14.2.

At first sight the marketer's model of the role of personal selling appears to allow for the replacement of selling with other (often IT-based) techniques. Since personal selling is regarded as an expensive option, this viewpoint is wholly understandable. An e-mailing which contacts 5,000 good prospects for a cost of £1,000 is a great deal cheaper than a sales rep. who would contact around half that number of prospects in a year at a cost of £50,000; even allowing for the sales rep's much better success rate, the cost advantage is obvious. If the marketers are right in thinking of selling as a communication tool, it is obviously cost-effective to seek other ways of communicating.

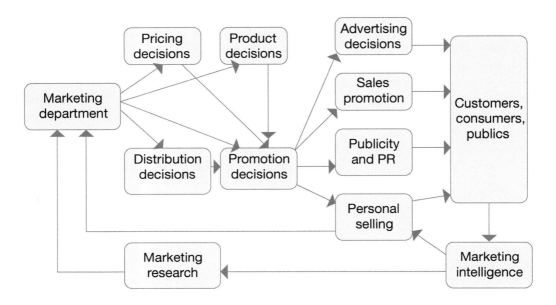

FIGURE 14.3 Marketer's view of the role of personal selling

TABLE 14.2 Replacements for salesforce functions	
Salesforce function	*Marketer's replacement method*
Prospecting	Bought-in database; database combination.
Evaluating prospects	Database scrutiny, credit referencing technology, response to direct mail.
Preparing	Combining databases to find most effective approach to the individual customer.
Approaching the customer	Initial mailing, Internet advertisement, direct-response advertising.
Making the presentation	Tailored direct-mail, Internet, or e-mail negotiation.
Overcoming objections	Interactive computer-based (Internet-based) information system.
Closing	Internet-based close, credit transfer, e-mail order forms.
Following-up	Direct mail.

Undoubtedly personal selling does have a major communications element, involving as it does a two-way dialogue between salesperson and prospect, but there is a great deal more to personal selling than this. An examination of what salespeople actually do will make this clearer.

THE SALESPERSON'S-EYE VIEW

Research into sales practice shows a somewhat different picture from that conveyed by most marketing texts.

The emphasis in selling practice is not on telling prospects about the products, but on asking questions about the prospect's needs. The salesperson's role in the sales presentation is not about delivering a persuasive sales talk, but rather is about using appropriate questions. The questions not only help in finding out what the prospect actually needs, but also help to lead the discussion and the subsequent negotiations in a particular direction. DeCormier and Jobber (1993) found a total of 13 different types of question in use by salespeople; some of these were for information-gathering purposes, others served to control and direct the discussion. Rackham (1991) categorized questions in four dimensions; situation, problem, implication, and need-payoff. In each case the emphasis is on asking the prospect about his or her situation, with a view to finding a solution from among the salesperson's portfolio of products. The three key elements in this are first, that the needs of the buyer are paramount; second, that the salesperson is asking questions not making statements: and third, that communicating the marketing department's "message" is not relevant to this core process.

Sales trainers and writers have emphasized the problem-solving aspects of selling for many years now, and salespeople are usually told that the most successful presentations are those in which the customer does most of the talking. Problem-solving is at the core of the activity rather than communication; if the customer is allowed to talk, he or she will (in effect) tell the salesperson how to sell the product.

In the case of services, the marketer and the salesperson will also be concerned with the people, process, and physical evidence (Booms and Bitner, 1981). Salespeople have a role to play here as well; for example, it is common practice for salespeople to leave something with the customer once the sale is closed (a copy of the order, a brochure about the product, etc.) The salesperson is the main individual in the "people" element, at least in most service industries, and also often has considerable input into the process.

In fact, a comparison of the salesperson's activities and the marketer's activities shows considerable common ground, as Table 14.3 shows.

The main difference between selling and marketing is that selling is concerned with individuals and individual relationships, whereas marketing is concerned with market segments. Although direct marketing and database marketing seek to target very small segments (even a segment of one) by using information technology, salespeople already do this, face-to-face and in real time, without the benefit of the marketing department's range of resources.

The salesperson's model of the relationship between marketing and sales will look more like that shown in Figure 14.4. From the salesforce viewpoint, it is the salesforce who do the "real" work of finding out the customer's needs and fulfilling them, with the marketing department providing the back-up services of advertising, public relations, and sales promotion. Marketers provide information

TABLE 14.3 Comparison of marketers' and salespeople's activities

Marketer's activities	Salesperson's activities
Research into the needs of consumers.	Needs analysis based on situation and problem questions.
Gap analysis.	Analysis of needs to identify problems.
New product development, designed to meet the consumers' needs.	Selection from among the existing range of products to find closest fit for prospect's needs.
Pricing: selecting a price which meets the needs and expectations of both the customer and the firm.	Price negotiation: negotiating a price which meets the needs and expectations of both the customer and the firm.
Promotion: developing an appropriate promotion strategy which will equate to the consumers' psychological and behavioral characteristics	Promotion: Explaining the features and benefits of the product in terms of the customer's needs, psychology, and behavioral characteristics.
Distribution decisions: ensuring that the product is in a convenient place for the consumer to buy it.	Distribution negotiations: ensuring that the product reaches the customer in the right quantities and at the right time.

(gained by market research) to the salesforce, and also to the production department, but the salesforce exists to identify and solve customer's problems. They do this using the range of products supplied by the production department.

In the salesperson's model, the marketing department occupies a subservient role. Since the salesforce are in the "front line", dealing directly with the customers, it is clear that every other department in the firm depends on them to bring in the business. They are, in fact, the only department which brings in money; everything else generates costs. Sales training programs sometimes emphasize this; salespeople are told that the average salesperson supports five other jobs, they are told that "nothing happens until somebody sells something", and they are encouraged to think of themselves as the most important people in the firm.

Many salespeople regard their relationship with their customers as being more important than their relationship with the firm that pays their salaries – further evidence that salespeople regard themselves as being the most important people in the firm. Research shows that salespeople are often defensive of their good relationships with customers even when this conflicts with instructions from the marketing department (Anderson and Robertson, 1995). This may be due to the belief that it is easier for salespeople to find a new company to work for than it is to find new customers.

While there may be some justification for the salesperson's model, the model ignores the interrelated nature of the firm's activities. Salespeople would have nothing to sell were it not for the efforts of the production department, would have no pay-packet and no invoicing without the finance department, would have no deliveries without the shipping department, and so forth. Salespeople may have been given a false view of their own importance, but trainers may feel justified in doing this in order to counteract the often negative image and low status that selling has in the eyes of other departments.

In this model, the salesforce collects information about the market from the marketing department's research, and information about the individual customer directly from the customer. Information about the product range, prices, and discount structures, delivery lead times and methods, sales promotions, and the use of advertising and PR materials (contained in the salesperson's "silent seller") are all used in negotiation with the customer. This is done with the aim of obtaining an acceptable solution for both parties, regarding both information exchange and product and price exchange.

For many salespeople, the marketing department also has the role of "softening-up" prospective customers by providing publicity and advertising; the salesperson feels more confident about making a call knowing that the prospect has already heard of the company, and has had the opportunity to form some favorable impressions. In this model the marketing department performs a support function, providing a set of products for the customer to choose from, a price structure for the salesperson and the customer to negotiate around, a distribution system which can be tailored to suit the customer, and promotional back-up in the form of advertising and publicity. Sales promotions might be useful as ways of closing sales (they are sometimes called deal-makers) but the basic problem-solving and decision-making is done by the salespeople when they are with the customer.

In fact, it is this problem-solving and decision-making function that distinguishes the salesforce from other "promotional tools." The salesforce do not think of themselves as being primarily communicators; they think of themselves as being primarily decision-makers – in fact, there is evidence that salespeople can and should have a role in developing the overall communications strategy (Flaherty and Pappas, 2009).

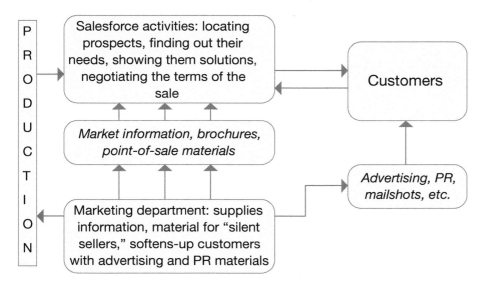

FIGURE 14.4 Salesperson's model of the relationship between marketing and selling

---

Talking Point

If customers are aware of their problems, why do we need salespeople at all? Why not simply provide all the information on a website, make it as interactive as possible, and let people get on with it? After all, the social side of selling is hardly worth bothering with – buyers are paid to buy, not to sit chatting to sales reps!

Not to mention that too cozy a relationship between salespeople and customers might lead to all sorts of complications – favoritism and so forth. So isn't it far and away the best and cheapest option to get rid of the salesforce and use the money to buy a really good website?

On the other hand, most of us like to socialize in work. We are social animals, are we not? And if that's the case, why do we limit corporate contacts just to salespeople and buyers? Why not expand out and get everybody to meet up?

If the salespeople are correct in this view, then it would be impossible to replace them with a database (at least, given the current state of the art). Computers can hold and manipulate information very effectively, but they are unable to solve problems creatively or negotiate effectively, or indeed establish a long-term relationship on a human level. For these functions a human being is necessary.

A problem that arises from this perspective is that salespeople tend to identify very much with the customers. They will, and indeed should, be prepared to represent the customers' views back to the company, and even fight the customer's corner for them within the firm, because this leads to a more customer-oriented attitude within the company. On the other hand, the firm is entitled to expect a certain amount of loyalty from its employees, so the salesforce's over-identification with the customers is likely to lead to conflict between salespeople and their colleagues back at Head Office.

For these reasons salespeople find it is easier and more beneficial to begin by finding out the customer's needs, and then apply a solution to those needs based on the firm's product range. Although marketing writers commonly refer to "the product," it is very rarely the case that a salesperson will only have one product to offer; in many cases, salespeople even have the capacity to vary products or tailor them to fit the customer's needs. For example, computer software houses selling to major customers are able to write customer-specific software for the client; services salespeople (for example selling training services) will almost always have to tailor the product.

TYPES OF SALESPERSON

Donaldson (1998) defined salesperson types as follows:

■ Consumer direct. These salespeople deal with consumers, and are therefore outside the scope of this book, but they are order-getters who rely on selling skills, prepared presentations (canned presentations), and conditioned response techniques to close sales.

- Industrial direct. These salespeople are also order-getters, but operate on a much larger scale. Usually these salespeople deal with one-off or infrequent purchases such as aircraft sales to airlines, machine tools, greenfield civil engineering projects, and so forth. The emphasis for these salespeople is on negotiation skills.
- Government institutional direct. Similar to industrial direct, these salespeople specialize in dealing with institutional buying. Because institutions typically operate by putting purchase contracts out to bid, these salespeople need special techniques: on the other hand, many of these organizations issue publications which explain how to sell to them, sometimes specifying the rules of business and acceptable profit levels. Often the salesperson's main hurdle is to become accepted as an approved supplier.
- Consumer indirect. These salespeople call on retailers. Selling is normally on a repeat basis to established customers, but the main thrust of the salesperson's effort goes into understanding the consumer market. This means that the salesperson needs to help the retailer sell more of the product, by using creative merchandising, by advising on sales techniques, and (in the case of fast-moving consumer goods) negotiating with the retailer for extra shelf space for the products.
- Industrial indirect. Most of the activity of these salespeople is in supporting distributors and agents. They need strong product knowledge, and will need to concentrate on defending existing business from incoming competition: this is because it is typically the case that product and price are similar between competitors. The service level the salesperson offers is therefore the main competitive tool.
- Missionary sales. Missionaries develop sales by influencing members of the decision-making unit who are not necessarily buyers. For example, missionaries work for drug companies, persuading doctors to prescribe certain drugs. The doctors do not buy the drugs themselves: pharmacists stock the drugs, but doctors decide which drugs to prescribe. This type of selling is most effective when the selling cycle is long but the information needs of potential specifiers are immediate, when other forms of communication cannot convey the whole picture, and when the buying process is complex.
- Key-account salespeople. A key account is one which is of strategic importance, which represents a substantial proportion of the supplier's turnover, or which is likely to lead to a change in the way the firm does business. Key-account salespeople need very strong negotiating skills, a high degree of confidence, and the ability to relate to people at many different levels in the organization (Cespedes, 1996; Millman and Wilson, 1995, 1996).
- Agents. A manufacturer's agent represents many different suppliers, but does not take title to the goods. Agents typically call on the same regular group of customers, but offer a wide range of goods: the skills required are therefore the ability to understand a wide range of products, the administrative ability to keep track of the orders and to meet the differing order formats of client companies, and the ability to work efficiently often on low margins. Good agents do not carry products which compete directly with each other, although there are exceptions to this general rule.
- Merchandisers. Merchandisers call on large and small retail outlets specifically for the purpose of maintaining in-store displays and point-of-sale materials. In some cases (for example Procter & Gamble) suppliers have their own employees stationed in supermarkets so as to improve the

coordination of their supply operations. These salespeople are sometimes called customer account managers, which more accurately describes the breadth of their role.

■ Telesales. Telephone selling can be either inbound or outbound. Inbound telesales involves responding to customer enquiries, often generated by advertising or exhibitions. Outbound telesales usually involves cold-calling prospects, or replacing a personal visit with a telephone call. The main advantage of telesales is that it is very much cheaper than personal calls: the main disadvantage is that it is considerably less effective on a call-for-call basis. Telesales people need good communication skills, including a clear speaking voice: on the plus side, the telesales operator usually has better access to customer information than a field salesperson would have, since he or she can be online during the call.

■ System selling. This involves teams of salespeople, each of whom brings a different skill to bear on the problem. Missionary salespeople, new-business salespeople, and technical salespeople may all be involved in selling to the same account.

■ Franchise selling. Franchising is much the same as licensing, but is much more extensive. The franchiser grants the franchisee the right to use its business system, and provides extensive support services and promotional input. In exchange, the franchisee pays a substantial royalty and an up-front franchise fee, and agrees to conduct the business exactly according to the instructions from the franchiser. An example of this in the business to business field is Snap-On Tools, which supplies tools to the light-engineering and motor trade.

There are, of course, many other ways of describing types of salesperson. Suggestions have included customer partner, buyer–seller team coordinator, customer service provider, buyer behavior expert, information gatherer, market analyst, forecaster, and technologist (Rosenbloom and Anderson, 1984; Wilson, 1993a). As personal selling develops in complexity, other classifications may well emerge.

THE SELLING CYCLE

Figure 14.5 shows the selling cycle.

The selling sequence is drawn as a circle to indicate that it is an ongoing process, although in practice each salesperson will divide up his or her day in such a way as to carry out several, or even all, of the separate processes at once.

Lead generation activities are sometimes also called prospecting, although in fact they differ considerably. Lead generation is concerned with finding people who are prepared to meet the salesperson and hear what he or she has to say. Prospects are potential buyers who have a need for the product, and the means to pay for it. Lead generation is a process of establishing first contact: leads are generated via advertising, cold-calling (making visits or telephone calls without an appointment), running exhibition stands, sending out mail shots, or by personal recommendation.

Prospecting is about establishing that the lead has a need for the product, and also has the means to pay for it. In some cases these issues cannot be clearly determined in advance of meeting the potential customer, but a good salesperson will try to investigate a prospect as thoroughly as possible before wasting time on making a sales call.

Preparing for the sale involves preparing both physically and mentally: wearing the right clothes, having the right presentation materials on hand, having the right mental attitude, and having the

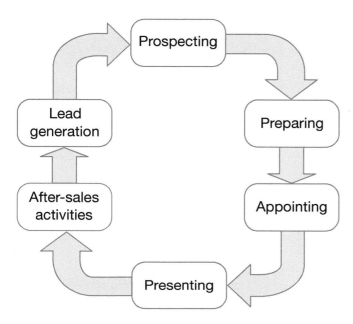

FIGURE 14.5 The selling cycle

appropriate knowledge of the prospect's company and circumstances. Preparing is likely to be complex, since in many cases the salesperson will be calling on several firms in one day, each with a separate set of data to remember, and each with a separate set of needs.

Appointing means making appointments to see the appropriate person or people in the firm. Salespeople are often advised to ensure that all the decision-makers are present, but in the modern business climate this is unlikely to be possible. Therefore the salesperson may well go through a process of using one appointment to generate the next until all the decision-makers have been seen.

The sales presentation is a process of conducting a directed conversation in which the prospect's need is established and agreed, the supplier's solution is explained and the sale is closed. Closing the sale may mean that the order is placed or it may not: the purpose of the presentation is to get a decision, which may or may not be in favor of purchase. There is a section on the sales presentation later in the chapter.

After-sales activities include calling on the customer afterwards to ensure that the process went smoothly, to learn lessons for the future, and perhaps to correct any shortcomings in the delivery or the product. Often salespeople are apparently afraid of carrying out follow-up calls, perhaps because of a fear that the customer will have a complaint: however, it is far better to find out from the customer that there is a problem than to be informed that the customer has complained to company headquarters. After-sales visits also offer opportunities for making further sales or asking for recommendations. Other after-sales activities include ensuring that the paperwork is correctly completed for the company's systems, ensuring that the products are delivered on time, representing the customer's views back to the company, and providing other appropriate market information.

KEY-ACCOUNT SELLING

A key account is one which possesses some or all of the following characteristics:

■ It accounts for a significant proportion of the firm's overall sales. This means that the supplying firm is in a vulnerable position if the customer goes elsewhere. This in turn means that the supplier may be expected to negotiate significant changes in its methods, products, and business practices in order to fit in with the customer's business practices and needs, which means an emphasis on change among the boundary-spanning members of the supplier's organization (Piercy, 2009).

■ There is cooperation between distribution channel members rather than conflict. This places the emphasis strongly on good, effective channels of communication, with the salesperson in the front line.

■ The supplier works interdependently with the customer to lower costs and increase efficiency. This again implies lengthy negotiations and frequent contact between the firms.

■ Supply involves servicing aspects such as technical support as well as delivery of physical products. Servicing aspects will often fall to the salesperson, and because of the intangible nature of services, good communication is at a premium.

Companies realize that key accounts need special attention (and a very different sales approach) as a result of both competitive pressure (when competitors are offering a better service) and their own intensity of coordination within the firm (Wengler et al., 2007). Unfortunately, the same authors found that around 80 percent of companies do not have a formal key-account management system in place, even though they do try to offer key accounts special attention in some way. Key-account selling techniques are aimed at bridging this gap in provision.

Key-account selling has the following features:

■ There will be many decision-makers involved, with very little likelihood of being able to meet all of them at one time.

■ It is frequently the case that the salesperson is not present when the final decision is made, and he or she may never meet the most senior decision-makers.

■ The problems which the salesperson is expected to address are complex and often insoluble in any permanent sense.

■ The consequences of the problem are often much more important than the immediate problem would suggest.

Traditional selling emphasizes objection handling, overcoming the sales resistance of the buyer, and closing the sale. This naturally tends to lead to a focus on the single transaction rather than on the whole picture of the relationship between the supplier and the buyer.

In itself, this may not matter for many purchases. A firm selling photocopiers, for example, has many competitors who are supplying broadly similar products. This means that a quick sale is essential, since otherwise the buyer will be getting several quotes from other firms and will probably make the final decision based on the price alone. In addition, repeat business will be unlikely to materialize, and will be a long time coming if it does, so the salesperson is not looking to establish a long-term relationship with the buyer, nor is the buyer particularly interested in establishing a long-term relationship with the salesperson. Both parties are mainly interested in solving the customer's immediate problems, then moving on to other business: in fact, for many customers, being accorded key-account status has little effect on their attitude to the supplier (Ivens and Pardo, 2007).

Selling to major accounts cannot follow the simplistic approach of finding out needs and closing which is used in traditional selling situations; it involves a much more drawn-out procedure. Buyers who are considering a major commitment to a supplier, either for a single large purchase or for a long-term stream of supplies, are unlikely to be impressed with a one-hour presentation followed by an alternative close. Also, the salesperson will need to sell the solution to his or her own firm, since major changes in products and practices are often needed. This means that key-account managers need to take a customer-oriented approach rather than a selling approach: also, there may need to be a team-selling approach, since this will lead to synergistic solutions which in turn engender greater trust in the customer (Guenz et al., 2009).

In major-account selling the emphasis shifts from objection handling toward objection prevention. The salesperson is concerned to ensure that objections do not arise, or at least if they do that the answers are already in place. This means that the questions that need to be asked are a little more sophisticated than just the open-or-closed dichotomy. The system of classifying questions as open or closed is inadequate in a key-account situation. As we saw earlier, Rackham (1995) identified four groupings of question types. These groupings can be further explained as follows:

1. Situation questions. These questions are about finding out the current situation of the prospective customer, in terms of the customer's strategic direction, financial position, status of the problem, and so forth.
2. Problem questions. These questions relate to the specific problem the buyer has at present. These questions help to develop mutual understanding of the problem and reveal the implied needs.
3. Implication questions. These explore the wider implications of the problem, and often reveal that the problem has much greater ramifications than were at first apparent. This makes the buyer feel the problem much more acutely.
4. Need-payoff questions. These questions enable the buyer to state explicit needs, which allows the seller to explain the benefits of the product.

This classification of questions has been registered as SPIN by Huthwaite Research Group Ltd. The process of covering all the implications of these questions and the proposed solution will involve many people, so the one-call approach to selling will not apply to major accounts.

From a sales management viewpoint this has major implications. In small-account sales, the one-call sale is the norm; typically, sales managers operate on the basis that the more calls the salespeople make, the more sales will result. On the face of it, this is perfectly logical. If a salesperson has a closing rate of one in four (one sale for every four calls) then twenty calls will produce five sales, forty calls will produce ten sales, and twelve calls will only produce three sales. Therefore most sales managers apply pressure to their salesforces to make more calls.

In major-account selling this approach would be disastrous. Encouraged (or compelled) to call on more customers, the salesperson will inevitably begin to call on only those customers who can be sold to quickly and easily, in other words the smaller accounts.

Sales productivity actually comes from two components; sales efficiency, and sales effectiveness. Efficiency is about getting in front of the maximum number of prospects for the minimum cost; sales effectiveness is about maximizing the sales potential once in front of the prospects. Both elements are important, but small-account selling puts more emphasis on efficiency, whereas major-account selling puts more emphasis on effectiveness.

In small-account sales, managerial involvement is not usually hands-on. The managers who are most successful concentrate on managing sales team activities, but do little or no selling themselves and do not become involved directly with customers unless there is a major problem (Rackham, 1995). In major-account selling, though, the sales manager is almost certain to become directly involved with the customer at some stage, if only because such a large commitment on the part of the customer demands that he or she should speak to the senior management of the supplier firm. Sales managers should follow these principles when becoming involved in major sales:

- Only become involved when your presence makes a unique difference. The salesperson involved on the account is probably very deeply immersed in it, and will know a lot about the customer and the state of the negotiation; you cannot possibly know as much.
- Do not make sales calls on a customer unless your salesperson is with you. You could upset a delicate stage of the negotiation, or at the very least introduce new factors.
- Before any joint call, agree on specific and clear selling roles with your salesperson. Again, control needs to be strongly with the salesperson who is responsible for the account, so it is essential to trust that person's judgement.
- Be an active internal seller for your salespeople. The solution arrived at for the client is likely to involve internal changes for the supplier, some of which will not be popular with the other people in the firm. They will need to be convinced, and the sales manager is the best person to do this.
- Always have a withdrawal strategy that prevents any customer becoming too dependent on you personally. Customers may prefer to deal with "the boss" rather than with the salesperson, but a sales manager cannot afford to spend all his or her time out of the office, selling to major accounts.

Problems arise for the sales manager in coaching major sales. In small sales, where the salesperson is perhaps making four or five calls a day, it is easily possible for the sales manager to accompany the salesperson for a day and observe what happens in calls. Corrections can be made to the salesperson's approach, and within a week or so the improvement in sales should become apparent. In major sales, the lead times between first contact with the client and the final agreement to the sale are likely to be very long indeed, often months and sometimes years; in those circumstances, coaching becomes difficult, to say the least. Improvements in methods may not show results for years, and therefore it may be difficult to motivate salespeople to make changes in their practices.

One of the biggest problems for the sales manager is that it is relatively easy to get people to work harder – extra incentives will usually motivate people to put in more hours, or otherwise increase sales efficiency. Increasing sales effectiveness, though, means getting people to "work smarter," and since most people are working as "smart" as they know how to already, extra incentives will probably not help.

THE KAM/PPF MODEL

The Millman-Wilson relational development model (Millman and Wilson, 1995) is a tool for examining the initiation, growth, and eventual demise of the relationship between firms. Linked to the PPF model of relational interaction (Wilson, 1993b), as shown in Table 14.4, it is possible to show that the types of problem being addressed and resolved by the partners in the relationship will vary according to the stage of the relationship.

Buyers and sellers will form closer relationships if they have similar business orientations (Hedaa and Ritter, 2005). Aligning the orientations of two disparate businesses requires a considerable investment in time and effort on the part of both organizations, and hence a collective focus on the problems facing those organizations. The PPF model postulates that the nature of dyadic organizational relationships is directly related to the nature of the problems that the parties focus on resolving. In dyadic business relationships these problems are hierarchical, in that a more distant relationship between the parties will only generate problems related to products. The higher order problems of process and facilitation will only become apparent as the relationship becomes closer.

The Millman-Wilson Stages of Relational Development model describes the stages firms go through as the relationship achieves key-account status (Millman and Wilson, 1995). In the pre-key account management (KAM) stage, the firms do not have a relationship but are assessing whether there is potential for establishing key-account status. In the early-KAM stage the supplying firm might develop preferred-supplier status. In the mid-KAM stage the partnership builds further, consolidating the preferred-supplier status. In the partnership-KAM stage the firms develop a spirit of partnership and build a common culture, and the supplier locks in the customer, becoming the

TABLE 14.4 The PPF model of problem characteristics

Problem category	Nature of problem
Product	Availability, performance, features, quality, design, technical support, order size, price, terms.
Process	Speed of response, manufacturing process issues, application of process knowledge, changes to product, projects management issues, decision-making process knowledge, special attention in relation to deliveries, design, quotes, cost reduction.
Facilitation	Value creation, compatibility and integration of systems, alignment of objectives, integration of personnel, managing processes peripheral to customer core activity, strategic alignment.

external resource base. In the synergistic-KAM stage the firms share rewards and become quasi-integrated. The final stage is the uncoupling-KAM stage in which the firms disengage.

The combined KAM/PPF model categorizes the types of problem, and shows how these can be related to the stages that firms go through when establishing a key-account relationship. Table 14.5 shows the PPF strategies mapped against the stages of relational development model (Wilson, 1999).

The strategic issues raised at different stages of the relationship connect with the firm's communication strategies, and particularly with the stated strategies of firms at trade fairs. In the early stages, communication might be dominated by outbound messages from the selling company, but in the later stages a true dialogue is likely to be the prevailing paradigm.

TABLE 14.5 KAM/PPF strategies

Development stage	Objectives	Strategies
Pre-KAM	Define and identify strategic account potential. Secure initial contact.	Identify key contacts and decision-making unit. Establish product need. Display willingness to address other areas of the problem. Advocate key-account status in-house.
Early-KAM	Account penetration. Increase volume of business. Achieve preferred supplier status.	Build social network. Identify process-related problems and signal willingness to work together to provide cost-effective solutions. Build trust through performance and open communications.
Mid-KAM	Build partnership. Consolidate preferred-supplier status. Establish key account in-house.	Focus on product-related issues. Manage the implementation of process-related solutions. Build inter-organizational teams. Establish joint systems. Begin to perform non-core management tasks.
Partnership-KAM	Develop spirit of partnership. Build common culture. Lock in customer by being external resource base.	Integrate processes. Extend joint problem solving. Focus on cost reduction and joint value-creating opportunities. Address key strategic issues of the client. Address facilitation issues.
Synergistic-KAM	Continuous improvement. Shared rewards. Quasi-integration.	Focus on joint value creation. Create semi-autonomous projects teams. Develop strategic congruence.
Uncoupling KAM	Disengagement.	Withdraw.

KEY-ACCOUNT MANAGEMENT IN A GLOBAL CONTEXT

Key-account management frequently involves dealing with multinationals: at the same time, the supplying company is often itself multinational. Because of cultural differences, the key-account manager in this situation has a much harder task than would normally be the case. The key-account process will need to accommodate different cultures, different needs in the local divisions of the multinational customer, supply difficulties across borders, and so forth.

Consider, for example, a truck manufacturer trying to win an order for delivery vans from a multinational soft-drinks producer. The vans will have to have different specifications to meet regulations in the countries in which they will be used, and will also have to be designed around local conditions: in Spain, delivery vehicles need to be able to negotiate the narrow streets of mountain villages for example, whereas in Germany they may need to be capable of travelling long distances on the autobahn. Buyers will require different approaches in each country – language is the least of the problems. In Germany, punctuality is essential, whereas in Spain it is far less important. The buyers in each country will probably have different priorities – up-front cost might be more important in Spain, whereas running costs and maintenance downtime might be more important in Germany where salaries are higher and so is the cost of diesel fuel.

These problems are likely to be multiplied dramatically when dealing across many countries and cultures, and could be even worse for some products. The overall result is that key-account selling in this type of situation, where both companies have a global presence, relies heavily on good teamwork. This in turn places an emphasis on excellent leadership and strategic planning.

MANAGING THE SALESFORCE

The salesforce is in some ways the hardest marketing tool to control. This is because it is composed of independently-minded people who each have their own ideas on how the job should be done, and who are working away from the office and out of sight of the sales managers.

Sales managers are responsible for recruitment, training, motivation, controlling, and evaluating salesforce activities, and managing sales territories.

Recruitment is complicated by the fact that there is no generally-applicable set of personality traits that make up the ideal salesperson. This is because the sales task varies greatly from one firm to another, and the sales manager will need to draw up a specific set of desirable traits for the task in hand. This will involve analyzing the company's successful salespeople, and also the less successful ones, to find out what the differences are between them.

Some companies take the view that almost anybody can be trained to sell, and therefore the selection procedures are somewhat limited, or even non-existent; other companies are extremely selective and subject potential recruits to a rigorous selection procedure.

Sources of potential recruits are; advertising, employment agencies, recommendations from existing sales staff, colleges and universities, and internal appointments from other departments.

Training can be long or short, depending on the product and the market. Table 14.6 illustrates the dimensions of the problem.

TABLE 14.6 Factors relating to length of training of sales staff

Factors indicating long training	Factors indicating short training
Complex, technical products	Simple products
Industrial markets with professional buyers	Household, consumer markets
High order values (from the customer's viewpoint)	Low order values
High recruitment costs	Low recruitment costs
Inexperienced recruits – for example, recruited direct from university	Experienced recruits from the same industry

The role the salesperson is required to take on will also affect the length of training; **missionary salespeople** will take longer to train than **order-takers**, and **closers** will take longer than **telephone canvassers**.

Typically, training falls into two sections; **classroom training**, in which the recruits are taught about the company and the products and may be given some grounding in sales techniques, and **field training**, which is an ongoing training program carried out in front of real customers in the field. Field training is often the province of the sales managers, but classroom training can be carried out by other company personnel (in some cases, in larger firms, there will be specialists who do nothing else but train sales people).

People tend to learn best by performing the task, so most sales training programs involve substantial field training, either by sending out rookies (trainees) with experienced salespeople, or by the "in-at-the-deep-end" approach of sending rookies out on their own fairly early in their careers. The latter method is indicated if there are plenty of possible customers for the product; the view is that a few mistakes (lost sales) won't matter. In industrial selling, though, it is often the case that there are fewer possible customers and therefore the loss of even one or two could be serious. In these circumstances it would be better to give rookies a long period of working alongside more experienced salespeople. Observing the sales manager carrying out adaptive selling is an extremely powerful tool in training and motivating sales people (Chakrabarty et al., 2008), probably because it generates respect for the sales manager as well as demonstrating the techniques of adaptive selling.

Ultimately, of course, salespeople will lose more sales than they get. In most industries, fewer than half the presentations given result in a sale; a typical proportion would be one in three. This means that sales managers have to accept that there will be failures, and sometimes customers will be lost forever.

Payment for salespeople traditionally has a commission element, but it is perfectly feasible to use a **straight-salary** method, or a **commission-only** method. Although it is commonly supposed that a commission-only salesperson will be highly-motivated to work hard, since otherwise he or she will not earn any money, this is not necessarily the case. Salespeople who are paid solely by commission will sometimes decide that they have earned enough for this month, and will give themselves a holiday; the company has very little moral power to compel them to work, since there is no basic salary being paid. Conversely, a salesperson who is paid salary-only may feel obligated to work in order to justify the salary.

Herzberg (1966) says that the payment method must be seen to be fair if demotivation is to be avoided, but the payment method is not in itself a good motivator. Salespeople are out on the road for most of their working lives and do not see what other salespeople are doing; whether they are competent at the job, whether they are getting some kind of unfair advantage, even whether they are working at all. In these circumstances a commission system does at least reassure the salesperson that extra effort brings extra rewards. The chart in Table 14.7 shows the trade-offs between commission-only and salary-only; of course, most firms have a mixture of salary and commission.

Motivation, perhaps surprisingly, tends to come from sources other than payment. The classic view of motivation was proposed by Maslow (1954). Maslow's Hierarchy of Need theory postulates that people will fulfill the needs at the lower end of a pyramid (survival needs and security needs) before they move on to addressing needs at the upper end (such as belonging needs, esteem needs, and self-actualization needs). Thus, once a salesperson has assured his or her basic survival needs, these cease to be motivators; the individual will then be moving onto esteem needs, or belonging needs. For this reason sales managers usually have a battery of motivational devices for salespeople to aim for.

For rookies, the award of a company tie might address the need to belong; for more senior salespeople, membership of a Millionaire's Club (salespeople who have sold more than a million pounds' worth of product) might address esteem needs. Many sales managers offer prizes for salespeople's spouses or partners. This can be a powerful incentive since salespeople often work unusual hours, and thus have disrupted home lives; the spouse or partner is sometimes neglected in favor of the job, so a prize aimed at them can help assuage the salesperson's natural feelings of guilt.

Sales territory management involves ensuring that the salesforce have a reasonably equal chance of making sales. Clearly a garage tools salesperson in a major city will have an easier task than one in a rural area, simply because of the shorter distances between prospects; such a salesperson would spend more time in presentations and less time driving. On the other hand, the city salesperson

TABLE 14.7 Trade-offs in salespersons' pay packages

Mainly salary	Mainly commission
Where order values are high	Where order values are low
Where the sales cycle is long	Where the sales cycle is short
Where staff turnover is low	Where staff turnover is high
Where sales staff are carefully-selected against narrow criteria	Where selection criteria for staff are broad
For new staff, or staff who have to develop new territories	For situations where aggressive selling is indicated (e.g. selling unsought goods)
Where sales territories are seriously unequal in terms of sales potential	Where sales territories are substantially the same

would probably face more competition and might also have to spend more time caught in traffic during rush hour periods.

Territories can be divided **geographically** or by **industry**; IBM divide territories by industry, for example, so that salespeople get to know the problems and needs of the specific industry for which they have responsibility. IBM salespeople might be given responsibility for banks, or insurance companies, or local government departments. This sometimes means that salespeople have greater distances to travel in order to present IBM products, but are more able to make sensible recommendations and give useful advice. Geographical territories are more common, since they minimize travel time and maximize selling time.

It is virtually impossible to create exactly-equal territories. Thus it is important to discuss decisions with salespeople in order to ensure that people feel they are being treated fairly. For example, some salespeople may be quite happy to accept a rural territory because they like to live and work in the country, even if it means earning less.

SALESPEOPLE AND INFORMATION TECHNOLOGY

As in any other profession, the sales role has been helped by the increased availability of information technology. While the cost of the average sales call declined by 15 percent over a decade, the remuneration earned by salespeople doubled over the same period (Tanner and Shipp, 2005). This huge increase in salesforce productivity was almost entirely due to the increased use of computers to smooth the sales process. This appears to be due to two factors: first, the operational efficiency created by having information readily available, and second the increased tendency for salespeople to sell adaptively when they have effective IT tools at their disposal (Robinson et al., 2005).

Having said that, a surprisingly large number of salesforce automation programs fail: around 55 percent to 75 percent are unsuccessful (Honeycutt et al., 2005). The reasons are failure in communication, failure in planning, and failure in evaluation. A lack of agreement between the salesforce and the senior management about the purposes and direction of salesforce automation also plays a leading role in ensuring that the projects fail (Gohmann et al., 2005), and certainly if senior management impose change on salespeople without consultation the result will be rejection (Wright et al., 2008).

Trust may also be a factor, in that salesforce automation may require salespeople to put their "black book" information into the system (Bush et al., 2005). This is the information they have acquired about the habits and attitudes of particular buyers, or about techniques they have adopted for dealing with particular firms. Obviously this information can be very sensitive, and in any case is usually regarded in a somewhat proprietary manner by salespeople – they are reluctant to share it.

Where salesforce automation has succeeded well, it appears to have done so because the salespeople themselves believe that the automation of their work will improve their performance (Bush et al., 2005). Salespeople's personal innovativeness (i.e. the degree to which they embrace new technology in their private lives) and the quality of their training also contribute strongly (Schillewaert et al., 2005). The same research indicated that sales managers have a crucial role to play, since salespeople will respond to the expectations of the sales manager. Perhaps surprisingly, the degree to which competitors' salesforces are using the technology was found to be less important:

however, many salespeople find that the process of adopting the new technology is stressful, and requires considerable effort to master (Rangarajan et al., 2005).

To sum up, the success of using information technology to improve customer relationship management (CRM) depends on the following factors (Avlonitis and Panagopoulos, 2005; Beuhrer et al., 2005):

- **CRM perceived usefulness**. If the salespeople believe that the system will help them perform better, and will be helpful to their customers, they will adopt it.
- **Setting of accurate expectations regarding system usage**. Provided the system performs as it was expected to, salespeople will be happy with it: if unreasonably high expectations were raised, they will tend to reject it.
- **Salesperson innovativeness toward new technological tools**. If individual salespeople are already computer-literate, they will naturally be less likely to find the new technology stressful or difficult to use.
- **CRM perceived ease of use**. As with any new product, ease of use will make it easier to adopt. If salespeople believe that the new system is over-complex, they will avoid using it wherever possible.
- **Supervisor encouragement and support**. As always, the sales manager has a strong role in supporting salespeople through changes in working practices.

Clearly, training plays a major role in the degree to which salespeople are able and willing to use the new technology – in fact, inadequate training will result in reducing salesperson performance (Ahearne et al., 2005).

CASE STUDY

O2

O2 is a subsidiary of Spain's national telephone provider, Telefonica, and is the UK's second largest provider of telecommunications services. The company is probably best known for its mobile telephone systems. In the corporate market, O2 faces strong competition from Vodaphone, T-Mobile, and Orange, and during 2003 it became clear that the company was being forced to compete on price. O2 senior management realized that competing on price is a sure route to losing profits or even going into negative territory, so they set themselves the task of shifting the customer mindset away from price and toward value for money.

Mia Nicoll, head of the sales department at O2, set up the O2 Sales Academy in conjunction with sales training company Imparta. The aims of the Academy were as follows:

- to increase revenue and profitability;
- to change behaviors through a holistic approach to building sales effectiveness;

. . . continued

- to differentiate O2 by creating value through sales;
- to build deeper, more strategic client relationships;
- to be recognized as world class in sales approach, customer service, and sales training.

Change takes time, and Imparta made it clear that this project would need to run for several years if it was to be truly effective. The first phase of the Academy was to change the mindset of the salesforce so that they would understand why their behavior in the field needed to change. For this, Imparta needed to ensure that senior and middle managers were fully on-board with the Academy idea. The second phase involved ensuring that people were applying the new thinking in the field: this involved extensive coaching and mentoring of field salespeople, and also some mentoring of managers to ensure that the new way of thinking would persist in future. Desk-based salespeople and support staff were included in the program, since salespeople trying to implement the new approach would need sympathetic support staff.

The third phase of the program provided individual learning programs for salespeople, designed to fill in any gaps and address any weaknesses in their skill base. Finally, the fourth phase was aimed at skilled salespeople, helping them to move on to Trusted Advisor status. This gave an opportunity for the high-flyers to gain greater recognition and to progress in their careers.

Customized programs were developed to reflect the experience level of the salespeople and the market segment they were expected to address. Inexperienced salespeople or those with low skill levels were offered a foundation course, for example. Training was delivered in three stages: activities before a workshop, then an interactive workshop, then field activities following on from the workshop, including online mentoring, coaching, and the use of application tools.

Ten years on, the program is still running. O2 customers enjoy many added-value privileges to back up the drive away from price competition. For example, in 2007 O2 bought the Millennium Dome (built for the 2000 Millennium celebrations in London) and converted it to the O2 Arena, which hosts concerts and exhibitions. O2 customers have priority for tickets, and can receive text messages giving advance notification of events. Inside the Arena there are dedicated private spaces available for customers, including the Blue Room bar and the O2 Lounge. Access to these areas is only available via barcodes sent to O2 customers' telephones, and once inside customers can change the wallpaper designs and music selections by sending text messages. For some business customers this provides a unique environment for holding meetings or entertaining clients.

Companies such as French maker and distributor of building materials Saint-Gobain use O2 to provide a complete telecoms package. Following an in-depth analysis of the company's telecoms needs, O2 salespeople were able to offer a complete redesign of over

. . . *continued*

CASE STUDY ... *continued*

13,000 connections, including mobile, land-line, and broadband. Special tariffs were developed which saved Saint-Gobain 33 percent across all services without compromising O2's profitability, creating a turnover totaling £2.3 million per annum for O2. Saint-Gobain say that "the greatest asset of O2 is its people. The network is a given, and is to a degree invisible, so it is people who make the difference."

O2 have certainly taken an integrated approach to their sales program. First, they have recognized a problem in the market in respect of their sales program. Second, they have provided salespeople with the necessary product adaptations to overcome the problem. Third, they have established a comprehensive and ongoing training program to ensure that salespeople are able to exploit the new approach to the maximum.

CASE STUDY QUESTIONS

1 Why might price be less important than value for money?
2 Why did O2 spend effort on training support staff?
3 What problems might occur in retraining experienced salespeople?
4 Why would a company like Saint-Gobain switch to O2?
5 Why does O2 have Trusted Advisor status for some salespeople?

CHAPTER SUMMARY

The salesforce is a major part of business to business budgets. In many cases, salespeople spend relatively little time actually selling, and a great deal of time filling in paperwork, travelling between appointments, and so forth. This means that much sales management effort is directed toward ensuring that the salespeople spend as little time on administration as possible, and are effective when they are in front of a customer.

Key-account managers take the relationship a step further. They establish long-term relationships with customers at many levels, and often never meet the actual decision-makers. Key-account managers play the long game, building up from initial contacts: this is essential since they are dealing with very large order values, or very important strategic decisions for the customer.

The key points from this chapter are:

- Relationships between firms operate at many levels.
- Conflict is not necessarily a bad thing: it often leads to creative solutions.
- Trust and person-to-person relationships are essential components of successful business to business relationships.

■ Selling is about solving problems for customers, it is not about persuasion.
■ Selling may not belong in the communications mix at all.
■ Salespeople often identify with customers.
■ After-sales activities are essential, but are often neglected.
■ Techniques used in small-scale accounts are counterproductive in key-account selling – and vice versa.
■ The same is true of management techniques.
■ Commission is a way of ensuring fairness: it is probably not a strong motivator.

REVIEW QUESTIONS

1   What are the main differences between key-account selling and small-account selling?
2   Which remuneration system would you expect to be more highly-motivating: a commission-only system, or a straight-salary system?
3   Why is conflict often a good thing?
4   Why do salespeople tend to identify with customers more than with the firms they work for?
5   Why are after-sales activities often neglected?

REFERENCES

Ahearne, Michael, Jelinek, Ronald, and Rapp, Adam (2005). "Moving beyond the direct effect of SFA adoption on salesperson performance: Training and support as key moderating factors." *Industrial Marketing Management*, Vol. 34, Iss. 4, May, 389–98.

Anderson, Erin and Robertson, Thomas S. (1995). "Inducing Multi-line Salespeople to Adopt House Brands." *Journal of Marketing*, Vol. 59, No. 2 (Apr.), 16–31.

Avlonitis, George J. and Panagopoulos, Nikolaos G. (2005). "Antecedents and consequences of CRM technology acceptance in the sales force." *Industrial Marketing Management*, Vol. 34, Iss. 4, May, 369–77.

Booms, B.H. and Bitner, M.J. (1981). "Marketing Strategies and Organisation Structures for Service Firms" in Donnelly, J. and George, W.R. (eds), *Marketing of Services*. Chicago, IL: American Marketing Association.

Buehrer, Richard E., Senecal, Sylvain, and Pullins, Ellen Bolman (2005). "Sales force technology usage – reasons, barriers, and support: An exploratory investigation." *Industrial Marketing Management*, Vol. 34, Iss. 4, May, 399–405.

Bush, Alan J., Moore, Jarvis B., and Rocco, Rich (2005). "Understanding sales force automation outcomes: A managerial perspective." *Industrial Marketing Management*, Vol. 34, Iss. 4, May, 379–88.

Cespedes, F.V. (1996). *Managing marketing linkages texts, cases and readings*. Upper Saddle River, N.J.: Prentice Hall.

Chakrabarty, Subhra, Oubre, Diana T., and Brown, Gene (2008). "The impact of supervisory adaptive selling and supervisory feedback on salesperson performance." *Industrial Marketing Management*, Vol. 37, Iss. 4, June, 471–83.

DeCormier, R. and Jobber, D. (1993). "The Counsellor Selling Method; Concepts, Constructs, and Effectiveness." *Journal of Personal Selling and Sales Management*, Vol. 13, No. 4, 39–60.

Dewsnap, B. and Jobber, D. (1998). "The Sales and Marketing Interface; Is It Working?" Proceedings of the Academy of Marketing Conference, Sheffield 1998.

Donaldson, W. (1998*). Sales Management Theory and Practice*. London: MacMillan.

Flaherty, Karen E. and Pappas, James M. (2009). "Expanding the sales professional's role: A strategic re-orientation?" *Industrial Marketing Management*, Vol. 38, Iss. 7, October, 814–24.

Geiger, Susi and Turley, Darach (2005). "Socializing behaviors in business-to-business selling: An exploratory study from the Republic of Ireland." *Industrial Marketing Management*, Vol. 34, Iss. 3, April, 275–9.

Gohmann, Stephan F., Guan, Jian, Barker, Robert M., and Faulds, David J. (2005). "Perceptions of sales force automation: Differences between sales force and management." *Industrial Marketing Management*, Vol. 34, Iss. 4, May, 345–54.

Guenz, Paolo, Georges, Laurent, and Pardo, Catherine (2009). "The impact of strategic account managers' behaviors on relational outcomes: An empirical study." *Industrial Marketing Management*, Vol. 38, Iss. 3, April, 312–23.

Hakansson, H. (1989). *Corporate Technological Behaviour – Co-operation and Networks*. London: Routledge.

Hakansson, H. and Gadde, L-E. (1992). *Professional Purchasing*. London: Routledge.

Hedaa, Laurids and Ritter, Thomas (2005). "Business relationships on different waves: Paradigm shift and marketing orientation revisited." *Industrial Marketing Management*, Vol. 34, Iss. 7, October, 722–31.

Herzberg, F. (1966). *Work and Nature of Man*. London: William Collins.

Honeycutt, Earl D., Thelen, Tanya, Thelen, Shawn T., and Hodges, Sharon K. (2005). "Impediments to sales force automation." *Industrial Marketing Management*, Vol. 34, Iss. 4, May, 323–36.

Ivens, Bjorn Sven and Pardo, Catherine (2007). *Industrial Marketing Management*, "Are key account relationships different? Empirical results on supplier strategies and customer reactions." Vol. 36, Iss. 4, May, 483–92.

Liu, Sandra S. and Comer, Lucette B. (2007). "Salespeople as information gatherers: Associated success factors." *Industrial Marketing Management*, Vol. 36, Iss. 5, July, 575–88.

Lynch, Joanne and de Chernatony, Leslie (2007). "Winning Hearts and Minds: Business-to-Business Branding and the Role of the Salesperson." *Journal of Marketing Management*, Vol. 25, Iss. 1–2, 123–35.

Madill, Judith J., Haines, George H., and Riding, Allan L. (2007). "Managing customer relationships: Account manager turnover and effective account management." *Industrial Marketing Management*, Vol. 36, Iss. 1, January, 21–8.

Maslow, Abraham (1954). *Motivation and Personality*. New York: Harper & Row.

Millman, A.F. and Wilson, K.J. (1996). "Developing key account management competencies." *Journal of Marketing Practice*, Vol. 2, Iss. 2, 7–22.

Millman, T. and Wilson K.J. (1995). "Developing key account managers." IMP 12th International Conference Proceedings. Manchester Federal School of Business and Management.

Moncrief, William C. and Marshall, Greg W. (2005). "The evolution of the seven steps of selling." *Industrial Marketing Management*, Vol. 34, Iss. 1, January, 23–37.

Piercy, Nigel F. (2009). "Strategic relationships between boundary-spanning functions: Aligning customer relationship management with supplier relationship management." *Industrial Marketing Management*, Vol. 38, Iss. 8, November, 865–71.

Rackham, N. (1991). *The Management of Major Sales*. Aldershot: Gower.

Rackham, N. (1995). *Spin Selling*. Aldershot: Gower.

Rangarajaran, Deva, Jones, Eli and Chin, Wynn (2005). "Impact of sales force automation on technology-related stress, effort, and technology usage among salespeople." *Industrial Marketing Management*, Vol. 34, Iss. 4, May, 355–68.

Robinson, Leroy Jr., Marshall, Greg W., and Stamps, Miriam B. (2005). "An empirical investigation of technology acceptance in a field sales force setting." *Industrial Marketing Management*, Vol. 34, Iss. 3, April, 203–10.

Rosenbloom, B. and Anderson, R.E. (1984). "The sales manager: Tomorrow's super marketer." *Business Horizons*, Vol. 27, No. 2, Mar.–Apr., 50–6.

Schillewaert, Niels, Ahearne, Michael J., Frambach, Ruud and Moenaert, Rudy K. (2005). "The adoption of information technology in the sales force." *Industrial Marketing Management, Vol. 34, Iss. 4*, May, 337–43.

Tanner, John F. and Shipp, Shannon (2005). "Sales technology within the salesperson's relationships: A research agenda." *Industrial Marketing Management, Vol. 34, Iss. 4*, May, 313–22.

Theoharakis, Vasilis, Saitos, Laszlo and Hooley, Graham (2009). "The strategic role of relational capabilities in the business-to-business service profit chain." *Industrial Marketing Management, Vol. 38, Iss. 8*, November, 925–36.

Wengler, Stefan, Ehret, Michael and Saab, Samy (2007). "Implementation of Key Account Management: Who, why, and how?: An exploratory study on the current implementation of Key Account Management programs." *Industrial Marketing Management, Vol. 36, Iss. 8*, November, 1022–34.

Wilson, K.J. (1993a). "A problem-centered approach to key account management." Proceedings of the National Sales Management Conference, Atlanta, Georgia.

Wilson, K.J. (1993b). "Managing the industrial sales force of the 1990s." *Journal of Marketing Management*, Vol. 9, Iss. 2, 123–39.

Wilson, K.J. (1999). "Developing key account relationships: The integration of the Millman-Wilson relational development model with the problem-centered [PPF] model of buyer-seller interaction in business-to-business markets." *The Journal of Selling and Major Account Management*, Vol. 1, No. 4, 33–46.

Wright, George, Fletcher, Keith, Donaldson, Bill and Lee, Jong-Ho (2008). "Sales force automation systems: An analysis of factors underpinning the sophistication of deployed systems in the UK financial services industry." *Industrial Marketing Management, Vol. 37, Iss. 8*, November, 1005–19.

Chapter 15

Sales promotion, exhibitions, and trade fairs

INTRODUCTION

Exhibitions and trade fairs are among the most widely-used business to business marketing tools, and yet at the same time they are the least well-researched. Even experienced exhibitors have very little idea of how, or even whether, exhibitions are effective.

Sales promotions allow free rein to the imagination of the manager. So many sales promotion activities are used by clever managers yet this area has received only limited attention from academics. In business to business marketing, sales promotions are often played down, yet they still have a potentially important role to play.

CHAPTER OBJECTIVES

After reading this chapter, you should be able to:

- describe the key benefits and drawbacks of using exhibitions
- explain how exhibitions can be used in key-account management
- explain ways of making exhibitions more effective
- describe the key benefits of sales promotions
- explain how sales promotions smooth out fluctuations in demand
- describe the main types of sales promotion, with their advantages and disadvantages
- describe ways of improving the effectiveness of sales promotions.

EXHIBITIONS AND TRADE FAIRS AS COMMUNICATION

Exhibitions and trade fairs represent a substantial commitment on the part of marketers. Total expenditure on exhibitions and trade fairs in the UK is consistently higher than the spend on advertising in the trade press, and is also higher than the combined expenditure on outdoor, cinema, and radio advertising. Yet few exhibitors assess the effectiveness of this activity in any realistic way, and there is continuing academic debate about whether exhibitions are actually effective in communicating with target markets. Attitudes are polarized among exhibitors: some believe strongly that exhibitions are excellent promotional tools, whereas others believe exhibitions are marginal at best (Blythe and Rayner, 1996). It is certainly the case that a successful trade show will depend on both the internal knowledge resources of the firm, and its existing external contacts (Ling-Yee, 2007).

One of the areas of dispute is the split between activities relating directly to making sales (generating leads, identifying prospects, even making sales pitches on the stand) and the non-sales benefits of exhibitions (public relations, enhancing corporate reputation, carrying out market research, etc.). Most exhibitors are concerned mainly with immediate sales (Shipley et al., 1993; Kijewski et al., 1992; Blythe 1997). Having said that, some exhibitors are more concerned with non-selling activities.

Exhibitions occupy a key role in business to business marketing, especially internationally, since they allow contact with buyers who otherwise might never meet due to geographical or time constraints. This is particularly the case with international trade fairs such as those held in Germany, where exhibitions occupy a more important role than in most other countries. Exhibitions such as these can bring together people who might otherwise not have known of each other's existence. Since contact at a fair takes place on neutral territory, both parties can feel more relaxed, so exhibitions offer an opportunity for the relationship between buying company and selling company to develop more fully, and perhaps develop in unexpected directions. Since many visitors are technical people or administrators rather than buyers, there are many opportunities for establishing contacts at all levels of the organization.

As a public relations exercise, exhibitions have much to offer. Since buyers are only a tiny minority of visitors to exhibitions (less than 10 percent at most) (Blythe, 2000; Gramann, 1994), selling objectives are probably not the most important activities to be undertaken. Yet, almost everybody who visits has some interest in the industry for which the exhibition is organized. This means that many of them will be influential in the buying decision, or at the very least might talk to people who are influential.

In terms of semiotics, trade fairs provide signs about the company and its products. For some firms, the sign is the main reason for exhibiting – being at the exhibition at all gives a signal that the company is at the forefront of the industry, or at least is not one of the laggards. In most cases, though, trade fairs are the vehicle by which signs are delivered. Sign systems of trade fairs are well-known – the stand, the suited personnel, the product samples, the free gifts, the product demonstrations, and set-piece displays are typical of trade fairs. Each system has an accepted etiquette, so that visitors and exhibitors know what their role is when attending the show.

Syntactically, trade shows tend to be stylized. The meaning of a brochure offered at a trade show is not the same as the meaning of a brochure offered by a salesperson at a customer's office. Because trade shows have a cultural context of their own, the resulting meanings differ from those encountered outside the exhibition hall.

RESEARCH INTO EXHIBITIONS

Most research into managers' perceptions of exhibitions confirms that managers tend to see them in terms of making sales. This is true of both US and UK shows: even when managers do not expect to take orders at the exhibition, they do see the exhibition as an opportunity to generate leads, qualify prospects, and open sales. This is particularly apparent in the staffing of stands: managers predominantly staff them with sales people, even though there is evidence to suggest that visitors do not like this (Tanner and Chonko, 1995; Skerlos and Blythe, 2000).

Shipley et al. (1993) identified thirteen reasons for exhibiting, of which seven were directly related to selling while six represent non-selling activities. Research conducted by Blythe (1997) showed that the selling aims were ranked highest in importance by the majority of exhibitors (see Table 15.1).

Attempts to determine whether exhibitions are effective or not are also colored by the assumption that they are primarily selling devices. Sharland and Balogh (1996) defined effectiveness as the

TABLE 15.1 Ranking of exhibition aims

Reason for exhibiting	Ranking
Meeting new customers	1
Launching new products	2
Taking sales orders	3
Interacting with existing customers	4
Promoting existing products	5
Enhancing the company image	6
General market research	7
Meeting new distributors	8
Keeping up with the competition	9
Getting information about the competition	10
Interacting with existing distributors	11
Getting an edge on non-exhibitors	12
Enhancing the morale of the staff	13

number of sales leads generated, followed up, and successfully closed, and efficiency as the comparison between the cost of trade show participation versus other sales and promotion activities. US research by Exhibit Surveys Inc. in 2011 put the cost of a trade show meeting at $276, which compares very favourably with the cost of a field visit by a salesperson (estimated at over $400 by Coe (2003)). Although a "useful contact" may not be the same as a sales lead, the general conclusion of researchers is that trade shows and exhibitions generate leads more cheaply than other methods.

The problem lies in determining the strength of these "leads." A useful contact may not be a buyer at all – which is not a problem if the individual might act as a gatekeeper or influencer in reaching the decision-makers. Even a qualified lead from a buyer may not be strong, since such a buyer will almost certainly be visiting the firm's competitors, who will undoubtedly be at the same venue.

Some early research by Kerin and Cron (1987) showed that some exhibitors do pay attention to the possibilities of non-selling activities. Although the emphasis was still on selling, other aims were present (see Table 15.2).

For this particular group of respondents, corporate image came out highest, although the next two highest-scoring aims were selling aims. The dissidents may well be right, since there is a discrepancy between the exhibitors' view of exhibitions and the visitors' view. If exhibitions are about communicating, it would seem reasonable to suppose that the visitors and the exhibitors should have compatible aims in attending: that is to say, their aims will not be the same, but they should be complementary. In the case of exhibitions, visitors are quite clearly seeking out at least some of the communication. Figure 15.1 shows the comparison between visitors' tactics and strategies, and exhibitors' tactics and strategies.

Personal selling clearly happens on exhibition stands, although probably not to the extent that exhibitors believe it does. Certainly exhibitions are good for market research – but it turns out that this works better for exhibitors than for visitors (Berne and Garcia-Uceda, 2008).

TABLE 15.2 Importance of trade show aims

Aim	Mean score (out of 10, with 10 as highest)
Enhancing corporate image	5.32
Introducing new products	5.14
Identifying new prospects	5.08
Getting competitive information	4.94
Servicing current customers	4.69
Enhancing corporate morale	3.75
Selling at the show	2.79
New product testing	2.17

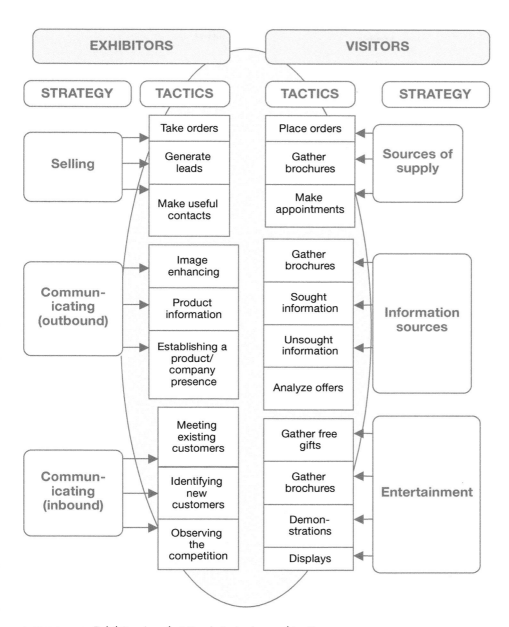

FIGURE 15.1 Exhibitors' and visitors' strategies and tactics

VISITOR EXPECTATIONS

Research conducted among visitors to trade fairs shows that most of them are not directly involved in purchase decisions, and many of them have no role whatsoever in purchasing (Skerlos and Blythe, 2000; Gramann, 1994; Bello and Lohtia, 1993; Munuera and Ruiz, 1999). The Skerlos and Blythe (2000) research showed the breakdown of job titles illustrated in Table 15.3.

When asked about their role in purchasing, 40 percent of the respondents said they had no role whatsoever. The respondents' reasons for visiting the exhibition were as shown in Table 15.4. Respondents were allowed to state more than one reason.

Those who stated that they had no role in purchasing were substantially more likely to be there to see new products and developments: this is not surprising, since they are likely to be technical people.

Visitors were invited to rate their overall satisfaction with the exhibition in terms of the extent to which their aims were met. Research and development people were significantly less satisfied with the outcomes than were the sales and marketing people, and engineers showed a similar pattern.

TABLE 15.3 Visitor job profiles

Job	Percentage of respondents
Sales and marketing	24
General administration	26
Design	14
Engineering	22
Research and development	14

TABLE 15.4 Reasons for attending

Reason for visiting	Percentage citing
To see new products and developments	54
To try new products and go to demonstrations	23
To obtain technical or product information	21
To see new companies	12
To discuss specific problems and talk with the experts	10
To compare products and services	7
To make business contacts	6
To see a specific company or product	5

Visitors' experience of the trade show is therefore clearly related to their jobs, since the job will tend to dictate the visitor's needs and requirements from the show. Failure to meet these needs will result in visitor dissatisfaction with the show.

EXHIBITIONS AND KEY-ACCOUNT MANAGEMENT

Key-account management is about creating long-term relationships with other firms (see Chapter 14). As we saw in that chapter, relationships go through stages, at each stage of which the focus is on a different type of problem.

In the context of key-account management, exhibitions offer an opportunity to initiate relationships by approaching influencers and users, for example technical people and administrators: these opportunities are much greater than the opportunity to meet buyers, simply because of the numerical preponderance of these people. Opportunities to deepen existing relationships by meeting key-account firms' technical or administrative people are obviously present, and may represent the real strength of exhibitions. In some cases these people may not have been involved directly with the supplying company as the relationship is being established, but are able to become part of the process by meeting people on the exhibition stand.

Using the KAM/PPF model outlined in Chapter 13 (Wilson, 1999), it is possible to map visitors' and exhibitors' reasons for attendance (Blythe, 2002). Table 15.5 shows this mapping.

For key-account managers, trade fairs offer three main opportunities:

1 first contact at the pre-KAM or even early-KAM stage;
2 building partnerships and establishing a common culture at the mid-KAM and partnership-KAM stages;
3 a shared voice at the synergistic-KAM stage.

The first contact is far more likely to be with a technical person or an administrator than with a buyer or decision-maker, which means that the key-account manager needs to use these people as product champions in order to enter the prospective customer's firm. Given that these technical people are at the trade fair for the purpose of finding out what is new in the field, exhibitors might be well advised to put some of their own technical people on the stand in order to explore possible synergies. In the pre-KAM stage, when the parties are feeling each other out, it appears that exhibitors place a high importance on finding new customers and launching new products. Unfortunately, only 12 percent of visitors cite seeing new companies as a reason for attending, only 6 percent cite making business contacts, and 7 percent cite comparing products and services.

At the early-KAM stage, when the parties are aiming to increase the volume of business and build a social network, the exhibitor's aim of interacting with existing customers will be most appropriate. The 21 percent of visitors who cited obtaining technical information as a reason for attending will also probably be catered to. Where the prevailing strategy is concerned with building networks, the trade fair offers a neutral territory on which people who would not normally have the chance to meet are able to network with the exhibiting firm. For the exhibitor, the key strategy here is to ensure that the partner firm's technical, administrative, and marketing people are

TABLE 15.5 Exhibitions and the KAM/PPF model

Development stage	Visitors' reasons for attendance (percentage citing in brackets)	Exhibitors' reasons for attendance (importance ranking in brackets)
Pre-KAM: defining and identifying strategic account potential	See new companies (12%), to make business contacts (6%), to compare products and services (7%)	Meet new customers (1), launch new products (2), meet new distributors (8), promote existing products (5)
Early-KAM: account penetration, seeking preferred supplier status	Obtain technical or product information (21%)	Interact with existing customers (4), interact with existing distributors (12), enhance the company image (6), take sales orders (3)
Mid-KAM: building partnership, consolidate preferred-supplier status	Discuss specific problems/talk with the experts (10%).	Interact with existing customers (4), interact with existing distributors (12)
Partnership-KAM: develop spirit of partnership, build common culture, lock in customer	Discuss specific problems/talk with the experts (10%)	Interact with existing customers and distributors (possibly by sharing exhibition space)
Synergistic-KAM: continuous improvement, shared rewards, quasi-integration	No real role. At this stage the companies are very close together, and may even be sharing their promotional activities, including exhibiting at trade fairs	No real role
Uncoupling-KAM: disengagement	To see new customers, products, developments, and companies	To meet new customers and distributors, and to take sales orders

Talking Point

Gosh, it hardly sounds as if it's worth bothering to exhibit at all! If there are so few buyers, and even the ones who are there aren't ready to buy, how do we justify the expense? Are we mad?

Or is it just that the visitors are not quite ready for us yet, but would like to know more? In which case, why don't they just visit our corporate website, instead of turfing out of the office and driving 300 miles to spend the day in a stuffy exhibition hall?

specifically invited to the stand, possibly with the objective of meeting their opposite numbers. Interaction between these individuals is likely to encourage the identification of problems, the finding of creative solutions, and a closer relationship between the organizations. However, research indicates that many technical people's needs are not being met – the opportunity to discuss specific problems, which is a common reason for visiting the exhibition, is unavailable because the exhibiting firms tend to concentrate mainly on selling activities.

In the mid-KAM stage, visitors may wish to discuss specific problems (and 10 percent gave this reason for attending). Exhibitors will wish to interact with existing distributors and customers, the latter of which aims is rated fourth in importance by exhibitors.

At the partnership-KAM stage the two parties are probably too closely intertwined to need to meet in an exhibition hall, and may even be sharing stand space. Nevertheless, social activities built around the exhibition such as dinners together can help cement relationships.

At the synergistic-KAM stage, firms develop strategic congruence. At this point, trade fairs provide the opportunity to share a voice. This is, of course, true of other communications media, but trade fairs allow congruence across a broader spectrum of activities than most because of the interactive nature of the medium. For example, trade fairs can be used for concept testing of new products, allowing the partners to obtain quick feedback on the market viability of the product.

At the uncoupling-KAM stage, when the partnership is dissolving, the parties are likely to use the trade fair to seek new partners. Obviously there is likely to be considerable overlap between the separate stages and activities, but as the relationship deepens the role of trade fairs is likely to become less important.

Using trade fairs effectively as a tool in key-account management means understanding how trade fairs work and who the visitors are. As in any other area of marketing, the key issue is to meet the needs of those visitors effectively in order to facilitate exchange. Using the courtship analogy, the exhibition hall is the business equivalent of the local bar. It is a place for chance encounters that may lead to romance, or it is a place to go to on a date? Whether chance or pre-arranged, the key-account manager can only make the best of the event by setting objectives and being clear about achieving them.

An important issue here is to ensure that the right people are on the stand in order to discuss issues with the visitors. If the exhibitor intends to relate to technical people, it would seem sensible to ensure that some of the exhibitor's technical people are on the stand to answer questions. If the intention is to establish links with key accounts at other levels in the organization, it may be sensible to arrange for senior managers to be on the stand, at least for part of the time: these people frequently have few opportunities to meet customers.

WHY EXHIBITIONS FAIL

Exhibitions frequently do not work for firms. In most cases, this is because exhibitors have not thought through their strategies clearly enough, have not set objectives, and have not evaluated their activities sufficiently rigorously (or at all, in many cases) (Blythe, 2000). As in any other area of marketing, failure to meet the needs of the customer (in this case the visitor) will result in a failure to communicate effectively and hence a failure of the exhibition.

In other cases, exhibitions fail because the exhibitors have inappropriate objectives. Although orders are sometimes placed at exhibitions or shortly afterwards, going to an exhibition with the sole objective of making sales is almost certainly unrealistic in most cases because so few buyers are present as a proportion of visitors. Even when buyers are present, they are likely to be in the information-gathering stage of the buying process and are unlikely to be in a position to place an order anyway.

As in other areas of business, much of the risk of failure can be reduced by planning ahead. Unfortunately, many exhibitors leave the planning of the exhibition to the last minute and do not prepare sufficiently in advance.

When sales are made at exhibitions (as does happen in Germany, for example) the actual sale is usually the culmination of a long period of preparation on the part of the salesforce. In Germany, buyers will typically make appointments to visit specific stands at specific times, and since it is common practice there for senior managers to be present on exhibition stands, buyers may well only place orders when they have had the opportunity to meet the managing director and chief engineer of the supplying company. Exhibitions are very big business in Germany.

PLANNING FOR EXHIBITIONS

Failure to plan an exhibition may be caused by the view that exhibitions are merely flag-waving exercises aimed at showing the corporate face and nothing more. In other cases, companies do not plan because they regard the exhibition as a one-off event, and so do not wish to impose extra burdens on the marketing team. In some circumstances, however, failure to plan is simply a result of lack of knowledge or lack of the will to take trouble over ensuring that the exhibition is successful.

Planning an exhibition properly can easily take up six months or more, if pre-preparation and post-exhibition activities are taken into account. The stages of planning an exhibition are as follows:

1   Decide on the objectives. This goes beyond merely deciding what the reasons are for exhibiting: the objectives need to be measurable (and systems need to be in place to do this), achievable (within the context of the firm's resources), and realistic (considering the visitor profile and competitive pressures at the exhibition).
2   Select which exhibition to attend. This relies on the range of choice, the visitor profiles (obtainable from the organizers, though the figures may have been massaged), the cost of exhibiting, the availability of suitable space in a good location, the timing of the exhibition relative to the firm's business cycle, the competitive level, and the prestige value of the exhibition. It is a good idea, where possible, to attend an exhibition in person before committing to a corporate effort (usually the following year).
3   Plan the staffing of the stand. Most managers tend to use the salesforce to staff the stand, but often this is inappropriate: much depends on what the objectives of exhibiting are. Using salespeople also has the disadvantage of taking them off the road at a time when enquiries are likely to be at their highest. Since visitors are likely to be in the information search stage of the buying process, it is probably too early to involve salespeople anyway.

4 Plan the support promotions. These may include social media, direct mail to visitors, advertising campaigns in advance of the exhibition, press releases in the trade press, and salesforce activity before the exhibition (inviting existing customers to visit the stand) and afterwards (following up on enquiries), including a wide variety of social events.

5 Decide on the layout of the stand and its contents. Since visitors are usually information-gathering, the layout needs to be attractive and eye-catching but should also convey solid information. It is often a good idea to have a quiet area so that customers can discuss business in private: this area can double as a rest area for stand personnel. Refreshments can be made available within this area: opinions are mixed as to whether alcoholic drink should be available.

6 Arrange the follow-up activities after the exhibition. A surprising number of exhibitors fail to do this, with the result that the salesforce is not able to follow up on leads generated; the company is not in a position to send information out to those who requested it, and the PR momentum obtained from the exhibition is wasted (Blythe and Rayner, 1996). The biggest problem with delaying follow-ups is that prospective customers will almost certainly have contacted the firm's competitors at the same exhibition, so a delay is likely to mean that competitors will get the business.

7 Plan the logistics of the exercise. Ensure that sufficient promotional material has been produced, that the staff are transported to the exhibition, that the hotels are booked and are of a suitable standard, that stand personnel are briefed and prepared, that equipment, furnishing, samples and so forth all arrive at the right time and in the right condition.

Once the exhibition is over, evaluation needs to take place. Many firms do not evaluate their activities effectively (or at all) which seems perverse considering the amount of money and effort which is expended on exhibition attendance. The reasons for not evaluating might be as follows (Blythe, 1997):

■ the firm lacks the resources to carry out the evaluation;
■ the activity is not important enough to warrant evaluation;
■ the evaluation would be too difficult or expensive;
■ the firm is owner-managed and therefore the owner feels able to estimate the effectiveness of the exhibition without formal evaluation.

MANAGING THE EXHIBITION STAND

Stand management is straightforward provided the planning has been carried out effectively and the necessary equipment and staff have arrived. Designing the layout of the stand is an important part of the process; most exhibitors tend to make the company name the most prominent feature of the stand, with brand names and product specifications lower on the list of priorities. This is a reasonable policy if the purpose of the stand is to raise the corporate profile, but in most circumstances the visitors' need for solid information will dictate the design and layout of the stand.

In many cases, firms assume that the visitors will recognize the company's name and will know what products are available. This is something of a leap of faith; overseas visitors to exhibitions may not be familiar with the firm and its products, and even domestic visitors may be more familiar with brand or product names than with company names, since they are what is usually given the heaviest promotion.

Exhibitions are tiring for the visitors as well as for the exhibitors, so visitors usually only spend significant time at a few stands. This may be as few as 10 or 12, and this figure does not rise if the exhibition is larger since most visitors only spend one day at an exhibition. This means that large exhibitions with many stands do not increase the number of visitors who will see the stand; statistically, large exhibitions actually reduce the chances of particular visitors seeing a particular stand since there are more to choose from. The problem of clutter is probably greater at exhibitions than in any other environment, as exhibitors all compete for the visitors' limited attention. For this reason the stand must be designed with the visitors' as well as with the exhibitor's objectives in mind.

For example, if the exhibition objective is to raise corporate awareness the company name needs to be prominent, and a plentiful supply of brochures and leaflets needs to be available. Temporary promotion staff could be employed to hand out leaflets in other parts of the exhibition so that exhibitors who do not plan to visit the stand might be encouraged to do so, or at least go away with some information about the firm. The stand might have some kind of stunt or gimmick to raise awareness; a product demonstration or some spectacular event will attract attention.

On the other hand, if the aim is to make sales or generate leads the stand should show the brand names prominently, with plenty of information on product benefits. The stand should be staffed with some technical people and some sales people, and brochures should only be given to visitors who are prepared to leave their names and addresses (some exhibitors will only mail out brochures rather than give them out on the stand). This ensures that follow-up calls can be carried out. Promotions and stunts should be used to collect names and addresses; for example, a free draw for a prize. Special "exhibition-only" discounts or promotions can be used, and pre-publicity can reflect this in order to get buyers onto the stand. In these circumstances, casual non-buying visitors are less important and might even be actively discouraged – although (for the reasons outlined earlier in the chapter) this may be a short-sighted policy since most exhibitions are probably not good selling venues, and the casual visitors may be the exhibitor's best future customers.

The following is a checklist for organizing the stand itself.

- Ensure that displays are easily accessible and are informative.
- Check that stand members have a clear brief.
- Have clear objectives in place and, where possible, set targets for stand members.
- Have an area where prospects can be taken for a private conversation if necessary.
- Ensure an adequate supply of drinking water and other refreshments.
- Establish a manning schedule for stand staff to ensure regular breaks.
- Have a record-keeping system for leads and useful contacts.
- Have a feedback system for visitors' comments.
- Set up some "fun" activities for stand staff.

It is useful for stand staff to have the opportunity to tour the rest of the exhibition (this also gives them a break) and it is worthwhile to give them objectives for doing this, for example, making it the time for gathering information about competitors. Staff will need a break at least every hour; long periods of standing, smiling, and relating to large numbers of people is both physically and psychologically exhausting. This requires careful planning to ensure that there are enough suitably-qualified people left to man the stand during breaks.

The main problem concerning stand staff is maintaining their motivation over the period of the show. After a few hours on the stand the visitors seem to meld into a single mass, most of the enquiries seem like a waste of time, and the smile begins to wear a little thin. For this reason it is a good idea to have some activities running which keep the stand personnel interested. For example, a competition for collecting business cards, with an appropriate small prize, can keep staff interested. Demonstrations throughout the day can help to break the monotony for staff as well as visitors, particularly if the demonstrations are given by stand members in rotation. Again, a small prize could be offered for the best demonstration.

Exhibitions are often held away from the firm's home base, and therefore away from the staff's homes and families. Sometimes it might be appropriate to allow staff to bring their partners with them, but in most cases this is problematical, so every opportunity should be given for staff to telephone home, and it almost goes without saying that their accommodation and meals should be of a high standard – this compensates to a small extent for being away from home, but in any case it reflects better on the firm.

Overall, exhibitions need to be planned in fine detail, with everything leading toward the planned objectives. Choice of exhibition, pre-publicity and post-follow-ups, stand design, staffing, and choice of what to exhibit should all be chosen with clear objectives in mind.

ALTERNATIVES TO EXHIBITIONS

Because of the cost and commitment attached to exhibiting, not least the disruption to the exhibitors' normal routine, firms are beginning to look for alternative routes for meeting buyers and promoting their products. Since one of the major advantages of exhibitions is the "neutral territory" aspect, allowing buyers and sellers to discuss matters in a more relaxed way, many exhibitors are moving toward private exhibitions or road shows to exhibit their products.

PRIVATE EXHIBITIONS

Private exhibitions are sometimes run at venues near to the public exhibition, and coinciding with the main event. Typically such events are held in hotels or small halls where the buyers are invited.

The main advantages are as follows:

- the atmosphere is usually more relaxed and less frenetic than that found in the main exhibition
- no competitors are present to distract the visitors
- the exhibitor has much more control over the environment than would be the case at the public exhibition, where the organizers may impose irksome regulations

- superior refreshment and reception facilities are available
- if the event is held in a hotel the staff will have access to their rooms and can easily take breaks
- sometimes the overall cost is less.

The main drawback of the private event is that visitors will only come to it if they are given advance warning, and even then may decide only to visit the main exhibition. The invitations need to be sent out early enough so that visitors can make allowance for the event, but not so early that they forget about it, and some incentive to make the necessary detour may also need to be in place. It is extremely unlikely that the list of desirable visitors will be complete – one of the main advantages of the public exhibition is that some of the visitors will be unknown to the exhibiting company, and a first contact can be made.

Private exhibitions work best in situations where the company has a limited market, where the costs of the main exhibition are high, and where a suitable venue is available close to the main site.

ROAD SHOWS

A road show is a travelling exhibition which takes the product to the buyer rather than the other way round. In some cases these are run in hotels, in other cases trailers or caravans are used. Road shows are useful in cases where large numbers of buyers are concentrated in particular geographical areas, and where many of them would not make the journey to visit a national exhibition. In some countries (for example the United States) industries may be geographically concentrated (e.g. the film industry in California or the machine tool industry in Illinois), making a road show more economical.

Like private exhibitions, road shows allow the exhibitor to control the environment to a large extent. Road shows can be run in conjunction with other firms, which reduces the cost and increases the interest level for the visitors; this can be particularly effective if the firms concerned are complementary rather than competing.

In common with private exhibitions, the roadshow's organizer is entirely responsible for all the publicity. In the case of a major public exhibition the exhibition organizers and even the firm's competitors will ensure that a certain minimum level of visitors will attend; in the case of a road show the exhibitor will need to produce considerable advance publicity and even send out specific invitations to individual buyers and prospects. Social media can be very effective here as well. This adds to the risk as well as the cost.

SALES PROMOTION

Sales promotions are intended to create a short-term increase in sales and allow free rein for the creativity of marketers. They can take many forms, from short-term discounts through to extra quantities, free packs, and free gifts. These extra incentives should be aimed at the corporation, not at the buyer in person, of course.

Sales promotions are typical of push strategies. A push strategy is one in which the goods are heavily promoted to distributors rather than to the end customer: the theory is that the distributor will, in turn, promote the product heavily, thus pushing the goods through the distribution chain. The converse of a push strategy is a pull strategy, in which the goods are promoted heavily to the final users in order to create demand which will pull the goods through the distribution chain.

Sales promotion expenditure has increased in recent years as producers find that push strategies can be more accurately targeted and are less prone to clutter (the effect of too much advertising vying for the customer's attention). One of the major benefits in a business to business scenario is that it deflects interest away from price as a competitive tool, particularly if the promotion is not of the "extra discount" variety. Creating the campaign should be based on the "who do I want to do what?" question (Cummins, 1998).

Sales promotions can be used to encourage end customers to trial, to trade up (buy the more expensive version of the product), or to expand usage: when aimed at distributors, they can encourage distributors to increase stock levels (load up). This may only move sales from the future to the present: when the promotion is over, the distributor may destock and therefore reduce purchases for a period. This may not matter if the purpose of the promotion is to even out demand in order to schedule factory production better, or if the purpose is to lock out competitors from shelf space at the warehouse, but it is important to understand that sales promotions usually have a short-term effect.

Sales promotions can sometimes be used in creative ways. An example is the promotion run by Osram, the light-bulb manufacturer, when the company first began to produce long-life light bulbs. These bulbs are much more expensive than ordinary filament bulbs, but last many times longer. Osram identified a market among factory and warehouse operators, where the cost of replacing a light bulb is often high: apart from the man-hours involved just in changing light bulbs, the bulbs were often inaccessible, high in the roof spaces of the company premises. The problem in marketing the bulbs lay in the fact that many factory maintenance managers had a fixed budget allowance for buying light bulbs, and were unable to exceed this even when the labor savings were obvious. Appeals to the finance directors to increase the budget were usually met with a flat referral to the maintenance manager. Osram somehow had to get the two individuals together to discuss the new bulbs, so they used a creative sales promotion. Osram mailed a cashbox to the finance directors with a note saying that there was information inside which would save them 50 percent on light bulb replacement: Osram mailed the key to the cash box to the maintenance manager. This meant that both parties had to get together to access the information, and would presumably discuss the outcome.

Another creative approach used in business to business sales promotion was that adopted by the German hair cosmetics manufacturer, Goldwell. Goldwell deals exclusively with hairdressing salons, and when the firm entered the UK market they found themselves facing an established market in which L'Oréal, Schwarzkopf, Wella, Clynol, and Clairol had sewn up the bulk of the market between them. Goldwell countered this by giving away free samples of product – but if a salon placed an order, the free samples would be of a different product in the Goldwell range. Salon owners would use the products, and perhaps order them next time – thus obtaining free samples of yet another product. This approach bought Goldwell a substantial share of the professional market in the UK, and coupled with its rapid delivery system made the company a major player within five years of entering the market.

Talking Point

Are hard-nosed industrial buyers really swayed by such things? Why would a gift of something you don't want make any difference at all to your thinking? Wouldn't a nice fat price discount be a lot better?

Yet people do seem to respond to this type of promotion. Is it a solid business decision, or is it the feeling of getting something for nothing – or even (dare we say it) the warm glow one gets from putting one over on the sales rep?

Joint promotions are a way of reducing the costs of promotions by sharing them with another (related) firm. Entering into a joint-promotion agreement with another company allows the firm to gain in several ways: the cost of the promotion is reduced, the scope of the promotion is increased because the other firm will contact its own customer base, and the customer's perception of value is often increased. For example, a firm manufacturing engineering lubricants might offer a joint promotion with a firm selling industrial cleaning materials. The products are complementary in that using lubricants often creates a cleaning problem, but they may be dealing with different firms and therefore might open up a new customer base for each other.

In capital-goods markets, reduced-interest or zero-interest deals can be powerful incentives, as can leasing deals. These incentives can overcome situations where the corporate budget is spent out, or where the finance director has declared a moratorium on expenditure. The problem for the supplier can lie in working out the cost of such deals, so many firms involve an outside bank or finance company to handle the details. Finance companies judge the supplier against the following criteria:

- the goods need to be durable, identifiable, and movable (in case of repossession);
- the goods should have a value greater than the outstanding debt at all times, which means there should be a well-established second-hand market;
- the supplier must itself be a reliable, well-established business.

Some suppliers are large enough to act as their own finance companies. This was notably the case for IBM, which from its foundation up until the mid-1980s did not sell any of its equipment outright: everything was leased. This meant that IBM retained ownership of all of its equipment throughout the world, which gave the company a substantial measure of control over its customers, though at the cost of cash flow problems in the early years.

CATEGORIES OF SALES PROMOTION

Sales promotions in the business to business environment fall into three categories: promotions aimed at the sales team, promotions aimed further down the value chain at middlemen, and promotions aimed at the customer.

Promotions aimed at the salesforce are part of the motivational program, covered in Chapter 14. Prizes, cash rewards, and extra benefits such as "salesman of the month" status all come under this category, and can be considered as sales promotions since they are aimed at gaining a short-term increase in sales. Such promotions work well in single-transaction type selling, but can be seriously counterproductive in key-account management, since salespeople are encouraged to go for quick results rather than build long-term relationships.

Sales promotions aimed at channel intermediaries (as opposed to end users) form part of a push strategy. Early in the product life cycle, incentives to middlemen may be necessary to gain acceptance of new products by channel members. This can be an important consideration for the customer, since onward sales of the goods needs to be assured. Incentives to encourage distributors to carry the product will also help in shutting out later competition. For example, a manufacturer of an artificial sweetener may want to encourage food manufacturers to incorporate the sweetener. In order to do this, a sales promotion encouraging retailers to stock products containing the sweetener would clearly help. Promotions aimed at customers might be used to shift the time of purchase, stimulate trial, or encourage continued use of a product. These probably represent the mainstream of sales promotions.

Sales promotion is less widely-used in business to business markets than it is in consumer markets. The reasons for this are obscure: it may be that business buyers are less likely to be swayed by temporary promotions, or it may be that a sales promotion is not conducive to building long-term relationships. There is, however, a role for sales promotion in the business to business arena, even if only in the form of "deal sweeteners" which are available to salespeople to cement orders and build relationships.

CASE STUDY

The Farnborough Air Show

The Farnborough Air Show had its origins in the 1920s when British aircraft manufacturers put together an exhibition to showcase British aviation technology. Following on from a six-year break (to accommodate World War II) the show restarted in 1946 at Handley-Page's Radlett airfield: Handley-Page was then Britain's leading aircraft manufacturer.

In 1948 the show moved to its present location, Farnborough, which was home to the Royal Aircraft Establishment. The RAE was the official aviation research unit in the UK, now replaced by the Air Accidents Investigation Branch of the Civil Aviation Authority, and the airfield is also conveniently located near to BAE Systems, the country's largest aerospace manufacturer. The airfield itself has one runway (06/24) which is 2,000 meters long. Normally this is only used for light aircraft and business jets, but during the airshow even the largest aircraft fly in (the Airbus A380 being the latest). The show is held in five display

. . . continued

buildings, and there is a static display of aircraft parked outside for potential buyers and suppliers to inspect.

Currently, the show happens in even-numbered years (the Paris Air Show occupies odd-numbered years) so the latest show was held from 9 to 15 July 2012. The first five days of the show are reserved for trade delegates, but the show is opened up at the weekend to the general public: this is when displays by the Red Arrows (the RAF display team) as well as other aviation displays take place. The rest of the week is devoted to serious business talk, with airlines, component suppliers, manufacturers, and dealers working out multi-million-pound (or dollar, or yen, or ruble) deals.

The 2012 show welcomed delegates from all over the world. Especially popular was the Meet the Buyers event, at which potential suppliers could meet interested buyers and make an initial pitch. Each supplier paid £195 for between four and seven 15-minute meetings with buyers. Suppliers' representatives could state their preferences in advance as to which buyers they would like to meet, and the exhibition organizers would book in for as many as could be arranged: for someone angling to make sales in the millions, the fee was negligible. Naturally potential suppliers would know exactly which companies might be interested in their products – and the buyers represented corporations involved in every aspect of aviation, from defense contractors to component suppliers to security organizations to aircraft manufacturers.

For buyers, the Meet the Buyers event is not only free, but participants were given free hotel accommodation, free entry to the show, and free meals. Buyers who wished to bring a colleague were encouraged to do so, and free food was provided for the colleague (not, unfortunately, a free hotel room). More than 40 buyers participated in the event, which ran for two days: each buyer met an average of 20 to 30 sellers over the two days of the event.

Of course, it would be entirely unrealistic for any exhibitor to expect to make sales at the show, even if (sometimes) firms place orders as the culmination of a long pre-show negotiation process. At Farnborough 2012, Boeing announced deals worth \$35 billion in total: all of these deals would have been months, or even years, in the making but Farnborough offers the opportunity to win some publicity for the company by announcing the final contract. The show exists to strengthen links with buyers with whom the firm already does business (or is about to), and to make new contacts with potential business partners. For all delegates, buyer or supplier, the show offers an opportunity to see the latest developments, meet the movers and shakers in the aviation business, and perhaps revitalize one's excitement at being involved in such a dynamic industry.

CASE STUDY QUESTIONS

1 Why would buyers be given free hotels and meals, whereas suppliers are made to pay?
2 What alternative promotions might an aerospace supplier seek to use?
3 How might an aircraft manufacturer maximize exposure to potential buyers?
4 What other benefits, apart from meeting buyers, might a supplier gain from visiting the airshow?
5 Why might the show only be held in alternate years?

CHAPTER SUMMARY

Although exhibitions and trade fairs are often considered a form of sales promotion, they do in fact have totally separate features and advantages. Exhibitions offer a wide range of communications possibilities between all levels of the organizations which exhibit, and those which attend. Like an old-fashioned marketplace, exhibitions allow all interested parties to meet if they so wish, but this opportunity is often squandered by an over-emphasis on making immediate sales.

Sales promotions occupy a small but useful role in business to business marketing by smoothing and facilitating the decision-making process. The key points from this chapter are as follows:

- Buyers are very much in the minority at most, if not all, exhibitions.
- Most visitors are on an information search, not on a shopping trip.
- Most exhibitors are focused strongly on selling, whereas they should be focused on making useful contacts.
- Exhibitions and trade fairs offer an unrivaled opportunity in key-account management.
- The dissonance between exhibitors' aims and visitors' aims often results in disappointment for both parties.
- Exhibitors should establish objectives for their activities, but rarely do so.
- Sales promotions can be useful as deal sweeteners or facilitators.
- Sales promotions can be used for the salesforce, for intermediaries, for customers, or for the customers of customers.

REVIEW QUESTIONS

1 How might an exhibitor evaluate the aim of enhancing the company image?
2 What objectives might be appropriate for a first-time exhibitor?
3 What would be the most appropriate staffing approach for an exhibitor seeking to relate to existing customers?
4 What type of sales promotion would be most effective for a firm entering a new market?
5 How might salespeople use sales promotions to close deals? What might be the dangers of doing this?

REFERENCES

Bello, D.C. and Lohtia, R. (1993). "Improving trade show effectiveness by analyzing attendees." *Industrial Marketing Management*, Vol. 22, Iss. 4, 311–18.

Berne, Carmen and Garcia-Uceda, M.E. (2008). "Criteria involved in evaluation of trade shows to visit." *Industrial Marketing Management, Vol. 37, Iss. 5*, July, 580–92.

Blythe, J. (1997). "Does size matter? Objectives and measures at UK trade exhibitions." *Journal of Marketing Communications*, Vol. 3, Iss. 1, 51–9.

Blythe, Jim (2000). "Objectives and measures at UK trade exhibitions." *Journal of Marketing Management*, Vol. 16, No. 1, 203–22.

Blythe, Jim (2002). "Using Trade Fairs in Key Account Management." *Industrial Marketing Management*, Vol. 31, No. 7, 627–35.

Blythe, J. and Rayner, T. (1996). "The evaluation of non-selling activities at British trade exhibitions – an exploratory study." *Marketing Intelligence and Planning*, Vol. 14, Iss. 5, 20–4.

Coe, John (2003). *The Fundamentals of Business-to-Business Sales & Marketing.* New York: McGraw-Hill Professional.

Cummins, J. (1998). *Sales Promotion: How to Create and Implement Campaigns That Really Work.* London: Kogan Page.

Gramann, J. (1994). "Independent market research." Birmingham: Centre Exhibitions with National Exhibition Centre.

Kerin, R.A. and Cron, W.L. (1987). "Assessing trade show functions and performance: an exploratory study." *Journal of Marketing*, Vol. 51, Iss. 3, July, 87–94.

Kijewski, V., Yoon, E., and Young, G. (1992). "Trade Shows: How Managers Pick their Winners." Institute for the Study of Business Markets.

Ling-Yee, Li (2007). "Marketing resources and performance of exhibitor firms in trade shows: A contingent resource perspective." *Industrial Marketing Management, Vol. 36, Iss. 3*, April, 393–403.

Munuera, Jose L. and Ruiz, Salvador (1999). "Trade Fairs as Services: A Look at Visitors' Objectives in Spain." *Journal of Business Research*, Vol. 44, No. 1, 17–24.

Sharland, A. and Balogh, P. (1996). "The value of non-selling activities at international trade shows." *Industrial Marketing Management*, Vol. 25, Iss. 1, 59–66.

Shipley, D., Egan, C., and Wong, K.S. (1993). "Dimensions of trade show exhibiting management." *Journal of Marketing Management*, Vol. 9, Iss. 1, 55–63.

Skerlos, K. and Blythe, J. (2000). "Ignoring the Audience: Exhibitors and Visitors at a Greek Trade Fair." Proceedings of the Fifth International Conference on Corporate and Marketing Communication, Erasmus University, Rotterdam, 22 and 23 May.

Tanner, J.F. and Chonko, L.B. (1995). "Trade show objectives, management and staffing practices." *Industrial Marketing Management*, Vol. 24, No. 4, 257–64.

Wilson, K. J. (1999). "Developing key-account relationships: the integration of the Millman-Wilson relational development model with the problem-centred (PPF) of buyer-seller interaction in business-to-business markets." *Journal of Selling and Major-Account Management*, Vol. 1, Iss. 4, 11–12.

Chapter 16

Corporate reputation management

INTRODUCTION

Corporate reputation has been defined as the aggregate perceptions of outsiders about the salient characteristics of firms (Fombrun and Rindova, 2000). In other words, an organization's reputation is composed of the overall view that people have about the organization. Reputation is important for two reasons: first, it has a direct effect on the bottom line because organizations with good reputations are more likely to attract customers, and second a good reputation acts as a buffer should a crisis occur.

CHAPTER OBJECTIVES

After reading this chapter, you should be able to:

- identify the features that characterize an organization's reputation
- explore the key events and characters that create and influence an organization's reputation
- understand how reputation is valued and why it is significant to the performance of the enterprise
- identify different categories of image
- explain how image is managed
- understand the interplay between different categories of image within the organization.

CREATING AND MANAGING A REPUTATION

Reputation, along with image, is a component of the attitude people have toward the organization (see Chapter 2 for more on attitude formation and change). Reputation is the set of expectations which the organization's publics have of its future behavior, and is therefore closely related to the cognitive element of attitude. Organizations with a good reputation are expected to act well: organizations with a bad reputation are expected to behave badly.

Of course, reputation is more than simply good or bad. Typically, the organization's reputation will be good in some respects and bad in others, or it may be that the organization has a reputation for a particular type of behavior that is perceived as good by some people and bad by others. This perception is often culturally-based: for example, research shows that corporate reputation is affected by local cultures in overseas markets since some cultures have a higher regard for innovative companies than do others (Falkenreck and Wagner, 2011). For the manager, therefore, the problem is not so much one of creating a good reputation rather than a bad one, it is rather a problem of creating the right reputation so that the organization's publics are clear about what to expect. Attempts to create the wrong reputation (good or bad) will result in frustrated expectations.

Managing reputation is more than just an exercise in spin-doctoring. Spin-doctoring is a process of putting a good face on unacceptable facts, whereas managing reputation is a process of ensuring that the facts themselves are acceptable. It is about ensuring that everyone's experience of the organization is in keeping with the reputation the organization has or hopes to build. This means that everyone within the organization has a role to play: each member of staff has the power to work well or badly, each shareholder has the power to affect the share price, each customer has the power to buy or not to buy. More importantly, each stakeholder has the power to make or break the organization's reputation simply by saying or doing the right things, or the wrong things, when dealing with those outside the organization.

The sources of knowledge which influence reputation are:

- direct experience of dealing with the organization;
- hearsay evidence from friends, colleagues, and acquaintances;
- third-party public sources such as blogs, social media, newspaper articles, TV documentaries, and published research;
- organization-generated information such as websites, brochures, annual reports, and advertising.

The degree to which the corporate communications officer has influence over these sources is in inverse proportion to the influence on attitude. This is illustrated in Figure 16.1.

Corporate reputation impacts on both customer trust and customer identification: customer commitment mediates these factors to create behavioral intentions (Tat Keh and Xie, 2009). This means that a good reputation coupled with customer commitment will have a direct effect on purchasing. The effects are even stronger in business to business services markets – corporate reputation has been shown to have a stronger effect on customer perceived value than information sharing, distributive fairness, or flexibility (Hansen et al., 2008). Corporate reputation also has a strong impact on customer loyalty, whereas brand image impacts more on perceptions of product and service quality (Cretu and Brodie, 2007).

Reputation affects decision-making on the part of all stakeholders however, so the reputation of an organization is both created and consumed by its members. There is an element of positive feedback involved – a particular reputation will attract people who feel positive about the organization and will repel those who feel negative about it. Once inside the organization, people will act in ways which reflect its reputation. For example, a company with a reputation for treating its staff well will attract managers who like to work in that type of managerial paradigm, and will therefore in turn treat their staff well. Figure 16.2 shows how these elements relate.

One of the problems with reputation management is that different reputations may be attractive to different stakeholders. Stakeholders are people or groups of people who are affected directly or indirectly by a firm's activities and decisions (Post et al., 2002). An employee may be attracted by an organization's reputation for paying its staff generously, but this same attribute might repel a shareholder. Likewise, customers might be attracted to a firm with a reputation for keeping its prices and profits at rock-bottom, but this would hardly attract either staff or shareholders. Ultimately it is not possible to please everybody, so managers need to identify who are the key players, and should seek to establish a good reputation with those people.

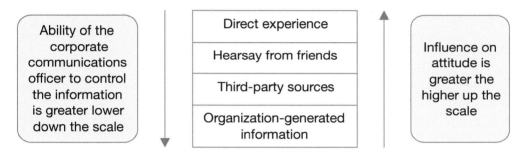

FIGURE 16.1 Hierarchy of information sources

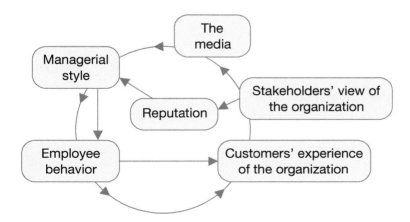

FIGURE 16.2 Creating a reputation

In practice, organizations acquire reputations rather than develop them. While it may be possible to re-establish a better reputation (or at least a more appropriate one) this is likely to be off-putting to some stakeholders, even if it is attractive to others. In practice managers are unlikely to create a reputation from scratch – they are much more likely to be tinkering with the organization's existing reputation to make it more attractive to some people, or to make it more explicit to the stakeholders.

Maintaining a strong reputation pays direct dividends for the enterprise. Research shows that investors are prepared to pay higher share prices for companies with good reputations, even when risks and returns are comparable with other firms in the same industry. Cordeiro and Sambharaya (1997) showed that earnings forecasts made by financial analysts were heavily influenced by the non-financial component of the corporate reputation. Surveys of MBA students show that they are attracted to companies with good reputations, which means that companies which are larger and more visible are apparently better to work for. Part of this attraction is the reflected glory of working for a high-profile company, and part of it is about a perception that working for a major company is likely to be more secure and better rewarded.

The reputation of the organization is important to all stakeholders, but there may be conflicts between the groups: what is good for shareholders may not be good for staff, and what is good for the board of directors may not be good for customers. This means that the board of directors often finds itself in the position of being a clearing house for pressures from different stakeholder groups. Even when stakeholders are in broad agreement as to where the company should be heading there will be differing opinions on how to get there.

For companies, there is a problem in meeting the differing needs of different market segments while still maintaining a consistent corporate reputation. For example, British Airways now offers a fully-reclining seat in business class, effectively giving each passenger a bed. While this provides an image of luxury for the business traveller (as anyone who has ever tried to sleep on an aeroplane can testify), it means less space in Economy, which is where many backpackers book seats. Backpackers are usually seen as a long-term investment by airlines, since they are often students taking time out from university, and are therefore the business class travellers of the future.

IMAGE

Image is the affective component of attitude toward the organization. It is the gut feeling or overall impression that the organization's name and brands generate in the minds of the organization's publics. There are five basic types of image, as shown in Table 16.1.

None of these images is likely to represent the whole truth. Mirror image can be confirmed by external market research, but members of the organization are often surprised or disappointed to find that the organization's external image is not what they had imagined. The current image may be more or less accurate according to whether it is based on misunderstanding or half-truths. It is likely to be less than accurate because outsiders do not have access to the information that people on the inside have.

Wish image is the image desired by management. Often it equates to a vision statement, defined when the organization was founded, and is the image the organization is working toward. Wish images are not always realized, of course. During the 1960s, town planners in Spain had the idea

TABLE 16.1 Types of image

Mirror image	How we think others see the organization. Sometimes this image is the result of self-delusion.
Current image	The actual view of us held by outsiders. This is not always as positive as we might wish it to be.
Wish image	How the organization wishes others to see it. This is something to strive for – often embodied in the mission statement.
Corporate image	The image of the organization, rather than the images of its brands.
Multiple images	The many images put forward by the individuals working within the organization.

of creating a quiet, respectable resort for the wealthier middle classes of Europe, foreseeing (correctly) that these people would have large disposable incomes and would be prepared to spend increasing amounts of their money on leisure, particularly as air travel became more widely available. The wish image of the resort was that of a peaceful town with an old quarter at its heart and upmarket, comfortable hotels around it. The result of these careful deliberations was Benidorm – now widely regarded as the epitome of rampant overdevelopment, and used as a byword for appalling resorts even by people who have never been there.

Corporate image is the image of the organization, as opposed to the image of its products and services. Corporate image is composed of organizational history, financial stability, reputation as an employer, history of corporate citizenship, and so forth. It is possible to have a good corporate image and a poor reputation for products and vice versa. For example, IBM has an exemplary corporate image although its products are not greatly different from those available elsewhere, whereas Rolls Royce has an outstanding image for its products despite a somewhat checkered corporate history involving several bankruptcies and relaunches.

Talking Point

Creating a standard corporate image is obviously desirable. Yet for most purchasing firms, the only real contact they have with the supplier is through the sales representatives – who are all individuals.

We are told that the strength of the sales function is the ability to provide a personalized, individual service. But if we insist on hiring a group of clones, how are we to individualize what we do? And even if the sales people are very similar, the simple fact of tailoring the company's service to each customer is bound to lead to variations in the image.

So is it really possible EVER to generate a consistent corporate image? Or are we left with the unpalatable truth that we cannot force our employees into neat little molds?

The multiple image occurs when separate branches of the business or even individuals within the business create their own image within that of the overall corporation. An obvious example is that of sales representatives, who each have a personal image and reputation with customers which may or may not accord with the overall corporate image. Organizations such as IBM try to overcome this by using very strict selection criteria when employing salespeople: at one time, IBM salespeople wore a company uniform of blue blazers and gray trousers, but this was discontinued after a "revolution" by French IBM salespeople, who simply refused to wear the uniform. Even now, IBMers tend to have a similar appearance, conforming to the strong corporate culture.

CORPORATE IMAGE AND ADDED VALUE

Corporate image is not a luxury. The image of a corporation translates into hard added value for shareholders, even if the firm's actual performance in terms of profits and dividends is no better than average. This is partly because of the effect that image has on the corporation's customers, but it is also a function of the effect it has on staff, and is very much a result of the influence the image has on shareholders. Since the central task of management is to maximize shareholder value, image must be central to management thinking and action.

Maximizing shareholder value is not the same as maximizing profits. Profit maximization tends to be short term, a matter of cutting costs, reducing investment, downsizing, increasing sales volumes at the expense of long-term customer loyalty, and so forth. Adding value to the shareholders' assets is about creating a secure, growing long-term investment. Since the dot.com bubble burst investors have become painfully aware that investments in firms with spectacular profits but little underlying solidity is a quick way to lose money. Investment analysts look more and more toward using measures such as customer loyalty, brand awareness, and investment levels in judging the long-term prospects for firms.

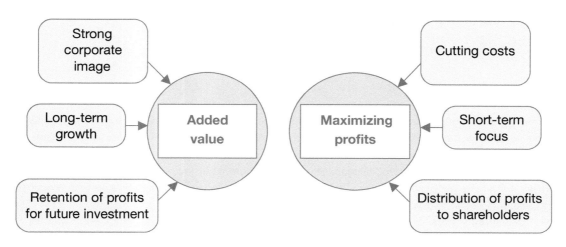

FIGURE 16.3 Comparison between adding value and maximizing profits

> ## Talking Point
>
> Boards of directors often use the stockmarket valuation of the company's shares as a barometer of the company's success. Yet this is rarely reflected in the corporation's mission statement. Most of these talk about caring for staff and customers.
>
> Does this mean that the mission statement is not strictly true? Or does it mean that staff and customers are mere instruments in attaining the goal of share value? And if a higher share value is independent of profit, does that mean that the wool is being pulled over shareholders' eyes? In short, are most boards of directors behaving in some Machiavellian way in order to shore up their own positions?
>
> Or are they perhaps merely trying to balance the needs of a wide group of people?

The counter argument for this is that the shifting global marketplace has reduced survival prospects for companies. The life expectancy of a firm was less than 20 years in 1997 (De Geus, 1997), and it seems likely that the rapid changes in the business environment since then will have shortened corporate life expectancy rather than increased it. Maintaining a profitable competitive advantage is also problematical. If a firm finds a profitable market niche, competitors respond rapidly and profits fall to the point where it is almost impossible to maintain an adequate return on the original capital investment (Black et al., 1998).

The value which accrues from image management has always been accounted for under the heading of "goodwill" on the firm's balance sheet. The goodwill element of the firm's value is the difference between the value of the firm's tangible assets and its value on the stockmarket. For some firms, the value of goodwill is actually the bulk of the firm's overall value. For example, Coca-Cola's goodwill value is more than 80 percent of the firm's total value. Much of this goodwill value comes from the Coca-Cola brand itself. This approach to valuing the firm's reputation and image is now regarded as being somewhat crude, and new measures are being developed to take account of brand value, customer loyalty values, and so forth to move away from the reliance on financial measures when assessing firms' successes.

PR AND EXTERNAL COMMUNICATION

Public relations or PR is the management of corporate image through the management of relationships with the organization's publics. Roger Hayward offered an alternative definition, as follows (Hayward, 1998).

> Those efforts used by management to identify and close any gap between how the organization is seen by its key publics and how it would like to be seen.

PR has more than just a role in defending the company from attack and publicizing its successes. It has a key role in relationship marketing, since it is concerned with building a long-term image rather than gaining a quick sale. There is a strategic relationship between publicity, PR, and press relations. PR occupies the overall strategic role in the relationship.

In some cases, firms use PR solely for crisis management, either by employing somebody with a nice smile and a friendly voice to handle complaints, or by waiting for things to go wrong before beginning to formulate a plan for handling the problem. This is a fire-fighting or reactive approach to public relations, and is generally regarded as being far less effective than a proactive approach, which seeks to avoid problems arising.

PR managers have the task of coordinating all those activities which make up the public face of the organization, and will have some or all of the following tasks to handle:

- organizing press conferences;
- staff training workshops;
- social events;
- handling incoming complaints or criticism;
- grooming senior management for TV or press interviews;
- molding the internal culture of the organization;
- managing social media.

PR people talk about "publics" rather than "the public." This is because they are dealing with a wide range of people, all with differing needs and preconceptions. The following publics might be part of the PR manager's remit:

- customers;
- suppliers;
- staff;

FIGURE 16.4 Publicity, PR, and public relations

- government and government departments;
- local government;
- neighbors;
- local residents;
- the general public;
- pressure groups such as environmentalists or trade unions;
- other industry members.

In each case the approach will be different, and the expected outcomes will also be different. The basic routes by which PR operates are word-of-mouth, press and TV news stories, and personal recommendation. The aim of good PR is to put the name of the firm and its products into people's minds in a positive way.

PR is not advertising, because it is not directly paid for. Advertising can be both informative and persuasive, but PR can only be used for conveying information or for placing the company before the public eye in a positive way. PR does not generate business directly, but achieves the company's long-term objectives by creating positive feelings. The ideal is to give the world the impression that this is "a good firm to do business with."

TOOLS OF PUBLIC RELATIONS

PR people use a number of different ways of achieving their aims. The list in Table 16.2 is by no means comprehensive, but does cover the main tools available to PR managers.

Of these, the corporate website, press releases, and sponsorship are probably the most important. Testimonials posted on the corporate website fall into three main groupings, as follows (Jalkala and Salminen, 2009):

- Discourse of benefits. These testimonials refer to the benefits the customer has received from dealing with the supplier. For example, a logistics firm might publish a testimonial in which a customer explains how the deliveries are more reliable, or more cost-effective, since giving the firm their business.
- Discourse of relationship commitment. This type of testimonial is about the "good people to do business with" type of statement. Extolling the quality of the relationship and the degree to which the customer feels that the supplier is on its side is the thrust of this type of testimonial.
- Discourse of technological expertise. This type of testimonial praises the skill of the supplier in meeting expectations, and is likely to be used in respect of firms which deal with highly-technical areas such as software design or bio-engineering.

A press release is a favorable news story about the organization, which originates from within the organization itself. Newspapers and the trade press earn their money mainly through paid advertising, but they attract readers by having stimulating articles about topics of interest to the readership. Broadcasters need to fill time and editors need to fill space, and are quite happy to use a press release to do so if the story is newsworthy and interesting to the readership or viewers.

TABLE 16.2 Tools of PR

Tool	Description and examples
Press releases	A press release is a news story about the organization, usually designed to put the firm in a good light but often intended just to keep the organization in the public eye. For example, a firm might issue a press release about opening a new factory in a depressed area of the country. Newspapers and broadcasters use this as news, since it is about creating jobs.
Sponsorship	Sponsorship of events, individuals or organizations is useful for creating favorable publicity. For example, many firms sponsor golf tournaments which provide opportunities for personal interaction as well as favorable publicity.
Publicity stunts	Sometimes firms will stage an event specifically for the purpose of creating a news story. Again, this is less common in B2B markets, since mass-media publicity is of less value.
Word-of-mouth	Generating favorable word-of-mouth is an important aim of PR. For example, Alex Lawrie Factors, a UK business financial services company, frequently invites financial intermediaries such as bank managers, business consultants, and financial advisers to sports events such as horse racing. The intermediaries are likely to raise this in conversation with clients, and thus remember to promote Alex Lawrie services.
Corporate advertising	Corporate advertising is aimed at improving the corporate image, rather than selling products. Such advertising is very common in the trade press, but occasionally appears in the mass media. British Airways have successfully used television to promote the company's image, aiming specifically at business-class sales.
Lobbying	Lobbying is the process of making representations to members of Parliament, congressmen, or other politicians. For example, an industry association might lobby Parliament to persuade MPs not to introduce new restrictions on the industry.
Corporate website	The website provides an opportunity for the company to publicize its mission statement, its success stories, and its corporate social responsibility. The website can include testimonials from satisfied clients, mini case studies of how the company has helped other firms solve their problems, and show what the company is doing to sponsor worthy causes or events.
Social media	The use of such media as Facebook, LinkedIn, and Twitter allows companies to create instant publicity with the exact audience they are trying to reach. As a bonus, such media also encourage viral marketing – "word of mouse" – if the post is especially interesting or amusing.

The trade press relies heavily on press releases, since industry news would be difficult to collect in any other way, but even business-oriented newspapers such as the *Financial Times* need companies to send news in, which is of course the essence of the press release.

The advantages of writing a press release are that it is much more credible than an advertisement, it is much more likely to be read, and the space within the publication is free. There are, of course, costs attached to producing press releases.

Table 16.3 shows the criteria under which the press stories must be produced if they are to be published.

Increasing skepticism and resistance to advertising has meant that there has been a substantial growth in the use of press releases and publicity in recent years. Press stories are much more credible, and although they do not usually generate business directly, they do have a positive long-term effect on building brand awareness and loyalty. It should be said that advertising alone also does not usually generate business immediately.

Editors do not have to publish press releases exactly as they are received. They reserve the right to alter stories, add to them, comment on them or otherwise change them around to suit their own purposes. There is nothing substantial that press officers can do about this. Cultivating a good relationship with the media is therefore an important part of the press officer's job.

Sometimes this will involve business entertaining, but more often the press officer will simply try to see to it that the job of the press is made as easy as possible. This means supplying accurate

TABLE 16.3 Criteria for successful press releases

Criterion	Example
Stories must be newsworthy, i.e. of interest to the reader.	Articles about your new lower prices are not newsworthy; articles about opening a new factory creating 200 jobs are.
Stories must not be merely thinly disguised advertisements.	A story saying that your new processing equipment is a bargain at only £23,000 is not news. A story saying that you have concluded a partnership agreement with a machine tool manufacturer in Poland probably is, in the trade press. A story that you are financing a new training initiative for underprivileged teenagers is probably news in the national media.
Stories must fit the editorial style of the magazine or paper they are being sent to.	An article sent to Cosmopolitan about your new machine tools would not be published. An article about your new female marketing director probably would.
Stories should be written in "reverse pyramid" style. The headline should contain the entire story in essence, and each paragraph should add a little more information.	Sub-editors need to trim stories to fill the available space, so they cut from the bottom. The reverse pyramid means that the story will still be complete and comprehensible, even if several paragraphs are cut.

and complete information, it means writing press releases so that they require a minimum of editing and rewriting, and it means making the appropriate corporate spokesperson available when required.

When business entertaining is appropriate, it will often come as part of a media event, press conference or trade show. This may be called to launch a new product, to announce some major corporate development such as a merger or takeover or (less often) when there has been a corporate crisis. This will involve inviting journalists from the appropriate media, providing refreshments, and providing corporate spokespeople to answer questions and make statements. This kind of event only has a limited success, however, unless the groundwork for it has been very thoroughly laid.

Journalists are often suspicious of media events, sometimes feeling that the organizers are trying to buy them off with a buffet and a glass of wine. This means they may not respond positively to the message the PR people are trying to convey, and may write a critical article rather than the positive one that was hoped for.

To minimize the chance of this happening, media events should follow these basic rules:

- Avoid calling a media event or press conference unless you are announcing something that the press will find interesting.
- Check that there are no negative connotations in what you are announcing.
- Ensure that you have some of the company's senior executives there to talk to the press, not just the PR people.
- Only invite journalists with whom you feel you have a good working relationship.
- Avoid being too lavish with the refreshments.
- Ensure that each of your senior executives, in fact anybody who is going to speak to the press, has had some training in doing this. This is particularly important for TV.
- Be prepared to answer all questions truthfully. Journalists are trained to spot lies and evasions.
- Take account of the fact that newspapers (and indeed broadcast media) have deadlines to adhere to. Call the conference at a time that will allow reporters enough time to file their stories.

It is always better from the press viewpoint to speak to the most senior managers available rather than to the PR people. Having said that, the senior managers will need some training in handling the press and answering questions, and also need to be fully briefed on anything the press might want to ask. In the case of a press conference called as a result of a crisis this can be a problem. Many major firms establish crisis teams of appropriate senior managers who are available and prepared to comment should the need arise. Press officers should be prepared to handle queries from journalists promptly, honestly and enthusiastically, and arrange interviews with senior personnel if necessary.

THE ROLE OF PR IN THE ORGANIZATION

Organizations, just like people, have needs. Some of these needs are common to all organizations, and have different levels of importance according to the circumstances of the organization, or the particular stage in its development. A hierarchy of organizational needs was developed by Pearson (1980). Table 16.4 shows how PR can help in satisfying those needs.

TABLE 16.4 The hierarchy of organizational needs

Organizational need	Requirements	Typical PR activity
Output	Money, machines, manpower, materials	Staff programs to attract the right people
Survival	Cash flow, profits, share performance, customers	Publicity aimed at customers; events publicizing the firm and its products
Morale	Employee job satisfaction	Staff newsletters, morale-boosting activities, etc.
Acceptability	Approval by the external stakeholders (shareholders, government, customers, suppliers, society in general)	External PR, shareholder reports, lobbying of government departments and MPs, events for suppliers and customers, favorable press releases
Leadership	Having a respected position in the company's chosen field; this could be customer satisfaction, employee involvement, industry leadership in technology, or several of these	Corporate image-building exercises, customer care activities, publicity about new products and technological advances, sponsorship of research in universities, sponsorship of the Arts

Source: Adapted from Pearson (1980).

Pearson's hierarchy is useful as a concept but less useful as a practical guide because so many firms deviate from the order in which the needs are met.

INTERNAL COMMUNICATIONS MEDIA

House Journals

House journals are printed information books or sheets, which are made available to employees. Journals may be of any of the following types.

- Magazines. Containing feature articles and illustrations, these magazines are relatively expensive to produce but have a professional, credible feel about them.
- Newspapers. These can be produced to resemble a tabloid newspaper, which makes them more accessible to some groups of employees. Content consists of news articles about the firm, with some feature articles.
- Newsletter. Common in small firms, a newsletter would probably be A4 or letter size, and contains brief items, usually without illustration. Newsletters are cheap and easy to produce, especially in small numbers.

- Wall newspaper. These look like posters, and are fixed to walls. They are useful for brief communications about events or changes in company policies.
- Electronic newsletter. Internal e-mail systems offer great potential for disseminating newsletters. The medium is cheap to use, effective, and often increases the likelihood that the newsletter will be read. Furthermore, it is possible to tell who has opened the newsletter and who has deleted it without reading it – although, of course, opening it is not the same as reading it.

When planning a house journal, you need to consider the issues shown in Figure 16.5.

- Readership. Different groups of staff may have different needs, so it may be necessary to produce different journals for each. Research workers are likely to have different needs from truck drivers, for instance.
- Quantity. The greater the number of copies, the lower the production cost per copy. If the number of employees is large, a better-quality journal can be produced: if the numbers are small, the firm may need to produce newsletters or wall newspapers instead.

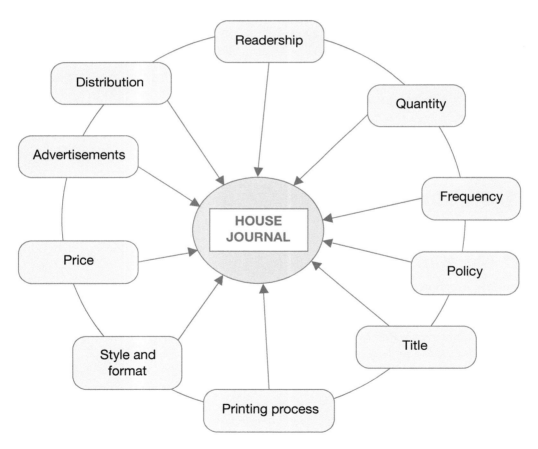

FIGURE 16.5 Issues in designing a house journal

- Frequency. Frequent publication means that the journal is more likely to become part of the daily routine of staff. Some large firms even publish such journals daily.
- Policy. The journal should be more than simply a propaganda device for senior management. It should fit in with an overall PR program, and should have a clear editorial policy to ensure the quality of content.
- Title. The title should be characteristic of the organization. Changing the title is difficult once it has become established, just as with any other brand name.
- Printing process. To an extent the printing process will affect the content, since simple, cheap printing processes cannot reproduce some illustrations. Cost will also affect the choice of process, as will the desire for a good-quality, credible journal.
- Style and format. Credibility is linked to the degree to which the journal resembles a commercial magazine. Style and format are part of the communication in the same way that packaging is part of a product.
- Price. Obviously the vast majority of house journals are free to staff, but it is feasible to make a charge if the journal is sufficiently interesting. There is no reason why a cover-price should not be put on the journal in any case, even if it is free. This conveys to the staff that the journal is valuable, and thus is more likely to be read.
- Advertisements. Carrying advertising may be a useful way to reduce costs. If the circulation is sufficiently large, outside organizations might be prepared to place advertising – this is particularly true if the firm is large and in a single location, since local shops, restaurants, and entertainment venues might well wish to promote their products. Employees may well want to advertise items for sale or forthcoming social events, and this also increases the readability of the journal.
- Distribution. Journals can be delivered by hand, by post to the employee's home address, or at distribution points within the firm (for example mail pigeonholes). The decision rests on the frequency of the journal, the location of employees, and the type of journal involved. Distribution via e-mail is probably the quickest and cheapest method.

House journals are often edited independently of senior management in order to ensure that the focus is on the employees' need for information rather than on the management's need to control or manipulate.

Websites

Most firms' websites are mainly geared toward external marketing. In some cases, firms operate internal websites aimed at employees. These sites are not accessible by outsiders, and they fulfill the same function as the house journal. The main advantage is that the costs are greatly reduced compared with producing a house journal. The disadvantage is that employees are unlikely to access the site except during working hours, and in some cases may not be able to access the site at all because the nature of their work does not involve using a computer.

Internal websites are most useful in organizations in which virtually all employees are provided with computers, and in which there is no problem about allowing employees to scan the website during working hours. Website design is a specialist area, but some rules have been developed. Sites need to be simple to access and use, graphics should be kept simple to minimize download time, and articles should fit onto one screen as far as possible.

Internal briefings and open meetings

Some organizations give staff the opportunity to have access to senior management at open meetings or briefings. These briefings have the advantage of allowing senior management to gain direct access to grass-roots views from the workforce, as well as allowing the workforce the chance to question senior managers about company policies.

The overall effect is to increase openness within the firm, and break down barriers. Employees (in general) work better if they understand why things are being done the way they are being done. This also enables them to use their initiative better if the system breaks down for any reason.

SPONSORSHIP

Sponsorship has been defined as "An investment, in cash or kind, in an activity in return for access to the exploitable commercial potential associated with this activity." (Meenaghan, 1991). Sponsorship of the Arts or sporting events is an increasingly popular way of generating positive feelings about firms.

Sponsorship in the United States reached $17.2 billion in 2010 (IEG, 2011). This figure was up 3.9 percent on the previous year, and worldwide sponsorship was up 5.2 percent. This colossal increase is largely due to the problem of cutting through advertising clutter. Companies sponsor for a variety of different reasons, as shown in Table 16.5 (Zafer Erdogan and Kitchen, 1998).

TABLE 16.5 Reasons for sponsorship

Objectives	% Agreement	Rank
Press coverage/exposure/opportunity	84.6	1
TV coverage/exposure/opportunity	78.5	2
Promote brand awareness	78.4	3
Promote corporate image	77.0	4
Radio coverage/exposure/opportunity	72.3	5
Increase sales	63.1	6
Enhance community relations	55.4	7
Entertain clients	43.1	8
Benefit employees	36.9	9
Match competition	30.8	10
Fad/fashion	26.2	11

The basis of sponsorship is to take the customers' beliefs about the sponsored event and link them to the company doing the sponsoring. Thus a firm wishing to appear middle-class and respectable might sponsor a theater production or an opera, whereas a company wishing to appear to be "one of the lads" might sponsor a football team. As far as possible, sponsorship should relate to the company's existing image.

Sponsorship will only work if it is linked to other marketing activities, in particular to advertising. Hefler (1994) estimated that two to three times the cost of sponsorship needs to be spent on advertising if the exercise is to be effective. The advertising should tell customers why the firm has chosen this particular event to sponsor, so that the link between the firm's values and the sponsored event is clear. A bank which claims to be "Proud to sponsor the Opera Festival" will not do as well as they would if they were to say "We believe in helping you to enjoy the good things in life – that's why we sponsor the Opera Festival." A recent development in sponsorship is to go beyond the mere exchange of money as the sole benefit to the sponsored organization or event. If the sponsored organization can gain something tangible in terms of extra business or extra publicity for their cause, then so much the better for both parties.

For example, Lincoln-Mercury (a Ford subsidiary) sponsored a mini-tour of the Canadian circus company, Cirque du Soleil. The tour was linked to the new-model Lincoln luxury car, but Cirque du Soleil were able to use the mini-tour as a publicity exercise for their later major tour of the United States. This in turn led to more publicity for Lincoln, so that the two organizations developed a symbiotic relationship beneficial to both. This type of sponsorship is a way of creating a new type of business to business relationship in which neither business is a customer of the other.

Successful sponsorship relies on trust and commitment. Commitment tends to lead to greater economic satisfaction from the relationship, while trust also leads to some non-economic benefits – a feeling of pride at being associated with the event (or, in the other direction, with the sponsoring firm) (Farrelly and Quester, 2005).

There is evidence that consumers feel gratitude toward the sponsors of their favorite events, but there is no evidence regarding business buyers. Any feelings of gratitude may be an emotional linking between the sponsor and the event rather than a feeling of gratitude that the sponsor made the event possible. The difference between these emotions is merely academic in any case – if sponsorship leads to an improvement in the firm's standing with customers that should be sufficient. There are also spin-offs for the internal PR of the firm; most employees like to feel that they are working for a caring organization, and sponsorship money often leads to free tickets or price reductions for staff of the sponsoring organization:

The following criteria apply when considering sponsorship (Hefler, 1994).

- The sponsorship must be economically viable; it should be cost-effective, in other words.
- The event or organization being sponsored should be consistent with the brand image and overall marketing communications plans.
- It should offer a strong possibility of reaching the desired target audience.
- Care should be taken if the event has been sponsored before; the audience may confuse the sponsors, and you may be benefiting the earlier sponsor.

In the business to business arena, one of the main benefits of sponsorship of sports events and arts events is the availability of tickets or reserved seating for sponsors. This enables the sponsoring firms to offer seats as a relationship-builder or deal-sweetener to possible customers.

Talking Point

Anyone watching a major sporting event such as the Wimbledon tennis tournament will have noticed many empty seats. Anyone wanting to obtain tickets for such events finds them hard to get. So why does this happen?

Corporate sponsorship is the culprit. Corporations are given many free seats which they are unable, or unwilling, to use on the days they are available, and therefore seats are empty while real sports fans are unable to obtain tickets. This naturally causes a degree of resentment among fans – and a feeling that "Big Business" is acting against the interests of ordinary people.

So how do corporations gain by this? What does this achieve for enhancing the corporate reputation? Perhaps in the business to business environment there is no need to care about Joe Public, but isn't that attitude somewhat cynical?

Or perhaps there is an opportunity for someone. Could corporations make unwanted seats available to the public on a first-come-first-served basis?

RISK MANAGEMENT

No matter how carefully PR activities are planned and prepared for, crises will develop from time to time. Preparing for the unexpected is therefore a necessity. Some PR agencies specialize in crisis management, but a degree of advance preparation will certainly help if the worst should happen. Preparing for a crisis is similar to organizing a fire drill. The fire may never happen, but it is as well to be prepared.

Crises may be very likely to happen, or extremely unlikely. For example, most manufacturing firms can expect to have a product-related problem sooner or later, and either need to recall products for safety reasons, or need to make adaptations to future versions of the product. On the other hand, some crises are extremely unlikely. Assassination or kidnapping of senior executives is not common in most parts of the world, nor are products rendered illegal without considerable warning beforehand.

Crises can also be defined as within the firm's control, or outside the firm's control. Many firms have been beset by problems which were really not of their making: however, very few problems are entirely outside the firm's control. In most cases, events can at least be influenced, if not controlled. Sometimes, however, the cost of such influence is out of all proportion to the level of risk involved.

ESTABLISHING A CRISIS TEAM

Ideally, the organization should establish a permanent crisis management team of perhaps four or five individuals who are able to take decisions and act as spokespeople in the event of a crisis. Typical members might be the human resources manager, the safety officer, the factory manager, the PR

FIGURE 16.6 Elements of good crisis management

officer, and at least one member of the Board of Directors. Keeping the crisis team small means that communication between members is easy and fast.

The team should meet regularly to review potential risks and formulate strategies for dealing with crises. It may even be possible to rehearse responses in the case of the most likely crises. Importantly, the team should be trained in presentation techniques for dealing with the media, especially in the event of a TV interview.

The team should be able to contact each other immediately in the event of a crisis, and should also be provided with deputies in case of being away on business, on holiday, off work sick, or otherwise unavailable. The essence of planning for crises is to have as many fall-back positions as possible. Having a Plan B is obvious, but it is wise to have a Plan C or even Plan D as well.

DEALING WITH THE MEDIA IN A CRISIS

One of the main PR problems inherent in crisis management is the fact that many crises are newsworthy. This means that reporters will be attracted to the company and its officers in the hope of getting comments or newsworthy statements which will help to sell newspapers. The situation has been exacerbated in recent years by 24-hour news on TV and the creation of the blogosphere – bad news travels extremely quickly via blogs and forums, without the intervention of journalists. This means a rapid response through the firm's own blogs and social networking becomes of paramount importance.

Provided the groundwork has been laid in advance, the company should have a good relationship with the news media already. This will help in the event of a crisis. However, many managers still feel a degree of trepidation when facing the press at a crisis news conference. The journalists are not there to help the company out of a crisis, they are there to hunt down (or create) a story. Their objectives are probably not compatible with those of the company, but they are under an obligation to report the news reasonably accurately.

Preparation is important. As soon as the crisis breaks, the crisis team should be ready to organize a press conference, preferably on the company's own territory. The press conference should be held as soon as is reasonably possible, but it allows the spokespeople sufficient time to prepare themselves for the journalists and gives a reasonable excuse for not talking to reporters ahead of time. The crisis team should remember that they are in charge. It is their information, their crisis, and their story. They are not under an obligation to the news media, but they are under an obligation to the company's shareholders, customers, employees, and other publics. The media may or may not be helpful in communicating with these publics in a crisis situation, which is another good reason for maintaining regular inputs to blogs and social networking sites.

Another important consideration is to ensure that the situation is not made worse by careless statements. Insurance and legal liability may be affected by what is said, so this should be checked beforehand.

Crisis teams need to have a special set of talents, as well as the training needed to perform their ordinary jobs. Rapid communication, and rapid response, is essential when the crisis occurs. Good relationships with the news media will pay off in times of crisis.

Crisis management should not be left until the crisis happens. Everyone involved should be briefed beforehand on what the crisis policy is. This enables everyone to respond appropriately, without committing the company to inappropriate actions – in simple terms, being prepared for a crisis will help to prevent panic reactions and over-hasty responses which might come back to haunt the company later.

USING OUTSIDE AGENCIES TO BUILD CORPORATE IMAGE

Outside public relations agencies are frequently used for developing corporate image. The reasons for doing this might be as follows:

- the firm is too small to warrant having a specialist PR department;
- external agencies have expertise which the company lacks;
- the external agency can provide an unbiased view of the firm's needs;
- external agencies often carry greater credibility than internal departments or managers;
- economies of scale may make the external agency cheaper to use;
- one-off events or campaigns are more efficiently run by outsiders, without deflecting attention away from core activities.

The Public Relations Consultants' Association lists the following activities as services that a consultancy might offer.

- establishing channels of communication with the client's public or publics;
- management communications;

- marketing and sales promotion related activity;
- advice or services relating to political, governmental, or public affairs;
- financial public relations, dealing with shareholders and investment tipsters;
- personnel and industrial relations advice;
- recruitment, training, and higher and technical education.

This list is not exhaustive. Since outside agencies often specialize, the firm might need to go to several different sources to access all the services listed above. Even firms with an in-house public relations department may prefer to subcontract some specialist or one-off activities. Some activities which might involve an outside agency might be as follows.

- Exhibitions. The infrequency of attendance at exhibitions (for many firms) means that in-house planning is likely to be disruptive and inefficient. Outside consultants might be setting up four or five exhibitions a week compared with the average firm's four or five a year, so they will quickly acquire strong expertise in exhibition management.
- Sponsorship. Outside consultants will have contacts and negotiating expertise which is unlikely to be available in-house. In particular, an outside firm will have up-to-date knowledge of what the "going rate" is for sponsoring particular events and individuals.
- Production of house journals. Because of the economies of scale available in the printing and publishing industry, house journals can often be more cheaply produced by outsiders than by the firm itself.
- Corporate or financial PR. Corporate PR relies heavily on having a suitable network of contacts in the finance industry and the financial press. It is extremely unlikely that a firm's PR department would have a comprehensive list of such contacts, so the outside agency provides an instant network of useful contacts.
- Government liaison. Lobbying politicians is an extremely specialized area of public relations, requiring considerable insider knowledge and an understanding of current political issues. Professional lobbyists are far better able to carry out this work than a firm's public relations officer would be.
- Organizing one-off events. Like exhibitions, one-off events are almost certainly better subcontracted to an outside agency.
- Overseas PR. Firms are extremely unlikely to have the specialist local knowledge needed when setting up public relations activities in a foreign country.

Choosing an appropriate agency or consultancy begins with the agency's ability to carry out the specific tasks you need. Deciding which tasks the agency should do can be a process of elimination. Begin by deciding which tasks can be completed in-house, then whatever is left is the task of the agency.

Unless the outside agency has been called in as a result of a sudden crisis (which is possibly the worst way to handle both PR and consultants), the consultancy will be asked to present a proposal. This allows the consultancy time to research the client's situation, and its existing relationships with its publics. The proposal should contain comments on the following aspects of the problem:

- analysis of the problems and opportunities facing the client company;
- analysis of the potential harm or gain to the client;
- analysis of the potential difficulties and opportunities presented by the case, and the various courses of action (or inaction) which would lead to those outcomes;
- the overall program goals, and the objectives for each of the target publics;
- analysis of any immediate action needed;
- long-range planning for achieving the objectives;
- monitoring systems for checking the outcomes;
- staffing and budgets required for the program.

Client firms will often ask several agencies to present, with the aim of choosing the best among them. This approach can cause problems, for several reasons. First, the best agencies may not want to enter into a competitive bidding situation. Second, some agencies will send their best people to present, but will actually give the work to their more junior staff. Third, agencies in this position may not want to present their best ideas, feeling (rightly in some cases) that the prospective client will steal their ideas. Finally, it is known that some clients will invite presentations from agencies in order to keep their existing agency on its toes.

Such practices are ethically dubious and do no good for the client organization's reputation. Since the whole purpose of the exercise is to improve the firm's reputation, annoying the PR agencies is clearly not an intelligent move. To counter the possibility of potential clients stealing their ideas, some of the leading agencies now charge a fee for bidding.

Relationships with external PR consultancies tend to last. Some major firms have used the same PR consultants for over twenty years. Changing consultants frequently is not a good idea. Consultants need time to build up knowledge of the firm and its personnel, and the firm needs time to develop

FIGURE 16.7 Example of task division between in-house staff and agency staff

a suitable atmosphere of trust. Consultancies need to be aware of sensitive information if they are not to be taken by surprise in a crisis, and the firm is unlikely to feel comfortable with this unless the relationship has been established for some time.

DEVELOPING A BRIEF

The purpose of the brief is to bridge the gap between what the firm needs and what the consultant is able to supply. Without a clear brief, the consultant has no blueprint to follow, and neither party has any way of knowing whether the exercise has been successful or not.

Developing a brief begins with the firm's objectives. Objective setting is a strategic decision area, so it is likely to be the province of senior management. Each objective needs to meet SMARTT criteria, as follows.

1 Specific, in other words it must relate to a narrow range of outcomes.
2 Measurable. If it is not measurable, it is merely an aim.
3 Achievable. There is no point in setting objectives which cannot be achieved, or which are unlikely to be achieved.
4 Relevant to the firm's situation and resources.
5 Targeted accurately.
6 Timed. A deadline should be in place for its achievement.

The objectives will dictate the budget if the firm is using the objective-and-task method of budgeting. This method means deciding what tasks need to be undertaken to achieve the final outcome, and working out how much it will cost to achieve each task. Most organizations tend to operate on the all-we-can-afford budgeting method, which involves agreeing a figure with the finance director. The SMARTT formula implies that, in these circumstances, the budget will dictate the objectives since the objectives must be achievable within the available resources.

Setting the objectives is, of course, only the starting point. Objectives need to be translated into tactical methods for their achievement, and these tactics also need to be considered in the light of what the company is trying to achieve.

The brief will be fine-tuned in consultation with the PR agency itself. From the position of their specialist knowledge, the agency will be able to say whether the budget is adequate for what needs to be achieved, or (conversely) say whether the objectives can be achieved within the budget on offer. The agency can also advise on what the appropriate objectives should be, given the firm's current situation.

MEASURING OUTCOMES

If the outcomes from the PR activities do not match up with the budgeted objectives, conflict between the client and the agency is likely to be the result. The most common reason for the relationship breaking down is conflict over the costs and hours billed, as compared with the outcomes achieved. From the agency's viewpoint, much of what happens is outside their direct control. Sponsored events might not attract sufficient audiences, press releases might be spiked as a result of major news stories breaking, and special events might be rained off. Many a carefully-planned reputation-enhancing exercise has foundered when the celebrity athlete involved has been caught taking drugs, for example.

Measuring outcomes needs to be considered at the objective setting stage. A good PR agency will not offer any guarantees of outcomes, but it should be feasible to assign probabilities to the outcomes and to put systems in place for assessing whether the objectives were achieved.

Table 16.6 shows some possible evaluation methods.

Evaluating activities is never an easy task. It is difficult to be objective, and some activities are too difficult or expensive for evaluation to be worthwhile, but without evaluation managers have no way of knowing what corrective action to take.

TABLE 16.6 Evaluating PR

Activity	Possible evaluation methods
Press campaign to raise awareness.	Formal market research to determine public awareness of the brand/ company.
Campaign to improve the public image.	Formal market research. Focus groups for perceptual mapping of the firm against competitors. Measures of attitude change.
Exhibition or trade show.	Records of contacts made, tracking of leads, formal research to determine improvements in image.
Sponsorship of a sporting event.	Recall rates for the sponsorship activity.

CASE STUDY

Fukushima Nuclear Disaster

On 11 March 2011 an earthquake and tsunami struck to the east of Japan's northeast coast. Waves up to 40 meters (120 feet) high rushed inland, killing at least 15,000 people (over 3,000 are still listed as missing). The earthquake and tsunami devastated vast areas around the coastline, destroying buildings and bridges, but perhaps the most frightening aspect of the disaster was the damage done to the Fukushima Nuclear Complex.

The six reactors at Fukushima were originally built by General Electric in the 1960s and early 1970s. They were owned and operated by the Tokyo Electric Power Company (TEPCO) and provided a significant proportion of electric power in Tokyo. When the earthquake hit, the plant survived

. . . continued

relatively well, but the subsequent tsunami broke the reactor's connection to the national grid, and also flooded the generator rooms where power to operate the plant itself was produced. With no electrical power, control systems at the nuclear plant could not operate, and in particular the electric pumps supplying cooling water to the reactor cores stopped working. The cores rapidly over-heated, and three of the reactors went into meltdown (in other words the reactor be-comes so hot the core melts completely, which sometimes releases radioactivity into the atmosphere). To prevent further radio-active contamination, the Japanese govern-ment stepped in and ordered that seawater be pumped in to cool the remaining reactors, which of course ruined them entirely and made it impossible to repair the damage later.

At first, Japanese officials stated that the disaster was Level 4 on the international scale of nuclear disasters. In fact it was subse-quently found to be Level 7. Significant radioactivity was released into the air, causing a general evacuation of anyone living within 12 miles of the plant: later, significant levels of radioactivity were found as far as 30 miles from the plant, causing the government to ban sales of food grown in the area. Even higher radioactivity was released into the sea, following the use of seawater to cool the reactors: the long-term effects are unknow-able at this time.

During the effort to control the reactor there were several hydrogen explosions, but no-one was killed or injured: several workers accumulated more than the lifetime dose of radioactivity, and as a result may suffer cancer or other radiation-induced diseases in later life. It was only in December 2011 that the government declared the plant stable, although it will take decades to decontamin-ate the surrounding area.

From a corporate reputation viewpoint, TEPCO handled the problem badly from the start. As long ago as 1976 the company was accused of falsifying safety records, a scandal which led to the resignation of several TEPCO executives: one GE designer testified that design flaws had been reported to GE, but nothing had been done about them. In 1991, a back-up generator flooded as a result of a burst pipe: a former TEPCO employee, in an interview with Japan Broadcasting news service in December 1991, said that he had reported this to senior management and given his opinion that the plant could not stand a tsunami, but management did not move the generators to higher ground. In 2008, a study showed that the plant could not withstand waves of 10 meters in height, but this study was ignored since management did not accept that such waves could ever happen (although they had in 1896 in a previous tsunami in the area).

At first, TEPCO denied that fuel at the reactor had been exposed to the atmosphere. They played down the scale of the disaster, and had grossly underestimated the risk from tsunamis (according to a Japanese government report). There was a lack of trust between the three major players in the disaster – TEPCO, the Japanese government, and the plant management team – and communication was poor, action taken too late, and confusion over what should be done and when.

. . . *continued*

A report in *The Economist*, published in 2012, said: "The reactors at Fukushima were of an old design. The risks they faced had not been well analyzed. The operating company was poorly regulated and did not know what was going on. The operators made mistakes. The representatives of the safety inspectorate fled. Some of the equipment failed. The establishment repeatedly played down the risks and suppressed information about the movement of the radioactive plume, so some people were evacuated from more lightly to more heavily contaminated places" (*The Economist*, March 2012).

Public anger over the disaster has led to a pressure group, Safecast, setting itself up to monitor radiation throughout the country. The Japanese government says that it will ignore any such activity, since it will not accept non-government measurements of radioactivity. This has, not surprisingly, angered the public even more. The net result is a very strong anti-nuclear lobby, with former Prime Minister Naoto Kan joining in the call for fewer, and eventually no, nuclear reactors (despite having been very much pro-nuclear power prior to the disaster).

The overall impression given, from the perspective of foreign journalists, is one of panic, denial, and cover-up. A report published by the National Diet of Japan Fukushima Nuclear Accident Independent Investigation Commission, published 5 July 2012, stated that Japanese culture was the fundamental cause of the disaster – a reluctance to lose face, a reluctance to report bad news to superiors in the organization, and a god-like belief in the technology were blamed as the main causes.

Meanwhile, the clean-up continues. Robots supplied by the United States, and clean-up teams from France, are in action around Fukushima. This, of course, has contributed even further to TEPCO's embarrassment – that a nation renowned for its robot technology should have to ask for outside assistance is almost beyond belief. In the longer term, it seems unlikely that nuclear power will survive in Japan, and already the search is on for alternative, sustainable power generation.

CASE STUDY QUESTIONS

1 What should TEPCO have done as soon as the tsunami hit?
2 What did TEPCO do wrong in the ensuing weeks?
3 What should TEPCO do now to restore public trust?
4 Why would the Japanese government have to step in?
5 What is the role of the pressure group Safecast?

CHAPTER SUMMARY

Corporate reputation goes beyond merely putting spin on the corporation's activities. It is a coordinated effort to influence communications to and from stakeholders, and also between stakeholders, in order to improve the corporation's position in the minds of its publics. In this sense, corporate reputation has a strategic role, because it involves positioning the corporation in the public consciousness: this has real pay-offs in terms of share values, employee satisfaction and behavior, and customer perceptions of the firm.

The key points from this chapter are as follows:

- corporate reputations are not built through spin-doctoring.
- corporate reputation has a stock market valuation.
- public relations has internal and external roles.
- crises will happen: having a crisis team in place is prudent.
- outside agencies are often cheaper and more effective than carrying out PR tasks in-house.
- between two and three times the cost of sponsorship should be devoted to other communications efforts in order to support the sponsorship expenditure.

REVIEW QUESTIONS

1 Why might a firm prefer to handle its corporate reputation activities in-house?
2 What are the key issues in building a crisis team?
3 If corporate reputation has such a strong effect on the firm's stock market valuation, why bother with other activities?
4 What are the main criteria for deciding to sponsor an event or organization?
5 How might a company avoid PR disasters such as that resulting from the Fukushima disaster (see case study)?

REFERENCES

Black, Andrew, Wright, Philip, and Bachman, John E. (1998). *In Search of Shareholder Value*. London: Pitman.

Cordeiro, J. J. and Sambharaya, R. (1997). "Do corporate reputations influence security analyst earnings forecasts?" *Corporate Reputation Review*, Vol. 1, No. 2, 94–8.

Cretu, Anca E. and Brodie, Roderick J. (2007). "The influence of brand image and company reputation where manufacturers market to small firms: A customer value perspective." *Industrial Marketing Management*, Vol. 36, Iss. 2, 241–8.

De Geus, Arie (1997). *The Living Company*. Boston MA: Harvard Business School Press.

Falkenreck, Christine and Wagner, Ralf (2011). "The impact of perceived innovativeness on maintaining a buyer–seller relationship in health care markets: A cross-cultural study." *Journal of Marketing Management, Vol. 27, Iss. 3–4,* 225–42.

Farrelly, Francis J. and Quester, Pascale G. (2005). "Examining important relationship quality constructs of the focal sponsorship exchange." *Industrial Marketing Management, Vol. 34, Iss. 3,* April, 221–34.

Fombrun, C.J. and Rindova, V. (2000). "The road to transparency: Reputation management at Royal Dutch Shell" in Schultz, M., Hatch, M.J., and Larsen, M.H. (eds), *The expressive organization: Linking identity, reputation, and the corporate brand.* Oxford: Oxford University Press.

Hansen, Havard, Samuelson, Bendick M., and Silseth, Pal R. (2008). "Customer perceived value in B-to-B service relationships: Investigating the importance of corporate reputation." *Industrial Marketing Management, Vol. 37, Iss. 2,* 218–27.

Hayward, R. (1998). *All About PR.* London: McGraw-Hill.

Heffler, Mava (1994). "Making sure sponsorship meets all the parameters." *Brandweek,* Vol. 35, Iss. 20 (16 May), 16.

IEG (2011). "Sponsorship spending: 2010 Proves Better Than Expected; Bigger Gains Set for 2011." Press release 6 Jan. 2011. Accessed at http://www.sponsorship.com/About-IEG/Press-Room/Sponsorship-Spending–2010-Proves-Better-Than-Expe.aspx

Jalkala, Anne and Salminen, Risto T. (2009). "Communicating customer references on industrial companies' Web sites." *Industrial Marketing Management, Vol. 38, Iss. 6,* 599–607.

Meenaghan, J. A. (1991). "The role of sponsorship in the marketing communications mix." *International Journal of Advertising,* Vol. 10, Iss. 1, 35–47.

Pearson, A. J. (1980). *Setting Corporate Objectives as a Basis for Action.* Johannesburg: National Development and Management Foundation of South Africa.

Post, James E., Lawrence, Anne T., and Weber, James (2002). *Business and Society: Corporate Strategy, Public Policy, Ethics.* New York: McGraw-Hill.

Tat Keh, Hean and Xie, Yi (2009). "Corporate reputation and customer behavioral intentions: The roles of trust, identification and commitment." *Industrial Marketing Management, Vol. 38, Iss. 7,* 743–56.

The Economist (2012). "Blow-ups happen: Nuclear plants can be kept safe only by constantly worrying about their dangers." *The Economist,* 10 March 2012.

Zafer Erdogan, B. and Kitchen, P.J. (1998). "The interaction between advertising and sponsorship: uneasy alliance or strategic symbiosis?" Proceedings of the 3rd Annual Conference of the Global Institute for Corporate and Marketing Communications, Strathclyde Business School.

Chapter 17

Marketing planning, implementation, and control

INTRODUCTION

Coordinating marketing activities has been a problem for marketers since the beginning of marketing thinking. In any organization, individuals act according to ideas of their own: media buyers operate with one set of rules, salespeople and advertising planners with another. Since all employees go home, and almost all talk about their work and their company, the possibilities for controlling all marketing communications are strictly limited. Having said that, planning is essential if there is to be any common direction in the organization.

CHAPTER OBJECTIVES

After reading this chapter, you should be able to:

- explain the processes involved in planning
- describe ways of obtaining feedback
- explain how to combine elements of the marketing mix to attain goals
- describe some of the problems of implementing marketing plans
- describe ways of developing control systems for marketing plans.

MARKETING PLANNING

As we saw in Chapter 3, planning is an essential part of management. Nevertheless, much planning is carried out in a haphazard or ad hoc manner: strategic plans are often produced and then ignored (a practice which Nigel Piercy has dubbed SPOTS, or "strategic plan on the shelf").

The basic process of planning is shown in Figure 17.1. Having decided on a strategic direction and position, marketers need to consider how to marshal the tools at their disposal in order to achieve the desired strategic outcome.

The firm will already have made the basic strategic decisions, which are:

- Which market should the firm be in?
- What strengths and weaknesses is the firm bringing to the marketplace?
- How can the firm's networks help it achieve its goals?
- Where does the firm intend to be in 5 to 30 years' time?
- What will the firm's competitors do in response to the market and to the firm's activities?
- Does the firm have sufficient resources to achieve the objectives decided upon?

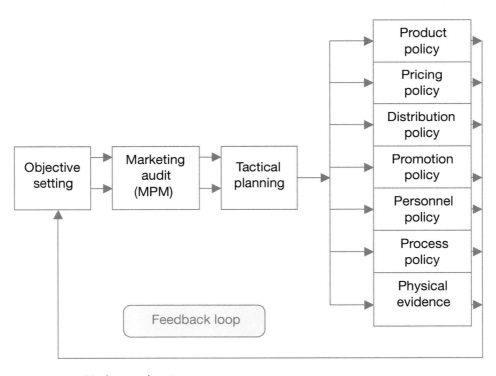

FIGURE 17.1 Marketing planning process

This in turn will have led to setting more specific objectives, giving the detail of how the strategy is to be achieved. The next stage in the planning process is to determine where the firm is now. This can be carried out by using the marketing audit.

THE MARKETING AUDIT (MARKETING PERFORMANCE MEASUREMENT)

The marketing audit is a comprehensive review of the firm's current position in terms of its marketing activities. It is, in effect, a snapshot of the firm's marketing, but like a snapshot it inevitably represents a past position since matters will have progressed while the situation is being analyzed. This means that the audit should be carried out on a regular basis if the firm is to be able to see whether progress is being made. Taghian and Shaw (2008) find that there is no single recognized method for conducting the marketing audit. Nevertheless they conclude that implementing recommendations developed from the audit are positively associated with changes in market share. However these benefits are realized only by firms conducting these audits periodically rather than on an ad hoc basis. Obviously the frequency of the audit will depend on a number of factors:

- The amount of time that can be spared from actually carrying out marketing tasks.
- The cost of carrying out the audit, in both man-hours and resources generally.
- The nature of the market. In a volatile market, the audit may need to be carried out more frequently than would be the case in a stable, mature market.
- The nature of the corporate objectives. Some objectives need constant monitoring, and also some objectives impact greatly on other parts of the marketing effort.

Taghian and Shaw also found no difference in the results based on the audit method used, indicating that using internal resources may be just as effective as contracting with outside consultants.

The audit breaks down into seven main areas, with several sub-sections in each. The main areas are:

- The macro environment audit. This takes account of all the factors which impact on the industry as a whole, including the economy, technology, political-legal, cultural, and ecological factors.
- The task environment audit. This is concerned with factors which impact on the company itself, for example markets, customers, competitors, distribution and dealers, suppliers, facilitators, and publics.
- The marketing strategy audit. This area is concerned with the appropriateness of the business mission, marketing objectives, and strategic aim.
- The marketing organization audit. This area is about the formal structure of the marketing function, functional efficiency, and interface efficiency.
- The marketing systems audit. This is concerned with the marketing information systems, marketing planning systems, control systems, and new product development systems.

■   The marketing productivity audit. This section brings in financial measures such as profitability analysis and cost-effectiveness analysis.
■   The marketing function audit. This audits the seven Ps and determines how effective the company is in each of those areas. A refinement of this focuses on Marketing Performance Measurement (MPM). O'Sullivan and Abela (2007) identify 15 marketing activities and 4 performance metrics (financial, non-financial and benchmark indicators of marketing performance) to be measured in an MPM system. They find that using an MPM measurement approach improves firm performance as well as marketing's stature within the organization and CEO satisfaction with marketing.

McGovern et al. (2004) advise that Boards of Directors choose metrics for the key business drivers of the firm. They point out that a firm need not participate in all areas of marketing but only those that support its main business drivers. These might include performance measures versus competition (share of expenditures on a particular product/service), customer experience, and growth of existing customer business. They also recommend a review of the marketing skills required by the company compared to the inventory of talent. Many firms are now using the marketing dashboard to graphically display the performance and operational metrics discussed above. Borenstein (2009) says the marketing dashboard is an "essential tool for every CEO," and recommends the following four guidelines for establishing an effective tool:

1   choose five key performance indicators (KPIs);
2   add qualitative metrics to assess each KPI;
3   establish quantitative metrics to measure each KPI;
4   develop open-ended textual area for innovation and/or reinvention.

Putting together an effective dashboard presents a number of challenges as shown by Karpinski (2006). First of course is developing the most meaningful metrics as described above; second the need to coordinate with other departments – sales, finance, and operations; and third finding sources of data and ensuring these are accurate. The development of the actual dashboard tool requires graphic as well as data management skills. Although there are many dashboard services available on the Web (entering "marketing dashboard software" into Google yields more than 14 million hits), both Borenstein and Karpinski advise that an effective dashboard cannot be bought "off the shelf." Interestingly, the study by O'Sullivan and Abela (2007) "questions the merit of the current high level of practitioner enthusiasm for marketing performance dashboards." They find no effect from dashboards on the relationship between MPM and firm performance or CEO satisfaction with marketing.

The marketing audit can be time-consuming: it involves a degree of subjectivity, and a considerable amount of introspection. This can make it an expensive exercise, both in time and in emotional labor. For the audit to be effective, it has to be more than a simple "tick the box" exercise.

The marketing audit has been criticized because it tends to lead people into the trap of thinking of all the activities as being separate from each other, whereas of course everything impacts on everything else. This means that problems are likely to be complex: such complexity has three characteristics, as follows (Mason and Mitroff, 1981):

- Any policy-making situation comprises many problems and issues.
- These problems and issues tend to be highly interrelated, so that the solution to one problem creates other problems elsewhere, or at least requires a more global solution.
- Few if any problems can be isolated effectively for separate treatment.

Complex problems cannot be solved by simple means. Variations in one element of the system causes reverberations throughout the system: many corporate problems display this level of complexity. Rittel (1972) referred to this type of problem as a wicked problem. Wicked problems have the properties shown in Table 17.1.

The existence of wicked problems means that the marketing mix approach, sometimes called the "silo" approach because everything is placed in separate containers, falls far short of providing a useful model for problem-solving. In the same way, the marketing audit implies that each activity is separate and can be treated in isolation.

Another criticism of the audit is that it tends to view the company as a discrete entity, surrounded by an environment which is mainly hostile. In the business to business world, it is more likely that the company has a number of strategic alliances and long-term relationships which are largely benevolent in nature. On the other hand, any assessment of the organization's current position needs to start somewhere.

Despite the criticisms, the marketing audit does have the advantage of focusing the minds of the marketers, and it is certainly a useful checklist.

Talking Point

The marketing audit, like the balance sheet, offers an instant picture of where the company is. Of course, by the time the audit has been carried out and all the information has been collated, several months might have elapsed and the company will have moved on greatly. The audit therefore tells us where we used to be, not where we are now.

Yet shouldn't we be looking forward? What is the point of looking backward? This would be a poor way to drive a car, so why do we think it's a good idea when we are driving a company? If the world is changing as fast as we are told it is, we can't afford to be backward looking!

On the other hand, what choice do we have? We can never know exactly where we are, and the future is always hard to predict.

TACTICAL PLANNING

Because marketers are looking for a competitive edge, they will usually try to offer their customers something that is unavailable elsewhere. In this respect, marketing differs from other business disciplines. If the legal directors were swapped from one competing firm to another, they would have little difficulty in continuing with their jobs. The law remains the same throughout the industry.

TABLE 17.1 Properties of wicked problems

Property	Explanation and Examples
Ability to formulate the problem	Tame problems can be formulated and written down. Wicked problems have no definitive formulation. For example, the problem of buying a house can be formulated in terms of writing down price range, location, and size. Desirable (but not essential) features such as a south-facing garden might be added. This is a tame problem. On the other hand, planning to buy a house to retire to in thirty years' time is a wicked problem because of the huge number of variables that will affect the individual, and the property market.
Relationship between problem and solution	Tame problems can be formulated separately from any implied solution. The formulation of wicked problems cannot be separated from statements of the solution, in other words understanding the problem in itself creates the solution.
Testability	Solutions to tame problems can be tested, and judged either correct or false. There is no single way to tell whether the solution to a wicked problem is correct or false, because solutions can only be good or bad relative to each other.
Finality	Tame problems have a closing point, at which they can be deemed to have been solved. The stopping-point can be tested, in other words. Wicked problems, on the other hand, have no end: there is always room for improvement, and each solution generates more problems.
Tractability	There is a large range of possible solutions for a tame problem, and these can be listed. For a wicked problem, there is no exhaustive, numerable list of possibilities.
Explanatory characteristics	A tame problem can be stated as a gap between what is, and what ought to be, and there is a clear explanation for every gap. Wicked problems have many possible explanations for the same discrepancy.
Level of analysis	Tame problems have identifiable, natural form: there is no argument about the level of the problem. The proper level of generality can be found for bounding the problem and identifying its root cause. Wicked problems are symptoms of another problem, and have no identifiable root causes. Would-be problem solvers cannot be sure that they are not attacking the symptoms rather than the root causes of the problem.
Reproducibility	A tame problem can be abstracted and modeled, and attempts to solve it can be tried out until one is found that appears to fit. Wicked problems are all one-shot propositions: there is no trial and error.
Replicability	Tame problems tend to repeat themselves in different organizations or at different times. Wicked problems are essentially unique.
Responsibility	No-one can be blamed for failing to solve a tame problem, but people are often praised. Would-be solvers of wicked problems are often blamed for causing other problems, but are unlikely to be praised because wicked problems are rarely solved in any final sense.

The same is true for financial directors, personnel directors, production managers, and so forth. If the marketers were swapped, however, they may well feel completely lost since each firm within an industry adopts its own approach to the market. Each firm should be addressing the needs of different segments, dealing with different distributors and different clients, and using different promotional campaigns.

The tactical possibilities for a marketing campaign are huge in number. Most of the tactics of marketing involve creativity on the part of marketers, so it is virtually impossible to lay down any hard and fast rules about approaching different marketing problems. However, the following is a list of useful guidelines for practitioners:

- try to do something that the competition has not thought of yet;
- always consult everybody who is involved in the day-to-day application of the plans;
- do not expect instant results from anything you do – but monitor the results anyway;
- ensure that the messages you give to customers, suppliers and other publics are consistent;
- be prepared for a competitive response, and try to anticipate what it might be when formulating plans;
- communication tools cannot be used to achieve marketing objectives. They can only achieve communications objectives.

The dividing line between strategy and tactics is often blurred. One of the key identifying features of tactical decisions is that they are relatively easy to reverse, which means that tactics can be adapted in unstable circumstances. For a strategy to be converted into tactics, the following four elements need to be put in place:

1 a specific action (what is to be done);
2 an accountability (who is to do it);
3 a deadline (when it is to be done by);
4 a budget (what it will cost to do it).

Usually a set of tactics is developed to implement the strategy, and these tactics will need to be coordinated. An example in marketing is the development of an integrated marketing communications package, which will involve the coordinated efforts of a great many individuals. In the business to business environment the process is similar but the elements include the sales force, trade shows, catalogs, and websites rather than relying mostly on media advertising.

Having decided what is to be done, managers are in a position to implement the program.

DEVELOPING UNIQUE CAPABILITIES

Competency to achieve a given strategic objective is derived from the way resources are combined and utilized. Efficiency in the use of resources is the key to effectiveness in strategic success derived from unique capabilities and usually expressed as competitive advantage. If resources are to be adequately utilized, managers must know what resources are available: in order to ensure that those resources are being used effectively, competency auditing is also essential. But, there are problems in translating theory into practice.

There has been considerable research into the importance of resources for the firm (Penrose, 1958; Wernerfelt, 1984; Barney, 1991; Leinwand and Mainardi, 2010). There is a problem of definition here, however: some authors prefer not to use the term "resources" when writing of the range of means at the disposal of the planners and managers, but instead refer to "assets" or "capabilities." This means that there is currently no generally-agreed classification of capabilities, resources or assets within the strategic management field.

Certainly some major distinctions can be made. First, resources may be tangible or intangible. Tangible resources and capabilities may be divided into financial, physical, technological, and organizational categories (Peng, 2009). They include the ability to raise money or generate external funds, machinery, buildings, vehicles, raw materials, work in progress, possession of patents trademarks and copyrights, planning, command-and-control systems, and management information systems which can be measured. Intangible resources include human, innovation and reputation resources and capabilities. Of the two, it is the tangible assets which are the easiest to identify and value; the intangible assets are more fragile (in that they can easily be lost) and are harder to value (since future income streams can be hard to predict). Intangible assets often represent the major part of a firm's stock-market valuation, on the other hand.

Intangible resources include relational resources and competences. Relational resources are all of the means available to the firm derived from its relationship with its environment (Lowendahl, 1997). These might include special relationships with customers, distributors, and consumers, and also the firm's reputation and brand equity. Eng (2008) shows that a firm can derive intangible and tangible assets through its network relationships. This researcher recommends management choose carefully which relationships it wishes to develop for sources of sustainable competitive advantage. Eng concludes, "managers must develop skills and knowledge of their business networks, combined both tangible and intangible resources, and integrate resources and processes . . . to enhance performance."

Leinwand and Mainardi (2010) say "a capability is something you do well that customers value and competitors can't beat." Durand (1996) has drawn a distinction between knowledge, capability, and attitude. These are shown in Table 17.2.

Leinwand and Mainardi offer the idea of "the coherence premium," a capabilities system supporting firm strategy and aligned with the correct product/service offering. They suggest the firm choose three to six interlocking capabilities for this coherent approach. Their research shows that firms with higher levels of coherence report higher profits.

From the viewpoint of auditing resources and competences, there are considerable conceptual difficulties. As far as tangible assets go, accountants have evolved some straightforward techniques for arriving at a value: however, these values are only valid in particular circumstances. For example, a fixed asset such as a piece of machinery might be valued in one of three separate ways. First, there is its value in terms of what it can produce, or the income stream that might be expected from it. This is also a function of the business environment, since the value of the production might vary or the demand for the product may shift dramatically. For example, a mold which produces plastic components is only valuable as long as the demand for those components continues – as soon as the demand is removed, the value of the mold drops to zero.

TABLE 17.2 Knowledge, capability, and attitude

Knowledge	The set of rules (know-how, know-what, know-where, and know-when) and insights (know-why) that are used to make sense of information (Dretske, 1981). This knowledge is contained in the heads of the employees for the most part, but is collective: examples are marketing insights, knowledge of competitors, technological expertise, and understanding of political issues.
Capability	This is the organization's potential for carrying out specific activities. Capability bases might include rapid response to market changes, or specific abilities to create new products (Stalk et al., 1992).
Attitude	This is the shared tendency to respond in a particular way to outside stimuli. Some firms are known for an aggressive attitude, or a litigious attitude, or even a caring and sharing attitude (Hewlett-Packard being an example of the latter). This attitude is shared by the employees, at least during working hours. Such attitudes, when seated firmly within the organizational culture, can represent substantial assets (Barney, 1986).

Second, tangible assets might be valued in terms of their purchase price and expected life. Thus a vehicle might depreciate by a calculable amount over a given period: the firm's accountants are usually able to calculate the value of, for example, the salesforce's company cars in this way.

Third, tangible assets can be valued according to their resale value. This can be higher than the original purchase price (for example, buildings or office premises) or lower than the original purchase price (for example vehicles or machinery), or in some cases might be virtually zero (for example, some of the tunneling machinery used to build the Eurotunnel).

Each of these valuation methods will arrive at a different answer. Clearly the difficulties inherent in auditing intangible assets are likely to be greater, particularly if there is pressure to audit in financial terms. Therefore few organizations do this: this is one of the problems faced by marketers when trying to justify expenditures on (for example) brand-building.

Auditing knowledge is likely to be judgment-based, since knowledge has a high rate of decay in a changing environment. A linked audit might be to consider the firm's ability and disposition toward maintaining its knowledge base: this is a function of the training of staff, of staff development initiatives, and of the firm's propensity to spend money on research and development. This audit can be assessed qualitatively by making benchmarking comparisons with other firms in the same industry.

Auditing capability is likewise a judgment-based activity, though there may be some objective elements involved. Capability might be judged by events in the recent past (for example, an exceptionally effective new-product development and launch) or might be judged by assessing the individual capabilities of the firm and aggregating them to give an overall view of capability (i.e. what we should be able to accomplish). This latter method has the advantage of being more up-to-date, but has the major drawback of not taking account of possible synergies or unforeseen weaknesses.

Corporate attitude is probably subject to more instances of self-delusion on the part of senior managers than any other element in the competences framework. Often the attitude of senior

---

Talking Point

Corporate attitude is an interesting concept. It seems to imply that the whole organization has the same attitude – yet how can this be? Organizations are not separate from their members: each member presumably has a set of attitudes on all sorts of issues. In some cases they will agree with their workmates, in other cases not – this is what makes those round-the-photocopier discussions interesting!

So how can we talk about a corporate attitude? Do people perhaps have one set of attitudes in private, and another set when in work? Does the organization have that much influence over us?

If so, doesn't each member's attitude affect the whole corporation to some small extent? How can we possibly expect to control that?

---

management is not reflected further down the hierarchy, and (worse) employees may be at some pains to conceal their real attitudes for fear of appearing to be out of step with the management. This is likely to have a severely damaging effect on the coordinating function of the strategy, since employees are likely to act in one way while trying to convince senior management that they are in fact acting in a different way. For this reason, corporate attitudes need to be monitored at grass-roots level: attitudes are difficult to measure at best, because behavior is not a good guide and self-reports may conceal political agendas.

Relational resources are even harder to pin down: with whom does the organization have a relationship, and what is the value and status of the relationship? Relationships often break down, in business as in real life. What is the value of the firm's reputation? This can sometimes be arrived at in general terms by looking at the difference between the firm's balance-sheet asset value and its stock-market valuation, but this is a somewhat nebulous measure, relying as much on factors such as the general state of the economy, the general state of the industry, and the state of competing investments, as on the current state of the firm.

Valuing a brand is not as straightforward as might at first appear, either. A well-established brand tends to have a less elastic demand curve: in other words, it is less price-sensitive (Hamilton et al., 1997). This means that a price increase on a strong brand will have less effect than a price increase on a weak brand. This implies that a strong brand will have a much better chance of weathering a recession, for example, than a weak brand: this is in itself a valuable characteristic, and is one that is well worth investing in.

The resource audit will cover the areas shown in Table 17.3.

The resource audit should include all the resources the firm can tap into, even when these are not actually owned by the firm: network relationships, intangible resources, and financial resources which can be called upon if needed fall into this category. Particular weight should be given to unique resources – those resources which competitors are unable to duplicate, for example patented products or other intellectual property.

Competence analysis cannot be measured in absolute terms: it always has to be measured against competitors' provision and customers' expectations. In particular it is important to identify the

TABLE 17.3 Elements in the resource audit

Element	Examples and explanation
Financial resources	This should include the sources of money (whether internal or external), the liabilities the organization has, and the possible availability of capital or loans should it become necessary to acquire more funding – this is essentially the firm's credit rating.
Physical resources	A list of the fixed assets of the organization, for example machinery, buildings and equipment. The audit needs to include the age and condition of the assets, their location, and their capability as well as their financial value (which is often calculated in an arbitrary manner in any case). This is to determine their usefulness in achieving strategic advantages.
Technological resources	This includes patents, trademarks, copyrights, and trade secrets. Lists of these can be made but establishing future value for each can be quite difficult.
Human resources	This can be a problematical area, since much of the value of staff depends on their motivation and commitment rather than on their paper qualifications and the numbers of them within the organization.
Innovation	This relates to research and development capabilities and the capacity for the organization to innovate and change. Obviously this is extremely difficult to measure.
Reputation	This includes customer perceptions of product quality and reliability, and company reputation as a good employer and responsible corporate citizen.

organization's core competences – the particular competences that ensure that the organization can outperform its competition in some respects.

Identifying core competences will vary from one industry to another. Threshold competences are those which any business in the industry would need to have in order to survive: any machine tool manufacturer needs a threshold competence in engineering and in design, but some manufacturers have developed core competences which single them out from the competition. For example, Abbott Toolfast Pvt. have a core competence in producing clamping equipment, Sharma Machine Tools has a competence in presses, and Galaxy Machinery Pvt. has a core competency in lathe manufacture. All of these companies are Indian, and in the global context they share a competency in low-cost manufacture. Core competences only have relevance when compared with competitors, and with market segments.

Core competences might also be linked to critical success factors. The critical success factor in an industry is the basic elements that have to be right if the firm is to succeed, rather than merely survive. For example, Internet-based firms need a threshold competency in information technology, but the critical success factor is likely to be the design of the Web page. A well-designed page will encourage business, whereas a poorly-designed one is frustrating to visit. Examples of poor design abound: websites which use complex images which take too long to download, websites which require in-depth knowledge of the company's systems in order to navigate, websites which do not give hard information but instead concentrate on sales pitches, and websites which do not allow the visitor to escape by any other means than rebooting the computer.

Because competences involve combining many elements, the process involved is perhaps crucial to a successful outcome. For example, a chef may take basic ingredients such as flour, eggs, apples, sugar, and so forth and make an apple pie. A great chef will use the same ingredients to create a confection which is a work of art: a bad chef might create an inedible mess. In the business world, every process combines the following four resources:

- Basic assets. These are the tangible and intangible assets of the business, as expressed in the financial reporting systems. Tangible assets would include plant and machinery, cash, work in progress, buildings, fixtures and fittings. Intangible assets include reputation of the firm, reputation of brands, and goodwill.
- Explicit knowledge. This is knowledge which can be written down or otherwise recorded. Much of this would be in the public domain: the legal restrictions that companies in the industry need to work within, the technical problems associated with the industry, or the published market research which forms the basis of the tactical marketing planning. Some explicit knowledge might be in the form of customer databases or patents.
- Tacit knowledge. This is knowledge which is difficult or impossible to codify, and usually resides in the heads of employees. For example, skilled workers or professionals within the organization may have particular abilities which cannot be written down: skilled welders, toolmakers or machinists have honed their skills over many years of practice. Likewise, a skilled buyer or corporate lawyer will develop skills (such as the ability to read another person's true intentions) which cannot be taught in college. Some tacit knowledge might be disseminated throughout the organization, for example customer-care skills.
- Procedure. This is the mechanism by which the basic assets, explicit knowledge, and tacit knowledge are brought together.

Procedure can easily be mistaken for process, but the two differ. A good procedure which lacks the necessary staff skills to carry it out will not produce an effective process, nor will a bad procedure be compensated for by (for example) an abundance of basic assets. The procedure must therefore take account of the available assets, explicit knowledge, and tacit knowledge.

Procedure is the element which is most easily changed by management, and therefore it is the element which most commonly changes. This is often unsettling for staff, and requires a degree of relearning and reordering of knowledge. From a tactical point of view, this can prove to be severely counter-productive.

When processes are linked together to deliver a set of benefits to customers they become the components of a capability. A capability should be more than the sum of the individual processes: synergies should result from the combination of the processes as described earlier as capability coherence. This will not happen if the processes are inappropriately linked or mutually damaging in some way (Stalk et al., 1992). An organization may combine its processes in different ways in order to develop different capabilities, either at the same time or in order.

For example, a company may have developed effective processes for recruitment, for stock purchasing, for delivery, and for efficient invoicing. These processes might all arise from having combined an asset base of state-of-the-art computer equipment and the tacit knowledge of a group of IT experts within the firm. This is shown diagrammatically in Figure 17.2.

Obviously different managers might combine the same components in a different way in order to generate new processes and competences. This is a more complex management task than simply altering procedures, so it is somewhat rarer and also it is a valuable ability for a manager to have. An example of this is the nuclear waste reprocessing plant at Sellafield in Cumbria. Originally this was a facility which was used in conjunction with the nearby nuclear power plant, but managers realized that the firm's resources would be better spent on developing the waste reprocessing facility rather than expanding the power plant. British Nuclear Fuels now has a world reputation for reprocessing nuclear waste.

Generating new capabilities from existing components is in itself a process, involving creative thought as well as the ability to identify which components are available and which processes they can be diverted from in order to strengthen other components. From the viewpoint of the end customer, the process is a major part of the benefits of the product, and forms a large part of the perception of both company and brand. For most firms, improving the firm's competitive position will mean developing new capabilities, which in turn means either changing processes in some way or recombining processes in order to generate new capabilities.

For example, a computer software company moving into a foreign market will need to develop the capability to service that market. This may mean changing the process of recruitment to include foreign-language speakers, it may mean changing the training process to encompass training in the foreign software protocols (or at least learning the usual jargon in the foreign language). Conversely,

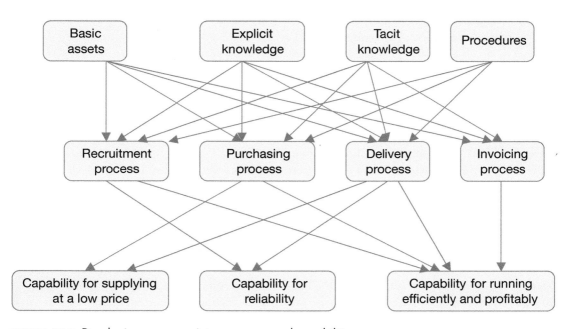

FIGURE 17.2 Developing resources into processes and capabilities

it may mean combining an existing process for translating foreign-language documents into English with an existing capacity for writing software, so that the translation is simply carried out in reverse. In practice, it probably means a combination of all these changes, plus several more. In addition it will involve the use of the firm's network to offer full capabilities to customers.

MONITORING AND EVALUATING MARKETING PERFORMANCE

Feedback is essential for monitoring performance, and (in an ideal world) no marketing activity would be undertaken without having a monitoring and evaluation system in place beforehand.

There are two basic groups of approaches for performance analysis; sales analysis and marketing cost analysis. Sales analysis looks at the income generated by the firm's activities, whereas marketing analysis looks at the costs of generating the income. Table 17.4 illustrates some sales analysis measures.

Considerable amounts of information will be needed if the firm is to make effective use of sales analysis to monitor activities. This may involve the firm in substantial market research expenditure, since market research is the cornerstone of monitoring and evaluation.

The other part of the picture is to examine the cost of achieving the goals which have been specified. Marketing cost analysis is a set of techniques for breaking down the costs of the firm's activities and associating them with specific marketing objectives. Costs can be broken down (broadly) into direct costs such as salespersons' salaries which can be directly attributable to a given activity, traceable common costs such as costs of advertising which can be traced back to specific products, and non-traceable common costs such as the cost of PR or corporate advertising which cannot be allocated to any particular product range or brand.

The main problem with marketing cost analysis lies in organizing the firm's accounting systems in such a way as to permit analysis. For example, payroll records may not be easily broken down by job function; it may be difficult to sort out which of the administration staff spend most of their time on marketing-related tasks, or even to find out what the pay bill is for the salesforce. Likewise, defining which jobs constitute marketing jobs and which do not also presents problems. Clearly the cost of servicing customers in remote areas is a marketing cost – so should the transportation costs be taken into account as well as the salesforce mileage costs? Also, if a given product is not performing well, should we be looking at the costs of production?

For the dyed-in-the-wool customer-oriented firm these answers are obvious, since all the activities of the firm are regarded as marketing activities. In other firms, not all managers agree with the basic premises on which marketing is based. At the very least, many people find it difficult to translate the theory into practice and to gear the organization's activities toward a consumer orientation.

A problem with all of the above approaches is that they are financially-based and predicated on the assumption that marketing is about making sales rather than about achieving strategic marketing objectives. For example, a firm may have a legitimate marketing objective to improve customer loyalty. While this may increase sales in the long run, the appropriate measure of success would be the degree to which customers make repeat purchases, which in the short term may actually lead to a reduction in sales as the firm shifts the emphasis away from recruiting new customers toward retaining existing ones.

TABLE 17.4 Methods of sales analysis

Analysis method	Explanation
Comparison with forecast sales	The firm compares the actual sales achieved against what was forecast for the period.
Comparison with competitors' sales	Provided the information is available, the firm can estimate the extent to which marketing activities have made inroads into the competitors' business. The problem here is proving that the difference has been caused by the high quality of the firm's marketing activities, rather than by the ineptness of the competitor.
Comparison with industry sales	Examination of the firm's performance in terms of market share. This is commonly used in industries where a relatively small number of firms control the market; for example, the car industry.
Cash volume sales analysis	Comparison of sales in terms of cash generated. This has the advantage that currency is common to both sales and costs; it has the disadvantage that price rises may cause the company to think it has done better than it has.
Unit sales analysis	Comparison of sales in terms of the number of units sold, or sometimes the number of sales transactions. This is a useful measure of sales force activities, but should not be taken in isolation; sometimes the figures can be distorted by increased sales of cheaper models.
Sales by geographic unit	Sales are broken down regionally so that the firm can tell whether one or two regions are accounting for most of the sales, and whether some less-productive regions are not worth what they cost to service.
Sales by product group or brand	This is particularly important for judging the product portfolio. This serves two purposes; it is possible to identify products which should be dropped from the range, and it is also possible to identify products which are moving into the decline phase of the product life cycle and should therefore be eliminated.
Sales by type of customer	Can reveal, for example, that most effort is being expended on a group of customers who make relatively few purchases. May reveal that the firm's customers tend to be aging, and may therefore be a declining group in years to come.

BALANCED SCORECARDS

The balanced scorecard approach was suggested by Kaplan and Norton (1992). The authors suggest that the organization should measure performance using a limited, specific set of measures which are derived from the success factors which are most important to the stakeholder groups.

The measures to be used can be grouped in the following categories:

- Financial measures. These would include return on capital employed, cash flow, growth in share value and so forth.

- ■ Customers. These measures would include perceived value for money (not necessarily cheapness), competitive benefits package, and so forth.
- ■ Internal processes. These might be enquiry response time, conversion rate from enquiry to order.
- ■ Growth and improvement. This would include the number of new products on offer, the extent of employee involvement and empowerment, employee attitudes to the firm, and so forth.

The balanced scorecard is an attempt to integrate all the factors which would impact on the organization's long-term success so that the strategy does not become unbalanced. To be most effective, managers need to apply some weighting to each of the factors in order to ensure that attention is paid to those areas which are most closely allied to the corporate mission or vision.

FEEDBACK SYSTEMS

When a discrepancy appears between the expected performance and the actual performance, the marketing manager will need to take action. This will usually take the following sequence:

1 Determine the reason for the discrepancy. Was the original plan reasonable? Have the firm's competitors seized the initiative in some way, so that the situation has changed? Is someone at fault?
2 Feed these findings back to the staff concerned. This can be in the form of a meeting to discuss the situation, or in the form of memos and reports.
3 Develop a plan for correcting the situation. This will probably involve the cooperation of all the staff concerned.

Feedback should be both frequent and concise, and any criticisms should be constructive; managers should never (for example) go to a sales meeting and offer only criticisms since this sends the salesforce out with negative feelings about themselves and the company.

Marketing strategy and planning is much like any other planning exercise; it relies on good information, a clear idea of where the organization is going, and regular examination of both outcomes and methods to ensure that the plan is still on target.

CONTROL SYSTEMS

The purpose of any strategic control system is to decide whether the current strategy is correct, and should therefore be retained, or whether circumstances have altered in such a way that the strategy should be scrapped and a new one formulated.

Most control is reactive: it seeks out variances in performance, and applies a correction to redress the variance. Such feedback is called negative feedback, because it acts against the trend of the variance in order to reduce it. Feedback which tends to increase the variance is called positive feedback, and is generally considered to be counter-productive since it creates a situation where the system runs away with itself entirely in one direction. In some cases a variation which is self-correcting, i.e. a temporary blip in performance, may be over-compensated for so that variance increases rather than decreases. This comes about because of time delays in the feedback systems. Figure 17.3 illustrates how this works in practice.

In Figure 17.3, the first arrow shows how feedback applied too late will send sales rocketing too high. This may seem like a good outcome, but it is likely that the feedback applied will have been a costly sales-boosting exercise such as a major sales promotion or an advertising campaign, the result of which is a fall in profits, possibly a fall in competitive position, and at worst provokes an insupportable competitive reaction. The second arrow shows a correctly-applied negative feedback, which helps the fall in sales to bottom out and return to normal.

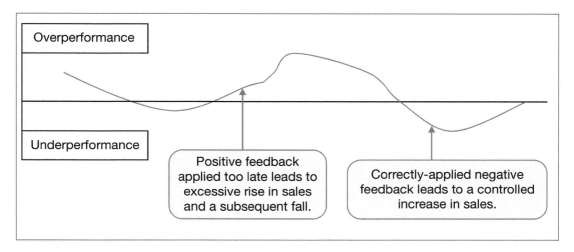

FIGURE 17.3 Positive and negative feedback

Talking Point

Feeding back into the system seems to be fraught with risks. Too early a feedback increases the problem, too late a feedback seems to be wasted effort. And if we look at the most important fluctuation of all, the economic cycle, we must wonder whether it's worth bothering at all.

Since the 1930s, governments have sought to control the boom-and-bust cycle, taking the credit when the economy booms and passing the buck when the economy crashes. Yet all the feedback, government initiatives, job-creation schemes, and rhetoric seem to have done nothing whatsoever to cure the problem.

Maybe there is no problem. Maybe fluctuations are just a natural part of life: the process of sleeping and waking, applied to business. In which case, why are we bothering with feedback at all?

Some fluctuation is inevitable. Minor deviations from the plan will always occur sooner or later: the difficulty for managers lies in judging the extent to which such deviations are permissible before action must be taken.

The concept of feedback and control is borrowed from engineering. The controls for a machine are intended to maintain the status quo: some controls are automatic (for example the governor on a steam engine) while others are designed for used by a machine operator (for example the accelerator on a car). In either case the machine will obey the control systems, because that is what it has been designed to do.

Human beings are not machines. The most difficult management issues concern the control of human beings, and this is the area where the feedback systems most often break down. For the purposes of feedback and control, processes can be divided into systematized processes such as repetitive clerical or assembly-line tasks, and unstructured processes, which are activities requiring judgment (Dermer, 1977). Examples of the second type would include professional activities such as the law or accountancy, and within the firm they would include senior managerial tasks and one-off projects. For most twenty-first century firms, unstructured processes are in the majority, simply because repetitive clerical work has been taken over by computers and most factory work has been automated. Since Dermer first formulated this division in 1977, the number of people working in manual jobs has more than halved: at the same time, the number of clerical tasks such as filing and typing have dramatically reduced due to the use of computers. It is unlikely that any firms nowadays have a typing pool, but in the 1970s such systems were commonplace.

DIFFICULTIES WITH CONTROL SYSTEMS

The type of thinking that applies to engineering problems is not necessarily applicable to human problems. Each has its own set of assumptions which may not hold true for the other: certainly many of the assumptions made by managers prove to be false when attempts are made to put them into practice. Finlay (2000) says that there are four assumptions borrowed from engineering which do not transfer to management. These are shown in Table 17.5.

Because of these problems, firms need to use adaptive controls. While much of the control system can be automatic, managers need to use human judgment to override the system when necessary, otherwise long-term change is unlikely to happen. Hofstede (1978) uses a biological analogy to explain this in terms of a living cell, but it may be more appropriate to think of a more complex organism. Fluctuations in outside temperature can be compensated for by the body's natural homeostatic mechanisms – sweating when the temperature is too high, shivering when it is too cold – but beyond certain limits of comfort a human being will exercise judgment and either go somewhere cooler or wear something warmer, as appropriate. In a similar way, organizations need to exercise judgment when the environment behaves in a way that is beyond the control system's capacity.

Two methods of control exist: first, to change the organization's behavior in some way to overcome the difficulty and reach the objective, or secondly to change objectives and aim for something that is achievable rather than something that is not. The ancient Greek philosopher Diogenes was perhaps the greatest exponent of the latter course: in order to avoid the problems of

TABLE 17.5 Assumptions underlying control systems

Assumption	Problems with this view
Objectives can be devised and can be stated precisely.	Most organizations do not have clear objectives, but rather have broad goals. For example, it is almost impossible to set objectives for a personnel department or a legal department, and in many cases it is difficult to do so for a marketing department. Companies led by visionaries neither have nor need objectives – the vision is sufficient.
Achievement can be measured and a measure of variance can be calculated.	Without measurable objectives, achievement cannot be measured. Even if there is a measurable objective, the reason for the variance may be difficult to calculate – a fall in sales may be due to a great many factors, some of which are beyond the marketer's control.
Variance information can be fed back.	Unstructured activities involve judgment and are often unique, so feedback for one activity is unlikely to be directly applicable to another. Indirect feedback is about accumulating knowledge and extrapolating from it, not about applying a set, known correction.
The feedback is sufficient to maintain control.	The system will only work if the applied feedback is bigger than the environmental shift. For example, a company selling carburetors might decide that a fall-off in business should be followed by a major advertising campaign, but if the fall-off has been caused by a dramatic fall in the demand for cars, the campaign is unlikely to be effective.

earning enough money to live in a house, he chose to live in a barrel instead. This option may not always be the optimum one.

Controls come in hierarchies, and levels of control are exercised at different levels of the organization. Three generic ways of controlling the course of events in the business are available: firstly, changing the inputs to the system; second, the process itself can be controlled; third, the objective of the organization can be changed.

TACTICS OF CONTROL

There are three basic types of control, as shown in Table 17.6 (Johnson and Gill, 1993).

Administrative control is often exercised through planning systems which control the allocation of resources and monitor the utilization of resources against the plan. Planning systems might be top-down, centralized systems in which the standardization of work procedures is paramount. Such centrally-planned systems often use a formula approach, for example setting budgets as fixed percentages of sales or allocating resources on the basis of numbers of customers dealt with. This tends to place an emphasis on bargaining within the organization to vary the formula in some way.

TABLE 17.6 Types of control

Type of control	Explanation and examples
Administrative control	Based on systems, rules and procedures, administrative control is typical in hierarchical organizations which often have large numbers of rules and regulations.
Social control	The control exercised by workmates and the organizational culture. This is common in organismic organizations and smaller organizations.
Self-control	Control exercised by individuals on themselves, based on their own interpretation of correct behavior. This is common in organizations composed of professional people, who may be working to a professional code of ethics rather than a set of rules laid down by the employer.

Within a devolved organization structure, administrative control is more likely to center on bottom-up planning, carried out within an overall set of budget constraints. In these circumstances, each division needs to reconcile its activities with other divisions in order to ensure consistency: this becomes the main role of senior management within the organization. The risk of bottom-up planning is that key strategic issues are left out of the equation, because each division focuses on its own part of the problem without seeing the overall picture. Again, coordination is a function of senior management: the center needs to establish the boundaries and reconcile the plans of the divisions, which may in turn mean that the center should benchmark in order to establish best practice.

Control through direct supervision is common in small organizations, where one person is able to control resources effectively. In large organizations it is only really possible in conditions of stability, or during times of crisis (for example if the survival of the organization is threatened). Autocratic direct control by one person might be the only way the necessary changes can be forced through – although, of necessity, this is a route which is likely to lead to considerable resentment among lower-grade staff who are displaced or undermined.

Control through performance targets has become popular during the 1990s, especially as a way of controlling the newly-privatized natural monopolies of power supply, railways, telephone systems and so forth. Setting the correct performance indicators is far from easy: indicators often give only a partial view of the overall situation, and it is usually the case that activities which are measured are the ones that get done, regardless of the real-life situations faced by the staff and managers in the organization.

Responsibility for marketing is likely to be devolved to the divisions, since marketing (in a customer-oriented firm) pervades all the activities of the organization. An organization given to using financial controls is likely to establish such divisions as profit centers, which rather complicates the issue for the divisions since they will be working toward marketing-based objectives, but will be judged on a finance-based objective. Strategic planning based organizations will be more likely to use cost or revenue centers, with marketing planning being carried out at the center.

Social and cultural control comes from the standardization of norms of behavior within the organization. In such organizations, administrative controls have a lower priority: people behave in the way they do because it is the right way to behave, not because they have a boss applying the yardstick at every stage. In the twenty-first century organization, this type of control is likely to become much more prevalent: people are becoming more individualistic and more idealistic, and less inclined to obey orders blindly. Also, social controls are much more effective in organizations which are facing chaotic situations or circumstances of rapid environmental change, in which it is impossible to lay down fixed procedures for dealing with every possible eventuality.

Social controls can sometimes work the other way, by hindering senior management when changes become necessary. The reason is that cultural norms are difficult to change, and people who regard themselves as professionals are likely to prove difficult if asked to do something which they feel impinges on their professional prerogatives.

In some respects, the twenty-first century workplace is likely to be less about controls and more about influences. Managers may not be able to impose fixed procedures on workers, partly because such procedures will be difficult to formulate, and partly because a well-educated, independent-minded workforce is unlikely to be as prepared to accept management by diktat as workers were fifty or a hundred years ago. Influence can come from many sources, but the greatest influences are likely to be social ones, created by and in turn creating obligations between the staff. This implies that managers will need to be charismatic rather than autocratic, and lead rather than drive the workforce. Beverland et al. (2007) examined what needs to be done to make a firm more market oriented. Since market orientation is a corporate culture these researchers recommend management undertake a number of initiatives. One important aspect is to involve a number of firm employees as well as customers. Marketing management must build coalitions within and outside the organization. They will also need to develop a market-oriented learning style, systems and structures including educational materials, reward systems, and clear feedback on performance. All of this requires top management and cross-functional support.

CASE STUDY

Micron Technology

In 2012, Micron Technology bought out the bankrupt Japanese company, Elpida Memory Inc., for a reported $2.5 billion. This gave Micron 35 percent of the global manufacturing capacity for DRAM (dynamic random access memory) chips for computers and (currently) 24 percent of the market, putting them in second place to Samsung, who currently have around 41 percent of the market. Approval for the deal had to come from the Tokyo District Court, since there is a risk of creating an oligopolistic market, and also purchases of Japanese companies by foreign companies require court approval. This acquisition was the latest example of Micron's ability to succeed and prosper in one of the most volatile markets in the world.

Micron was founded in 1978, in the unlikely location of Boise, Idaho. Boise is the capital of Idaho, but is a small city of around 200,000 people surrounded by one of the least-populated states in the US. It is a long

. . . continued

way from the IT hothouse of Silicon Valley, California, and even further from the financial resources of New York. Sixty years ago Boise had a tenth of its current population, so growth has been rapid: Micron has certainly played its part in this by establishing two manufacturing centers in Boise, and is the city's largest employer.

Micron's own rapid growth has been largely technology-driven. The company has a low cost base (partly due to its location) and has managed to survive many downturns in what is, by all accounts, a volatile market. Apart from the natural volatility involved in any cutting-edge technology, the global nature of the business means that competitors might appear from anywhere: for example, in 1985 Japanese manufacturers were accused of dumping chips onto the market at prices below the cost of manufacture. This crisis led Intel to leave the DRAM market altogether, but Micron survived and prospered. As might be expected, the volatility of the market and the high investment in research and development encouraged firms to look for ways of cooperating rather than competing: unfortunately, this took the form of an international price-fixing agreement which was exposed by major computer manufacturers such as Dell and Gateway. The US Justice Department investigated the allegations in 2002, and to date five manufacturers have pleaded guilty to the charges. Micron cooperated fully with the investigation, and will not suffer any penalties.

In 2005, Micron announced a new joint venture with Intel to establish a NAND flash manufacturing facility in Lehi, Utah. Micron also has a track record for merging by acquisition – the company bought Rendition, a graphics chip manufacturer, in 1998: Internet firm HostPro was bought in 1999: Qimonda's stake in Inotera was bought in 2008: flash-chip maker Numonyx was bought in 2010: and Micron continues to expand its association with former competitor Intel by building new plants in Singapore and China. The company's willingness to cooperate with former, or current, competitors has been a strong plank in its ability to ride out market volatility.

The effects of the company's cost-cutting and acquisition policies have resulted in job losses in Boise, however. More than 3,500 jobs have gone so far this century as work has moved to lower-cost countries and joint-venture plants elsewhere. The company even has production facilities in the UK, south of London in the rural county of Sussex. Presumably this was a way of establishing a presence in the European Union, rather than a cost-cutting exercise.

Micron faces a "perfect storm" of factors creating massive swings in demand. First of these is the technology, which changes rapidly due to new discoveries and new ways of using scientific breakthroughs. The second factor is the global nature of the market – competition might come from anywhere in the world, and might come from countries where the government is more than willing to subsidize companies in their quest for market domination. Third, Micron is in the component supply business, so derived demand will amplify movements in the end-

. . . continued

user markets. Finally, it is a market in which it is absolutely essential for firms to cooperate (or collude) because new developments in software will require new developments in hardware. This makes it easy for a firm to find itself shut out of the market altogether, as has happened to many firms: it also makes it easy for firms to find themselves in trouble with monopolies regulators.

Provided Micron remains well-run, with a management which is close to the market, the volatility will become a strength – after all, the Elpida acquisition has only been possible because Micron kept a close eye on the market, and Elpida's management didn't. Provided Micron can continue to understand its market, and watch for the nasty surprises, it will grow and prosper – much like its home town, Boise.

CASE STUDY QUESTIONS

1 Identify some of the problems faced by Micron. Are any of these "wicked problems?"
2 What are the critical institutional and industry factors Micron should consider?
3 What are Micron's most important capabilities or resources? (Use the VRIO approach described in Chapter 3).
4 What would be the key factors in a marketing audit for Micron?
5 How should Micron measure their marketing effectiveness? If you were to develop a Dashboard for Micron what would it include?

CHAPTER SUMMARY

Planning and implementing marketing tactics is complex because so many activities impinge on each other, and almost all the activities of the firm and its employees impact on customers in one way or another. Controlling the process is far from simple, and planning in advance often seems to be a Herculean task, when one considers the number of factors to be taken into account.

Of course, planning has to happen, and it has to be sufficiently flexible to allow for change: it also needs to be flexible enough to allow individuals some leeway in what they do for the organization.

The key points from this chapter are:

- The marketing audit is a snapshot, and is therefore out of date as soon as it is completed.
- Wicked problems are common in marketing, and may not have a single, final solution.
- For a firm to be successful it requires the right knowledge, capability, and attitude.
- Combining resources creates unique capabilities for competitive advantage: resources may be tangible, intangible or relational.
- MPM and the marketing dashboard are new ways of measuring marketing performance.

- Controls may be administrative, social or self-control.
- Activities divide into systematized processes, and unstructured processes. In the twenty-first century, the latter are becoming more common.

REVIEW QUESTIONS

1 What are the factors which would determine the frequency of marketing audits?
2 What are the major approaches to establishing control systems?
3 Why is brand evaluation difficult?
4 What are the differences between tame problems and wicked problems?
5 How would you classify employees: as tangible resources, or as intangible resources?

REFERENCES

Barney, J.B. (1986). "Organisational culture: can it be a source of sustained competitive advantage?" *Academy of Management Review*, Vol. 11, Iss. 3, pp 656–65.

Barney, J.B. (1991). "Firm resources and sustained competitive advantage." *Journal of Management*, Vol. 17, No. 1, 99–120.

Beverland, Michael B. and Lindgreen, Adam (2007). "Implementing market orientation in industrial firms: A multiple case study." *Industrial Marketing Management*. Vol. 36, Iss. 4, May, 430–42.

Borenstein, Gal S. (2009). "Building a Meaningful Executive Marketing Dashboard: A Prerequisite to Corporate Survival and Growth." *Mworld*, Vol. 8, No. 2/3, 18–21.

Dermer, J. (1977). *Management Planning and Control Systems: Advanced Concepts and Cases*. Homewood, IL: Irwin.

Dretske, F. (1981). *Knowledge and the flow of information*. Cambridge MA: MIT Press.

Durand, T. (1996). "Revisiting key dimensions of competence." Paper presented to the SMS Conference, Phoenix, Arizona.

Eng, Teck-Yong (2008). "Customer Portfolio Planning in a Business Network Context." *Journal of Marketing Management*, Vol. 24, No. 5/6, 567–87.

Finlay, P. (2000). *Strategic Management*. Harlow: Financial Times Prentice Hall.

Hamilton, W., East, R., and Kalafatis, S. (1997). "The measurement and utility of brand price elasticities." *Journal of Marketing Management*, Vol. 13, No. 4, 285–98.

Hofstede, G. (1978). "The poverty of management control philosophy." *Academy of Management Review*, Vol. 3, No. 3, July, 450–61.

Johnson, P. and Gill, J. (1993). *Management Control and Organisational Behaviour*. London: Paul Chapman.

Kaplan, R.S. and Norton, D.P. (1992). "The balanced scorecard – measures that drive performance." *Harvard Business Review*, Vol. 70, Iss. 1, Jan.–Feb., 71–80.

Karpinski, Richard (2006). "Making the most of a marketing dashboard." *B To B*, Vol. 91, No. 3, 17.

Leinwand, Paul and Mainardi, Cesare (2010). "The Coherence Premium." *Harvard Business Review*, Vol. 88, No. 6, June, 87–92.

Lowendahl, B.R. (1997). *Strategic management of professional business service firms.* Copenhagen: Copenhagen Business School Press.

Mason R. and Mitroff, I. (1981). *Challenging Strategic Planning Assumptions,* New York: Wiley.

McGovern, Gail J., Court, David, Quelch, John A., and Crawford, Blair (2004). "Bringing Customers into the Boardroom." *Harvard Business Review,* Vol. 82, No. 11, 70–80.

O'Sullivan, Don and Abela, Andrew V. (2007). "Marketing Performance Measurement Ability and Firm Performance." *Journal of Marketing,* Vol. 71, No. 2, April, 79–93.

Peng, Mike W. (2009). *Global Strategy.* Mason OH: Southwestern Cengage Learning.

Penrose, E.T. (1958). *The theory of the growth of the firm.* New York: Wiley.

Rittel, H. (1972). "On the planning crisis: Systems analysis of the first and second generations." *Bedriftsokonomen,* No. 8, 390–6.

Stalk, G., Evans, P., and Shulman, L. (1992). "Competing on capabilities." *Harvard Business Review,* Vol. 70, No. 2, March/April, 57–69.

Taghian, Mehdi and Shaw, Robin N. (2008). "The Marketing Audit and Organizational Performance: An Empirical Profiling." *Journal of Marketing Theory & Practice,* Vol. 16, No. 4, 341–9.

Wernerfelt, B. (1984). "A resource-based view of the firm." *Strategic Management Journal,* Vol. 5, Iss. 2, April/June, 171–80.

Chapter 18

Organizing for maximum effectiveness

INTRODUCTION

Once the hard work of segmentation has been completed and a strategy has been chosen, the basics of marketing must be put in place. Nothing is more basic than the organization structure. The design and implementation of this structure can empower employees to make the strategy work or place insurmountable obstacles in the way of this success. As Day (1990) says, "above all, the structure must mirror the segmentation of the market so that responsibilities for serving each major market segment are well defined."

CHAPTER OBJECTIVES

After reading this chapter, you should be able to:

- describe organization structure alternatives
- discuss the strengths and weaknesses of centralization versus decentralization
- discuss the advantages and disadvantages of the product or market manager form of organization
- discuss the benefits and drawbacks to the matrix form of organization
- understand the considerations in choosing the most effective structure
- explain how to react to turbulent markets
- know when to restructure the marketing department
- understand how to manage organizational change.

STRUCTURAL ALTERNATIVES

Marketing can be organized around functions, product lines, target markets, or some combination of these. The five broad ways to organize marketing tasks are shown in Table 18.1.

In smaller firms, there may be no specific marketing department, and of course in some firms marketing is not very high on the agenda because the firm has little control over the variables of the marketing mix. Such firms may have a marketing department, but it may only be concerned with running the occasional advertisement and organizing trade fairs. Figure 18.1 shows a simple functional organization normally used in businesses which provide single product lines to a limited number of markets.

A major advantage of this approach is simplicity. Decision-making is centralized. However, where a firm has multiple products or markets to be addressed, this approach becomes unwieldy. In the functional design, it is difficult for a particular product or market to get the attention it needs from the various functions in marketing. This has led to the establishment of product or market-based organizations as shown in Figure 18.2.

While this seems to solve the problem of the functional organization it also puts a great amount of strain on the top marketing executive who needs to be an expert in several different lines of business or differentiated market segments. This approach creates a great deal of duplication.

A combination approach is shown in Figure 18.3 where marketing is organized on a functional basis but the sales organization is organized by product.

TABLE 18.1 Organizational alternatives

Alternative	Description
Functional (Fig. 18.1)	Each marketing activity has a specialist in charge of it. This structure would have an advertising manager, a product development manager, a market research manager and so forth.
Product (Fig. 18.2)	Each manager is responsible for all the marketing decisions concerning a particular product. The firm may also employ specialists to advise and assist, but each product manager would have overall responsibility.
Segment or market (Fig. 18.2)	Here each manager is responsible for a given market segment. For example, a glass manufacturer might have one manager in charge of marketing to the automotive industry, another for marketing to the building trade, another marketing to the bottling industry, and so forth. Each manager would thus be able to develop specialist knowledge of the customers' needs.
Geographic or area (Fig. 18.4)	This approach usually is used in international markets, but can be used elsewhere. Managers are each responsible for all the marketing activities within their own geographical region.
Matrix (Fig. 18.7)	Here there is joint decision-making between the specialist market researchers, sales managers, product managers and all the other functional managers. No one manager is in overall control, and decisions are made by balancing each person's role and demands.

FIGURE 18.1 Simple functional organization

The difficulty with this organization is the obstacles it presents for functions such as manufacturing and engineering to interact with product line experts. It should be noted that this structure would be the same organized around markets rather than products.

The geographic or area organization is represented in Figure 18.4.

This structure is best employed by companies with short or similar product lines with vastly different conditions in its geographic markets. The structure allows local managers to adapt their marketing programs very well to specific markets. However, it limits the exchange of information from one area to another and adds a level of complication to rationalizing the product line. Once again, duplication and inefficiency are evident.

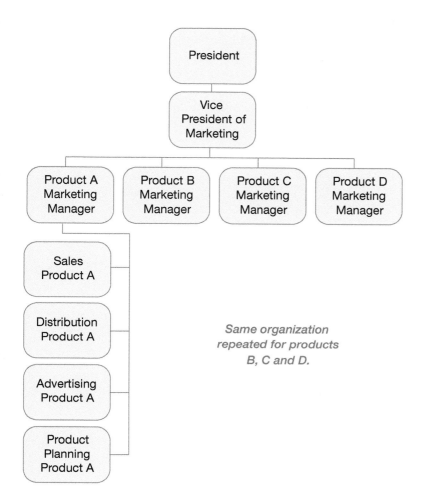

FIGURE 18.2 Product or market organization

Talking Point

The least expensive way to organize is to keep the functions together – all sales grouped in one department and all the marketing functions in another, and so on.

If this is true, then why do some firms devise such complex organization structures? Why not just tell the functional managers to cooperate with one another to serve the most important product areas and market segments?

Figure 18.5 shows yet another permutation where the sales organization is organized in the traditional geographic way, but product managers are established to focus attention on the needs of the particular product line.

This organization is best used where a single sales organization serves one set of customers with a varied line of products. Again, this structure may be organized around markets rather than products. While this organization approach is quite common in B2B firms, the difficulty here is that product

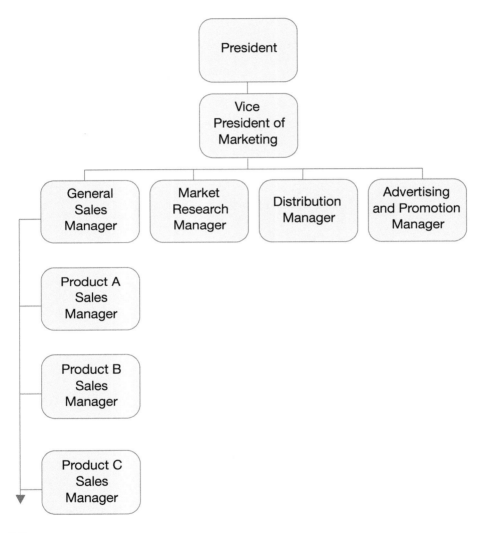

Other
Product Sales
Managers

FIGURE 18.3 Product or market sales organization

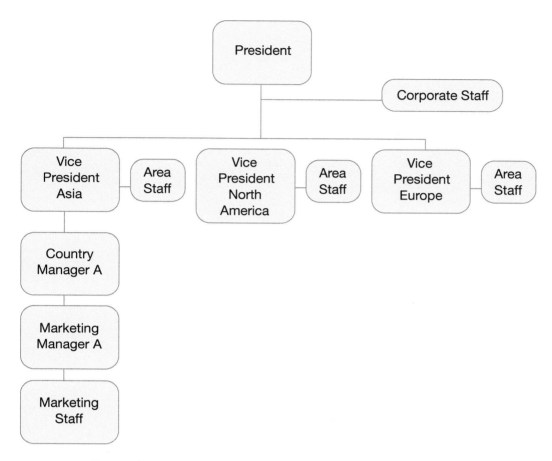

FIGURE 18.4 Geographic or area organization

managers do not report to a level high enough in the organization so that they can affect the basic decisions of other functions. We shall discuss this in some depth later in this chapter.

The overlay of serving international markets adds more complexity to the organization design. The simplest approach for handling international business is the export department as an extension of a functional organization. This is seen in Figure 18.6.

This organization is effective only for a firm with very limited sales outside its home market. Once a firm begins to have significant international sales, the export sales department is overwhelmed and the firm may move to various other types of organization. There are six basic types of international organization structures according to Czinkota and Ronkainen (2010):

- Global product – product divisions are responsible for all manufacturing and marketing worldwide.
- Global area – geographic divisions are responsible for all manufacturing and marketing in their area.

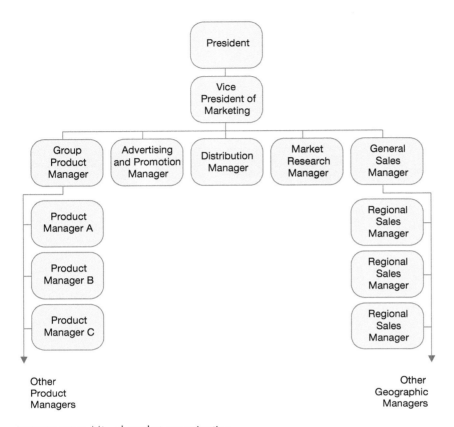

FIGURE 18.5 Mixed market organization

- Global functional – each functional area is responsible for worldwide operations.
- Global market – similar to the global product structure but based on customer segments.
- Mixed or hybrid – combining features of all the alternatives listed above.
- Matrix – for large multinational corporations attempting to give equal emphasis to functional and geographic aspects of the organization.

These organizations look similar in a general way to the simple organizations shown in Figures 18.1 through 18.7.

The most common structure used by multinational organizations is the product structure. The benefit of this approach is centralization and ease of decision-making. A global product structure assigns the international responsibility to each product division, therefore, there is no central pool of international expertise. In many cases, several product-oriented organizations in the firm are marketing simultaneously to the same customer with little or no coordination between them. In addition, some activities such as market research are often not given adequate attention, especially on an international basis since the critical mass of projects does not develop within each product organization. Centralizing functions like research is sometimes the solution to that problem. The

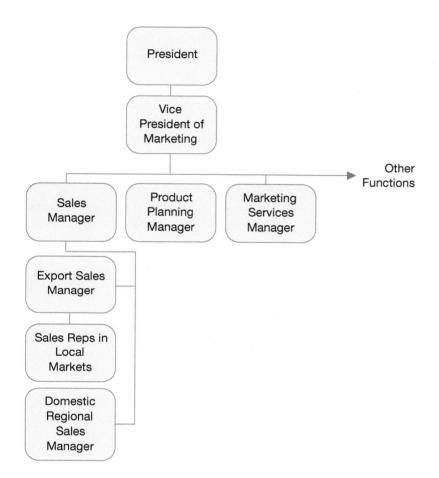

FIGURE 18.6 Export department

market structure allows the firm to focus on specific market segments and has the same advantages and disadvantages as the product structure.

Day (1990) calls the product-oriented organization an impediment to "market-driven thinking." He says these organizations tend to be competitor-centered and to over-emphasize cost. Day prefers the market-oriented organization with its ability to clearly align sales and marketing toward customer segments. He adds that functionally-organized firms who have semi-related products suffer because no individual takes the responsibility for a customer group or a prospective new segment.

The area or regional structure is the second most frequently used approach internationally. In this case, the firm is divided geographically and all activities related to the particular area are planned and executed within the area organization. For firms whose customers exhibit great variations by geography, this approach can work well. Here again, duplication is a possible negative effect. Another problem is a possible lack of information transfer from one country organization to another. Cost-effective product standardization is often downplayed in favor of regional differences. Some firms group countries together into regions to capture some of that synergy.

The mixed structure combines aspects of all the organizational types mentioned above. It is similar to Figure 18.5, which presents this form in a very simple way.

Figure 18.7 shows the essentials of the matrix organization.

In this case, a French product manager and a sales manager located in France report to their respective managers located in a regional or centralized headquarters location. At the same time, they also report to a country manager for France. This dual reporting relationship violates the basic principle of management, that an individual should have only a single supervisor. But this approach has been devised to cure the ills of functional, product-only or area-only focus in the other organizational alternatives. Many large firms such as GE, Eriksson, Boeing, and Philips have used this approach successfully over many years. The matrix structure has been criticized because the dual reporting causes problems with each supervisor (functional and country) demanding different actions from an individual. The very complexity of the matrix organizational approach can make decision-making clumsy.

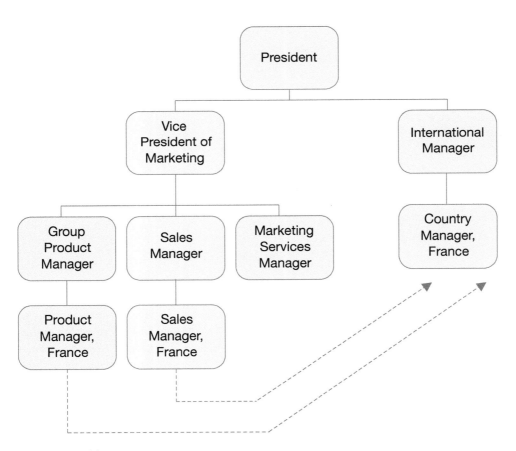

FIGURE 18.7 Matrix organization

Yip (2003) predicted that many corporations would be heading in this organizational direction. Czinkota and Ronkainen (2010) claim the matrix structure helps a business meet the challenges of global markets. This approach allows true integration of the global strategy.

Bartlett and Ghoshal (1990) provide three principles for changing organizational psychology in a way that will make the matrix organization work:

■ the development and communication of a clear and consistent corporate vision;
■ using human resources to broaden individual perspectives and develop identification with corporate goals;
■ integration of individual thinking into the overall corporate agenda. Success lies in developing in a manager's mind flexible perspectives and relationships that allow individuals to make the proper judgments and trade-offs to achieve an overall strategic objective.

Kesler and Schuster (2009) identified six strategies to make the matrix organization more effective:

■ clarity of authority and ownership to be given to a specific function;
■ developing optimal balance of vertical and horizontal power across units;
■ consideration of organizational units which generally act as catalysts for innovation (product development) versus those responsible for constraining opportunities (finance) in assigning formal power;
■ understanding whether practices should be introduced which are culture-challenging or culture-friendly;
■ balancing the cost of management time versus allowing more input;
■ allowing management to be open to new ideas rather than overly focused on internal matters.

Peter Drucker probably said it best when he advised that to make a complex organization work requires clear goals, self-discipline, and top management that takes responsibility for relationships and communications (Drucker, 1973).

In 1999 Boeing regrouped its design and manufacturing engineers in the commercial transport area into a matrix organization based around five specific aircraft model teams (or platforms) (Proctor, 1999). Boeing made the change from a product-based organization after a year of benchmarking with various other firms including BMW, Daimler-Chrysler and Toyota. The new organization is responsible for the design, planning, parts, and tools required to build a specific aircraft type. To keep the platform teams from going off in their own direction, experts from each function interface with the teams to aid in consistency and knowledge transfer. In this organizational structure, an individual employee belongs both to a functional group such as structures, payloads or systems and to a platform team.

An extension of the matrix organization structure is the organismic structure. Unlike the traditional mechanistic or bureaucratic pyramid, there is no clear "boss." Each individual contributes expertise (and effort) toward achieving the organization's objectives. The leader for each task is determined by the project being tackled at the time. This type of structure is typical of small consultancy firms who may be dealing with a wide range of disparate tasks, but can be found in larger organizations or departments of larger organizations. The main advantage of the organismic structure is that it is extremely flexible, which makes it a more appropriate structure for dealing with changing environments.

Organismic structures have the following characteristics:

- Communications flow evenly between all the members of the organization.
- There is no fixed leadership: leadership devolves to the person best fitted to deal with the situation facing the organization at the time.
- Status in the organization comes from knowledge and skill rather than from qualifications and experience.
- The organization makes use of a broader range of skills from each individual than would be the case in a hierarchical organization.

These characteristics mean that an organismic structure is able to react quickly to external changes, and thus does not need to go through the painful readjustments that a hierarchical organization would need. Organismic organizations can react extremely quickly. Of course, they also have drawbacks, as follows:

- A great deal of time is spent in discussions, and in resolving leadership issues.
- Career paths can be difficult to identify.
- The bigger the organization, the more complex the communications become.
- In periods of stability, managers tend to become confirmed in their leadership roles. In other words, the organization tends to become hierarchical if conditions remain stable.

Talking Point

Change is a constant, or so we are told. If that is the case, why aren't all organizations organismic? How can hierarchical organizations survive at all? And yet most organizations are hierarchical – this seems to be a natural law!

So why do we like hierarchies? Is it because we like to think someone else will take responsibility? Do we feel more comfortable being told what to do? Are people really that lacking in initiative? Or (moving to the dark side of the Force) is it that we like to boss people around, show our power over others, not allow other people to have their say in decision-making?

There is an old saying – "uneasy sits the butt that bears the boss." So why not let someone else share some of the responsibility? Maybe because we are afraid to let go!

CENTRALIZATION VERSUS DECENTRALIZATION

One key decision to be made in international marketing is the degree of independence to be given to local organizations. Decentralized organizations allow a high degree of independence for local subsidiaries while highly centralized organizations concentrate decision-making at the head office.

In reality, firms are a mix of centralization and decentralization, often by function. Some functions, such as R&D or human resources may lend themselves to centralization while local marketing functions are often decentralized. Wise management allows a high level of local marketing decision-making so that products and approaches can be adapted to the needs of the local customers. If a firm faces severe challenges by competitors on a global basis, it may wish to set strategy on a global basis while allowing local decision-making within that strategy. This is called coordinated decentralization (Czinkota and Ronkainen, 2010).

In the past, country managers played a significant role in international organizations. But as Yip (2003) says in a semi-serious way, "the country manager has been made obsolete by the fax machine and the Internet." In truth, the role of the country manager while continuing to be important has changed significantly. Today, rather than having unquestioned power, the country manager is often the most visible representative of the parent company especially under matrix organizations. In general, the hierarchical, colonial form of management organization has fairly well disappeared and has now been replaced by a mix of organization types more suited to the particular needs of individual firms.

While most marketing organization theories show the sales department reporting to a senior marketing executive, in truth sales often does not report to marketing. In a study of 47 German and US firms, Workman et al. (1998) did not find one sales manager reporting to a marketing manager.

CHOOSING THE MOST EFFECTIVE STRUCTURE

In deciding how to design the organization, several factors come into play. These are seen in Figure 18.8.

The first and most important driver of organization structure is strategy. Hult at al. (2007) found that "suitable structure and processes need to be instituted to realize the fruits of global strategy." Obviously the products and services offered have a significant effect upon the organization. Should the products require installation and maintenance with highly skilled technical people, a more centralized organization would be required. Firms with single, or a limited number of, products or services can use the least costly and easiest to manage functional approach. Firms with multiple product lines selling to multiple segments will more than likely have to use the product or market-based organizational structures.

For international firms, the degree of internationalization is an important factor in making the structure decision. A firm that simply sells a few products outside its home market can have an export department within a functional organization and this will work perfectly well. But a firm with a global strategy will eventually move to a complex matrix or other hybrid type of organization with all of the advantages and disadvantages this provides.

Both market and technological environments can have a major effect upon the structure decisions. Where rapid and unpredictable changes in government regulation, customer needs, competitive actions or distribution are occurring frequently, the need is for a structure that can respond rapidly. This may take any of the forms described depending on the other variables the firm must face (human resources, size of firm, products, segments, etc.). Firms facing hyper competition especially need

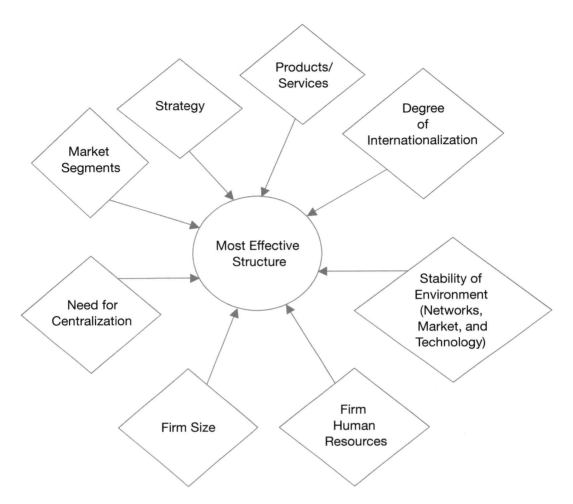

FIGURE 18.8 Factors affecting organizational structure

Source: adapted from Czinkota and Ronkainen, 2010; Workman et al., 1998; Hult et al., 2007; Hult, 2011.

adaptable organizational structures. Network alliances and collaborations (Hult, 2011) can make organizations more complex but also are important in the development of strategic resources.

A key question affecting firm organization is its human capabilities. As we have seen, the matrix organization works best where management and employees understand how to make it work. The experience, knowledge, and capabilities of individuals must be understood when an organization type is chosen.

Firm size was found to be a key determinant by Workman et al. (1998). In their study, smaller firms tended to have marketing and sales together in one unit which was functionally organized. Medium-sized firms organized marketing and sales in a strategic business unit along with a corporate marketing group. The largest firms placed marketing in a business unit but employed shared salesforces which sold more than one business unit's product. Alternatively they placed sales and marketing in a "distribution business unit," an entity essentially devoid of R&D and production capabilities. We have discussed the need for centralization or decentralization in a previous section.

Nohria et al. (2003) found that despite the fact that management spent considerable effort trying to find the ideal structure for their firms, the keys to success were simplicity, cooperation, and exchange of information across the company, putting the best people "closest to the action" and establishing systems for easy knowledge sharing.

In the 1950's the Westinghouse Electric Corporation, one of the world's first global conglomerates, established an international company in New York City. This subsidiary in effect purchased and resold products for more than 100 product divisions. Westinghouse International established country organizations throughout the world and hired individuals both at headquarters and outside the US who were experts in their respective markets. By the late 1960s, it was clear that the corporation was losing share to firms with more product expertise in the local markets. So the firm dissolved the international company and placed all international activities within each product division. While this improved the product focus for the larger divisions such as nuclear power, the smaller divisions ignored international opportunities since the critical mass required to address these opportunities was lacking in those smaller divisions. Ten years on, the firm realized that a new organization was required and so a matrix approach was instituted.

None of these organizational alternatives was entirely satisfactory. Obviously, the changes were significant and costly, both in terms of resources and morale and yet no final ideal organization had been achieved. Some firms, such as GE, have successfully used the matrix approach but have adapted it to give lead responsibility in a particular country to the product group with the most interest in that country. For instance, in the late 1980s, the lead divisions for GE in the People's Republic of China were the aircraft engine and nuclear power divisions. While the company had a strong country manager organization, these divisions also provided leadership and had a major input into decision-making for the PRC.

PRODUCT/MARKET MANAGER CONSIDERATIONS*

As has been pointed out, functional organization often underplays the importance of particular products or markets, since each functional manager has to allocate his human and financial resources among many competing products and markets without detailed knowledge of any of them. Therefore, the product manager form of organization was instituted some years ago, first in consumer products firms and then more commonly in business marketing organizations. This form of organization is most often used by firms with a number of uniquely different products produced in the same facilities, marketed by a functional marketing organization and sold through a common salesforce. Where the product line is quite similar but the products are sold to a number of highly differentiated market segments, the market manager approach would be more appropriate. However, there is little difference between these approaches in terms of organization. In both cases an individual is assigned to the task of getting special attention for either a product or a market without any direct authority over any of the line managers he/she needs to accomplish his/her objective.

There are a number of cases where the product management form of organization is not ideal. First, where a product group has grown to the size where it can support its own production and marketing, it is more appropriate to set up a separate division for that product. In some cases where divisionalization is not feasible but marketing requirements for each product are quite different, it may make sense to set up separate marketing groups but keep all other operations centralized. In other cases, separate sales groups are the most logical approach where specific customer segments must be served or when the business of each product is too small for divisionalization.

Often firms begin to use product managers with the hope that they will focus the company on improving the product. But firms have frequently been disappointed with the change to the product manager approach. A most important aspect of success for this approach is setting realistic expectations. The product manager is by definition an anomaly. In many firms he or she has the responsibility for the profit and loss of a particular product line without the authority over any of the departments required to deliver that profitability. A firm must carefully construct the product manager's job description and explain to all other departments how this product manager will function. Another major problem is selecting the wrong person. Since the product manager has no authority to order anyone to do anything, he/she must convince other managers to act on programs which they may not be enthusiastic about. Thus the product manager must have extraordinary powers of persuasion and be able to assemble the most information about this product line available anywhere in the company.

Another key to success is proper orientation and training for product managers. One should think of a product manager as a mini-general manager, especially in a B2B firm. These individuals must develop an understanding of all the functional aspects of the firm including engineering, manufacturing, finance, and human resources as well as marketing and sales. A well-experienced person has a good head start on success. Realistic tests for the success of a product manager include his/her ability to:

- accurately interpret the changing needs of the product/service line of business;
- draw together complete and imaginative plans;
- develop specific programs for product improvements;
- devise a follow-up system so that plans can be modified should the objectives not be met.

In some firms, neither product managers nor market managers adequately serve the needs of customers. In these firms, both market and product managers have been established. While this creates more complexity, it is possible to make this organization work well. The critical factor in the success of a combination product and market manager organization is to clearly define the activities each should concentrate on. Product managers should focus on protecting the pricing integrity of their product, maintaining product leadership, and providing in-depth technical or product knowledge to support sales efforts. In general, product managers should be held accountable for long-term profitability for their product line.

Market managers, on the other hand, should be responsible for developing a full understanding of customer needs, identifying opportunities, and developing a reputation for industry expertise among key customers. The inevitable conflict which arises from having both product and market managers can be regarded as a positive force if properly managed. This approach both uncovers market opportunities and provides a mechanism for sorting those opportunities and pursuing only the most potentially rewarding ones.

Recently, organizations have been dissatisfied with the results of traditional formal organization structures and have felt the necessity to change these organizations so that they are more customer focused. No consensus has emerged of the best approach but some recent examples follow. Homburg et al. (2000) describe the organization requirements for a "customer-focused" business. While there are similarities to the dual product/market manager approach, the key difference is that profit and loss responsibility shifts to customer (market segment) focused organizational units and more of the marketing activities take place within these units.

George et al. (1994) show the importance of cross-functional teams dedicated to major customers rather than the traditional product or brand manager approach. Cross-functional teams can include individuals from sales, manufacturing, R&D, finance, and several marketing functions. Challenges identified in instituting this approach include:

- roles and responsibilities of each team member must be sharply defined;
- team members often need to learn new skills;
- information systems need to be improved so that all can get information quickly;
- cross-functional career paths must be developed;
- incentives for success must be carefully aligned with team results.

* This section adapted from Ames, 1963; 1971.

REACTING TO TURBULENT MARKETS

Aufreiter et al. (2001) report that e-businesses doing well are able to re-direct their marketing very quickly. These researchers give the example of Staples.com which changes its marketing campaigns several times a day based on feedback from its websites. These authors recommend this for e-based businesses. They structure their marketing organizations to reflect stages of the customer lifecycle. One unit focuses on acquisition, another on retention/development. Individual managers are assigned to customer segments ranging from initial or casual respondents to frequent buyers. E-commerce businesses are seeking skills common in product managers. That is, the ability to integrate the functions across the company – since selling through the web yields instant feedback, highly flexible organizations and individuals are required for success.

Eisenhardt and Brown (1999) recommend "patching" – the strategic process by which corporate executives remap businesses in response to changing market opportunities. This is done by adding, dividing, transferring, exiting or combining parts of businesses. According to these researchers, "when markets are turbulent, patching becomes crucial." Managers in highly turbulent markets do not see organization structure as stable but as temporary. They are ready to make many small changes to keep their businesses flexible enough to respond to changing market conditions. These managers keep business units small and make changes quickly. They attempt to get the change approximately correct but the emphasis is on moving quickly rather than having all the details of an organization change worked out. Hult (2011) says that changing market conditions requires organizations to create "specialized subunits with differing structural features." He goes on to say that new organizational forms will arise to respond to new marketing strategies, networks, and markets and that organizations that do not adapt their culture, processes, and activities may be "selected out of the marketplace."

Patching does not work well in organizations with many shared services or cross-divisional committees and success depends upon clear business-level measurements and consistent company-wide compensation. Managers must have the basic facts of their business readily available so they can understand how to change and those involved in the change understand the rationale for it. Company-wide compensation is critical to allow the movement of individuals from one organization to another with a minimum of problems. Patching is a result of a detailed understanding of market segmentation and then the ability to create new products or services to address the needs of these market segments. Also important to success of this approach is picking the correct general manager and developing a detailed plan for the first 30 to 60 days after the patch is made. Often it is necessary to reward and recognize managers whose businesses have been cut or restructured.

WHEN TO RESTRUCTURE

Whether strategy dictates structure, or structure dictates strategy, is a somewhat vexing question. In their research, Hult et al. (2007) found that strategy "paves the way for appropriate organizational structure and processes." In most organizations, each will influence the other so that it will be difficult or impossible to tell which is cause and which is effect. From a planning perspective, the type of organizational structure which is most appropriate will depend on the volatility of the market and the degree of control the organization has over its environment. If the organization is hierarchical or mechanistic, a strategy which maintains the status quo is most likely to be effective, since the structure cannot cope with rapid change. Managers need to ask the following questions in order to know when to restructure the marketing department:

■ Is the marketing structure capable of implementing the plans?
■ Does the marketing focus the organization on priority markets or products?
■ Are managers suitably empowered?
■ Does the firm meet its sales and profit objectives?
■ Is the organization responding to customer needs or competitive actions?
■ Does the marketing department produce creative business strategies and plans?

If the answer to any of these questions is a negative, then either the structure of the organization is wrong or the strategy is wrong. Either one can be changed, but obviously the decision will rest on which is the easier (or safer) to change in order to ensure the organization's survival in the long run.

Before moving into a restructuring mode, a manager must determine whether the structure is the problem or whether the people filling the positions have been misplaced. Reorganizations are by necessity very disturbing and often cause productivity to plummet for a significant period of time. So all other alternatives should be reviewed before an extensive reorganization is undertaken. Some shifting of individuals to better utilize their inherent skills may solve the problems without formal reorganizing. Expecting reorganization alone to solve basic business problems can be quite naïve and lead to depressing results.

MANAGING CHANGE

Continual tinkering with the structure is not an optimum solution in most cases, because employees will become unsettled by the changes: it is probably better to build in the required degree of flexibility when first designing the corporate structure. The downside to changes in the structure (from the staff viewpoint) are as follows:

- changes in structure mean that people's career paths become unclear;
- effort which has been put into building relationships with colleagues can be wasted;
- changes often mean learning new roles. This means that the benefits of the structural changes will be slow in arriving;
- learning new roles means that more mistakes will be made at first;
- if a staff member is being forced through a change, this might be seen as an opportune moment to change jobs;
- the people who are most able to change jobs are usually the most talented;
- changes in structure inevitably mean changes in status: those whose status improves might be happy about this, but those whose status is lowered will not.

If staff do not support required changes, feel threatened by them, and feel that their status or job security is threatened, they are likely to sabotage the changes. This may happen officially, through industrial action or through union representation, or it may happen covertly through non-cooperation with the changes. Managements in hierarchical organizations can easily acquire the reputation of being bullies, and it is common for firms in trouble to bring in "hatchet men" who use force of personality to push changes through, often with little regard for casualties. The tactics outlined in Table 18.2 might be useful in reducing the problems outlined above.

Sometimes replacement of staff is unavoidable. Some skills become obsolete; others become essential and are unavailable from within.

Strategic changes will be easier to implement if managers (and indeed staff) feel that they own the mission and corporate strategy. Suitably empowered managers and staff will be able to be more innovative, more flexible, and more able to take risks in order to improve the outcomes of environmental threats and opportunities.

Failure to predict the amount of time implementation will take and the problems which will arise, failure to take account of other problems which will divert attention and resources elsewhere, and failure to forecast correctly the bases on which the strategy was formulated will also affect the outcomes (Alexander, 1985).

Quinn (1989) shows that managers use an approach of "logical incrementalism" in making major strategic changes such as a reorganization. Managers must move more slowly and opportunistically toward an overall goal while keeping in mind the capabilities of the people and the requirements of new roles they may be placed in. They will selectively move people trying to meet an organizational goal that will be modified along the way and rarely publicly announced or discussed.

TABLE 18.2 Tactics for improving the acceptance of structural change

Problem	Tactical alternatives
Career paths become unclear	New career opportunities under the new regime will exist, and these should be pointed out early on the process. For example, a document which begins, "Due to our ongoing commitment to improving the organization, a restructuring will be implemented. This will mean that the following new posts will be created, and priority will be given to existing staff in making appointments to these posts." This positive approach is more likely to be supported than an approach which says that posts will disappear.
Networks with colleagues will disappear	Time spent in building networks is never wasted. People who are well-networked should be identified, as they are often the best drivers for the new structure since they are usually influential in the organization.
New roles take time to learn	Before the new structure is implemented, an audit should be taken of staff to find out who already has the necessary skills for the new structure. These people should be given status, and preferably also the task of teaching others whenever this is possible. Obviously managers should be tolerant of mistakes at this early learning stage.
More mistakes will be made	Tolerance of mistakes is of course essential, but also managers need to be extra vigilant during transition periods. Training is only partly effective: often people will do well in the training sessions, but only apply the learning correctly once they have actually started trying to do the job they have trained for.
Staff may feel that this is an opportune moment to leave	Change is always disruptive, even when it is beneficial. Staff who can see that the change will be beneficial to themselves are more likely to accept the changes: emphasising the career benefits and medium-term improvements that the changes will bring will certainly help. Emphasizing the ways in which the firm will benefit is likely to be counterproductive, since it signals that the management are more concerned with the shareholders than with the staff. Although this might be obvious to staff anyway, it is tactless to make it explicit.
The most talented people will find it easiest to leave	Any strategic changes should (ideally) benefit the most talented staff most directly. These people need to be brought into the confidence of senior management: in fact, if possible everybody in the organization should be kept as fully informed as is reasonable.
Some people will lose status	Ideally, this should not happen but if it does happen then such people should either be compensated in some way, or should be offered the chance to take redundancy payments. They would almost certainly be entitled to this anyway in the UK, as a reduction in status would be regarded as a constructive dismissal by an industrial tribunal. Perhaps surprisingly, however, some people may be prepared to downshift in status if this also means a quieter life.

CASE STUDY

KIS

Dr Khaled Ibrahim is a successful entre-preneur in Delhi. Ten years ago he saw an opportunity to use the scientific knowledge being developed in Indian universities to start a scientific instrument business. That firm, KI Scientific (KIS), provides scientific instruments in many areas, focusing on hospitals and industrial processing as well as environmental monitoring. KIS is a manufacturer of a number of these instruments, but purchases and resells instruments from various other manufacturers as well.

During the past year, its turnover reached $40 million (US), with most of the revenues coming from markets in the Middle East and Africa. Dr Ibrahim was now dissatisfied with the level of success he was achieving in several key markets. When KIS began, it had a clear lead over competitors both in cost of manufacture and in technology. The firm

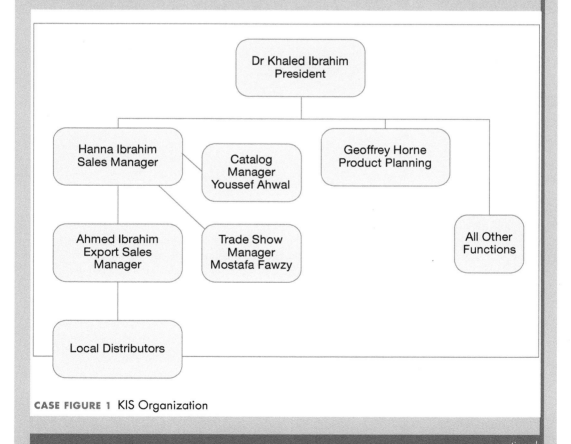

CASE FIGURE 1 KIS Organization

. . . continued

CASE STUDY

was easily able to make inroads with the most important customers in Nigeria, South Africa, and several of the smaller African nations as well as Jordan, Iran, and Saudi Arabia. Now the competition appears to be moving forward more quickly and closing the gap, and in some cases even developing superior products to KIS's. KIS's current organization is shown in Case Figure 1.

Dr Ibrahim has been reading lately about the importance of organization to success and wonders whether he should change the organization. His daughter is the sales manager. She is a 35-year-old doctoral student at Amity University. His brother is in charge of international sales and a number of young people populate the various marketing departments. He has recently hired an ex-patriate British manager to oversee product development and suspects that this individual may be able to handle more responsibility.

CASE STUDY QUESTIONS

1 What should Dr Ibrahim do first in his quest to improve the results for his firm?
2 What organizational alternatives might there be for KIS?
3 If Dr Ibrahim decides not to reorganize, what other moves might he make to improve his firm's competitiveness?

CHAPTER SUMMARY

Achieving the optimum marketing organization is a difficult task. Many approaches have been tried and each has its advantages and disadvantages. Understanding the capabilities of the individuals in your firm will go a long way to improving the results, but designing the proper structure is a key way that individuals can be empowered to do their best. The most important points from this chapter are as follows:

- Organization ranges from the simple functional structure where all similar functions such as market research, advertising or distribution are gathered together to the complex matrix or organismic organization structure where lines of authority are blurred.
- The trade-off in organization design is usually simplicity versus a proper level of concentration on product or market segment.
- Many combinations of organization are possible and managers tend to develop their organization in an incremental way to satisfy an overall idea of the most effective organization form.

■ The needs of the global firm add another layer of complexity to organization.

■ A major question in global organizations is the need for centralization versus decentralization of marketing functions.

■ Decisions about the most effective organization are based upon a number of internal and external factors.

■ The best organization structures probably have these characteristics: simplicity, easy exchange of information, and putting the best people closest to the customers.

■ The debate about product or market managers has evolved into the "customer-focused organization" where market segment-oriented organizations take precedence over product organizations.

■ For fast-moving markets, major reorganizations have been replaced by "patching," where small changes are made quickly to meet the needs of a rapidly changing market.

■ It is often more effective to leave the structure the way it is and move individuals into positions where they can succeed.

REVIEW QUESTIONS

1 Describe the major alternative forms of organization.
2 How do the export manager and matrix forms differ? Why would a firm choose the matrix organization?
3 When is it appropriate to use product or market managers?
4 What are the most important considerations in deciding how to design the organization structure?
5 What is patching? When is it best used? Describe how patching might be employed.
6 What questions would you ask before changing the organization structure?
7 What tactics could you use to improve the acceptance of structural changes?

REFERENCES

Alexander, L.D. (1985). "Successfully Implementing Strategic Decisions." *Long Range Planning*, Vol. 18, Iss. 3, 91–7.

Ames, B. Charles (1963). "Payoff from Product Management." *Harvard Business Review*, Vol. 41, Iss. 6, 141–52.

Ames, B. Charles (1971). "Dilemma of Product/Market Management." *Harvard Business Review*, Vol. 49, Iss. 2, 66–74.

Aufreiter, Nora, Ouillet, Pierre-Yves, and Scott, Mary-Kate (2001). "Marketing Rules." *Harvard Business Review*, Vol. 79, Iss. 2, 30–1.

Bartlett, Christopher A. and Ghoshal, Sumantra (1990). "Matrix Management: Not A Structure, A Frame of Mind." *Harvard Business Review*, Vol. 68, Iss. 4, 138–45.

Czinkota, Michael and Ronkainen, Ilkka A. (2010). *International Marketing*, 9th ed. Mason, OH: Southwestern Cengage Learning.

Day, George S. (1990). *Market Driven Strategy*. New York: Free Press.

Drucker, Peter (1973). *Management: tasks, responsibilities, practices*. New York: Harper & Row.

Eisenhardt, Kathleen M. and Brown, Shona L. (1999). "Patching: Restitching Business Portfolios in Dynamic Markets." *Harvard Business Review*, Vol. 77, Iss. 3, 72–82.

George, Michael, Freeling, Anthony and Court, David (1994). "Reinventing the Marketing Organization." *The McKinsey Quarterly*, No. 4, 43–62.

Homburg, Christian, Workman, John P., and Jensen, Ove (2000). "Fundamental Changes in Marketing Organization: The Movement Toward a Customer-Focused Organization Structure." *Journal of the Academy of Marketing Science*, Vol. 28, No. 4, 459–78.

Hult, G. (2011). "Toward a theory of the boundary-spanning marketing organization and insights from 31 organization theories." *Journal Of The Academy Of Marketing Science*, Vol. 39, No. 4, 509–36.

Hult, G., Tomas, M.S., Cavusgil, Tamer, Kiyak, Tunga, Deligonul, Seyda, and Lagerström, Katarina (2007). "What Drives Performance in Globally Focused Marketing Organizations? A Three-Country Study." *Journal Of International Marketing*, Vol. 15, No. 2, 58–85.

Kesler, Gregory and Kates, Amy (2010). "Designing Strategic Organizations: The New Work of Executives and HR." *Human Resource Planning*, Vol. 33, Iss. 3, 14.

Kesler, G. and Schuster, M.H. (2009). "Design Your Governance Model to Make the Matrix Work." *People & Strategy*, Vol. 32, No. 4, 16–25.

Nohria, Nitin, Joyce, William, and Roberson, Bruce (2003). "What Really Works." *Harvard Business Review*, Vol. 81, No. 7, July, 43–52.

Proctor, Paul (1999). "Boeing Shifts to Platform Teams." *Aviation Week and Space Technology*, Vol. 150, No. 20, 63.

Quinn, James Brian (1989). "Strategic Change: Logical Incrementalism." *Sloan Management Review*, Vol. 30, No. 4 (Summer), 45–60.

Workman, John P., Jr., Homburg, Christian, and Grunner, Kjell (1998). "Marketing Organization: An Integrative Framework of Dimensions and Determinants." *Journal of Marketing*, Vol. 62, Iss. 3, 21–41.

Yip, George S. (2003). *Total Global Strategy II*. Upper Saddle River, NJ: Prentice-Hall.

Chapter 19

The future of business marketing

INTRODUCTION

Predicting the future is easy – predicting it accurately is not. This chapter aims to examine the trends in thinking about business to business marketing, and to consider some of the possibilities implicit in current developments.

CHAPTER OBJECTIVES

After reading this chapter, you should be able to:

- explain the three major trends affecting business to business marketing
- describe some of the new marketing approaches now developing as a result of those trends
- explain how postmodernism is affecting marketing thought
- describe value-based marketing
- list the new insights developed in relationship marketing.

Business to business marketing will be strongly affected by three major trends – globalization, rapidly changing technology, and increased visibility. These trends can be seen in Figure 19.1 and, in fact, the trends affect each other as well.

Globalization is made possible in part by rapidly changing technology and these changes in technology measurably increase the visibility of marketing actions; and because globalization exists, companies are more visible as well. One can make the case that each of these three trends would be weaker without the other.

Talking Point

A medium-sized manufacturer of hip joint replacements has provided its products to hospitals throughout North America and Europe. The director of marketing suddenly sees comments on various websites accusing the firm of supplying defective products. The director knows these defective units are supplied by a competitor.

How do the major trends in B2B marketing affect this rumor? If the report isn't true why should the marketing director care? Why not just do nothing?

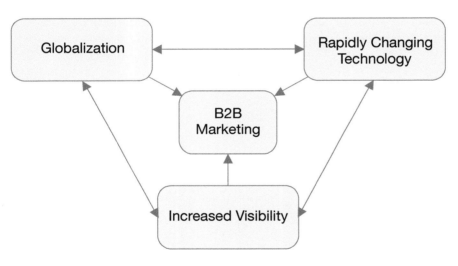

FIGURE 19.1 Major trends affecting B2B marketing

GLOBALIZATION

Globalization is a commonly used but poorly defined term. Definitions range from the all encompassing (Friedman, 2000) –

Globalization is the inexorable integration of markets, nation-states and technologies to a degree never witnessed before – in a way that is enabling individuals, corporations and nation-states to reach around the world farther, faster, deeper and cheaper than ever before, and in a way that is enabling the world to reach into individuals, corporations and nation-states farther, faster, deeper, and cheaper than ever before.

to the very succinct (Dunning, 2003) – "connectivity of individuals and institutions across the globe or at least over most of it." Czinkota and Ronkainen (2010) say that globalization results in the belief that "distinctions between national markets are . . . fading and, for some products, will eventually disappear." Dunning makes the distinction between globalization, the global marketplace, and global capitalism. He believes that globalization by itself is a neutral concept, but that the global marketplace and global capitalism are criticized for failing to provide goods and services at fair and affordable prices in an equitable way and for allowing multinationals too much power. No matter what the definition, most agree that globalization is a permanent fixture of the twenty-first century.

Czinkota and Ronkainen (2010) identified the drivers of globalization – market factors, cost factors, environmental factors, and competitive factors:

- *Market factors* –more and more the world customer is becoming a real factor and products can be designed to meet similar needs of customers throughout the world. In addition, customers are expecting both higher quality of service as well as customization. They see fewer real product differences and are less brand loyal (Kotler, 2003).
- *Cost factors* – cost efficiencies and the avoidance of duplication of effort are two important drivers of globalization. Developing new products has become more and more expensive so that firms must look to a very large market in order to justify the cost of development.
- *Environmental factors* – the removal of various barriers to trade and improved communications is also driving firms toward seeing markets globally.
- *Competitive factors* – when a competitor is marketing its products in many nations throughout the world a firm must react to match these competitive strategies and tactics and prevent the competitor from securing an unassailable advantage. A firm must seek global competitive advantage rather than just national advantage.

Recent developments call into question the continued pace of globalization. Frequently, emerging economies ask for major changes in the ways that the developed world deals with them in trade agreements. Also, the trend toward global outsourcing has limitations – there are drawbacks to outsourcing, and therefore there is a point at which outsourcing leads to poorer performance. Some researchers have concluded that any company has an optimal level of outsourcing: more, or less, will reduce performance (Kotabe et al., 2008). Especially important factors for developing countries are:

- government agricultural subsidies given to farmers in the EU, the United States and Japan which essentially keep out agricultural products exported from the developing world;
- anti-dumping regulations (which have also been used to protect indigenous industries in developed countries);
- intellectual property rules which also have the same effect (Czinkota and Ronkainen, 2010).

Protectionist pressure is seen in the US as well as the EU (especially in the wake of the 2008 financial crisis) and the new, more aggressive approaches from Asian and Latin American countries may slow the pace of globalization considerably. Should this pace slow, the business marketing manager will have to recognize the opportunities some trade barriers may provide for securing protected markets through intelligent selection of the market entry strategy. While in the long run increasing globalization might make marketing business products around the world more effective, a wise manager will watch these trends carefully and take advantage of opportunities which present themselves.

RAPIDLY CHANGING TECHNOLOGY

A second important trend is rapidly changing technology, especially in electronics and tele-communications. One need only pick up any newspaper or view any television program in nearly any part of the world to see the impact of communications technology. The Internet, of course, is the most important technological event impacting business marketing. But the advent of the smartphone, faster and lower cost computers, and the continuing reduction in the size of components of every kind, are all critical technological advances. These technologies improve communications and management within the firm and with suppliers and distributors. They also allow for higher quality products and customization to meet customer needs.

Improved technology not only makes products better and adds to visibility, but it also provides many more vehicles for contacting the customer. Only a decade ago, tried and true methods of marketing communications like trade shows, catalogues, trade magazine advertising, and mailings were adequate to reach potential customers and provide leads to the sales force. Now, a good website is an absolutely essential weapon in the marketing communications arsenal. Unfortunately, the advent of the website has not reduced the need for the other forms of communications. In fact, one of the ironies of the Internet is that other forms of communications are required to drive customers to the firm's website.

In other words, a website alone is not enough. One of this book's authors carried out research with architects which showed that they expect up-to-date and user-friendly websites while continuing to want printed catalogues and the ability to get specific advice from a manufacturer either through a local sales rep or factory technical support on the other end of a toll-free telephone line. The Internet does not remove the human element of business either – one of the most important factors for buyers in e-business is that of the reliability of the supplier's employees (Lai and Yang, 2009).

A well-designed website also helps a firm most effectively serve a large number of smaller volume customers. If these customers can be convinced to order direct from the website, the sales force can be focused on the largest volume opportunities.

One intriguing new trend is that of webcasting, sometimes called push technology. Webcasting has been defined as a way of updating news or other selected information on a computer user's desktop through periodic transmission over the Internet (WhatIs.com). However, the Hyper Dictionary (2003), defines web casting as "real-time transmission of encoded video under the control of the server to multiple recipients who all receive content at the same time (in contrast to normal web browsing)." In some definitions, webcasting implies sending information to be viewed by users at their own convenience. In any event, this new and more powerful way to send information is used by B2B marketers who, once they have established an e-list of their most important customers and other buying center members, can announce new products or services or provide other important information to selected segments as required.

Online auctions and exchanges have received some attention lately, as providing a model for future business to business dealings. Service providers such as Covisint provide a cloud-based purchase and supply service: in the UK, some government departments use a tendering service provided by Proactis. These exchanges allow buyers to source products at the lowest prices, and to have access to a very wide range of potential suppliers. However, the exchange model for B2B transactions on the Internet is flawed (Wise and Morrison, 2000). First, the emphasis on obtaining the best price runs counter to the relationship marketing paradigm which is regarded as the best current thinking on how buyer–seller relationships should work. Second, these online exchanges offer little to suppliers. Although they gain access to a wide range of new buyers, the transactions are likely to be unprofitable since the lowest bidder gets the sale. Third, the firms running the online exchanges often have very little understanding of the needs of the buyers or the sellers.

E-marketing is not always successful. An attempt to establish an e-marketplace for steel in Taiwan led to failure because the system did not meet expectations. Steel buyers were looking for a safe, secure platform to conduct transactions, and were less concerned about cost savings or management efficiency improvements. Unfortunately, the system failed to meet these expectations since it was too heavily focused on providing industry information (on which it scored highly with buyers) rather than meeting the core needs of its users (Tao et al., 2007).

SOCIAL NETWORKING

The huge growth in social networking sites (Facebook, Twitter, LinkedIn, etc.) during the last decade has opened up many opportunities for promoting consumer goods. Business to business marketers have been a little slower in accessing these new media, but are now realizing the possibilities for communicating through social networks. The slow take-up rate of the new media in B2B markets probably stems from the difficulty of measuring return on investment or tracking success. In fact, these objections apply to traditional promotional methods as well, but because of the newness of the medium (Facebook and Twitter are both less than ten years old) there is a degree of caution applied by managers.

In fact, firms are realizing the possibilities of using YouTube to demonstrate new products or supply training to distributors and their salespeople, of using blogs or Twitter to inform stakeholders of new developments and ideas, and (perhaps most importantly) of monitoring social networking sites for trends in the market, shifts in attitude, and new possibilities for product development.

Zimmerman (2012) found that there have been substantial increases in the use of social media and other new technologies in recent years. Between 2010 and 2012, use of YouTube for work purposes rose by 27 percent among architects.

Currently there appear to be four basic strategies adopted by firms seeking to exploit social networks (Wilson et al., 2011):

- The predictive practitioner. This strategy is used by firms which seek to avoid uncertainty, and wish to deliver measurable results.
- The creative experimenter. These companies seek to learn from social media, taking on board the feedback they get from customers and others on Twitter and Facebook.
- The social media champion. This is a firm which uses social media in a very large way for specific projects (for example, a new product launch). The company operates on the basis that results will be predictable, so in that respect it is similar to predictive practitioners.
- The social media transformer. This strategy involves both internal and external stakeholders, with a strong emphasis on using social media to transform the way the firm operates.
- The differences between the strategies are shown in Table 19.1.

Firms which follow a mixed strategy tend to end up losing focus and (more importantly) losing the knowledge gained from each encounter. Whichever strategy the firm adopts, it will almost certainly need to have the support of staff: even the social media champions, who establish a central department to handle social media, need to use influencers and evangelists to spread the word among the employees.

TABLE 19.1 Social media strategies

Type of approach	Objectives and rationale	Tactics and techniques	Internal organization	Outcomes
Predictive practitioner	Each project has a clear business objective.	There is little or no cross-functional coordination among projects.	Social media projects are owned by specific departments.	Each project's impact can be measured with existing metrics.
Creative experimenter	The overall objective is to learn from social media projects.	The aim is to enable engagement and to learn from different projects.	Projects are regarded as experiments within discrete departments.	Outcomes are not usually predefined.
Social media champion	Policies and guidelines are developed by the central group.	Executive champions and other influencers promote and participate in projects.	Has a centralized group with specific leaders to manage social media efforts across departments.	Best practice and experience are shared throughout the organization.
Social media transformer	Social media technology is closely integrated with how the firm learns and works.	Social media projects involve both employees and external stakeholders.	Projects typically encompass multiple functions and departments.	Centralized groups think about new ways of using social media.

INCREASED VISIBILITY

There is no question that firms are now being subjected to far greater visibility. The growth in the number of media outlets corresponding to the growing number of investors have made business a popular subject for far more individuals than in the past. Institutions are responding, providing firms with the ability to show their good intentions. The web allows facts or rumors to spread very quickly across the world. Firms concerned about reputation management monitor the web and are proactive in providing corrective information.

As we saw in Chapter 4, interest in marketing ethics is markedly greater than ever before. Perhaps one of the most obvious ways in which firms' actions are becoming more visible is the establishment of the UN's Global Compact. The Global Compact, first proposed by Kofi Annan, Secretary-General of the United Nations in 2000, lays out nine principles in the areas of human rights, labor, and the environment which firms are invited to adapt as core values "within their sphere of influence" (*International Herald Tribune*, 2001). A tenth principle on corruption and bribery was later added. According to the United Nations, there are now 90 local networks of companies throughout the world committed to advancing the Global Compact (United Nations, 2011). While the Compact has no regulatory mechanism or enforcement capabilities, the basic idea is to establish worldwide peer pressure for firms so that the adoption of these principles is a prudent action. According to Jagdesh Bahagwati (*International Herald Tribune*, 2001), the Global Compact is one of a series of actions to increase social responsibility by companies. The others include mandatory and voluntary home and host country codes.

Sustainability has become another important issue related to visibility. The World Business Council for Sustainable Development is one business association focusing on this issue and the Global Reporting Initiative allows firms to say what they have been doing to address sustainability or environmental problems throughout the world (Kolk, 2002).

Unfortunately, the increasing visibility has also encouraged terrorists. A small band of dedicated suicidal individuals can gain worldwide attention by attacking business targets, especially those which are seen as icons of a particular nation. In today's world, marketing executives must give at least some thought to security when planning events and attempt to balance clever creativity in communications with possible negative reactions.

Partly as a response to the trends described above, marketing scholars and managers have been rethinking some of the basic assumptions about marketing. In the sections that follow, we have described some newer thinking which may change a manager's perspective on the future of marketing.

PRODUCT DEVELOPMENT

The acceleration of the international product lifecycle (which is now reduced to as little as months or even weeks) means firms must speed up product development. In addition, management must design for a global market when moving new products through the development process. This does not necessarily mean complete standardization, because technology allows for customization even for narrow market segments. Responding to the challenge of faster development requirements, the most advanced firms have dramatically reduced the time they need to bring a product from the idea stage to commercialization.

The basis of this new approach, according to Holman et al. (2003) is the way product and process information is used throughout the development cycle. Instead of a sequential process, these firms have adopted a flexible approach. Holman et al. claim that by using a standard product development approach as much as one-third of the time is spent doing unnecessary work or waiting for information. To optimize the process, the team decides on the most important information it will need and attempts to get those answers as quickly as possible.

One example is the development of prototypes. In the standard approach, the prototype team would attempt to make the best possible model of the product. In order to do this the team needs detailed product specifications which are normally available only late in the development cycle. It will then require some time to construct the model. However, in the more efficient approach, the team decides what information it requires from the prototypes and they are designed to elicit this information. This may result in a simpler model which can be produced at a much earlier stage in the cycle.

Another key to the success of this process is the leader. Leaders of the process are vital since they must decide which are the most important activities the team should undertake and also which activities are unnecessary (Czinkota and Ronkainen, 2010; Holman et al., 2003).

POSTMODERN MARKETING

Postmodernism as a philosophical movement appears to cause considerable confusion; Stephen Brown's book on this subject (Brown, 1998) makes a brave attempt to clarify the topic, but he admits the difficulty of doing so in a mere 100,000 words. Even the avowed founders of the postmodernist movement have subsequently repudiated their involvement with it, which is in itself a typically postmodernist action.

The modernist view that the world holds certainties which can be discovered by the scientific approach has been called into question; chaos theory implies that the future is unpredictable, and that therefore planning should be replaced by preparation, for example. Postmodernism, on the other hand, has the features shown in Table 19.2.

While it is inextricably modernist to do so, it is feasible to examine the marketing philosophy and developments in marketing and recognize postmodernist features. For example, markets have become more fragmented and individualistic, and relationship marketing (and database marketing) try to recognize this and provide working day-to-day solutions. De-differentiation is evidenced in marketing campaigns using classical music or great works of art, and indeed the reverse (marketing imagery displayed as art – e.g. Andy Warhol's soup cans). The borderline between advertising and entertainment has long been eroded by television, and in the business to business arena has been eroded by exhibitions, trade fairs, and seminars or conferences which take place in exotic locations. Hyperreality is evidenced by virtual reality, and also by retailers who indulge in a hyperreal price war which isn't really taking place (Brown and Quinn, 1994).

The chronology issue is increasingly exemplified by some marketers' obsession with the past; the nostalgic re-creation of old designs, of "traditional recipes," and of "real" products is typified by

TABLE 19.2 Features of postmodernism

Feature	Explanation
Pastiche	Most human activities are composed of elements of many disciplines, and are usually made up of previously-known elements. Nothing is new: everything has already been written, and we are merely recombining old ideas in different ways.
Fragmentation	There is an omnipresence of disjointed moments and experiences in life and sense of self. The world is dynamic, and therefore people cannot be permanently assigned to groups: people shift attitudes, behavior, and intentions too frequently. In other words, life is not a coherent dialogue, but is rather a series of sound bites.
Hyper-reality	There is a constitution of social reality through hype or simulation, and this is powerfully signified and represented. There is a confusion of the borders between reality and simulation (Baudrillard, 1983).
Chronology	Time is often reversed: the latest model might be based on an old design (e.g. the Chrysler PSV or the BMW Mini), or the latest fashion in design becomes futuristic. Much depends on era: in the 1950s and 1960s design fashions were futuristic, whereas in the early twenty-first century the fashions are retro. The world is not progressing towards anything: everything happens in the "now."
De-differentiation	The differences between aspects of society are gradually being eroded. The distinction between chemistry and physics, between art and science, between music and the written word, are all broken down in the postmodern view. In other words, there is a blurring of boundaries.
Reversal of consumption and production	The current cultural assumption is that we define ourselves by what we consume, not by what we produce. Production is low in importance, consumption is high in importance.
Anti-foundationalism	This is also described as anti-authoritarianism. Established rules and models are seen as suitable targets for attack, lampoon, and satire.
Pluralism	The acceptance of difference in styles and culture without making judgements about superiority or inferiority. This has become a feature of Western societies, growing out of the hippy movement of the late 1960s and early 1970s.
Acceptance of disorder and chaos	Unlike modernists, postmodernists accept that chaos is a natural concomitant of change. It is therefore the natural order of things, the common state of existence. Modernists seek to create order out of chaos: postmodernists see this as futile.
Emphasis on form and style rather than content	Meaning is determined by the form rather than the content. An academic paper may contain the same information as a novel, but the message to the reader is different, and the values conveyed are vastly different.

the replacement of "new improved" on packages with "as good now as it's always been." In business markets, some firms promote themselves as being "newer than tomorrow" while others (notably financial service providers) emphasize their traditional values and solid background.

In the business to business arena, postmodernism can explain the blurring of boundaries between companies. Traditional thinking has been that one company is a buyer, while the other is a seller. The current trend toward establishing long-term relationships between firms means that some companies are in buyer–seller relationships whereas others have progressed to the point of being joint-venture partners in establishing a value chain. This is much more in accord with postmodern views. Boundaries are further blurred by the fact that the same firms may collaborate in one market while they compete in another for example, the Ford Galaxy (Ford's European multi-purpose vehicle) is the same vehicle as the Seat Alhambra and the Volkswagen Sharan. Volkswagen make engines for all three models, and the companies collaborate on the design of this car while competing in (for example) the compact car market. No one firm has the ability to fully compete in all markets – as a result, smart managers are choosing their opportunities for both cooperation (through strategic alliances or other arrangements) and competition.

Anti-foundationalism commonly expresses itself in avant-garde marketing techniques and innovative approaches to doing business. Since most marketers aim to differentiate their products by doing something the competition is not doing, there is an emphasis on achieving competitive advantage by breaking the rules – the essence of anti-foundationalism.

The postmodernist view is not easily understood, and still less is it easy to apply to marketing issues. As a philosophy it has much to offer in understanding current trends, however.

VALUE-BASED MARKETING

Value-based marketing is the almost single-handed creation of Peter Doyle (2000). Starting from the premise that the central task of management is to maximize shareholder value, the theory goes on to look at how this affects marketing thinking and action.

As discussed maximizing shareholder value is not the same as maximizing profits. Maximizing profits is often a short-term, tactical process involving cutting costs, reducing investment, downsizing, increasing sales volumes at the expense of long-term customer loyalty, and so forth. Shareholder value is about creating a long-term, secure, and growing investment. Increased sophistication among investors has led them to look for long-term growth prospects rather than short-term profits. The risk of speculating in firms with spectacular profits but little underlying substance has become well-known, and City analysts look more and more toward using measures such as customer loyalty, brand awareness, and investment levels in judging whether stocks are likely to increase in value in the long term. Because speculation is so dangerous, investors look for stocks which they will own for the long term.

Unfortunately for the investors, the shifting global marketplace means that companies do not survive long. Maintaining a profitable competitive advantage is likely to be even more elusive: as soon as it becomes apparent that a firm has found a profitable niche, competitors enter the market and profits are rapidly eroded until they reach the point where the company is unable to maintain an adequate return on its original capital investment (Black et al., 1998). This problem becomes a great deal worse during times of economic turbulence: financial crises, recessions, and political turmoil recur with monotonous regularity, making long-term planning all but impossible.

Obviously some companies are exceptions to this general trend. Large, well-established firms seem able to maintain their shareholder value year after year, using profits to increase capital value rather than pay dividends. Such blue-chip companies are regarded as safe investments because they maintain steady growth, even if the dividends are unexciting. In fact, for some investors a small dividend is a sign that the company is reinvesting profits rather than distributing them imprudently. Even such companies are not immune from environmental shifts, and often the weight of their carefully-calculated strategic plans helps to bear them down. Recent examples include UK supermarket chain Tesco which (despite being in an industry which is regarded as virtually bullet-proof) was forced to issue a profit warning to its shareholders in 2011.

For marketers, the idea that the company exists to increase shareholder value may seem to fly in the face of the customer-oriented, high-service approach which has been advocated by marketing academics for the past 50 years. In fact, customer orientation does not necessarily mean that the company gives the customers everything they want: it does mean that the company ensures that customers are satisfied and loyal in order to maximize the long-term survival potential of the firm.

Because marketers have focused almost exclusively on the customers, while other (often more senior) managers have focused on the shareholders, marketing thinking has not realized its early promise, and has been met with suspicion at boardroom level. In fact, marketing can and will fulfill the objective of maximizing shareholder value once marketers accept that the customers and consumers are the means to an end rather than the end in themselves.

Doyle (2000) has offered an alternative definition of marketing which encompasses this view.

> Marketing is the management process that seeks to maximise returns to shareholders by developing and implementing strategies to build relationships of trust with high-value customers and to create a sustainable differential advantage.

This definition has the advantage of removing profitability from the equation and substituting shareholder value. It also includes an oblique reference to the relationship marketing perspective. However, it is certainly not hard to imagine successful firms which do not bother to build long-term relationships, and which do very nicely from dealing with a large number of low-value customers. The point here is that loyalty is important for building shareholder value (hence the relationship marketing focus) and low-value customers tend not to be loyal.

Relationship marketing has also not fulfilled its early promise in consumer markets, although it has been successful in business to business markets. Establishing relationships of trust is easier in an environment where the benefits are obvious to all concerned: in consumer markets the benefits are often obscured. Consumers do not necessarily want to establish a relationship with the companies which supply their needs, and many people are irritated by firms' attempts to move the relationship beyond the business level. In business to business markets, the advantages of forming close strategic alliances are much more obvious.

Growth is essential in a shareholder-driven company, because growth in the value of the shares (rather than the dividends) is what investors seek. Therefore it is the central factor in creating shareholder value. For marketers, this means an emphasis on two possible strategies: first, recruiting more customers, and second, selling more to the customers who are already on board. In the past, transactional marketing has concentrated on the former, whereas relationship marketing focuses on the latter. It seems likely that both are necessary if the firm is to achieve the levels of growth that shareholders require. In these conditions, the use of existing customers as recruiters for other customers becomes a desirable tactic, and thus the emphasis again shifts to delighting customers.

This does not necessarily mean offering customers more and more for less and less – that way lies bankruptcy. For example, Viglen is the UK's largest computer manufacturer, but the company only deals with business markets. The computers supplied for educational establishments are cheap and basic, with few frills or refinements – they are widely used in education because budgets are tight, and the need for all the "bells and whistles" is small. Viglen's customers are, however, delighted to be able to obtain the basic equipment at a low price.

Much of the value that will be added to the shareholders' assets will be through growth in the brand value. This is the key area which marketers are able to influence. Increases in brand value reveal themselves in four ways, as shown in Table 19.3.

The difference in orientation between aiming for an increase in brand value and aiming for an increase in customer satisfaction is a small one. It is really a difference in focus rather than a new philosophy altogether: a key focus for marketers is the twofold problem of how to increase the brand value, and how to cash in on the increased value in the long term. Simply harvesting profits is not the way forward – reinvesting profits in further building of the brand, or in other ventures, is realistic and will increase the shareholder value.

Possibly the most important of the tactical decisions that spring from this difference in perspective is that of deciding which brands to keep and which to drop. Previously this decision would have been made on the basis of the BCG Matrix or some similar tool, but under a value-adding regime the decision will more likely be made on the basis of the growth potential for each brand rather than the current profitability or sales status. This may give different answers from those obtained from a BCG analysis.

TABLE 19.3 Aspects of brand value

Aspect	Examples and explanation
Obtain higher prices	A well-known brand can command higher prices because it reduces risk for customers. Most major brands follow this approach to deriving value from the brand: Mercedes trucks and IBM computers are more expensive than their competitors, but the companies justify this by offering a high-quality, reliable product. Mercedes trucks require less servicing than cheaper brands, and also break down less often, so downtime is minimized and a fleet owner can, consequently, operate with fewer vehicles.
Higher volume growth	By keeping prices competitive, a brand owner can increase the amount of business done. This is the approach taken by Dell, and Iveco trucks.
Lower costs	If a brand achieves a large market share, many of the marketing costs are amortized across a larger production run. The marketing costs for a major brand may well be lower per unit of production than the costs for a less well-known brand.
Higher asset utilization	A major brand which follows a high-volume strategy will make better use of production assets. A brand which goes for a high-price strategy will generate greater returns on assets.

Talking Point

When asked to outline his company's mission statement, Sir Alan (now Lord) Sugar once said "We just want your money!" This refreshing honesty toward customers is rare – most firms talk about customers as if they owned the place, which of course they don't – shareholders do.

So if shareholders own the firm, why aren't we more honest about this? Why should mission statements not say, "Our shareholders come first. We want to please them more than anything – so what do we have to do for you, so you will help us please our shareholders in return?"

In business, most people accept that everybody is out for themselves – it's a dog-eat-dog world. Are customers so sensitive that we need to mollycoddle them? Or is it just that we are following the marketing dogma and paying lip service to the idea of customer centrality?

Value-based marketing offers a somewhat different perspective, and at the very least a change of emphasis. In fact, earlier definitions of what marketing is all about centered on profit – all value-based marketing has added is the concept of substituting shareholder value for profit. In this scenario, customer satisfaction is seen as a means to an end, but whether the end is profit or capital growth is debatable. Either way, it may explain why the marketing concept has not really been accepted at Board level.

RELATIONSHIP MARKETING

Currently, relationship marketing has failed to deliver in consumer markets, but it appears to have scored notable successes in the business to business arena. Recent research has offered a number of new insights, as follows:

- Relationships can be developed almost accidentally, by firms which have never heard of the theory but simply believe in looking after their customers (O'Driscoll, 2006).
- Exchanges of information, and more importantly knowledge, increase both the stock of relationship-specific knowledge and the capacity for innovation. In other words, if companies exchange not only information, but also the ideas that derive from that information, the relationship becomes a great deal more effective (Fang et al., 2011).
- Relationships between supplier and purchaser need to be complemented by developing effective internal relationships in both firms. This will enable a closer fit between the firms (Piercy, 2009).
- The relationship between satisfaction and customer loyalty appears to be weaker in a highly-relational exchange (Homburg et al., 2003). This implies that establishing a long-term, deep relationship has more effect on loyalty than offering customer satisfaction in terms of product or service delivery.
- Organizational infrastructures have a marked effect on salespeople's ability to establish relationships with other firms (Dubinsky et al., 2003).

■ The marriage analogy continues to be used when discussing relationship marketing (Stoltman and Morgan, 2002).
■ Relationships can be regarded as an asset of the firm, albeit a risky asset (Hogan and Armstrong, 2001). Interestingly, this paper also regards increased shareholder value as being the main aim for the corporation.

This focus on relationship marketing may be a result of an increasing desire to create stability in an unstable world, or it may be a way of simplifying the complex problems created by managing the value chain.

Of late, there has been a great deal of academic interest in the Chinese concepts of *renqing* and *guanxi*. This is because these two basics of Chinese culture equate strongly to relationship marketing in the B2B context. *Guanxi* is about personal connections, either between two people who accept that they have obligations to one another, or through a network which can be called upon to cooperate in performing specific tasks. Sometimes a person with a *guanxi* connection to an individual can call on that individual to use his or her connections through the network. Reciprocal favors bind the members together: such favors do not necessarily happen in a direct one-to-one exchange, in other words a favor might be given with no return asked or expected: the person accepting the favor is under an obligation to return it at a future date if asked. Since *guanxi* obligations are personal, they do not apply to companies: thus, if a buyer moves from one company to another, he takes his *guanxi* network with him. This has a clear implication for corporate relationship marketing, since the relationship is between the individuals not between the firms, and a salesperson who leaves to work for a competitor will take the business with him.

Guanxi can create corruption where it cuts across government regulations. This is clearly a problem when dealing on a global scale: many US businesses dealing in China have violated anti-corruption laws without actually doing anything that would be seen as morally unacceptable in China. The moral obligation to maintain the relationship is called *renqing*, and violations of *renqing* would certainly be considered immoral, which often creates dilemmas for Westerners.

Although similar concepts occur in Western business (the Old Boy Network in the UK, which refers to those prominent people who were in upper-class schools together, and the Good Ol' Boy Network in the United States, which has more working-class origins) there is no exact parallel. The implications for global relationship marketing are, of course, profound especially as China becomes a more open, global marketplace.

THE TWENTY-FIRST CENTURY MARKETPLACE

In the B2B area, four formative trends have been identified (Wise and Morrison, 2000). These are:

■ The move from simple to complex transactions. Twenty years ago, a typical business to business transaction involved a single purchase, paid for with money. Currently, transactions may involve several companies on the supply side (offering a single product made up of service and physical attributes) and even several cooperating companies on the purchasing side, each wanting something different from the deal. For example, consider the position of the consortium of civil engineering companies that built the Channel Tunnel. The financing package for the Tunnel involved corporate shareholders, private individuals, and banks. This meant that a wide range of finance industry companies needed to become involved in the deal, each of whom hoped to establish a longer-term relationship with the various consortium members in order to transact deals in other parts of the civil engineering world. The situation was made more complex by the fact that the consortium was drawn from both French and British companies.

■ The move from middleman to speculator. As profit margins are driven down by intensifying competition, the online exchanges will need to consider speculating in the products on offer online. Instead of merely brokering deals, they are likely to become involved in the actual transactions themselves, as a way of generating revenue. One of the difficulties of trading on the Internet is that people have the perception that it should be free, which leaves Internet providers without an income. Speculation may be the answer.

■ The move from transactions to solutions. Creative companies can use the Internet, and their relationships with the rest of the value chain, to offer more than just a product. Integrated firms can (and will) offer tailored solutions to their customers' problems.

■ The move toward sell-side swaps. Rather than go through the procedures for setting up a buy–sell transaction, some firms are now using the Internet to exchange products or services. For example, the trucking business is one in which trucks often travel empty or with part-loads. This is clearly inefficient: the cost of running the truck is virtually the same whether it travels empty or full, so several Internet sites now exist where trucking companies, instead of competing against each other for loads, are able to exchange loads to ensure that the trucks run full. This is especially important for small operators, some of whom are owner-drivers with only one truck. These online swaps enable them to compete with the major haulage companies.

If these predictions are correct, the B2B world is likely to become less competitive and more cooperative, less transactional and more relational, less secretive and more sharing.

THE IMPORTANCE OF BASICS

Despite the trends described above, the findings of one important study focus on the basics. In its Trends Study 2005, the Institute for the Study of Business Markets (ISBM) at Pennsylvania State University asked leading B2B marketers in the US to identify the most important challenges facing them (ISBM, 2006). The respondents identified the following things they needed to do (included in order of importance):

■ better organize and market the marketing function itself;
■ get right the basics of market segmentation, targeting, and positioning;
■ refine the marketing budget process and metrics;
■ build markets through higher-customer value solutions;
■ better manage changing distribution channel relationships;
■ deploy the power of business to business brands;
■ compete more aggressively in global markets;
■ master eBusiness tools.

Source: The Institute for the Study of Business Markets,
Smeal College of Business, Penn State.

The need to improve the marketing function, to "sell" the benefits of the function and to be able to successfully implement the most basic marketing tasks – segmentation, targeting, and positioning – have been consistent themes of these studies conducted every other year.

CONCLUSION

Overall, B2B marketing in the twenty-first century presents many new challenges. Shrinking markets, green issues, runaway advances in communications technology, and rapidly-changing public attitudes toward consumption and communication predicate major changes not only in marketing techniques but in corporate strategy. The role of marketing is still, at the end of the day, to meet customers' needs in the most effective, efficient, and sustainable way possible for as long as it is possible to do so. Marketers will need to re-examine their models of marketing strategy many times; in an era where change is the only constant, marketing cannot afford to stand still. Ultimately, the firms who take the greatest care of their customers' interests are the ones most likely to maintain their competitive edge in a cut-throat world. Yet the basics will always be vital to success.

The rapid change in the marketing environment and the many responses to it indicate that a good marketer must have a combination of skills. He/she will not only need specific knowledge of the marketing techniques which we have described throughout this text but will also need to develop timeless skills, identified by Chonko (2004) as written and verbal communication, decision-making, analytical skills, listening, creative and critical thinking. An individual who has these skills and the ability to learn will not be at a disadvantage when new environments present themselves. He/she will be able to combine the skills and knowledge already learned with the new skills required to address the problems of these new environments.

CASE STUDY

Formica Group

Mark Johnson FAIA, principal of MARKITECT.me)

Formica Corporation's legacy dates back to the invention of "Formica®" in 1913. By the 1950s, its decorative laminates were used for the kitchen and bathroom countertops in one out of three new American homes. In the same decade Formica® Brand-topped dining tables with chrome legs became an icon of mid-century American furniture design.

The second half of the 1900s presented greater challenges to Formica Corporation. Competing decorative laminate manufacturers, changing consumer preferences for up-scale tile and stone countertops, the product's lifecycle maturity, and its perception as a commodity, all challenged its market leadership.

. . . continued

Now a global company, Formica Corporation is the North American entity of the Formica Group of companies. It has introduced hundreds of new patterns and surfacing innovations in recent decades. Yet, laminate, the brand's core product offering, had an inherent design limitation – "the brown line," the dark edge of laminate that is visible in many installations. In addition to eliminating its design challenge, Formica Group tackled the significant task of "greening" its product line, a priority for designers looking to specify sustainable products in the new millennium. The Formica® Brand's relevance within the B2B design community hinged largely on these two R&D initiatives.

In 2012, Formica Group introduced IdealEdge™, decorative laminate edges suitable for curved, clipped or 90-degree corner installations. IdealEdge™ profiles transcend the customary limitations of laminate by eliminating flat edges and brown seams. In addition to introducing this laminate industry breakthrough, Formica Group made tremendous strides in its sustainability initiatives in recent years by completing a lifecycle assessment (LCA) on key products, achieving FSC® certification on its laminates and developing the first major-branded solid surfacing material to contain post-consumer recycled content.

The rise of B2B social media marketing coincided with Formica Group's introduction of these new products and achievements. The company's marketing team speculated if its product launch, in conjunction with its new app for the iPad, could be optimized using social media marketing campaigns and events at two major North American trade shows, the International Builders' Show and the Kitchen & Bath Industry Show. If implemented, the team needed to formulate and execute a social media strategy to reach the design and building community in record time. There were several key questions Formica Group had to consider before committing additional resources to B2B social media marketing:

- Did Formica Group have the leverage to reach the B2B community even though its current social media presence was largely B2C?
- What social media networks beyond Facebook and Twitter should it consider using, if any?
- The team had heard of on-line crowdsourcing using live "Twitter chats" and "TweetUps" but had no experience organizing them. Would a combination of live and online social media marketing for Formica Group's new product launch and iPad app be effective leading up to and during the trade shows?
- Should it seek support from bloggers within the ranks of designers and builders? Formica Group knew about the growing readership of trustworthy bloggers as product specifiers and considered tapping their influence.
- The Cool Energy House, a "green model home," was being planned to showcase sustainable products at the International Builders' Show. Should Formica Group

... continued

participate and how could social media be used to create added value for the sponsorship?

■ With designers' increased desire to use online, interactive tools to design and present product options to clients, Formica Group invested in developing the free "eChip™" app for the iPad and making its products available as free downloads at the Trimble 3D Warehouse, powered by Google. Could Formica Group take advantage of these online assets to create "buzz" for its new product launch with designers, builders, remodelers, and architects at the trade shows? Would social media be an effective use of resources to reach an audience of B2B influencers who were "virtually" attending the trade shows online?

Formica Group and its agency tackled each of these social media marketing opportunities and challenges in the first four months of the year during the building industry trade show season. The strategy and tactics evolved as the team uncovered key learnings from each venue. As with any new initiative, mistakes were made and lessons learned.

CASE STUDY QUESTIONS

1 What were the possible risks attached to using a new medium at a time when the company was also launching a new product?
2 What combination of social media networks should Formica Group use?
3 How could Formica Group integrate its marketing campaign and events by cross-promoting on multiple social media networks to optimize ROI?
4 How might Formica Group reach out to the designer and builder bloggers attending the trade shows to leverage their influence?
5 How can Formica use social media to create an effective "content marketing" message about their sustainable products and leverage the Cool Energy House at the International Builders' Show?
6 Online design apps, software, and 3D product models are a way that building product manufacturers differentiate themselves from competitors and create brand loyalty within the design community. How can Formica Group leverage its investment in this technology with designers attending the trade shows?

CHAPTER SUMMARY

Three major trends will be affecting business to business marketing in the foreseeable future: globalization, rapidly changing technology, and increased visibility. Each of these trends will have an impact on how marketing is accomplished and each of the trends affects the others as well. The key points from this chapter are:

- While described in many ways globalization essentially means improved, less-difficult trade, and growing similarities of market segments.
- Four drivers of globalization are market, cost, environmental, and competitive factors.
- Technologies and improving communications will allow for higher quality products which more closely meet customer needs.
- The website is a critical tool in marketing communications because good or bad information can be passed around quickly.
- A firm must pay more attention to what is said about it on the web. Increased visibility means a firm must think about the impression it is making.
- There are many avenues available to firms to show their good intentions. One important one is the UN's Global Compact.
- Product development is speeding up as a result of the pressures for faster introductions of new products.
- Postmodernism is a factor in today's marketing. According to postmodernism, planning should be replaced by preparation.
- Postmodernism reinforces the idea that good managers know when to collaborate and when to compete.
- Value-based marketing is another important trend which emphasizes the building of long-term shareholder value rather than short-term profit maximization. This requires building customer loyalty and brand awareness.
- Relationship marketing continues to be vital in the B2B area. Relationships should be seen as an asset of the firm.
- The old idea that manufacturers dominate markets is being replaced by the domination of customers.
- The basics of marketing – segmenting, targeting, and positioning remain as important today as at any time.
- The best-prepared marketing executive will have developed specific skills about marketing but also "timeless skills" which he/she can use to learn about new environments as they present themselves.
- The presence of social media probably represents the biggest shift in business to business marketing in the last twenty years.

REVIEW QUESTIONS

1   Describe the three major trends affecting B2B marketing.
2   What are the specific effects of each one of these trends?
3   What is postmodern marketing and how can it affect marketing decisions?
4   How has product development been changed to meet the needs of fast-changing global markets?
5   What is the difference between a shareholder-driven and a profit-driven company?
6   What are the essential ingredients of improving shareholder value?
7   What are some new developments in relationship marketing?
8   Describe the use of social media in B2B marketing.
9   What marketing basics did B2B marketers feel were critical in 2005?
10 What are the most important timeless skills?

REFERENCES

Baudrillard, J. (1983). *Simulations*. New York: Semiotext(e).

Black, Andrew, Wright, Philip, and Bachman, John E. (1998). *In Search of Shareholder Value*. London: Pitman.

Brown, S. (1998). *Postmodern Marketing 2*. London: Thomson.

Brown, S. and Quinn, B. (1994). "Re-inventing the retailing wheel: a postmodern morality tale" in Goldrick, P.J. (ed.), *Cases in Retail Management*, London: Pitman.

Chonko, Lawrence B. (2004). "Marketing Education in the 21st Century: A look to the future of marketing education: observations of one teacher-researcher curmudgeon." *Marketing Education Review*, Vol. 13, No. 1, 1–18.

Czinkota, Michael R. and Ronkainen, Ilkka A. (2010). *International Marketing*. Mason, Ohio: Cengage South-Western Publishing.

Doyle, P. (2000). *Value-Based Marketing: Marketing Strategies for Corporate Growth and Shareholder Value*. London: Wiley.

Dubinsky, A., Chonko L.B., Jones, E.P., and Roberts, J.A. (2003). "Development of a relationship selling mindset: Organizational influencers." *Journal of Business to Business Marketing*, Vol. 10, No. 1, 1–30.

Dunning, John H. (2003). "The Moral Imperatives of Global Capitalism: An Overview" in Dunning, John H. (ed.), *Making Globalization Good*, Oxford: Oxford University Press.

Fang, Shyy-Rong, Fang, Shih-Chieh, Chou, Chia-Hui,Yang, Shu-Mi, and Tsai, Fu-Sheng (2011). *Industrial Marketing Management*, Vol. 40, Iss. 5, July, 754–62.

Friedman, Thomas L. (2000). *The Lexus and the Olive Tree*. New York: Anchor.

Hogan, J.E. and Armstrong, G. (2001). "Toward a resource-based theory of business exchange relationships: the role of relational asset value." *Journal of Business to Business Marketing*, Vol. 8, No. 4, 3–28.

Holman, Richard, Hans-Werner, Kaas and Keeling, David (2003). "The future of product development." *McKinsey Quarterly*, Iss. 3, 28–40.

Homburg, C., Giering, A., and Menon, A. (2003). "Relationship characteristics as moderators of the satisfaction-loyalty link: findings in a business to business context." *Journal of Business to Business Marketing*, Vol. 10, No. 3, 35–62.

Hyper Dictionary (2003). Accessed 12th June 2003 at http://www.hyperdictionary.com/computing/webcasting

International Herald Tribune (2001). "Rallying firms for UN goals: The advocate: Kori Annan" in "The global compact: Business and the UN," *International Herald Tribune*, 25 January 2001, pp. 11–14.

ISBM (2006). *ISBM Trends Study in 2005* (Olivia, Ralph 2005). Unpublished. ISBM.org

Kolk, Ans (2002). "Multinational and Corporate Social Accountability." *Insights* (Academy of International Business), Vol. 2, No. 4, 12.

Kotabe, Masaaki, Moi, Michael J., and Murray, Janet Y. (2008). "Outsourcing, performance, and the role of e-commerce: A dynamic perspective." *Industrial Marketing Management*, Vol. 37, Iss. 1, January, 69–82.

Kotler, Philip (2003). *Marketing Management*. Upper Saddle River, NJ: Prentice-Hall.

Lai, Jung-Yu and Yang, Chun-Chieh (2009). "Effects of employees' perceived dependability on success of enterprise applications in e-business." *Industrial Marketing Management*, Vol. 38, Iss. 3, April, 275–82.

O'Driscoll, Aidan (2006). "Reflection on Contemporary Issues in Relationship Marketing: Evidence from a Longitudinal Case Study in the Building Materials Industry." *Journal of Marketing Management*, Vol. 22, Iss. 1/2, 111–33.

Piercy, Nigel (2009). "Strategic relationships between boundary-spanning functions: Aligning customer relationship management with supplier relationship management." *Industrial Marketing Management*, Vol. 38, Iss. 8, November, 865–71.

Stoltman, Jeffrey J. and Morgan, Fred W. (2002). "Extending the Marriage Metaphor as a Way to View Marketing Relationships." *Journal of Business to Business Marketing*, Vol. 9, No 1, 49–75.

Tao, Yu-Hui, Chen, Chia-Ping, and Chang, Chia-Ren (2007). "Unmet adoption expectation as the key to e-marketplace failure: A case of Taiwan's steel industry." *Industrial Marketing Management*, Vol. 36, Iss. 8, November, 1068–81.

United Nations (2011). Accessed 2012 at http://www.unglobalcompact.org/

Whatls.com (2003). Accessed at http://iroi.seu.edu.cn/books/ee_dic/whatis/webcasti.htm

Wilson, H., Clark, M., and Smith, B. (2011). "Justifying CRM projects in a business-to-business context: The potential of the Benefits Dependency Network." *Industrial Marketing Management*, Vol. 36, Iss. 6, pp. 784–98.

Wise, Richard and Morrison, David (2000). "Beyond the exchange: The future of B2B." *Harvard Business Review*, Vol. 78, No. 6, Nov.–Dec., 86–96.

Foreign Exchange

Marketing managers operating around the world will frequently be faced with the prospect of selling in a local currency. While the letter of credit is a common form of payment (described elsewhere in the text), it is often necessary to sell product in the currency of the buyer. Therefore, an international manager must be familiar with the foreign exchange process.

In the simplest terms, the exchange rate shown everyday online or in some newspapers is the price of one country's currency in terms of another country's currency.

There is no single foreign exchange rate for trading one currency into another and there is no single place of exchange such as a stock market where this takes place. In reality, the exchange of currency takes place electronically, mostly between banks throughout the world. At any one time the exchange rate between currencies may vary slightly for each transaction. Nevertheless, many online sites and newspapers print rates derived from particular sources at a particular time.

Rates may be found on Oanda.com (http://www.oanda.com/currency/converter/)

There are two types of exchange rates, spot and forward rates. The spot rate is that given for immediate delivery of a currency. However, settlement is usually required within two business days.

The formula for converting any amount of currency into US dollars (US$), for example, would be (where Sd is the spot rate in US $ terms and FC is the amount of foreign currency to be converted):

$$Sd = \frac{US\$}{FC}$$

To make the calculation in foreign terms (Sf), the formula is reversed.

So, for instance, if we wish to know what the value of HK$50,000 in US dollars would be for spot delivery, we would use the formula as follows:

Take the spot rate for the Hong Kong dollar (in US Terms) given on OANDA as 0.12895. The simple math shown below converts the HK$50,000 to $6,447.50 in US dollars.

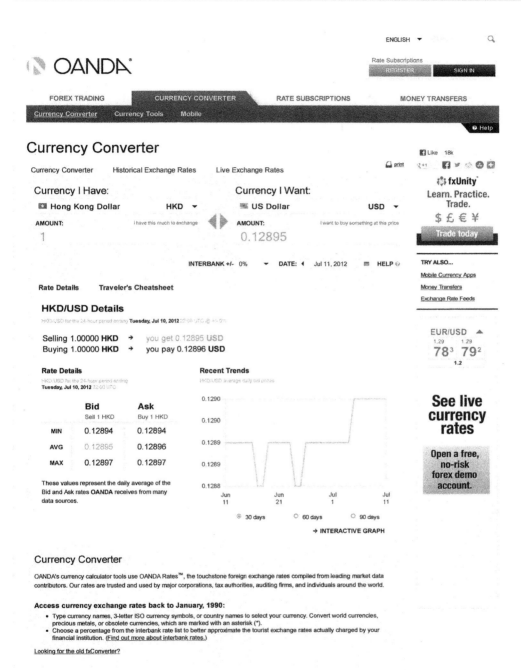

APPENDIX A FIGURE 1.1 Screen shot of Oanda website

© 2012 OANDA Corporation. Used with permission

$$0.12895 = \frac{US\$}{HK\$50,000}$$

$HK\$50,000 \times 0.12895 = \$6,447.50$
$\$ = US \$6,447.50$

Some firms can profit from slight differences in the exchange rate between various currencies. This involves selling one currency for another, selling that for a third, then converting back to the original currency. These calculations are based on the cross rates. OANDA has made this convenient by providing the capability of creating custom cross rate tables of some currencies.

Often, when a sale is made, payment will be completed at a later time. Should the contract be negotiated in a foreign currency, the manager may wish to assure payment of a certain amount by contracting with a financial institution to receive his or her local currency at a future date. Rates in the future are called forward exchange rates and are also shown on OANDA. For major currencies these are available for one-month, two-month, three-month, and one-year terms. A manager may arrange with this institution to deliver a certain amount of foreign currency at a particular date and receive a contract or option from the financial institution assuring that a fixed amount of domestic currency will be delivered.

For instance, were a firm to sell 500 computers to Japan at $US500 each, the manager would expect to receive $US250,000 in payment. Let us assume it takes 90 days to make and ship the product and the manager has quoted the contract in yen. To make this example simple, we will assume that the exchange rate when the contract is made is 100 yen per dollar. In this case, the manager expects to receive ¥25 million in payment. Should the yen weaken to 110 per dollar, a simple calculation would show that the firm would now only receive $US227,272. (We have used the formula for foreign terms in this calculation.) So, if the manager wishes to be assured of receiving $US 250,000, he/she would arrange for a forward contract or option and pay the required fees. The financial institution will use the forward rates in determining how much currency must be delivered to yield the $US 250,000 required by the selling firm.

Having this rudimentary knowledge of foreign exchange can enable a manager to sell in local currency when it is commercially desirable to do so while also preventing serious erosion in receipts.

Marketing Plan

Marketing managers are often called upon to write plans for their particular lines of business. There are any number of templates available online for these plans. The outline presented below is a result of the authors' many years' experience in developing both domestic and international marketing plans. It may be used as a starting point since every business varies, but it is particularly useful combining international and business to business aspects of marketing.

The marketing plan should be a one-year plan. We find that, especially on a global basis, environmental factors, including country economic and political conditions, technology, and competition can change very quickly. Therefore one year is a good time horizon. Making plans for longer time ranges is usually not worth the effort. In fact one-year plans must have built-in contingencies as seen in the outline below.

Note that the country information in the Situation Analysis has been reduced to the absolute minimum. A manager may decide to add more information about country markets. A good rule to follow is to address only those topics which will have an impact on the business in question.

Within the Action Plan section we have provided a heading called Sourcing. This is very important for international marketers but is not something that needs to be considered when marketing just within the home country. An international marketing manager must know how and where the product will be made (or the services delivered) to devise many aspects of the plan including positioning, pricing, availability, installation, and after-sale service. Therefore we have included Sourcing in the plan outline.

Experience shows that senior management has limited time for reading lengthy reports. Therefore an Executive Summary is absolutely essential. We strongly recommend that after completing all of the other sections, the marketing manager should prepare a two-page (maximum length) summary of the major points and place it at the front of the report. The purpose of an Executive Summary is to give the reader a brief glance at the critical points in your report.

INTERNATIONAL MARKETING PLAN OUTLINE

EXECUTIVE SUMMARY

I. SITUATION ANALYSIS

    A. Business/Economic Environment for Selected Market(s)

        1. General economic position

            a) GDP and GDP per capita; trend
            b) Income distribution
            c) Currency vs. US dollar; trends

        2. Major exports and imports

            a) Products and dollar value

        3. Government import and foreign investment policies/laws affecting foreign businesses (for example: tariffs, quotas, joint venture limits, capital controls).
        4. Key business and labor laws

            a   Protection of intellectual property

        5. Brief overview of infrastructure (physical and financial)
        6. Near-term economic outlook and assessment of overall business climate.

            a) Critical problems/opportunities

    B. Analysis of Market Segment(s)

        1. Description
        2. Size and growth
        3. Buyer motivations/needs

            a) Important cultural characteristics

        4. Product requirements
        5. Market trends affecting our business positively or negatively
        6. Competition

            a) By key market segment
            b) Strengths and weaknesses

    C. Summary – Company's Current Position

        1. Summary of past programs (if relevant)
        2. Key company strengths and weaknesses vs. competition

II. COMPANY MARKETING OBJECTIVES AND STRATEGIES

    A. Objectives (must be measurable and attainable)

B. Positioning of the Product/Service

C. Market Entry Strategy

    1. Rationale for choosing this strategy

III. KEY MARKETING ACTION PLANS – BY PRODUCT OR SEGMENT

1. Product Offering
2. Sourcing
3. Pricing and rationale for pricing approach
4. Distribution channels
5. Marketing communications
6. Logistics
7. Pre and post-sale customer service
8. Additional research
9. Marketing staffing/organization
10. Marketing budgets
11. Summary schedule and assignments

IV. MEASUREMENT/CONTROL AND CONTINGENCY PLANS

V. APPENDIX

Comprehensive case

The Frankfurt Pump Company GmbH (FPC)

The Frankfurt Pump Company (FPC) was founded in 1965 in Frankfurt am Main, Germany, by Heinz Hoffman, a mechanical engineer. FPC initially manufactured specialty tools for the oil and gas industry. The specialty tools provided capital for Hoffman to design and manufacture a quality high-pressure patented pump. By the mid-1980s, the patented FPC pump enjoyed a reputation as the best high-pressure injection pump available. The pump was particularly well suited to the requirements of secondary oil and gas recovery with steam injection. FPC soon captured a dominant market position in the oil and gas industry. After Hoffman's death in 1979, his son Frederick was in charge of the rapidly growing company. However, Frederick had interests in car racing and sold the company in 1995 to a group of eight investors. The company's growth and high profits continued, and its pump was still considered the best quality high-pressure pump in 2000, when the company was sold for the second time to a major coal company. In 2001, the coal company was losing money and needed the cash FPC Pump was generating, but in 2003 the coal company sold FPC for 2.5 times what it had paid for it. The buyer was one of the largest steel companies in the United States. FPC Pump was again sold in 2008 to a large multinational integrated oil company based in Europe. Division sales for 2008–2011 are shown in Exhibit 1.

FPC's pumps were regarded as the "standard of oil patch high-pressure injection pumps." The pumps were widely recognized as the best engineered for high pressure steam injection and corrosion problems in the oil fields. The company was managed by leading engineers.

The frequent buying and divesting of FPC Pump had many negative effects on the business. Initially, the division was primarily bought as a financial "cash cow," which meant it was milked for cash, with little reinvestment. Much of the company's manufacturing was inefficient, and FPC was believed to be a high-cost producer. The new owners knew little about the high-pressure injection pump business, which had no technical, manufacturing or marketing unity with their other operations. Relationships with customers and distributors were neglected, especially when energy booms allowed FPC to ride the growth curve and sell all it could produce.

Account Type	2008	2009	2010	2011
Stocking distributor	€15.2	€19.0	€25.1	€18.5
Nonstocking distributor	4.1	5.2	7.3	4.1
Direct sales	9.9	13.7	18.7	9.7
Interdivisional	1.1	1.0	1.4	2.3
Reverse osmosis	0.6	0.9	1.2	2.4
	€30.9	€39.8	€53.7	€37.0

APPENDIX C EXHIBIT 1 Divisional sales by type of account (in millions of euros)

Note: Stocking and nonstocking distributors sold both pumps and parts. The remaining types of accounts were nearly all pump unit sales.

With a sharp decline in new orders and a rapidly diminishing backlog, the oil company parent saw the need for a new management team. In 2011 it hired a bright and aggressive 39-year-old general manager, Fritz Schmidt, from another company to build up the existing business and to find new uses for FPC pumps. Schmidt was the first non-engineer to head the division. He had had 15 years of experience selling specialty piping to oil and gas companies. The organizational chart is shown in Exhibit 2. As soon as Schmidt obtained an understanding of the company, he was going to take a hard look to see if it was properly organized around market opportunities. One of the first personnel changes Schmidt made was to dismiss the marketing vice president and hire Greta Klaus, an engineer he had worked with three years earlier.

PRODUCT LINES

FPC was the largest manufacturer of high-pressure injection pumps. The pumps and parts had been made at the original location since 1970. As the company grew, adjacent land was acquired and extensions added to the original building.

A centrifugal pump line FPC manufactured was usually selected for applications that require high pressure. FPC's pumps had a high volumetric efficiency and consumed less energy than other types of pumps. The rated or recommended speed of pumps is important when a design engineer selects a pump to go into a new installation. Most pump manufacturers use the term "rated" speed interchangeably with "recommended" speed. The customer's design engineer selects a rated speed that will provide sufficient suction and discharge performance in moving the material. The recommended speeds of the FPC lines of pumps are shown in Exhibit 3.

Because FPC pumps were well engineered, they were often operated at much higher RPMs than competitive pumps, which would fail or need parts more frequently. FPC pumps were the only ones that held up in the severe operating conditions of the South African gold mines. The head of engineering stated:

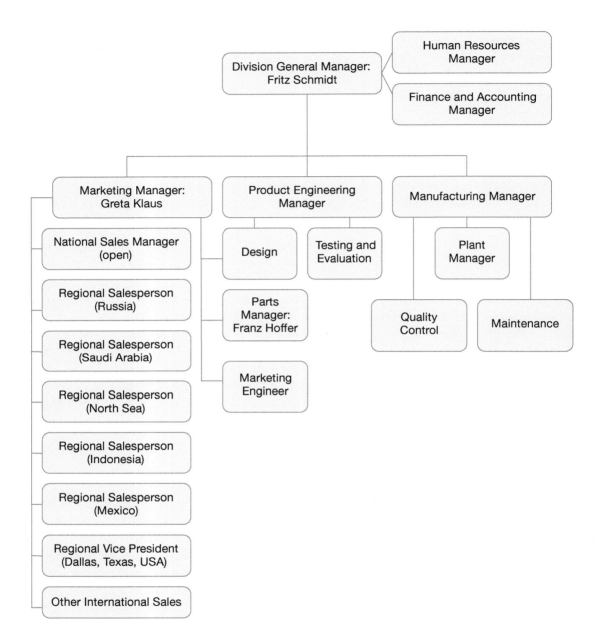

APPENDIX C EXHIBIT 2 FPC pump division organization

Pump series	Stroke	Recommended speed	Maximum speed
E-10, E-50, E-100, E-200	2 ³/₁₆"	400 RPM	500 RPM
E-330, E-300	3 ⅛"	400 RPM	500 RPM
E-125	3 ½"	400 RPM	500 RPM
E-100	4 ½"	400 RPM	500 RPM
E-165	4 ½"	360 RPM	400 RPM
E-160	6 ⅛"	324 RPM	360 RPM
E-250, E-360, E-600	7 ⅛"	324 RPM	360 RPM

APPENDIX C EXHIBIT 3 Recommended speeds of FPC pumps

Our pumps can be run at the highest RPMs with no problems. We use the highest-quality Timken bearings and have the strongest crankshafts. A helicopter literally drop-shipped one of our pumps into an oil-gathering field in Kazakhstan with no damage whatsoever. Our 100 percent inspection is another check to make sure no defects leave our shipping dock.

FPC had 16 product lines or series, as shown in Exhibit 4. Within each of the 16 series there were 2 or 3 different models, for a total of 48 different pumps. Exhibit 4 also shows the quarterly shipments of all pumps for the 2009–2011 period. One FPC oil field distributor described FPC's product line as:

> . . . the best and broadest in the industry. But at €12,000 to €100,000 per pump, depending on the size, I can't stock many of them. Some of them are hot items and others rarely ever fit a customer's steam injection pumping requirements.

Competition

In addition to FPC, four other companies produced high-pressure injection pumps. Two were divisions of major steel companies that also owned large chains of oil field supply stores. The third competitor, Oilflo, was the only one that carried a full line which competed with FPC across the board. Oilflo was founded in the mid-1960s. Located in Dallas, Texas, it was a privately held firm with sales believed to be about 35 percent less than FPC's. The fourth competitor was a UK manufacturer of industrial pumps that recently began selling in the oil field market.

Many more competitors produced parts for high-pressure oil field pumps. In addition to the four producers of pumps that also produced parts, there were 18 to 20 pump parts suppliers. Most of these were small two- to five-person firms. However, four of the parts firms were believed to be €20 to €30 million businesses. These suppliers were called "parts pirates." The parts suppliers did little or no repair or service work, but were essentially small machine shops that made standard parts for the more popular models of high-pressure injection pumps.

Pump Series	2009					2010					2011					2012
	1st	2nd	3rd	4th	Total	1st	2nd	3rd	4th	Total	1st	2nd	3rd	4th	Total	1st
E-10/E-15	58	26	39	76	199				25	25	3	13	9	30	55	41
E-50 series	79	28	67	77	251	84	107	37	36	264	31	20	9	10	70	7
E-100 series	42	42	79	59	222	73	58	56	41	228	36	14	8	8	66	20
E-200 series	36	27	14	19	96	70	97	75	47	289	41	33	15	22	111	26
SE-200 series	118	97	69	75	359	23	50	21	41	135	84	53	53	54	244	76
E-300 series	11	6	10	17	44	112	115	95	114	436	176	101	26	33	336	34
SE-300 series	-	-	5	9	14	18	19	38	32	107	4	2	2	3	11	2
6X-100 series	52	37	89	59	237	13	29	41	40	123	32	16	8	11	67	7
6X-125 series	12	3	2	5	22	58	65	50	69	242	49	16	25	8	98	9
6X-160 series	-	-	1	3	4	12	16	11	15	54	14	8	5	-	27	
6X-165 series	-	2	1	2	5	6	8	18	28	60	30	9	4	6	49	2
6X-250 series	-	-	-	-	-	7	1	8	4	20	7	5	-	-	12	1
6X-300 series	1	3	3	-	7	-	-	-	-	-	3	2	3	1	9	2
6X-360 series						1	1	1	5	8	1	-	8	3	12	
6X-600 series											1	-	2	-	3	
3L-450/5L-750						1	-	3	1	5	1	1	-	1	3	
TOTAL	409	271	379	401	1460	478	566	454	498	1996	513	293	177	190	1173	227

APPENDIX C EXHIBIT 4 2009–2011 quarterly pump unit shipments

Note: The major difference among these lines is the size of the basic design. The E-10 is the smallest model and the 3L is the largest.

Product warranty and guarantee

All FPC pumps are guaranteed for one year from the date the end user received the product. The pumps are repaired or replaced free of charge within the one-year period. All FPC pumps are sold with a warranty card. This might be filled in by hand or online. Often the warranty information was completed by the distributor and contained only the distributor's name. The distributor usually did not identify the end user by name or location because of concern that the customer and FPC might do business directly and bypass the distributor. Even if the end user did complete the warranty information, the customer sometimes bought the pump as a spare for one or two years and did not immediately place it in service. This situation caused FPC to have a problem enforcing its one-year warranty. Exhibit 5 shows the information required to activate the warranty and provide end-user information to FPC. There was no warranty on parts because of the lack of a serial number and the errors caused by independent repair people in the field.

Since FPC pumps were engineered to perform above the recommended speeds, there were few warranty claims. But since most of the warranty cards were inaccurately or not completed, FPC had little knowledge of where its pumps were operating and what material was being pumped at each location.

END USERS

Oil and gas systems

The largest current use of FPC pumps was in the oil and gas industry. Steam flooding was a specific technique for which most FPC pumps were used in oil and exploration. Steam flooding is a method of secondary oil recovery where steam is pumped down and forces more oil out of the well. Steam flooding injection oil recovery systems always require a high-pressure pump. Natural

---

Pump Figure No. _____   Serial No. _____

Distributor   _____
Address   _____
End User   _____
Location   _____
Date shipped from factory   _____
Date shipped from distributor   _____
Date pump installed on location   _____

If pump was altered in any manner from the way it was shipped from the factory, please describe alterations below:

_____
_____
_____

APPENDIX C EXHIBIT 5 FPC pump warranty activation

gas plants treat gas by taking the hydrogen sulfide and water out of the gas. High-pressure injection pumps are used for this purpose. Natural gas by-products like LPG are then injected into a pipeline, and high-pressure injection pumps are also used to perform this task. A new and important market is hydraulic fracturing, known as "fracking," which requires pumping high-pressure water into underground natural gas reserves, breaking up the rock and making the gas easier to extract. Many environmentalists expressed concerns about this method. There were claims of contamination of water and soil in areas where extensive fracking had been used.

Car wash systems

Automated high-pressure car wash systems need high-pressure pumps. Two of the largest automated car wash builders were located near FPC's factory. In the late 1990s, FPC pumps were designed into many of the original car wash equipment systems. FPC was a major factor in the car wash pump market. But as the automatic car wash business became more cost-sensitive, FPC lost most of the OEM business to lower-priced pumps and was subsequently "designed out' of most new systems. The average car wash system needs water pumped at 700 to 800 PSI, whereas FPC pumps operated at 2000 PSI. FPC's engineering manager, stated:

> We could have built low-pressure pumps for car washes, but we were more interested in the high-pressure needs of oil and gas. We once had a committee to rethink this market. We never had anyone do a study or take responsibility for the car wash market. The pump we sold to car washes was the same one that went to the oil and gas folks. We never had the car wash replacement pump or parts business. Once in a while we'd get a phone call here in Frankfurt from one of the car wash people, but we didn't have distributors to serve that replacement market. They do a lot of car washing in the snow and frost belt, where people take salt off their cars. Those aren't the same areas or distributors as where there are oil fields. Furthermore, after we'd sell the car wash builders a pump, we had no idea where they were shipping and installing the finished system, which might later need parts or a replacement pump.

Reverse osmosis market

FPC had had an interest in the reverse osmosis market for the last 15 years. Reverse osmosis (RO) is a process in which salt or brackish water is pumped with high pressure against a membrane filter. The fresh water migrates to one side of the membrane, and the salt water stays on the other side. The company that developed the membrane came to FPC for the first pumps used to test the membranes. When the membrane producer's design engineers wrote technical papers in this area, they referred to the FPC pumps. That helped establish FPC's name in the RO market, where high pressure was necessary. Some FPC pump sales had been going to RO systems builders for the last five years, as shown in Exhibit I. Since this was also a different market for FPC, it did not have distributors that repaired pumps or supplied parts. A few replacement unit and part orders were received by telephone. About 90 percent of the RO sales were direct, and not through distributors. The size and growth prospects of the commercial RO market were not known to FPC.

Additional end users

Over the years, a few FPC pumps had been sold as sewer cleaning pumps in municipal waste systems. This was believed to be a very price-sensitive market. A long-time FPC engineer stated:

> We have received inquiries for a lot of strange applications that are foreign to us. That's how the car wash systems business came in, through the window. Since the pumping of oil and gas is what we know best, other applications took a low priority.

The marketing manager, Greta Klaus, walked into the room and heard the last part of the conversation and added:

> We don't even have good market data on the oil and gas market we are supposed to know. I just wish we had market shares by geographic oil and gas regions. Since we sell to distributors who build systems for oil and gas end users, we don't have enough contact and feedback from our ultimate customers. Our distributors don't know where many of the customers are either, especially if they didn't sell them the original pump, and we are really in the dark about the location and size of the parts market for high-pressure injection pumps.

Oil and gas OEM installations

The large oil companies have engineering departments that write specifications and sometimes specify a brand to the pump distributor that builds the OEM system. The high-pressure injection oil field pumping system typically consists of a pump, a diesel or electric motor, and a V-belt chain drive all mounted on a "skid." The specifying of the type and size of pump is guided by what is being pumped, how much per day, and at what pressure. The OEM system builder uses the end user's technical performance parameters to select the pump brand. The pump manufacturer had to call on both the end user and the OEM builder to sell the system.

THE AFTERMARKET

The repair and replacement pump purchase was somewhat less formal than the OEM buying decision. However, the larger oil company maintenance departments would frequently specify the general type of pump and quantity desired and then put the business out to bid for quotes. If a large end user had 20 pumps of one brand in an oil field, the twenty-first would most likely be the same brand to reduce repair problems and the number of parts needed. The smaller independent company maintenance departments usually bought one pump at a time from the pump distributor they had bought from before. Normally they did not ask for quotes from multiple distributors. They also did not plan the purchase and usually waited until the last minute to repair or replace a pump. During the oil boom years, customers did not have the time to conduct preventive maintenance on their high-pressure injection pumping systems. They waited until the pressure fell or visible leaks occurred. A few large oil companies were now beginning to conduct preventive maintenance on all their equipment.

When a high-pressure system breaks down, the oil company needs a replacement pump or part immediately because the cost of downtime could be between €6,000 to €15,000 per hour in a secondary recovery well. Either the oil company's maintenance personnel or an independent pump service firm did the repair work. Approximately 70 percent of the repair work was done by independent repair firms. Since competitive high-pressure units and parts were interchangeable, the repair person did not have to specify original equipment and part brand names.

OEM pump demand

The number of OEM oil pump installations is a function of the price of oil and the resulting amount of exploration activity. The number of geophysical survey teams prospecting for oil and gas is an early leading indicator of new oil and gas construction. The oil and gas equipment repair market or aftermarket, however, is more dependent on the number of in-place and operating pumping jacks and offshore platforms. The demand for aftermarket replacement equipment material and parts is considerably less cyclical than it is for items going into oil and gas OEM equipment. When an independent repair firm inspected a faulty high-pressure injection pump in the field, it usually informed the oil firm of the cost of the needed repairs. As the cost of repairs approached the cost of a new pump, the repair firm suggested that a new pump be installed. A pump repair was an oil firm maintenance expense item, but a new pump was usually categorized as a capital equipment appropriation.

Pump and component parts aftermarket

The size of the pump and component parts aftermarket depends on the in-place pump population and age of each unit. Since FPC had the largest oil field population of any manufacturer of high-pressure injection pumps, there was considerable potential for replacement pumps and parts. Due to the incomplete warranty card information, FPC did not have information on the location or age distribution of in-place units. To help FPC's planning, the engineering department had attempted to determine the average life of a pump and the wear-out life for parts. But because of wide variances caused by differences in viscosity, the chemical content of the crude oil, suction pressures and the RPMs at which the oil firm operated the machine, it was very difficult to identify "average life" and recommend repair and replacement schedules. However, it was common for FPC's high-pressure injection pumps to be in continuous operation for 20 to 35 years.

Pumping speeds, suction conditions and the nature of the fluid being pumped determined the life of these parts. FPC produced nearly 800 parts, many of which were different sizes of the same basic design. FPC's wide product line created the need for a larger number of parts. Most of the parts made by the five competitors were interchangeable. This interchangeability also created an attractive opportunity for parts "pirates" and allowed distributors to sell products to the parts pirates.

The fluid end parts were the major part of a pump repair bill. In a typical repair situation, 20 to 30 percent of the cost was labor, with possibly some machine shop time, and the remaining 70 to 80 percent was for parts, usually always at the fluid end. For example, a purchase price of €15,000 for a new high-pressure injection pump would require yearly fluid end parts costing between €1,500 and €3,200. The plungers would cost €450 to €600 each, and a pump would have three or five of them. Valves for the pump would cost approximately €90 each, × three or five per pump. Packing was €150 to €180 for the pump. Every two or three years, a major overhaul was usually needed. Over a conservative 20-year pump life, it was common for the parts cost to be two or three times the initial purchase cost.

Historically, all the major manufacturers of high-pressure injection pumps neglected the parts market. As one FPC pump distributor stated:

> The previous management at FPC was more interested in selling pumps or metal tonnage rather than pursuing parts. Some producers saw the pump parts business as a nuisance, and therefore let in the parts pirates. I never understood why they all favored the higher revenue but lower profit margin pump business over the higher margin parts business.

Franz Hoffer was the manager of the aftermarket parts business. He was 59 years old and had been an FPC salesman for 29 years before taking this position. Hoffer was also independently wealthy from the sale of his FPC stock in 1995 to the group of investors.

Parts "pirates"

The higher profit margin in parts, the large pump population needing parts, and neglect by the major pump producers attracted a large number of parts pirates to the injection pump business. Only a few of the parts were protected by patents in various markets. Many pirates were previously employed in the machine shops or sales areas of the pump sales and service distributors. It was easy to enter the parts market, since it only required a machining tool, usually a used one, and a small inventory of metal stock from which to machine parts. Most were located in the center of major oil field areas in simple structures with two or three employees. One pump distributor described the parts pirates:

> These bootleggers are everywhere. Most were once pump repair service people who saw the prices, profit, and potential in the parts side of this business. They also know where all the pumps are in the area. They sell to anyone. They literally have little over their heads; often there is only an old barn or open shed with a roof to shelter them from the sun. They play havoc with parts prices. We can't buy parts from FPC at the prices the parts pirates sell them for and still make an attractive profit.

The parts pirates were in many cases producing at 50 to 60 percent below FPC's current costs, and an increasing number of their parts were of excellent quality, A small number of the parts pirates in the oil fields were beginning to do pump repair work, often working through the night or the entire weekend to put a pump back in operation for an oil producer.

Since these independent parts suppliers were low-cost producers, they sold most of their output to distributors at prices that were 30 to 50 percent below the prices distributors paid the five major producers. The pirates published parts substitution sheets to make it easy for distributor counter people to substitute their products for the manufacturers' items. This situation encouraged many FPC distributors to stock the lower-priced parts as well. The pump producers often "shared the shelf" with competitive parts producers. FPC had no policy or position on this common occurrence.

The independent parts producers sold to three types of accounts. The bulk of their production was sold to the same specialty pump distributors FPC sold its pumps through. The parts producers also sold a significant amount of their output to the five injection pressure pump manufacturers. Finally, a small but increasing amount of the high-volume parts were sold by the independents to the oil field supply houses. The oil field supply houses were considered general stores in the oil production field, selling a wide range of maintenance and supply items. They did little repair work and were essentially similar to a "walk-in auto supply distributor." Pump salespeople referred to the supply houses as "Rope, dope, and soap stores." FPC did not sell parts directly to the supply houses, but rather sold to its distributors, who in turn were supposed to resell the high-volume items to the supply houses. Some FPC distributors sold parts to supply houses on a consignment basis. When Greta Klaus asked one FPC distributor why he sold parts to supply houses on consignment, the distributor stated:

> It's nice to have samples of what you're selling. They only have our more popular parts. They usually sell the samples and then we ship them more. This is no different than what your nonstocking distributors do when they repeatedly sell the pump demos you give them on consignment.

The FPC distributors made relatively few parts sales to the supply houses. Since the FPC distributors did not separately report pump and parts sales by account to FPC, the precise amount of distributor sales of parts to supply houses was unknown.

On 30 April 2011, the FPC Pump Company parts manager, Franz Hoffer, was called into Fritz Schmidt's office to discuss the reasons why the FPC parts business had declined for the last three quarters. Hoffer said he would prepare a memo on the situation within a week. Exhibit 6 shows Hoffer's response, dated 5 May 2011.

DISTRIBUTION

FPC sales force

FPC Pump had six salespeople who were responsible for both pumps and parts sales in their territories. The six were based in St. Petersburg, Russia; Riyadh, Saudi Arabia; Edinburgh, Scotland; Jakarta, Indonesia; Mexico City, Mexico; Dallas, Texas, USA. They were also responsible for sales through distributors and sales served direct by FPC's factory. The salespeople spent most of their time calling on the direct accounts. They sometimes helped FPC's pump distributors call on end-use customers. FPC did not have an established policy regarding which accounts should be sold direct or through a distributor. If a distributor located a customer whose technical problems it was not able to solve or one geographically outside its area, FPC did not compensate the distributor for the lead. FPC's Scottish salesman said:

> It really angers the distributors when we sell any account direct or don't pay them for a sale outside their geographic area. It causes some distributors to play down our line and

May 5, 2011

To: Fritz Schmidt, Division General Manager

From: Franz Hoffer, Parts Manager

Subject: Reasons for and Possible Solutions to our Parts Decline

Reasons for Parts Decline

I. *Parts Pirates*
Like FPC's pumps business, the parts pirates' business has tapered off. To counter this lower level business situation, the pirates have put on a concentrated effort to penetrate distributors, supply stores, and service shops.

2. *FPC Parts Suppliers*
Some of the same suppliers that sell us OEM parts are making very strong efforts at penetrating our markets (i.e., setting up master distributors and contacting our distributors in an effort to sell to them). The discounts given to their master distributors are approximately the same given to us and other OEMs.

3. *Lack of Distributor Inventory*
The distributor, in most cases, does not have the proper inventory mix of parts in stock to sell what the customer wants.

4. *Distributors Not Selling to Supply Stores*
This is the situation with a majority of our distributors. They feel they cannot sell to supply stores at a 20 percent discount. Therefore, the parts pirates are getting this business.

5. *Lack of Distributor Training*
Many distributors lack technical pump knowledge and therefore miss sales opportunities.

6. *Lack of FPC and Distributor Salespeople in the Field*
Companies and distributors that have salespeople in the field are making the contacts. This includes both old and new contacts.

Possible Solutions to Parts Sales Decline

I. Sell direct to supply stores, giving them a 20 percent discount off list.
2. Take a stronger stand with distributors regarding the carrying and selling of parts made by parts pirates.
3. Sell parts on consignment to distributors and/or supply stores. This would be a fixed amount.
4. Hold a meeting with the Distributor Council to discuss their problems and possible solutions.
5. Redesign parts for lower costs and improve performance.
6. Have more sales concentration in the areas of our large pump population.
7. Have distributors hire separate outside sales parts personnel.
8. Conduct an in-depth analysis of each of our distributors and determine who needs help, who should be dropped, and where we need to add new ones.

APPENDIX C EXHIBIT 6 Parts business memo

not pass on leads to us when they are not in their territory. However, FPC does not have a history of taking a distributor account and selling it direct. But an OEM, regardless of its annual purchase, can approach FPC and usually be sold direct. There is no set rule.

It took about seven to ten months for a new salesperson to learn the FPC line and trouble-shooting expertise in oil and gas applications. The FPC salespeople were considered good trouble-shooters and were known for conducting excellent technical seminars for design engineers and maintenance personnel. The salespeople were paid on a combined base and commission schedule for pump sales. The sale of parts was not in the quota or compensation plan. Their quotas were set every year on aggregate pump sales, whether they were sold through distributors or direct. FPC's salespeople were paid a commission on what the distributor bought. Some distributors believed this compensation method encouraged the salespeople to overload distributors with pump inventories. Most of FPC's stocking distributors had large inventories. The marketing manager, division general manager and marketing engineer each spent 15 to 20 percent of his or her time in the field working with customers and distributors.

The FPC salespeople spent most of their time with direct OEM accounts. The marketing manager, Greta Klaus, believed there was a need for a sales incentive system for both pumps and parts, but she was not sure what the percentage should be between the two.

Pump distributors

Greta Klaus described the typical FPC distributor as follows:

> Since FPC makes a high-quality technical pump, we need very specialized distributors. These guys are both systems fabricators and component and parts distributors. They provide engineering, fabrication, parts, replacement units, and repair service for oil and gas operators. They can build a system for the customer or sell the components to end users. They put the pumps, torque converters, clutches, couplings, drive unit and controls on a platform or skid. They also sell compressors, diesel and electric engines, and all that is needed to build the system. Our pump distributors have engineers who go in and evaluate an end user's requirements and specifications before submitting a price quotation. The fabricators, engineers, and draftsmen work closely with the customer in all stages of a job. Every situation is carefully analyzed to assure that the proper components are on the skid.
>
> The fabricators' engineers prepare a schematic flow and bills of material for each job. On more complex projects, in-depth conferences are held between the client's engineering personnel and the fabricator's engineers. The distributors usually have testing facilities to test and break in the completed system.

The specialty distributors usually had one to three outside salespeople and an inside salesperson. All had a parts counter for walk-in business. One distributor described its business as follows:

> We are a very technical distributor that performs a lot of value-added. We are not just order takers or inside salesclerks. We have graduate engineers who design a system from a

concept or a customer's specs. We then fabricate the appropriate package, install it, and service it until it's running to the customer's satisfaction. We have a counter, but we are not an auto parts store that does everything across a counter with catalogs.

All of FPC's stocking distributors are shown in Exhibit 7 along with their annual purchases from FPC (2009–2011), the year-end euro value of their FPC pumps and parts, inventory, and the number of branch locations. Where there are multiple or branch locations for one distributor, they are usually in different cities or states. The 16 distributors in Exhibit 7 account for the majority of FPC distributor sales. The average stocking FPC distributor had annual total sales (systems, components, parts) of between €10 and €50 million. The remainder of FPC distributor sales were through nonstocking distributors.

	PUMPS AND PARTS				
Distributor's Main Location	**Sales**			**Inventory**	**Number of Branches**
	2009	2010	2011		(12/31/11)
1. Oil and Gas Equipment St. Petersburg, Russia	€ –	€ –	€ 349,700	€ 215,700	1
2. Bakersfield Pump Co. Bakersfield, CA, USA	–	–	161,000	5,400	1
3. Eastern Pump and Supply Astana, Kazakhstan	324,540	851,329	817,210	46,210	4
4. Cook Industries Edinburgh, Scotland	2,082,100	3,315,900	2,504,400	934,530	7
5. United Industries London, England	178,710	132,201	205,604	36,370	2
6. Western Equipment Kiev, Ukraine	215,901	355,216	423,404	66,410	1
7. Jakarta Pump and Supply Jakarta, Indonesia	344,770	489,276	1,778,701	469,270	1
8. Maracaibo Engine and Equipment Maracaibo, Venezuela	379,110	697,117	1,551,501	83,090	1
9. Oil Service Mainheim, Germany		188,624	1,243,060	154,156	1
10. Lopensa Equipment Mexico City, Mexico	455,333	657,845	645,761	205,650	9
11. Flow Equipment Jeddah, Saudi Arabia	486,650	716,100	740,799	115,110	3
12. LaPine Equipment Longview, TX, USA	74,203	277,701	1,340,234	67,515	1
13. Saudi Industries Riyadh, Saudi Arabia	815,090	1,374,267	1,715,100	569,450	6
14. Gulf Supply Dubai, UAE	–	1,397,401	2,375,400	835,170	6
15. Fluid Pumps Bakersfield, CA, USA	115,217	287,171	1,077,191	172,660	1
16. Rucker Engine and Pump Oklahoma City, OK, USA	374,104	360,991	413,876	148,420	1

APPENDIX C EXHIBIT 7 FPC pump stocking distributors

Many of the FPC distributors stocked nothing and sold very little each year. The non- stocking distributors had all the FPC catalogs and literature. FPC had no distributor stocking policy for pump units or parts. If a non-stocking distributor got an order, it would still collect the 20 percent standard commission on FPC pumps. When the marketing manager asked one distributor why he didn't stock FPC products, the distributor replied:

> We must know the business is out there before we'll put anything in stock. Plus, FPC has many dead lines and parts that never sell. That really impacts a distributor who lives on inventory turnover. Without knowing the market potential for their product lines, they can't tell us what and how much to inventory.

The Gulf Supply distributor, with six branches and headquarters in Dubai, commented:

> I wish FPC was able to have the oil field maintenance people come in and demand FPC pumps and parts. As it is now, they usually come in, say what their pumping requirements are, and our counter people can sell them whatever they think will do the job. FPC provides very little direction to its distributors and does even less for end users. Just email or call FPC in Frankfurt for technical help sometime. Sometimes no one calls back for days. FPC comes around and makes promises, but nothing happens. They have no set policies for distributors. Some of the manufacturers of rotary and low-pressure pumps we carry have very clear rules on how to work with and help distributors.

Distributor territory coverage

In the early 2000s, FPC rarely had more than one distributor in larger geographic areas. But as oil and gas drilling expanded and the older in-place pumps needed more repair and parts, and as more distributors wanted to represent FPC, additional distributors were signed up.

Greta Klaus described the distributor territory coverage:

> In many geographic areas, we now have double or overlapping coverage and in some areas little or none. But I like dual coverage because if we drop one or he drops us, we still have a guy there carrying our lines.

FPC had no mechanism for resolving the inevitable conflict that occurs when one FPC distributor opens or acquires a branch where another FPC distributor already has a branch. FPC did not provide any distributor with protection or assurance that there would be no other distributor nearby. None of its distributors had specific territories or designated areas of geographic responsibility.

Greta Klaus asked many FPC distributors two questions: How large a geographic radius can you travel to effectively and profitably service? How far does the typical walk-in customer drive to buy from you? The answer to the first question was usually stated in terms of driving times. Based on the distributor responses, it appeared that a 100- to 125-km radius was about the maximum for a one-day service job. The drive there would take about 11/2 hours, work on the pump would take 3 to 5 hours, and a return trip was another 11/2 hours. Longer distances were inefficient for the pump service distributor and increased the downtime cost of a problem oil well. The maximum driving time and radius for walk-in customers was about 75 km.

Most of FPC's larger distributors, especially those with multiple locations, believed FPC had too many distributors in many markets that were now competing for a smaller total amount of business. This was less of a problem in boom times, when every distributor had a lot of business.

Distributor relationship

Klaus was aware she had serious problems with distributors. She decided to spend the next week in the field traveling with FPC salespeople. One salesperson stated:

> We are lucky these distributors stay with us. Many would leave if they had another product line with FPC's quality image and customer acceptance.

Klaus traveled with the US salesman for a day, and at dinner that evening the rep summarized to her how he thought distributors in his territory viewed FPC:

> The distributors in California see all the end users as their private customers, rather than as our common customer. Many of the distributors out here don't like me to call on end users in their territory. Even though we don't have a history of taking distributor accounts direct, most won't even show me "their" customer or mailing lists. However, when there is a technical problem at an end user, then it's an FPC problem and not theirs. The better distributors are just beginning to see us as partners.

In June 2011, Greta Klaus decided to call a distributors' meeting, which all FPC salespeople would also attend. FPC had not held a distributor council meeting for many years. She called the meeting to get to know the distributors better and to get feedback from them. All but one stocking distributor attended the meeting. A summary of the meeting was put into the Distributor Council minutes (Exhibit 8).

PRICING AND PROFIT MIX

FPC had a company target of 30 to 40 percent gross margin on pumps; the floor was a 30 percent gross margin. Specialty Pump orders were to be priced at a 65 percent gross margin. There were no quantity discounts for OEM or distributor sales. For parts, FPC had a 70 percent gross margin pricing objective and was the highest priced parts supplier. Recent competitive action by pirates had caused FPC to price all parts at a 60 percent gross margin. Historically, 40 percent of FPC's sales were from parts, but 60 percent of profits. In 2012, FPC believed parts would be about 60 percent of sales and 80 percent of profits. OEMs that were sold direct by FPC were given discounts of 20 percent for both parts and pumps.

I. FPC should clean up its distribution situation.

2. What is FPC's policy on selling to nonstocking distributors?

3. FPC's distribution policy appears ruthless and arbitrary.

4. Distributors need direction from FPC to expand market applications for existing pumps, i.e. sewage, mining, reverse osmosis.

5. New application case histories that solve common application problems in expanding markets need to be written and shared with distributors.

6. Need a clear written definition of what an OEM is, along with an OEM policy statement.

7. A quarterly distributor newsletter might be published by FPC, including:
    a. Case histories.
    b. Competitive information.
    c. Distributor personnel changes.
    d. FPC personnel changes.
    e. New distributor appointments.
    f. Service tips.
    g. Application photos and stories.

8. The council thought there should be a limited number of OEMs and that:
    a. Before signing on an OEM, current distributors need to be given a chance to see if they can meet the OEM's needs.
    b. If FPC decides to sign on a OEM even if the local distributor can meet its needs, the distributor needs to receive some type of compensation.

9. If a particular distributor is not doing the job expected, it should be canceled with sufficient notice. FPC should not just surround an existing distributor with more distributors to get the coverage needed. FPC should be careful not to over saturate an area with distributors.

10. What is FPC's intention for the reverse osmosis market? Will this be a direct market or a distributor market?

II. Marketing Communications
    a. FCP must improve "user friendliness" of its website.
    b. Direction should be toward testimonials/applications, with reprints available for distributors to use.
    c. Co-op advertising programs in regional and local publications and trade shows were suggested.
    d. When responses are received from ads or the website, all distributors in that particular geographic area should be sent copies of the request for information.

APPENDIX C EXHIBIT 8 Minutes: distributor council meeting

FPC's pump distributors received a discount of 35 percent on parts and 20 percent on pumps. A typical pump unit sale by a distributor in 2011 sold at a suggested list price of €15,000. Many distributors believed their 20 percent discount from list price on pumps was insufficient. The typical pump distributor's total profit was approximately 40 percent from parts, and 30 to 40 percent from parts and service work. The remaining 20 to 30 percent came from pump unit sales. Greta Klaus and Fritz Schmidt were considering a quantity discount of 5 percent for distributors that placed a combined pump and parts order of €300,000 or more. Klaus was concerned that the quantity discounts might encourage distributors to hold back orders until they had accumulated enough for the discount.

The FPC suggested resale price for distributor parts to the supply houses was 20 percent off list. That left the distributor with 15 percent from the 35 percent discount. Many distributors believed it would be costly for them to sell to supply houses from their stock. To solve this concern, Klaus was considering shipping direct to the supply houses and then providing the distributor with 10 percent for doing the paperwork. However, because of the parts pirates' low prices, it was doubtful that FPC's prices could be at all competitive with the no-brand parts. The supply houses generally did not stress a brand, for which FPC could receive a premium. The supply houses were often disloyal buyers that sold fast-turnover pump parts on a generic basis. Some pirates were selling private label parts to the supply houses at 50 percent below FPC's supply house list price. If FPC sold parts direct to the supply houses, it was concerned about receiving more complaints from distributors, since the FPC parts were very profitable for the distributors.

Price on application program (POA)

To be more competitive, FPC announced a new distributor pricing program on 1 May 2011, which was already bringing many complaints from distributors. As part of the POA program, if a distributor had a prospect for a new pump, it could call the factory to see what price FPC would allow to be competitive. For example, if a competitor submitted a €13,000 price for a pump that normally sold at list for €16,000, FPC would usually meet or match it and give the distributor a 15 percent commission on the sale price. The stocking distributors complained that the program was reducing the value of their inventory, and many now wanted rebates. Many of the POA prices to the end user were less than the cost of the pump to the distributor. The POA program temporarily stopped the use of all pump price sheets.

On 12 July 2011, Greta Klaus met with Schmidt to discuss the POA program and other marketing issues. Klaus first commented:

> We aren't really managing our sales and distribution. Many of the distributors are managing us and acting more like reps than distributors. In fact, in some territories we have competition between our distributors; if they sell someone else parts, we are competing with our own distributors. We need to agree on firm policies and put them into a new distribution agreement. This means we will have to evaluate, cancel, restrict, and add new distributors. There will be a lot of hot tempers because we've kept so many on for decades. We will also have inventory return problems. If our distributors don't give us the coverage, penetration, and customer service, why keep them?

Schmidt:

> Our sales and distribution emphasis should follow our product-market strategy. We must get this sorted out fast because this morning I got bad news from our accountant. This last quarter the first red ink in FPC's history appeared on the books. The loss isn't as bad as it looks, because most of it is due to depreciation charges. The fact that they paid two times book value for this business caused management to write up the assets and now write off large depreciation expenses. But our cash flow is still not healthy. We are extending payables from 30 to 60 days. We really can't lay off any more people. The burden is on you to improve our top line so we can show a better bottom line.

Klaus:

> I believe we need a full look at our strategies and resulting policies. I will begin a detailed analysis immediately and have specific recommendations to you in no more than 30 days.
>
> Source: adapted from Hlavacek and Ames (1986),
> used by permission of Random House, Inc.

CASE QUESTIONS

1. What are the major problems FPC faces and what are the causes of these problems?
2. Are there any ethical problems FPC should be concerned about?
3. What internal and external market information does FPC need in order to analyze, develop, and implement better strategies for pumps *and* parts?
4. Should you suggest a custom market research study for question 2 above, what information should FPC attempt to get?
   What method(s) should be used?
5. What strategies should FPC establish in specific product-markets?
6. Are FPC's pricing and cost structures competitive for pumps and parts? What actions should management take to improve pricing and costs?
7. What changes should FPC make to improve results in the parts business?
8. What distributor policies does FPC need to develop?
9. Where are the weaknesses in FPC's organization and how could the company improve the organization?
10. What actions should management take regarding the current product line and new product development?
11. What new country markets might FPC consider and how would management assess opportunities in each?

Index